THE COLLECTED
WORKS OF
JEREMY BENTHAM

General Editor

F. Rosen

Correspondence

Volume 8

This is the eighth volume of the *Correspondence* produced in the new edition of *The Collected Works of Jeremy Bentham*. During the years covered by this volume, Bentham's Panopticon penitentiary scheme was finally rejected by the government; and his efforts to secure its implementation, and then to gain adequate compensation, form a major and recurring theme. But the letters do much more than complete the Panopticon saga. They give an insight into Bentham's relations with his editors and followers Étienne Dumont and James Mill, and provide information on the writing, editing, and in some cases, printing and publishing of works on law, politics, religion, and education. Just as important is the clear impression the correspondence gives of his contacts, especially with the legal and political reformers of the day.

The Collected Works of Jeremy Bentham

The new critical edition of the works and correspondence of Jeremy Bentham (1748–1832) is being prepared and published under the supervision of the Bentham Committee of University College London. In spite of his importance as jurist, philosopher, and social scientist, and leader of the Utilitarian reformers, the only previous edition of his works was a poorly edited and incomplete one brought out within a decade or so of his death. Eight volumes of the new *Collected Works*, five of correspondence, and three of writings on jurisprudence, appeared between 1968 and 1981, published by the Athlone Press. Further volumes in the series since then are published by Oxford University Press. The overall plan and principles of the edition are set out in the General Preface to *The Correspondence of Jeremy Bentham* vol. 1, which was the first volume of the *Collected Works* to be published.

Volumes published by Oxford University Press

Constitutional Code
Volume 1
Edited by F. Rosen and J. H. Burns 1983

Deontology, together with A Table of the Springs of Action and Article on Utilitarianism
Edited by Amnon Goldworth 1983

Chrestomathia
Edited by M. J. Smith and W. H. Burston 1983

Correspondence, volume 6: January 1798 to December 1801
Edited by J. R. Dinwiddy 1984

Correspondence, volume 7: January 1802 to December 1808
Edited by J. R. Dinwiddy 1988

The CORRESPONDENCE *of* JEREMY BENTHAM

Volume 8
January 1809 to December 1816

edited by
STEPHEN CONWAY

CLARENDON PRESS · OXFORD
1988

Oxford University Press, Walton Street, Oxford OX2 6DP
Oxford New York Toronto
Delhi Bombay Calcutta Madras Karachi
Petaling Jaya Singapore Hong Kong Tokyo
Nairobi Dar es Salaam Cape Town
Melbourne Auckland
and associated companies in
Berlin Ibadan

Oxford is a trade mark of Oxford University Press

Published in the United States
by Oxford University Press, New York

British Library Cataloguing in Publication Data
Bentham, Jeremy
The correspondence of Jeremy Bentham.—
(The Collected works of Jeremy Bentham).
Vol. 8: January 1809 to December 1816
1. Bentham, Jeremy 2. Philosophers—
England—Biography 2. Civil procedure—England
I. Title II. Conway, Stephen III. Series 192
B1574.B34

ISBN 0-19-822615-2

Library of Congress Cataloging in Publication Data
(Revised for vol. 8)
Bentham, Jeremy, 1748–1832.
The correspondence of Jeremy Bentham.
(The Collected works of Jeremy Bentham)
Vol. 3—edited by I.R. Christie; v. 4–5 edited by Alexander Taylor Milne; v. 6 edited by J.R. Dinwiddy; v. 8 edited by Stephen Conway.
Contents: v. 1. 1752–76.—v. 2. 1777–80.—[etc.]—v. 8. January 1809 to December 1816.
1. Philosophers—Great Britain—Correspondence.
2. Bentham, Jeremy. 1748–1832—Correspondence.
I. Sprigge, Timothy L.S., ed. II. Christie, Ian R., ed.
III. Title. IV. Series. V. Series: Bentham, Jeremy, 1748–1832. Works. 1983.
B1574.B34A4 192 68–84119

ISBN 0-19-822615-2

Printed in Great Britain
at the Alden Press, Oxford

PREFACE

This is the first volume of Bentham's correspondence prepared for the press with the financial support of the Leverhulme Trust. A generous grant from the Trust enabled the Bentham Committee to appoint a full-time editor and a half-time research assistant to work on this and subsequent volumes in the correspondence series. The Committee and the editor wish, therefore, first and foremost to record their thanks to the Leverhulme Trust. In addition, we acknowledge with deep gratitude the financial contribution made by the British Academy, the Economic and Social Research Council, the Pilgrim Trust, and University College London.

We are also grateful to the institutional and private owners or custodians of manuscripts printed in this volume. In particular, we are indebted to the British Library; the Public Record Office; the Bodleian Library, Oxford; King's College Library, Cambridge; the Linnean Society of London; the London Library; Devon Record Office, Exeter; Archives Nationales, Paris; Staatsbibliothek Preussischer Kulturbesitz, Berlin; Bibliothèque Publique et Universitaire, Geneva; Library of Congress, Washington D.C.; William R. Perkins Library, Duke University, Durham, North Carolina; Yale University Library and the Beinecke Rare Book and Manuscript Library, Yale; the Carl H. Pforzheimer Collection of Shelley and his Circle, the New York Public Library, Astor, Lenox and Tilden Foundations; the New-York Historical Society; Haverford College Library, Haverford, Pennsylvania; the Historical Society of Pennsylvania, Philadelphia; Boston Public Library, Boston, Massachusetts; Central State Archives of Ancient Acts, Moscow; Academia Nacional de Historia, Caracas; Mr D. R. Bentham; Mr George Clive; Mrs B. Hyde-Smith; the late Professor G. N. Ray; and Mr Hamish Riley-Smith.

The completion of this volume would have been impossible, or at least much delayed, without the assistance of a great many people. My principal debt as editor is to Ms Catherine Atkinson who, as my half-time research assistant, checked many of the transcripts and gathered valuable information for the footnotes. Dr Philip Schofield assisted in the same capacity before Ms Atkinson's arrival at the Bentham Project and his own appointment as editor of a volume in the *Collected Works* edition. Dr

Cyprian Blamires and Ms Marilyn Morris kindly consented to assist me with the proof-reading, and made useful suggestions that have improved the volume. Mrs Rosamine Hayeem typed the prelims, index, and parts of the text, while Mrs Paula da Gama Pinto typed all of the notes. For earlier work in helping to establish the texts of the letters I am indebted to Professor Pedro Schwartz, Dr Michael Harris, Dr Ivon Asquith, Dr Martin Smith, and Mrs Claire Daunton (née Gobbi). I should like also to thank the General Editor of the *Collected Works*, Dr Frederick Rosen, for his unfailing encouragement and support, and Dr J. R. Dinwiddy, editor of the preceding two volumes of correspondence, for his advice and experienced judgment.

Lastly, I should mention those who have given me information on particular points: Dr Michael Beddows, Dr Lea Campos Boralevi, Professor J. H. Burns, Professor W. E. Butler, Professor Ian R. Christie, Professor Michael Crawford, Mr Alan Griffith, Mr A. D. E. Lewis, and Professor W. L. D. Ravenhill. Their expert knowledge made my task immeasurably easier.

University College London S. R. C.

CONTENTS

LIST OF LETTERS IN VOLUME 8

LIST OF LETTERS IN VOLUME 8

LIST OF LETTERS IN VOLUME 8

LIST OF LETTERS IN VOLUME 8

LIST OF LETTERS IN VOLUME 8

LIST OF LETTERS IN VOLUME 8

LIST OF LETTERS IN VOLUME 8

LIST OF LETTERS IN VOLUME 8

INTRODUCTION

1. THE LETTERS

This volume contains all the letters known to have been written by and to Bentham between January 1809 and December 1816. Papers enclosed in letters have also been published when appropriate, either after the relevant correspondence, or in editorial footnotes. Letters drafted but evidently not sent have been omitted, as have Bentham's observations on letters received. In many cases, however, these items are mentioned in footnotes, and their location recorded.

Nearly four-fifths of the letters are produced from original manuscripts, the vast majority of which have never before been published. The most important source, as in previous volumes in this series, is the collection of Bentham papers in the British Library. This contains a large number of letters written to Bentham, several of his autograph letters to his brother Samuel (or Sir Samuel as he was known from 1809), and drafts and copies of some of Bentham's letters to other correspondents. A significant portion of this material relates to Bentham's Panopticon penitentiary scheme, particularly to his attempts to secure its adoption and then to obtain compensation for its non-implementation. But most of Bentham's letters on Panopticon can be found in two other important collections, both housed at the Public Record Office. The first of these is the treasury papers (which also include some letter-book copies of items sent to Bentham), and the second, the papers of the crown estates office, where many of Bentham's letters were deposited by treasury officials in December 1813. Another major manuscript source is the Bentham papers at University College London. The bulk of this collection comprises manuscripts relating to Bentham's works, but it includes some letters to Bentham and drafts or copies of his own correspondence. Also important are the Dumont MSS at the Bibliothèque Publique et Universitaire, Geneva, which contain a number of Bentham's letters to Étienne Dumont, his Genevan editor, and the Koe MSS in private hands, which include letters from Bentham to his secretary and protégé, John Herbert Koe, and a few items to Bentham from Sir Samuel and Lady Bentham. The remaining letters reproduced from manuscripts have been assembled from more than twenty other public repositories and private collections in the United Kingdom, the USA, the USSR, France, Germany, and Venezuela.

Where the letters Bentham actually sent or received have survived, these have been used. Copies or drafts have been employed only when the originals have proved untraceable. If no manuscript is available, letters have had to be reproduced from printed sources. By far the most important of these is Sir John Bowring's *The Works of Jeremy Bentham*, 11 vols., Edinburgh, 1838–43, particularly volumes x and xi, which contain selections from Bentham's correspondence. Bowring's editing, it must be said, was not of a high standard. Whenever reliance has had to be placed on his edition for the text of a letter, every effort has therefore been made to rectify its shortcomings. Items have sometimes had to be redated, letters that he obviously conflated have been divided, and his scanty and often misleading footnotes replaced with fuller information.

Several other published sources, generally more accurate than Bowring, are also worthy of note. Matthew L. Davis's *The Private Journal of Aaron Burr*, 2 vols., New York, 1838, despite its title, contains a number of letters. So too does Alexander Bain's *James Mill*, London, 1882, which has the virtue of printing in full many items from which Bowring printed only extracts. Bentham's own *Papers Relative to Codification and Public Instruction* and its *Supplement*, both published in 1817, are useful too, for they contain printed versions of many of his letters to statesmen in Europe and America, together with their replies.

Inevitably, the letters published in this volume represent only a portion of Bentham's correspondence for the years 1809–16. Many letters have either not survived or not been found. Nevertheless, readers will be able to gain a valuable insight into Bentham's life and work. Much of the correspondence relates to Panopticon, especially in 1810–13, and presents a detailed picture of Bentham's struggles and the numerous frustrations and disappointments he faced. But however time-consuming, Panopticon was not Bentham's only concern. During this period he researched and wrote, and in some cases had edited, printed, and published, works on the law, education, politics, and religion. A number of letters shed light on these activities. Bentham's correspondence with his editors Étienne Dumont and James Mill is particularly illuminating, while a fascinating glimpse of Bentham's research methods is provided by the set of letters to John Herbert Koe. The correspondence also gives an impression of the circles in which Bentham saw himself operating, and, just as important, of those whom he sought to influence. His close contact with leading political and legal reformers such as Henry Brougham, Francis Horner, Sir Samuel Romilly, Sir James Mackintosh, Sir Francis Burdett, John Cartwright, Thomas Northmore, and Joseph Hume, emerges clearly. So too does his desire to play a prominent part in law reform overseas, whether in the United States through Governor Simon Snyder of Pennsylvania and

President Madison, or in Russia and Poland through Emperor Alexander and Prince Czartoryski. But not the least interesting aspect of the correspondence is the personal one. Bentham's character, habits, and way of life are all to some extent revealed in these letters.

2. OUTLINE OF BENTHAM'S LIFE
JANUARY 1809 TO DECEMBER 1816

1809 Nearly fifty letters have survived for this year, and many of them relate to Bentham's writings, or to the editions of them produced by Dumont and James Mill. In January Bentham was consulted by Dumont about the material he was using for the work published in 1811 as *Théorie des peines et des récompenses.* This was discussed again in February, when Dumont also mentioned his manuscript of *Tactique des assemblées législatives.* Unpublished until 1816, it seems that this manuscript was examined in March by Aaron Burr, the former vice-president of the United States, who had taken a keen interest in Bentham's writings. A third work occupied Dumont too. Letters written in May, July, and August reveal that he was making use of Bentham's manuscripts on evidence, though it was not until 1823 that Dumont's *Traité des preuves judiciaires* appeared in print.

While Dumont laboured to translate and recast Bentham's writings, Mill was also engaged in editorial work. Considering the important role Mill was to play in Bentham's life, it is particularly regrettable that the date of their first meeting is unknown. The first surviving letter between them is from Mill and dated 27 April 1809, but they had clearly been in contact before this. By the summer of 1809 Mill was busy, like Dumont, with Bentham's voluminuous writings on evidence, portions of which were to be printed in 1812. In late September Bentham wrote that editing the evidence material 'forms Mill's sole business'. Small wonder then, that several of Mill's letters are largely concerned with the difficulties this considerable task entailed. 'I am immersed in old Circumstantial', he told Bentham on 31 October, '—and not a little non plused, on more occasions than one, whether to take or reject—unwilling to lose, and yet unwilling to overload'.

Bentham himself was involved with other projects. In April he was seeking information from William Cobbett on libel cases for use in *The Elements of the Art of Packing.* In May we find him receiving information from Francis Horner on sinecures, a subject that was to occupy Bentham's pen in the following year (see UC cxlvii). About three months later, in August 1809, Bentham started to work on material on parliamentary reform, writing a substantial quantity of manuscript sheets that formed the basis of the works he subsequently published on this topic. By September he was able to report to his brother that 'Parliamentary Reform' had grown into 'a capital constitutional work'. At the same time he noted that his writings on fallacies would soon be complete.

Many matters besides writing and editing are discussed in the correspondence of this year. An exchange of letters in late January between Bentham and William Huskisson, then secretary to the treasury, introduces Panopticon at an early stage. But there are few further references to it in 1809. Apart from an apologetic letter from William Wilberforce in June, and Dumont's suggestion in December that Panopticon might interest the Corporation of London, little is heard of Bentham's model penitentiary. A more prominent theme is Bentham's wish to visit Mexico. He had approached Lord Holland in October 1808 (see *Correspondence*, vii), explaining that he was looking for a more hospitable climate and the chance to work in seclusion. Through Lord Holland he was able to make contact with the Spanish authorities, but for the most part his correspondence on Mexico was discouraging. In February Peter Mark Roget, the young scientist who had helped Bentham with refrigeration experiments in 1800, declined an invitation to accompany him, while in September Bentham received a letter from Don Gaspar de Jovellanos, the Spanish reformer, which described the difficulties he was likely to face.

In late November and early December the main topic of discussion in Bentham's correspondence with Mill and Dumont was the article in the *Edinburgh Review* on Scipion Bexon's *Application de la théorie de la législation pénale*, Paris, 1807. Bexon's work, written for the King of Bavaria, seems to have owed much to *Traités de législation civile et pénale*, 3 vols., Paris, 1802, Dumont's first and most famous recension of Bentham's writings. The piece in the *Edinburgh* was originally written by Mill, but was substantially altered by the editor, Francis Jeffrey. All but one of Mill's flattering references to Bentham were cut out. Bentham, while professing to be unconcerned, was deeply hurt. 'As to Mr. Jeffrey', he wrote to Dumont on 5 December, 'he has made no secret of his *disposition*—I should rather say his *determination*—to persevere in doing whatsoever may be in his power to keep down the reputation of whatever work I either have published or may come to publish in future: and you see he is not over scrupulous in the choice of his means.'

On a personal level, it should be noted that Bentham spent much of 1809 closeted at Queen's Square Place, Westminster. At the close of the year, however, he stayed for more than a month with his brother at Hall Oak Farm, Hampstead, and during much of the summer and autumn he was at Barrow Green House, near Oxted and Godstone, Surrey. Barrow Green was the home of Bentham's former secretary John Heide Koe, who had acquired the property through his elderly wife Sarah Chicheley Koe. Bentham was a regular visitor for many years to come.

It was while he was at Barrow Green in September that he learned of the death of his stepmother. Neither the letter he received from her son, Charles Abbot, nor Bentham's reply have survived, but he included the substance of these letters in his own letter to Sir Samuel telling him the news. Signs of grief on Bentham's part are hard to detect, but then he was never very close to his stepmother. His main concern appears to have been to rescue from her papers the letter he had written many years before to his father, in which he asked permission to devote himself to the study of legislation rather than practice at the bar.

1810 Only twenty-three letters have been traced for this year, and their chronological distribution is uneven. Nevertheless, they provide information on Bentham's writings and Dumont's editorial work, on Bentham's following of political developments in Britain and the Iberian world, and, perhaps most importantly, on Panopticon.

The first letter of the year is from Sir Samuel Romilly and it advises Bentham not to publish *The Elements of the Art of Packing* for fear of prosecution by the government. In November there is correspondence relating to several of Bentham's other works. Dumont was in contact again about his work on Bentham's writings on evidence, and he was sent the manuscript version of 'Scotch Reform', which Bentham described as much fuller than the 'abridgement' published under the same title in 1808. Bentham also wrote to Cobbett, asking him to include in his *Weekly Political Register* a chapter of the work later published as *Plan of Parliamentary Reform*. Cobbett, however, required time to consider, and Bentham withdrew his request.

A few days later he urged Dumont to write a short piece he had promised for the first number of *The Philanthropist*. The article was to be on the Edinburgh Bridewell, which had been inspired, in part at least, by the Panopticon plan. Bentham had made a similar attempt to publicize his work in the previous month. On 25 October he wrote to Joseph Blanco White, editor of *El Español*, seeking to secure a mention of the code on 'Liberty of the Press' that he had drawn up for the use of the Venezuelan patriot, General Francisco de Miranda. This code, and Miranda's progress in Venezuela, are also discussed in a letter of 1 November to Bentham's old friend, John Mulford. Mexico, Bentham explained, no longer attracted him as a place of residence, but Venezuela was a quite different matter.

This interest in events in South America was matched by a close attention to domestic politics. George III's illness and the prospect of a regency are mentioned in several letters. Bentham was able to obtain detailed and up-to-date news as a result of his connection with the Baillie sisters, Joanna and Agnes, whose brother Dr Matthew Baillie was physician extraordinary to the King. Another contemporary political issue that interested Bentham was the Droits of Admiralty. The Droits, which secured for the crown a share of the prizes captured by British seamen, were the subject of debate in the Commons in May. From early November until well into the following January Bentham wrote sheet after sheet on the cognate subject of the Prize Acts, and in December apparently received useful information from Brougham, who had played a prominent part in the May debate.

To a much greater extent than in 1809, Panopticon is a major topic in the correspondence. In early May Bentham told Wilberforce that Romilly had promised to call for the implementation of the penitentiary system. Bentham was reluctant to allow himself to become too hopeful, however, for Romilly had expressed the same intention on many earlier occasions without translating it into action in the Commons. Moreover, having spent much time lobbying ministers to no avail, Bentham viewed the prospect of a further attempt with some trepidation. He had no wish, he explained to Wilberforce in an allusion to his earlier humiliations, to pass 'the short remainder of my life among the Treasury Porters'. Wilberforce replied most positively. Bentham should forget the treasury porters. Although he was wise to be cautious until the 'way is smoothd and the doors thrown wide open for yr triumphant passage', Wilberforce was confident of success. 'I am delighted by seeing with my minds Eye, your Honour like a great Spider, sealed in ye Center of yr Panopticon'.

In early May the government also showed itself to be interested. On the 7th Bentham received an enquiry from Richard Wharton, secretary to the treasury, and he replied promptly that he was ready to proceed with the plan, 'notwithstanding all I have suffered'. There the matter stood, it seems, until 25 August, when Bentham wrote to Wharton about an alarming new development. The agents of the Vauxhall Bridge Company had begun work and were bound to infringe upon the land acquired at Millbank as a site for Panopticon. In October the Company's lawyers informed Bentham that they had made an agreement with Samuel Cooke, one of the tenants at Millbank, empowering the Company to occupy land near his house to facilitate its operations.

1811 This was a crucial year in the story of Panopticon, and a good many of the fifty-four letters relate to this subject. On 4 January Bentham was asked by George Harrison, assistant secretary to the treasury, whether he was prepared to undertake the scheme on a limited scale, for 500 convicts rather than the 1,000 originally agreed, and whether he would expect remuneration if the plan were 'relinquished altogether'. In addition, Harrison made enquiries about the buildings on the Millbank site. Bentham replied in two letters. The first, sent on 18 January, dealt with the questions regarding the buildings. In the second, dated 2 February, Bentham argued at length for the adoption of the full plan, but acknowledged that he was willing to proceed on the reduced scale.

On 4 March a House of Commons Committee was appointed to examine the laws pertaining to penitentiaries. Bentham was questioned by the Committee for the first time on 27 March. At the close of the meeting he was handed a note from George Holford, the chairman, asking if he would be prepared to accept 400 male and 300 female convicts, or 700 males and 300 females. After first telling Holford that he could no longer undertake to build Panopticon at his own expense, but that he was still willing to take charge of its supervision, Bentham replied on 1 April to the queries about the female prisoners. He was willing to take the 300 women, but argued that it would be best to have 1,000 men as well. He also accepted the idea of building a temporary Panopticon for the females, which 'would serve as a sort of school of experiment with a view to the permanent one'.

At this stage Bentham had reasonable grounds for optimism. He was disturbed, it is true, by the presence on the Committee of Charles Long, the former secretary to the treasury. Long had been closely involved with earlier Panopticon negotiations, and Bentham saw him as 'Sitting over me as Judge to pronounce himself guiltless and me guilty'. But Bentham had some friends on the Committee who could be expected to counter Long's influence. One was Wilberforce, with whom Bentham seems to have conferred on tactics before his second examination on 1 April. Another was James Abercromby, who approached Bentham in late March and provided him with information on the disposition of his fellow Committee members.

When Bentham wrote again to Holford at the beginning of May, he did so confidently. Moving beyond the immediate issue of his own contract, he addressed the broader question of how to cater for convicts from outside the metropolis. He reviewed a number of options, but recommended that a second Panopticon be built in London. By the time that he next wrote on Panopticon, however, his mood had changed completely. On 17 May Holford presented the Committee with his own report rejecting Bentham's plan. Anxiously trying to rally his forces in an effort to defeat Holford's surprise attack, Bentham wrote to Sir Evan Nepean, an absent Committee member, imploring him to attend the next meeting and voice his support for Panopticon. But on 25 May Bentham learned that the Committee had discussed Holford's report without considering any other proposal. On the 31st the report was presented to the Commons. 'It is very long and I understand very unfavourable to your Contract', Romilly reported the next day. By 4 June Bentham was convinced that the Committee had been a sham. There was, he wrote to Dumont, 'an originally preconcerted plan for setting aside Panopticon, concerted I mean before the appointment of the Committee'. Wilberforce, Bentham suggested darkly, had been a party to this deceit.

Panopticon clearly absorbed much of Bentham's time and energy—emotional as well as physical—but the correspondence once more provides evidence of the breadth of his interests and activities. In April, at the height of the Penitentiary Committee excitement, he was trying to persuade Sir Samuel to join in a plan to fit out a privateer. This, naturally, was to be no ordinary privateer, but, so it seems, a primitive form of submarine. Bentham was also busily involved in writing and giving advice and assistance to Dumont. At the start of the year he sent Dumont the manuscript of what became *Plan of Parliamentary Reform*, and promised to give him a copy of the material on liberty of the press that Miranda had taken to Venezuela. Later in January Bentham told Burr about his progress on the writings on parliamentary reform and the fallacies material, and reported on Dumont's work on the evidence manuscripts. A note of 8 June relating to Bentham's views on colonies was presumably meant to be used by Dumont in another work, though how and where it was employed remain unclear. A letter from Lord Holland in December refers to a further product of Bentham's pen—a paper calling for the adoption of the name 'Brithibernia' to describe the United Kingdom. Holland, who had been sent the paper by Bentham, carefully couched his response in polite and complimentary language, but reminded Bentham that changes of a more fundamental nature would be necessary to conciliate the Irish. Undeterred, Bentham used the term 'Brithibernia' for many years to come.

His communication with Lord Holland points to Bentham's continuing contact with political and legal reformers. In August and early September he exchanged letters with the veteran Major John Cartwright on abuses in New South Wales. In May and June he wrote on delays in the court of chancery and the possible appointment of a third judge, chiding Sir Francis Burdett for his failure to attend the Commons when a motion on chancery delays was introduced on 17 May. But Bentham also concerned himself with law reform abroad, and by far the longest letter of the year is addressed to President James Madison. In it Bentham offered to codify the laws of the United States, or any one of them, by drawing up a complete body of laws or 'Pannomion'.

1812 More than fifty letters have been found for this year, and as in 1811, Panopticon is the most important theme. In January Bentham was worried about the plans to build a road to the Vauxhall Bridge across the Millbank site. In February he was engaged in a tedious correspondence with treasury officials about the deeds and papers relating to Millbank. The treasury, it transpired, had lost the copies of the documents made with Bentham's co-operation in 1811, and now wanted to obtain new ones. The letters for March turn to Romilly's attempts to amend the Penitentiary Bill for Bentham's benefit. The Bill, introduced in January, was in effect the legislative enactment of the Penitentiary Committee's report. A penitentiary for convicts from London and Middlesex was authorized, but not on the Panopticon model. Bentham, for his part, was to receive compensation fixed by arbitrators appointed by himself and the treasury. Pending the final determination of the arbitrators, he would be paid provisional compensation money. Romilly's efforts seem to have been at least partly successful, but Bentham remained bitterly aggrieved. What particularly angered him was the role played by Holford. That the chairman of the committee that had condemned Panopticon should apparently be intimately involved in the new penitentiary that was proposed in Panopticon's place struck Bentham as deeply suspicious.

Yet even at this late stage, he had not given up all hope of seeing Panopticon itself constructed. The Penitentiary Bill received the royal assent on 20 April, but on 18 June Bentham met the new home secretary, Lord Sidmouth, and, in Bentham's view, extracted from him a promise that no further steps would be taken in the 'Penitentiary business' until Bentham had been given the chance to present his case. Contact with Sidmouth was resumed in September. Bentham sent him a letter complaining that Panopticon had been rejected by the Penitentiary Committee without sufficient reason, and enclosed a long paper on its advantages over the proposed new penitentiary, together with copies of his relevant printed and published works.

Bentham's letters to Sidmouth, so full of expectation of assistance, contrast sharply with his correspondence with the treasury, with which he continued to have an unhappy relationship. As the Millbank site had become crown property under the provisions of the Penitentiary Act, Bentham was requested in September to surrender the deeds and papers relating to the land. He replied that many of these documents had already been deposited in the office of woods and forests, and that he was most reluctant to part with others that might be necessary for the pursuit of his compensation claim. Preparations for this claim are the subject of the remaining Panopticon letters for this year. Bentham consulted Romilly in November about a suitable arbitrator, and in

December he submitted a memorial to the treasury praying for payment of the first instalment of his provisional compensation money.

An issue arising from the Panopticon scheme was the construction of Vauxhall Bridge. The problems this posed for Panopticon have already been mentioned. Some of the correspondence for 1812 suggests, however, that Sir Samuel was indirectly connected with the building of the bridge. His letter of 4 January reveals that he was in contact with James Grellier, a manufacturer of Roman cement at Millwall, who was seeking an agreement to supply materials for the bridge. By the time that Bentham wrote to Mill on 25 July Sir Samuel appears to have been more involved, while Grellier was about to sign a contract with the Vauxhall Bridge Company.

As in earlier years, Bentham kept a close eye on political developments. The negotiations to form a new ministry in May and June were reported to him by Mill. Bentham himself gave an account of recent events to John Mulford on 9 July, providing information on Sir Francis Burdett, on Brougham and his part in the revocation of the Orders in Council, and on the *Examiner* and its editor Leigh Hunt. Hunt, Bentham told Mulford, 'has taken me under his protection, and trumpets me every now and then in his paper'. Given this connection, it is unfortunate that the correspondence between Bentham and Hunt for this period is fragmentary and bears primarily on dinner invitations and arrangements for other meetings. Another letter to Mulford, written about 21 December, gives further news of current politics, particularly of Brougham's misfortunes in the 1812 elections and Romilly's eventual return for Arundel.

Close as his relationship with many of the reformers unquestionably was, Bentham was always prepared to work directly with ministers to forward his schemes. Besides contacting Sidmouth about Panopticon, he sent him a draft of the letter to Madison on codification. To this he added a proposal to draw up a penal code for Britain. 'Since the days of Lord Bacon', Bentham announced grandiloquently, 'the sort of offer I am making to your lordship is what has never, from that time to this, been made to any public man'. Nor was Bentham reluctant to approach the court. In July we find him persisting with the 'Brithibernia' proposal, despite Lord Holland's discouragement, and reporting to Mill that Lord St Helens was to mention it to the lord chamberlain, who in turn would inform the Prince Regent.

An interesting minor theme is the early education of John Stuart Mill. Bentham and James Mill communicated on this matter in July, when Mill expressed the hope that John Stuart would be 'a successor worthy of both of us'. John Stuart himself wrote to Bentham at the end of the month, relating his progress in reading Nathaniel Hooke's

Roman History. A letter to Sir Samuel in late September refers again to the young Mill's reading: this time Mitford's *History of Greece* and d'Anville's *Compendium of Ancient Geography* are mentioned as needed for John Stuart's use.

Among the miscellaneous letters, two perhaps deserve particular note. The first is from Henry Rhodes of the land revenues office. Its subject is the occupation by Bentham's father of a small portion of St James's Park next to Queen's Square Place. Bentham's father had agreed to a rent of two guineas per year, but had neglected to pay a penny. Rhodes therefore requested Bentham to settle the twenty-eight years' arrears within a month. Sent in January, while he was in the midst of his struggle with government over Panopticon, this demand must have been particularly irksome to Bentham. Indeed, he could have been forgiven for interpreting it as an act of bureaucratic revenge. But the most curious letter of the year is from Bentham to John Reeves, the superintendent of aliens and commissioner of bankrupts whom Bentham had probably met through Aaron Burr. Dated 21 March, the letter concerns a 'Miss C': almost certainly Amelia Curran, an Irish artist and friend of Burr. She appears to have been a tenant of Bentham's, but the nature of their relationship is difficult to judge.

1813 Bentham's compensation claim for the non-adoption of Panopticon dominates this year's sixty letters. In January the treasury named John Hullock, a lawyer and legal writer, as its arbitrator and threatened Bentham with prosecution if he failed to hand over all the papers concerning Millbank. Bentham explained again that the deeds had been delivered to the office of woods and forests in the previous September, and asked to be allowed to keep the instrument appointing him feoffee, which had been signed by Pitt, 'as a sort of family memorial'.

February saw the extinguishing of Bentham's flickering hopes that Lord Sidmouth might save Panopticon, and thereafter he concentrated on securing his compensation. He finally named his own arbitrator, after much prompting from the treasury, on 25 March. His choice was John Whishaw, a lawyer in Lord Holland's circle. A few days later Bentham reminded the treasury that the second instalment of his provisional compensation was due. The treasury board authorized this to be paid in early April, but took the opportunity to criticize Bentham for his delay in appointing an arbitrator, which had set back the settling of the definitive compensation.

Bentham had certainly taken a long time selecting Whishaw. But at this stage it was Hullock's absence on the northern circuit that was causing the delay. When he returned to London in the middle of May the arbitration started in earnest. The arbitrators met the solicitors for both parties on 1 June and continued their deliberations for more than a month.

On 9 July the award was made. The arbitrators recommended that Bentham should be paid £23,000 clear of all deductions for fees. Five days later, however, Bentham was sent news that must have diminished whatever pleasure he felt at this outcome. The treasury announced that, despite the requirement in the Penitentiary Act that the definitive payment be made a month after the award, the money could not be paid out of the consolidated fund until the end of that quarter. To make up for this, Bentham was promised interest on the sum from 9 August, the date on which it should have been paid, to 10 October, the date on which the treasury now proposed to pay him.

There, after so many years of effort on Bentham's part, the issue might have been expected to rest. But Bentham was unwilling to give in until he had obtained all that he considered he was owed. He sent a memorandum to the treasury on 28 August requesting that the costs he had incurred during the arbitration be taken into account. More than a month later Harrison replied, enclosing the treasury minute rejecting Bentham's supplementary claim. Apparently undeterred, Bentham returned to the fray on 27 October, arguing that the compensation he had been paid fell short of the sum expected by £779. 3*s*. The causes of this underpayment, he explained, were his having to pay higher fees than had been allowed for, and the treasury's failure to include a number of days' interest. The docket on Bentham's letter, together with a note from the receiver of fees at the treasury, indicate that Bentham's dogged determination was rewarded with at least part of the additional money he requested.

While these last shots in the compensation battle were being fired, another long-running struggle was drawing to a close. In early September Bentham received a further demand for the Millbank papers. Again he replied that the deeds had been delivered some months earlier, and that only one relevant document remained in his hands—the greatly-cherished instrument of enfeoffment signed by Pitt. Since this was what the government seemed to want, he agreed, with undisguised reluctance, to deliver it on his return from Barrow Green. Accordingly, on 27 October the last of the papers relating to the land at Millbank was handed over to the treasury.

In view of the quantity of correspondence concerned with Panopticon, it comes as something of a surprise to learn that Bentham had time to consider other matters in 1813. Yet, notwithstanding the considerable distraction of the compensation claim, the letters of this year show that he continued to take a keen interest in the editing and preparation for the press of his writings. On 18 May Dumont wrote to Bentham about the manuscript of what was later published as *Traité des sophismes politiques*, while in July Sir James Mackintosh urged Bentham to soften the tone of '*Swear not at all*', his recently printed work on oaths.

During 1813 Bentham also endeavoured to further his brother's interests. In April he is to be found reading the proofs of Sir Samuel's *Services Rendered in the Civil Department of the Navy*. Three months later Bentham was distributing copies and urging Sir Samuel to offer to construct a new naval establishment at Northfleet, rather than allow the work to be undertaken by his great rival, John Rennie. In July Bentham also discussed the building of Vauxhall Bridge, confirming the impression given in the 1812 correspondence that Sir Samuel had been involved in this project. The building techniques that Sir Samuel had developed at Sheerness in 1811 were to have been used, and the material was to have been supplied by Grellier. By 1813, however, the Company had abandoned the original plan to build a masonry bridge, and had adopted James Walker's cheaper iron design instead. No doubt partly to console Sir Samuel, Bentham told him that Walker's work had proved disappointing to many members of the Company's Committee, adding that only fear 'of the imputation of fickleness' prevented them from returning to the original plan.

Another letter to Sir Samuel, written a few days later, introduces a different topic. Armed with the promise of his definitive compensation money, Bentham was looking for a new summer retreat. When he wrote to Sir Samuel the West Country seemed to be uppermost in his mind, but by September he was in contact with his old friend Lord St Helens, making enquiries about a property near Maidstone owned by Lord Aylesford. In October he was offered a house by St Helens near Dorking, which, St Helens remarked, had the advantage of 'being in the close vicinity of our friends the Romillys'.

A cheerful letter to Sir Samuel and Lady Romilly, arranging a visit later that same month, suggests that Bentham might have found such proximity congenial. At any rate, he appears to have had no desire to distance himself from current political preoccupations, which, as in earlier years, were never far from his thoughts. In April, for instance, he alluded to Queen Caroline's difficulties in a letter to Mrs Susannah Chicheley Koe, and wrote further on the subject to John Mulford. He also informed Mulford of his own contribution to the debate about Caroline. He had three letters, signed 'An Ex-Lawyer', published in the *Examiner* in late March and early April in which he supported Samuel Whitbread's arguments about the impropriety of recording only the answers of witnesses, and not the questions put to them, during the enquiry in 1806 into Caroline's conduct.

Several of the miscellaneous letters are worthy of note, either because they complete old themes, or start new ones. Bentham's offer to draw up a penal code, sent to Lord Sidmouth in June 1812, received a discouraging, or, at best, non-committal, response in December. And even this seems to have been forthcoming only as a result of Bentham's request that Sidmouth return his letter to President Madison. Sidmouth sent back the letter 'with many Thanks' but without further comment. But as this codification offer reached its unsuccessful conclusion, another was just beginning. On Christmas Day Bentham wrote to Sir Samuel telling him of a 'letter designed for Emp. Alexander'. This had been read by Iakov Smirnov, a Russian clergyman in London, and he had recommended various changes. The letter was now about to be sent to Dumont to be put into French. To further the offer, Bentham was also hoping to enlist the services of Pavel Chichagov, the Russian admiral and former navy minister, who had been in contact with the Benthams for many years. Chichagov's standing with the emperor was in some doubt, however, because he had been dismissed from the command of the Russian Danube army following the battle of the Berezina. Chichagov's attempts to exonerate himself were soon to be the subject of a friendly correspondence with Bentham. Another topic touched upon briefly in 1813 but more thoroughly documented in later letters is Bentham's wish to trace his family history. In his letter to Mulford of 21 April he explained that Sir Samuel 'does not care about these things near as much as I do', and continued: 'anything you could favour me with on that head would be very interesting to me'.

Mention should also be made of two figures who were to assume greater importance for Bentham in the future. One is Edward Blaquiere, then a lieutenant in the Royal Navy, who wrote to Bentham in July. The other is Robert Owen, whose New Lanark Mills are discussed as an investment opportunity in a letter from James Mill of 3 December. (For Bentham's involvement in the New Lanark concern see his letter to Owen of 25 March 1815.)

1814 Forty-two letters have been found, and they relate to a wide range of subjects. Panopticon, its fate sealed in 1813, is hardly mentioned, though a communication in December from W. D. Evans, the Manchester magistrate, shows that he and his colleagues were interested in Bentham's proposals.

Far more prominent is Bentham's determination to become a codifier. The opening letters from Dumont, dated 17 and 22 January, are concerned with Bentham's letter to the Emperor Alexander, which Dumont seems to have had a hand in bringing to a finished state. The letter itself apparently was dispatched later that month. In 1814 Bentham made another codification offer, this time to Governor Simon

Snyder of Pennsylvania, after the way had been prepared by Albert Gallatin, the secretary to the United States treasury. It should also be noted that in June Bentham had a two-hour conversation with Prince Adam Jerzy Czartoryski about codification for Poland.

Work on Bentham's writings is frequently discussed in this year's correspondence. In August Bentham asked his brother to send him some papers on geometry—probably those composed by the two of them as long ago as the 1770s and the 1790s—for use in his work on logic, which he described as 'making Giant strides or rather Dragon's brushing in and gathering up with its tail as it goes on every part of the field of thought and action'. The geometry papers were also required for the major enterprise engrossing Bentham's attention in 1814, the writing of what was later published as *Chrestomathia*. The idea of establishing a school for the education of children of the 'middling and higher ranks' of London society seems to have originated with Edward Wakefield and Francis Place. It was adopted by Bentham early in the year, and the book was designed to set out the curriculum and teaching methods to be used. In March and April Bentham was undertaking research for this project, asking William Salisbury about lectures at his Botanic Garden and John Pickton about the commands employed in the Lancasterian school in the Borough Road. In July David Ricardo agreed to subscribe to the proposed Chrestomathic school, apparently after reading a manuscript edition of part of Bentham's work. Bentham continued to gather information, however, and in December he reported to Koe that he was indexing Dr Andrew Bell's *Elements of Tuition*, an influential work on the monitorial system.

Bentham was able to spare time to encourage Chichagov to write a defence of his conduct at the battle of the Berezina. An undated letter, probably written in May, shows that Bentham gave the admiral detailed guidance. Further references to this matter can be found in the correspondence for July. Chichagov, Bentham told Sir Samuel, had 'in pursuance of my advice, brought with him to England an ample provision of documents'. An evening at Queen's Square Place was devoted to Chichagov's reading out a French account of the battle, penned by General Guillaume de Vaudoncourt.

Many of the letters between Bentham and Chichagov mention plans for Chichagov to visit Ford Abbey, Bentham's new country home near Chard. We have already seen that Bentham was searching for a summer residence in 1813, and by early July 1814, after concluding arrangements with the abbey's owner, John Fraunceis Gwyn, Bentham was ready to depart for Devon. He arrived on the 17th and two days later gave Sir Samuel a full and enthusiastic description of the property. During the summer, autumn, and winter months he entertained many friends and acquaintances, including Joseph Hume, Francis Horner, Thomas Northmore, David Ricardo, and Jean-Baptiste Say.

Bentham's time at Ford Abbey was not entirely trouble-free. On 1 July his amanuensis, Henry Tonkin Coulson, was admitted to Queen's College, Cambridge, and he left to start his studies in the following October. This meant that Bentham needed a new secretary, and several of his letters in August and September contain appeals for help in finding a suitable replacement. A potentially more serious problem was the deterioration of the relationship between Bentham and Mill. A letter from Mill, written at Ford Abbey on 19 September, recommends that they see less of each other. 'I cannot help perceiving,' Mill commented, 'either that you are growing more and more difficult to please; or that I am losing my power of pleasing'. Although we have only Mill's account of the episode, it seems that his riding with Hume rather than accompanying Bentham on a walk in the abbey grounds was the immediate cause of the upset. But Mill could not believe that this was the only or even the main reason for Bentham's coolness. That he attributed to their 'too long, and uninterrupted intimacy'.

Bentham's enjoyment of Ford Abbey was probably lessened also by his brother's departure for France, where he and his family were to stay until 1827. There are several indications that Bentham regretted Sir Samuel's leaving. In July Bentham asked him to come to Devon before going to France, explaining that 'it may be the last time we ever spend together'. In August he told Sir Samuel that 'Virtue, supreme virtue' would consist in his keeping a journal 'and sending it off to me sheet by sheet', adding that 'postage whatever it may come to will not be grudged'. That Sir Samuel did write is clear, but none of his letters from France survive for this year. We do have, however, a short letter from Sir Samuel's son, George, written at Le Havre in August, and a much longer and more detailed one from Lady Bentham which was sent in October.

1815 At the start of the year Bentham gave notice of his intention to give up the tenancy of Ford Abbey at the end of the following June. But although he returned to Queen's Square Place in late March, he seems to have changed his mind about quitting the abbey. By the beginning of July he was back in Devon. He remained there for the rest of the year, and in December, judging by an enthusiastic letter he sent to Koe, he concluded a fresh agreement with Gwyn.

None of the twenty-nine letters that have been traced sheds any light on why Bentham decided to stay at Ford Abbey or on his life there. For the most part the correspondence relates to Bentham's work and interests. His codification offers are discussed in several letters. In

January we find him writing to Gallatin about the letter sent to Governor Snyder, and this is also the subject of a communication from Romilly in May. But by this time Bentham's attention had turned to Russia. On 22 April Alexander replied to Bentham's letter of January 1814. He sent Bentham a ring as a token of his approval, and promised to instruct his law commission to seek Bentham's advice. Bentham wrote back in June, returning the ring and criticizing the work and personnel of the law commission. Bentham dismissed as jealous its effective head, Baron Gustav Rosenkampf. 'Ever since he began his career,' Bentham claimed, 'he has beheld in my name an object of terror'. Rosenkampf could therefore hardly be expected to allow Bentham to assist. It would be better if Bentham were permitted to present the emperor with a printed outline code, the details of which could be filled in by local experts trained at a school of legislation. Around the same time, Bentham wrote to Prince Czartoryski, renewing his offer to work on a constitutional code for Poland.

In this letter to Czartoryski, Bentham also mentioned the Chrestomathic school that was to be set up in the garden of his home in Queen's Square Place. He told Czartoryski that if Alexander would send money to the value of the ring Bentham had returned, it would be used for the school. Other correspondence also bears on the proposed school. In July a letter from John Herbert Koe explains how the power of the subscribers to interfere in the running of the school can be circumscribed, and effective control can be vested in the hands of the managers.

The prospects for the Chrestomathic school were, of course, closely tied to the completion of Bentham's *Chrestomathia*. In January Bentham explained to Gallatin that this was nearly finished, and asked him to supply the names of Americans to whom copies could be sent with advantage. In March Bentham was busy with the proofs of the first part of the work and, apparently, the separate tables designed to accompany it. By June he was able to report to Czartoryski that 'everything which it is necessary to publish in the first instance, is either already in print or in the printers hands'. A letter to the printer, John McCreery, reveals that Bentham sent him about half of the manuscript of the second part of *Chrestomathia*—comprising the 'Essay on Nomenclature and Classification'—in the middle of December. In the intervening months Bentham distributed copies of the first part and the tables, and started to receive favourable responses: Jean-Baptiste Say and the comte de Lasteyrie, the French educationalist, both wrote letters of thanks in August.

Some of Bentham's other works and Dumont's recensions are discussed in the letters of this year. In February Admiral Chichagov asked to see Bentham's writings on parliamentary reform, to which

Bentham had been making additions and amendments. Correspondence in September and October relates to the proofs of *A Table of the Springs of Action*, printed by Richard and Arthur Taylor in July and August, but not published until 1817. Earlier, in June, Bentham had sent a copy of his *Essay on Political Tactics* to the French minister of the interior, Lazare Carnot, for the use of the Chamber of Deputies. This work, which had been printed in 1791 but never published, formed merely a part of Bentham's writings on the subject of legislative procedure, and he took the opportunity to announce the imminent appearance of Dumont's much fuller *Tactique des assemblées législatives*.

Bentham's timing was particularly unfortunate. When he wrote his letter Napoleon was still undefeated, but within a short period the Bonapartist regime was to collapse. Carnot and many others were driven from office. Bentham followed these events closely. In July he told Koe that 'Mill and I are mourning the death of all hopes of a free government in France'. Letters in August from Say and Madame Gautier, referring to the so-called 'white terror' that followed the second restoration of Louis XVIII, can have done little to change this view. In the meantime, the future of Poland had become a matter of great interest to Bentham. No doubt his wish to see his codification proposals acted upon lay behind this interest, but he appears to have discussed Polish affairs in a more general way with Chichagov during the summer.

Bentham's correspondence with Chichagov later in the year touches upon other matters. Once again, the writing of Chichagov's exculpatory narrative of the battle of the Berezina is mentioned, and there are references in November to Chichagov's reading of various autobiographies, apparently recommended by Bentham, as a preparation for Chichagov's writing his own 'self-biography', as Bentham termed it. By the following June Chichagov had made some progress, but it is impossible to tell whether the material he had written was included in the versions of his *Mémoires* published in extracts in 1855 and in fuller form in 1860.

1816 Several of the thirty-nine letters provide interesting glimpses of Bentham's life at Ford Abbey, where he stayed for much of the year. On 2 January, for instance, he described to Koe the festivities in the Great Hall over Christmas and the New Year, while in a letter to Aaron Burr of 23 February he wrote of the Abbey as 'uniting antique with modern magnificence', adding, by way of comparison, 'Barrow Green a doghole to it'. Bentham also proudly informed Burr that he played fives every morning, 'beating a boy of 18'. This, it appears, was the nephew of Joseph Hume, James Hume, who had been in Bentham's service since

March 1815 at the latest. In November 1816 Hume left Bentham to gain medical experience prior to taking up a post in the East India Company. Before this, however, another secretary, a few years younger than Hume, had been recruited. He was John Flowerdew Colls, denominated 'sub-reprobate' in the letters to differentiate him from Hume, who had been termed 'his Reprobacy' and now became 'Super-Reprobate'. In August Bentham wrote that Colls was 'deficient in general instruction' but read well as he was now working under Mill's direction. This and other references to Mill's being with Bentham at Ford Abbey suggest that the rift between them revealed in Mill's letter of September 1814 was only short-lived.

Equally interesting on a personal level, are the letters from Bentham's near neighbour at Ford Abbey, John Bragge of Sadborow House. Written between September and December, they are about Bentham's wish to investigate a possible connection with James Bentham, a merchant of Charleston, South Carolina, who had been born in Dorset. Taken together with Bentham's remarks to Mulford in April 1813, to which reference has already been made, these letters show that Bentham took a keen interest in genealogy.

Other items of correspondence tell us a little about Sir Samuel and his family in France. Three letters written in March were occasioned by the death of Samuel Bentham junior. But even though Sir Samuel was evidently distressed by the loss of his eldest and much-loved son, he still found himself able to spare a thought for his brother's financial affairs. He was anxious, he wrote, about Bentham's suffering from a connection with Grellier, whose Millbank cement works have been mentioned earlier. Grellier had by this time acquired a lease on a marble quarry at Babbacombe in South Devon. Bentham, it seems, had invested money in the quarry and had proposed that Sir Samuel do the same. Later in the year there is another allusion to Grellier's enterprises. In July Bentham discussed both Babbacombe and Millwall with Koe—who had also invested money—explaining that James Hume was probably 'going to Mill wall with a view to Partnership'. Even at this stage Grellier was in difficulties, but the damaging consequences of Bentham's connection with him were not to become fully apparent until early the next year.

During 1816 Bentham's hopes for Panopticon revived. In May he wrote both to Sir Samuel and Dumont about the prospects of a Panopticon being built at Bristol and the possibility of another at Manchester. Manchester was probably mentioned because of the interest shown by W. D. Evans and his colleagues, but Bristol offered the better opportunity as a bill was at that time passing through Parliament authorizing the construction of a new prison in the city, and Bentham had a staunch local supporter in Miss Morgan of Clifton, a

Quaker philanthropist. By August no more was being said about Manchester, but a new prospect was exciting Bentham. The Committee for Investigating the Causes of the Alarming Increase of Juvenile Delinquency in the Metropolis, which included among its members Koe, Mill, Ricardo, William Allen, and Basil Montagu, had issued a report critical of the existing system of prison discipline. When the Committee's secretary, Samuel Hoare junior, wrote to Bentham in late July it seems that he asked him about a Panopticon for young offenders. Planning for this 'Juvenile Panopticon' occupied much of Bentham's attention during the following weeks.

Another of Bentham's long-running ambitions was given a boost in 1816. In February Bentham was lamenting the disappointing responses to his various codification offers, but on 8 May President Madison at last replied to Bentham's long letter of 1811. He explained that 'a compliance with your proposals would not be within the scope of my proper functions' and cast doubt on the practicability of Bentham's intentions. Still, he conceded that some reform of American law was certainly necessary, and he expressed the hope that Bentham's labours might be of assistance in this respect. Bentham chose to interpret this as 'highly gratifying' and 'in substance . . . a recommendation to the several states'. His determination to send printed copies of his codification correspondence to leading Americans, he explained to Koe on 19 August, was thus 'confirmed and accelerated'. This material was to form part of the *Papers Relative to Codification and Public Instruction* and its *Supplement* published in 1817.

Bentham's writings and Dumont's recensions are often mentioned in the letters. *Traité des sophismes politiques* and *Tactique des assemblées législatives* appeared at Geneva and Paris in 1816, and in July Brougham told Bentham that the *Sophismes* was 'a very magnificent work indeed'. Bentham, meanwhile, was busy with the second part of *Chrestomathia*, which he described to Dumont in May as 'that commenced and alas! not yet finished work: for, though the brouillon has been gone through, yet I find that the revisal *always* takes me up a much longer time than the brouillon'. By July and August, however, Bentham was giving instructions for the distribution of copies of *Chrestomathia*.

Concurrently, Bentham was researching and composing material for *Church-of-Englandism*. In July he wrote from Ford Abbey that the work was experiencing 'a deplorable delay' because his papers on the subject had not been collected from the London coach and had ended up in Exeter. A series of letters to Koe, written between August and the close of the year, show that Bentham was making enquiries about relevant statutes and seeking information from a wide variety of published sources. By the end of November he was ready to send 'an immense mass of between 40 and 50 pages in two sections' to the printers. In the last months of the year many of the letters to Koe refer also to the two articles 'Defence of Economy Against the Late Mr. Burke' and 'Defence of Economy Against the Right Hon. George Rose', which appeared in *The Pamphleteer* in 1817.

KEY TO SYMBOLS AND ABBREVIATIONS

SYMBOLS

/ In /	In the text this means an alternative version, usually interlinear. In the footnotes it indicates new lines in dockets, addresses etc.
| |	Space left in MS.
[to]	Word supplied by the editor according to sense.
⟨so⟩	Conjectural restoration of mutilated word.
⟨. . .⟩	Word torn away or hidden in binding of MS.
[?]	Reading doubtful.
[. . . ?]	Word proved illegible.

ABBREVIATIONS

Apart from the standard abbreviations, the following should be noted:

Bain:	refers to Alexander Bain, *James Mill: A Biography*, London, 1882.
BL I, II . . . etc.:	refers to the main series of Bentham papers in the British Library, Additional MSS 33537–64, the volumes of which are numbered from I to XXVIII. Thus BL VIII and BL IX, the volumes in the collection most frequently cited in these years, refer to Add. MSS 33544 and 33545.
Bowring:	refers to *The Works of Jeremy Bentham*, published under the superintendence of . . . John Bowring, 11 vols., Edinburgh, 1838–43.
Bowring 'Memoirs':	refers to Bowring's own specially bound copy of the 'Memoirs of Bentham' in vols x and xi of *The Works of Jeremy Bentham*. This copy is interleaved with original manuscripts, and can be found at British Library shelfmark C.61c.15.
Davis:	refers to *The Private Journal of Aaron Burr*, ed. Matthew L. Davis, 2 vols., New York, 1838.
D. R. Bentham MSS:	refers to MSS in the possession of Mr D. R. Bentham of Loughborough, Leicestershire.
Koe MSS:	refers to MSS in the possession of Mrs B. Hyde-Smith of The Old School, Balsham, Cambridgeshire.
PRO CRES:	refers to the papers of the crown estates office, at the Public Record Office.
PRO T:	refers to the papers of the treasury, at the Public Record Office.

KEY TO SYMBOLS AND ABBREVIATIONS

UC: refers to the Bentham papers in the Library of University College London. Roman numerals refer to the boxes in which the papers are placed, Arabic to the leaves within each box.

NOTE

Apart from sources cited in the notes, the following standard works have been in frequent use and have not usually been cited:

Dictionary of National Biography.

Joseph Foster, ed., *Alumni Oxonienses . . . 1715–1886*, 4 vols., Oxford and London, 1887–8.

John and John Archibald Venn, comps., *Alumni Cantabrigienses*, Pt. I (to 1751), 4 vols., Cambridge, 1922–7. Pt. II (1752–1900), 6 vols., Cambridge, 1940–54.

Sir Lewis Namier and John Brooke, *The History of Parliament. The House of Commons 1754–1790*, 3 vols., London, 1964.

R. G. Thorne, *The History of Parliament. The House of Commons 1790–1820*, 5 vols., London, 1986.

J. C. Sainty and J. M. Collinge, comps., *Office-holders in modern Britain*, vols. i–, London, 1972– . In progress.

J. F. Michaud, ed., *Biographie universelle, ancienne et moderne*, 52 vols., Paris, 1811–28.

J. C. F. Hoefer, ed., *Nouvelle biographie générale*, 46 vols., Paris, 1856–67.

Allen Johnson and Dumas Malone, eds., *Dictionary of American Biography*, 20 vols., New York, 1928–36.

Correspondence January 1809 to December 1816

2022

From Étienne Dumont

12 January 1809

Dear Bentham

Si vales, bene est, ego valeo.[2]

Mon hypercritique Ashdonien[3] a lu les *Peines*[4] il en approuve beaucoup l'impression,—quoiqu'il n'en attende pas un succès de vogue. Je voudrois en causer avec vous, si vous me faites une visite antejentaculaire, je vous exhiberai les Mss.

Pouvez-vous me renvoyer le VIIe vol. de l'Edin. review et le No XVIII.[5]—cela n'est point pressé. Vale et me ama.[6]

Jeudi. 12.

2022. [1] BL VIII. 404–5. Autograph. Docketed: '1809 Jany 12 / Dumont Hay Mar⟨ket⟩ / to / J.B. Q.S.P. / J.B. to see *Peines*'. Addressed: 'Jeremy Bentham / Queen Square Place / Westm'.

Pierre Étienne Louis Dumont (1759–1829), Bentham's Genevan editor, had used Bentham's MSS as the basis for *Traités de législation civile et pénale*, 3 vols., Paris, 1802. For Dumont's earlier contact with Bentham see *Correspondence*, iv, v, vi, and vii, as index.

[2] i.e. 'If you are well, that is good, I am well.'

[3] A reference to Dumont's friend the Revd John North (1746?–1818), rector of Ashdon in Essex 1791–1818, for whom see *Correspondence*, v, vi, and vii, as index.

[4] Dumont was at this time preparing his edition of *Théorie des peines et des récompenses*, 2 vols., London, 1811, the first volume of which was to be concerned with punishment.

[5] The *Edinburgh Review*, vii (1805–6), no. xiv, 413–36 contains a review of Robert Forsyth's *The Principles of Moral Science*, London, 1805, a book which offered a critique of utilitarianism. The reviewer defended the idea of happiness as the end of human action. Vol. ix (1807), no. xviii, 462–92 is a review of 'Pamphlets on the proposed Reform of the Court of Session in Scotland.' Bentham and his *Draught of a New Plan for the Organisation of the Judicial Establishment in France*, London, 1790 (Bowring, iv. 285–406) are mentioned on pp. 483–5.

[6] i.e. 'Farewell and love me.'

2023

From Aaron Burr

13 January 1809

Edinburgh, January 13, 1809.

Have patience, and I will pay thee all. Not all, but all that I can. The defects of the head will be redeemed by the warmth of the heart.

I have a good deal of stuff for your amusement, but most of it in a form not transmissible by mail, for want of *frank*. My friend Arbuthnot[2] receives letters free, but cannot frank, which disappoints me, and has saved you some time and expense of eyesight. I lead a life of the utmost dissipation. Driving out every day, and at some party almost every night. Wasting time, and doing many silly things, as you will see. But, in the midst of folly and dissipation, some little, little thing has been effected in the way of business. The friend and correspondent of your tenant[3] enters into my views, and takes an interest in my progress. Has actually written on the subject to a great man now near you.[4]

I am seeking (courting; it is a lady) the influence of another personage. Shall wait here K.'s[5] reply to the above, and then wherever the gods may direct. You will, in the mean time, receive some 'sketches,' etc.

2023. [1] Davis, i. 135. Aaron Burr (1756–1836), attorney-general for New York 1789–91, senator 1791–7, and vice-president of the United States 1801–5. Involved in a scheme to establish a new independent state, including both Spanish territory and southern and western states that would secede from the Union, he was tried for treason but acquitted in 1807. In the following year he sailed for England and until his return to the United States in 1812, travelled extensively in Europe. For his earlier contact with Bentham see *Correspondence*, vii, as index.

[2] William Arbuthnot (1766–1829), secretary to the Board of Trustees of Edinburgh University, later lord provost of Edinburgh, created baronet 1822. See Davis, i. 134.

[3] Bentham's tenant and next-door-neighbour at Queen's Square Place was the Hon. Andrew James Cochrane Johnstone (1767–1834), soldier, politician, and adventurer. On 21 December 1808 Cochrane Johnstone wrote to the lord justice clerk, Charles Hope, Lord Granton (1763–1851) introducing Burr. See Davis, i. 121.

[4] i.e. Henry Dundas, 1st Viscount Melville (1742–1811). Burr started his letter on the night of 13 January, but completed it on the next day, after he had heard that Granton had written to Melville. The relevant entries in Burr's journal are not included in Davis, but see *The Private Journal of Aaron Burr*, ed. William K. Bixby, 2 vols., Rochester, New York, 1903, i. 55–6.

[5] John Herbert Koe (1783–1860), Bentham's secretary and protégé.

Theodosia[6] has written you a note,[7] which I hold, as not being worth postage. That, with her letter to me, will be transmitted in some way. Her health is the same. My American letters contain little more than is found in the newspapers. A chiffré has not yet been translated. Do not despair of me.

A. Burr

2024
FROM ÉTIENNE DUMONT

21 January 1809

Observations[2]

1. Definition—deux chapitres dans les Mss. sur ce sujet-j'ai pris celui que j'ai le mieux entendu.[3]
2. Ch. X. Discretionary power of the Judge—je ne sai où placer ce chapitre—il n'est pas fini—ce n'est qu'un fragment dans le Mss.[4]
3. Mesure des peines et qualités désirables—je garde ces deux chap. que je n'ai pas finis.[5]
4. Forfeitures quasi pécuniaires—c'est un chap. de jurisprudence

[6] Theodosia Burr Alston (1783–1813), only child of Aaron Burr, and wife of Joseph Alston (*c.*1779–1816), the governor of South Carolina 1812–14. She was hoping to translate Dumont's *Traités de législation* into English

[7] Missing. Burr's journal mentions a letter of 3 January which might be this one. Davis, i. 151.

2024. [1] BL VIII. 406–7. Autograph. Docketed: '1809 Jany. 21 / Dumont Haymarket / to / J.B. Q.S.P. / Observations on J.⟨B's⟩ / *Punishment*, occasioned / by Dumonts translation / of it'.

[2] Written after this, in Bentham's hand: 'par Et. Dumont sur la traduction du treatise on Punishment, de Jeremie Bentham'.

The first volume of *Théorie des peines et des récompenses* (later published in revised form in English as 'Rationale of Punishment', Bowring, i. 388–525) was based on Bentham's writings on punishment which can be found in UC cxl–cxliii, clix, and clxvii. Some of these MSS were written in French in the 1780s, but most are in English and date from the previous decade. They presented Dumont with considerable problems, for, as he explained in his introduction: 'Ils m'offraient souvent, sur le même sujet, différents essais dont il fallait prendre la substance pour les réunir en un seul. Je n'avais, pour me diriger dans quelques chapitres, que des notes marginales.'

[3] 'Définitions et Distinctions' were the subjects of the first chapter of the first book of *Théorie des peines* as published.

[4] 'Choix de la peine—latitude à laisser aux juges' was to be the eleventh chapter of the first book.

[5] These became the fifth and sixth chapters respectively of the first book.

generale—est-il nécessaire au sujet?—il est d'une metaphysique ardue.[6]

5. Forfeitures affectant la condition—caret dans le Mss.[7]
7. Analyse des maux resultant de ces forfeitures—je garde l'article du Mss., je ne l'ai pas traduit.[8]
7. Peines religieuses—Examen—R. conseille la suppression de ces deux chapitres.[9]
8. Corruption du sang—caret dans le françois.[10]
9. Represailles—ce n'est qu'un fragment—je ne sai où placer.[11]
10. L'appendice est de la Jurisprudence Angloise, très important, mais très difficile à traiter en françois.[12]

Dans les *Principes* V. II. c. VII. il est question de peines *pénitentielles.*[13]—il n'en est pas fait mention ici. cette classification n'étoit pas bonne, mais elle étoit populaire—il me paroit manquer quelque direction sur les petites peines à appliquer aux délits inférieurs.

11. Il y a quelques morceaux intitulés *fragments.* Ce sont des pierres d'attente qui n'ont pas encore trouvé leurs places.

2025

From Aaron Burr

23 January–1 February 1809

Edinburgh, January 23, 1809.

This sheet of paper is large enough in truth, but how and with what it will be filled, I am as unconscious as the whiskey-bottle on my table. I set out, as you know, resolved to write to you daily, and

[6] 'Peines pécuniaires et quasi-pécuniaires. Déchéances de propriété' formed the fourth chapter of the third book.

[7] 'Déchéances affectant la condition' became the fifth chapter of the third book.

[8] 'Maux inévitables dérivés de la peine' became the second chapter of the fourth book.

[9] 'R' was probably Sir Samuel Romilly (1757–1818), who had known Dumont since 1781. Romilly was solicitor-general 1806–7 and at this time MP for Wareham. In the published work there is ony one chapter that deals with religious punishments; the second of book five, entitled 'Excommunication'.

[10] The fifth chapter of the fourth book, 'Peines transitives', contains a discussion of 'corruption du sang'. Significantly, Dumont wrote in his introduction: 'Pour le quatrième livre de la *Théorie des peines*, j'ai été réduit à rassembler et mettre en oeuvre des fragments'.

[11] 'Du Talion' formed the eighth chapter of the first book.

[12] Possibly material that appeared in the fifth book of the published version, described thus in a footnote: 'Ce livre se rapporte principalement à la jurisprudence anglaise.'

[13] 'Peines pénitentielles' are discussed in *Traités de législation civile et pénale*, ii. 412 ('Principes du Code Pénal', III. vii. 5).

2025. [1] Davis, i. 166–70.

to write you everything, and the resolution has been pretty well kept; but, in the first place, I had commenced on too large a scale (a sheet is enclosed by way of sample); and then, on my arrival, the disappointment in the franking matter was fatal to the execution of my plan. Yet on every evening I have written you something. Every hour of every day I have conversed with you. In solitude, in company, at dinners, routes, balls—during the discussion of things the most remote from all association with you, you appear and look me in the face, but eminently in the midst of my follies. Why is it so? You are present; yet always with a look so benign and complacent that cheers; sometimes, perhaps, admonishes. Once, indeed, though still a smile, there was a look of inquiry and surprise. 'What the d—l do you do here?'

Since leaving London I have not written a letter to any human being, save that to Koe,[2] and three lines of business to Graves,[3] except trifling matters of courtesy in this vicinage. Not a line to any American friend by the last packet; not even to Theodosia. In my state of nullity I wish to be forgotten till I can rise to view in a shape worthy of the hopes of my friends. This, however, is not applicable to you nor to Theodosia, and yet I am silent to you both, as far as either of you know! And now, just returned from passing two hours, intensely occupied in researches into *Natural History* (zoology), sublimed and tranquillized by the acquisition of much useful and curious knowledge, on this Tuesday night, being the 23d of January, anno dom. 1809, at the silent and hallowed hour of *one*——nay, then, it must be Wednesday the 24th, at one A. M. What a fatal interruption to a fine poetic sentence, which was to tell you, what could never have been otherwise known, that I was writing to you. So the great Virgil begins, 'I am going to sing you a song;' which all the world admires.[4] But at this rate, this vast surface may be filled without telling you anything. As you seem a little impatient to know something of where I am and what about, you may skip over all till the next line. Very practicable in Ireland.

I was provoked to this understanding by a conversation lately had, of which you were the subject. It has been my daily practice, not avowing my own opinions, still less my feelings, to throw out, incidentally, something to sound. When I find a man who knows nothing of you, which (with blushes be it said) has sometimes happened, I pity him; but when one, pretending a knowledge of your works, uses 'very able, very ingenious,' or any such trite epithets, I

[2] Burr wrote to Koe on 13 January. See Davis, i. 134.

[3] William Graves, merchant and broker of 18 Wallbrook, London.

[4] *Aeneid*, i. 1; *Georgics*, i. 5.

hate him, and am disposed to quarrel. This has often happened. We were fifteen at table. Two physicians, a judge, four advocates, seven ladies (women are here a part of society), and one anomaly, the Moheigungk.[5] I had talked a good deal, and apparently to the satisfaction of the hearers. Not to satiate, and with other views, I changed the subject to Scotch reform.[6] (Point de physique.) How amiable was that trait; how it has sunk into my heart! Where was the friend who would have had the candour, the sensibility the boldness? Mr. Ferguson, an advocate of respectable standing (author of a book on national defence), without prompting, spoke of you and your work on that subject (Scotch reform) in terms which pleased me.[7] The occasion being suitable, and the company in good-humour with me, 'I made a speech.' Ferguson supported me. Most of those present took a list of your works, etc., and I came home in good humour with myself. F. called on me the next morning. While we were sitting together, Sir Hay Campbell, formerly president of the court of sessions, and now one of the committee on the reform, came in.[8] Ferguson, being full of you, began to talk. Told Sir Hay that your pamphlet had given him quite a new view of the subject, and said many handsome things, and expressed a very strong wish that your attention could again be called to it.

Tuesday, January 31. You will not be able to conceive any good reason for this intermission of *eight days*. To account for it satisfactorily might consume eight more. Leaving, therefore, for the present, my reputation to its fate, we proceed. The lord advocate, M. P. for Edinburgh, has sought me out.[9] If there were time, I think we should become friends. He professes to be one of your admirers. Says that, as often as he has been in London he has in vain endeavoured

[5] i.e. Burr. In an earlier letter (2020, *Correspondence*, vii) Burr had referred to himself as 'Gilblass Mohsagungk de Manhattan'. Gil Blas was the central character of the picaresque novel *The Adventures of Gil Blas of Santillane* by Alain René Le Sage (1668–1747), first published in 1715–35 and translated into English in 1749. The Moheigunk Indians had inhabited Manhattan Island.

[6] Bentham's *Scotch Reform; Considered with Reference to the Plan Proposed in the Late Parliament, for the Regulation of the Courts and the Administration of Justice in Scotland*, London, 1808 (Bowring, v. 1–53).

[7] James Ferguson (1769–1842), Scottish judge and legal writer, the author of *Letters upon the establishment of the Volunteer Corps and Domestic Military arrangements of Great Britain*, Edinburgh, 1806.

[8] Sir Ilay (Hay was probably a mistranscription by Davis) Campbell (1734–1823), solicitor-general for Scotland 1783, lord advocate 1783–9, lord president of the court of session 1789–1808.

[9] The lord advocate 1807–16 was Archibald Campbell-Colquhoun (d. 1820). He was MP for Elgin Burghs (Edinburgh is probably a mistranscription by Davis) 1807–10 and for Dumbartonshire 1810–20.

to get access to you. I rather indiscreetly tendered my services to procure him that honour when he should be next in London (a fortnight hence). The vanity of pretending influence with the great is quite an English foible, and I hope venial. In justice to myself, it must be added, that the overture was qualified with reservations regarding your health, your habits, and the importance of your time. Before you decide against the interview, I must be heard.

You have several new female friends here. Among them one a little prone to writing, who may possibly assail you in that way. If so, and you should design to reply, which I have rendered extremely doubtful, say nothing of A. B., unless, if necessary, in those commonplace terms, of which you may borrow for the occasion from your tenant,[10] who has a fine collection. Many of the ladies of this place are enthusiastically engaged in promoting benevolent institutions, and it is on these topics that I have gained importance with them, by strutting about adorned with shreds stolen from you; but without giving you any sort of credit—though I am greatly afraid they will find me out when they come to read. Now for something of self. In truth, this has been the principal subject all along; but now more exclusively.

I have got on pretty well here, and with rather more discretion than usually falls to my lot, not having said or done, publicly, more than twenty outrageously silly things. Avoiding all ugly, naughty topics. From any man, save one, if I cannot vanquish, I can escape. In the hands of that one, I am just what Theodosia is in mine. This was perceived after the first two hours; and seeing no retreat, nor anything better to be done, I surrendered, tame and unresisting, to be disarmed, stripped, hacked, hewed, dissected, skinned, turned inside out, at the will and mercy of the operator. Much good may it do him.

My late friend Charles Williamson[11] was greatly esteemed by persons of the first distinction in this region, and had their confidence. He had talked much of me, and had done full justice. Full justice, allowing the utmost claims of vanity. The gentleman to whom your new tenant wrote in my behalf has entered into my concerns with intelligence and with zeal.[12] He has written to Lord

[10] Cochrane Johnstone.

[11] Charles Williamson (1757–1808), American land promoter. Born in Scotland, he resumed his allegiance to the crown in 1803 and later contacted the British government about Burr's plans to invade Mexico. In 1808 he was sent on a mission of trade and goodwill to the Spanish West Indies, but contracted yellow fever and died on the return voyage.

[12] i.e. Charles Hope, Lord Granton.

Moira,[13] and has received answers of an auspicious tenour. You may thank the new tenant for me, if you think proper, though, in fact, his friend made advances, and asked me to his house before I had announced myself. Yet I have no very confident hopes. This friend of the tenant says I must be off; that I shall be in demand yonder. I have a further little purpose in view, auxiliary to the same object. When that shall fail or be accomplished, I go. You will hear from me again from this place, but you cannot write to me. The residue of my projected tour is for the present given up. Within four or five days I shall be on my way to London, by sea or land.

Theodosia's note is enclosed, for I have found a frank. I could choke her for her 'one of.' I never did class you with any man or description of men; but poor, dear little soul, it is a new evidence of debility. Indeed, I almost despair of her recovery. The capture of the Hopewell[14] is, on many accounts, vexatious; but distressing, as it will prevent her from receiving, perhaps until this day, my advice as to a voyage to England. Her letters shall be sent too, if I can find them. Only see with what enthusiasm she has caught the idea of translating, etc. I said nothing of it; have not given the remotest hint or allusion. It has originated wholly with herself. If she were well, she would do more justice to the original than any one who is likely to engage in the task.

February 1. After half an hour's search, Theodosia's note to you cannot be found. It will appear in the general scrutiny which is to take place a day or two hence. Her letter of December is sent, and, by way of indemnity, a note from Madame d'Auvergne.[15] My frank has come in, and this must now go.

A. Burr

[13] Francis Rawdon-Hastings, 2nd Earl of Moira (1754–1826), later 1st Marquis of Hastings, soldier and politician. A general since 1803, he had served as commander-in-chief in Scotland 1802–6 and as master general of the ordnance 1806–7. He was a close friend of the Prince of Wales.

[14] The American ship on which Graves had sent letters to Burr, and Burr to his daughter. For the capture of the *Hopewell* see Koe to Burr, 17 January 1809, Davis, i. 136.

[15] These letters are missing. Madame d'Auvergne is identified by Davis (i. 149) as Leonora Sansay, Burr's mistress. She was the wife of Louis Sansay, a French-born merchant resident in America. See *Political Correspondence and Public Papers of Aaron Burr*, ed. Mary-Jo Kline and Joanne Wood Ryan, 2 vols., Princeton, 1983, i. 317, ii. 703.

2026

From William Huskisson

26 January 1809

Sir

I am commanded by the Lords Commissioners of His Majestys Treasury to desire you will transmit to me forthwith, your Account and Vouchers for the Expenditure of the sum of £12.000. Issued to you in November 1799. for the purchase of Ground for erecting a Penitentiary House for Convicts, in Order that their Lordships may give such Directions for the Examination thereof as they may think fit.

I am
Sir
Your most obedt Servant
W. Huskisson.

Treasury Chambers.
26. Janry 1809

Jeremy Bentham Esqr.

2027

To William Huskisson

28 January 1809 (Aet 60)

Queen Square Place Westmr
28 Jany 1809.

Sir

In obedience to the commands, signified to me on the part of the Lords Commissioners of his Majesty's Treasury, by your letter, dated the 26th but not till this day delivered,[2] in which I am required 'to transmit to you forthwith my account and Vouchers for the Expenditure of the sum of £12,000, issued to me for the purchase of ground for erecting a Penitentiary House for Convicts', what I have to say is as follows, viz.

2026. [1] BL VIII. 408. In the hand of a copyist, but autograph signature. Docketed: '1809 Jan 26. / Panopt. / Huskission Treasury / to / J.B. Q.S.P. / For account of the £12,000.'

William Huskisson (1770–1830) was at this time secretary to the treasury.

2027. [1] PRO CRES 2/675. In the hand of a copyist, with the exception of the valediction, signature, and Huskisson's name and address. Autograph draft at UC cxxii. 103–4.

[2] Letter 2026.

In strictness of speech, no such sum or any sum was issued to me at any time for that purpose, and therefore it is that I have neither '*account*' nor 'vouchers' to produce for the expenditure of it.

True it is, that, according to my recollection, a *form of receipt* was signed by me, acknowledging the receipt of that sum: which document (I make no doubt) is forthcoming, and may be obtained by application made from the proper quarter to the proper hands: equally true it is, that the sum so received can not but have been applied to the purpose abovementioned, being the purpose to which at the issuing it was destined.

Signing a document by which acknowledgment was made of my having received a sum of money which in fact had not come into my hands, was unquestionably an irregularity; nor did its being so escape my observation at the time. But, at the time in question, I had experienced too many difficulties in my endeavours to bring the transaction to a conclusion, to be disposed to make of myself any unnecessary addition to the number, on a point of mere form, from which no mischief or inconvenience in any shape could result.

It was at the instance, and at the Chambers, of *Mr White*,[3] at that time Solicitor to the Treasury, that I wrote *that* signature: Of that document; which at this time can not but be in the possession of that gentleman, or in some other proper hands, my *charge* in respect of the sum in question is (I presume) composed.

My *discharge* would (I suppose) consist—in the first place, of a separate instrument of *receipt*, for that sum, signed by the Marquis of Salisbury,[4] the noble Lord of whom the purchase in question was made: in the first instance, (I say) of *that* document, and *subsidiarily* (I mean supposing the *other* not forthcoming) (I presume) of the instrument of *conveyance*, on the back of which the receipt of that sum, in the character of purchase money, is indorsed. If any *separate* receipt was taken, as in respect of the stamp duty (besides the demand for it in the character of a Voucher, and to be kept as such, in custody different from that of the conveyance) I should rather expect to find it was, it must have been taken from his Lordship by the said Mr White; in whose possession, or that of some other proper person, I can not but presume it would now be found to be. The instrument of conveyance, dated on the 12 of October 1799, is in *my* custody, and ready to be *produced* if deemed necessary, which I should not expect it to be. But, as to the *transmitting* it to you, which is what an obedience to the *letter* of your commands, if

[3] Joseph White (d. 1815), treasury solicitor 1794–1806.

[4] James Cecil, 7th Earl and 1st Marquis of Salisbury (1748–1823), who sold his Millbank estate in October 1799.

applied to that document, would require, I flatter myself it is what would not be regarded by you as either necessary or proper: at least, if the fate of this document would in that case have to follow that of some other documents which I had lately occasion to send in to the *Audit Office* to serve as Vouchers, on the occasion of an Account connected with the one now in question: on which occasion, having applied for the temporary return of certain of those documents, (being Books of Account that had been kept for a *different* purpose) I received for answer (14 July 1808) that it was 'contrary to the rules of that Office to part with any Vouchers that had been delivered in support of an Account.'[5]

I am, with all respect,
Sir,
Your most obedient Servant
Jeremy Bentham.

W. Huskisson Esqr:
Secretary to the Treasury.

2028
From Aaron Burr

2 February 1809

Edinburgh, February 2, 1809.

Within an hour after forwarding my despatches of the 1st instant,[2] I had the good fortune to finish, to my satisfaction, that little negotiation mentioned as the pretence for delay. And now, having no other plausible excuse to offer to myself; and as well my right honourable friend,[3] as the brother of my deceased friend,[4] urging my departure as a thing of moment—I obey. Yet of that importance I believe not one word. Nevertheless, I go; to-morrow, adieu to Edinburgh. One day is allowed to see the minstrel[5] at York; and, if Cambridge should not entice me out of the road, I shall take tea with you on Wednesday evening. But, before writing, I must set

[5] See letters 1977 and 1979, *Correspondence*, vii.

2028. [1] Davis, i. 155–6.

[2] Letter 2025.

[3] Probably the lord justice clerk. Granton had urged Burr to go to London on 20 January. See Davis, i. 146.

[4] David Williamson, Lord Balgray (b. 1761), a prominent attorney in Edinburgh and the sheriff of Sterling.

[5] Presumably a mistranscription of 'minster'.

to work to pack up, assort and burn papers, etc. During the which operation, that little billet doux will undoubtedly be found. No, no, I can never see your face till that is found. From gallantry, you know, you must rave, and storm, and scold. This must be forestalled, and I go forthwith to work.

It is found; but after such labour! You, who have seen the beautiful order observed in a certain room in Q.S.P., may form some judgment. I have gone over, and burned or filed, and marked every paper in my possession; and this little billet was the last that came to my hands or view. Again I have heaped some maledictions on that '*one of*.' I have cut out of her letter to me one sentence. The whole is too long to be sent. I know you would read it, and it would only fatigue your eyes and waste your time. It will be always at your command. During the search, however, I made a very important discovery. K.'s letter of the 17th January was enclosed in a little piece of dirty printed paper.[6] Not suspecting that anything could be written on such a scrap, it was thrown aside, and it is surprising that it was not thrown into the fire. It was fortunately preserved, and it informs me that you have written me a long letter under cover to Dr. C.[7] How the receipt of that letter would have elevated and cheered me. The mere knowledge that such a letter had been written would have been consoling. I have a good mind to go round by Oxford to get it; but there will be time on the road to resolve. The same scrap mentions a letter enclosed to me by your friend, an M. P. That letter was received, and, after some hesitation, delivered. I never formed an acquaintance with so much reluctance.[8] I had resolved to hate him. After seeing the sort of man, I formed other views. We have become familiar acquaintances. If he should again have occasion to speak of one Jeremy Bentham, I am greatly deceived if it shall not be with more reverence.

You will not hear from me again before my arrival in London. I was about to write you some idle incidents, but this paper-hunting has consumed so much time that it is now one o'clock. I have half a dozen little notes of courtesy to answer, and all my baggage to pack up. In some of our walks, you will hear all that is worth hearing. You perceive that I intend reforming.

A. Burr.

[6] Koe's second letter of 17 January is published in Davis, i. 138.

[7] i.e. Dr. Septimus Collinson (1739–1827), Lady Margaret professor of divinity and provost of Queen's College, Oxford.

[8] Koe's letter mentions a letter directed under cover to Arbuthnot introducing Burr to Francis Jeffrey (1773–1850) later Lord Jeffrey, editor of the *Edinburgh Review*, but does not identify the writer.

2029

From Étienne Dumont

6 February 1809

Mon cher Bentham

Voilà un chapitre oublié et retrouvé par hazard[2]—je ne le vois pas dans la table des matières—il manque aussi l'*Examen* de ces peines—je ne sai si cela se trouve dans le Mss. original[3]—

Envoyez-moi, je vous prie, *Principles of morals and jurisprudence*, il faut que je revoye les deux chapitres *Properties* of a lot etc and *proportions*[4]—je ne vous le garderai que peu de jours. J'ai retrouvé mon exemplaire que je croyois perdu, mais il est entre les mains de Montagu,[5] et j'aurai peine à le ravoir.

Tout à vous

Mes compliments à Mr Koe. Je lui serai très obligé de me renvoyer mes mss, *Tactique des assemblées politiques*[6]

Lundi

2029. [1] BL VIII. 415. Autograph. Docketed; '1809 Feb 6 / Dumont Haymarket / to / J.B. Q.S.P. / For Tactique and Introd. / Sent.'

[2] i.e. a chapter of what was to become *Théorie des peines*. For Dumont's earlier communication with Bentham on this work see letters 2022 and 2024.

[3] It is unclear which 'examination' Dumont meant. Bentham's MSS on punishment include several examinations of various penalties. See UC clix. 148–9, 176–7, 193–204, 231–4, 235–6.

[4] Chapters XIV and XV of *Introduction to the Principles of Morals and Legislation*, London, 1789.

[5] Basil Montagu (1770–1851), legal writer and advocate of bankruptcy law reform, editor of *The Works of Francis Bacon*, 16 vols., London, 1825–36. He was to have translated Dumont's *Traités de législation civile et pénale* into English. See letter 1939 and n. 3, *Correspondence*, vii.

[6] Bentham's *Essay on Political Tactics* had been printed but not published in London in 1791. This formed only a portion of the whole work. Dumont was preparing a French version which appeared as *Tactique des assemblées législatives*, 2 vols., Geneva and Paris, 1816.

2030

From Lord Holland

18 February 1809

Dear Sir,

I am much afraid you must have thought me both negligent and rude, in neither promoting the object of your letter, nor answering it for so long a space of time; but the fact is, I have had no intercourse with the persons in government here till I arrived at Seville; and one of my first objects was, to place your petition in the hands of D^{a}. G^{r}. M. de Jovellanos,[2] than whom it is impossible to find a man more friendly or liberal, or whose protection and friendship can be more creditable. He espoused your cause most eagerly, as he is not unacquainted with your character, acquirements, and merits. Though he is the leading man of the Junta, there is, unfortunately, so little of a *lead* in the Government here, that he was unable to give an explicit answer, or to undertake to secure your permission to go to Mexico without any difficulty and hinderance. Indeed, I have taken his advice in the business, and presented a petition in your name to the Government, which Jovellanos was good enough to draw up himself; and if the answer should, unluckily, be delayed till I have left Seville, he will take the trouble of forwarding it to you.

He conceived that the character of *Jurisconsultus*, and writer on criminal law, might possibly be considered as a bad recommendation; and has, therefore, mentioned those circumstances as accidental, and ventured to ground your petition on your love of botany, and of antiquities, and on the precarious state of your health. I hope you will excuse me for dwelling so much on those trifles in the petition.—In representing your knowledge on any subject, one is very safe of finding sufficient to justify one's representations; but I hope that I have no ground for dwelling on your infirmities, but the goodness of the argument which it affords.

2030. [1] Bowring, x. 447. Henry Richard Vassall Fox, 3rd Baron Holland (1773–1840), Whig politician, lord privy seal 1806–7, chancellor of the duchy of Lancaster 1830–4, 1835–40.

[2] Ramirez-Gaspar Melchor de Jovellanos (1744–1811), Spanish reformer, professor of history and language at the University of Madrid, deputy for Seville 1767–78, minister of grace and justice 1797–8. Appointed a minister again in 1808 he declined to serve because of ill-health, but was described by Bentham in November of that year as 'an active member of the small body, the *Supreme Junta*'. See letter 2013, *Correspondence*, vii.

Lady Holland[3] and Mr Allen[4] are much flattered by your kind recollection,—and I hope, my dear Sir, you are convinced that it will be a source of lasting gratification to me, if I can contribute on this, or any other occasion, to promote your wishes, and to render the life of a man so useful to the world as yours, either longer or more comfortable than it would otherwise be.—I am, ever sincerely yours.

2031

From Peter Mark Roget

23 February 1809

Dear Sir,

Upon mature deliberation I have concluded to decline the offer in question. I am, for the present, quite nailed; having formed engagements here from which I cannot recede. A thousand thanks for your goodness in thinking of me.

Your's very faithfully
P. Roget.

[3] Elizabeth Vassall Fox, Lady Holland (1771–1845), married Lord Holland in 1797, three days after the dissolution of her marriage to Sir Godfrey Webster, bt.

[4] Dr John Allen (1771–1843), physician and political writer, from 1801 Lord Holland's assistant and a permanent resident at Holland House. See letter 1899, *Correspondence*, vii.

2031. [1] BL VIII. 422–3. Autograph. Docketed: '1809 Feb 23 / Roget | | Street [. . .] Square / to / J.B. Q.S.P. / Declines Mexico'. Addressed: 'Jeremy Bentham Esq. / Queen Square Place / Westminster.' Postmarks: '4 o'clock / 24 FE / 1809 ⟨. . .⟩' and 'Two Py Post / Unpaid Totten ⟨. . .⟩'.

Dr Peter Mark Roget (1779–1869), physician and compiler of the *Thesaurus*, 1852, nephew of Sir Samuel Romilly. For Bentham's earlier contact with Roget, see *Correspondence*, vi and vii, as index. This letter appears to be a response to an invitation to accompany Bentham to Mexico. No letter making such an offer seems to have survived, but the subject might have been discussed at a meeting Bentham arranged with Roget and Burr for 15 November 1808. See letter 2015, *Correspondence*, vii. In Burr's journal, however, no mention of Roget's presence is made: instead Burr noted that he and Bentham 'conversed of tatooing, and how to be made useful; of infanticide; of crime against Nature, etc., etc.' Davis, i. 88.

2032

To Aaron Burr

6 March 1809 (Aet 61)

Q.S.P. 6 March 1809.

Dumont has been applied to, and has brought himself, though not without some reluctance, to part with *Tactique* out of his hands.[2] The burthen which the shoulders of Etienne Dumont sunk under, and those of Jeremy Benthram shrunk from, is now waiting for those of Hercules Burr, on which it will sit as lightly as little Jesus, on those of Great St Christopher, in the cathedral of Notre Dame.

Meanwhile, and without any need either of prophecy or telescope, I behold Hercules with a distaff in his hand, spinning out—he would kill *me*, were I to say *killing*—time; now lying, now kneeling, at the feet of his Omphale.[3]

Logic and philosophy he is learning from a spick-and-span, spick and Span new horn-book. Life, no longer 'a *jest*', as Pope and Gay would persuade us,[4] is now a span, as somebody else, without much need, has taken the trouble to inform us.[5] *Ergo*, (says Logic,) they are, Life and Span are convertible terms: the *things* themselves, (quoth Philosophy) things of equal value: and so well-matched (adds Algebra) that, of each without the other, the value is = 0.

Such is the lesson learning and conning over, for the thousand-and-oneth time, by ever youthful Hercules. Meantime the midnight lamp is burning here in view, with the *Tactique* papers spread out before it. Say—tell us—what shall be done with them? Will the eye of Hercules vouchsafe to visit them? or shall they be consigned to the hands of the housemaid, to light fires?

2032. [1] Historical Society of Pennsylvania, Philadelphia. Autograph. Docketed: 'J. Bentham 6 Mar. 1809'. Addressed: 'To / P. Bartlett Esq / Little Gaddesden / Herts / A.B.' Postmark: 'MR / 6 / 1809'. Printed in Davis, i. 180. 'A.B.' in the address indicates that the letter was intended for Burr. Patrick Bartlett, who is mentioned frequently in Burr's journal at this time, was one of the friends with whom Burr stayed at Little Gaddesden.

[2] See letter 2029 and n. 6.

[3] Omphale was the Lydian queen whom Hercules served as a punishment for the murder of Iphitus. See Apollodorus, *Bibliotheca*, II. vi. 2–3.

[4] The English poets Alexander Pope (1688–1744) and John Gay (1685–1732). Bentham was probably thinking of Pope's *Epistles*, II. i. 18: 'The glory, jest, and riddle of the world', and Gay's 'My Own Epitaph', from *Poems on Several Occasions*: 'Life is a jest, and all things show it.'

[5] i.e. Shakespeare. See *Othello*, II. iii. 64. The same phrase was used by Sir John Davies (1569–1626), the law officer and poet, in his *Nosce Teipsum*, xlv.

2033

From Aaron Burr

8 March 1809

Little Gaddesden, March 8, 1809.

Your billet made *us* laugh. Since life is but a span, can anything better be done than to fill up that span with pleasure? I lead here a strict idle life, so congenial to savages. Lounge, smoke, read a little nonsense, sometimes walk or talk with the squaws. On my return to town, if I can summon the force to attempt anything useful, I will start myself off for eight days, and devote them to *Tactique*, but without the hope of adding one useful idea.

A. Burr

2034

From Étienne Dumont

March 1809

Nous avons mal combiné—il faut donner un exemplaire relié—je vous envoye les deux 1ers volumes[2]—il n'y a rien de si aisé pour un relieur que d'inserer dans le premier les titres et le discours preliminaire que vous tirerez de votre exemplaire.

2033. [1] Davis, i. 180–1.

2034. [1] BL VIII. 424–5. Autograph. Docketed: '1809 Mar / Dumont Hay Market / to / J.B. Q.S.P.' Addressed: 'Mr Bentham'. Bentham wrote at the top of this letter: 'March 1809 / With Dumont Principes for Mexico'.

[2] The first two volumes of *Traités de législation civile et pénale.*

2035

From Aaron Burr

1 April 1809

London, April 1, 1809[2]

I should like to know the author of 'The Progress and Practice of a Modern Attorney.'[3] Could it not be learned at Stationers' Hall? If so, ask Tom le Grand[4] to make the inquiry. It is written with feeling, with good sense, and with knowledge of the subject. Pity that the names of the parties were not given. The pamphlet is sent as an evening's pastime.

A. Burr.

2036

To Francisco de Miranda

1 April 1809 (Aet 61)

Mr. Bentham's compliments to Genl. Miranda and returns him with many thanks the Map of Columbia—Du Pons[2]—the Map of Mexico and the Mexican Guide.

2035. [1] Davis, i. 193.

[2] In Davis '1808': clearly a typographical error.

[3] *The Progress and Practice of a Modern Attorney; exhibiting the Conduct of Thousands towards Millions! To which are added, the different stages of a Law Suit, and attendant costs, with Instructions to both Creditors and Debtors; together with Select Cases of Individuals who have suffered from the Chicane of Petty fogging Attornies, and the Oppression which flows from the present law practice: concluding with Advice to young Tradesmen*, London [1794?]. The author was Alexander Grant.

[4] Thomas Coulson junior (1791–1813), at this time Bentham's amanuensis.

2036. [1] Archivo del General Miranda, Academia Nacional de Historia, Caracas, vol. xvi. fo. 1. In Koe's hand. Printed, with various errors, in *Archivo del General Miranda*, 24 vols., Caracas and Havana, 1929–50, xxii. 256.

Francisco Sebastian de Miranda y Rodriguez de Espinola (1750–1816), born in Caracas, served in the French army during the American war of independence and the French Revolutionary war, reaching the rank of general. He spent much time trying to enlist European support for the liberation of Latin America, and in 1806, with British help, landed in Venezuela. His forces were overpowered, however, and Miranda was compelled to withdraw. At this time he was living in Grafton Street, London.

[2] François Raimond Joseph de Pons (1751–1812) was the author of *Voyage à la partie occidentale de la terre-firme dans l'Amérique meridionale, fait pendent les années 1801, 1802, 1803 et 1804*, Paris, 1806.

If Genl. M. has done with it Mr. B. would be much obliged to him for *Jovellanos.*[3] It will always of course be at the Genls command if he should ever wish to look at it again.

1 Apl
Queen Sq Place
To Genl Miranda.

2037

From Étienne Dumont

7 April 1809

Si vous êtes libre aujourd'hui, mon cher Bentham, je serai chez vous à cinq heures; si vous ne l'êtes pas, il nous faut prendre un jour fixe, par example, mercredi, sans quoi nous aurons plus de peine à nous rassembler qu'un congrès de Ratisbonne.[2] Adieu.

Dimanche

2038

From Étienne Dumont

8 April 1809

Voilà qui est très bien—j'aime l'homme—il dit son sentiment à voix haute et intelligible—il n'est pas comme des *tièdes* que je connois—des admirateurs honteux—qui vous disent vingt belles

[3] Jovellanos had written *Informe de la Sociedad Económica de esta Corte al Real y Supremo Consejo de Castilla en el expediente de ley agraria*, Madrid, 1795, which appeared in translation as *L'identité de l'intérêt général avec l'intérêt individuel est la vraie source des richesses des nations*, trans. M. Rouvier, St Petersburg, 1806. For earlier references to this work, see letters 2013 and 2014, *Correspondence*, vii.

2037. [1] Caroline Archer Clive Autograph Collection, in the possession of Mr George Clive, Whitfield, Allensmore, Herefordshire. Autograph. Docketed: '1809 Avr. 7 / Dumont Hay Market / to / J.B. Q.S.P.' Endorsed: '7 April 1809. Answer Mercredi'.

[2] The old imperial diet or *Reichstag* had met at Ratisbon (Regensburg) before the dissolution of the Holy Roman Empire in 1806.

2038. [1] BL VIII. 426–7. Autograph. Docketed: '1809 Apl 8/Dumont Hay-market / to / J.B. Q.S.P. / Returns Annual Revs'. Addressed: 'Jeremy Bentham Esqr / Queen Square Place'. A translation of part of this letter is in Bowring, x. 449.

choses dans une chambre et qui n'osent pas ou ne veulent pas en exprimer une seule dans un écrit—[2]

Je suis très content de mon petit tour de campagne—si vous me voulez demain à diner, je suis à vos ordres—Sinon, quelque jour de la semaine, Mardi par exemple ou Mercredi. Tout à vous

Samedi Et. D.

2039

To William Cobbett

8 April 1809 (Aet 61)

A writer, who is preparing for the press, to be published with his name, a work on the subject of Libel Law, in which great use will be made of the cases of the King against Cobbett, and Do. against Johnston,[2] finds himself in great need of the information which the attorney's bill in the former case would afford, and this partly in respect of the sum total of the pecuniary burthen—partly in respect of the *items* of which it was composed. The mode of communication by which the purpose would, beyond comparison, be best answered, is, the printing an exact copy in Mr Cobbett's *Register*; because, by

[2] Dumont was referring here to the author of the article on *Scotch Reform* that appeared in *The Annual Review, and History of Literature*, vii (1808), 198–203. On p. 198 the writer stated: 'Every thing which comes from the pen or from the mind of Mr Bentham is entitled to profound regard. Of all men, in all ages, and in all countries, who have made the philosophy of law their study, he has made the greatest progress'. The author of this review has been identified as James Mill (1773–1836), the philosopher, economist, and historian, who was to become one of Bentham's most influential followers. See Bain, p. 95.

2039. [1] Bowring, x. 448–9. Introduced by Bowring: 'Bentham made to Cobbett (April 8, 1809) the following anonymous communication, to which I do not find any written reply in his papers:—'

William Cobbett (1762–1835) was the editor of *Cobbett's Weekly Political Register* from 1802.

[2] In November and December 1803 Cobbett published libels on Philip Yorke, 3rd Earl of Hardwicke (1757–1834), the lord lieutenant of Ireland; John Freeman Mitford, 1st Baron Redesdale (1748–1830), the Irish lord chancellor; Charles Osborne (*c.*1759–1817), one of the judges of the king's bench in Ireland; Alexander Marsden (1761–1834), Irish under secretary; and William Plunket (1764–1851), later 1st Baron Plunket, the solicitor-general. On 24 May 1804 Cobbett was prosecuted for criminal libel and fined £500; two days later he was sued by Plunket, who was awarded damages of £500. On 23 November 1805 Robert Johnson (*c.*1745–1833), judge of the court of common pleas in Ireland, was tried as the author of the libels. See George Spater, *William Cobbett: The Poor Man's Friend*, 2 vols., Cambridge, 1982, i. 128–31.

Bentham made reference to these cases in *The Elements of the Art of Packing, as applied to Special Juries, particularly in cases of Libel Law*, London, 1821 (Bowring, v. 61–186), which he was writing at this time and which was printed in 1810.

this means, the text being in everybody's hands, the comments that would be made upon it would find, readily laid down for them, an authenticated basis, universally intelligible. But lest the publication of a document of this nature should not be found suitable to the plan of the *Register*, the writer finds it necessary to indicate a private mode of correspondence for this purpose.

A *Mr Davies*,[3] as it may happen to Mr Cobbett to know, has, during Mr Cochrane Johnson's absence on his expedition to Seville and Mexico for dollars,[4] the direction of the repairs and alterations that are going forward at the house he has lately taken in Queen Square Place, Westminster. To him Mr Cobbett is desired to have the goodness to direct any private communication which, on this occasion, he may be disposed to make. The writer is not personally known to Mr Cobbett; and as Mr Cobbett will understand in the sequel, it may be material to a purpose which Mr Cobbett cannot but approve, that he may have to say, and that with truth, that there has not been any personal intercourse, nor exists any connexion between them. But for a token that the degree of confidence necessary to the purpose in question is not likely to be abused, nor the trouble, that on Mr Cobbett's part may be necessary, altogether thrown away, he thinks it may be of use to mention that not long ago he partook of a brace of partridges at No. 13, Alsop's Buildings.[5]

Other articles of information wanted, are—

1st. Defendant's sentence in King *v.* Cobbett.—Imprisonment, if any.—If fine, amount of the fine.

2d. Bill of costs in King *v.* Johnson; but as to this, there does not seem any probability of its lying within Mr Cobbett's reach.[6]

The writer wishes, if possible, to get out his work before any of the twenty-six prosecutions on the ground of Major Hogan's pamphlet[7] come on for trial; or will before Lord Ellenborough's[8] death, which, he understands from good authority, is expected to be not far

[3] Perhaps Daniel Davies (d. 1819), surveyor, of 11 Bloomsbury Square.

[4] Cochrane Johnstone obtained a contract for supplying the Spanish government with muskets and arranged with the *junta* that he should be paid by an order on the royal treasury at Vera Cruz. A British frigate was accordingly appointed to take him to Mexico.

[5] Cochrane Johnstone's residence at New Road, Marylebone.

[6] In Trinity term 1806, the crown entered a *nolle prosequi* upon Justice Johnson's indictment, and Johnson retired from the bench with a pension for life.

[7] Denis Hogan was the author of *An Appeal to the Public and a Farewell Address to the Army, by Brevet-Major Hogan, late a Captain in the Thirty-second Regiment of Infantry*, London, 1808, in which he complained of the ill-treatment he had received from Frederick Augustus, Duke of York and Albany (1763–1827), the commander-in-chief 1798–1809, 1811–27, and criticized the promotion system in the army.

[8] Edward Law, 1st Baron Ellenborough (1750–1818) was lord chief justice 1802–18. He had been the judge in the cases of the *King* v. *Cobbett* and the *King* v. *Johnson*.

distant. Should the information in question, viz. the bill of costs, be destined for a place in the *Register*, the earlier the better,—in the next number if possible; meantime, should my notice of this be destined for a place in the *Register*, the writer may be designated by the letters A Z.

2040

From Étienne Dumont

10 April 1809

Mon cher Bentham

Je viens de recevoir un billet qui me rappelle un engagement que j'avois pris pour demain et que j'avois oublié. Je vous avois proposé le Mercredi avec la même étourderie, ayant oublié que ce jour étoit pris pour aller voir le London dock avec Mr Vaughan[2] et dîner avec lui. Je vous écrirai le premier matin libre. Pardon, mon cher Bentham, de la liberté grande—Allez voir le Panorama du Caire.[3] J'avais cru, d'après force descriptions, m'en être fait une idée—tout a été aussi nouveau que si je n'avois rien lû. Tout à vous

Et. D.

Lundi matin

2040.[1] BL VIII. 428–9. Autograph. Docketed: '1809 Apl 10 / Dumont Haymarket / to / J.B. Q.S.P. / Declines dining here Tuesday.' Addressed: 'Jeremy Bentham Esqr. / Queen Square Place'.

[2] William Vaughan (1752–1850) was a merchant and the author of a number of tracts published between 1793 and 1797 advocating the building of docks for the Port of London. For his earlier contact with Bentham see *Correspondence*, iv. 426, v. 3 and n., and vii, as index. He was the younger brother of Benjamin Vaughan (1751–1835), the politician, political economist, and associate of the Marquis of Lansdowne with whom Bentham had corresponded in the early 1790s. See *Correspondence*, iv, as index.

[3] An advertisement in *The Times* of 15 March 1809 announced that at the Panorama, Leicester Square, the View of Gibraltar was to close on 25 March and be replaced by 'a splendid view of GRAND CAIRO'.

2041

From Aaron Burr

19 April 1809

London, April 19, 1809.

After leaving you last evening I saw one of the Philistines. He was all suavity and good-humour. Drunk, perhaps. He had not the least doubt of the cheerful concurrence of Lord Liverpool[2] in the voyage to Gottenburg, and requested that I would write to his lordship. He engaged that the letter should be delivered, and read, and answered this morning; and lo! the result. When I came to write '*my* lord,' penna digitis hoesit.[3] I tried in vain, but could not get it out; so I adopted the stiff diplomatic third person. *My* lady or *his* lordship does not stick in my savage throat; but '*my* lord'—the Lord deliver me. Resolving, however, that if I did quarrel, it should be for rem and not for modum; and having already given up the rem, I tax your eyes with the perusal of the note, to see if it be secundum (or juxta) consuetudinem.[4] It must be in before ten, and has to come all the way back here first. Erase or add as you like.

A. Burr

2042

From James Mill

27 April 1809

My Dear Sir

I made enquiries yesterday about the channel of intelligence for promotions—I was referred to the publisher of the Court Calendar—who told me that *the Companion to the Court Calendar*, published by Stockdale in Pickadilly, is the book—the Court Calendar containing only the names of the happy persons who are in, not the dates of their coming to that happiness.—Perhaps the best plan

2041. [1] Davis, i. 202–3.

[2] Robert Banks Jenkinson, 2nd Earl of Liverpool (1770–1828), was at this time home secretary.

[3] i.e. 'the pen stuck to my fingers'.

[4] i.e. 'according to custom'.

2042. [1] BL VIII. 432–3. Autograph. Docketed: '1809 Apl 27 / Mill Rodney St / to / J.B. Q.S.P.' An extract of this letter is published in slightly different form in Bowring, x. 450, where it is misdated 27 September 1809, and in Bain, p. 102.

would be for Mr. Koe to call at Stockdales, and there look over the volumes, till he come to what he wants.—A list of promotions I find is given too in the Annual Register, into which I have looked, and find the manufacture of Sir John Mitford into a peer, and his appointment to the Chancellorship of Ireland was on the 13th. of February 1802.[2] If it would be any use to you to see that vol. of the Ann. Reg. have the goodness to let me know by the two-penny post and I will bring it in my hand on monday.

I offer up my devotions to heaven every morning for the prosperity of Libel-law. I hope that like the young Messiah it is growing rapidly 'in stature and in favour with God and man'[3]—for never had the earth more need of such a Messiah,—After the feeble and timid talk on the subject of the freedom of the press in the House of Commons on Monday night,[4] I am more impatient than ever. Pure fear of the lawyers seemed to tie up the tongues even of Sir F. Burdett,[5] and of Whitbread,[6] who otherwise appeared willing to speak. They were afraid they should commit some blunder in regard to the requisite provisions of law, and therefore eat in their words. Oh, God! if they but knew what law is, and ought to be, as well as you can tell them, on this most interesting of all points, we shall find the boldness, I trust, on the other side to that of the lawyers.

I am dear Sir
Your zealous pupil
J. Mill.

12 Rodney Street
Pentonville
Thursday Morg

[2] Mitford had been knighted in 1793 on becoming solicitor-general. He was created Baron Redesdale on being appointed Irish lord chancellor.

[3] Luke 2:52.

[4] On 24 April a petition was presented to the Commons from Henry White, proprietor of *The Independent Whig* newspaper, who had been convicted of libel and was imprisoned in Dorchester gaol. White complained that the criminal investigations against him had been filed before the king's bench at Westminster rather than a grand jury of the City of London, that the special jury was packed, that there had been other irregularities in his trial, and that he had been mistreated in prison. See *Parliamentary Debates*, xiv. 175–82.

[5] Sir Francis Burdett (1770–1844), radical MP for Westminster.

[6] Samuel Whitbread (1758–1815), Whig MP for Bedford. He had presented White's petition and moved that it lie on the table.

2043

From Francis Horner

2 May 1809

My Dear Sir

You will find Lord Hardwicke's patent place stated in page 294 of the Third Report,[2] which I send you; but which I will thank you to return to me in a day or two, as it will form the subject of some important motions in the House next week.[3]

I send likewise the accounts respecting writs of error;[4] I have not had time since I saw you yesterday to examine them myself.

Yours ever faithfully
Fra Horner.

11 Manchester Buildings
May 2d 1809.

2043. [1] BL VIII. 434–5. Autograph. Docketed: '1809 May 2 / Horner / to / J.B. / Sends Appeal / Accounts etc'. Addressed: 'To / Jeremy Bentham Esq / Queen Square Place / Westminster'.

Francis Horner (1778–1817), one of the founders of the *Edinburgh Review*, was MP for St Ives 1806–7, Wendover 1807–12, and St Mawes 1813–17. For his earlier contact with Bentham see *Correspondence*, vii, as index.

[2] The *Third Report from the Committee, appointed to examine and consider what regulations and checks have been established, in order to control the several branches of the Public Expenditure in Great Britain and Ireland*, 29 June 1808, p. 294, records that a patent of 21 September 1805 gave the Earl of Hardwicke the reversion of the post of clerk of the common pleas in the courts of exchequer in Ireland, which had an annual value of £11,094. At that time the clerkship was held by Robert Hobart, 4th Earl of Buckinghamshire (1760–1816).

[3] On Monday 8 May Henry Martin (1763–1839), MP for Kinsale, proposed resolutions urging the necessity for the strictest economy in the disposal of public money, and calling for the annual publication of all grants of places. See *Parliamentary Debates*, xiv, 420.

[4] Horner was probably referring to the case of Henry White and the printer of the *Independent Whig*, John Harriot Hart, mentioned in letter 2042. The writ of error in this case was presented to the Lords on 16 May and two days later the judgement of the king's bench was affirmed. See *Parliamentary Debates*, xiv. 583–607.

2044
From Étienne Dumont

11 May 1809

Le mien, mon cher Maître, a grand besoin de révision—d'abord le stile à soigner—mais cette guerre aux mots ne peut se faire qu'avec l'espérance d'imprimer—puis, des fragments à incorporer—etc.[2]

Si vous le lisez de suite, tant mieux—vous m'en diriez votre avis comme de l'ouvrage d'un autre.

Mais comme vous ne le lirez pas, je vous serai très obligé de me le renvoyer, quand vous aurez vu ce que vous voulez voir.

Les notes en crayon de votre frère.[3] Il étoit fort content de l'ouvrage. Il auroit souhaité seulement qu'on eût moins attaqué l'Eglise, et un peu plus, d'autres départements.

Je voudrois bien retirer du gouffre mes cahiers sur l'ordre judiciaire que vous avez depuis trois ans.

J'ai encore deux ou trois articles about *rewards* que je vous enverrai incessamment.[4]

N'oubliez pas Paley.[5]

Tout à vous.

Si vous voulez que je ne sois pas oisif à la campagne, donnez-moi de *l'Evidence*.[6]

2044. [1] BL VIII. 436–7. Autograph. Docketed: '1809 May 11 / Dumont Hay market / to / J.B. Q.S.P. / Demands back two / Judic Establisht / Papers'.

[2] Dumont was again consulting Bentham about what was to become *Théorie des peines et des récompenses.*

[3] Samuel Bentham (1757–1831). He was usually known as 'Sir Samuel', and will be referred to in this manner hereafter, because he had been awarded the Russian cross of St George for his part in the Russo-Turkish war of 1788–92. From 1807, when he became a commissioner of the navy, his friends urged him to use the title, and he seems to have adopted it for official purposes from 1809. See M. S. Bentham, *The Life of Brigadier-General Sir Samuel Bentham*, London, 1862, p. 257.

[4] Reward was the subject of the second volume of *Théorie des peines et des récompenses.*

[5] Dumont was probably referring here to the essay on the death penalty that Bentham was writing, entitled 'Law versus arbitrary power; or A Hatchet for Dr. Paley's net'. This critique of the ideas of William Paley (1743–1805) archdeacon of Carlisle and author of *Principles of Morals and Political Philosophy*, London, 1785, can be found at UC cviib. 193–277, dated January, February, and July 1809. It is headed 'Peines', which suggests that it was originally intended for inclusion in the writings on punishment that Dumont used in *Théorie des peines et des récompenses.*

[6] Dumont was engaged in work on Bentham's evidence MSS; see below, letter 2049. His efforts finally bore fruit in *Traité des preuves judiciaires*, 2 vols., Paris, 1823.

2045

To Pavel Chichagov

20–5 May 1809 (Aet 61)

Queen's Square Place Westmr 20 May 1809

Sir

To save circuity, I intrude myself thus on your correspondence

My Brother having communicated to me the desire you had expressed of his choosing for you some modern English publications, I recommend to him, besides some of these which are accordingly sent to you, the Edinburgh Review and the Monthly Magazine, as being in by far higher estimation and more extensive circulation than any others in their respective classes. In this he agreed with me: but declined sending them, under the persuasion that they could not but be accessible to you somewhere at Petersburgh, if not already in your possession. The Edinbg Review prints now *11,000* / eleven thousand / copies. It comes out once a quarter: at 5d, just now increased to 6d. It began in 1802.

The Monthly Magazine at 1s. 6d per number began in 1796. The information it affords is valuable and infinitely diversified.

My Brother having communicated to me the terms in which you were pleased to speak of such of my works as through the medium of M. Dumont's translation had found their way into your hands, I profit by this opportunity to beg the honour of your acceptance for such of them as are at present in print and accessible to myself.

Nasmyth's treatise on agriculture[2] has been added to the books sent to you at the suggestion of an intelligent friend, on the ground of its uncommon merit and utility, confirmed from other quarters. He is a practical working farmer, who in consideration of its subservience to *Agriculture*, made himself acquainted with *chemistry* and is said to have derived from it information of practical utility, communicated in his work: and far from being a vain speculatist, he has

2045. [1] Staatsbibliothek Preussischer Kulturbesitz, Berlin. Draft, part autograph, part in hand of a copyist. Docketed: '1809 May 20 / J.B. Q.S.P. / to / Tchitchagoff Petersburgh / With Books'.

Pavel Vasil'evich Chichagov (1767–1849) was a Russian admiral and former minister of the navy. He was later to command Russian armies during Napoleon's invasion of 1812. For his earlier contact with the Benthams see *Correspondence*, vii, as index.

[2] John Naismith wrote several works on this subject, but Bentham was probably referring to his *Elements of agriculture; being an essay towards establishing the cultivation of the soil and promoting vegetation on steady principles*, London, 1807.

enriched himself—I mean in hard money—by following the practices recommended in his book. Should it happen to you to find it useless with reference to yourself, you would oblige me by transmitting it in my name to Admiral Mordvinoff,[3] who used to be ⟨. . .⟩ ⟨. . .⟩

Along with this you will receive a list of my printed works: distinguishing such as are herewith sent from such as could not be sent being out of print; and among both such as have not from such as have been made public in the ordinary way of sale.

I have the honour to be,
Sir
Your most obedient Servant
Jeremy Bentham

Admiral Tchitchagoff
etc etc etc.

M. Mordvinoff used at one time to amuse himself with causing translations to be made of such books as promised to be of use in Russia. By the account I have heard of Nasmyth I should expect to find it interesting to him in this point of view. You would oblige me by communicating to him so much as bears relation to him in this letter. The occupations that press upon me make me shrink from the idea of commencing another.

P S 25 May 1809

An additional extent of funds and time having been announced by Mr Smirnow[4] an addition has in consequence been made to the number of Books sent.

1 Thorntons Account of Turkey[5] being the Book which Mr Etons whose pamphlet is herewith sent took for the subject of his remarks[6] was ordered, but is unfortunately out of print.

[3] Nikolai Semënovich Mordvinov (1754–1845), Russian admiral and friend of Sir Samuel Bentham. See *Correspondence*, iii, iv, and vii, as index.

[4] Iakov Ivanovich Smirnov (1754–1840), chaplain of the Russian embassy and pastor of the Russian church in London. For Bentham's earlier contact with Smirnov see *Correspondence*, iii. 163n. and iv. 415n.

[5] Thomas Thornton (d. 1814) was the author of *The Present State of Turkey*, London, 1807.

[6] Thornton's work attacked William Eton's *Survey of the Turkish Empire*, London, 1798, and therefore drew from Eton a pamphlet entitled *A Letter to the Right Honourable the Earl of D***, on the Political Relations of Russia, in regard to Turkey, Greece, and France; and on the means of preventing the French establishing a permanent control over Russia: with strictures on Mr. Thornton's Present State of Turkey*, London, 1807. Eton (or Eaton) had been in contact with Bentham in the 1780s, after his meeting with Samuel in St Petersburg. See *Correspondence*, iii, as index.

2 Edinburgh Review is now sent in consideration of the sensation it makes as mentioned in the Letter.
3 Cobbetts Register for the current Year, and the last preceding is sent on account of the encreased importance it has acquired from its having in good measure originated the Attacks on the Duke of York[7] and for its being now the principle vehicle of the discussions brought on by the subject of Parliamentary Reform. Ten thousand is said to be now the number printed.
4 The Monthly Magazine is sent for the current year, and one or two years preceding by any future opportunity both this and Cobbetts Register might be completed from the beginning if desired.

2046

From Francis Horner

31 May 1809

My Dear Sir

We are to have very particular business in the House to-day, which will again deprive me of the pleasure of dining with you: the resolutions proposed by Mr Martin upon the Third Report of the Finance Committee,[2] the Bill for increasing the Salaries of the Judges,[3] and a resolution to prohibit the sale of offices in Courts of

[7] The Duke of York was obliged to resign as commander-in-chief on 18 March 1809 as a result of his involvement with Mrs Mary Anne Clarke. Mrs Clarke had made money out of her intimacy with the Duke by promising promotion to officers who paid for her recommendation. The radical MP Lieut.-Col. Gwyllym Lloyd Wardle raised the matter in the Commons on 27 January 1809 and an investigation was undertaken by a committee of the whole house. Although cleared of charges of corruption, the Duke felt it necessary to relinquish his post. He was reinstated in 1811.

2046. [1] BL VIII. 438–9. Autograph. Docketed: '1809 May 31 / Horner Linc. Inn / to / J.B. Q.S.P. / Postpones dining here'. Addressed: 'To / Jeremy Bentham Esq. / Queen Square Place / Westminster'.

[2] See above, letter 2043 and n. 3.

[3] On 31 May the Commons resolved to consider the augmentation of judges' salaries on the following day, 1 June. On 2 June it was decided that an augmentation bill should be prepared. See *Commons Journals*, lxiv. 368, 380. The bill passed into law on 20 June as 49 Geo. III, c. 127.

Justice.[4] I expect to get my freedom very soon, and the first use I shall make of it will be to wait upon you.

I am Ever My Dear Sir
Most Sincerely Yours
Fra Horner.

Lincoln's Inn
Wednesday
May 31.

2047

From William Wilberforce

14 June 1809

Kensingtn Gore or
New Pal Yd Hotel June 14
1809

My dear Sir

Though ye incessant Bustle in which I live during my residence in ye Neighborhood of London is such as to render it impossible for me to bestow much thought on any but urgently pressing Business, yet I can truly declare, that you, and the treatment you experienced have been often in my Mind; and that the Sense of it which I have formerly so often express'd to you remains utterly unalter'd—But in truth I always felt, that it was more than could be expected, (I might almost say out of Nature) for you to think that I had not neglected opportunities of pushing forward your Business, and therefore I was impress'd with ye persuasion, that howr. your good nature might prevent your opening your mind to me, you must

[4] During the discussion of judges' salaries on 2 June, Whitbread and Henry Bankes (1757–1834), MP for Corfe Castle, suggested that a clause should be inserted in the bill to prevent the sale of the office of clerk of assize. On 12 June Bankes proposed such an amendment but withdrew it after the chancellor of the exchequer, Spencer Perceval (1762–1812), had assured him that this office had not been sold recently and would not be sold in future. See *Parliamentary Debates*, xiv. 858–9, 988.

2047. [1] UC ix. 29–30. Autograph. Docketed: '1809 June 14 / Panopt. / Wilberforce Kensington / Gore or / N. Pal Yd Hotel / to / J.B. Q.S.P. / Disposition favourable to / Panopt. expressed by a / Minister. / Wilberforces panegyric / on J.B. in the House / unnoticed [?] by the Reporters.' Printed, but incorrectly dated, Bowring, xi. 147.

William Wilberforce (1759–1833), the evangelical and philanthropist, was MP for Hull 1780–4, Yorkshire 1784–1812, Bramber 1812–25. For his earlier contact with Bentham see *Correspondence*, iv, v, vi, and vii, as index.

number me among those who had usd you ill, and conseqy. not much relish my Society —I therefore satisfied myself with speakg of you, of your merits and cruel Sufferings, in ye way which Justice appeard to me to require, as often as opportunities occurr'd—at length an Occasion arose ye other day in ye Hos. of Coms. for publickly noticing your Plan,[2] and some private Conversat (tho' but a few words) with one of ye Treasury people, confirmed the opinion which various Circumstances had led me to form, that ye present was a favourable moment for carrying into Execution your great Project, and obtaining for ye public all ye Benefits it is calculated to produce—I have therefore ever since intendg to write to you, that I might learn whether you had still ye *Heart* to go forward after all your former disappointments. Indeed I hoped that what I said in the House wo'd have attracted ye public attention: But accordg to ye usual treatment which on principle I experience from ye Reporters of our debates (and which I expect will at length have ye Effect intended of ruining me with those of ye public to whom I am not personally known) not one word of what I said on this subject was mentiond in any N. paper I saw, and in one the Times, I was not even mentiond as havg spoken at all, tho' my Speech was (I will not say anythg of its *Quality*) more in *Quantity* than that of any other Speaker. I should be glad to confer with you on ye Buss. at any time and would either call on you or be happy to see you at ye Hotel or K Gore, at ye former I often am from abt 3 to 4 o Clock; at ye latter, till 12 o Clock in ye day from $\frac{1}{2}$ past 10 unless ye House has sat beyond 12 o Clock ye Night before in which Case I sleep in Westmr—Excuse ye Effects of extreme Haste and

Believe me, in Esteem and Regard My dear Sir
yours most truly
W Wilberforce

[2] i.e. Bentham's Panopticon prison scheme.

2048
From Gaspar Melchor de Jovellanos

27 June 1809

La honrosa memoria con que usted ha tenido la bondad de distinguirme en su carta escrita al respetable Lord Holland, mi favorecedor y amigo, y la justa idea que este señor me ha dado de la aplicacion y talento de usted y de su ardiente celo por el bien de la humanidad, no pudieran dejar de inspirarme, al mismo tiempo que una sincera gratitud, el mas íntimo aprecio de su persona y carácter, y como consecuencia de uno y otro la mas pronta disposicion á complacer á usted en cuanto deseare y cupiere en mi arbitrio. El designio de pasar en derechura y desde esa isla á la América para establecerse en ella puede ofrecer algun reparo. No así, si esta solicitud se entablase desde Cádiz y se expusiere por motivo de ella cualquier objeto de observacion y estudio relativo á la historia natural ó á las ciencias físicas.

La detencion de usted en Veracruz el tiempo necesario para cumplir con nuestros reglamentos de policía y economía es del todo indispensable, aunque deberá usted contar con que no le faltará recomendacion bastante para que sea la menor posible. Ni menos serán evitables otras formalidades prévias á la libertad que usted desea de establecerse y vivir tranquilo en lo interior de Méjico, pues aunque los reglamentos establecidos en aquel nuevo mundo sobre este y otros puntos ocuparán la atencion del Gobierno actual, no es este todavía el momento de alterarlos. En conclusion, señor, sin que sea visto que yo pretenda retraer á usted de su propósito de pasar á establecerse en aquel reino, no puedo dejar de decirle que el tiempo y las circunstancias no me parecen las mas propias para lograr en él la tranquila seguridad que desea. Pero sea la que fuere la resolucion de usted en este punto, espero y le ruego que viva seguro de que yo concurriré con el mayor gusto á complacerle, así como á acreditarle que soy siempre con las mas sincera estimacion y fina voluntad su mas afecto servidor que su mano besa.

2048. [1] *Biblioteca de Autores Españoles, desde la Formacion del lenguaje hasta nuestros dias. Tomo Quincuagésimo. Obras publicadas é ineditas de Don Gaspar Melchor De Jovellanos*, ed. Don Candido Nocedal, Madrid, 1859, ii. 319–20. The translation is taken from Bowring, x. 448. Jovellanos's letter was enclosed in Lord Holland to Bentham, 6 September 1809 (letter 2055).

TRANSLATION

The honourable mention you have been good enough to make of me to my distinguished patron and friend, Lord Holland, and the high opinion he has given me of your application, talents, and ardent zeal for the good of humanity, could not fail to inspire me with sincere gratitude and the highest esteem for your person and character, and the most earnest desire to serve you in all things at my disposal. Your design of passing directly from your island to our America may present difficulties: not so, if you were to address your representation from Cadiz, and present, as the object of your journey, something connected with researches or studies in natural history, or the physical sciences. Your detention in Vera Cruz the necessary time for fulfilling the exigencies of our police, is absolutely necessary, though you may reckon on all the recommendations for making it as short as possible. Other formalities will be necessary for the liberty you desire of establishing yourself and living tranquilly in the interior of Mexico; for though the rules established in the New World on this and other matters will occupy the attention of the government here, they cannot at this moment be changed. In conclusion, Sir, without desiring to induce you to change your purpose, I cannot avoid saying, that time and circumstances do not appear to me to promise you that tranquil security you seek. But be your resolution what it may, I hope and pray you to be assured, that I shall do all in my power to further your wishes.

2049

To Étienne Dumont

11 July 1809 (Aet 61)

Q.S.P. 11 July 1809

Dear Dumont

In regard to *Circumstantial*,[2] your best way will be to read in the first instance that part which was written Ao 1808, and is marked all

2049. [1] Dumont MSS 33 / I, fos. 133–4, Bibliothèque Publique et Universitaire, Geneva. Autograph. Addressed: 'To / Mr Dumont / 32 Haymarket.'

[2] Bentham was informing Dumont about his MSS on evidence. Dumont was to use these for his *Traité des preuves judiciares*, in which 'Des Preuves Circonstantielles' formed the fifth book.

along *Prospective View*. *Prospective View* was at first designed for an abridgment of the work at large, but having received as supposed some improvements is likely to become a substitute to it.[3] While Prospective View was writing, the Marginal Contents of the work at large were lying before me, and formed the basis of it.

In reading the old stuff of Years 1803 and 1804 (1804 was part of the way a 2d edition of 1803)[4] it would be an act of charity or of justice (place it to which account you please) if you would hold a *pencil* in your hand and mark by *cancelling lines* such passages as are clearly superseded by the edition of 1808, as on the opposite page:—[5]

still more if with pencil or better still if with pen you would, in such parts as may appear not superseded, make a memorandum indicative of the places in which they may with most propriety be respectively inserted: for example *in* such a Chapter: or *between* such and such a Chapter: viz in the edition of 1808 which contains 14 or 15 Chapters.

If in this way you amend the French, it will be ingratitude in you to grudge doing the same service to the English.

Of the edition of 1808 I have a notion you will find the whole of Book Circumstantial marginal-contented by Mr Koe: of course not exactly as I should have done it: for when I marginal-content I take care that not a single idea shall remain unindicated. These of his I dont think I ever looked at. They are distinguished by a K at the left hand corner of the top of the page. Pray do not omitt to return these Circumstantials to me / to Q.S.P. / all of them as soon as ever you return from *Bounds*.[6] I shall leave directions for them to be sent to me immediately to Barrow Green.[7]

Yours ever
J.B.

[3] '*Prospective View*', despite the similarity of its title, does not appear to have been a forerunner of the work partly printed in 1812 and later published in Bowring vi. 1–187 as 'An Introductory View of the Rationale of Evidence'. This latter work was written between autumn 1811 and August 1812. See UC xlva, xlvb, and xlvii.

[4] By 'edition' Bentham meant separate version of his work on evidence.

[5] To demonstrate, Bentham lightly crossed the opposite page of his letter with diagonal pencil lines.

[6] Bounds, near Tonbridge, Kent, was the country seat of Lord Henry Petty (1780–1863), MP for Camelford, who had travelled in Europe with Dumont in 1801–2. Petty was to succeed his half-brother as 3rd Marquis of Lansdowne in November 1809.

[7] Barrow Green House, Oxted, Surrey. In December 1806 John Heide Koe (1777–1842), Bentham's secretary in 1795–6 and the brother of John Herbert Koe, had married Susannah Chicheley Falkner, née Plowden (1739–1825). She was the widow of Captain Thomas Falkner of the Royal Marines, and had acquired Barrow Green through her first husband, Charles Hoskins (1728–68). See letter 1912, *Correspondence*, vii.

You asked for your own *Peines*.[8] I send it to you, with your own procedures.

P.S. Forget not to let me have the missing Chapter of *Récompenses*. I send you your own *Peines* with a modern scrap or two of *my* own.

2050

From James Mill

25 July 1809

12 Rodney Street, Pentonville,
July 25, 1809.

As to 'Elements,'[2] for the outcoming of which I appear to be far more impatient than you, I have been to give the man a lesson in reading Benthamic copy, and he is far less frightened than he formerly was, or pretended to be—and I expect that his experience will soon prepare some other bold-hearted man to take your stuff in hand. I have told Baldwin,[3] that it must be, through thick or through thin, *published* in six weeks. My motive for naming this time, was, that then it will be ready time enough for the *Edinburgh Review*, No. after the next—and I do not want it out much sooner, that no law *boa* may lick it over, and cover it with his slime, that it may glide the easier into his serpent's maw, and afterwards offer the excrement to Jeffrey, to the frustration and exclusion of an offering of my own.

What is to be, will be; what is not to be, will not be:—I hope I have here provided myself ground enough to stand upon. You see I have not turned my eye to the *pastoral office* so long for nothing:[4] had it been ever turned, like your own, to the equally reverend and pious office, the dispensation of law, the field of generalities would hardly have been more familiar to it.

Coming to Barrow Green on Wednesday, that is, to-morrow—under which of the clauses does that fall? Alas! under the latter. The

[8] Dumont was still working on what was to become *Théorie des peines et des récompenses*.

2050. [1] Bain, pp. 99–101. Partly printed in Bowring, x. 451.

[2] *The Elements of the Art of Packing, as applied to Special Juries, particularly in cases of Libel Law* (Bowring, v. 61–186). This work was not published until 1821, probably for fear of prosecution. See letter 2070.

[3] Either Charles Baldwin (1774–1865) or Robert Baldwin (*c.*1780–1858), of Charles and Robert Baldwin, printers, of New Bridge Street, Blackfriars.

[4] Mill had been licensed as a preacher in 1798.

reason? So it was in the womb of Providence. Who can command what is in the womb of Providence? As Jonah was three days and three nights in the whale's belly,[5] so must we be three days and three nights in the darkness of Pentonville before we can emerge into the light of Barrow Green. Saturday is the day decreed. The causes various. 'Flounces and furbelows,' if among them, are latent. Those set forward to view, if by the art of description I can give them dignity requisite, are as follows:—1. The duty of detersion—a great household abomination, of twelve times recurrence in the year, for which Monday before last was the regular day—but the wedding[6] on the said day delayed, after the fashion of the great expedition which is now a-going,[7] a-going, till Monday last. This, with all its appendages, goes for a great part of the week. Then there is another mischief—there are two aunts,[8] one of whom is necessary to take charge of the brat to be left behind, and they have first to be pulled home from Margate. To pull women from their pleasures, you know too much not to know is not a trifling task. Saturday is the earliest day we can expect them. Another reason concerns myself. Having consented to review this book on China for Jeffrey,[9] I had intended to carry it to Barrow Green, had we gone there on Monday—but now I am anxious, as there is so little time, to have done with it before I leave town. In the meantime, I hope the lilies and roses will be generous and delay their departure for a few days. It will be dreadful to lose them.

By-the-bye, in a note I received from Mr. Koe on Saturday, he desires me to bring *Motive Table*, and *Evidence Exclusion Table. Motive Table* I have, and *Table des Délits*, but no such table as *Evidence Exclusion Table* did I ever see.[10]

When I received your letter on Monday,[11] John,[12] who is so

[5] Jonah 1: 17.

[6] Whose wedding is unclear.

[7] A reference to the Walcheren Expedition. Since the end of June British troops had been gathering in the principal southern ports and the newspapers had been discussing the 'Grand expedition' for some time, although its destination was then unknown. On 28 July the forces finally embarked for the Scheldt to attack the French bases at Flushing and Antwerp.

[8] Presumably sisters of Mill's wife Harriet.

[9] *Voyages à Peking, Manille, et l'Île de France, faits dans l'intervalle des années 1784 à 1801*, 3 vols., Paris, 1808, by the French orientalist Chrétien-Louis-Joseph de Guignes (1759–1845). An article on this work appears in the *Edinburgh Review*, xiv (1809), 407–29, and has been attributed to Mill.

[10] The items in italics appear to be parts of Bentham's writings on evidence, on which Mill was working at this time.

[11] Missing.

[12] John Stuart Mill (1806–73), James Mill's eldest son.

desirous to be your inmate, was in the room, and observed me smiling as I read it. This excited his curiosity to know what it was about. I said it was Mr. Bentham asking us to go to Barrow Green. He desired to read that. I gave it him to see what he would say, when he began, as if reading—'Why have not you come to Barrow Green, and brought John with you?'

The prospect of the pleasures to come keeps up our spirits under the vexation and delay of the days we must lose. The pleasures you are in the actual enjoyment of, ought to keep up yours.

Mrs. Mill desires me to offer her very best respects, and to say that she promises to make up in good behaviour when she comes, for what of the delay in coming is layable at her door.

I am, my dear Sir,
With the highest regard,
Yours, etc

Devil take them! Since writing the above, has the mother[13] of these aunts come into the house, telling us she has heard from them—that they will be in town on Sunday, spite of fate, but not before. It will be Monday morning therefore, before we can be with you. We shall set off, however, before breakfast. We shall breakfast at Croydon, and be with you to the enjoyment of the day—not, however, to break in upon you, till your own dinner-hour—the intermediate time shall be spent in getting acquainted with the place. We shall come in a post chaise, by which means we shall avoid the trouble we should otherwise occasion in sending for us, as Mr. Koe had the goodness to mention, to Godstone. John asks if Monday is not to-morrow.

2051

From Étienne Dumont

31 July 1809

Vous voilà, mon cher Bentham, réhabilité dans mon esprit, je me presse de vous rendre justice, vous n'êtes pas si bête que je l'ai cru depuis trois ans, et s'il y a une bête dans cette affaire, ce n'est pas

[13] Presumably Mrs Harriet Burrow of Hoxton, Yorkshire, Harriet Mill's mother.

2051. [1] UC clxxiv. 69. Autograph. Docketed: '1809 July 30 / Dumont Bounds / to / J.B. Barrow Green / On Circumstant. Evidence'. Addressed: 'Jeremy Bentham Esq. / Queen's Square / Westminster'. Readdressed: 'Barrow Green House / Godstone / Surry'. Postmark: 'FREE / I AU I / 1809'. Stamped: 'TUNBRIDGE / 31'. Franked: 'Tunbridge July thirty / first 1809 / He Petty'. Also written in the same hand as the new address: '[. . .?] Monthly publications will be sent by coach [?]'.

vous—mais aussi qui auroit soupçonné qu'après tant de fait, il y avoit encore tant à faire, et que vous iriez fouiller à mille pieds sous les rochers?—

Vous m'aviez dit de lire 1808 et de prendre ensuite 1804 et de crayonner les superfluités de cette première édition—j'ai voulu et je n'ai pas pu procéder ainsi—j'ai fait mieux—en trois semaines d'un travail ardu, j'ai traduit, autant que traduire m'étoit possible, les 14 chapitres de *prospective view*, cela fait soixante et dix de mes grandes pages.—ainsi en possession des idées principales, en lisant l'édition de 1804, je verrois immédiatement, soit ce qui n'est pas entré dans celle de 1808, soit ce qui est plus développé ou mieux traité dans l'ancienne que dans la nouvelle—je n'aurois qu'à faire des additions—sauf à y ajouter un petit travail subséquent pour fondre les matériaux et incorporer le tout ensemble—Ç'auroit été une occupation pour le bord de la mer—mais il faut renvoyer à un autre temps puisque vous avez besoin des manuscrits[2]—Si ceux de 1808 pouvoient vous suffire, je garderois les autres et j'irois en avant—Je serai en ville le 7 du mois prochain.—Je tâcherai de n'y rester que trois jours—si vous ne me répondez pas, je ferai remettre tous les papiers en QSP.—

Traduit—imaginez les tourments d'un pauvre traducteur à qui les mots essentiels manquent dans la plus gueuse des langues pour la philosophie—j'ai hazardé sans scrupule les mots qui avoient déjà quelque analogue comme infirmatif—inculpatif—exculpatif—criminatif—confessorial—jactantieux—mais que faire de ceux-ci—self desserving, self inculpative—deportment—disprove, un-trustworthiness —concealment—misrepresentation—inference—latentcy latitancy—avoidance of justiciability, conclusiveness—veracious, mendacity, extraneous evidence, authorship—to purport—responsion—forthcoming, incompleatness, et beaucoup d'autres j'ai hazardé *inférence*—(en attendant), car il me semblait que *conséquence* ne rendoit pas bien l'anglois—au reste, je n'ai pas fixé la terminologie, on fait quelquefois en fait de langue des découvertes auxquelles on ne s'attendoit pas.

Je ne m'aventure point à juger le fonds—je suis disciple, j'apprends, il faut voir le tout—mais je puis bien vous dire que cette manière d'opposer les faits infirmatifs aux faits inculpatifs m'a paru un des procédés les plus lumineux et les plus simples.

Quant à la forme, j'ai trouvé quelques endroits obscurs par trop de précision—mais en voyant l'immensité de la matière que vous embrassez, je comprends que jamais vous n'auriez pu vous en tirer,

[2] Presumably for Mill's use. See above letter 2050, and below letter 2058.

en vous livrant aux développements. Il y a tel chapitre qui entre les mains d'un auteur ordinaire, donneroit de l'étoffe pour un volume. Voila la mine—on y puisera comme on voudra—il faudra cent ans pour que toutes ces richesses entrent dans la circulation. Adieu, Tout à vous.

My best compliments to Mr Koe
Bounds—31 Juillet 1809.

2052

To Étienne Dumont

11 August 1809 (Aet 61)

Barrow Green House near Oxted Surry
11 Aug. 1809.

Dear Dumont

Just received yours of yesterday:[2]—answer instantaneously. Take *Impossibilities* in God's name: much good may do you with it: I thought it would have plagued my heart out. I grew tired of it, and bid it go to the Devil. Was it you that he sent for it? For the sake of symmetry and precision, I tried at first to put *impossibilities* and *improbabilities* one after another, *impossibilities* of course first. But to draw the line between them requires *omniscience*: which, for want of having served an apprenticeship to *Omniscient Jackson*[3] (a King's Counsel sort of lawyer in whom I remember that *quality*—*endowment* I mean—used to be recognized) I make no pretensions to: therefore they must go together, and, for the chapter which they denominate, form one *title*.[4] You owe me something for the pains I have taken to tell you of this: to save you from the pains which it cost me.

I intended of course to have resumed the subject, with a view of abridging what I had written on it: written as I believe you will see at different times, attempting it on different plans. When you have worked at it sufficiently, pray let me see what you make of it.

2052. [1] Dumont MSS 33/I, fos. 135–6. Autograph. Addressed: 'To / Mr Dumont / 32 Haymarket / London.' Postmark: 'B / AUG 11 / 1809'. Stamped: 'GODSTONE / 19'.

[2] Missing, but Bentham's response indicates that it contained queries about his evidence writings.

[3] Richard Jackson (d. 1787), lawyer and politician, agent for various American colonies 1760–70, secretary to George Grenville 1763–5, lord of the treasury under Shelburne 1782–3. He was nicknamed 'Omniscient' or 'all-knowing' Jackson.

[4] In Dumont's *Traité des preuves judiciaires*, these subjects are dealt with together in the eighth book, 'De l'improbable et de l'impossible'.

Thank you kindly for your intentions about Lord Holland and his gleanings: I look with hope for the effect.

Yours ever
J.B.

2053

To Francisco de Miranda

25 August 1809 (Aet 61)

Barrow Green House near Oxted and
Godstone Surrey 25 Aug. 1809.

Dear General

I have commissioned Mr Mill, in quality of my Chargé d'Affaires, auprès de Votre Excellence, to say whatever may appear to him most conducive to the purpose of procuring for us the honour of a visit from you to the farm-house denominated as above: requesting of you to give credit to whatever shall have been said by him to that purpose though nothing of it will be seen by me, as if said by myself: which said, after assuring you of my high consideration—(I should have said begging of you to receive the assurance of the same) and praying God to take you into his holy keeping, as also that you may, by his grace live a thousand years—I say no more, than that I am

Jeremy Bentham

To General Miranda etc. etc etc.

2054

From Francisco de Miranda

31 August 1809

My dear Sir,

On my arrival from Richmond last Evening, I found your kind invitation inclosed in a letter of the 25th Inst. from our mutual friend Mr. Mill—Nothing could certainly afford me more pleasure than to spend some time at Barrow Green House, and to partake of

2053. [1] Archivo del General Miranda, vol. xvi, fo. 297. Autograph. The letter is written on the same sheet as Mill to Miranda of the same date. Printed in *Archivo del General Miranda*, 24 vols., Caracas and Havana, 1929–50, xxiii. 52.

2054. [1] Archivo del General Miranda, vol. xvi, fo. 274. Autograph draft. Partly printed in *Archivo del General Miranda*, xxiii. 57–8.

your learned and instructive Conversation;—but it is out of my power at the present moment to obtain that satisfaction, being obliged to attend to some essential Business in Town.

Have the goodness to accept my best thanks for your friendly invitation—and (Excusing Diplomatic form) to believe me always with sincere regard

Grafton Street
Augst. 31st. 1809

Jeremy Bentham Esqr.

2055

From Lord Holland

6 September 1809

Holland House
Septr 6
1809

Dear Sir

Don Gaspar M Jovellanos was so delighted with your letter and so anxious to give you every assistance and advice that though worn out with business he preferred dictating a letter to you (which I inclose and which will be a good Spanish lesson to you) to entrusting any verbal message to me[2]—His signature he said would sufficiently account for his employing an amanuensis as he was provided with that assistance and it was not equally certain that you had a decypherer—You might visit Seville any time after this month with perfect security from agues but whether that circumstance does not render a visit from the French more probable also you will be able to determine for yourself better than I can advise you—you would if at Seville find them I hope in the midst of the work of legislation and reform to the object of establishing or renewing a free Constitution your Correspondent Jovellanos dedicates all his time and directs all his zeal and eloquence

I am Dear Sir
Ever Yrs
Holland

Did you get my letter from Seville?[3]—

2055. [1] Ogden MS. 62(1),59, University College London. Autograph. Docketed: '1809 Septr 6 / Ld Holland Kensington / to / J.B. Q.S.P. / Reced at Barrow / Green 14 Septr / Inclosing Jovellanos to / J.B. June 27th 1809'.

[2] Letter 2048.

[3] Presumably letter 2030.

2056

From Aaron Burr

13 September 1809

Gottenberg, 13th Sept, 1809.

To-morrow I go to Copenhagen, where I shall see the father of the Comités Conciliateurs,[2]—the communication is quite open,—pray afford me a few lines; but do not scold too much,—I could not bear it just now.—Tell me of your health, and what you are about.—Have you finished the 'Essay on Libels, and Liberty of the Press?[3] —It is wanted here,—for they are willing to do, on this head, what is right, but are quite in a quandary as to the 'how.' It is wanted in the U. S.—It is wanted everywhere, except in England, where no improvement will be tolerated.—Innovation! But I see that one of your great friends is likely to come into the ministry.[4] I am glad, for your sake,—not that he can do you any good,—but that it will gratify you.

My new sovereign treats me with civility; that is, he lets me alone.[5]—One of his ministers, however, D'Engerström,[6] has been constant and assiduous in active civilities towards me.

2056. [1] Bowring, x. 451–2.

[2] Christian Colbjörnsen (1749–1814), the Danish statesman and jurisconsult. For his role in the founding and development of the reconcilation courts—which were established by royal ordinance on 10 July 1795—see Andreas Bjørn Rothe, *Mémoire sur l'origine et l'organisation des Committés Conciliateurs en Dannemarc*, Copenhagen, 1803, pp. 118–19.

[3] Mill was trying to get *The Elements of the Art of Packing* published at this time (see letter 2050) but Burr seems to have been referring to another work. Bentham had written part of his proposed law for the establishment of the liberty of the press in Venezuela in 1808 (UC xxvi. 2–11), and in UC lxvii. 29–43 there are marginals and other MSS dating from 1809 on libel law and liberty of the press. Further writings on liberty of the press appear in Bentham's other papers (UC xxvi. 12–65, 137–42; UC lxv. 138–70; UC cvi. 238–50).

[4] Probably an allusion to Romilly. On 6 September William Henry Cavendish Bentinck, 3rd Duke of Portland (1738–1809) had resigned as first lord of the treasury. Burr correctly foresaw that the ministers would approach the opposition leaders to strengthen the government, and perhaps thought Romilly would return to office. In the event, Perceval's invitation to talks was refused by Charles Grey, 2nd Earl Grey (1764–1845) and William Wyndham Grenville, Baron Grenville (1759–1834).

[5] Burr's new sovereign was Charles XIII, proclaimed king of Sweden on 5 June 1809.

[6] Baron Lars von Engeström (1751–1826), Swedish diplomat and statesman, appointed president of the chancellery earlier in 1809.

2057

To Sir Samuel Bentham

29 September 1809 (Aet 61)

Barrow Green near Oxted Surry 29 Sept. 1809.

Alas! my poor dear Sam, you have had a tedious bout of it I for my part have thought as little of you as ever I could.

The Speaker's[2] letter you shall have on the other leaf: mine will be still shorter, but with nothing of uncivility or unkindness.

Our Father's[3] picture will now probably be at a loss for house-room. Of course Abbot will not set any value on it. On account of the brats it might be as well that you should have it: suppose you were to call on him and beg it for them.

Another thing there is, which possibly some of them might set more value on than the picture of a man they never saw. On my Father's death, the widow[4] with my consent took away bodily the bundles of letters for a number of years: the object was manifest and reasonable, viz. that letters of her's to him before marriage might not get into other hands. But in one of those bundles *were*—*should have been* at least—a number of letters of mine, and amongst them one in particular, written from Lincoln's Inn, in which I begged leave to decline practising at the bar, for the purpose of devoting myself to the study of legislation.[5] Pity that should perish. Possibly all the bundles may have been already burnt. Possibly however those letters of mine may have yet survived.

Perhaps at your request he would let you look over the bundles, and from the endorsements, in his presence, or without that ceremony, pick-out those letters which purport to have come from me. The sooner you apply the better, (for fear of their being burnt, for he has a quick hand at such riddances) and better in person than by writing, on account of the sort of expansion of mind which an interview on such an occasion is apt to produce.

2057. [1] BL Add. MSS 36,524, fos. 27–8. Autograph. Docketed: '1809 Septr 29 / JB–SB. / mention of his / declining the / practice of the Law'. Addressed: 'To / Sir Saml Bentham / etc etc etc / Navy Office / London'. Postmark: 'B / SEP 30'. Stamped: 'GODSTONE'.

[2] Charles Abbot (1757–1829), later 1st Baron Colchester, speaker of the House of Commons 1802–17, was Bentham's stepbrother.

[3] Jeremiah Bentham (1712–92).

[4] i.e. Sarah Bentham, whose death on 27 September 1809 was the occasion of this letter. Her first husband was the Revd John Abbot. After he died she married Jeremiah Bentham in 1766.

[5] Missing.

'*Packing*', unfortunately can not be sent you till ready for publication:[6] we have tried to get duplicated sheets here for our own use and failed. The Printer's people (of Mill's choice for very good reasons,) have proved very incapable: worse ⟨at⟩ reading my scrawl than any others had been: which has been a great retardment: but I shall now apply where I had before been better served. Something of it must be got out before the first day of term 6 Novr: and therefore I believe I shall publish first Part the 1st, giving the titles of Chapters and Sections of Parts 2. 3. and 4. which together are about equal to it, and saying that they are in the press.

'*Parliamentary Reform*' is grown into a capital constitutional work:[7] the particulars of the reform proposed have been long ago settled, and reduced to the form of a Table. '*Fallacies*' necessarily wait for it but will soon follow it.[8] Evidence—the editing it forms Mill's sole business, and the business of striking out various sections so to fit it for the press goes on prosperously. I hope to see it ready for the press before Christmas—yes considerably before.[9]

Aye do, get my stove ready, there's a good boy. I am already suffering loss of time as well as uneasiness from the cold: in other respects well.

C. Abbott to J.B.

I have to acquaint you my dear Sir that my poor Mother died this day. Amongst her papers she has always marked one which concerned you, and I now send it you enclosed. Although her time of life and long illness precluded the hope of her continuing much longer with us, yet the want is to me very afflicting. God bless you.
Palace Yard
Wedy Night 27 Sep. 1809

J.B. to C.A. in answer.

I have to thank you, my dear Sir, for the melancholy token of your kind remembrance, which reached me here y⟨ester⟩day, too late for acknowledgment on that day ⟨. . .⟩ this place.

[6] i.e. what was to be published as *The Elements of the Art of Packing*. See above, letter 2050 n. 2.

[7] 'Parliamentary Reform' was the title of a work for which Bentham drafted many pages around this time, but which he never published. These writings provided material for his later published works on the subject. See L. J. Hume, *Bentham and Bureaucracy*, Cambridge, 1981, p. 180.

[8] Material that formed part of what was to be published as *The Book of Fallacies; from Unfinished Papers of Jeremy Bentham*, London, 1824 (Bowring, ii. 375–487). Dumont published these writings, together with the 'Anarchical Fallacies' in *Traité des sophismes politiques*, which appeared with *Tactique des assemblées législatives*, 2 vols., Paris and Geneva, 1816.

[9] See letters 2050, 2051, and 2058.

For the paper in question I am the more ⟨. . .⟩ as the existence of it, as well as of the other docume⟨nts⟩ which upon former occasions you had brought to my view, had been suffered to slip out of my memory, confiding in the custody in which I presumed them deposited. Of the transaction I had of course a general remembrance.

To S.B. I shall send you by a man who goes on Sunday to London a letter I received t'other day from Ld Holland with the letter it incloses from Jovellanos.[10]

In the next Edinburgh Review (early in Novr) you will probably see, what I have not seen nor shall see till you do, a palaverification of Dumont principes, on the occasion of a proposed Code of laws which being confronted with it is but [?] ragged: a Code of penal law drawn up by Bexon a French man for the dominions of Bavaria in the Introduction to which Code Dum princs cuts the principal figure.[11]

I hope soon to have to congratulate you on the extirpation of the Admiralty nuisances.

2058

From James Mill

26 October 1809

My Dear Sir,

When I engaged to dine at Hampstead on Friday I did not recollect, nor thereafter until I was informed by my wife, that there were certain of her friends engaged to come here on that day—from whom it would not be civil in me absolutely to run away. But nevertheless I shall not fail to be with you (saving always the Generals[2] saving clause, that the Lord be willing) on Saturday morning by nine o Clock—that so the expedition to Hendon may be shared in by me, no less fully than by the best of you.—My review went yesterday—so that this shall be a hard day at Circumstan-

[10] See letters 2048 and 2055.

[11] Scipion Jérôme François Bexon (1750–1825), French lawyer and legal writer, was the author of *Application de la théorie de la législation pénale, ou code de la sureté publique et particulière, fondé sur les règles de la morale universelle, sur le droit des gens ou primitif des sociétés, et sur leur droit particulier, dans l'état actuel de la civilization; rédigé en projet pour les états de sa majesté le roi de Bavière*, Paris, 1807. For the *Edinburgh Review* article see letters 2061, 2062, and 2064.

2058. [1] BL VIII. 449–50. Autograph. Docketed: '1809 Oct.26 / Mill Pentonville / to / J.B. Hampstead'.

[2] i.e. Sir Samuel Bentham, brigadier-general in the Russian service.

tial[3]—and tomorrow I mean to repair to Q.S.P. for the sake of importing what follows Circumstantial.

By the bye—of the copy I brought with me the other night, a page, it appears to me, must be wanting—viz. page marked 26—containing, I conjecture, the copy of Mac's letter.[4]

Trusting the righteous business of Packing Juries goes on prosperously in your learned, as in other learned hands, I remain ever, as in duty bound—Yours most faithfl. etc.

J. Mill

12 Rodney Street
Pentonville
Thursday Morning

2059

From James Mill

31 October 1809

Pentonville
Tuesday 8 o clock A.M.

My dear Sir

The thick mist of this morning—which some treacherous appearances of last night led me not to expect, and drew me on to continue in my design of being with you this evening—sets before my eyes, in such horrible array, the terrors of my walk of the other evening from Hampstead, a walk of Stygian darkness, 'with perils and with tremblings 'vironed round',[2] (a night in a watchmans box by the side of the road being the last of the evils with which it threatened)—that my 'stomach stout', however I smite upon it like Hudibras,[3] and Ulysses, and however I cry with the latter, *τέτλαθι δή, κραδίη κ.τ.λ.*[4] gives way, and bids me with imperious voice wait for clearer

[3] i.e. 'Circumstantial Evidence', part of Bentram's writings on evidence that Mill was looking over at this time.

[4] Probably a reference to the letter from Sir Archibald Macdonald (1747–1826), lord chief baron of the exchequer, to Sir Richard Phillips (1767–1840), sheriff of London, which appears on pp. 135–44 of the 1821 published version of *The Elements of the Art of Packing* (Bowring, v. 125–30).

2059. [1] BL VIII. 451–2. Autograph. Docketed: '1809 Oct. 31 / Mill Pentonville / to / J.B. Hampstead / Hodie non venturus'. Partly-printed in Bowring, x. 452, with the addition of a paragraph from a later letter. See below, letter 2061.

[2] Samuel Butler, *Hudibras*, I. iii. 1.

[3] ibid., I. ii. 739.

[4] i.e. 'Bear up, my heart. You have had worse to endure before this'. Homer, *Odyssey*, xx. 18.

weather. Then comes your spirit, and cries, a bed—a bed—Hall-oak-farm[5] is such a kind of a place in which there is such a kind of a thing as a bed.—But then again there comes the spirit of a Doctor—who was it?—Boerhaave[6]—was it not?—and it cries *Vita brevis, ars longa*[7]—and then there is an internal spirit that whispers to self, 'what a devilish deal, master of mine, you have yet to do, before you are good for much'—and all this raises such a tumult that I am puzzled what to do. Virtue, however, asserts, that she cannot sanction the bed—because that interferes with not one day but two—and that so many are the little teasing interruptions I meet with while in this London, that I do not get on as I ought to do.—What I wish is—and that most earnestly—that this said Cochrane Johnstone, may have finished with this lady of his, and that I may get his meretricious house some time soon.[8]

I propose friday at 5 O Clock to be with you—tomorrow and the next day it is impossible for me.

I am immersed in old Circumstantial[9]—and not a little non plused, on more occasions than one, whether to take or reject—unwilling to lose, and yet unwilling to overload.

Your affectionate pupil
J. Mill

P.S.

How you have worked the three learned correspondents of our friend Sir Richard[10]—I am more and more impatient every day to have it in the hands of the public—though I understand there is no chance of any of the trials coming on—I have written to Baldwin along with the copy to put another hand upon it—and have offered to go and read it over with the said man, any time he chuses to send me word—assuring him, as I found to be the case—that the last copy is by no means difficult to read.

[5] Sir Samuel Bentham's house at Hampstead.

[6] Herman Boerhaave (1668–1738), Dutch physician and professor at Leiden, FRS.

[7] i.e. 'Life is short, art is long'. See Hippocrates, *Aphorisms*, I. i; Seneca, *De Brevitate Vitae*, I. i.

[8] Cochrane Johnstone was absent from the house in Queen's Square Place on business in Spain and Mexico. See above, letter 2039 and n. 4. Cochrane Johnstone's 'lady' has not been identified. He was already divorced from his second wife, Amelia Constance Gertrude Etienette Godet, whom he had married in March 1803.

[9] See above, letter 2058 n. 3.

[10] i.e. Sir Richard Phillips. See above, letter 2058 n. 4. Besides Sir Archibald Macdonald, Mill was referring to an unnamed member of the Temple and another of Lincoln's Inn who had written to Phillips. See *The Elements of the Art of Packing*, pp. 174–91 (Bowring, v. 143–52).

2060

From James Mill

6 November 1809

My dear Sir

I begin to be ashamed of writing apologies for breaking engagements—but here I am in that pretty office again. The case is this—tomorrow I must go, and that on pain of nullity early in the morning, to Q.S.P.—I counted on being ready to go to day—but this Pre-appointed, which is a remarkably interesting part, is not for that reason a part the sooner to be got through. Now going to Q.S.P. in the morning, and going to Hampstead in the afternoon presented themselves to my imagination as swallowing up a whole day, and tempted me to think of postponing the Hampstead journey till another day—especially as so much of my time is at present squandered away—my northern friends making use of the shortness of their intended stay in London as a ground to refuse any apology for not being with them almost every day.[2]

Baldwin has sent me word—that as the man engaged with our printing is now familiarized with the hand, and as they will urge him to stick close to the work, they expect that he will get on so fast, that the time spent in getting another man initiated in the business would be nearly as much as the other will require to finish the job. I have not sent them any intimation about the putting of the latter part into the hands of another printer, because I have not yet sufficiently talked with you upon the subject. That we can do on friday, the day on which I propose to see you—and if you are anxious for greater expedition, you or Mr. Koe may write me a line, as to the person who, and the manner in which, as far as you have any directions to give, and they shall be executed immediately.

With all a pupils best regards
ever and faithfully yours
J. Mill

Pentonville
6th. Novr. 1809

2060. [1] BL VIII. 453–4. Autograph. Docketed: '1809 Nov. 6 / Mill Pentonville / to / J.B. Hampstead'.

[2] The identity of Mill's 'northern friends' is unclear. He knew a number of Scotsmen resident in London, but among his visitors might have been David Barclay, the tenant of the farm on which Mill's father lived. Bain, p. 110, states that Barclay came to London to see Mill sometime in 1810.

P.S. on second thoughts, and recollection that Sir Samuel[3] will be in town tomorrow I shall carry this with me, that Tom[4] may give it to his Commissionership at the office.

2061

From James Mill

27 November 1809

The *Edinburgh Review* was sent me yesterday morning,—Bexon sadly mangled.[2]—The mention of you struck out, in all but one place,—and there, my words, every one of them, removed, and those of Mr Jeffrey put in their place: the passage is still complimentary, but with a qualifying clause.[3] What is to be done with this concern?—I am, indeed seriously at a loss.

2062

From Étienne Dumont

3 December 1809

Holland house
3 December

Il y a quelques jours, mon cher Bentham, que j'accompagnai Mr le Sheriff Wood[2] dans sa visite de Newgate, et cette prison amena naturellement la conversation sur le Panoptique qu'il ne connoissoit

[3] Sir Samuel Bentham was a commissioner of the navy 1807–12.

[4] Thomas Coulson junior.

2061. [1] Bowring, x. 452, where this is printed as the last paragraph of Mill's letter of 31 October (letter 2059). Bentham's second letter to Dumont of 5 December (letter 2064) quotes part of this and states that it is an extract from a letter dated 27 November.

[2] Bexon's *Application de la théorie de la législation pénale* was reviewed in the *Edinburgh Review*, xv (1809), 88–109. In letter 2064 below, Bentham has 'mauled' instead of 'mangled'.

[3] A paragraph on pp. 101–2 is devoted to Bentham, who is described as the only author who has attempted the difficult task of tracing the ramifications of good and evil through the whole field of human action and devising clear and accurate rules to increase the good and diminish the evil. Although his success has necessarily been 'imperfect', he has done 'more to elucidate the true grounds of legislative interference, than all the jurists who had gone before him'.

2062. [1] BL VIII. 455–6. Autograph. Docketed: '1809 Dec 3. / Panopt. / Dumont Haymarket / to / J.B. Hampstead / Panopticon for City / thro' Sheriff Wood / Bexon article in / Edinbgh Review / Plagiarism charged'. Endorsed: '2pd'. Addressed: 'Jer. Bentham Esqre. / at Sir Samuel Bentham's / Hampstead.' Postmark: '7 o'Clock / 4 DE / 1809 NT'.

[2] Matthew Wood (1768–1843), sheriff of London and Middlesex 1809–10, lord mayor 1815–16, 1816–17, MP for the City 1817–43, baronet 1837.

point, et dont il fut d'autant plus frappé qu'il s'agit à présent de construire une nouvelle prison pour la Cité de Londres—il en a parlé au Comité[3]—et il paroit croire qu'il seroit possible de profiter de cette circonstance pour réaliser ce plan—Je reçois de lui un billet par lequel il me demande de nouvelles informations, mais il désire surtout de voir le modelle—Seroit-il possible, en votre absence, de le satisfaire sur ce point—Je retourne Mardi en ville et j'y resterai trois ou quatre jours.

L'article *Bexon* dans le dernier Ed. review m'a paru d'abord un très impudent plagiarisme, toutes les bonnes observations étoient empruntées de vous sans rendre justice à l'auteur, excepté par un éloge très maigre et qui ne s'applique qu'à un seul point[4]—j'en étois fort indigné—mais j'ai vu des personnes qui prétendent savoir ou du moins qui soupçonnent très fortement que cet article a été fait sous votre direction,—si cela est, il faut qu'il y ait en cela quelque vue profonde qui m'échappe—Adieu Tout à vous

Et Dumont.

No. 19. Hay-Market
at Mr Lawler's.[5]

2063

To Étienne Dumont

5 December 1809 (Aet 61)

Hampstead 5 Decr. 1809

My dear Dumont

Just and but just received your's of the 3d.[2] As to the models you speak of, the one which was upon the largest scale, and on account of the largeness of the scale but a partial one, was on that same account necessarily taken to pieces. Others probably exist in some

[3] Probably the committee for general purposes of the Corporation of London, which was asked by the Common Council on 21 June 1809 to examine allegations respecting London gaols in Sir Richard Phillips's *A Letter to the Livery of London Relative to the Duties and Office of Sheriff*, London, 1808. A sub-committee of the general purposes committee drew up a report which accepted Phillips's arguments and was submitted to the Common Council in May 1810. This report is printed as appendix 9 of the *Report from the Committee* [of the House of Commons] *on the State of the Gaols of the City of London, etc. Ordered, by the House of Commons, to be printed, 9 May 1814.*

[4] See above, letter 2061 n. 3.

[5] T. Lawler was the owner of a glass and Staffordshire warehouse, 19 Haymarket.

2063. [1] Dumont MSS 33/I, fos. 141–2. Autograph.

[2] Letter 2062.

repository of lumber at Q.S.P.—one, two or three—but all of them more or less in a state of *delabrement*: however such as they are they certainly might be rendered visible supposing it to be worth while. But for my part unless a determination were actually taken to pursue the general idea, it scarce appears to me how it could be worth while. A building so contrived as to have in it one room from which the inside of every other room and place in it may at any time by any number of persons [. . . ?] sitting in that room be viewed at pleasure. I don't see, unless for the information of the Architect, how by any models the general idea could be rendered much clearer, or the utility of it if it has any much more manifest than by the above. In a state more improved than that which is exhibited in any of the models a plan, section and elevation are to be seen in the wooden print inserted in those 'Outlines of Pauper Management' that were published in Young's Annals of Agriculture,[3] and of which you have a copy. I have still I believe a few copies left, and if so, and if the intention be serious, one should be at the service of the gentleman you speak of, and another of that of the Chairman for the use of the Committee: moreover of the Panopticon book in two or three volumes, a copy would at any rate be at the service of each of the Members.

As to any good coming of it, it depends altogether upon the influence which the Architect whoever he is for whom the business is destined may have on the Committee whoever they are: for of every thing belonging to it I am in a state of compleat, and at present invincible, ignorance. So great would be the saving to the public, and consequently so great the loss to the Architect, that be he who he may no expectation more irrational could be entertained, than that he should omitt any exertion that in his view presented any chance of enabling him to prevent it.

Twenty years ago, upon my applying to *Blackburne*[4] (Howards[5] intended Architect) for his eventual assistance, he demanded of me an extra price, alledging as a reason that if that idea were to be

[3] Bentham's essays on 'The Situation and Relief of the Poor' appeared in seven letters published by the agriculturalist Arthur Young (1741–1820) in his *Annals of Agriculture*, xxix (1797), 393–426, xxx (1798), 89–176, 241–96, 457–504, xxxi (1798), 33–64, 169–200, 273–88. These were reprinted, but not published, as *Outline of a Work entitled 'Pauper Management Improved'*. In 1812 they appeared as *Pauper Management Improved: particularly by means of an Application of the Panopticon Principles of Construction* (Bowring, viii. 360–439).

[4] William Blackburn (1750–90), the architect who received first prize in the competition for designing a male prison organised by the commissioners appointed by the Penitentiary Act of 1779 (19 Geo. III, c.74).

[5] John Howard (1726–90), the prison reformer and author of *The State of the Prisons in England and Wales*, Warrington, 1777.

carried into execution in the proposed single instance, no prison would ever be built upon any other plan, and the saving and consequent loss to himself would be prodigious.

In planning the Edinburgh prison, Adam[6] had before him the Panopticon book,[7] a copy of which he had obtained from me through the medium of Mr Pole Carew.[8] When he had got it, he wrote me from Scotland a letter which I have somewhere begging of me not to let any other copy find its way out of my hands into Scotland, for that it would set ignorant gentlemen there upon grounding on it discordant and unskilful plans by which confusion would be produced and the business delayed.[9]

2064

To Étienne Dumont

5 December 1809 (Aet 61)

Hampstead 5 Decr
1809

My dear Dumont

Of the article about *Bexon* in the Edinburgh Review I neither saw nor heard any more than you did: and herein you have an answer to—'*Si cet article a été fait sous votre direction, il faut qu'il y ait en celà quelque vue profonde qui m'èchappe.* Thus far, it is true the '*soupçons*' you speak of were not ill-grounded: viz. that the author of it, or rather he who but for falsifications would have been the author,[2] was not unknown to me. As to *direction* from me he had no more than he had from you or Bexon himself. Of the whole article I neither suggested a single syllable, nor before it was sent did I either see or hear read or reported to me so much as a single syllable.

As to the cause of what you call *un très impudent plagiarisme*, the following extract from a letter I received a few days ago from the writer in question may serve to throw some light upon it. Its date is Novr 27th: your's is Decr 3d.

[6] Robert Adam (1728–92), who started work on the Edinburgh prison in 1791 but did not live to see it completed.

[7] *Panopticon; or, the Inspection-House,* Dublin and London, 1791 (Bowring, iv. 37–172).

[8] Reginald Pole Carew (1753–1835), MP for Fowey. For the sending of a copy of *Panopticon* to Adam see Letters 771, 777, 784 and n., 789, and 792, *Correspondence*, iv.

[9] See letter 792, *Correspondence*, iv.

2064. [1] Dumont MSS 33/I, fos. 139–40. Autograph.

[2] i.e. Mill, whose work was amended by Jeffrey. See above, letter 2061.

'The Edinburgh Review was sent me yesterday morning. Bexon sadly mauled. The mention of you struck out in all but one place, and there my words, every one of them removed, and those of Mr. Jeffery put in their place. The passage is still complimentary, but with a qualifying clause.'—This, except an expression of his vexation, is all he says about it. Meantime here, by a providential anticipation you have the aetiology of the '*éloge très maigre, et qui ne s'applique qu'à un seul point.*' The communication you have just been reading was entirely spontaneous: no questions put by me. It gave me the first intimation I received of the arrival of the Review in London. The article I have not read; and seeing no inducement probably never shall read.

As to Mr. Jeffrey, he has made no secret of his *disposition*—I should rather say his *determination*—to persevere in doing whatsoever may be in his power to keep down the reputation of whatever work I either have published or may come to publish in future: and you see he is not over scrupulous in the choice of his means. He has for this purpose tried his influence in conversation with more than one person by whom it has been reported to me. As to the fact of the alterations there is at least one other witness,[3] though I am not of the number.

Ever Yours
Jeremy Bentham

2065

FROM AARON BURR

5 December 1809

Altona, December 5, 1809.

Please to deliver to the order of Professor Ebeling[2] my map of North Carolina. It is in three or four sheets, and will be found in the large trunk. If you should not have the key of that trunk, let K.[3] open it by force or by gentle means, as he may see proper.

A. Burr.

[3] Koe. See letters 2066 and 2067.

2065. [1] Davis, i. 352.

[2] Christoph Daniel Ebeling (1741–1817), professor of history and Greek at Hamburg Akademische Gymnasium.

[3] John Herbert Koe.

2066

To James Mill

5 December 1809 (Aet 61)

Hampstead, 5th December, 1809.

From the enclosed letter of Mr Dumont, you will see the sensation made by the *Bexon* while at Holland House.[2]

To preserve the person most immediately *injured*, it seemed to me that nothing better could be done than to send to Mr Dumont a copy of so much of your letter of the 27th November as related to that subject.[3] Under so serious a charge as that of a 'most *impudent plagiarism*,' it was no small satisfaction for me to have in my possession an anticipated exculpation, and that so complete a one for your defence; and it was an additionally fortunate circumstance that I was enabled to add the existence of at least one witness, (meaning, though not mentioning,) Mr K. by whom the groundlessness of the charge, in so far as you were concerned, could be attested. For my own part, not a single syllable of the attack having either been seen or heard, read or reported to me, it seemed to me that I could do no less than say as much: viz. in answer to which it said of the *personnes qui prétendent savoir, ou du moins qui soupçonnent très fortement, que cet article a été fait sous votre direction*; with the observation—'*si celà est, il faut qu'il y ait en celà quelque vue très profond qui m'échappa.*'

On account of what is said about Panopticon, as soon as you have given Mr Dumont's letter a sufficient perusal, I will beg the favour of the return of it by post.

2067

From James Mill

6 December 1809

December 6, 1809.

Your communication to me of Mr Dumont's letter though the intelligence imparted by it was not of the most agreeable sort, found it difficult to add to my anger, which was near its maximum before.

2066. [1] Bowring, x. 452. Partly reprinted in Bain, pp. 103–4.
[2] Letter 2062. [3] Letter 2061.

2067. [1] Bowring, x. 453–4. Reprinted in Bain, pp. 104–6.

Under this oddly generated surmise, I feel gratitude to Mr Koe for his very lucky expression of his desire to read the article in MS. before it was sent off, and the very moment before it was sent off; for it came out of his hands; and was sealed up that very instant under his eye. The contradiction of this—not very measured accusation—would otherwise have rested on my self-serving testimony; for it was not my intention to have troubled Mr K. with the reading of it, as I thought he would so much more easily satisfy himself with it when he could see it in print.

It is no less satisfactory to me in respect to another of the said wisely conceived surmises, viz. *that of the article's being drawn up under your direction, etc.*, that you neither saw it, nor heard it,—a circumstance owing entirely to the same cause, viz. a reluctance to encroach with it upon your time, and the reflection that all you might desire to know about it, you would know, with most pleasure, when it should come to be read to you in print.

Notwithstanding, however, the passage in which I endeavoured, not only to do justice to your merits, but to point you out, in as distinct a manner as I could, to the public, as the only man from whom light was to be got on legislative matters, I own that I, after knowing the dislike which Mr Jeffrey had to praise, studiously made use of your doctrines, at the same time sinking your name; and in more places than one, as I dare say Mr Koe remembers, I had originally named you as the author of what I was saying, and afterwards struck it out. This was done upon the exhortation of Mr Lowe,[2] who said, that from what he knew of Jeffrey,—from what Mr Jeffrey had said to him about what he called my propensity to *admire*, and in particular to admire you, as also what he said about his own (Jeffrey's) propensity *not to admire*, that he would not admit the mention of you in such terms to stand in so many places, and that it would be best to retain it in two or three of the places where I thought it of most importance, and strike it out in the rest, when the probability was, he would not meddle with it. As there appeared to be reason in this, I allowed myself to be governed by it,—and after all this caution, we still see what has come of it.

To come, however, to a more aggreable subject,—after thanking you, as I most heartily do, for your zeal to exculpate me,—I have

[2] Joseph Lowe (d. 1831), Scottish school-friend of Mill. In 1808 he was living at 31 Charter House Square. He subsequently moved to Ludlow in Shropshire (see below, letters 2277 and 2285). He may have been the Joseph Lowe who wrote *An Inquiry into the State of the British West Indies*, London, 1807.

this day got to the end of *Exclusion.*[3] *Impossibility* then is all that remains; and I am at the end of the principal stage of my labours, viz. my operations upon your text,—*i. e.* among your various lections, the making choice of one—the completing of an expression, when, in the hurry of penmanship, it had been left incomplete, etc. Editorial notes, of which we have so often talked, are only thus far advanced, that a variety of rudiments are set down, with references to the places of the work where they should be introduced. But it has often happened to me to find, what I had thought might be added as a note in one place, was given admirably by yourself in another place, and a better place. And in truth, having surveyed the whole, the ground appears to me so completely trod, that I can hardly conceive anything wanting. It is not easy, coming after you, to find anything to pick up behind you. My memory, too, is so overmatched by the vast multiplicity of objects which the work involves, that I am afraid to trust myself in any kind of notes, save suggestions of cases, illustration by instances,—lest what I say should be an idea brought forward in some other part of the work. All this, however, is not intended to operate as an apology or pretext for indolence. Notes there shall be written, and very full ones,—whether these notes shall be printed, is another question. My feet are still lumber—still of no use. They seem slowly bringing themselves back to that state in which use may again be made of them. When they will accomplish that desirable object, it is not yet for me to say.

2068

From James Mill

10 December 1809

Pentonville, 10th December 1809

Though I hesitated at first whether the *fides literarum*[2] permits me to shew to you the accompanying letter—a letter which would certainly not have been written, at least not as it is written, had it been supposed that it would be shewn to you—yet as I think there is real utility as between you and me that it should be shewn to you,

[3] 'Exclusion of Evidence'. Mill was referring again to Bentham's writings on evidence.

2068. [1] Bain, pp. 107–8. Partly printed in Bowring, x. 454, where it is undated.

[2] i.e. 'confidentiality of letters'.

and as no harm can thence arise either to the author or any other body, the reasons for shewing it to you appear to me to preponderate. It appears to me at the same time to be proper that it should not be known to any other body that you have seen it; or if you think proper to communicate it to Mr. Koe, to which I have no objection, let this restriction be at the same time made known to him.

The letter which is marked No. 1 was sent first. I answered it by saying that I was unable to visit the gentleman as invited, but begged he would give me a foretaste of what he had to say by his pen, to stay my stomach, till we could meet. I received in answer the letter I have marked No. 2.

These two letters you had better here read, and the few words I have to add afterwards, as they will be in the nature of commentary upon the said letters.

Forcibly did the reading of that last letter strike me with the truth of an observation, which you yourself have somewhere made —that the man who has anything of great importance for the good of mankind to propose, must be dead before his beneficent proposals have any tolerable chance for a favourable reception, or so much as a fair consideration. The man who gets the start too much of his contemporaries, I see, must be an object of jealousy; and while he lives, must have eyes and ears purposely shut against him. I own, in the present quarter, I am disappointed and grieved. One of the most liberal-minded, and enlightened, and one of the most amiable men I know—and yet, such is the letter he writes to me![3] Let us not, however, be discouraged—let us go on cheering one another; and, as I shall find nobody when you are gone—why, you must, just for that reason, live for ever.

When you have sufficiently perused the said notes, have the goodness to let me have them again.

I have made a sort of discovery. In a piece of Voltaire's, the title of which caught my eye the other day, 'Essai sur les probabilités en fait de justice,' he makes use of figures (numerals) for expressing the different degrees of probative force in different articles of evidence. He applies it merely as an instrument for a particular purpose, and in a particular case; and seems to have had no idea of a scale for general use. But it may be useful for you to see it, and to say when and how you have seen it; as the fashion seems to be to impute plagiarisms where the imputation is not shut out by bolts and bars,

[3] The author of these letters might have been Henry Brougham (1778–1868), later Baron Brougham and Vaux, one of the founders of the *Edinburgh Review*. Bowring (x. 454) and Bain (p. 106) print extracts of a letter from Brougham to Mill, 10 December 1809, critical of Mill's praise of Bentham in the Bexon article.

and a guard of soldiers. The vol. is the 30th in my edition, and it is the second of those entitled Politique et Législation.[4] If you have it not, I will send it you per first conveyance.

2069

To John Mulford

1809 (Aet 61)

I am hard at work, trying whether I cannot get the public, or some part of it, to turn its attention to the corruptions in the law department;[2] in comparison of which, the commander-in-chief's office, make the worst of it, was purity itself.[3] It is perfectly astonishing to see how, by comparatively trifling instances of misgovernment, the current of public opinion has been turned against the Ministry, or rather against all Ministries, and in favour of Parliamentary Reform as the only remedy.

2070

From Sir Samuel Romilly

31 January 1810

January 31, 1810.

I have read a good deal of 'Elements of Packing,' and I do most sincerely and anxiously entreat you not to publish it,—and I have not the least doubt that Gibbs[2] would prosecute both the author and the printer. An attorney-general, the most friendly to you, would probably find himself under a necessity of prosecuting, from the representations which would be made to him by the Judges,—but Gibbs would want no such representations, and would say, that not

[4] See *Oeuvres complètes de Voltaire*, ed. P. A. Caron de Beaumarchais *et al.*, 70 vols., [Kehl] 1785–9, xxx. 415–49.

2069. [1] Bowring, x. 449. John Mulford (1721–1814) was Bentham's mother's first cousin. For earlier contact between Mulford and Bentham see *Correspondence*, i–vii, as index.

[2] Probably an allusion to *The Elements of the Art of Packing*.

[3] A reference, presumably, to the Mrs Clarke scandal, for which see letter 2045 n. 7.

2070. [1] Bowring, x. 450–1.

[2] Sir Vicary Gibbs (1751–1820), attorney-general 1807–12.

to prosecute such an attack upon the whole administration of justice, would be a dereliction of his duty.

Recollect what you say yourself,—that it is much easier to attack King George, than King Ellenboro' etc.; and, with all the heroism and disregard of changing your own comfortable climate for that of Gloucester or Dorchester, which, whatever you may feel, you will hardly, I think, reconcile to yourself the involving your printer in the same calamity.

2071

To John Mulford

24 April 1810 (Aet 62)

24th April, 1810.

As to Lord Holland, saving your presence, Doctor,[2] you misconceived me—Oh, no! that is not polite. I am glad I did not say so—I mean—I must have misexpressed myself. Lord Holland never has been in Mexico; in Spain, indeed, he was till lately, and from thence sent me those letters which you saw.[3] The man who has been in Mexico, is not a lord, only an honourable; Cochrane Johnson, my next door neighbour and tenant; one of the uncles of the Lord Cochrane, Member for Westminster,[4] whom, if you ever read papers, you are so continually reading of in the papers. Twitting me with what you acknowledge to be but a half promise, you call upon me for stories;—after Lord H., I should not be afraid of telling stories; but after my tenant, I am, a little. What say you to a shrub or tree, about the stature of a lilac, covered from top to toe with flowers, in form like a *Canterbury bell*, in size as big as a quart bottle, (he would not bate a hair's breadth,) in odour strong and delicious, in colour of the purest white, giving to the whole tree, when in blossom, the appearance (to an eye at a certain distance) of a mount of snow? This (he says) is among the weeds that grow there, and *floripundia* is its name. If circumstances would not admit of bringing

2071. [1] Bowring, x. 454–5.

[2] Mulford, an amateur surgeon, is often referred to as 'the Dr' in Bentham's letters. See *Correspondence*, i. 19 n.

[3] Probably letters 2030 and 2048.

[4] Thomas Cochrane, known as Lord Cochrane (1775–1860), was the son of Archibald Cochrane, 9th Earl of Dundonald, Cochrane Johnstone's brother. Lord Cochrane was MP for Honiton 1806–7, Westminster 1807–18. He served in the Royal Navy (and was knighted for his services), then in turn as commander-in-chief of the Chilean, Brazilian, and Greek navies. He became 10th Earl of Dundonald in 1831.

growing plants or cuttings, why not bring seeds at least? *whys*, more might be put in plenty. Plants or cuttings, he indeed professes to expect—but with other expected things in abundance, what those who know him, fear much will never come. A plant, with flowers about the size of those of a honeysuckle, and growing in a manner not unlike to one, but in each stalk, exactly in number and shape, like *a thumb and four fingers*. This I myself saw, he having imported a specimen, preserved in a bottle with spirits. Also, besides snakes, lizards, and other such vermin, specimens of the *stones*, and the *woods* of the country, cut in squares. Item, a sort of painting in oil, say, about fifteen inches by ten, and not ill executed, exhibiting the inhabitants, as they exhibit themselves, in all the varieties that result from the intercopulation of European Spaniards, American Indians, and African negroes. Moreover, a most magnificent, recently published, map of Mexico the capital—the number of inhabitants about 200,000—the first that ever came to Britain; another copy I have a promise of, but I will sell it you at a cheap rate.[5]

But alas! the paper will hold no more.

2072

To William Wilberforce

5 May 1810 (Aet 62)

Q.S.P. 5 May 1810

My dear Sir

Permitt me now to avail myself of your kind offer of calling upon me.

Yesterday evening, through the medium of a third person, in

[5] Perhaps *Plano General de la Ciudad de Mexico, levantado par el teniente coronel de dragones Don Diego Garcia Conde en el año de 1793, y grabado en el de 1807. De orden de la misma noblisima ciudad.* (BL Map Library ref. 76900(5).) This was not the first map of Mexico City to be available in Britain, but it is a large detailed map, with an index of streets and various important buildings marked.

2072. [1] MS Wilberforce d.15, fos. 147–8, Bodleian Library. Autograph. At BL VIII. 459–60 there is an autograph draft in the same words docketed: '1810 May 5 / Panopt / J.B. Q.S.P. / to / Sr C. Bunbury / (as supposed) / Romilly, notice to / J.B. of his intention / to move about Peni- / tentiary Establishment'. Sir Thomas Charles Bunbury, 6th Bt. (1740–1821), MP for Suffolk, was one of the supervisors appointed to buy land for the penitentiary houses under the 1779 Act. He had long taken an active interest in the Panopticon scheme. See *Correspondence*, iii–vii, as index. Whether Bentham actually sent Bunbury the same letter as he sent to Wilberforce, or decided to write to Wilberforce instead after drafting the letter to Bunbury, is unclear.

consequence of an accidental interview, I received a message from Sir S. Romilly, importing, as far as I could learn, that it was his intention on Tuesday, or so soon after as might be, *possibly* even on Monday, to move for an Address for carrying into effect the Penitentiary System,[2] and that on communication with the Sollr Genl.,[3] he had offered to second it: the offer however being limited some how or other to the Act of 1779 putting thereby an implied exclusion on that of 1794.[4] Tomorrow morning early, I propose to call on R. to hear his explanation. On former occasions, more than one, he had expressed to me his intentions of making such a motion, as soon as his Bills were disposed of: on my part, so far from solicitation, no expression but that of reluctance: having no such ambition as that of passing the short remainder of my life among the Treasury Porters.

If therefore it should happen to be consistent with your more important engagements, Monday, you see, or at least Tuesday, would be preferable to any other day: and, to make sure, if you can favour me with a previous line, mentioning the hour, so much the better.

Yours most truly
J. Bentham.

W. Wilberforce Esqr.

2073

From Richard Wharton

7 May 1810

Sir

I am commanded by the Lords etc. to transmit you a copy of Mr. Long's letter to you dated 24th. March 1801,[2] and to request that

[2] Romilly moved an address for carrying into execution 19 Geo. III, c.74 on 9 May. See *Parliamentary Debates*, xvi. 947.

[3] Sir Thomas Plumer (1753–1824) was solicitor-general 1807–12.

[4] 34 Geo. III, c.84, 'An Act for erecting a Penitentiary House or Houses for confining and employing convicts', which was based on Bentham's own penitentiary bill of 1794.

2073. [1] PRO T 27 / 66, p. 211. Letter-book copy. Endorsed: J. Bentham Esqre. / with copy / Mr. Long's lre. to him of / 24th. March 1801— / Respg. contract for a / Penitentiary House—'. Richard Wharton (1764–1828) was junior secretary of the treasury 1809–14 and MP for Durham City 1806–20.

[2] Letter 1619, *Correspondence*, vi. Charles Long (1761–1838), later 1st Baron Farnborough, was junior secretary of the treasury 1791–1801.

you will call on me at the Treasury Chambers tomorrow between the hours of 12 and 2 for the purpose of communicating with me on the subject of that letter—

I am etc. 7th. May 1810. R. Wharton

2074

From William Wilberforce

7 May 1810

Kensn. Gore
12 o Clock Monday May 7th. 1810

My dear Sir

When and where, yr Note of Saturdy's date,[2] came to my Quarters whether here or in Westmr at ye New Pale. Yard Hotel, I know not —I never saw its Exterior till ysty Eveng and owing to an accident, (partly from havg a House full of friends) I have only perusd it within the last 5 Mins.—I will try to call on you today betn 2 and 3 but I dare not positively promise—yes I think I can do all but promise absolutely—But my dear Sir, dont talk of Treasury Porters—I agree with you—After all you have experienced Unless ye way is smoothd and the doors thrown wide for yr triumphant passage, I would not have you stir from ye Chimney Corner—But if ye Hos. of Coms does awake from its long Slumber and wish to establish a System in ye highest degree beneficial and humane, Surely you will not refuse to tend yrself to those who are eager to bring it forward—nor is it fair to yr friends, if you are yourself indifferent to Credit, that you should lose ye just praise of originating or at least devising ye Means of carrying into Effect, ye true principles of penal Jurisprudence—I scribble in extreme Haste—But I am delighted by seeing with my minds Eye, your Honour like a great Spider, sealed in ye Center of yr Panopticon—

yours ever sincly
W Wilberforce

P S
I have found that my Copy of yr *little* Book is incomplete and must beg you to perfect it.[3]

2074. [1] BL VIII. 461–2. Autograph. Docketed: '1810 May 7 / Panopt / Wilberforce Kensington / to J.B. Q.S.P.' Endorsed: 'Mem. Visit accordingly from Mr. W. to Q.S.P. that same morning'.

[2] Letter 2072.

[3] Apparently *Panopticon; or, the Inspection-House*. See below, letter 2096.

2075

To William Wilberforce?

7 May 1810 (Aet 62)

Q.S.P. 7 May 1810
Monday afternoon

My dear Sir

Within this half hour has been delivered at this House of mine a letter from Mr Secretary Wharton,[2] a copy of which I here inclose: together with the also inclosed Letter of Mr Secretary Long[3] written upon the occasion of Mr Pitt's exit from the Office Ao 1801,[4] and which was afterwards among the Papers printed by order of the Ho of Commons.[5] My answer, not yet written, is intended to be in very general terms—to say that Compensation is and ever has been out of the question with me, that I stand bound to execute the business upon terms as near, as the vast change of circumstances will admitt, to those agreed upon, but that as to Mr Wharton the business is of such complexity, and he so perfectly a stranger to the whole of it, that out of respect for his time, I forbear consuming so much of it as would necessarily be consumed, were I thus early to accede to his appointment, before I had endeavoured to learn by means of some of my friends what could be the real drift of it. These will not be my words, but this is the meaning to be conveyed.

As to Long's letter it was a direct breach of promise, announcing virtually more and more such to the end of the chapter.

If they be really in earnest, Nepean[6] (who always votes with them, does not he?) and who knows all about the business from first to last, and who always has been that honest man that Long would be thought to have been, would be the man, through whom they would be ready to deal with me. I can make no doubt of *his* readiness: though I have not exchanged four words with him for these four years.

2075. [1] Duke University Library. Autograph.

[2] Letter 2073.

[3] Letter 1619, *Correspondence*, vi.

[4] William Pitt (1759–1806), first lord of the treasury 1783–1801, 1804–6.

[5] See *Proceedings and Measures of Government, 1798–1803, on the Finance Reports of 1797–1798*, section F, ordered to be printed, 12 June 1801.

[6] Sir Evan Nepean (1751–1822), government office-holder 1782–1806, at this time MP for Bridport, in 1812 appointed governor of Bombay. For his earlier contact with Bentham concerning Panopticon see *Correspondence*, iv–vii, as index.

This is the Mr Wharton, who wrote the silly empty pamphlet, as if to advertize the Edinburgh Review.[7]

My eagerness to see the *Dominus*[8] would not be great—my reluctance to throw away my time upon this *Fur*[9] is extreme.

I imagine this has some connection with Romillys Motion;[10] and perhaps they may wait to hear what I say before they determine what on that occasion they shall say in the House.

Possibly by speaking to Mr Percival[11] you might learn and be kind enough to inform me what is their purpose in sending me a letter written 9 years ago, and which has for these 9 years been receiving so many answers from my silence.

2076

To Richard Wharton

8 May 1810 (Aet 62)

Queen's Square Place Westmr
8 May 1810.

Sir

I have to acknowledge the honour of Your Letter of yesterday's date, with the inclosure announced by it.[2]

If, on the part of the present Lords of the Treasury, there exists a disposition to give execution to the Acts in question, relative to the

[7] *Remarks on the Jacobinical Tendency of the Edinburgh Review, in a Letter to the Earl of Lonsdale*, London, 1809.

[8] i.e. 'master'.

[9] i.e. 'thief'.

[10] See letter 2072, n. 2.

[11] Spencer Perceval, who had become first lord of the treasury in succession to the Duke of Portland.

2076. [1] PRO CRES 2 / 675. In the hand of a copyist, with the exception of the signature and Wharton's name. The postscript is in the hand of another copyist. Docketed: '8th May. 1810 / Mr. Bentham / in reply to Mr. Whartons / Letter of the 8th: Inst, / rel. to the Penitentiary / Establishment. / No 5443 / Rd: 14th May 1810 / Read 15 May 1810 / 4 Div. 3 Sht. / Write to Mr. Beckett / immediate'. John Beckett was under secretary at the Home Office 1806–17. Autograph draft at BL VIII. 463–5. Docketed: '1810 May 8 / Panopticon. Brouillon. / J.B. Q.S.P. / to / Secry Wharton Treasury / Answer to his of the 7th / requesting interview. / Signed copy sent by Walter / to Treasury ½ after 2. / Same time by do Copy / to Wilberforce, and ano- / ther to Romilly.' Walter was Walter Coulson (1794?–1860), the brother of Thomas Coulson junior. Walter succeeded his brother as Bentham's amanuensis and then became parliamentary reporter for the *Morning Chronicle*. He was later editor of the *Traveller*, and then gave up journalism to read for the bar.

[2] Letter 2073.

once intended Penitentiary Establishment—viz. the Act of 1799 and that of 1794, the latter of which was passed, in consequence of the arrangements which, at my own expence, I had by the late Mr Pitt and the present Lord Melville been called upon to make, and made accordingly, as stated by me in communications printed by authority and never questioned, (not to speak of the subsequent purchase, at the expence of the public, of a portion of the ground intended or professed to be intended for the purpose) their Lordships may rest assured, that notwithstanding all I have suffered, I hold myself still bound to meet that disposition, and as far as depends upon myself to give effect to it.

If, in the event of such an assurance on my part, there exists, on the part of their Lordships, any such further intention as that of concurring in the motion which I understand is intended to be made by Sir S. Romilly for an Address to His Majesty praying an execution of those Acts,[3] the assurance hereby given by myself and under my signature, will, in my humble conception, be still more satisfactory to their Lordships than any report, which, from a verbal communication with me, any intermediate person could make to them.

As to the printed Letter dated 29th March 1801,[4] a written copy of which forms the enclosure above spoken of as received by me, it had not any other purpose than the placing the business in the situation in which it has remained ever since: and, considering the manner in which in that Letter the word *compensation* is connected with my name, it may be proper, Sir, that you should know, that not so much as any the remotest hint about compensation had ever been dropped from me before my receipt of that Letter, or has been since.

Another thing it may likewise be proper on this occasion you should hear from me, is that there never has been on my part any such intention as that of receding from any terms that ever were agreed to by me: and that no such conception ever was, or ever could have been, really entertained by any body else.

Less than what is above would I think hardly have been sufficient for the Parliamentary purpose above spoken of. More I could not expect you to look upon as any thing better than superfluous.

I am
Sir
Your obedient Servant
Jeremy Bentham.

Richard Wharton Esqr
etc etc etc.

[3] See above, letter 2072 n. 2.

[4] Letter 1619, *Correspondence*, vi. For the printed version see letter 2075 n. 5.

PS
On turning to my Examination, as printed in the 28th Report of the Finance Committee of 1796–8, you might see if it were worthwhile, what at that time my answer was on the subject of compensation, when forced upon me by a question put to me by the Committee.[5]

2077

To Sir Charles Bunbury

18 May 1810 (Aet 62)

Q S P Saty. 18 May
1810

Dear Sir,

In your quality of eventual '*Fundator incipiens*'[2] of future contingent Panopticon, I have just been able to muster up the exertion necessary to the sending you the inclosed papers, which when glanced over you will have the goodness to return to me.[3] In the account given in the Times of last Tuesday sennight or Wednesday? of the conversation that took place on the subject on the preceding day on the occasion of Sir S Romilly's motion, it is stated as being to come on again on the 21st. instant?[4] by which time Mr Secry. Rider[5] is to have made up his mind. Since that time I have received no private information. Sense of obligation, in addition to memory of experienced kindness, extorts from me this communication to you.

[5] *Twenty-Eighth Report from the Select Committee on Finance, etc. Police, Including Convict Establishments, Ordered to be printed 26th June 1798*, p. 77. In reply to an omnibus question about terms and indemnification if the scheme were not put into practice, Bentham said that in view of the difficulties put in the way of his proposals, and the length of time taken to consider them, he had long expected 'Execution and Indemnification for Non-execution will glide away together'. He was reluctant to make claims 'such as I could not myself represent as otherwise than purely burthensome' and had no wish to see himself 'fastened as a dead weight upon the Public I had hoped to serve'.

2077. [1] BL VIII. 466–7. In the hand of a copyist. Docketed: '1810 May 18 / Panopt / J.B. Q.S.P. / to / Sir C. Bunbury / Pallmall / sending the recent Treasury / Correspondence'.

[2] i.e., literally, 'the founder beginning'.

[3] i.e. the letters discussed in letter 2075.

[4] *The Times* of Thursday 10 May 1810 reported Romilly's motion in the Commons on the previous day and noted that Romilly 'after a few observations on what had occurred in the debate, stated his intention of withdrawing the motion for the present, in conformity to the advice of some of his friends. He then fixed it for the 25th of May'.

[5] Richard Ryder (1766–1832), home secretary 1809–12.

As to my own part whether I consider myself or the public, I know not whether to wish or to deprecate.——At any rate the age of attendance-dancing as you will see is over with me. I am, till I lay myself down to sleep for the last time——(I am already very drowsy)

My Dear Sir,
Yours,
Jeremy Bentham

Sir C. Bunbury.

2078

From Sir Charles Bunbury

19 May 1810

Pallmall
May 19th 1810

My dear Sr,

I am much obliged by your Note,[2] and Papers which I return.

Tired with the fatiguing attendance, I was out of Town when Sr S Romilly made his Motion, and am going into the Country directly or would have called upon you, which I will do as soon as I return, in abt a Fortnight.

I am, like yourself, tired of dancing attendance on Ministers, who *do not know their own Minds*. I wish Sr S. Romilly good Success, and shall be happy for the Public Benefit, and for yours, to see The Panopticon firmly established, and filled with *improving* Inhabitants.

Yours truly,
Chas Bunbury

2078. [1] BL VIII. 468–9. Autograph. Docketed: '1810 May 19 / Panopt / Sir C. Bunbury / Pall Mall / to / J.B. Q.S.P'. Addressed: 'To / Jer: Bentham Esqre'.

[2] Letter 2077.

2079

To Richard Wharton

25 August 1810 (Aet 62)

Queen's Square Place, Westminster,
25 August 1810.

Sir

In consequence of the communication, with which I was honoured by your Letter to me of the 7th of May last,[2] inclosing the copy of a letter to me Dated Treasury Chambers 29th March 1801, and signed by Mr Long, at that time one of the Secretaries to the Board, to which Letter of your's answer was returned by me, dated and transmitted the next day,[3] it seems incumbent on me to take this method of submitting to the notice of the Lords Commissioners of his Majesty's Treasury, that the Agents of the *Prince's Bridge Company*[4] have begun their operations, and *that* in such a direction as if pursued, would *cut in two*, and contribute in a very material degree to render less fit for its intended purpose, the ground at Milbank purchased under the direction of the Board about the year 1799, in part of the intended site of the intended Penitentiary establishment.

They are, (I understand from themselves,) conscious of their inability to carry on the concern, in that direction at least, without the concurrence of government: and it is by this consciousness that they were led to an application which, (I understand from them) they made not long ago to Mr Secretary Ryder.

Their concern is, (I understand from the public prints,) at a discount of 5 per Cent: and it is for the obvious purpose of preserving it from ulterior depression, that they made a sort of formal show of commencement on the side of Milbank, as above, with firing of guns, and other ceremonies, accounts of which I see inserted in the public prints: on which occasion, to the injury of an occupant, they took, or attempted to take, possession of some land without consent,

2079. [1] PRO CRES 2 / 675. In the hand of a copyist, except for the valediction, signature, Wharton's name and address, and minor corrections. Autograph draft at BL VIII. 472–3, docketed: '1810 Aug. 25 / Panopt / J.B. Q.S.P. / to / Secry Wharton Treasury / Notice of trespass without / tender by | |'.

[2] Letter 2073.

[3] Letter 2076.

[4] i.e. the Vauxhall Bridge Company, incorporated by 4 Geo. III, c. cxlii on 3 June 1809. The bridge was first known and projected as the Regent's Bridge, which might explain Bentham's description.

or so much as tender of recompense: and I observed yesterday evening piles driven and driving, and materials deposited.[5]

Had it been my fortune to possess at present any assurance or well-grounded expectation, of support, from that quarter from which, in relation to the establishment in question support was at one time considered as my due, I should, I believe, have deemed it advisable to cause to be made public such counter information as the nature of the case appeared to call for:—but, as matters stand at present, the taking the liberty I am hereby taking is quite as much as I can find any warrant for doing in human prudence.

The cause of this address is the communication which I was so lately honoured with from their Lordships, as above.

For the opposite reason, I forbear taking any such liberty with *Mr Secretary Ryder*. If, in their Lordships' judgement, it should be found to appertain to the cognizance of that Gentleman's Office, they will of course take the proper orders for apprizing him of it.

I am,
Sir,
Your most obedient Servant,
Jeremy Bentham,
Feoffee of the Land at Milbank
purchased A° 1799, for the
purpose of the intended
Penitentiary Establishment.

Richard Wharton Esqr.
etc etc etc
Treasury Chambers.

2080

From Étienne Dumont

3 September 1810

3d September, 1810.

I do not know of your having been informed that I have been carried away, suddenly carried away—that I had been conveyed, half in the air, in a certain machine—that I had seen a multitude of lakes and a multitude of mountains—that one day I found myself

[5] *The Times*, 24 August 1810, records that 'The first pile of the Vauxhall Bridge was driven on the Middlesex side of the River yesterday, about two o'clock . . .'

2080. [1] Bowring, x. 455. A translation.

in the capital of metaphysics—that I dined there with the literary people of the country—that I colloquized in all good humour with our enemies—that afterwards I went from castle to castle—that I have now a firm faith in enchanters, and still more in enchantresses. Alas, that in the midst of that world, and of its attractions and its illusions, I should have abandoned my faith and denied my master! But my good genius—my good genius has saved me—and—I will dine with you to-morrow. Your silence says Yes!

2081

From Henry Goulburn

24 September 1810

Mr. Goulburn presents his Compliments to Mr. Bentham and would be much obliged to him to call upon him either to morrow or Wednesday at any hour most convenient to himself.

Home Department
Whitehall
Sept. 24th. 1810

2082

From Wilson, Chisholm and Monday

19 October 1810

Sir,

The Vauxhall Bridge Co. having entered into a treaty with Mr. Cooke[2] for the Occupation of a portion of the Ground lying contiguous to his House for the purpose of laying and working the

2081. [1] BL VIII. 476–7. In the hand of a copyist. Docketed: '1810 Sept 24 / Goulburn Home / Department / to / J.B. Q.S.P. / Visurit / Reced at Barrow Green / Sunday 30th Septr / Mrs. Stoker to H.K. Sept. / 29 Friday. The enclosed / "was brought here on Monday / and the same Gentleman / called again this day / and asked for a direction / to write to Mr. B."—He / had one.'

Mrs Elizabeth Stoker was Bentham's housekeeper until 1822. 'H.K.' was John Herbert Koe. Henry Goulburn (1784–1856) was at this time under secretary at the home office 1810–12. He was later chancellor of the exchequer 1828–30, 1841–6 and home secretary 1834–5.

2082. [1] BL VIII. 478–9. Autograph. Docketed: '1810 Oct 19 / Panopt / Wilson and Co Linc / Inn Field, / to / J.B. Q.S.P. / Reced at Barrow / Green 23. / To enquire about Cookes / lease'. Addressed: 'J: Bentham Esqre. / Queen Square / Westmr'. Re-addressed: 'Mr. Koe's / Barrow Green House / Godstone / Surry'. Postmarks: 'Two Penny Post / Unpaid / [. . .?]' and 'OC / 19 / 1810'.

[2] Samuel Cooke, a tenant at Millbank.

materials for the Bridge upon, he has proposed to grant them a Lease thereof for four or five Years; Mr. Cooke states that he holds his Property under you and your Brother on a Lease for 14 Years and an additional term of 9 Yrs. subject to your joint Lives, but as he has hitherto declined, after repeated Applications either to furnish an Abstract or permit an inspection of his Lease, and we having understood from Mr. Koe that it contains a Proviso enabling you to put an end to the Term, if the Land should be wanted for Building on by giving six Months Notice, We take the liberty on behalf of the Company of apprizing you of this treaty and to request you will have the goodness to inform us whether the particulars stated by Mr. Cooke are correct and whether he can grant such a Term as proposed we would be further obliged by your favouring us with a description of the Premises as set forth in Mr Cooke's Lease. I am

Sir

Your mo Obedt. humble Servts.
Wilson Chisholm and Monday

47 Lincolns Inn field
Oct. 19th. 1810.

2083

From Joseph Blanco White

24 October 1810

I am confident, from the knowledge I have of your philanthropy, that you will favour the cause of my country with the further communication of such of your observations as you may consider most beneficial to it. Meantime, I feel myself bound to contribute to that satisfaction, which is the purest reward of every man who consecrates his labour to the amelioration of mankind, by bearing testimony to the good effects of your works in Spain. Though thwarted in their circulation by prejudice and ignorance, they were looked for and read with avidity: they were mentioned as a leading rule for the amendment of our laws, when a committee was appointed to that purpose, during the Central Junta; and I venture to foretell, they will have a material influence in the future code of Spanish laws, if we ever come to possess such a blessing.

2083. [1] Bowring, x. 456. Joseph Blanco White (1775–1841), a Spaniard who had studied at Seville University, settled in England in March 1810. He was the editor of *El Español*, a periodical published in England and distributed in Spain and South America.

2084

To Joseph Blanco White

25 October 1810 (Aet 62)

Oxstead, 25th October, 1810.

Your favour of yesterday's date having just come to hand,[2] I take the earliest opportunity of stating something, which possibly may not yet be too late for a brief mention in the last sheet of your next *Español*.

In the account of the proceedings of the Cortes, on the 27th September last, I see mention made of the appointment of a committee of eight, for drawing-up a law relative to the *Liberty of the Press*.[3] At the request of a common friend of ours,[4] so it happens, that I have of late been occupied—I am ashamed to say for what length of time—in drawing up a Code upon that subject, including what to me seemed the necessary explanations. Though the principles were fully settled, the text was not quite finished when he left this country; but as much was finished and put into his hands, as there could be any practical use for, for some time to come.[5]

He had been several times attacking me on that subject. My answer was, that the accomplishment of it was precisely the most difficult of all problems discoverable in the field of legislation; and amongst other reasons for this, that the whole field of legislation is comprised in it: that, in a word, in my view of the matter, everything else within that field was child's play in comparison of it. Such was the difficulty I expected to find, and such was the difficulty I actually found: accordingly, without its being yet quite finished, about two months of my time were completely occupied by my attempt. You know, without my telling you, the latitude for which my draught was calculated; but a very trifling alteration would, I believe, suffice for rendering it as fit for the purpose now in question, as for that for which it was designed.

It would not be without emotion, and possibly for a moment, not

2084. [1] Bowring, x. 456–7.

[2] Letter 2083.

[3] See *El Español*, ii (1810), 81.

[4] Miranda, who had left London on 10 October for his second landing in Venezuela.

[5] MSS for Bentham's proposed law for liberty of the press in Venezuela, dating from 1808 and 1810, can be found at UC xxi. 7–56 and UC xxvi. 2–11. Material for his press codes of 1809 and 1810 is at UC xxvi. 12–65, 137–42. According to Letter 2094, Miranda took with him a 'fair transcript' of relevant papers.

altogether without regret, that our friend would view, one of these days, so early a mention of a work which he had in some measure been entitled to consider as his own; but if things go on well where he is gone, he would have given it its chance there before your next *Español* can probably have reached his hands; and whatsoever, if any, may be the value of it, I have too high a sense of his liberality to suppose him capable of considering it a proper subject for engrossment.

My arrival in town is fixed for Monday next; after which, I flatter myself with the hope of an early opportunity of paying my personal respects to you, at a sociable time of the day, at the place to which your letter was directed.

2085

From Étienne Dumont

1 November 1810

Nov. 1, 1810.

I return you this tissue of abomination—employ me to reëstablish torture—anonymous accusations—religious excommunications! force a man into the company of executioners—tyrants—inquisitors,—how *can* anybody publish such horrors?[2] I wash my hands of them. I have put it all into barbarous French. The academy will only condemn me: but you will be burnt alive, at the first philosophical and legal *auto da fe*.[3]

I am *forthcoming* on a simple invitation, without any compulsory application of a physical or a religious nature: Friday, or Saturday, or Monday, at choice,—but not later, for I decamp on Tuesday or Wednesday for Ashdon.[4]

After such a succession of horrors, I am hardened, and you may d— me and out and out by some diabolical service—exclusion of evidence, for instance. There will be sulphur enough to consume Lincoln's Inn and the Temple. Farewell, monster!

2085. [1] Bowring, x. 457. A translation.

[2] Dumont was referring to Bentham's writings on evidence, which he was working on and was later to use in his *Traité des preuves judiciaires*.

[3] *Auto da fé* was the ceremonial procedure of the Inquisition in sentencing heretics prior to handing them over to the secular authorities for punishment.

[4] Ashdon was the home of Dumont's friend the Revd John North. See above, letter 2022.

P.S. Dumont's criminal style, wanted to imitate the Monitorial formulary, to be issued without delay.[5]

2086
To John Mulford

1 November 1810 (Aet 62)

1st November, 1810.

You may know, or not know, that the king's illness you read of in the newspapers, is the *old madness*. Sir S.,[2] in his way hither, met two members of the House of Commons: one of them ministerial, the Comptroller of the Navy,[3]—of course with a long face; the other, Sir Samuel Romilly, an oppositionist—the man you read of in the newspapers—mighty brisk and alert. It had never been intended that the House should have met this day: probably not till after Christmas. It would have been prorogued of course; but the king's signature being necessary, could not, under these circumstances, be conveniently obtained. Not that it was regarded as altogether impracticable; but Mr Perceval, the minister, acquainted the House that he feared to make the experiment. Since the king has become blind, those who have seen his signature report it a mere scrawl, without the similitude of a letter. The House having power to adjourn itself, did so; but for not more than a fortnight. You may imagine now what an uproar all our politicians are in on both sides. If he is not mended by that time, there will be battling about the Regency, as before.[4]

You mention Mexico. Mexico I have no longer any thoughts of. But another country still more charming, the province of Venezuela, *alias* the Caracas, so called from the capital, I have very serious thoughts of. Mexico is very scantily watered, both by rains and rivers,—Venezuela abundantly. The temperature is delightful, summer temperature all the year round. Within sight of the sea, though almost under the line, you have a mountain topped with ice, so that

[5] The *Gazette Nationale ou le Moniteur* was described earlier by Bentham as 'the semi-official fountain of French truth'. See *Correspondence*, vi. 416 and n.

2086. [1] Bowring, x. 457–8.

[2] Sir Samuel Bentham.

[3] Sir Thomas Boulden Thompson (1766?–1828), comptroller of the navy 1806–16, was MP for Rochester 1807–18.

[4] A reference to the regency crisis of 1788–9, when the then first lord of the treasury, William Pitt, had opposed the Prince of Wales's desire to exercise the full regal powers during the period of the King's insanity.

you may absolutely choose your temperature, and enjoy the vegetable luxuries of all countries. If I go thither, it will be to do a little business in the way of my trade—to draw up a body of laws for the people there, they having, together with a number of the other Spanish American colonies, taken advantage of the times, and shaken off the Spanish yoke, which was a very oppressive one.

General Miranda, a native of Venezuela, who rose at the time of the French Revolution to the command of an army in the French service, and whose life has been employed in the endeavour to emancipate the Spanish colonies, left this country about a fortnight ago, by invitation, to put himself at the head of them. He took with him the draught of a law which, at his solicitation, I drew up for the establishing of the liberty of the Press.[5] He is to write to me immediately on his arrival; and if things are in a peaceable state, I shall probably take a trip thither not long after I have received his letter. The province has agents here in the style of ambassadors, who, though on account of our connexion with Spain, they cannot be openly recognised, are well received. One of them was sent here t'other day in a king's ship sent on purpose. I am flattered with the hopes of a similar conveyance to be granted at their solicitation. I should prefer it much to a common packet, not only for safety, but for comfort.

I see nothing that can prevent my going if I am alive and well; but either their falling into confusion, or Miranda's immediate loss of that ascendancy, which there can be no doubt of his possessing at present there: both of them, effects for which no probable cause is as yet discernible. A number of our considerable political characters, and even women too, are already looking to that country, and longing to go there. Lady Hester Stanhope, who was niece to minister Pitt, and used to live with him,[6] promised Miranda, that if he found things there settled to his wishes, she would go over to him, and superintend female schools for him. This was before she heard of the above-mentioned revolution. At present, she is among the Greek Islands, or at Constantinople; but the news of the revolution will quicken her return. Even Wilberforce, who gave them an entertainment t'other day, talked, half jest half earnest, of paying them a visit. The good which I could do to mankind if I were in the House of Commons, or even if I were minister, is inconsiderable in comparison of that which I may hope to do if I go there: for having, by the ignorant and domineering Spaniards, been purposely kept in ignor-

[5] See above, letter 2084.

[6] Lady Hester Stanhope (1776–1839), Pitt's niece and housekeeper 1803–6. In February 1810 she left England and settled in the Levant.

ance, they have the merit of being sensible of it, and disposed to receive instruction from England in general, and from your humble servant in particular. Whatever I give them for laws, they will be prepared to receive as oracles: for the case is, though I have neither time nor room to give you particulars, that now at length, when I am just ready to drop into the grave, my fame has spread itself all over the civilized world; and, by a selection only that was made A. D. 1802, from my papers, by a friend, and published at Paris,[7] I am considered as having superseded everything that was written before me on the subject of Legislation. In Germany, as well as France, lawyers, commissioned by their sovereigns to draw new and complete codes of penal law, have sought to do themselves credit by references to that work.[8] In the Russian language, two translations of it were made by authority.[9] In Spain, it was received with enthusiasm, and was about to be made use of, had things turned out well there, by the constituted authorities. In my own country, of course, less said of me than in any other: but still my fame spreading, frequent references and quotations in books, and every now and then a panegyric in Parliament. Meantime, here am I sitting and scribbling on in this my hermitage, never seeing anybody but for some special reason, always bearing reference to the service of mankind. Farewell! my dear Doctor. I have given you a long dose. As I never see anybody, I don't know how soon I may be able to lay hold of a member to frank this.

2087

To Étienne Dumont

7 November 1810 (Aet 62)

Q.S.P. 7 Novr
1810

Dear Dumont

On reading my Scotch Reform Mr North,[2] you told me, complained that on the subject of the *Devices* of Lawyers my '*formes*'

[7] i.e. Dumont's *Traités de législation civile et pénale.*

[8] A reference to Bexon's *Application de la théorie de la législation,* for which see above, letters 2057, 2061, 2062 and 2064.

[9] Only one of these has been traced, *Razsuzhdenie o grazhdanskom i ugolovnom zakonopolozhenii. Spredvaritelnymi izlozheniem nachal zakonopolozheniia i vseobschchego nachertaniia polnoi knigi zakonov, i s prisovokupleniem opyta o vliianii vremeni i mesta otnositelno zakonov,* 3 vols., St Petersburg, 1805–11.

2087. [1] Dumont MSS 33/I, fos. 143–4. Autograph. Addressed: 'To / Mr Dumont / 19 Hay market.'

[2] The Revd John North.

were 'trop abrégées.'[3] I gave them on that occasion as much room as I could possibly spare for them, what I was in hopes would have been found sufficient. What was there given was an abridgement of a larger mass of paper which I believe you have never yet seen.[4] Mr Mill who not long ago went through it pronounced it not only readable but, with little need of revisal publishable. I fear this will hardly be found the case: and that in several places there are *lacunae* and solution of continuity. However such as it is I send it you. As to its title I find it bearing 'Exclusion II. Causes: II. Devices.' By this I perceive that it *grew* out of the topic of *Exclusion* as applied to Evidence. But in itself it relates solely to Procedure, and has nothing to do with Evidence, one Chapter of it excepted.

We agreed that any thing which was liable to be wanted to make use of before your return had better not go with you. Therefore I send you nothing that belongs to Evidence. But for this there can not till then be any demands. Much good may it do you! But it will not do you any. For your trunk will be too full, or its owner too lazy to open it. Forget not to send me back my other papers: especially Liberty of the Press for Venezuela.[5]

Since I saw [you] I have heard read the papers I told you of. The general result is that the P.R.[6] being in debt to this man Bolton[7] a Writing Master is with the advice of the Q.[8] and the D. of York struggling to evade ⟨pa⟩yment, yet without hope of ⟨su⟩ccess. The family is finely painted by its own hand.

[3] This appears to be a reference to Bentham's 'Corresponding Devices of Technical Procedure' that he placed next to 'Arrangements of Natural Procedure' in Letter I of *Scotch Reform* (Bowring, v. 8–14).

[4] See UC lxxxvii. 7–350; UC xci. 1–322; UC xcii. 1–478; UC xciii. 1–535; UC xciv. 1–555; UC cvi. 85–229; UC cix. 27–42; UC clxviii. 166–213.

[5] See above, letter 2084 n. 5. Presumably a transcript of this had already been made for Miranda's use.

[6] The Prince Regent. Since October 1810 the King had been deranged again, although George, Prince of Wales (1762–1830) was not officially made regent until February 1811.

[7] An attorney employed by the Royal princesses to manage their financial affairs but who was in fact cheating them. See A. Aspinall, ed., *The Correspondence of George, Prince of Wales*, 8 vols., London, 1963–71, vi. 494–6, 498–500, vii. 9 n.

[8] The Queen, Charlotte Sophia of Mecklenburg-Strelitz (1744–1818), George III's wife and the Prince of Wales's mother.

2088

To William Cobbett

16 November 1810 (Aet 62)

☞ The following introductory letter, it is desired, may beginserted, if the paper itself is.

Queen's Square Place Westmr
Novr. 1810.

Sir

The celebrity of your name, compared with the obscurity of my own, has suggested to me the idea of presenting you with the inclosed paper on Parliamentary Reform, for the chance of its obtaining through your Register a degree of circulation so much beyond what any such name as mine could give to it.

It forms but one chapter, in a work which I hope soon to have ready for the press.[2]

Bringing to view, in a concise and familiar form the chief of the *reasons* which presented themselves to my conception as pleading in favour of those fundamental arrangements which every body is acquainted with, it will be found to suggest some subsidiary arrangements which have in that character never as yet been submitted, I believe, to the public eye. I am, Sir,

Your very obedient Servant
Jeremy Bentham

Mr. Cobbet.

Copy of the Suggestions addressed to Mr Cobbet which were written on the 1st page of the Copy of the Catechism sent to him.

2088. [1] BL VIII. 482. Draft, part autograph, part in the hand of a copyist. Docketed: '1810 Nov 16 / J.B. Q.S.P. / to / Cobbet Newgate / with Catechism'. Partly printed in Bowring, x. 458–9, with the introduction: 'The following letter is thus endorsed—"With Parliamentary Reform Catechism for publication. Taken to Cobbett by Mr. K. Cobbett requiring a fortnight's time to consider of it, it was brought back, and never afterwards sent." '

Cobbett was sentenced to two years' imprisonment and fined £1,000 for seditious libel in July 1810; hence the reference in the docket to 'Newgate'. After only a few days in the prison proper he was moved, as a result of the intervention of Sheriff Matthew Wood, into the adjacent house of the keeper, from whose upper floor rooms Cobbett continued to edit his *Weekly Political Register*. See George Spater, *William Cobbett. The Poor Man's Friend*, 2 vols., Cambridge, 1982, i. 233–46.

[2] i.e. what was to become *Plan of Parliamentary Reform in the Form of a Catechism, With Reasons for Each Article*, partly written in 1809 and 1810, but not published until 1817. See Bowring, iii. 433–557.

Of the remainder, the part that would best bear postponement is the concluding Section 'Collateral Advantages' etc. If that be not sufficient the two Sections relative to Election Inconveniences might also be postponed.[3]—The Letter might be printed one day and the Catechism itself another

In regard to the division of the matter into Sections, and the insertion of the titles to the Sections, he is also requested to do as he thinks best.

☞ To Mr Cobbet. To make the surer of bringing the matter within compass, several passages, amounting together to about 4¾ out of 23 of these pages (equal to about 21½ full ones) have been marked with brackets, that they may respectively be *inserted*, or *postponed* to another No, or *omitted* altogether, as Mr C thinks best.

2089

TO ÉTIENNE DUMONT

19–20 November 1810 (Aet 62)

Dear Dumont

Friend Allen[2] duns me, and thereby forces me to dun you. This account of the Edinburgh Prison when is it to come?[3] He is in a state of distress about the next No of his Philanthropist for want of knowing whether he may count upon you, and for how much. If a tolerable guess could be given as to the quantity, and he could be assured of receiving it within a definitive length of time not greater than a fortnight from this day, his distress would cease.

Departure on so many points from the genuine Panopticon plan—imperfections resulting from such departure—considerable success notwithstanding such departure—these, according to my

[3] 'Collateral Advantages', 'Inconveniences Incident to Elections, and Election Judicature', and 'Election Inconveniences—Means for their Removal' formed sections xi, ix, and x respectively of *Plan of Parliamentary Reform* as published. See Bowring, iii. 546–52.

2089. [1] Dumont MSS 33/I, fos. 145–6. Autograph. Addressed: 'To / Mr Dumont / at / The Revd. Mr. North's / Ashdon / near Saffron Waldon / Essex'. Postmark illegible.

[2] William Allen (1770–1843), Quaker scientist and founder of *The Philanthropist*, which was to appear in 1811.

[3] Presumably what was to become 'Extract of a Letter on the subject of the Bridewell at Edinburgh', *The Philanthropist*, i (1811), 184–8.

recollection, were the topics which in the short account you were giving to me, you brought to view.[4]

The fact of the Architect (Adam's) having had the plan from me —viz. a copy of the Panopticon book in its three volumes you may mention boldly.[5] It was Pole Carew that got it of me for his use. I have by me some where a letter of his either to Pole Carew or to myself acknowledging the receipt of it, and entreating me not to make it public in Scotland.[6] The departure was studious, and could have had but one or both of two motives: the profit upon the extra expence, and the conveying the impression that his own scientific skill was necessary to set it to practice. To a question perfectly amicable and respectful, addressed as from a tyro to an adept for information, as to the reasons for the departure, he could not find so much as the shadow of an answer. *Bis deciens jam audivi*,[7] quoth Dumont in an Aside that makes the galleries ring again. No matter: it is but a page thrown away, and the ink flowed freely.

Paulet's Schools were mentioned,[8] according to your Reverends order,[9] to the Friend, by my Walter:[10] the dog had pirated the paper already: that is to say his myrmidon Lancaster[11] had, in some publication, solely or separately, not mentioned. He called them the Paris Schools.[12]

Toss up your hat, and cry Huzza! for the triumph obtained by the Liberty of the Press in the Cortes: though with the cursed restriction imported by the term '*political*'.[13] Out of 8, we had two disciples

[4] Bentham and his brother considered that James Adam (d. 1794), the younger brother of Robert Adam, had deviated from the original intentions of the Panopticon plan when he had taken over work on the Edinburgh prison on Robert's death in 1792. See letter 848 and n. (*Correspondence*, iv).

[5] See above, letter 2063.

[6] Letter 792, *Correspondence*, iv.

[7] i.e. 'I have already heard this twenty times'.

[8] Chevalier Paulet devoted his fortune to the establishment of a school in Paris in the 1770s which was broken up at the time of the Revolution. Bentham referred to this school and its monitorial system in his writings on penal law which were published by Dumont. See *Traités de législation civile et pénale*, iii. 156–7 (Bowring, i. 570).

[9] i.e. the Revd John North, with whom Dumont was staying.

[10] Walter Coulson.

[11] Joseph Lancaster (1778–1838), founder of the Lancasterian system of education. Since 1808 William Allen had been one of the trustees of Lancaster's model school in the Borough Road. See below, letter 2098.

[12] Lancaster was the author of *An Account of a Remarkable Establishment of Education at Paris, Extracted from the Literary Repository for April 16, 1788 . . . To which are prefixed, Queries Addressed to Doctor Bell, on his Claims to the Invention of the British System of Education*, London, 1809.

[13] See *El Español*, ii (1810), 149–63.

on the Committee: *Arguilles*[14] one of them: another man whose name, I believe, begins also with an A.[15] Thus B⟨lanco⟩ White said to me: and thus, I, for aught I know, m⟨ight⟩ have already said to you. I have already ripened into the inevitable compound of garrulity and forgetfulness.

Remember to write in English: with power only to substitute French here and there, at the suggestion of the improba Syren should it happen to the pen to stumble upon a Remora.[16]

Give me sixpennyworth by return of post: so will you punish me by an analogous fine.

19 Novr 1810

My Brother heard yesterday from some of the matadores I believe chiefly in the Opposition, that Perceval makes no secret that should there be no decided convalescence by the meeting of Parliament he shall then give the matter up: because if so there must be a Regency: and if a Regency there can be no permanent recovery.[17]

20 Novr. Tuesday. Bulletins exhibited at 3 o'clock this day at St James's 'Evening $\frac{1}{2}$ past 8 Novr 19. His Mys fever has rather encreased in the course of this day.'

—Novr 20th

'His My. has had some sleep in the night, and has rather less fever this morning.'

Tuesday Nov. 20. Yesterday Mr K.[18] dined at the Miss. B.'s[19] who had been to see their brother the Dr at Windsor.[20] His expectations of perfect recovery are not now sanguine. The favourable circumstance was the union of fever with the madness: where there is no fever, few recover; where there is, many: when the fever is cured, the madness in general goes after it: and they know much better how to deal with the fever than with the madness. A.[21] has made a

[14] Agustin de Arguelles (1776–1844), Spanish politician and reformer.

[15] Unidentified.

[16] 'Remora' is Latin for 'delay', but Bentham might also have been thinking of the sucking fish (*Echeneis remora*), believed by the ancients to have the power of staying the course of a ship to which it attached itself. For the Sirens that attempted to allure Ulysses with their songs see Homer, *Odyssey*, xii.

[17] See above, letter 2087 n. 6.

[18] Koe.

[19] Joanna Baillie (1762–1851), the poet and dramatist, and her sister Agnes Baillie (1762–1861).

[20] Dr Matthew Baillie (1761–1823), physician extraordinary to the king. For his earlier contact with Bentham, see *Correspondence*, vii, as index.

[21] Princess Amelia, youngest daughter of George III. She died on 2 November 1810, aged twenty-seven.

will and left every thing to Gen. Fitzroy.[22] The K. it seems was not apprized of the connection: for when the news of her death was brought to the K. Fitzroy being present, the impression it made on him becoming audible, the K. spoke of it aloud, as an odd circumstance. Executor, the P. of W.[23] He and the Dukes[24] have written to Fitzroy telling him that they shall not prove the Will, but that it shall be the care of all of them that whatsoever she left shall be faithfully delivered to him.

2090

From Étienne Dumont

22 November 1810

Eh bien, mon cher Bentham,—je n'ai pas grand chose à vous dire, mais vous m'ordonnez de jaser—et je jase—d'abord en vous remerciant de vos petites nouvelles sur A et F[2]—qui m'ont fait briller à un diner—en les introduisant avec un peu d'art—une belle dame me croit des correspondence à la Cour—

L'article Panoptique du Brid. Ed.[3] est fait—cela pourra tenir 3 ou 4 pages de leur petit caractère du philantropiste—la ressource n'est pas grande—je tiens que le morceau Paulet doit entrer dans cette collection—j'y ferai des changements et cela suffira pour en justifier la réimpression, mais il vaudra mieux peut être renvoyer au 3e numero—remember to write in english—l'avis est venu trop tard, le fait est qu'en Anglois mon stile est gêné, constipé ou fort plat—il y a bien ça et là quelques mots Anglois—when I stumbled upon a remora—j'essayerai de me traduire—vous aurez cela incessamment, c- à d- que je retourne à Londres le 2 ou 3 de Decembre au plus tard.

Vous avez compris que ma malle étoit faite—et vos papiers dans

[22] Lieutenant-General Lord Charles Fitzroy (1764–1829), second son of the 3rd Duke of Grafton, aide-de-camp to the king 1795, served on the English staff 1799–1802, 1803–9, MP for Bury St Edmunds 1787–96, 1802–18.

[23] i.e. the Prince of Wales.

[24] i.e. the Royal Dukes, George III's sons and the Prince of Wales's brothers.

2090. [1] BL VIII. 480–1. Autograph. Docketed: '1810 Nov 22 / Dumont Ashdon / to / J.B. Q.S.P. / Press Law Part. Codes.' Addressed: 'Jeremy Bentham Esqr / Queen Square Place / Westminster / London'. Postmark illegible. Stamped: [. . .?] WALDON / [. . .?]'.

[2] i.e. Amelia and Fitzroy. See letter 2089.

[3] i.e. the Edinburgh Bridewell.

le fonds—ce que j'avois (les Codes particuliers)[4] est traduit, mais ma curiosité n'est qu'excitée—ce n'est pas le palais, ce ne sont que les cuisines—j'y trouve une originalité piquante—cette impartialité imposée aux Editeurs périodiques—bonne aubaine pour Sydney S.[5] —Dieu sait combien il s'égayera—un Journaliste Caton[6]—les vertus d'un Juge requises d'un marchand de paragraphes—et les *échantillons*, j'entends mes hommes pâmer de rire et puis—Comment Perry[7] balancera-t-il épigramme contre épigramme—une plaisanterie de Jekyll[8] en vaudra-t-elle deux de Canning[9]—ou faut-il qu'un papier pour être impartial, soit aussi grave qu'un sermon—

Mais raillerie à part, on vous opposera un des principes que vous suivez partout—pourquoi ne pas se fier en ce genre de commerce à l'intérêt des entrepreneurs, ils savent mieux que personne ce qui leur convient—S'il y a deux partis chacun aura son papier, chacun plaidera sa cause—et voilà la seule chance d'impartialité possible —après tout les lois seront inefficaces, car à moins d'un tribunal littéraire, l'Editeur n'est-il pas toujours maître de rejetter ce qui lui déplaît—Qui le jugera—

J'examine—je ne rejette pas—L'idée n'est pas Utopienne—Cobbett l'a mise en pratique—mon doute est sur la convenance d'en faire une loi,—une loi générale—s'il pouvoit y avoir un gouvernement assez éclairé, assez courageux pour l'admettre relativement à son papier officiel, ce seroit un modelle pour les autres—peut-on l'espérer? oui, peut être d'un gouvernement neuf et encore pur, je ne vois pas d'inconvénient à le proposer—l'engagement solennel est si beau qu'il suffiroit pour porter un homme respectable à se charger de l'entreprise.

[4] Probably a reference to Bentham's 'Particular Codes' relating to the press, for which see UC xxvi. 137–42 and above, letter 2084.

[5] Sydney Smith (1771–1845), one of the founders of and a frequent contributor to the *Edinburgh Review*.

[6] See Plutarch, *Life of Marcus Cato*, iii. 2: '[they told Valerius] many other instances of Cato's fairness and moderation'.

[7] James Perry (1756–1821), editor and proprietor of the Whig newspaper the *Morning Chronicle*.

[8] Joseph Jekyll (1754–1837), lawyer and MP for Calne 1787–1816, noted for his witty contributions to newspapers, particularly the *Morning Chronicle* and *Evening Statesman*. For his earlier contact with Bentham see *Correspondence*, iv and vii, as index.

[9] George Canning (1770–1827), politician and author, foreign secretary 1807–9, 1822–7, president of the board of control 1816–20, prime minister and chancellor of the exchequer 1827. While under secretary for foreign affairs 1796–9, he had founded and contributed to *The Anti-Jacobin or Weekly Examiner*, which ridiculed Whigs and reformers. He was one of the projectors of the *Quarterly Review*, which appeared as a rival to the *Edinburgh Review* in February 1809.

Mr N. est à son menage—plus de ferme—un charbonnier de Chancery lane l'a achetée—et l'a décorée à sa manière dans le vrai goût de Fleet Street—tous les arbres abattus—la haye coupée—une palissade blanche—la maison blanche—tout nud et rasé comme un boulingrin—

On m'a mis en requisition sur votre santé—sur vos travaux—vous êtes le héros du Docteur[10]—et votre persévérance est un objet d'admiration. Il est fort bien, il travaille un peu à la logique médicale, mais cela n'avance pas comme je voudrois. Adieu.

Tout à vous

Jeudi. 22.

2091

To Martin and Co.

5 December 1810 (Aet 62)

Messrs. Martin and Co London 5 Decr. 1810.
Pay Mr. Cuthberson[2] or Bearer twenty seven pound 15s : 10 d for

Jeremy Bentham[3]

£27 : 15 : 10.

2092

From John Beckett

10 December 1810

Mr. Beckett presents his Compliments to Mr Bentham and is directed by Mr Secretary Ryder to request that he will take the trouble to call at the Secretary of State's office for the Home Department any time on Wednesday morning which may be most convenient to him.

Whitehall Monday night 10th Decr.

[10] Either Dr Edmund Goodwyn (1756–1829), a neighbour of the Revd. John North, or Peter Mark Roget. See below letter 2146.

2091. [1] Historical Society of Pennsylvania, Philadelphia. Autograph. For Bentham's earlier dealings with the banking firm of Martins, Stones, and Foote of 68 Lombard Street, see *Correspondence*, v. 268, 295, vi. 149–50.

[2] Perhaps John Cuthbertson, mathematical instrument maker of 54 Poland Street.

[3] Another autograph bill presented to Martins, dated 3 July 1811, instructing payment of £25 to Bentham himself or to the bearer, is at the Pierpont Morgan Library, New York. It appears to have been cashed by Herries, Farquhar and Co., bankers of St James Street.

2092. [1] BL VIII. 483–4. Docketed: '1810 Dec 11 / Panopt. / Becket Secry State / Office / to / / J.B. Q.S.P. / For J.B. to attend / there next day. / Verbal answer in / the affirmative.' For Beckett see letter 2076 n. 1.

2093

To James Mill

13 December 1810 (Aet 62)

December 13th, 1810.

But just received yours dated yesterday morning.[2] Concerning *Droits*, what you tell me is altogether new to me, and the best news possible. I am delighted to see it in such good hands. Oh, yes; get the documents by all means. Those which consist in House of Commons' papers, printed last session, I have of my own, or, at least, ought to have. But let me have the whole *tote*, whereupon all that I have of my own, I return instantly,—and the others speedily, that is, as soon as I have done with them, and as much sooner as they are wanted. Not having yet received my *Cobbett's Debates* for the last session, I remain in total darkness. I feared it had been in no hands but inept and unpractised ones, such as those of the seafaring members.

2094

To Étienne Dumont

4 January 1811 (Aet 62)

Q.S.P. 4 Jany. 1811

Dear Dumont

Herewith you have my Catechism.[2] On Monday[3] before 9 P.M. I must again borrow from you *Liberty of the Press Law*:[4] when I

2093. [1] Bowring, x. 460.

[2] Missing, but it appears that in it Mill informed Bentham of the contents of a letter of 10 December 1810 that he had received from Brougham. Brougham, who was at this time MP for Camelford, had written (Bowring, x. 460):

'I trust that Mr. B. will consider the great question of Droits of Admiralty, as worthy of his attention. I don't know if he is aware of what was done in it last session. As I had a principal share in pressing it,—and in threatening to press it more generally this session,—I could explain its situation easily to you, the first time we meet, and give you the documents.'

For Brougham's involvement in the debate on Droits of Admiralty on 30 May 1810 see *Parliamentary Debates*, xvii. 217–18. Bentham would have been interested in Brougham's offer because since the beginning of November he had been writing on the Prize Acts, a project that occupied him well until into the following January. For Bentham's notes see BL XI.

2094. [1] Dumont MSS. 33/I, fos. 147–8. Autograph. Addressed: 'To / Mr. Dumont'.

[2] i.e. part of what was to be published as *Plan of Parliamentary Reform, in the Form of a Catechism*. See above, letter 2088 and n. 2.

[3] Monday was 7 January.

[4] See above, letter 2087.

return it, you may have in company with it the papers of *Marginals*,[5] such as they are: (they were never fully compleated and put in order): item a Bolton's Press copy[6] of a considerable part of the fair transcript that was taken by Miranda to Venezuela.[7]

Monday being so near you may perhaps prefer taking the present opportunity for returning what you have.

Yours ever
J.B.

2095
From George Harrison

4 January 1811

Sir

In answer to your Lr: of the 15th Ulto.[2] on the Subject of the Erection and Maintenance of a Penitentiary House at Milbank; I am commd. by the Lords etc: to acqt. you that before H.M. Govt. come to any decided Determn. in regard to the Erection of the sd. Penitentiary House, My Lords desire to be expressly informed by you whether you would undertake to carry the Plan into Execution and enter into a Contract for building a Penitentiary House upon the limited Scale for 500 Persons and upon what Terms?, and whether you would expect any and what remuneration in the Event of the Penitentiary Plan being relinquished altogether? and I am to desire you will also inform My Lords whether any and what Buildings have been erected upon the Land at Milbank purchased in 1799 since you became Trustee, who has recd. the Rent of any such

[5] Marginals relating to liberty of the press, some dating from 1809, others from 1817, can be found in UC lxvii.

[6] i.e. a copy made by a press technique invented by Matthew Boulton (1728–1809) and James Watt (1736–1819). See Bowring, vi. 576 n.

[7] See above, letter 2084.

2095. [1] PRO T 27/67, p. 495. Letter-book copy. Endorsed: 'rel. to a Penitentiary / House at Milbank.'

George Harrison (1767–1841) was assistant secretary to the treasury 1805–26. He was knighted in 1831.

[2] See letter 2100, where Bentham denied having written the letter to which Harrison referred.

Buildings as may have been erected thereon, and upon what Terms the Tenants of such Houses or Buildings hold possession of the same.

Geo: Harrison

4th. Jany. 1811

2096

To William Wilberforce

16 January 1811 (Aet 62)

Q.S.P. 16 Jany 1811

My dear Sir

Along with this goes a set of *Panopticon* Plates, which were dug out not long after I had the pleasure of seeing you here, but which I postponed sending, in expectation of some more material demand for intercourse, which has not presented itself till now.[2]

I have now got a Treasury Letter,[3] in relation to which and some incidents that led to it, it would be highly useful to the cause for me to be favoured with your advice. If, without inconvenience you could give me a call at this place, we should be much more secure against interruption for half an hour than in any place of yours, besides the constant need of a momentary reference to documents not portable. In the opposite case, I will attend you at your place in Palace Yard.

In either case I would thank you for at least half a day's notice.

Yours most truly
Jeremy Bentham

W. Wilberforce Esqr.

2096. [1] MS Wilberforce d.15, fo. 149, Bodleian Library. Autograph.
[2] See the postcript to letter 2074.
[3] Letter 2095.

2097

To George Harrison

18 January 1811 (Aet 62)

Queen's Square Place Westminster
18th Jany. 1811.

Sir,

I have to acknowledge the receipt of a Letter under your signature, dated Treasury Chambers 4th Jany. 1811.[2]

This letter having two distinct parts,—viz. one in which questions are put to me in relation to the once intended Penitentiary establishment, the other calling on me for information relative to certain buildings supposed to have been erected on part of the ground purchased for that purpose in the year 1799, and in my possession in the character of feoffee, I take the liberty of giving a separate answer to this latter part, reserving my answer to the other for a separate address.[3]

In the part to which I am now paying my obedience, I observe three questions: to which I hereby submitt the answers thereto respectively subjoined.

1. Question 1. 'Whether any and what Buildings have been erected upon the Land at Milbank purchased in 1799 since you became Trustee.'

Answer. Not one, with any previous consent or knowledge on my part. I understand that in two or three instances, under the notion of repair, some enlargement or other has been made, viz by making addition of a room either at top, in front or on one side.

Unless it be a wooden shed capable of being removed at any time; there is but one building which I suspect to have been erected on a foundation altogether new: and *that* is a slight building, on one floor only, which is now furnished and used as a Confectioner's shop, and was, I imagine, erected for that purpose.

The Map that was taken of the Estate for the purpose of the purchase is not in my custody. It is kept in the Office of the

2097. [1] PRO CRES 2/675. In the hand of a copyist, with the exception of the signature and Harrison's name and address. Docketed: '18 Janry 1811 / Mr. Bentham / in reply to Mr. Harrison's / Letter of 4th: In on the / Subject of the Penitentiary / Establishment / No 678. / Rd. 19th Jany. 1811 / Read 25 Jany 1811. / 4 Div. 1 Sht. / Note to the Comrs. of Crown Lands and Mr / Beckett'. Autograph draft at UC cxviib. 264–7. Endorsed: 'Fair copy sent same day by Walter.'

[2] Letter 2095.

[3] The answer to the other part, on the penitentiary establishment, is letter 2100.

Surveyor-General of Crown Lands (if that be the proper stile of the Office—I mean that which was the late Mr Fordyce's[4]) at Whitehall.

With that document in his hand, on comparing the present state of the premises with the state of them as exhibited on the map, the proper professional Officer, whosoever he may be, would, under their Lordships' orders, afford, in relation to this question, information much more correct and appropriate than any which it is in my power to give.

2. Question 2. 'Who has received the *Rent* of any such Buildings as may have been erected thereon?'.

Answer—Whether, in respect of any such new Buildings, any rent has or has not been received by any body else, is more than I know or ever heard. What I know of my own knowledge, is—that *I myself* have never either received or asked any emolument in the shape of rent, fine, or any other shape, in respect of them or any of them.

3. Question 3. 'Upon what terms the Tenants of such Houses or Buildings hold possession of the same?'

Answer. If there be any such new buildings, the terms on which the Tenants respectively hold possession are such as subject such possession to be divested at a very short warning (one Month's) should the Estate of which they form a part be ever applied to its intended purpose.

I have the honour to be,
Sir,
Your most obedient Servant
Jeremy Bentham.

Mr Secretary Harrison,
Treasury Chambers.

[4] John Fordyce (1738?–1809) was surveyor-general of the land revenues of the crown from 1794 until his death. He was succeeded by Henry Dawkins (1765–1852) former MP for Boroughbridge 1806–8, later MP for Aldborough 1812–14.

2098

To Aaron Burr

19 January 1811 (Aet 62)

London, Q. S. P., January 19, 1811.

Your short note, dated 30th December, 1810,[2] through M. J.,[3] has strongly excited my sensibilities. In point of information from yourself it leaves a sad void, but a void which, in your situation, could not, consistently with prudence, be filled up. You speak of two or three little notes, as written to me at so many anterior periods 'from this place' (Paris). Not one of them have I received.

The last communication received from you was dated Gottenburg, October 14.[4] It was preceded by one of October 2, 1809,[5] speaking of a 'trunk or box with books,' etc., as about to come with it, but which, unfortunately, never came. I forget by what means came certain fragments of *journals*, which, coming from the quarter they did, had their value; but they were little in comparison of the views of the interior of the microcosm, which could not be hazarded.

I embrace this opportunity to send you such letters from *Theodosia*,[6] two in number, as came hither since your departure; one dated Oaks, April 20, 1809; another of two sheets, dated May 31, 1809. Being addressed to myself, I opened them. I also send, 1. One directed 'Mr. Lewis de Sevilly, care of Mr. George H. Edwards,'[7] marked (Pernelles) in the corner. 2. Another directed 'M. L. Sevilly, care of Hon. George Henry Edwards, London.' 3. One directed 'Hon. George Henry Edwards.' All these unopened.

In what you say about Germany, you seem not to be aware that, in his code for Bavaria, *Psixon*[8] has said much about Dumont's book; though, if there be anything good in it, he has profited from it very little. In a line with Montesquieu[9] and Blackstone,[10] *J. B.* is

2098. [1] Davis, ii. 435–9.

[2] Missing.

[3] Unidentified.

[4] Also missing.

[5] Also missing, but see letter 2065.

[6] Burr's daughter. The letters are missing.

[7] A pseudonym used by Burr. See Davis, i. 21–2. Edwards was the maiden name of Burr's mother.

[8] i.e. Bexon. See above, letter 2057 n. 11.

[9] Charles Louis de Secondat, Baron de la Brède et de Montesquieu (1689–1755), author of *De l'esprit des lois*, 2 vols., Geneva, 1748.

[10] Sir William Blackstone (1723–80), author of *Commentaries on the Laws of England*, 4 vols., Oxford, 1765–9.

also mentioned as one of the authoritative codes that have lately been published at Paris.[11] '*Protest against Lawgivers*,'[12] and '*Fragments on Government*,'[13] have not either of them been republished. Since your departure, various works have been put upon the anvil, but none are out yet. 1. Necessity of Parliamentary Reform. 2. Influence Analyzed. 3. Plan of Parliamentary Reform, with reasons for each article.[14] 4. Catechism of Parliamentary Reform (in questions and answers), an abridgment of No. 3, ready for the press.[15] 5. Political Fallacies; distinguished into, Part I., Fallacies of the Ins. II., Do. of the Outs. III., Either side Fallacies. In Part I., all the commonplace arguments against doing good are gibbeted.[16] This last is the only one that contains much chance of exciting general interest. In America—English and Spanish—the others might, perhaps, in some points be thought applicable. *Evidence* may perhaps find in Dumont a zealous disciple.[17] An Edinburgh Reviewer, enlisted since you were here, and divers others (collaborators), are civil and serviceable. He keeps plying Jeffrey with articles containing elogia on J. B., which Jeffrey either leaves out or bedevils, yet still grows civiller and civiller.[18] J. B. has another disciple in Blanco White, who edits the Spanish Monthly Political Miscellany—*El Espagnol.* He tells me of an individual (priest) who had formed a little school in Spain to preach to, upon Dumont's book for text: and from him as well as the Hollands, I find it has made great sensation in Spain.

I send you, as a curiosity, a book called '*Elements of Packing*,' that has been put into my hands. Romilly, without reserve, approves

[11] *Traités de législation civile et pénale.* Bexon mentioned Bentham with Montesquieu, Blackstone and others in the first part of the introduction to his *Application de la théorie de la législation pénale*, p. i. *Traités de législation civile et pénale* is referred to in the second part of Bexon's introduction, pp. iv, lxxxvii, cxxii.

[12] A mistranscription, surely, of *A Protest Against Law Taxes*, Dublin, 1793; London, 1795 (Bowring, ii. 573–83).

[13] *A Fragment on Government; Being An Examination of What is Delivered, On the Subject of Government in General in the Introduction to Sir William Blackstone's Commentaries; with a Preface, in which is given a Critique of the Work at Large*, London, 1776. (See *A Comment on the Commentaries and A Fragment on Government* (*CW*).)

[14] These were the various parts of Bentham's unpublished work 'Parliamentary Reform', for which see above, letter 2057 n. 7. Relevant material survives in the MSS at UC cxxvi and UC cxxix.

[15] i.e. part of *Plan of Parliamentary Reform, in the Form of a Catechism.*

[16] *The Book of Fallacies*, was not published in English until 1824, but appeared as part of *Traité des sophismes politiques* with *Tactique des assemblées législatives*, ed. Dumont, 2 vols., Paris and Geneva, 1816. For the parts identified by Bentham see Bowring, ii. 381.

[17] See above, letters 2044, 2049, 2051, 2052, 2085.

[18] i.e. James Mill. See above, letters 2061, 2062, 2064.

of the plan therein proposed; but says that, if it were published, both author and printer would be presented as libellers, and convicted.[19]

A set of people, chiefly Quakers, keep palavering me in a quarterly publication called the 'Philanthropist,' which I send. The principal of them, William Allen, is a fine fellow; shopkeeping chymist, lecturer in chymistry and natural philosophy at the Royal Institution and Guy's Hospital, ardently benevolent, and increasingly rich. Besides other donations, he gave four thousand pounds the other day towards Lancaster's school plans, which are growing every day in popularity and utility. An account of the spoiled *Panopticon,* at Edinburgh, is translated from a paper written by Dumont for that purpose.[20] Perhaps there may not be room for this.

B. White preaches to the Cortes my ideas, and the proposed law which I have been drawing up by desire for another quarter, about the liberty of the press.[21] But they are such fools that many people, for their own good, wish *Bony*[22] had them quietly, and I for one.

Thanks for your intended *Code Napoleon*; it is here have-able, or at least accessible.[23]

Should you happen to come across any of the Rochefoucault family, especially the head of it,[24] assure them of my respectful and affectionate remembrances.

If you see any of the De Lessert family (now a ci-devant great *banquier*),[25] greet them in my name. Worship for me Madame Gautier, who is one of them.[26] Tell them the Romillys are all well and flourishing. Doubts whether Romilly is or is not to be chancellor.[27]

[19] See letter 2070.

[20] See letter 2089 and n. 3.

[21] i.e. for Miranda in Venezuela. See above, letters 2084 and 2087.

[22] i.e. Napoleon Bonaparte (1769–1821), Emperor of France, whose armies were fighting in Spain.

[23] '*Code Napoléon*' was the name usually given to the *Code civil des Français*, first published at Paris in 1804. An English translation, in two volumes, *The Code Napoléon, verbally translated from the French*, appeared in 1811.

[24] François Alexandre Frédéric de La Rochefoucauld, duc de Liancourt (1747–1827). President of the National Assembly in 1789, he came to England in 1792 after the murder of his cousin Louis Alexandre, duc de La Rochefoucauld d'Enville (1743–92), and took the title duc de La Rochefoucauld. He corresponded with Bentham from the United States in 1795. See letters 1075 and 1085 and *Correspondence*, iv and v, as index.

[25] Gabriel Étienne Delessert (1735–1816) was the French banker who had translated Bentham's *Defence of Usury* as *Lettres sur la liberté du taux de l'intérêt de l'argent, traduites de l'anglais de Jeremy Bentham*, Paris, 1790.

[26] Madame Madeleine Gautier was the daughter of Gabriel Étienne Delessert, and the wife of Jean Antoine Gautier, a Genevan banker in Paris.

[27] With the Prince of Wales about to become regent it had been expected that he would dismiss the Perceval ministry and instal the opposition. On 1 February, however, he announced to Grenville and Grey that he would not require their services, and three days later told Perceval that he intended to continue his father's servants in office.

If you come across Dr. *Swediaur*,[28] an eminent German physician, who now or once lived in the Rue Jacob, tell him that the books he wrote for were packed up at the time by *Callow*[29] (a bookseller), at whose house they lie, it is supposed, still ready for him; but the persons of whom it was expected they would take them, declined it. Swediaur will not be sorry to hear tidings of me, i. e., if alive, for he was a man about my age.

For my part, I am as well in general health as when you saw me last, and my eyes somewhat better.

To know that you were in any situation that would turn talents such as yours to the benefit of any considerable part of mankind would afford me the most heartfelt pleasure. In any other I should have said, on the opposite expectation, I cannot even profess to give you any good wishes. For the trade of *throat-cutting* I cannot see any openings. *Cabbage-planting* would be better, if, haply, any ground were to be got for it.

I wonder whether Theodosia perseveres in her intended translation. No such thing is yet going forward here. Two attempts have been progressed in considerably, but ultimately given up, and, because by inept hands, happily.[30]

Do not be immoderately surprised if you should hear from or of me one of these days from some distant quarter of the globe. There exist climates preferable to that of Mexico. Jovellanos, through Lord Holland, gave me a civil put-off.[31] A temperate climate is rendered matter of less necessity to me since my brother filled up my workshop upon the principle of a floreal conservatory. It has been much more than a conservatory to my comfort and recreation. What a delight it would be to me to meet you anywhere, supposing you there upon any such errand as I should call a good one! I do believe that, of the regard you have all along professed for me, no inconsiderable part is true. But a man must have his eyes well about him when he has to deal with leaders of factions and professed men-catchers.

Jeremy Bentham.

[28] François Xavier Schwediauer or Swediaur (1748–1824), for whom see *Correspondence*, ii, iii, vi and vii, as index.

[29] John Callow, medical bookseller, of 10 Crown-court, Soho.

[30] Probably a reference to Montagu's abortive attempt to translate *Traités de législation civile et pénale* into English. See letters 1939 and n. 3 (*Correspondence*, vii) and 2029.

[31] See letters 2048 and 2055.

2099

To William Wilberforce

1 February 1811 (Aet 62)

Queen's Square Place, Westminster, February 1, 1811.

Dear Sir,

Having lost the hopes with which I had been led to flatter myself,—that I may not have to reproach myself with being ultimately wanting either to the public or to myself,—I find myself reduced thus to attempt troubling you, under much disadvantage, with the mention of a favour which, subject to your approbation, I had, since my last, settled with myself to request at your hands.

You had been already apprised, I believe, of my having received a letter from the Treasury. It came to me dated on the 4th instant. To a part, the answer to which did not seem to me to admit of any further postponement, I sent an answer on the 18th.[2] The other part I was led to defer answering by the above-mentioned lost hope.[3]

As to the views with which the letter was written,—though, or rather because, it contains a question about undertaking on a reduced scale,—if I were obliged to lay a wager on the subject, I should lay about ten to one that a determination had been taken not to set the business on foot upon any scale; and that the letter is but one step in a plan for my ruin, in which more steps than one had been taken already; but, not holding myself justified in acting upon probabilities as if they were certainties, I planned, on my part, as above, for the purpose of reducing them to certainties, the *experimentum crucis*,[4] which I now proceed to state.

Sir Evan Nepean, you will presently recollect, has from first to last been fully possessed of the whole business.[5] Of the height occupied by that truly right honourable man, in public estimation, it were needless to say more. To the present administration, if what I heard some time ago, and from satisfactory authority, be at present true, viz., that his votes in the House have been habitually on their side, the choice of such a person for referee should, naturally speaking, if they mean what they would be thought to mean, be in a

2099. [1] *Correspondence of William Wilberforce*, 2 vols., London, 1890, ii. 203–6. An autograph draft of this letter is at BL VIII. 492–7, docketed: '1811 Feb 1 / Panopt. / J.B. Q.S.P / to / Wilberforce Kensington / Gore / In[. . .?] [. . .?],/ To propose Nepean.'

[2] Letter 2097.

[3] Letter 2100.

[4] i.e. 'the experience of misery (or torture)'.

[5] See letter 2075 and n. 6.

particular degree acceptable. Many years ago, when Panopticon was still, in appearance at least, depending, he informed me of a spontaneous offer he was then about to make to Mr. Pitt, to take upon himself, in, as well as out of the House, the whole responsibility of setting it on foot, if such were Mr. Pitt's pleasure. As towards me, who am less than nobody, and who, except for a moment in the street (I think it was last spring), have not had any sort of intercourse with Sir Evan, direct or indirect, for I know not how many years,—whether any thing of undue partiality can be supposed to exist on his part, especially in opposition to the leanings of men in their station, with whom he is in the sort of connection above spoken of, and with all of whom he cannot but be more or less in personal habits of intercourse, is a question upon which I am ashamed to observe how many words I have consumed.

What occurred to me then in relation to him was that, some day or other, when in the House, you might, perhaps, have no objection to the mentioning him to Mr. Perceval in the above view. I mean proposing, as from yourself, or in what other manner might seem most proper, the referring the whole matter to Sir Evan, for him to settle with me, as above. Which to speak to first, him or Mr. Perceval, that would be another point for you to determine.

As to any body else, a Secretary of the Treasury, for instance, who, at this time of day, should take up the business *de novo* . . . having it in charge to deal with the sort of troublesome man which it has been my fate to be converted into . . . a person in every such situation would, if sincere, find in real ignorance, a perpetual source of embarrassment, or, if insincere, in affected ignorance, a perpetual cloak for injustice. For settling the terms of the contract, (that is to say, for gaining time, for they were afterwards to be settled again, as if nothing had been settled,) Mr. Long, then Secretary to the Treasury, turned me down to Mr., afterwards Sir Richard Good, then not in any office, unless it were that of police magistrate, or justice of the peace.[6]

On the part of the administration, should this proposal be declined, my intended fate with them will be no longer a secret to me. I shall then have to carry on against Mr. Perceval the same sort of cause that Sir Thomas More, according to his own report of the case, had to carry on against Henry VIII.[7] In defence of my own

[6] Sir Richard Ford (1758–1806), MP for East Grinstead 1789–90, Appleby 1790–1, chief magistrate at Bow Street 1800, knighted 1801.

[7] Sir Thomas More (1478–1535), author and lord chancellor of England 1529–32, executed for treason on account of his refusal to accept Henry VIII's supremacy over the Church of England. Bentham was probably alluding to More's claims during his trial that the solicitor-general, Sir Richard Rich, had committed perjury.

character, I shall find myself under the miserable necessity of exposing divers others, though, unhappily, with not much greater prospect of advantage to the public from any such exposure, than from a similar exposure at the expense of Buonaparte.

Ever since I received yours of the 23d,[8] I have been confined to the house by indisposition, which has been one cause of my not endeavouring to profit by a hint, which I am not quite sure of my having rightly understood, about Kensington Gore; but I think of recommencing my usual early walks to-morrow.

Entreating your indulgence for the liberty I have thus been taking,

I remain,
Dear Sir,
Your most obedient servant,
Jeremy Bentham.

2100

To George Harrison

2 February 1811 (Aet 62)

Sir

I now take up the pen in obedience to the first part of the Letter under Your signature dated the 4th instant[2] viz. what is therein said to me in relation to the proposed Penitentiary Establishment.

Permitt me Sir in the first place to observe that in relation to a supposed letter of mine some little misconception has / seems / some how or other to have taken place. Your abovementioned Letter sets out in these words.—'In answer to your Letter of the 15th ulto on the subject of the erection and maintenance of a Penitentiary House at Milbank, I am commanded' and so forth. Thus far Sir Your Letter.

The only Letters I ever addressed to his Majestys Treasury on this or any other subject since the entrance of the present Administration into office bear date the one of them the 8th of May 1810,[3] the other the 25th of August 1810:[4] this of August having no other

[8] Missing.

2100. [1] UC cxviib. 268–88. Autograph rough draft, dated 17 January 1811. Fragments of the letter actually sent (dated 2 February 1811) are at PRO CRES 2/675. See also PRO T 2/58, where the receipt of a letter from Bentham dated 2 February is recorded on 4 February, and letter 2099, which confirms that the letter had not been sent by 1 February.

[2] Letter 2095. [3] Letter 2076. [4] Letter 2079.

object than the giving information of a trespass committed on the land in question, and that of May being in answer to a letter with which I had been honoured on the preceding day by Mr Secretary Wharton,[5] and of which the subject was that mentioned by you as above. I take the liberty of considering this of the 8th of May 1810 as being that which you had in view.

In this Letter I observe two distinct questions

1. In the first you say to me as follows 'before his Majesty's Government come to any decided determination in regard to the erection of the said Penitentiary House, My Lords desire to be expressly informed by you, whether you would undertake to carry the plan into execution, and enter into a contract for building a Penitentiary House upon the limited scale ('*limited*' is your word) for 500 persons, and upon what terms?'

In answer to this, Sir, it is not without extreme / much / regret that after so explicit an assurance as in my letter of May had been given of my doing what depended on myself toward the carrying the Penitentiary Plan into execution, instead of any corresponding assurance of a corresponding disposition on the part of their Lordships, I find nothing more encouraging than a repetition of a question put to me under a former Administration,[6] and which in my abovementioned address to their present Lordships I had stated as having, to my own compleat understanding, 'no other purpose than the placing the business in the situation in which it has remained ever since'.[7]

With so discouraging a circumstance under / in / my eye / communication before me / I wish rather than hope it were in my power to persuade myself that this question by which the questioners are bound to nothing and in which the individual questioned beholds his fate hanging over his head had any other object than the affording an *occasion*, or to use the word which the nature of the case if separated from the consideration of the persons would call for the pretence, for 'relinquishing' the once settled plan called for this purpose by those whose steps they are thus treading in 'the *project*' altogether: viz. on any other supposition can find any use or motive / [. . . ?] or cause or use / for the question about eventual remuneration that immediately follows.

Under these circumstances, it does appear to me that instead of giving answer to any such question, and to save myself from so burthensome and ungracious a task as it seeks to impose upon me, I

[5] Letter 2073.

[6] i.e. in Charles Long's letter of 24 March 1801 (letter 1619, *Correspondence*, vi).

[7] Bentham was quoting from his own letter of 8 May 1810 (letter 2076).

should not have been unwarranted in humbly requesting to know as a preliminary whether on the part of their Lordships there does really exist any such disposition as that of carrying / enabling me to carry / the plan into execution in any event and upon any terms. Since if really no such disposition does exist, any such task as that of sitting down to make calculations for which a long train of mercantile enquiries would be an indispensable preliminary, would be a useless addition to a train of sufferings which long ago even in the estimation of those who were occupied / concerned / at the time in inflicting them had when they were not a quarter part of what they have been since, [exceeded] by much the utmost length that consist either with humanity or justice.

Nevertheless forasmuch as the pen is already in my hand and that the commands / desire / of their Lordships to receive *express* information have put in your hands, Sir, this / so / peremptory aspect I proceed,[8] with that simplicity / plainness / which I hope will not be deemed inconsistent with the respect / this respect / due to their Lordships station the express information so desired.

In the first place, Sir, the term '*limited*' which I am sorry to see adopted from as / the / former administration above spoken of, is by far too important / material / an one to be passed over without observation.

Limited, with submission, Sir, is a term which is [. . . ?] very far from being expressive of the real nature of the case. A scale for 2000 persons the number I was at one time flattered with—a scale for 1000 persons the number of the assurance of which my property and my expectations in life were embarked—both these, Sir, were limited scales. A scale for 500 persons was likewise, it is true, a limited scale, but what is truer it was a *reduced* scale. Why then not call it a reduced scale? Why not call it by this its proper name? Because: if expressed by that its proper name it would have expressed and laid open to view / the light /, the act of irrevocable and arbitrary power, by which in breach of an engagement too notorious to admitt of dispute, and without any the smallest pretence that ever durst venture into the light, one half of that engagement was in substance violated, and this for the undisguised purpose of paving the way to a violation of the whole.

The way being thus prepared by this observation, I proceed now to submitt my answer.

1. I most decidedly will not upon any terms undertake to carry what is called the plan but which in fact would be but half the plan into execution, in any other case than that of finding it taken out of my

[8] The rest of this pararaph is crossed through in pencil.

power to carry into execution the whole of it. No personal advantage to myself should any such be offered to me is capable of inducing me to deprive out of the number of 1000 persons in that unhappy situation half that number of the benefits which I am as confident as ever of being able to bestow which with unabated confidence the plan continues to present itself to my eyes as perfectly calculated to bestow.

The waste of public money which would be the inseparable concomitant / consequence / of such a reduction is a circumstance which I am sorry it should in this course prove necessary for me to present to their Lordships view.

No small part of the expence would be exactly the same for the greater number as with the lesser and could neither be reduced in the same proportion with the greater number nor in any proportion at all.

1. In this case is a great part of the official Establishment: all the superior branches, and an indeterminate number of the inferior ones. The constantly resident Deputy Governor: the constantly resident / attendent / Chaplain: the constantly resident / attendent / Medical Curator: Turnkey, Porters at the Gates: Instructors, nature and number not determinable antecedently to experience.

Savings such as could be made out of the bread money were the fund and the only fund out of which this part of the expence could be defrayed. If the whole was / be / not too great and it was pared down as low as possible, the half would be too small by half.

2. To no inconsiderable portion of the building does this same observation apply, and with equal force. To the central and characteristic part for example 1. the scene of visitation, the Inspector's Lodge: 2 to the walls by which the Approach would require to be bounded: 3 to the walls by which the square in which the building would be to be set down would be to be inclosed. 4. to the commanding turrets at two of the angles:[9] on which occasion may here be mentioned as another part of the official establishment, the persons / watchmen / who in the night time at least would have to watch the four exterior walls on the outside of the square: 5 the occasionally discernible room apparatus for the Chapel: besides other apartments which in the present stage of the business it would be equally difficult and unnecessary to enumerate. 6 amongst others the private apartments appropriated to the use of the several members of the official establishment. Last but not least the surrounding wall with which, as could be done, it would be necessary that the whole spot of ground allotted to the establishment, (quantity originally

[9] The rest of point 4 is crossed through in pencil.

demanded and engaged for, for the 1000 79 Acres: quantity at present purchased about 51 or 52 acres) [be enclosed].

The difference, which I pray and trust I shall not be reduced to calculate, is a sum which it would be absolutely necessary should be made good at the public expence. But any sum so employed is what it is impossible for me to set down to any other account than that of public money spent in waste.

On occasion similar to this I have sometimes been told / heard observed / that considerations of this sort are no business of mine. To no such observations, Sir, could I / can I / ever subscribe. I hope to find their Lordships of opinion that in point of a public duty it concerns them not to be principals in the offence of public waste. I am sure it concerns me not to be an / a willing / accessory to any such offence. I have not less than their Lordships or any other Lord a conscience to guard / keep pure /. I have not less than their Lordships or any other Lord a character to keep from being sullied / spotless /.

I know not whether after the above it will be worth submitting / adding / further to their Lordships consideration, that if in consideration of any time and trouble, (for, as to any thing devoid of all estimable value as any talent that I could pretend to I feel but too sensibly can never have place in the / any such / account), I say, if in consideration of any such expenditure as just mentioned, the whole advantage / retribution / in all shapes together, possible emolument, reputation, consciousness of service rendered to the public and mankind was not too much, in any such supposition the mere half of that allowance in these several shapes can never be sufficient.

As to '*compensation*', on that score, none has ever been so much as hinted at. It might have been / Without much expence to the public it might however have been / not only hinted at but offered: for by me most assuredly nothing on that score either would now or ever would have been accepted.

The tutelary influence of the public eye was among the foremost / constituted no inconsiderable article on the list / of the securities to which I had trusted for the goodness of the management. The degree / share of interest and / of attention with which it would be regarded by the public eye / an establishment of this kind would experience on the part of the public / could not but depend and that in a variety of accounts, on the magnitude of the scale: The greater the object the greater the share of attention it would draw of course were it on no other account than that of its mere magnitude: and since the greater the magnitude the greater the quantity of money which it would place at the disposal of the Manager, the greater would be the power / means / it would afford him of adding to the number and variety of the sources of attraction / attractions / which it might be enabled to afford.

Here then is another point / way / of view in which it is impossible that the proposed reduction / any such reduction as that which is proposed / in the scale of magnitude should not be attended with a proportionable reduction in its beneficial influence.

Of such an innovation what would be the effect upon the reputation of the author of the plan and upon that of the plan itself? The terms per man / head money / being necessarily so much the higher, the variation produced in the other part, produced to my prejudice, and against my remonstrance, would be charged upon me.

Be the nature of the establishment what it may no great advantage to it can reasonably be expected from any such circumstance as that of a mark / token / of desertion imprinted / cast / in the character of him under whose / to whose / management it is placed / entrusted/.

In the year 1792, eighteen / nineteen / years ago, when you first gave in your proposal for the establishment 1000 being the number stipulated for in your proposal, it was our hope and expectation, to find in you qualities of all sorts moral and intellectual adequate to the management of the whole. The nineteen years that have elapsed since have indicated / warned / us of the danger we should bring on / that would be brought upon / the public by any government / administration / which should continue to you so large a share of confidence. Proceeding with the caution the necessity of which has been imposed upon us by a fuller knowledge of your character we now in your old age and even now not without great hesitation venture to trust you with half that measure of confidence of which your middle age had with too little circumspection been thought capable of being entrusted with.

There was a time when it was thought and hoped and thought that you might have been trusted with the whole. But that time is no more: and now such as you have been proved to be by your conduct for these last nineteen years, the half of that whole is quite as much as the prudence so necessary in our situation will endure our trusting you with.

I do think, Sir, that it will hardly be said, that a mark of Suspicion and desertion that public can in itself have any great tendency to add to the power / efficiency / effective powers of him / of doing well on the part of him who is the declared object.

Necessity and that of no weak or obscure complection must be the plea / cause / justification / cause / that if any thing can / must / can alone / be made / adduced / to justify it. But whether this / such necessity is among those things / matters of fact / which to the prejudices of an individual any person even in their Lordship's high situation, will be considered as warranted in taking for / assuming / as a matter of course, and without need of alledging / reference / any one matter of fact in the character of a ground for the support of it, is what I must beg leave to present to their Lordships serious consideration / mature reflection /.

It may be a light matter to cast such an imputation it can not be a light matter to be the object of it.

For the purpose / any such purpose as that / of paving the way to what has been called '*the relinquishing of the project*' the talk about reducing it to half the scale agreed upon may / might / serve for aught I shall presume to say as well as any other course. But, upon any one who should bring upon the carpet any such proposition with any view of carrying it / seeing it carried / into effect, it would rest to shew—why, being fit to be carried on upon the exact scale that was agreed upon.[10] This no more easy to shew than that a causeless violation of agreement is consistent with honour or justice.

After so much has been said, an expectation that may not be unapt to present itself, and looked for not impossibly perhaps by some eyes, not altogether without impatience,—is a refusal on my part to undertake the business on any such reduced terms.

But no, Sir, no such refusal, will their Lordships receive from me. The expedient is of the number of those that were tried long ago, that have been tried over and over again, but were seen through from the very first, have all along been most cautiously and I beg leave to assure you, Sir, successfully guarded, and never in any the smallest degree have in any one instance, succeeded. By irresistible force / main / I have indeed been dragged and thrown headlong into this net, but never have I been enticed into it as, for so much as a moment nor so much as a single step towards it.

But first to last Sir it has been an / a Cherokee / Indian trial, Sir, on the one part which shall inflict most, on the other part which shall bear most: and I will venture to appeal to all or any of the several Gentlemen Right Honourable and Honourable to whose lot in the course of so many years / almost these twenty years / it has fallen to bear a part in the ceremony, whether I have ever flinched.

While the trial of a man whose services were too great to be

[10] A marginal note, apparently intended to continue this point, is incomplete. It reads: 'and upon the faith of which'.

forgiven I mean Mr Palmer[11] was going on, the trial of another man in whom the faculty of rendering service had been [. . . ?] in the bad, was going on upon the same principles and in the same hands, Mr Palmer in a moment of weakness sunk under the torture and great was the relief / comfort / afforded to the surrounding court. As for my part what I have wanted in merits I have made up in services. with the benefit [of] his example before my eyes in the character of a warning, I still have to give them trouble / am still upon my legs/.

No / Yes /, Sir: when after month upon month spent in distress and consultation, Gentlemen have felt or conceived themselves under the necessity of charging upon me the deserting the cause of the prisoner and of him who hath come to help him they have taken shame and prudence into counsel they have hid their faces; they have given in papers without a name No one Gentleman being to be found whose reason would enable him to advance a fact with the most pointed proofs to the contrary put for that very purpose into his hands a paper without signature, was put together and sent out upon that purpose / errand /. Yes, Sir from the very board at which this will find you an anonymous paper, the very first paper of that description which I am inclined to think and have some reason to think was yet issued from that source, and which I am not less inclined to hope may be the last.

Had passion / the different passions / been my guide, and the gratification of them my first object, materials / fuel / machinery /, it is no secret have / has / never been wanting, and whatsoever accommodation might be afforded to some persons / this and that Right Honourable person / by any such refusal would have been afforded to them some sixteen or seventeen or eighteen years ago and more. But my not being able to do above half the good the means of which even once, and for such a length of time / so many years / continued to be promised to be, will not in this instance, any more than from the beginning of my life till now it ever has in any other instance, be regarded by me as a sufficient warrant for doing service [?]: as a sufficient warrant for refusing at any time to do whatsoever little good it may at that time have been in my power to do.

Yes, Sir, even now I am ready, if so it be that it is presented to

[11] John Palmer (1742–1818), MP for Bath 1801–18, post office reformer. His scheme for conveying mail by stagecoaches was adopted in 1784 and in 1786 he was appointed comptroller-general of the post office. In 1792, however, he was dismissed following disputes over remuneration for his scheme. He was given a pension of £3,000 per annum, but continued to press his claim. In 1799 a Commons committee decided in his favour, only to be overruled by the government. Palmer was eventually paid £50,000 in 1813.

me in earnest, to take up / in hand / and drink down the cup of contempt that is presented to me. I will, if such be their Lordships inexorable command set about making calculations grounded on this reduced scale.

But, Sir, the credit / admiration / praise / whatsoever it may be, that belongs in justice to such prudence, be assured, Sir, that it shall be my special and effectual care not to rob any person whatever, of any / the smallest / part of it. It will not be my fault if it is not known, and known to every individual who shall have ever seen the establishment or heard of its existence, that the prudence which exercised / has thus displayed / itself at the expence of good faith and justice, displayed itself against / was exercised not only without / my consent, but in spite of my most strenuous remonstrances / protestations / that in my declared view of the matter there was no one reason for it, there was every reason against it, and that as to any such persons, if any such there be, by whom in / from / the seat of power, reason or any thing in that shape is looked upon as any thing better than surplusage and waste of words, to / it is to / the seat of power that in the present instance they must address themselves for what they want / look for /, and not to me.

Gentlemen may forget but really, Sir, it is not in my power to forget that all this prudence is a most pointed and even acknowledged / condoned / violation of good faith: that the scale of 1000 which I am now so coolly called upon to see reduced / join in reducing / to half, is a scale that was acceded to eighteen years ago, formed an indispensable part of the proposal acted upon on both sides for a long course of years / year after year/, stated as acceded to, stated as binding as far as any thing can be binding on those whose station is above law, stated so / in this way / over and over again never denied by any of those who if it had not been true were by every call of conscience and reputation continually called upon to deny it.

That for these | | years I who have now the honour thus to address you have stood upon record; recognized from the Board at which you sit, and by the signature of those whose place / seat / you occupy, in the number of the public Creditors and that except the circumstance that for the payment of this debt no special day was / had been / fixt, there is nothing to save that Honourable Board / firm / from the imputation, and that a just one, of having committed an Act of Bankruptcy, as decided as that which on the indication made / given of it / in the House, comes out so much to the surprise, and not a little to the perplexity, of the Right Honourable and Honourable Gentlemen who [were] then sitting on it.

Yes, Sir, so clearly in every other particular than the antecedent fixation of the day and the responsibility of the firm subjection to the law (I mean in the burthensome sense of the word responsibility) does the appellation / do the characters / of Bankruptcy belong to the transaction, that time and for no other reason than that the / my / Debtors are within the *rules*—10s in the pound, and that not promised is held out to me as the composition the utmost composition that I am allowed so much as to think of.

Well, Sir, 10s in the pound I will accept, if no more will be paid, and only if no more will be paid, and because no more will be paid and because half a loaf is better than no bread: but I do not accept it, but for these reasons and declaring these to be my reasons, and because it has been my misfortune to have for my debtors a firm whose shop is within the rules / of the Kings Bench /, and whose seat is above the law, and to whom it is matter of pride and / as well as / safety to be above the rules of good faith and honesty as well as those of law.

When in that secrecy which is so favourable / convenient / to guilt and so useless to innocence, condemnation was passed upon the establishment, it was altogether without a hearing. On that occasion as[?] for that purpose, From first to last no such faculty as human reason ever was employed. / no such thing as a reason was ever attempted to be brought to view: / rummaged up /. It was all will, pure will: and by what motives and considerations that will was determined will not be mentioned by those whose will it was, and neither need / needs / any more than durst be mentioned by any body else.

Lastly As to remuneration the last point in your letter—It is only in the event of the plans / 'project's / being 'relinquished' altogether that there can be any use in my speaking more explicitly than I have done on the subject of '*remuneration*,' to employ a / the / term / this being the word / which I see in the letter that lies before me. On this subject, I humbly hope that untill some '*express information*' has been afforded to me, in answer / reply / to the observations already submitted, what in my examination before the Finance Committee of 1797–8 as printed in their 28th Report is there said on the subject of *compensation* (for alas! Sir! where service has not been permitted, remuneration is not possible) may, for the present, at least I hope suffice.[12]

[12] See the postcript to letter 2076.

2101

From Étienne Dumont

16 February 1811

February 16, 1811.

The man in the moon takes as much interest in my labour as you do.—I am a working slave,—the whip would not be so afflictive as so much indifference. Massa is a very bad massa. Not one poor visit in the antejentacular perambulations. Read the fable of La Fontaine, 'L'âne et le jardinier.'[2] I regret my former master.

I threaten you with an invasion,—but I give you fair warning, —to-day, if you choose, or Tuesday,—petit régime, remember,—je suis un sage, je ne mange ni ne bois, je travaille, je maigris à vue d'œil, j'ai besoin de causer avec vous avant d'entrer en conférence avec l'imprimeur, et je suis impatient de commencer pour être libre, si possible, à la fin de Mai.[3]

Samedi. E. D.

2102

From William Wilberforce

8 March 1811

New Pal Yd Hotel
Fridy March 8th

My dear Sir

I have been wishing to call on you, and once I did write to you, but owing to an Accident my Letter was mislaid, till its Contents were superseded. I shall be glad to see you soon either Chez vous, or Chez Moi—

2101. [1] Bowring, x. 460.

[2] A reference to the *Fables* of Jean de la Fontaine (1621–95) and more particularly to 'L'âne et ses maîtres', *Fables*, iv. 11, in which a gardener's donkey wants a different master because the gardener works him too hard. He then finds that his new masters, first a currier, then a coalman, are just as unsatisfactory as the gardener.

[3] Probably a reference to the printing of *Théorie des peines et des récompenses*.

2102. [1] BL VIII. 498. Autograph. Docketed: '1811 Mar 8 / Panopt / Wilberforce Pal. Yd / to / J.B. Q.S.P. /For letters to Ld Pelham / and Plea for Constitution / sent by his Messenger do / with / Views of Hard Labour Bill / and / Pauper Management.' The last two works mentioned in this docket are *A View of the Hard Labour Bill*, London, 1778, and what was to be published in 1812 as *Pauper Management Improved: Particularly by Means of an Application of the Panopticon Principle of Construction.* See above letter 2063 n. 3.

Meanwhile havg changd my Amanuensis lately I cannot find my Copy of your Letters to Ld Pelham[2]—May I beg you to give me another, because I cannot buy it—

I hope to buy your 'Plea for ye Constitution'[3] and if it be out of print I must trouble you for that also—

I am w. cordial regard
My dear Sir
Yours sincerely
W Wilberforce

2103

From Robert Boucher Nickolls

12 March 1811

Stanton, 12th March, 1811.

Sir,

I do remember a Greek, with a Hebrew name, my opposite neighbour in the inner Quadrangle, of our *Alma Mater*, Coll. Reg. Oxon., whose retired and studious habits rendered him hermetically sealed at the time, though I was persuaded that he would open to advantage at some future season: in this persuasion I have not been disappointed; and the receipt of his last publication, on the Reform of the Laws of our Judicature,[2] which came to hand a few days since, has shown me how much he has studied, to his own honour, and incalculable advantage to the cause of justice, and humanity, and good government, if he should be attended to; as indeed he must eventually be under such patronage, if the highest reason and equity retain any friends in power. The difficulty, the anxiety, distress, and sometimes ruin, which attend the repetition of right in our courts of law, imperiously demand redress; and from the sovereign ruler, if

[2] *Letters to Lord Pelham, giving a comparative view of the system of penal colonization in New South Wales, and the Home Penitentiary System, prescribed by two Acts of Parliament of the years 1794 and 1799*, London, 1802.

[3] *A Plea for the Constitution: shewing the enormities committed, to the oppression of British subjects, . . . in and by the Design, Foundation, and Government of the Penal Colony of New South Wales*, London, 1803 (Bowring, iv. 249–84).

2103. [1] Bowring, x. 460, introduced: 'Extract of a letter from The Rev. R. B. Nickolls to Bentham.'

The Revd. Robert Boucher Nickolls (b. 1744?), was educated, like Bentham, at Queen's College, Oxford.

[2] Nickolls was probably referring to *Scotch Reform*, the second edition of which was published in 1811.

not remedied by the proper powers, *must* bring down just retribution in national visitations, and *do even now greatly cool the regards of many to our political constitution.*

2104

From George Holford

27 March 1811

Mr. Bentham

Can you state the Terms on which you would now undertake the building and superintendance of a Penitentiary House to contain 400 Male and 300 female Convicts?

The same on a Calculation for 700 male and 300 female Convicts.

If you cannot—state any Terms upon which you would now enter upon a Contract for carrying your plan into execution and if the whole should therefore with respect to yourself be relinquished Can you state the Amount of Compensation you conceive yourself intitled to under such Circumstances?

2105

From William Wilberforce

29 March 1811

New Pal Yd Hotel
Fridy 29th March

My dear Sir

I was extremely sorry for not being able to attend the Committee on Wedny[2] and indeed knowing I could not be there, I had desired ye Chairman[3] to put off ye Examinatn to another day; but He [said]

2104. [1] UC cxviib. 315. Autograph. Docketed: 'Panopt Penitentiary Committee Wedny 27 March 1811 / Paper delivered to J.B. by Abercromby at breaking / up of the Commee—This served as a basis to / J.B.'s two letters to Chairman Holford.'

On 4 March 1811 a Committee on laws relating to Penitentiary Houses was appointed (*Commons Journals*, lxvi. 144) and Bentham was examined by the Committee on 27 March. George Holford (*c.*1768–1839), MP for Lostwithiel, was chairman and James Abercromby (1776–1858), later 1st Baron Dunfermline, at this time MP for Midhurst, was another member of the Committee. Bentham's two letters to Holford are 2106 and 2110.

2105. [1] D. R. Bentham MSS, Loughborough. Autograph. Docketed: '1811 Mar 29 / Panopt / Wilberforce / N. Pal Yd / to / J.B. Q.S.P.' Addressed: '⟨. . .⟩ Bentham Esq / Queen's Square Place / Westmr'.

[2] The meeting of the Penitentiary Committee on Wednesday 27 March. See letter 2104.

[3] Holford.

that He could not. I mean to be there, and would have called on you previously, but that havg been very late up last night, I am only just going to Breakfast—If there be anythg you wish to say to me before yr Examinatn commences[4] let me know, and I will with pleasure receive you here or retire with you into a private Corner at ye House of Coms abt 1 o Clock

I am my dear Sir
yours sinly
W Wilberforce

Jere Bentham Esq

2106

To George Holford

29 March 1811 (Aet 63)

Queen Square Place, Westminster,
29th March 1811.

Sir,

A written intimation with which I was favoured,[2] together with such recollections as I have been able to preserve of what passed at the Committee in the course of my examination on Wednesday last, have suggested to me the propriety of bringing to view, in this shape, some matters of fact, the nature of which, I am inclined to hope, will for this day at least be found to supersede the demand for my personal attendance. Whatever be the time which it may occupy in reading, will, I trust, be found less than what would be requisite to the committing to paper, during the sitting of the Committee, an equal quantity of matter, if delivered in the shape of *viva voce* and impromptu statements, together with the questions and explanations that would necessarily arise out of a mode of communication so ill adapted to the nature of the case.

Question 1. Can you state the terms on which you would now undertake the building of a Penitentiary House, etc.?

Answer. What concerns the *Building*, I could not *now* undertake, at my own risk in point of expense, on any terms. The cause of my inability is, in brief, my being deprived, by death and other incidents, of the necessary assistance.

[4] Bentham was due to be examined again on the following Monday 1 April.

2106. [1] *First Report from the Committee on the Laws relating to Penitentiary Houses Ordered, by the House of Commons, to be printed, 31st May, 1811*, pp. 67–9.

[2] Letter 2104.

1. In respect of the details of construction, I myself having no professional acquaintance with the subject, and my own attention being necessarily devoted to other parts of the business, my dependence was altogether upon my brother, Brigadier *General Samuel Bentham* (now Commissioner of the Navy) with whom the general idea of central inspection, together with the system of mechanical inventions by which employment was to be found for such of the prisoners as could not be employed in works they had been accustomed to, had originated; and whose life interest in the concern was, according to the terms agreed upon[3], made to succeed mine. He is at present stationed at Queenborough or Sheerness: his time altogether engrossed, as I understand, by urgent official business. In respect of prices of materials and labour, and the assurance of no unnecessary enhancement by sinister professional interest, his and my dependence was upon a most ingenious as well as trustworthy man, at that time Architect to the Naval Works, a *Mr. Bunce*, who is since dead.[4] It had been settled by me with him, and to his perfect satisfaction, that whatever remuneration he was to receive for his part in the business, should be not in the usual shape of a per centage of the expenditure, encreasing consequently with the expenditure, but in the shape of an annuity, which was not to commence till the means of payment had been extracted from the concern by success. Besides his inbred probity, of which from intimate acquaintance I had derived full assurance, it was thus by the terms of the engagement rendered his interest to put the completest exclusion possible upon all unnecessary expense. It was on the ground of his continual assurances, together with those of my brother, that I, in my ignorance, ventured to charge myself with the expense of erecting the necessary buildings for so small a sum as £.19.000, money of that time. Neither I, nor my Brother know at present of any person by whom that loss could be replaced. And in regard to my brother, whatever occasional advice and information, in case of a fresh contract actually entered into, I might be able to obtain from him, in the present state and complexion of the business, he would, I am certain, be as far from being willing, as consistently with his offical duties he would for some time be from being able, to give any the least time to it.

2. Another professional man, on whose unremitted attention, as

[3] A marginal note reads: 'Finance Committee 1797–8 Rep. 28. Draught of Contract, p. 71.'

[4] Samuel Bunce, appointed architect and engineer of naval works by Sir Samuel Bentham in 1796, died in 1802.

well as skill, in the character of foreman, our dependence was, and in particular for the putting together the frame-work, which was to be of iron upon a plan never before attempted, and whom, upon the stoppage put to the works, we found ourselves under the necessity of parting with (a Mr. Lloyd) has since given proof of his capacity, by making a very ample fortune in a very extensive concern of his own, which engrossing the whole of his time, deprives me of all hope of his assistance in any such character as above.[5]

With respect to one part of the engagement, and that entered into in consequence of my own offer, and that so material a one, finding myself thus under the necessity of declaring it to be no longer in my power to fulfil it, to preserve myself from any such mortification as that of seeing inevitable misfortunes imputed to me as faults, it seemed necessary to me to be particular in shewing that this inability on my part has had for its cause incidents altogether out of my own control, and such as were among the natural and obviously probable results of the delay which I was destined to experience.

So far then as concerns the erection of the building, all that at this time I could possibly do towards the business would be (after applying my mind to the subject and getting what occasional information I could from my brother and other persons, for example the above-mentioned Mr. Lloyd) the using my own endeavour towards keeping down the expense: in which case, to give the best possible and most manifest security for my so doing, I should be ready and desirous of concurring in any efficient measures that should be suggested, for bringing my own personal interest in that respect as near as possible into coincidence with the interest of the public purse in that behalf: viz. upon some principle analogous in this respect to that which suggested the agreement, entered into as above, with the late *Mr. Bunce*.

Not that, in point of economy, any more than a comparatively small advantage need be lost by this change. If the principles of the plan itself be not disapproved, the great saving is upon the *plan*: that saving would be retained. As to the difference between an Architect taken upon intimate acquaintance and with the advantage of such mode of remuneration and adjustment of interests as has been mentioned, and an Architect taken at a venture and without any such advantage, a difference which would be ruinous to an individual, would to the public purse be no more than a deduction from the saving which would otherwise originally have been made.

[5] John Lloyd, millwright, who made some of the parts for Sir Samuel's steam-pump engine in 1800. See *Correspondence*, vi, as index.

Mr. Blackburn's[6] *minimum* was £.200,000. for 1,000 prisoners: my *maximum* was £.19.000 for 1,000 prisoners.[7]

2. *Question* 2d. If you cannot undertake the building, state any terms upon which you would now enter upon a contract for carrying your plan into execution.

Answer. What concerns the *building* being (as per answer to question 1, out of the question) as to what concerns *superintendence* (what I mean by it is, the entire *management*) the answer I have to submit is as follows:

Should it be the pleasure of the Committee to give a correspondent recommendation to the competent authorities, I should be ready and willing to undertake the superintendence of the number before agreed upon, to wit, 1,000 male prisoners; viz. upon terms such as should not vary at all in substance, and in language should vary no otherwise than by the substitution of the real present value of the sum then agreed upon, viz. £.12. per head, to that value which by the rise of prices is become no longer real, but nominal. Merely for illustration, let me take a certain sum for an uncertain, and say £.20. Whether any such given sum (£.20.) money of the present day, 29th March 1811, would in the purchase of articles such as is in question in the contract, go just as far, or not so far as, or further than the sum of £.12. money of that day, August 1795, is a question which there is not (I suppose) a single gentleman in the Committee who is not at this moment better qualified to give a precise answer to than, at this same moment, after so many years, during which my endeavour was to keep as far as possible out of my thoughts every thing that could bring into them so many painful sensations, I can pretend to be.

Should it be pressed upon me, and insisted upon, (which I hope it will not be) that at present, and antecedently to any Report made by the Committee, I should set about making the necessary enquiries and calculations, this is a task I should beg leave to decline, and for the following reason:

For the purpose of determining the eligibility of the plan, any such translation of *then* present into *now* present money, would not afford the Committee any real information beyond what they

[6] William Blackburn, for whom see letter 2063 n. 4.

[7] In his original letter Bentham had put different figures: £27,000 and 900 rather than £19,000 and 1,000. An autograph note of the correction is at BL VIII. 514, docketed: '1811 Apr 20 / Panopt / Corrections / made in J.Bs Letter I. / to Penitenty Comm / for £27,000–£19,000 / for Prisoners 900–1000. / made by Beeby / at the suggestion of / and in presence of / J.B. at the Journal / Office H. of C. / the inserted / figures being at the suggestion of J.B. / preserved in an unobliterated state'. Thomas Beeby was a clerk in the office of the chief clerk of the House of Commons 1803–36.

already have without it. *Certum est* (says the law maxim) *quod certum redai potest:*[8] and if there be any cases to which this maxim is reasonably and truly applicable, surely, in my humble apprehension at least, this is of the number.

To be explicit, so far as concerns prices and expenses, and pecuniary means and resources of all sorts, I must beg leave to decline, once for all, entering into any particulars beyond what are contained in the contract that was agreed on. Of the consequence of the discussions which any such specification would bring on, I am not altogether without experience. 'A special good bargain you are making for yourself,' says one. 'It will never do: it can't be done for the money: you will ruin yourself,' says another. Such was the language I used continually to be hearing in conversation among friends. Now, to apply this to the case of a Committee of Parliament, consisting, suppose, of a score of Members. By a majority out of one half score, the price is deemed excessive, and such that on *that* account the contract ought to be set aside. In a majority out of the other half score, the same sums are deemed deficient, and so deficient as to shew the undertaking to be impracticable, and such that on *that* account the contract ought to be set aside. In the case of each Member, as in the case of any individual taken singly, the chances are infinity to one that the quantum will not exactly quadrate with his views of what it ought to be. It is thus that a whole assembly, composed of two equal divisions, opposite to each other in every opinion about particulars, may as to the whole be unanimous against what may all this while, and without any imputation upon any one of them, have been perhaps the golden mean.

In settling the terms of the contract with the Treasury, no such enquiries were ever made. I should not expect to hear that any such had ever been made in any other instance. If it had been said to me, 'After having been settled with us, the terms will be to be examined into and settled anew by a Committee of Parliament,' I should immediately have declined the business. *Competence* being altogether out of doubt, I should not expect to find that, in point of *fact*, any such Committee had ever thought fit so to employ itself. In case of suspicion of fraud or delinquency in any shape, yes: but that is, I flatter myself, not the present case.

By the next meeting of the Committee, if it should *not* be so early as to-morrow, I hope to be able to submit the remainder of such

[8] A misprint, presumably, for 'Certum est quod certum reddi potest', i.e. 'That is certain which can be rendered certain'. See *The Ninth Part of the Reports of Sir Edward Coke, Kt. Chief Justice of the Common Pleas*, London, 1738, fo. 47.

answers as I shall have been able to find, to the questions that are before me.

I hope nothing like disrespect towards the Committee will be imputed to me, for having thus forborne to present myself, as if ready to give sudden answers to questions for which it has been impossible to me, notwithstanding my utmost exertions, to put myself in a state of tolerably adequate preparation. When these answers have been received and considered, I shall be ready to give, to the best of my power, present answers to any such ulterior questions as may have been suggested by them, the Committee signifying to me their order for that purpose.

I hope by that time to have sufficiently matured the expedient that has occurred to me, for meeting what I understand to be the wishes of the Committee, as to the accommodating the original plan to what appears at present the most pressing exigency; viz. the reception of *females*.

I have the honour to be, with all respect,
Sir,
Your most obedient and humble Servant,
Jeremy Bentham.

George Holford, Esq.
Chairman of the Committee on
Penitentiary Houses.

2107

From William Wilberforce

30 March 1811

Saturday
morng.

My dear Sir

I had carefully put all together ye papers I last received from you exceptg. one, viz ye Copy of ye Letter to the Speaker[2] If you wish for it also, be so good as to send to me at Kens. Gore betn 4 and 5 today or later

ever yours sincerely
W Wilberforce

2107. [1] UC clxxiv. 123. Autograph. Docketed: '1811 Mar 30 / Panopt / Wilberforce / to / J.B. Q.S.P. / Returns J.B.'s / Letter to Speaker'. Addressed: 'Jere: Bentham Esqr.'

[2] Charles Abbot. Which letter is unclear.

2108

To Sir Samuel Romilly

31 March 1811 (Aet 63)

31 Mar 1811.

Dr Romilly

The Comforter promised for Saty Mg: this is Sunday Aftn and no Comforter came.[2] Here am I with a whole host in league agt me and not so much as one confidential friend. What is to be done? For reasons unscrutable to me it looks as if we were unwillg. If so even shd he call on Monday there wd not be time for assistance that I might have wished to derive from him.[3] But any thg is better than nothg.

I know not whether I may not enclose with this the intended introduction of a once intended publication Picture of the Treasury.[4] It is nothg for you to read but if he were well disposed wd not perhaps be for him. The use wd be to judge whether proof being made of the probanda[5] therein mentioned there wod be any use or need of it for the present purpose viz. the keeping of Panopt. on its legs.

Sitting over me as Judge to pronounce himself guiltless and me guilty here is a man (L)[6] who for these 16 years and more has been the instrument of all the evil that has been done to me:

2108. [1] BL VIII. 499–500. In the hand of a copyist. Docketed: '1811 Mar 31 / Panopt / J.B. Q.S.P. / to / Romilly Russ. Sq / —Abercromby non / venit.'

[2] The 'Comforter' was Abercromby, judging by the docket.

[3] i.e. time before Bentham's examination before the Penitentiary Committee on the afternoon of Monday 1 April.

[4] Bentham never completed the account of his dealings with government entitled 'A Picture of the Treasury, with a Sketch of the Secretary of State's Office under the Reign of the Duke of Portland, under the Administrations of the Rt. Hon. W. Pitt and the Rt. Hon. H. Addington'. Only a part of it was published as *Letters to Lord Pelham*.

[5] i.e. 'things to be tested or approved'.

[6] Charles Long, who was a member of the Penitentiary Committee.

2109

From James Abercromby

31 March 1811

Sir,

Sir Saml. Romilly did some time ago at my request ask your permission for me to wait upon you, which request I was inclined to make, with the hope of having your assistance, to enable me to do all the good I could do in the Committee, when we came to discuss the details of the plan which we are to recommend to Parliament. The discussions which have taken place in the Committee, have so much retarded our progress, that we are not yet arrived near to that point, and therefore I did not conceive that it was yet time for me to apply to you for that assistance which you had so kindly promised.

I mentioned to Sir S. Romilly at the Committee on Friday, that I should take the liberty of waiting on you to explain as far as I could do so, the views of the Committee, but I subsequently heard that both Sir Even Nepean and Mr. Wilberforce had waited on you for that purpose, and therefore I conceived that my calling for the same purpose, might be considered as an unnecessary intrusion. But as I find by a Note which I have this Evening from Sir S. Romilly, that you would wish to see me,[2] and as that is the Case, I most eagerly embrace the opportunity thus afforded to me of communicating with you on a subject which I consider as one of very great public importance, and shall have the pleasure of waiting on you tomorrow soon after 10 o Clock if that hour is not inconvenient to you. I have the Honor to be

Sir

Yr. most Obedt. Servt.

Jas. Abercromby.

6 New St.
Spring Gardens.

If it would be inconvenient to you I am quite at liberty this Evening, and would wait upon you tonight.

2109. [1] BL VIII. 501–2. Autograph. Docketed: '1811 Mar 31 / Panopt / Abercromby New Str / Spring Gardens / to J.B. Q.S.P. / Visitabit cras.' (i.e. 'he will visit tomorrow'.)

[2] See letter 2108.

2110

To George Holford

1 April 1811 (Aet 63)

Queen Square Place, Westminster,
1st April 1811.

Sir,

In my letter of Friday last, March 29th,[2] I contracted a sort of engagement to submit 'an expedient that had occurred to me, for meeting what I understood to be the wishes of the Committee, as to the accommodating the original plan to what appears at present the most pressing exigency; viz. the reception of females.'

What follows, is the result of my humble endeavours to fulfil that engagement.

One circumstance that has been mentioned to me, as presenting a difficulty relative to any such addition, is the difficulty which it has been supposed might attend the adjustment of the *terms*. 'From the labour of the males, you would have (it has been said to me) your expected profit; from that of the females, you can have no equal expectation; taking 300 for the supposed number, what encrease of terms then will you, in this latter case, demand for the supposed encrease of numbers?'

To any such question I give this short answer—I desire no encrease of terms.

Give me the number of males specified in the contract, viz. 1,000, and then under the same roof (preserving at the same time perfect separation) I will, at the same price per head, give accommodation to the 300 females. If at that price any profit be made upon any work done by these females, such profit rests with me. If loss be the result, at the same time that profit is made upon the males, I shall still be able to bear such loss, and I am content to bear it. If I make no profit upon the males, or if the profit made upon the males falls short of covering the loss upon the females, then and then only it is that I call for any addition at all; nor in that case do I call for any greater addition than what shall be sufficient to make me whole.

But you may have miscalculated (say honourable gentlemen) and the loss upon females may be to any degree greater than you can cover by all your profit upon the males. Possibly, answer I, and in

2110. [1] *First Report from the Committee on Laws relating to Penitentiary Houses Ordered, by the House of Commons, to be printed, 31st May, 1811*, pp. 70–4.

[2] Letter 2106.

that event the sooner the account is out of my hands the better, But my accounts will be kept in the plainest and clearest manner;[3] and to a degree of copiousness and minuteness as yet without example. They shall at all times be open to the inspection of any lawful authority that shall be named; and if nobody comes to inspect, so soon as the symptoms of failure become visible to me, so soon will I of my own accord point them out. What should hinder me? In point of purse, in point of reputation, what should I get or save by plunging deeper and deeper into debt and disgrace? Disgrace, in respect of probity as well as intelligence, would be the result of improper perseverance; disgrace in respect of probity at least, would be saved by prompt disclosure.

But the exigency respecting the females is (I understand) a very pressing one. If so, I am solicitous to do whatever may be in my power towards meeting the exigency with the utmost promptitude.

Gentlemen's apprehensions (I understand) are pretty much alive to the danger of insurrection and forcible escape on the part of the males; such apprehensions will not (I suppose) be excited in equal strength by the females.

On the supposition of a surrounding wall of sufficient height, without ladders or any thing within to climb over by, and, if gentlemen please, with a parallel ditch on the outside to let in the water upon any one who should attempt to escape by undermining: with this security, added to that of the inspection principle (a principle just as easily built upon in such a case as any other principle) in my humble view of the matter, the slightest temporary building that, with a view to dispatch, could be suggested, might be trusted to in such a case for safe custody. On the outside, in exterior watch-houses (such as one of my plans exhibits) in addition to the two which I should think proper to provide, gentlemen in whose view of the matter the above provisions would not yet be sufficient, might station as many additional guards as in their view might seem necessary. Of these guards, it being the destination not to see the prisoners, or any of them, but in the event and at the moment of eruption, there would be no objection, I suppose, to their being of the stronger sex. Might not such a place as Chelsea Hospital be resorted to for this purpose?

As to a *site*, land which would be capable of being put to this use, would (I should expect to find) be to be had at a very short warning; certainly at a month's warning, probably at even less. What I have

[3] Written in the margin: 'For the plans relative to this subject, see the Papers on Pauper Management, published in Young's Annals of Agriculture, Vol. XXX. anno 1797. pp. from 99 to 112'.

in view is, a part of the land already purchased. Though there exists a part in it which I have heard called by the name of *The Hill*, I cannot indeed but wish it had been higher than it is. But if there be any thing in it dangerous to health, it is more than I ever heard from any inhabitant of it. To learn exactly how this matter stands, is in the power of the Committee. In former days, I remember hearing it said, that it was by the advice of his Physicians that the residence of the present Lord Grosvenor (then Lord Belgrave)[4] was continued so long in this very spot. For assuredly there is no part of the ground in question lower than the spot which not many years ago he took in and converted into pleasure ground; and which from the ground in question is separated by nothing but a wall or ditch.

In the providing of this receptacle, I should be happy in the assistance of any one gentleman whom the Committee, or any other authority recommended by the Committee, would be pleased to name; indeed I should not be willing to undertake the business without some such assistance.

Let the money, for example, be lodged in the Bank of England, or if that cannot be, in the hands of some Banker, not named by either of us; at any rate they should not be those of any Banker of mine. No money to be drawn for but on our joint draft, specifying in each the person in whose favour, and the nature of the service.

What I assume is—that, by this *my Guardian*, (such I take leave to call him) the Panopticon principle is approved. This being the case, supposing any difference between us, the ground of it would probably be, that he, as not being the inventor, would not have all the confidence in the potency of the principle that I, the inventor, should have. Such elements of security as to me would seem sufficient, I should accordingly state. Supposing them in his eyes insufficient, let him add such others as to him would seem sufficient, and at the same time necessary. These I offer to join in the provision of, on this single condition; viz. that whatever expense I should find myself unable to reconcile myself to, I should be at liberty to exempt myself from the responsibility of.

The *management* might go on in the same way. I, not standing to profit or loss, always understood that the permanent establishment shall go on in its own train, and the sufficient means of dispatch shall be in my hands.

This *temporary* establishment would serve as a sort of school of experiment with a view to the permanent one.

[4] Robert Grosvenor, 2nd Earl Grosvenor (1767–1845), later 1st Marquis of Westminster. He was styled Viscount Belgrave until he succeeded his father, Richard Grosvenor, 1st Earl Grosvenor (1731–1802).

Should it succeed, there would be no reason why the buildings should not be suffered to continue in use for the same purpose, as long as the charge of repair would render such continuance consistent with economy. Should it fail, Government might derive from experience sufficient reason for keeping out of my hands, or myself for forbearing to take into them, the *permanent* establishment; always supposed, that, by the now proposed temporary establishment, the permanent establishment shall not be delayed.

Should it succeed, the *official* establishment, consisting principally at least of females, might either, as above, continue on the management in the *same* receptacle, or, fraught with experience, be transferred to the *permanent* establishment: if continued, there would be so much the more room left for the reception of an eventual addition to the number of the male prisoners.

All this while, upon the face of the questions that lie before me, the alternative that I see, is—not between the number of 1,300 prisoners, that would be composed of the *agreed-on* number of males, viz. 1,000 and the now proposed or supported additional number of females, viz. 300,—but between a total of no more than 1,000 (whereof 300 females, leaving 700 males) and a total of 700, whereof 300 females, leaving but 400 males.

The proposed reduction being so considerable, looking out for the reason, what I have been able to collect, is—an apprehension about safe custody, in respect of the numbers and the vicinity of the metropolis.

On this subject, what I have said elsewhere and in print, there can be no need of repeating here. If it has had the honour of being read, the result must be—that it has not had the good fortune to prove, at least for the present, satisfactory to the gentlemen here in question. Nothing that is in my power towards rendering it so shall be wanting.

Let but room, sufficient for the number agreed on, viz. the 1,000 males *plus* the *now* proposed 300 females, be provided,—let but a possibility of coming back to the agreement be preserved,—the *immediate* fulfilment shall be waved.

I hope honourable gentlemen will not insist on precluding themselves from the possibility of seeing the agreed-on number provided for on this plan, even though by themselves it should be ever so much approved. In good faith is there any thing so mischievous or so odious, or in economy, if economy be really adverse, any thing so much superior to good faith, that gentlemen should make a point of rendering the keeping of good faith impossible? This is what on the part of any honourable gentleman I can never believe, till I have the mortification of seeing it from his own pen, or hearing it from his own lips.

As to the introducing the whole number all at once, what seems probable to me is, that, when the time for opening came, it is more than I myself should venture on. What then (it may be said) is the number you would introduce at once? My answer is, that, at this distance from the time of action, the fixation of a precise number would not, in my humble view of the matter, be consistent with the rules of human prudence. The building being erected, and the circumstances of the *moment* observed and considered, *then* would be the time for fixing on the first number. This for the *first* experiment: the experiment succeeding, then it would be, that, in proportion to the degree of confidence indicated by experience, the number would be enlarged.

Seven hundred seems to be the greatest number of *male* prisoners, the existence of which, under one roof and one system of inspection, seemed, in the eyes of the honourable gentlemen in question, capable of being endured: 400 is the number to the idea of which in the same minds, a greater portion of satisfaction seems to be attached. Let them then take either number, or any intermediate number at pleasure. Let them fix for me a *time of probation*: let them say and cause it to be ordained, that, till the expiration of the probationary *time*, the probationary *number* shall not be exceeded. Let them do this, or any thing else that to them seems reasonable and necessary, rather than secure to themselves the regret of seeing 300, or 600 prisoners, precluded from the possibility of being provided for, upon a plan which, by the supposition, they do not even *now* disapprove, and the utility and security of which will, by the same supposition, have been demonstrated by experience.

But, if your agreed-on number of 1,000 males is reduced (it may be said) to 700, you will have so much the less profit wherewith to cover the above supposed loss upon the 300 females whom, unless your proposed *temporary* establishment be rendered *permanent*, you are to have at all events: and, if reduced to 400, you will have still less: while, on the expense of the official establishment, the reduction, if any reduction there can be, will be far indeed from being proportionable.

All this I am fully aware of; and to this my answer is the same as to that respecting the introduction of the females, as above. Let the profit, so long as there is any, upon the 700, or though it be upon no more than the 400 *effectives*, be employed in covering the deficiency produced by the *non-effectives*.

The superintendence bestowed by the promiscuous assemblage of *unknown*, and therefore unpaid, ungarbled, and uncorruptible Inspectors, or in a word, by the Public at large, that is, by such individuals as curiosity and love of amusement (the most universally operative springs of action that apply to such a case) mixt with any better and rarer motives, may happen to attract; this is what, from first to last, I have all along spoken of as being among my principal dependencies, viz. for security against abuse and imperfection in every shape. But the banquet offered to curiosity, will be attractive in proportion to the variety, and (if such a term may here be endured) even the *brilliancy*, of the scene. This will on a twofold account be as the magnitude of the establishment: first, in respect of mere physical magnitude, one acknowledged and principal ingredient (ask Edmund Burke else) in the composition of the *sublime*:[5] then again in respect of the *expense*, that would be required for giving to it whatever subsidiary attractions it might be found susceptible of.

Even on the supposition, that, either on or before the completion of the permanent Panopticon, the use of the proposed temporary one would be discontinued, the expence of it would not be altogether lost. As materials, the materials would have more or less saleable value, and the consideration of such value might be taken into the account in the choice of them: wood for example, or iron, as far as it can be applied, removable with least loss: brick not without more loss: lath and plaster total loss. The selection might have a professional Report to warrant it.

Of the four surrounding walls of the square, one might perhaps be so situated, as to be capable of constituting, with or without addition to the height, one of the walls of the *permanent* Panopticon: and, if, of the parallelogram containing the temporary Panopticon, one pair of sides were longer than the other, one of the longer pair might be taken for this purpose.

I come now to that part of the question which concerns the difference in point of *terms* between Panopticons for the accommodation of the several numbers 1,300, 1,000 and 700 prisoners.

For the reasons that were submitted in my former letter, numbers of pounds, arithmetical details in general, are a sort of answer which it is out of my power now to give. But, what cannot be detailed in *figures*, may be rendered sufficiently clear by being stated in principle.

The reduction in the expense of the building—was this, among

[5] A reference to Edmund Burke (1729–97) and his early work *A Philosophical Enquiry into the Origins of our Ideas of the Sublime and Beautiful*, London, 1757, pp. 51–2 (II. vii 'Vastness').

the considerations, that suggested the wish to see the proposed reduction made upon the number for which provision should be made?—Upon a second glance, any saving that by any such reduction as is proposed could be made under this head, would be found much less considerable than, on a first glance, may have been supposed.

To understand this,—two thousand was at one time,—but let us now, for the standard number of prisoners to be accommodated, take no more than the above proposed number of 1,300. From this standard number let the two several proposed reductions be measured. By reducing it, in one case to 1000, in another to 700, the saving in expence would be far less than in proportion to the number. Why? Because there would be so many parts,—so many masses of brick, or iron, or wood,—that in dimensions would require to be nearly the same in all three cases.

I. BUILDING.

1. In the first place, the Inspection Tower, including the Inspector's Lodge, which is at the same time the proposed room for the reception of visitors from the public at large. The need of visitors, and consequently of a comfortable and spacious apartment for their reception, would be the same in all cases.

2. In the second place, the like may be said, and with little or no difference, of the *surrounding wall*, and of the walled *avenue* or *approach* that would be to be cut through it.

3. The like may be said, and without any variation, of the proposed external *guard houses*, as per Plan; and of the proposed *ditch* or *canal* which, except where cut by the approach, was to surround the surrounding wall.

II. OFFICIAL ESTABLISHMENT

In its principal and most expensive parts, the numbers of the persons in the Official Establishment, and consequently the expense, would be the same. 1. Sub-Governor constantly resident. 2. Chaplain. 3. Medical Curator. 4. Chief Book-keeper. 5. Chief Jailor. 6. Turnkeys, one at every entrance. 7. Porter at the entrance, for the reception of persons at large in the character of spectators. 8. Watchmen or Patroling Guards for the external Guard-houses. 9. Chief Schoolmaster, if any such official character were introduced.

These I believe are the principal, though assuredly not all, the items of expense, which would be the same on all three scales, on the smallest as on the largest; and, the fund for this expense being to decrease in exact proportion to the numbers expressive of the three scales, a proportionable supply would be to be provided: the amount of the supply, it being to be provided at the public expense, would give the degree of disadvantage which, in point of economy, would be the respective results of the two several reductions. Upon the standard scale, number expressive of the source of supply, 1000: upon the two several reduced scales, numbers expressive of the source of supply, 700 and 400.

Note, that, in case of the proposed addition of female prisoners, an official establishment composed of persons of that sex would also be to be added.

I have spoken of 2,000, as being, without impropriety, capable of being taken for the *standard number*, with reference to which any proposed lesser scales may be termed *reductions*. My reason for speaking thus is as follows:

The number agreed on per contract in | | 1795 being 1,000[6] on the 25th March 1800 it was, that I received a letter from the Treasury, mentioning the concurrence of the Duke of Portland (then Secretary of State) and 'acquainting me (such are the words of it) that the proposed building of a Panopticon is to be calculated to accommodate two thousand persons.'[7]

The date of my first proposal is 15th January 1791.[8] There had then been nine years and upwards passed in consideration, or at least applicable to the purpose of consideration, and, in very high places no want of desire to find grounds, had such been to be found, not merely for reduction, but for annihilation: and, at the end of these nine years, what is the result?—not any *subtraction* from the number originally agreed on;—not any *subtraction* from it, but a *multiplication* of it.

In the character of a testimonial,—declaring that whatsoever confidence had, five years before this, been reposed in me and my plan, was at this time doubled,—a testimonial not the less valuable in effect for not being such in form,—this letter is of no small value to me.

True it is, that, to this *multiplication*, succeeded, and at no very long interval of time, an operation of the opposite kind, viz; *division*:

[6] See *Twenty-Eighth Report from the Select Committee on Finance, etc. Police, Including Convict Establishments. Ordered to be printed 26th June 1798*, appendix (F.3) 'Draft of a Contract between the Lords Commissioners of the Treasury and Jeremy Bentham, Esquire', p. 69

[7] Letter 1530, *Correspondence*, vi.

[8] Why Bentham wrote 15 January is unclear. He sent a letter to Pitt on his Panopticon proposal on 23 January 1791 (letter 738, *Correspondence*, iv) and had been discussing plans for a Panopticon in Ireland with the Irish chancellor of the exchequer, Sir John Parnell (1744–1801), since the summer of 1790.

division of the 2,000 by 4; quotient 500: hesitation between this number and number 0.

Three-fourths struck off?—one-half from the number originally agreed on? three-fourths from the number indicated by second and maturer thoughts? Struck off, and for what reason?

To extract a complete answer to this question, if such were the pleasure of the Committee, would (I suppose) be within the competence of the Committee. All that *I* shall presume to say is,—what to the present purpose it seems necessary for me to say,—viz. that any abatement of confidence, either in the Plan itself, or in the Author of it, would (I think) not be found to be in the number.

Of the several questions that lie before me, that which regards eventual *compensation* is the only one to which it remains for me to submit my answer.

But, considering that the rescission of the contract is the only event in which any provision on this head will come to be made, I hope to stand excused for wishing to defer giving any answer on this head, until intimation of a determination to that effect shall have been given to me.

I have the honour to be, with all respect,
Sir,
Your most obedient and humble Servant,
Jeremy Bentham.

George Holford, Esq.
Chairman of the Committee on
Penitentiary Houses.

2111

From Sir Samuel Bentham

3 April 1811

Sheerness 3d April 1811.

The Panoptic drawings are perhaps in the office if so Mr Ainslie[2] can give them to you, and if they are at Hampstead it is by his means they can be easiest procured. Walter however might [see] him

2111. [1] BL VIII. 503. Autograph. Docketed: '1811 Apr 3 / Panopt / S.B. Sheerness / to / J.B. Q.S.P. / Panopt drawings / with Ainslie.' Addressed: 'H. Koe Esqre / Lincoln's Inn / Old Buildings / London.' Koe had been admitted to Lincoln's Inn in 1804, and called to the bar in 1810.

[2] George Ainslie, draftsman to the civil architect and engineer and to the surveyor of buildings at the navy board 1809–15.

there or go with them there to bring them away, they would be to be found in the bottom drawer, or the next above it, in the press under the window in the paper room.

Mr Ainslie also begun with a drawing for a Panop. prison in c⟨. . .⟩ of its being asked for a few months ⟨. . .⟩ by Sheriff Wood[3] so that he is most apprized of my ideas on the subject.

I shall be very glad to receive the parliamentary papers you speak of and have accordingly written to desire them to be sent immediately.

I enclose a draft for £50 it is of old date for reasons.

I rejoice to hear that poor Panop. appears once more to be raising its head: but there will [be] much to rearrange.

2112

To George Holford

4 April 1811 (Aet 63)

MS. Minutes p. 28.

4. April 1811.

Sir

—(Written upon my Examinations being brought to me for revisal.) What follows was not stated by me at the time of my examination. But being to several Members of the Committee then present known to be true, and being in my view of the matter material I should suppose for giving admission to it no such formality as a fresh examination would be deemed necessary.

The place for the insertion of it might be, I suppose, the commencement of p. 28. of the MS. Minutes.

Jeremy Bentham

The construction of the intended building being such as rendered it in a peculiar degree difficult to form any adequate conception of it from graphical representations, models representing it in various points of view occupied for several years a room in my House. It was

[3] See above, letter 2062 and n. 2.

2112. [1] BL VIII. 504–5. Autograph draft. Docketed: '1811 Apr 4 / Panopt. No. 3 / J.B. Q.S.P. / to / G. Holford Chair- / man of the Penitenty / Committee, through / Beeby Clerk of the Jour- / nal Office etc as per / Nos 1 and 2. / Proposed Addition 3 / (not numbered?) viz to / MS. Minutes p. 28 / respecing models of / Panopticon / Brouillon.' Bentham's letters '1 and 2' are the letters to Holford published in the *First Report* of the Penitentiary Committee, letters 2106 and 2110 above.

in the view of these models or most of them that the then First Lord of the Treasury and the Secretary grounded their acceptance, as stated in my Examination before the Finance Committee of 1797–8.

Long before the drawing up of the Draught of Contract these models had been, amongst other persons viewed by Members of both Houses, to the number (I suppose) of some scores: amongst the rest by a considerable proportion (I remember) of the present Committee.

At the same time a Book intituled *Panopticon* etc which gives ample details concerning the essential parts of the plan, together with no less ample reasons for every thing that was proposed to be done, as well in respect of plan of management as in respect of plan of construction, and which has in part been published in Ireland, under the direction of Government there,[2] was put into several hands. A copy of it is in the hands of the Committee.

2113

From Sir Samuel Bentham

5 April 1811

Sheerness 5 April 1811

You will receive by this post a plan and letter from your Nephew Sam[2] giving such a description as he thought proper you should have of our proceedings on the first *Mass.*[3] the intention was his own and I had not seen it till he brought it to be forwarded. He has had but very little experience yet in drawing plans but I am surprised at his readiness of comprehension and his invention but still more at the circumspection exhibited by his observations, so that I think I can now recommend him as your Engineer and Architect for the revived Panopticon.

I have desired the pressed Copy of a letter I have sent a few days

[2] *Panopticon; or, the Inspection-House*, was published at Dublin and London in 1791. For Bentham's contact with Sir John Parnell and Major Robert Hobart (subsequently 4th Earl of Buckinghamshire), the Irish chief secretary, see *Correspondence*, iv, as index.

2113. [1] BL VIII. 506–7. Autograph. Docketed: '1811 Apr 5 / Panopt / S.B. Sheerness / to J.B. Q.S.P. / Retiraturus?' Addressed: 'Jer^y Bentham Esqr / Queen Square Place / Westminster.'

[2] Samuel Bentham (1799–1816), Sir Samuel's son. The letter and plan are missing.

[3] Sir Samuel had devised a method of constructing a sea or river wall at Sheerness which involved a series of hollow masses of brickwork, 21 feet square, which were to be covered in Roman cement and floated to their intended site. Once in position they would be filled and sunk into the mud. Ten days after writing this letter, Sir Samuel informed the navy board that the first 'mass' was ready to be floated off, and on 16 April he reported that it had successfully been sunk in place. See M. S. Bentham, *The Life of Brigadier-General Sir Samuel Bentham*, London, 1862, pp. 270–1, 278–80.

ago to my Colleagues in reply to one of theirs (the Copy of which is likewise sent) breathing the suspicions and want of confidence at the Admiralty. This letter I am endeavouring to follow up with two or three others to my Colleagues and one to Mr Yorke[4] which will bring my concerns to a crisis. I have to state the impossibility of continuing the duty of my present situation with such advantage to the public as can be satisfactory to myself and to prepare accordingly in what manner I conceive it would be proper to treat me at my dismissal. I made up my mind first to the retiring to Berry lodge[5] and living upon the smallest allowance which I conceive it possible they should give me. I have given notice of not keeping horses any more and as I have learnt here to ride on a mule the transition to an ass will not be great and that will [be] a *monture* which may well answer our purposes in our retirement. If building in masses should be brought into repute Sam or I may profit by it so as to enable me to have all the luxuries I have ever had. so you may say Panop: revived may contribute to the same effect. In regard to that without knowing what your intentions may be in that respect and having forgotten in what manner it was intended my name should appear in the Contract it has occurred to me that possibly Sam's name might be inserted instead of mine which on account of his age would be much more valuable. If however this were practicable you would probably have thought of it, at any rate *thy will* be done. I feel today something very like an approaching ague but on the receipt of Koe's letters[6] speaking of the female immediate Establishment (which we cannot understand how far it is to [be] considered as an Experiment previous to the commencement of the Male Establishment) we too could not help revolving projects for employing in *Washing*. I have been making Convicts do house Carpenter's work more industriously than the workers of the dockyard but by means by which I am liable to I know not what.

[4] Charles Philip Yorke (1764–1834), first lord of the admiralty 1810–11.

[5] Sir Samuel's residence near Gosport.

[6] Missing.

2114

To Thomas Beeby

8 April 1811 (Aet 63)

Q.S.P. 8. April 1811

In conformity to the desire expressed by Mr Beeby, Mr Bentham wrote his amendments on this 2d. paper of Minutes (as he had done those on the 1st.) in pencil only. But his pencils happening to be bad, and his hand writing not very good, he found upon experiment that there was considerable hazard of its appearing in this last instance illegible, or (what would have been worse) being misread. He has therefore procured it to be copied in ink. But this mode can not be productive of any injurious alteration in the recorded minutes, care having been taken that the obliterations to which it became necessary to subject them should be performed not, as in the case of Mr Bentham's additions in ink, but in pencil, as desired.

The state of his eyes not very well admitting of an immediate revisal of the words in ink which have been written to serve as copies of those which were written by himself in pencil, and understanding Mr Beeby to have called or sent this morning for this 2d paper of minutes, he sends it at a venture.

If at the time of the impression, (should it happen to this paper to be sent to the press) Mr Beeby would have the goodness to send him the *proofs*, the security for correctness would be still greater than any that could be afforded by the revisal of the M.S. in its present state.

2114. [1] BL VIII. 508–9. Copy. Docketed: '1811 Apr 8 / Panopt / J.B. Q.S.P. / to / Beeby Journal / Office. H. of C⟨.⟩ / Returning / Minutes of J.B.⟨'s⟩ / 2d Examination / with J.B.s cor- / rections. In ink / obliterations. in / pencil.'

2115

From Sir John Sinclair

20 April 1811

Dear Sir,

I have read over the inclosed volumes, in so far as regards The Code of Health.[2] The Editor proposed to give an Abstract of several Chapters of that work, in plain and intelligible French, and he seems to have succeeded.[3] With many thanks, I remain,

Faithfully
Yours
John Sinclair

5. Terrace
Palace-yard
20th April

2116

To Sir Samuel Bentham

24 April 1811 (Aet 63)

24 Apr. 1811. Wednesday.

Abercromby (the Honble James) M.P. (son of the General[2] whose widow he being killed in Egypt was made a Peeress in her own right with succession etc[3]) being a Member of the Penitentiary Committee

2115. [1] BL VIII. 510–11. Autograph. Docketed: '1811 Apr 20 / Sinclair Sir J. / to / J.B. Q.S.P. / Letter 2d / of this / day. Returns Esprit des ⟨. . .⟩'. Addressed: 'Jeremy Bentham Esqr / etc etc etc'. Franked: 'J. Sinclair'. Sir John Sinclair (1754–1835) was the president of the board of agriculture and MP for Caithness. He was the author of *The History of the Public Revenue of the British Empire*, 2 vols., London, 1784, and *The Statistical Account of Scotland*, 21 vols., Edinburgh, 1791–9.

[2] Sinclair's *Code of Health and Longevity; or a Concise View of the Principles Calculated for the Preservation of Health, and the Attainment of Long Life*, 4 vols., Edinburgh, 1807.

[3] Extracts of the *Code of Health* appeared in French translation in *L'esprit des journaux, Français et étrangers, par une société de gens de lettres* between August 1809 and January 1811.

2116. [1]BL VIII. 512–13. Autograph. Docketed: '1811 Ap 24 / JB–SB'. Addressed: 'To / Sir Samuel Bentham / etc etc etc / Queenborough / Sheerness.' Readdressed: 'His Majys Dock Yard / Sheerness.' Stamped: 'AP / C / 24 / 811'.

[2] James Abercromby was the third son of Lieut.-Gen. Sir Ralph Abercromby (1734–1801), who had died of wounds received while leading the British forces at the battle of Alexandria.

[3] In recognition of her husband's services, Lady Mary Anne Abercromby was created Baroness Abercromby of Aboukir and Tullibody on 28 May 1801.

is the person to whom the charge of Panopticon was committed by Romilly. Having just been with me on that business, he asked me in the way of conversation whether in a call I had made a few days ago at his House, I had observed a man who went out as I went in. On my answering in the negative That says he is Johnson—the famous Smuggler and Prison-breaker.[4] He then proceeded to state to me what Johnsons business with him was.

By this Johnson an offer had been made to Government—viz to somebody in Office—but I do not know who, to make an attempt to destroy Bony's fleet in the Scheldt etc: stating that the plan he meant to pursue for that purpose was *Fulton's*:[5] which you can not but have heard more or less of.

From principles of sentimentality, this Mr Government had refused to give him any encouragement. But not being easily abashed, he had addressed himself to certain individuals of the mercantile class who were disposed to assist him, in case any probable prospect of pecuniary advantage could be found: and for that purpose the plan was to fit out a Privateer.

What brought him to A. was to learn from him as a lawyer[6] (what the opening that led him to A. was I did not learn) what probability of remuneration might be derived from the provisions in the Prize Acts and Proclamations.

In answer to the objections on the score of sentimentality he produced parallel cases which are in daily practice. A. was going to mention them—or some of them: but they are so obvious, that to save migration I stopped his mouth.

Now then suppose it could be so managed—what say you to the taking a part in this business—in the way of advice? viz. as to the most effectual and secure mode of proceeding etc.

You have it in contemplation I understand to come to town ere long. A. can not but know where to meet with the man. He at my desire would I make no doubt direct him to Q.S.P. at which place

[4] 'Captain' Thomas? Johnson (1772–1839) was imprisoned in 1798 following an affray with Revenue officers. He escaped and received a pardon after he offered to pilot the expedition to Holland led by Sir Ralph Abercromby in 1799. In 1802 Johnson was again imprisoned, this time for debt, and charged with further smuggling offences. He escaped and was pardoned for a second time when he piloted the Walcheren expedition in 1809.

[5] Robert Fulton (1765–1815), American civil engineer, inventor, and painter. After recommending the use of a submarine and torpedoes to the French, Fulton advised the British in 1804 to use his craft to attack the French fleet. A raid on Boulogne was unsuccessful owing to the failure of Fulton's torpedoes to explode. He returned to the United States in 1806.

[6] James Abercromby was called to the bar in 1801.

you might meet him, in any way you liked: I present, or not present; cognizant or not cognizant.

You see there is no time to be lost. Whether you approve or disapprove of this idea answer me by return of post.

For my part not only on the score of patriotism, but on ⟨. . .⟩ of humanity I can not but look upon it with ⟨. . .⟩ favourable eye. Drowning is the easiest of all Deaths. If this man fails and perishes, he can be better spared than a better and less mischievous man. As to retaliation it can not be but that they who are first at assault will be best prepared for defence. In all our military inventions, the advantage is to the first practiser. After that all nations are upon a par: and the more destructive the particular operation, the less destructive war so carried on has been found to be upon the whole.

2117

From Thomas Beeby

3 May 1811

Journal Office
House of Commons
3 May 1811.

Sir,

Herewith I send you a proof print of your Evidence taken before the Committee on Penitentiary Houses——Mr. Holford has made some observations thereon which he will be obliged to you to peruse and settle as soon as you can possibly make it convenient and return it to me that the printer may work it off without delay the Committee being extremely anxious to get the proceedings before the House with as little delay as possible I am Sir your most obt

hble Servt.
Thos. Beeby.

2117. [1] BL VIII. 515–16. Autograph. Docketed: '1811 May 3 / Panopt / Beeby Journal / Office / to / J.B. Q.S.P. / Sends J.B.s Evidence / etc for Correction of the / press / Returned it next day / at 12 by Walter.' Addressed: 'Jeremiah Bentham Esqr.'

2118

To George Holford

6 May 1811 (Aet 63)

Queen's-square Place, Westm
6th May 1811.

Sir,

Understanding at different times, from different Gentlemen, Members of the Committee, that in calling me before them, the object of the Committee has been—not merely to scrutinize into the Contract to which I am a party, but also, for the purpose of forming their judgment concerning the most eligible mode of disposing of such part of the Convict Population of the Country, as it may not be thought fit to confine in Hulks or employ in colonizing, to collect any such information as, in any shape, I might be found capable of affording—I take the liberty of submitting in this mode, to your consideration and that of the Committee, a few suggestions on the subject of the *Country Convicts*.

For such of the Convicts, whose conviction shall have taken place in London or Middlesex, with or without the addition of a few other Counties nearly contiguous to the *Metropolis*, such as those for instance which are comprized in the *Home* Circuit, the provision made by the existing Contract may, it seems to be supposed, suffice.

On this supposition, what, in some mode or other of the Penitentiary plan, remains to be provided for, is—that as yet indefinite part of the Convict population, which may be expected to be furnished by the more or less distant Counties:—say, for example, the five *remaining Circuits*.

For this large remnant of that population the question then is—What is the best mode?

To this question the answer presents three options—

1. *Panopticons* in the *Metropolis*, over and above the one supposed to be determined upon: viz. in number, one at least, and as many more, if any, as the number of convicts to be provided for shall be deemed to require.

2118. [1] *Second Report from the Committee on Laws relating to Penitentiary Houses Ordered, by the House of Commons, to be printed, 10th June 1811*, pp. 124–131. Reprinted in Bowring, xi. 152–9. In the *Report* it is noted that a corrected copy of this letter was received on 10 June. A very rough autograph draft, dealing with similar topics, headed 'Letter IV' and dated 9–10 April 1811 is at UC cxviib 304–13. For Bentham's three earlier letters to Holford see 2106, 2110, and 2112.

2. *Panopticons*, upon an equal scale, and consequently in equal number, in the *Country*. These two plans belong alike to what, for distinction sake, I would beg leave to call *the open mode upon a large scale*.

3. *Penitentiary Houses*, in the *existing* mode, one in and for each *County*; or, in such cases in which the convict population afforded by a single County would be manifestly too small, one in each *aggregate* of contiguous Counties, to be associated together for the purpose.

This last mode I would beg leave to distinguish by the appellation of *the close mode upon a small scale*.

As to the question between *the open mode upon a large scale*—viz. the Panopticon mode upon the Panopticon scale—and *the close mode upon a small scale*—my *opinion* has been already submitted, and not my opinion only, but the *considerations*, or the ground on which it was formed.

Management, in every imaginable point, better; *expense* less:—in these few words all those considerations will be found comprized.

On the question between Panopticons all in the Metropolis, and Panopticons one in the Metropolis and others in the Country, (in each case in *the open mode upon the large scale*) neither are the points of distinction so manifest, nor the importance of them so great.

On the whole, however, the result of my enquiry is—that *Panopticons* all in the *Metropolis* present a decided title to preference.

What presents itself to me as the principal reason is—that the Metropolis affords beyond comparison *the best public*. Here whatsoever matter proper for consideration comes into existence, is with the minimum of trouble, brought instantaneously to the *ear*, laid open even to the inspection of the *eye*, of the whole body of *constituted authorities*: of the Members of the *Administration*, of the immediatly superintending *judicial authority*: of every Member *of the Legislature*.

Not that *objections* are altogether wanting: but neither from report nor from imagination, have I been able to collect any, the united force of which seems sufficient to constitute a preponderant one.

1. *Danger* to the Metropolis, from *forcible* and general *eruption*, increased.
2. Inordinate *accumulation* of Convicts for whom provision may be to be made *after discharge*.
3. *Remoteness* of the Convicts from their respective *desired abodes*, at the time of their *discharge*.

4. Inordinate *expense* of *conveying* the Convicts from the place of conviction to the place of punishment.
5. Supposed unsuitableness of the *fund*, upon which, on this plan, the expense of maintenance, with or without the expense of conveyance, would be to be charged.

These are all the *objections* which I have been able to discover: and to these I proceed to submit such answers as the nature of the case has suggested.

I. Objection 1. *Danger of general and forcible eruption.* Answer. In my own particular it will readily enough be conceived, considering the peculiar *guards* which the peculiarities of the *Panopticon* plan provides, this danger cannot appear very considerable in either case.

But, if it be considerable, the *Metropolis* is the spot in which it should naturally appear much *less* considerable than in any *other* place:—in any other town or towns at least, to which, otherwise, this part of the Convict population would be to be consigned.

Milbank and *Tothill Fields* being, by the supposition, the spot fixed upon already for *one* Panopticon, I see not what should hinder its being made to receive as many *others* as can be required.

Within a few hundred yards of Tothill Fields is constantly stationed a body of *regular troops*, to the amount of some *thousands*:[2] the distance, so small, that, in case of commotion, communication might be made by *signals* of both sorts: signals not only to the *ear*, but even to the *eye*, if an apparatus to that effect were thought fit to be provided.

In *Tothill Fields*, at one end of *Rochester Row*, stands, and has stood for (I think it is) about eight or ten years, a *Military* Infirmary,[3] in which is constantly stationed a military *Guard*, consisting, as I have just been informed on the spot, of nine soldiers. On one side, the Waste called Tothill Fields has for its boundary this *Rochester Row*, on the opposite side the parcel of ground already purchased for the *Panopticon* Penitentiary House. On no part of this ground is there any building but what may at present be actually seen from the Infirmary just mentioned, and by the Guard there stationed.

On a subject so plain I should never have thought of troubling the Committee with so many words, but for the recollection, that some 18 or 19 years ago, at the commencement of my negotiations, to an observation of mine pointing to the military force in the *Park* as an obvious source of security, the answer returned, by a Gentle-

[2] i.e. at St James's Park Barracks, to the south of Birdcage Walk, later to become the Wellington Barracks.

[3] At 37–9 Rochester Row.

man then in office, was an inexorable negative. What the objections were, I enquired in vain: with the Gentleman himself they did not originate. Be they what they may, they would now be found, I should hope, no longer in existence. If the *Panopticon* contained within its Lodge an acting *Magistrate*, this Military Guard, being actually in his view, would, on any such occasion as that in question, be actually under his command. I mean by Common law, to which no order from any War Office, would, I presume, be opposed.

By the constant *sight* of a similar Guard, stationed, if thought necessary, close to the spot;—for example, three or four at the entrance into the *Panopticon* ground through the *walled avenue* that leads to the House,—two or three at each of the two elevated *Watch-houses*, which command, each of them, by night as well as by day, the inside as well as outside of two of the four *surrounding walls*,—by the constant *sight* of this *small guard*, coupled with the *knowledge* of the arrangements that might so easily be made for instantaneous communication with the *great body* stationed in the neighbouring Park, it would be extraordinary indeed, if in the imagination of the most refractory prisoner, all chance of success in any such attempt, would not be rendered hopeless,—manifestly as well as constantly hopeless. Further observations on this head, may be seen in Panopticon Postscript, Part II. §. 15. pp. from 201 to 208.[4]

Against every danger of this sort, such are the means of security afforded by the Metropolis in general, but in a more particular degree by the particular spot in question. In any of the provincial situations, what security comparable to this, could be afforded: and that too, as in this case, without any special allotment of military force for this particular purpose?

True it is, that spite of military guards, French and other *Prisoners of War* have, from time to time, and but too often, and in too great numbers, contrived to make their escape.

But, against the escape of Convict Prisoners, the Panopticon plan presents securities in abundance, few of which, if any, would (I believe) be found employed on any existing plan, in the case of foreign Prisoners.

1. *Uniform* conspicuously distinctive.
2. *Close dress*, in which the concealment of any weapon suited to the purpose of offence or defence, would be impracticable.
3. *Mark*, by which on the mere baring the habitually covered arm, (the other being habitually uncovered) the condition of the person in question—viz. the fact of his being a person

[4] *Panopticon: postscript, Part II, Principles and Plan of Management*, London, 1791 (Bowring, iv. 164–5).

belonging, in the character of a Prisoner, to the prison in question—would, for weeks at least after escape, be manifested.

4. Constant *division* of the Prisoners into small, and these assorted companies.
5. The Prisoners rendered distinguishable at a distance, each of them by a *number*, marked upon his *clothing* at the back and at the breast.
6. No *outlet* for the Prisoners into the enclosed area, but through *a passage* commanded by a *guard*; and so *narrow*, that no more than one can make his exit at a time, nor then but under a horizontal bar, so stationed, as, by obliging each person to *stoop*, to render impossible any acquisition of *conjunct force* by *running*.
7. *Light* kept constantly thrown, by *night* as well as by *day*, not only upon every spot to which the Prisoners have access within the prison, but upon the whole surface of the four surrounding walls.
8. For the purpose of *inspection*, eyes in considerable numbers constantly availing themselves of that light: viz. some in the *centre* as well as other parts of the circularly polygonal building within the walls, others stationed in the commanding watch-houses above mentioned, on the outside of, and in part above, those walls.
9. On the top of the walls all round, a range of *spikes*, iron or wooden, of such *slightness*, that, in the attempt to set a ladder against them or throw a rope over them to get up by, they would give way and break, and in either case strike against a range of wires, by which a number of *bells* would be set a ringing.
10. A *conversation-tube* from the central lodge to each of the exterior *guard-houses*.
11. On the outside of each of the surrounding walls, a *ditch*, the water of which would, on any attempt to undermine the contiguous wall, *inundate* the miners, and, while it betrayed their operations, render an exit, if not absolutely impracticable, at least impracticable without such noise as would give abundant warning to the Guard-house.
12. To each such Guard-house, a dog or *dogs*, of the sort of those which in the night are set a *barking* by any the least noise.

In the eyes of the Committee the enumeration of these several resources may be perhaps the more pardonable, if they should appear, any of them, capable of being applied with advantage to the giving additional security to those modes of confinement of which in the present state of things the inefficiency has so frequently been seen to betray itself.

To such of the Convicts as it might be thought fit to give employment to in the Panopticon *ground at large*, and thence *without* the limits of the enclosed area, true it is, that no more than a part of the above securities, nor that the most considerable part, would be found applicable.

But, considering, that the time of day-light would be the only time at which the demand or use for any such employment would present itself;—considering that in fact, on the many public works on which Convicts have now for so many years been employed, they have been employed in large numbers, and (as supposed) without any particular means of selection or anxiety on that head, and that too under slight guard, and yet, at those times at least, without any instances (I believe) of escape;—considering, that the passion by which a Prisoner is prompted to seek, by violent means and at the hazard of his life, a relief from durance, is not likely to be found in equal strength in the breast of every individual member, of a society so numerous and so miscellaneous, the members of which may, with less danger of injustice than any where else be rendered responsible for each other;—considering, that in the mode of treatment which is essential to a system of commercial operation conducted upon the plan in question, there is nothing that seems to present a probability of its being productive of any exertion more violent and desperate than in the case of a prison upon any of the ordinary plans:—all these things considered, the conclusion may (it is hoped) be—that in a case where by any failure of human prudence the party failing would, as in the present case, be in so many shapes and in so high a degree a sufferer, *that* same human prudence, on which, in spite of all possible securities of every other kind, reliance must in every case be placed, is not, in the present case, to be considered as destitute of all claim, to that sort and degree of confidence, which is so unavoidably bestowed upon it in all other cases.

To make use of every one of these securities, at all events, and under all circumstances, without any exception in any case, is more than I see any necessity of pledging myself for: nor yet do they constitute a complete list of *all* the securities, to which it might eventually happen to me to have recourse. Many of them will be attended with an expense which, if incurred without necessity, would be so much waste; but for which the *justification*, as well on the score of *necessity* as of *good economy*, will be the more complete, the *larger* the *scale* is on which the establishment is conducted.

The faculty by which these securities were devised, will not, I presume, be considered as putting an exclusion upon the kindred faculty, by which the decision on the question—how many and which of them to employ—will from time to time be to be pronounced.

I proceed with the objections.

II. Objection 2d. *Inordinate accumulation of Convicts for whom provision may be to be made after discharge.*

Answer. Upon the Panopticon plan, there will be the *Subsidiary Establishment*, open to as many as may choose to take the benefit of it. Some will, some will not;—but, whatever may be the proportion of the one number to the other, and whatever may be the sum of the two numbers, the exclusive choice of the Metropolis does not, to my apprehension, present itself in the shape of an inconvenience.

In the character of a reservoir for the influx in question, the option lies between the Metropolis and some Country-town:—some other Town within the Circuits of South Britain. The Metropolis will, it is true, already have to provide for the influx from its own Panopticon. But, taking into the account the magnitude of the influx in both cases, compare the magnitude of the mass of population into which the influx will have to discharge itself in this case —(say in round numbers a million) with the magnitude of the largest mass into which it can be set to discharge itself in the case of any other such Town—say 80,000:—by this comparison, all apprehension on this score will, it should seem, be dissipated.

III. Objection 3d. *Remoteness of the Convicts from their respective desired abodes, at the time of their discharge.*

Answer 1. Merely for the purpose of facilitating, on the part of Prisoners after their discharge, the return to their places of *birth* or subsequent *settlement*, in *the open mode on the large scale*, it would hardly, I presume, be deemed worth while so much as to build *one* additional *Panopticon* as above, much less, as in *the close mode upon the small scale*, to establish, in each County or set of associated Counties, a Penitentiary House or improved Prison, on any *other plan* or plans. On this occasion, the object ultimately and intrinsically aimed at, would be, I suppose, not the *birth-place* of each person, nor yet his place of *last settlement* as such, but the place, wherever it were, of his *choice*. But, take either of those places of presumed preference, the stain upon his character considered, it might not less probably be the spot, that, of all others, he would be the most *averse*, than that which he would be most *desirous*, to fix upon for his residence.

2. The *Subsidiary Establishment*, which, under the Panopticon

plan, the Governor would stand bound to provide for the purpose of making provision for all such as chose to accept of it, has for its basis the supposed *non-existence* of any such place of *former* abode, or the *unwillingness* to fix in it: and the least that this provision does is—to remove from the ground of *necessity* to that of mere *inclination*, the demand for means of conveyance to any other spot.

3. Whatsoever be, in preference to employment in the above-mentioned Subsidiary Establishment, the object of each man's desire, that portion of the *earnings* of his whole term, which by the contract is secured to him, must be small indeed, if it does not afford him ample means of gratifying such desire.

4. If after all, it were deemed necessary, that to each such discharged Convict means of *conveyance* to the place of his choice, whatever it be, should be afforded at the public charge, a mode beyond comparison less expensive, than providing, though it were no more than a single prison, in this sole view, would be the putting into his pocket a sum of money, under the *expectation* of its being applied to this purpose. But, as the ascertaining, upon any satisfactory evidence, the spot *really* desired, would be plainly impossible, the spot *assumed* could be no other than the spot most distant from the Penitentiary House in question, for, as that *most distant* spot is the spot that would command *most money*, *that* would of course be the declared spot of each man's choice.

But even *this maximum*—meaning the annual sum of all these *maximums*—would be a trifle, in comparison of the expense of an additional prison, to be built and kept up on purpose. As to *conveyance*, the means of loco-motion derived by each man from the bounty of nature, would for this purpose be, I presume, regarded as sufficient: of the *maximum* in question, the expense would therefore be neither more nor less, than the supposed necessary expense of subsistence, during a journey begun, continued, and ended, in the *pedestrian* mode.

IV. Objection 4th. *Inordinate expense of conveying the Convicts from the place of conviction to the place of punishment.*

Answer. Supposing the convicts to be conveyed from the several *Assize* and *Quarter Session* Towns to the Metropolis, the *expense* (it must be acknowledged) could not but be greater, than it would be, upon the supposition of a plurality of Panopticons, of which, the number being determined by the largeness of the scale, the situations should be exclusively adapted to this one purpose: say one allotted to each of *three* points of the compass—East, North, and West. But—

1. Suppose, that in addition to the *one London* Panopticon, only

two such *Country* receptacles were required,—place these two in any *two* of the three above-mentioned points of the compass, to the exclusion of the third,—in the East and North only—or in the East and West only—or in the West and North only,—it seems questionable whether any such saving as supposed—even to any the minutest amount would really take place.

2. Even supposing *each* of those *three* points of the compass to have its Panopticon, and thence, in respect of length of *journeys* and magnitude of *travelling expenses*, a corresponding *saving* produced, the advantage produced on this score would, on calculation, be found (I am inclined to think) so *small*, as to go but a very little way towards counteracting the disadvantage already indicated as having place, on the more important score, above mentioned.

Being, as to a more or less considerable portion of it, unavoidable, we have here an expense which, as to so much cannot be *saved*. But that which may be done, and in point of justice (it should seem) ought to be done, is—to *equalize* it:—to equalize it, I mean, in such sort that upon a County, the Assize or Quarter Session Town of which is more *distant* than that of another County from the place of permanent confinement, man for man, the burthen of conveyance may not, on that account, be rendered, or left to be, the *heavier*, in its pressure on the first-mentioned County,—viz. in the proportion of the *distance*.

Now as to the *mode of equalization*. On the contract plan, whosoever carries on the management of that Panopticon receptacle which is the common reservoir for the Convicts of all the several counties in question, in his contract it might be made a *condition*, that, for a sum certain, he should take upon him the conveyance of the Convicts from *all* the several Assize Towns and Quarter Session Towns in the district:—for which purpose, an average would of course be taken, viz. by taking the *sum* of the *distances*, and dividing it by the *number* of the *Towns*:—charge of conveyance, so much per mile.

V. Objection 5th. *Supposed unsuitableness of the fund, upon which, on this plan, the expense of maintenance, with or without the expense of conveyance, would be to be charged.*

To this objection two answers present themselves:

I. That, for the expense in question, the fund in question is *not* an unsuitable one: but, on the contrary, a *more* suitable one, than the fund upon which it would, in the other case, be charged.

II. That, supposing the *rival* fund a *more* suitable one, there would be no difficulty in *transferring* the expense to that rival fund.

I. First then, *the proposed fund is not an unsuitable one.*

1. The proposed is the common *national* fund. It is the *same* fund, on which the expense is charged, in the instance of all that portion of the convict population which is sent to *colonize*. It is the same fund, on which the expense is charged, in the instance of all that portion of the same population which is consigned to the *Hulks*.

If, as yet, of that portion which has hitherto been consigned to prisons,—to improved or not improved prisons,—the expense has hitherto been charged on the *Counties*, that is on the contributors to the *Poor Rates*, the disposition thus made, had, I should suppose, for its *cause*,—not any such opinion, as that the Poor Rates constituted a fund *more suitable* than the National fund, but merely *this circumstance*, viz. that the Poor Rates of each County constituted the *only fund*, out of which it was possible to obtain money for defraying the expense of the sort of prison in question; viz. a prison situate within the County, and appropriated to the use of *that* County, to the exclusion of every other part of the Kingdom.

To save the trouble and responsibility of making provision, at the charge of the *national* fund, for an expenditure to a certain amount, a public man would hardly, I should suppose, be desirous of imposing upon this or that class of his fellow-subjects, such as the contributors to the *Poor Rates*, an expense for example of *double* that amount.

But my calculation as well as my expectations will have greatly indeed deceived me, should the difference in point of expense between *the open mode upon a large scale*, and *the close mode upon a small scale*, turn out to be as little as to the amount of two to one to the disadvantage of the *small* scale.

In the case of *Poor Houses*, in the tract entitled *Pauper Management improved*, etc. published in *Young's Annals of Agriculture*,[5] in p. 43. may be seen a calculation, made by a professional and official hand, in which, under the head of *construction*, for a system of Poor Houses on that *small scale* which then was and actually is in practice in the *Suffolk Poor Houses*, the expense for all England being £.10,275,250. money of that time, the expense of the Central Inspection plan, on the scale of 2000 inhabitants to a House, is stated at no more than £.2,357,000; considerably less than a *fourth* part;—amount of saving, £.7,918,250:—and upon the *Official Establishment*, (an annually recurring expense) the amount of the *annual*

[5] The essays on 'The Situation and Relief of the Poor', which appeared in Arthur Young's *Annals of Agriculture* in 1797–8, were reprinted (but not published) in 1798 as *Outline of a Work entitled 'Pauper Management Improved'*. This was published in 1812 under the title *Pauper Management Improved: particularly by means of an Application of the Panopticon Principles of Construction* (Bowring, viii. 360–439).

saving is therein stated at £.408,131. 5*s*.—d° multiplied by 20 (to bring it, like the other expense, to principal money) £.8,162,625.—Number of persons maintained in each such supposed Panopticon Poor House, 2,000: being the exact number of the persons for whom, in the character of prisoners, above eleven years ago, viz. on the 25th of March 1800, as stated in a former Letter of mine now lying before the Committee, I was ordered to prepare.[6]

This is the case of *Poor Houses*: and, *both* being on the *Panopticon* plan, so far as concerns the influence of *magnitude of scale* upon *expense*, no difference will be found between the case of *Poor Houses* and the case of *Prisons*.

II. But, secondly, supposing the determination should be taken, to charge on the Poor-Rate-fund *this third* part of that *general* head of expense—the convict expense—of which the *two other* thirds are charged on the *national* fund,—on this supposition the *transference* might without difficulty be made. The average numbers of the Convicts, which, for a certain number of years back, the several Counties have respectively been in the habit of furnishing, being taken,—those numbers would serve for expressing the relative sums with which each such County might annually be charged, towards the expense of the common *Panopticon* or *Panopticons*, the station of which is supposed to be in the *Metropolis*:—I mean the Panopticons serving in common for the maintenance of the aggregate body of the Convicts receivable from those several Counties.

But, any such number as 2,000 would it not (I hear it asked) be an *unwieldy* number?—too unwieldy for good management? Oh yes:—on every *ordinary* plan,—too unwieldy by a great deal. *Nine hundred* was the number of the *prisoners*, that, on the original and supposed highly-finished Penitentiary plan, as per 19 G. 3. c. 74, were to have been confined in the *town* that was to have been built for that purpose at *Battersea-rise*:[7] and, as to *Houses, nine hundred*—(being the number of separate Houses, which, over and above such as were to be occupied in common, were to have been included in that town) was assuredly too great a number for good management: *two thousand*, consequently, in a much greater degree too great.

On every as yet exemplified plan of construction and management, the natural and naturally prevalent apprehension of unwieldiness has, therefore, very just grounds to stand upon.

But upon the *Panopticon* principle—whether it be for *Paupers* or for *Convicts*—for *free* and innocent men or for *prisoners*—though

[6] Letter 1530, *Correspondence*, vi. See also letter 2110 above.

[7] See 19 Geo. III, c.74 s.14.

the number of the *inhabitants* be 2,000, the *House* is but *one*: and that one House is capable of being pervaded in all directions,—pervaded by a single glance, and without so much as a change of posture.

Of the difficulties, which upon any *ordinary* plan of construction, for want of that source of simplification, attends the business of management, even in the case of a *Poor House*, and of a moderate size, an exemplification may be seen in *Pauper Management improved*, p. 43; in *Panopticon*, Letter VI. and in various parts of the Postscript; and, in the case of a *Prison*, in the instance of several *American* Prisons, in the tract intituled Panopticon versus New South Wales, Letter II. pages from 54 to 61.[8]

I have the honour to be, with all respect,
Sir,
Your most obedient Servant,
Jeremy Bentham.

George Holford, Esq.
Chairman of the
Committee on Penitentiary Houses.

2119

To Sir Francis Burdett

late May 1811 (Aet 63)

May, 1811.

Dear Sir,

Your presence was grievously missed on Thursday or Friday last, when M. A. Taylor's motion about Chancery Delays came to be made.[2] It *would* be so, still more deplorably, on Thursday next,—the day to which the debate was adjourned.[3] A parliamentary friend

[8] The title adopted in the 1812 published version of what had appeared in 1802 as *Letters to Lord Pelham* (Bowring, iv. 173–248). For Bentham's specific reference see Bowring, iv. 238–40.

2119. [1] Bowring, x. 460–1. From internal evidence this letter can be dated as written some time between Saturday 18 May and Wednesday 22 May 1811, and probably between Sunday 19th and Tuesday 21st.

[2] On Friday 17 May 1811 Michael Angelo Taylor (1757?–1834), MP for Ilchester, moved that a committee of the House of Commons be appointed to look into the causes of delays in chancery. See *Parliamentary Debates*, xx. 206–7.

[3] On 17 May a motion to adjourn the debate until the following Thursday was carried, but the matter was not discussed again in the Commons until 5 June.

of yours has just been with me.[4] His father is upon terms of the oldest and strictest intimacy with both the persons for whose accommodation the vile job threatened in the Lords is intended to be made; especially the one for the support of whose incapacity, the capacity of the other is to be called in.[5] In such a situation, is it for flesh and blood to *write* or to *speak* a single syllable? No: but he will be *there*; and being there, will give his honest vote. Is not this heroism?

Sir Francis Burdett has no such chains: and by Sir Francis Burdett shall the interest of the public be—I had like to have said, once more—sacrificed to the interest of the pillow?

The debates in the *Times*, and I fear in the other papers, presented but a very partial and altogether inadequate view of what was said on the occasion, especially by Romilly.

The pace of the present Chancellor in the making of *decrees* is more than ten times as slow as the average pace. Exactly this, in substance and effect, said Romilly in the House. In one term, (I think it was the last,) during which the Master of the Rolls made *one hundred and fifty* decrees, the Chancellor made—*not one*. This, too, if I do not misrecollect, Romilly said in the House: this, at any rate, he has said several times to me.[6] On Thursday he will move for documents, from which, what is above will be proved. This, then, in particular, is the motion which stands so much in need of support. In effect, I am not certain whether in *form* he gave notice of it on

[4] Probably William Pleydell-Bouverie, Viscount Folkestone (1779–1869), later 3rd Earl of Radnor, at this time MP for Salisbury.

[5] Jacob Pleydell-Bouverie, 2nd Earl of Radnor (1750–1828), Folkestone's father, was a member of the House of Lords Committee appointed on 5 March 1811 to consider chancery delays. On 20 May the Committee report was presented to the Lords by Radnor. In view of the business of the court, it recommended the appointment of a third judge in chancery (*Lords Journals*, xlviii. 110, 289). In letter 2132 below, Bentham argued that the beneficiaries of such an appointment would be the lord chancellor, John Scott, Baron Eldon (1751–1838), later 1st Earl of Eldon, and his friend Sir Thomas Plumer (1753–1824), the solicitor-general, whom Eldon wished to see made the third judge. When the post of vice-chancellor was created in 1813, Plumer was the first to occupy it. In this letter, however, Bentham seems to imply that Redesdale was likely to be appointed, and a later letter from Eldon to the Prince Regent suggests that the lord chancellor's original choice was indeed Redesdale, not Plumer. See A. Aspinall, ed., *The Letters of King George IV, 1812–1830*, 3 vols., Cambridge, 1938, i. 237.

[6] It seems unlikely that Romilly was this forthright in the Commons. He wrote with regard to this subject: 'My opinion is, that the Chancellor's hesitation and delays, and habits of procrastination are the principal, if not the only, causes of the evil; but it is impossible for me, who am constantly attending his Court as counsel, with any decency to state this to the House.' *Memoirs of the Life of Sir Samuel Romilly*, 3 vols., London, 1840, ii. 374–5.

Friday.[7] The few honest or half-honest lawyers, who, had they been there, would have given him their support, were, by this or that accident, kept away. Between personal and public considerations his situation was a most irksome one. I heard it from his lips, and still more impressively in his tone, (I speak of the closet, not the House,) as well as read it in his countenance. I called on him (it was but yesterday) for the purpose of spurring him to do the very thing he had declared his intention of doing in the House. What I am now writing, and whatever little else I have done, or may do on this subject, it is fit you should know is altogether without his knowledge. Since Lord Hardwick's time,[8] or earlier, the number of causes in the Court of Chancery has rather decreased than increased: so that, if a dozen of lawyers, having the most practice, were picked out, and the dice were thrown to obtain an *average man* among them, that average man being Chancellor, would have no need of the proposed coadjutor; so that the only use of the proposed job, except increase of the influence of the Crown over the lawyers, together with a few other etceteras, is to keep in that highest of places a man, of whom it will be proved by the rules of arithmetic, that he has not one-tenth part of the capacity that is necessary to enable a man to do his duty in it.

The Ministry looked wondrous grim: they are in a sad funk: their not venturing to do anything more than to adjourn the debate, seems sufficient proof of it. If duly and happily improved, opportunities may arise of uncovering more and more the nakedness and rottenness of the nursing mother of all abuse. Forgive all this liberty, and believe me,

most truly
dear Sir,
yours.

[7] In his speech on 17 May Romilly 'intimated that, if the Committee were refused, I should probably move for returns of the state of the Court of Chancery now and at some former periods, which would produce some of the information which it was intended should be got through the medium of a committee'. *Memoirs*, ii. 395. On 5 June, when the debate on chancery delays resumed, Taylor's motion concerning the appointment of a Commons Committee was successful, thus removing the need for Romilly to call for papers. See *Parliamentary Debates*, xx. 437–45.

[8] Philip Yorke, 1st Earl of Hardwicke (1690–1764), was lord chancellor 1737–56. The Lords Committee compared the business completed in the last ten years of his chancellorship (1745–55) with that in the period 1800–10, and this formed the basis for the recommendation that a third judge in chancery be appointed. See *Lords Journals*, xlviii. 290 (Lords Committee Report, Appendix B).

P.S.—My own situation considered, not to speak of other persons, you will understand without difficulty that I am casting myself on your generosity, and that no part of this is designed either for the tavern or the newspaper.

N.B.—Lord Redesdale, the ex-Chancellor of Ireland,[9] was for incapacity in this its worst shape, *indecision*, just such another. This appears from the most pointed facts printed in the debates of the time.

N.B.—Incapacity in *this* shape being proved by comparative arithmetic, is an element of unfitness which cannot but be accompanied by *mala fides*; since it is not possible, that, like *erroneous judgment*, it should be a secret to the man himself.

2120

To Sir Evan Nepean

21 May 1811 (Aet 63)

Dear Sir

Prepare your eyes for a troublesome man's letter. If Lady Nepean[2] is with you, as I suppose she is, summon her to the assistance of your old *protegé*, and set her opposite in readiness to smooth your brow, should the wrinkles become too deep. You bid *me* prepare t'other day to have my liver and soul plucked out—now for a piece of yours.

If, the building at—(I don't know what the name of your place in Dorsetshire is[3]—) being finished—and the embellishments at Fulham[4] clamouring for you, your carriage at the door in consequence, please place it to Panopticon account, all that is fair but if not, come you must and that 'without long tarrying'[5] or after what I took the liberty of saying of you in my Letter to the Treasury,[6] and

[9] Redesdale had lost his post as Irish lord chancellor in 1806, when the Ministry of All the Talents took office.

2120. [1] BL VIII. 519–23. Copy in Koe's hand. Docketed: '1811 May 21 / Panopt / J.B. Q.S.P. / to Sir Ev. Nepean / Designed for Dorsetshire / On advice of his return / sent to Fulham / Holford's adverse Report.' The second part of this letter, from the paragraph commencing 'yesterday', is at BL VIII, 522–3 and is separated from the first part, but both seem to belong to the same letter.

[2] Margaret Nepean (d. 1833), née Skinner, had married Nepean in 1782. For her exchange of letters with Bentham in 1799 and 1800 see *Correspondence*, vi. as index.

[3] Loders Court, near Bridport.

[4] For Nepean's house at Fulham see *Correspondence*, vi. 290–1.

[5] *Prayer-Book*, Psalms 40: 21.

[6] Nepean is mentioned in letters 2075 and 2099 above, but not in any surviving letter to the treasury.

what was done by the Treasury and said to you in consequence, those who know us both will perforce think less favourably of you or me than it is desirable they should.

'You made your *appeal* to Sir E. Nepean: he *could*' not say any thing for you: he *would* not say any thing against you:—he went to Dorsetshire: such will be language as to me. Now say, my dear Sir Evan, if it was under the assurance of your not accepting it, that they offered you the Chairmanship,[7] a preparation made for such language is in perfect accordance with every thing I have yet experienced. Be this as it may, the absence of Sir E.N. is actually and to my knowledge, a subject of notice and observation in the Committee.

I have just seen Mr *Abercromby*: the unknown member you were explaining to me. *He* makes no secret to me of his disposition, or his endeavours, in favour of Panopticon. He is the only acting Member of the Committee from whom since your departure, I have received any communication, or to my knowledge (except what I may have to mention presently) any assistance. His attendance has been constant without the omission I believe of so much as a single day.

On Friday there was a Committee.[8] Without any previous notice or conversation about the contents, out comes Mr *Chairman*[9] with a *Report* ready cut and dry recommending the execution of the Penitentiary system upon the original plan as per Statute 19 G.3: for the number of 600 males and 300 females, as therein mentioned.[10]—Panopticon slightly touched upon: reasons for putting it aside,—the *Contract* system and the *insufficiency* of the *degree* of separation.—Sir George and solitary Cells for ever![11]

I believe it has been since your departure (has it been? but no matter,)—that to the original *reference*, copy of which I have before me, has been added one calling for a Report upon propriety of continuing or discontinuing the *Hulks*. Per Report, as above, approbation given to the Hulks:—approbation pure and simple. Note that in the Hulks the supply is by *Contract*, and separation compleatly impossible: besides that as explained at large in the Panopticon Book etc whatever good effect can be expected from generally prevailing solitude, can not but be compleatly done away by frequent

[7] The chairmanship of the Penitentiary Committee, of which Nepean was a member. See *Commons Journals*, lxvi. 144.

[8] Friday 17 May.

[9] Holford.

[10] See Geo. III, c.74 s.14.

[11] An allusion to Sir George Onesiphorus Paul (1746–1820), designer of the Gloucester Penitentiary, built 1785–9, in which the prisoners were kept in solitary confinement.

occasional associations, neither preventible or proposed to be prevented. So much for *consistency*, and *sincerity*. It is exactly what I had been led to expect, and was accordingly prepared for.

Quoth Burton[12] 'I am for Panopticon' (Heaven bless his blind eyes! It was more than I expected) Quoth Wilberforce—something to the same effect. What Bragge Bathurst[13] or Sturges Bourne[14] said, *non constati*. Quoth Abercromby—'Here is a *Report* drawn up but no Resolutions debated or so much as drawn up—much less passed to *form a ground* for any such Report—Moreover here is an approbation passed upon the *Hulk* system: and yet not one tittle of *evidence* have we heard upon it. It seems to me that some *Resolutions* ought to be agreed upon: and in the mean time that since we are to Report upon the *Hulks* we should have some evidence about the Hulks' To this much, at any rate all agreed, except Mr Chairman, whose Report was accordingly for the present at least, put by.

Quoth Wilberforce before they parted, (but this must have been in a whisper to Abercromby alone, or to him and Burton) 'I must see about this—I must see what can be done,'—or 'what is to be done *innuendo* intriguing with the higher powers who are at the bottom of this Report.'

yesterday they heard evidence about the Hulks. Abercromby was prepared to find it bad (he sd) but not so bad. So far as concerns Panopt. the effect of his enquiry about the Hulks is the gaining a little time; and it is under favour of the time there gained that with the advice and consent of Mr A I am giving you this plague.

They cannot definitively carry an hostile report without an opportunity given to Romilly to be heard. When he is heard then will there be a little pulling and halling at some other livers and souls. I mean in the Committee; and if that will not do in the House.

Casting my eyes around me on my second examination I really did understand, that accordg to the concluding question wch you framed, it was the sense of the Committee, and even nem. diss. that the Contract was a Contract, and that so compleatly such as to preclude all further enquiry into the subject. But now you see the turn the business has taken.

Under these circumstances so far as depends upon the Committee, as the business might be lost for *want* of your Vote, so, for aught I know it might *possibly be carried* without your vote: but tho' it should be then carried yet as to ultimate success things wd not by any means be as if you were present. Before my abovementioned

[12] Francis Burton (1744?–1832), the blind MP for Oxford.

[13] Charles Bragge Bathurst (1754–1831), MP for Bristol.

[14] William Sturges Bourne (1769–1845), MP for Christchurch.

Letter to the Treasury the hostility of Mr Ryder had been put out of all doubt by the personal behaviour of his Mr Becket, who in the name of Mr Ryder had called me before him for no other purpose but to keep spitting in my face as he did for about half an hour, I wiping it off all the while with a good humour wch I had learnt from my twenty years experience, determined they should never have any such pretence as was sought for by that means.

But as to hostility all depends upon degrees. Your Mr Ryder I am well assured does not hate me whom he has never seen so much by a good deal as he loves himself: nor probably enough was the barking of his dog a correct echo of the masters voice. If it can be done with a certain degree of *pressure* then Panopticon is crushed: but if a certain degree of *counter pressure* is applied then so it may that *ease* (it may appear) will be better provided for by giving way than by carrying the annihilation plan with a high hand.

What is curious is that by several concurring circumstances in which I cannot help suspecting human ingenuity had its share I had been led to expect a report quite favourable: and so little have they to fear from reason that they have not only *received* but *printed* argumentative Letters from me (there are now three in all)[15] with a degree of liberality beyond what could have been naturally expected.

As to Wilberforce with his intriguing valeat quantum valere potest:[16] but trying is one thing: trying in such manner as to be *troublesome*, and thence *impressive* is another thing. From you one honest downright declaration in the Committee room, is what for my part I should expect more from than from all the whispering that is likely to be performed in other places.

One favour at any rate, one mark of friendship I do count upon —which is—and that by return of Post—a single line to say yes or no—and if yes on what day hope may fasten itself. Yes: on a single day if the whole business be not finally crushed at once the question may turn as between the present season, and some future one when I am no more. I have left myself no more room than just to say that as towards you I am still what you used to find me.

JB

PS. Just heard of your return—no matter off it goes

[15] Letters 2106, 2110, and 2118.

[16] i.e. 'Let it be worth as much as it can be worth.'

2121
From John Herbert Koe

22 May 1811

L.I.

I have not been able to get a sight of young Nepean[2] but I have seen his Clerk who tells me that Sir Evan has been and perhaps is in Dorsetshire, that he was not arrived from thence yesterday to the great surprize of his family who had been for the last four days expecting him and that now his arrival in Town was hourly looked for.

I dont send Walter on to the Bankers as was proposed, because I thought perhaps that under these circumstances you might possibly be for dispatching him to Fulham—I'll call on my way home at the Hour of 6 to learn whether he has been seen or if any tidings can be got of him there.

2122
From John Herbert Koe

23 May 1811

Linc. Inn

I saw Nepeans Clerk (Nepean himself not being at home) who tells me that he was at Fulham yesterday, where he learnt that Sir Evan had been heard from that Morning, his Letter being directed from his place in Dorsetsh., that he had been detained there by business, and should be in Town in a few days, but on what day in particular was not known.

2121. [1] BL VIII. 524–5. Autograph. Docketed: '1811 May 22 / Panopt. / H.K. Linc Inn / to / J.B. Q.S.P. / Enquiries after / Nepean'. Addressed: 'Jeremy Bentham Esq'.

[2] Molyneaux Hyde Nepean (1783–1856), eldest son of Sir Evan Nepean, entered Lincoln's Inn 1803.

2122. [1] BL VIII. 526–7. Autograph. Docketed: '1811 May 23 / Panopt / H.K. Lincs Inn / to / J.B. Q.S.P. / Nepean rediturus'. Addressed: 'J Bentham Esq'.

2123

From Richard Wharton

23 May 1811

Sir,

I am directed by the Lords Commissioners of His Majestys Treasury to request you will forthwith transmit to me for the purpose of being copied and afterwards returned to you the Feoffment under which you as Trustee for the Public hold certain Lands in Tothill Fields or in case you should be unwilling to let the said Feoffment pass from your Custody that you will name an early hour in the course of to morrow when a Person may attend from the Treasury at your House and in your presence take a Copy of the same,

I am,
Sir,
Your most obedient Servt.,
Rd Wharton

Treasury Chambers,
23d. May 1811
Mr. Bentham

2124

From Richard Wharton

24 May 1811

24 May 1811
Treasury

Sir

The Bearer, Mr Charles Woodforde[2] of this Office will receive from you the Deed of Feoffment, and will give you a receipt for it.[3]

2123. [1] BL VIII. 528–9. In the hand of a clerk, with the exception of the signature. Docketed: '1811 May 23 / Panopt. / Secry Wharton Treasury / to / J.B. Q.S.P. / For Feoffment of / Lord Salisbury's'. Letter-book copy at PRO T 27/68, p. 238.

2124. [1] BL VIII. 530–1. Autograph. Docketed: '1811 May 24 / Panopt / Secry / R. Wharton Treasury / to / J.B. Q.S.P. / Has commissioned / Charles Woodford to / give a receipt for / the conveyance of / Ld. Salisburys to / J.B.'

[2] Woodforde was assistant clerk of revenue 1805–21.

[3] The receipt is at BL VIII. 532, docketed: '1811 May 24 / Panopt. / Ld Salisburys / Charles Woodford / for Treasury / Receipt for *Release* / being the conveyance of / Ld Salisburys to J.B. / as Feoffee.'

It shall be returned to you on or before Wednesday next. I had gone to the House of Commons before your letter of yesterdays date reached the Treasury.[4] I am

Yr obedt servant
R Wharton

Mr J. Bentham

2125

From James Abercromby

25 May 1811

Dear Sir,

On my return home this morning I found your note, which being written in Pencil, and having been rubbed, I found it difficult to decypher.[2]

The Committee met yesterday, and they proceeded to consider Mr. Holford's Report, which I fear will not be, what you would have wished.

The remainder of the Report will be considered on Monday, and will probably be presented to the House early in next Week.[3]

I wrote to Sir C. Bunbury who was not in Town. Sir E. Nepean is still absent, and Mr. Morton Pitt[4] is in Town but has never been near the Committee.

I am going out of Town but return on Monday. I am very sorry indeed that I had not the pleasure of seeing you, when you was so good as to call, so I may not now be able to see you till after the Report is adopted. There is no other proposition under the consideration of the Committee at present except Holford's Report.

I remain
Dr Sir
Yrs. faithfully
J. Abercromby.

Saturday
May 25th
1811

[4] Missing.

2125. [1] BL VIII. 533–4. Autograph. Docketed: '1811 May 25 / Panopt / Abercromby New Street / Spring Garden / to / J.B. Q.S.P.' Addressed: 'To / Jeremy Bentham Esq. / etc. etc.' Franked: 'J. Abercromby.'

[2] Missing. See letter 2126.

[3] The report was presented on 31 May. See *Commons Journals*, lxvi. 388.

[4] William Moreton Pitt (1754–1836), MP for Dorset. For his earlier contact with Bentham see *Correspondence*, v, vi, vii, as index.

2126

To James Abercromby

27 May 1811 (Aet 63)

Monday. May 27th 1811

Yr Lre dated Saty May 25 reached this House betwn 8 and 9 of yt day and my hands abt 9 I am sorry my pencil scrawl gave you so much trouble. It was scrawled in ye passage of yr House for relying too much abt what you had told me of yr present habits of not going out before 10 I had been improvident enough not to make the requisite provision agt accidents to the contrary The object was to beg the favour of a previous sight of these Resolutns wch after what you had mentd to me on ye subject, I took for granted it was yr intention to move. As matters have turned out the only good effect a less degree of illegibility on the part of my afsd scrawl wd have had is the saving you the trouble of decyphering it.

Passing a previous string of Resols to serve as a basis for the Rept being in yr. opinion, if I understood you right, ye regular course I thought it had been yr plan to [. . .?] with Resols for yt purpose Mr Chairman finding himself alone or at least in a minority and havg in consequence put by his Rept, or at least postponed the continuance of the reading of it, till after the state of ye Hulks shd have been brought out by examinat of Witnesses

Rebus in stantibus[2] I had nothg left for it but to take yr Lre yesterday Morng to Romilly, who told me of yr endeavours to come to the speech of him before yr departure. All ye time on which the Comee will be sitting this day he will be in or about ye H of Lds and he makes no doubt of being able to look in and see to the matter. That sd Lre of mine wch after the required omissions was to have been printed and of course circulated had not reached him,[3] indeed he knew nothg of what had passed, since whatever it was that he heard when he last saw you. He seemed entirely to agree with you as to the propriety of bringing forward Resols He says it is contrary to all custom to present a Report till after it has been left for some days in the hands of the Clk for the inspection of ye Members in general and in particular of any such who may not have been present at the reading of the whole.

2126. [1] BL VIII. 535–6. Copy in Koe's hand. Docketed: '1811 May 27 / Panopt / J.B. Q.S.P. / to / Abercromby New Street / Spring Garden.'

[2] i.e. 'in the present circumstances'.

[3] Probably letter 2118, which was printed in the *Second Report* of the Penitentiary Committee.

If a motion were made in the Commee for bringing forward a set of Resols as above I do not very well see how they cod with any tolerable decency negative it; and even if they did, it appearing yt they did wd be so much gained. If communicatn were made of a design to bring forward a set of Resols accordingly, I do not see how they cod with any tolerable decency refuse to receive it. It was but t'other day yt delay seemed to be all yt I had to fear from: and yr fear, if I did not misconceive you, and that on my account was, lest it shd be found impracticable to go thro' what was necessary to be gone thro' in the Commee and the House time enough for any thing to be done this season in the land. Now what I have most to fear from is precipitation: or rather a delay seems to be my only chance.

Many thanks for yr trouble about Sir C Bunbury[4] as to the Lre my expectations from it are not sanguine—i.e. from any Letter in these circumstances If a particular day be fixt and it be sd and shewn to be near—every thing depends on that particular day—then perhaps an exertion may be made: but if ye length of attendance appears indefinite, then in the case of a man [cir]cumstanced like my old friend the chance is small indeed.

Nepean I wrote to ye same day on wch I saw you[5] It was in my head yt I must have mentioned yt to you before but if so, this instant I cannot recollect when or how.

Oh yes I did write to you about it mentioning his miraculous appearance in ye House to vote agt Brands then expected Parly Ref motion.[6] They were at yt time in daily expectation of seeing him at his House at Fulham: since then I have learnt that such expectations are no longer entertained

[4] See letter 2124.

[5] Letter 2119.

[6] Bentham's letter to Abercromby mentioning this subject is missing. The Hon. Thomas Brand (1774–1851), later Lord Dacre, MP for Hertfordshire, introduced motions respecting parliamentary reform on 21 May 1810 and again on 8 May 1812, but not in May 1811 despite his original intention to bring forward his motions annually. See *Parliamentary Debates*, xvii. 123–64; xxiii. 99–161. Bentham referred to these motions in the introduction to his *Plan of Parliamentary Reform, in the Form of a Catechism* (Bowring, iii. 517 n., 518 n., 519 and n., 521 n., 522 and n., 523 n., 525 and n., 532 and n., 535).

2127
From Charles Woodforde

28 May 1811

Mr Woodforde presents his Compliments to Mr Bentham and returns to him the Feoffment which he received from him a few days since —Mr Woodforde will thank Mr Bentham to give the Bearer the Receipt which Mr Woodforde left with him—
Treasury Chambers
28 May 1811.

2128
From Sir Samuel Romilly

1 June 1811

Dear Bentham

The Committee made their Report yesterday. I have not been able to see it. It is very long and I understand very unfavourable to your Contract I attended the last day but one of their meeting but found it quite impossible to do any thing. Except Abercromby and myself and Wilberforce no person friendly to you was present.

ever most sincerely
Yours
Saml Romilly

June 1.

2127. [1] BL VIII. 537–8. Autograph. Docketed: '1811 May 28 / Panopt Ld Salisbury / Woodforde Treasury / to J.B. Q.S.P. / Sends back the / Feoffment the return of / which was promised / for on or before 29th / with request for / a receipt from J.B. / Sent receipt accor / dingly by the Bearer / viz. Hatwell the / Messenger:— upon Hatwell being men- / tioned [?] in it.' John Hatwell was a treasury messenger 1793–1814.

2128. [1] UC ix. 31. Autograph. Docketed: '1811 June 2 / Panopt. / Romilly Russel / Square / to / J.B. Q.S.P. / Penitentiary Comms / Report delivered to / House June 1. / very unfavourable / to J.B.'s Contract'. Printed, with minor differences, Bowring, xi. 148. The *First Report* of the Committee was ordered to be printed by the Commons on 31 May.

2129

From Richard Wharton

3 June 1811

Treasury Chambers
1811 June 3.

Sir

I have to beg that you will favour me with a sight of the Counterparts of the Under Leases which you have granted of the several portions of the Premes in Tothilfields: and I will take care to return those instruments to you in the course of a few days. I am Sir

Yr obedt servt
R Wharton

Mr Bentham

2130

To Étienne Dumont

4–5 June 1811 (Aet 63)

Q.S.P. Tuesday 4 June 1811.

My dear Dumont

Just now a rencontre happened which gave compleat confirmation to the conclusion I had drawn as I was mentioning to you this morning of an originally preconcerted plan for setting aside Panopticon, concerted I mean before the appointment of the Committee.

Pole Carew must have been more or less known to you as the man who drew up the Report in favour of Panopticon which I think you can not but have seen——viz. the 28th Report of the Finance Committee (Abbot's) of 1797–8.[2] He was the man who procured for me a copy of the Panopticon Book for Adam, out of which I mean the Architectural Plan Adam extracted the spoilt extract which you saw and have described.[3] When the Committee was nominated P.

2129. [1] BL VIII. 539–40. Autograph. Docketed: '1811 June 3 / Panopt. / Secry Wharton / Treasury / to J.B. Q.S.P. / For Counterparts / of Lease of Ld / Salisburys —— / Answered 4th. / transmitting List / of do.'

2130. [1] Dumont MSS 33 / I, fos. 149–50. Part autograph, part in the hand of a copyist.

[2] The *Twenty-Eighth Report from the Select Committee on Finance, etc. Police, Including Convict Establishments, Ordered to be printed 26th June 1798.* For this report and Abbot's chairmanship of the Committee see *Correspondence*, vi.

[3] See letters 2063 and 2089.

Carew was still in the Country: upon his arrival, viz 2 or three days after, I wrote to him informing him of the business, and expressing my hope that the support he had afforded me on the former occasion, would not be withdrawn from me on the present.[4] No sooner had he received my letter, than he called upon me. What he said to me was in substance that he would go about immediately and endeavour to learn whether the plan they had in view was my plan: that if it was he would take measures for having his name added to the Committee, an arrangement about which as Romilly had before assured me there could be no difficulty. Nothing could be more explicit: nothing as I have since found reason to be satisfied, could be more sincere. In conversation, I mentioned to him the Philanthropist, as containing your account of Adam's Edinburgh Prison:[5] he expressed a desire to see it: I lent him my copy: he put it into his pocket. Since that till to day as I shall mention presently, I have never seen nor heard from him: taken by itself a worse omen (I mean than his silence) there could hardly be: but counter-appearance and even putative information in abundance, kept me in that state of delusion which you have witnessed.

This day walking in the Strand who should I meet but Pole Carew. We greeted each other and stopt and immediately he began accounting to me for his silence. I called on Wilberforce (says he) and saw him very soon after I saw you: the complexion of the Committee (he W said) was not favourable: I informed him of my wish to be upon it if there was a prospect that the cause in favour of which my opinion was so well known to him stood any chance of being served by it. He gave me to understand that there was not. Then said I (viz. J.B.) this was a thing settled before hand viz. before the appointment of the Committee—yes he said he supposed it was: his exact words I do not remember, but as to the import it is impossible I should entertain any the least doubt of it, looks and gestures being completely in confirmation. As the supposition all circumstances considered was not altogether favourable to that of Wilberforce's sincerity, I mean with respect to the protestations he had so recently and so repeatedly made to me in writing as well as in conversation, especially under the circumstance of his thus declining to receive the assistance thus proferred by a sure vote then would have been the time for Pole Carew (who is a friend of Wilberforces) to have been anxious to set me right and endeavour to do away that suspicion or rather supposition which I had been expressing so plainly.

[4] Missing.

[5] Letter 2089 n. 3.

5 June Wedny

With this you will [have] such part of the Appendix to the Penitentiary Committee's Report as I received yesterday from Abercromby, in answer to my request made to him that day: which part was of course all that had as yet come to his hand. Of the three Letters which I addressed at different times to the Committee it contains the two first: besides the Minutes of the two Examinations I underwent. You will also find some Papers relative to Panopticon that had been printed in the 28th Report of the Finance Committee of 1797: which Report you perhaps have never read, or have forgotten. In the 2d of those two recent Letters of mine and my 2d Examination together you will find the recent exertions made to wipe away cause of suspicion, etc. besides those that were before in print and that you are so well acquainted with.

2131

To Richard Wharton

4 June 1811 (Aet 63)

Queen's Square Place Westmr. 4 June 1811

Sir

Yesterday afternoon I received your letter of that days date expressive of your desire of 'a sight of the Counterparts of the Under Leases which' I 'have granted of the several portions of the Premes in Tothill Fields' meaning Milbank which is adjacent to Tothill Fields: adding that you 'will take care to return those instruments to' me 'in the course of a few days.'[2]

In obedience to your commands thus signified I inclose for the present, a list containing short descriptions of eight several instruments being five of them Counterparts of leases, the other three Agreements:[3] under which eight are comprised the whole of the estate conveyed to me as Feoffee to the purpose in question land and buildings included:

In quality of Co-granter along with myself my Brother Samuel Bentham (it may perhaps be observed) is mentioned. The short reason is—that under the contract as printed in the 28th Report of the Finance Committee of 1797, his life was to have succeeded mine.

2131. [1] BL VIII. 541–2. Autograph draft. Docketed: '1811 June 4 / Panop Ld. Salisbury / J.B. Q.S.P. / to / Secry. Wharton / Treasury / With list of Counter- / parts and Agreements / ready to be delivered / as desired by his / Letter of 3d.'

[2] Letter 2129. [3] The list immediately follows this letter.

In these descriptions the *terms* respectively granted are for shortness stated as if *absolute*. In the instruments themselves will be seen the care taken by appropriate conditions to secure the eventual immediate application of the land to the intended public purpose.

These documents I hold in readiness to be delivered to any person to whom you will be pleased to give it in charge to receive them from me, and who bringing with him the inclosed list will thereupon acknowledge his receipt of them, as before.

Should any explanations be desired, Mr Koe, of Lincolns Inn (Old Buildings No 19) a Gentleman of the Chancery Bar, who bore a part in the several negotiations will, on intimation received to that effect be ready to attend you at anytime for that purpose, your commands being addressed to him either at Lincolns Inn as above, or at this my House.

I am Sir,
Your most obedient Servant
Jeremy Bentham.

[List of Counterparts and Agreements][4]

1. Counterpart of a Lease dated 20th Decr 1803 and made between Jery. Bentham Esqr of the one part and Mr B. Hodges[5] for 21 years from the 25th day of Decr. then next of a Distillery and Houses at Milbank Westmr. at the yearly Rent of £107. And containing an Indorsement thereon made between the sd Jery. Bentham and Saml. Bentham Esqr of the one part and the sd B Hodges of the other part encreasing the sd Rent to £125.
2. Agreement dated 25th day of March 1805 and made Between the sd J. Bentham and Saml. Bentham of the one part and John White Esqr[6] of the other part being an Agreement for a Lease for

[4] BL VIII. 545–6. In Koe's hand. Docketed: '1811 June 5. / Panopt. / Bate Treasury Clerk Q.S.P. / to / J.B. ibid / Receipt for 8 leases and / Agreemnts from J.B. to / Milbank Tenants'. Endorsed; 'Received the several Instruments enumerated in the above List on the / part of Mr. Wharton of the Treasury this fifth day of June 1811 / Edward Bates'. Bates was an assistant clerk at the treasury. The docket and endorsement were added when he collected the documents on 5 June, bringing with him the list, which had been enclosed in letter 2131. A copy of the list is at BL VIII. 543–4, docketed: '1811 June 4 / Panopt. Ld Salisbury's / List of Counterparts / and Agreements / ready to be trans- / mitted to Secry Wharton / in pursuance of his / letter to J.B. of the / 3d: and transmitted / to him (the original / as drawn by Mr / Koe) via letter of / this date / J.B.'

[5] Benjamin Hodges, distiller. This document (together with many of the others listed) was later sent to the office of woods and forests, and can now be found at PRO CRES 2/675.

[6] John White, of Campbell and White, wharfingers and timber merchants, one of the owners of a wharf at Millbank.

14 years from the sd 25 day of March from the sd J. Bentham and Saml. Bentham to the sd J. White of the River Shore and 2 plots of Ground at Milbank Westmr. at the yearly Rent of £11. 18s. NB. The piece of Ground mentd. in this agreement as containing 2. Acres, 1 Rood was afterwards comprized in the Lease No 6.

3. Agreemnt dated 1. Augst 1805 and made Between the sd J. Bentham and Saml Bentham of the one part and the sd B. Hodges of the other part being an Agreement for a Lease for Seven years from 25th March 1805 from the sd J. Bentham and S. Bentham to the sd J. White of certain parcels of Meadow Ground situated at Milbank afsd at the yearly Rent of £63.——NB all except 3 Acres of the Land mentioned in this Agreement was afterwards comprized part in Lease No 5 and the remaining part in Lease No. 6.
4. Counterpart of a Lease dated 28th. Augt 1805 and made Between the sd Jery. Bentham and Saml. Bentham of the one part and Sam. Cooke[7] of the other part being a demise made by the said J. Bentham and Saml Bentham to the sd S. Cooke for Fourteen years from the 25th March then last past of Land and Houses at Milbank Westmr. at the yearly rent of £290—And containing an Indorsement thereon dated the 26th day of August 1807 made between the same parties extending the sd term in the sd Premises to 21 years from Midsummer day then last past:
5. Counterpart of a Lease dated 30th July 1807 and made Between the sd J Bentham and Saml. Bentham of the one part and the sd B. Hodges of the other part being a demise made by the sd J Bentham and S. Bentham to the sd B Hodges for $17\frac{1}{2}$ years from the Midsummer day then last of certain plots of Ground at Milbank aforesaid at the yearly Rent of £20. 6s.
6. Counterpart of a Lease dated 27 August 1807 and made Between the sd J. Bentham and S. Bentham of the one part and the sd Saml Cooke of the other part being a demise made by the said J. Bentham and S. Bentham to the sd S. Cooke for 21 years from Midsummer day then last past of certain Lands at Milbank aforesaid at the yearly Rent of £90. 2s. 9d. subject to the encrease therein mentioned.
7. Counterpart of a Lease dated 30 March 1809 and made Between the sd J. Bentham and S. Bentham of the one part and James Baker[8] of the other part being a demise made by the sd J. Bentham and S. Bentham to the sd J. Baker for Seven years from the 25 March then last past of a House and Garden Ground at Milbank aforesaid at the yearly Rent of £.95.

[7] See letter 2082 and n. 2.

[8] James Baker, gardener, of Neat Houses, Millbank.

8. Agreement dated 2. March 1811 and made between the sd J. Bentham and S. Bentham of the one part and the sd S. Cooke of the other part being an Agreement for Eight years from the 25th March then next ensuing from the sd J. Bentham and S. Bentham to the sd S. Cooke of the River Shore at Milbank aforesaid at the yearly Rent of £5.

2132

To Étienne Dumont

7 June 1811 (Aet 63)

7 June 1811

Since I saw you I have just been reading the Times of yesterday the 6th a Report of the debate on Lord Eldon's plan for getting his friend Plumer the Sollicitor General paid at the public expence for doing a part of that business for the whole of which he Eldon is so thoroughly incapable.[2] After a few words from M. A. Taylor; first speaker Sir S. R.[3] In line 9th comes the following sentence, 'The measure proposed of appointing another Judge to assist the Lord Chancellor in his Court; he considered of such importance, that he thought it impossible that it could be carried into effect at so late a period of the Session, when so thin an attendance was to be expected in both Houses of Parliament. An alteration in the Constitution of the Court, which would be productive of the most serious consequences required the most assiduous attention of both Houses. etc. etc.'

Delay therefore is not, in every case, even at the same period of a Session quite so bad a thing. It depends on circumstances. What the circumstances are is a different consideration, and not to be stated in the compass of a page. Mean time I can not but be curious to see (as I shall do by the Report) what the arguments are by which a conversion so sudden and so unexpected has been operated.

2132. [1] Dumont MSS 33/I, fo. 151. Autograph.

[2] i.e. the resumed debate in the Commons on 5 June on chancery delays. See above letter 2119 and n. 3.

[3] Romilly.

2133

To Étienne Dumont

8 June 1811 (Aet 63)

Q.S.P. 8 June 1811.

Utility of Colonies. Emancipation Pamphlet[2]

On this subject a loose observation of your's, repeating an equally loose one of my own on a former day, drew from me an equally loose answer.

So far as your proposed note is concerned,[3] a slight retrospect to the form and occasion of the pamphlet in question would, on the part of either of us, have suggested a different answer.

Had the occasion been other than temporary, and the form of the work *deductive*, possible exceptions would have been looked out for—and, from the constant habit I am in as you will know, of looking out for the differences producible, be the subject what it may, by the circumstances of *place* and *time*, I don't see how, it would have been natural I should have forborne stating as a possible ground for exception, the state of things similar in the respect in question, to that which has been since realised.

But the occasion was temporary and even momentary:—the form, (an Address to a representative Assembly) rhetorical, and I think your thought must have already have gone before my expression, in representing to you the incongruity there would have been in adding to so great a quantity of politico-economical matter, a sketch of a state of things the supposition of which must at that time of day appeared so perfectly ridiculous.

2133. [1] Dumont MSS 33/I, fos. 152–3. Autograph. Addressed. 'To / Mr Dumont / 19 Hay market.'

[2] A reference to what was printed in 1793 as *Jeremy Bentham to the National Convention of France* and was subsequently published as *Emancipate your Colonies!*, London, 1830 (Bowring, iv. 407–18).

[3] This note was perhaps intended for 'Des Colonies', the twelfth chapter of the fourth book of *Théorie des peines et des récompenses*, apparently based loosely on material in Bentham's 'Institute of Political Economy', which Dumont had intended to publish in French. See *Jeremy Bentham's Economic Writings*, ed. W. Stark, 3 vols., London, 1952–4, iii. 38, 352–7. Alternatively, it might have been for the treatise on international law for which Dumont gathered material but which he never completed. His papers at Geneva contain some preliminary writings on this subject (Dumont MSS 60). Some of Bentham's MSS on International law—on which Dumont based his own work—can be found at UC xxv and UC cix. They deal, *inter alia*, with colonies. Richard Smith edited this material for the essays on 'Principles of International Law' (Bowring, ii. 535–60). For Dumont's earlier, and apparently desultory, work on his own international law project see letter 1886, *Correspondence*, vii.

Suppose then your note were to say that the course of investigation I am in the habit of pursuing whatever be the subject, (as per . . . referring in some way or other to the Chapter in question in your book)[4] would naturally have led me to anticipate the sort of case that has since had place: that in that case a fresh account would have been to be taken of profit and loss by Colonies: that in that case on which side would have proved to be the probable ballance, could not have been known till after taking the account. But that in a tract written on the *occasion* and in the *form* in question any such dissertation could have been no better than a nuisance etc etc.

2134

To Sir Samuel Bentham

14 July 1811 (Aet 63)

Q.S.P. Sunday 14 July 1811

H.K.[2] called this morning on Dumont (I intirely in the secret) to sound him about visitation to Lord H.[3] It was evident, without any express mention that D. would not be prevailed upon, either with or without you, to go upon any such errand. But Ld H. he said, he had no doubt would be very glad to see you, and hear you upon that or any other subject. Twelve o'clock he mentioned as a time at which you might be sure of finding him any day: for that before that time he never stirs out.

It might not be amiss perhaps that if you do go you should first call upon Miss F[4] at Little Holland House: but if so, it might be advisable perhaps that such your call should well be known at the Great House; for at the time 10 days or so that Dumont was there, he saw nothing of them, though they (he understood) were all the while at their own House. However on this point you can not take better advice than hers. In my letter about Mexico[5] it was by her advice that I struck out a mention I had made of her name.

[4] Probably a reference to 'De l'influence des tems et des lieux en matière de législation' in Dumont's *Traités de législation civile et pénale*, iii. 323–95.

2134. [1] BL VIII. 547–8. Autograph. Docketed: '1811 July 14 / JB–SB'.

[2] Koe.

[3] Henry Richard Vassall Fox, 3rd Baron Holland.

[4] Caroline Fox (1767–1845), the daughter of Stephen Fox, 2nd Baron Holland (1745–74), and sister of the 3rd Baron. For her earlier contact with Bentham see *Correspondence*, iii, iv, v, and vii, as index.

[5] Letter 2014, *Correspondence*, vii.

Dumont by his own invitation, dines here tomorrow: of which opportunity you will of course avail yourself if it seems to you worth while.

But send me answer whether you intend so to do, by bearer.

At parting, Brougham gave me to understand that he should not on Monday (tomorrow) make any motion about your business; but that he should on that day make enquiries and feel his grounds with a view to the making a notice on Wednesday which would be the next day of the sitting of the House: and that on Tuesday he would send me a note, to tell me how it was to be.[6]

2135

From Étienne Dumont

7 August 1811

I have read Lord Charlemont's Life.[2] It may interest you more than it interests me. I found no amusement in it—too many generalities—too many allusions—too few anecdotes. It is rather a general view of Irish history, than a biography of the principal personage.

[6] The note, if written, is missing. On Thursday 18 July Brougham brought forward a motion that the minutes of a naval court-martial should be presented to the Commons and mentioned various other cases of the cruelty of officers towards sailors. See *Parliamentary Debates*, xx. 1027–38.

2135. [1] Bowring, x. 462. A translated extract.

[2] *Memoirs of the Political and Private Life of James Caulfeild, Earl of Charlemont*, by Francis Hardy (1751–1812), the Irish biographer, appeared in London in 1810. Charlemont (1728–99) was commander-in-chief of the Irish Volunteers, the armed force that induced the British government to grant first commercial concessions and then legislative independence to Ireland.

2136

FROM DAVID RICARDO

13 August 1811

Mile end 13th. Aug 1811

Dear Sir

I beg you to accept my thanks for your kind communication.[2] I should have been most happy to have passed a few weeks in your neighbourhood, as besides the pleasure of Mr Mill's society it would have afforded me the opportunity which I have long desired of procuring the gratification of your acquaintance, but there are obstacles in the way of my wishes which can not be surmounted. My family is large, and for Mrs. Ricardo's[3] comfort it would be necessary to have the whole of it with us. She would not be happy if one child were absent. At the present time this would be unattainable unless we were to withdraw the greatest part of our children from school, to which they have, after a long vacation but just returned. I regret that I have been the occasion of so much trouble to you. I trust that on your return to London, to compensate me for my present disappointment, you will give me your company at Mile end,—a pleasure which Mr. Mill has often flattered me with and to which your obliging letter appears to have given me a new claim

I am Dear Sir with great
esteem
Your obedt. Ser.
David Ricardo

J. Bentham Esqr

2136. [1] BL VIII. 549–50. Autograph. Docketed: '1811 Aug 14 / Ricardo (David) / Mile End / to / J.B. Q.S.P. / Declines the House / at Bletchingley.' Printed in *The Works and Correspondence of David Ricardo*, ed. P. Sraffa, 11 vols., Cambridge, 1951–73, vi. 46–7. David Ricardo (1772–1823), economist, was the author of *The High Price of Bullion, a proof of the depreciation of Bank Notes*, London, 1810. His main work, *Principles of Political Economy and Taxation*, was published in 1817. It seems that Bentham had asked him to stay at Bletchingley, near Barrow Green.

[2] Missing.

[3] Priscilla Anne Ricardo, née Wilkinson (1768–1849). She had married Ricardo in 1793.

2137

FROM JOHN CARTWRIGHT

29 August 1811

Thursday, 29th August, 1811.

My Dear Sir,

I yesterday heard of three free settlers of New South Wales, who are now in town, having come over with facts and documents to prove the enormous plundering of stores, etc. etc., in a case intended to have been brought to some inquiry in England, before the Privy-council, I suppose. But finding Ministers absolutely set their faces against any inquiry, these *free settlers*, after the expense, loss of time, and neglect of their settlements, are going *back again*, and in the course of seven or eight days. Thinking you might wish to converse with these men, who, after the treatment they have experienced, will probably be sufficiently communicative, and ready to produce their documents, I would not lose any time in giving you this information.

Possibly you might wish to converse with them without your name being known to them; in that case, I have no doubt I could get them to my house, where you might be present, and question them as you please; or I could contrive a meeting elsewhere, as you might like.

I am going this morning to Hackney to see the ascent of the balloon, a grand sight I have never yet witnessed.[2] In my way through the city, I will take my ground for an interview with the settlers, provided you should wish it, and contrive to have everything in readiness, that in case of meeting them you may lose as little of the country enjoyments as may be.

Yours, dear Sir, very truly
J. Cartwright.

2137. [1] Bowring, x. 463.

John Cartwright (1740–1824), former naval officer and major in the Nottinghamshire militia, was a consistent advocate of parliamentary reform.

[2] *The Times* of 30 August reported the ascent from Hackney on the previous day. The chief balloonist was James Sadler, one of the earliest British aeronauts, who had made his first ascent in May 1785 and was to fly from Birmingham to Boston in Lincolnshire in October 1811. Sadler was accompanied by Mr Beaufoy; probably Mark Beaufoy (1764–1827), the astronomer and physicist who lived at Hackney Wick.

2138

To John Cartwright

30 August 1811 (Aet 63)

Oxstead, Surrey, 30th August, 1811

My Dear Sir,

I have to acknowledge the favour of yours of yesterday's date.[2] Thanks in abundance for your kind remembrance of me. The business is interesting, and in altogether competent hands. Mine could not better it. But hands there are by which it might be bettered, viz., a Member of Parliament's; for example, (and if he could but bring himself to take the trouble of it, whose could be better?) Sir Francis Burdett's. Such and such are the facts which the persons in question were willing to depose to, and offered to such and such official persons (naming them) to give an account of; but those official persons would not hear them. At great expense and inconvenience to themselves they left the colony on such a day, staid till such a day; but finding that any further stay would be to no purpose, embarked on such a day on their return. This is what, according to your letter, a member of Parliament, who should have seen and examined them, would be able to say in his place.

In default of Sir Francis, who very probably is not within reach—viz., between Piccadilly and Wimbledon—but at some distant watering place, if this were a time in which any person were in town I might possibly have got some M.P. to see the men in question and act accordingly. This being hopeless, remains for consideration the next best thing to be done.

Objects two:—1. To collect the facts and preserve them from deperition; 2. To fix the ministry with *notice*, prove that the not proving the abuses and bringing them before Parliament and the public in the regular and usual manner is their fault—their wilful fault—and thus prove them guilty of connivance.

For the accomplishment of these objects, supposing motives on your part adequate, and the requisite means in your power, *i. e.* the persons in question ready to do their part, the following is the course that occurs to me:—

1. You to see them, (the sooner the better, since their departure is so near,) and to get out of them, and commit to paper, as particu-

2138. [1] Bowring, x. 463–5.
[2] Letter 2137.

larly as may be, all the relevant facts within their knowledge. For this purpose, by way of memento, the titles of the sections in that pamphlet of mine which you have, together with the running titles with which the pages are headed, might perhaps be found of some use.[3]

2 When the facts are before you, then to state them, or such parts of them as seem most material, in form of a letter, to be signed by the men in question, and addressed to Mr Secretary Ryder, within whose department it is, observation being made of the person to whom at his office it is delivered: the persons to mention the day fixed for their departure, *i. e.* for the departure of the ship in which they are to go, and their inability to retard it: likewise to state the preceding manifestations they had afforded of their readiness to give the information, and what steps, if any, were taken by the official persons in question (naming them) in consequence.

As to the once-intended inquiry, what I heard about the matter is as follows:—About the beginning of last session, I think it was, or earlier, an intimate friend of mine, M.P. (you may guess who: I don't like mentioning names, in black and white, without leave[4]) informed me, that some flagrant abuses in New South Wales had transpired, and that some members of Opposition had thoughts of trying to obtain a committee, for the purpose of bringing them to light. Some time afterwards, he informed me that the project was abandoned; for the person on whose evidence the principal reliance was placed, had, by means of a place, been satisfied and bought off by the Ministry,—under which circumstances, the prospect of his giving, before a committee, the same account that he had given of the matter, or any other account that would afford a justification for the inquiry, appearing hopeless, the design was given up. In answer to a question of mine, his name was mentioned; but I do not to any certainty recollect it. I have some notion that it was Fowel,[5] or some other name beginning with an F. I am certain of its not containing more than one or two syllables. I don't know whether it is not agent for the colony that he is made. Your settlers might perhaps ascertain this.

A friend of mine, whom you once saw at my house, but without speaking, and whom Mr Holt White[6] saw and spoke with, has mentioned to me a Mr *Brown*,[7] as having passed some years in the colony in quality of botanist, and living now in Gerard Street, where

[3] Probably Bentham's *A Plea for the Constitution*, London, 1803 (Bowring, iv. 249–84).

[4] Probably Romilly. See his *Memoirs*, ii. 319.

[5] Unidentified.

[6] Thomas Holt White (1763–1841), parliamentary reformer.

[7] Robert Brown (1773–1858).

he is librarian to the Linnæan Society, and moreover, librarian to Sir Joseph Banks.[8] He is mentioned as an honest, quiet man, but probably not very observant of anything but Natural History; and finding on his own personal account no grounds for complaint, not likely to have been very sharp in looking out for them.

By mentioning this Mr B. to your men, you might hear of some facts, in relation to which their testimony, when they are gone, would, upon occasion, receive confirmation from his. Mr MacArthur you must have heard mentioned as one of the most eminent and respectable of the free settlers.[9] In May or June, he was examined, on the trial of Lieut.-colonel Johnstone,[10] by a Court-martial, at the instance of Governor Bligh.[11] Mention was made of it about that time in '*The British Press*.'[12] Whether he is now in England, I have not heard. He has a brother, a mercer, in Plymouth, with whom, on occasion, communication might possibly be obtained.

Being in the office of the Secretary of State, the proposed letter might be *called for* in Parliament; and, against the connivers, the facts would be to be taken for true, since, if incorrect, it was their fault that the incorrectnesses were not ascertained and corrected. A copy should be preserved, that, without a committee, (which would not be granted,) any member having it in his hand might be enabled to speak to the facts with confidence.

Suggestion by Mr K.—Possibly these men, having heard how (Fowel?) was bought off, came hither on the like errand; but found the connivers tired of buying quiet at that rate. But this hypothesis depends upon there having been time for them to have heard of it, and come hither afterwards.

I take this only vacant place for assuring you, that I am, my dear Sir, ever most truly yours.

[8] Sir Joseph Banks (1743–1820), president of the Royal Society.

[9] John Macarthur (1767–1834), known as the 'father' of New South Wales. An ensign in the 68th Foot in April 1788, he joined the New South Wales Corps as a lieutenant in June 1789, and then settled in New South Wales and became a farmer and agricultural improver. He was made a captain in 1795 and retired from the service in 1804.

[10] George Johnston (1764–1823), lieutenant-colonel of New South Wales Corps April 1808. As a major he took a leading part with Macarthur in the 'Rum Rebellion' of 26 January 1808 when he marched on the governor's house with his troops and arrested the governor. Johnston and Macarthur returned to England and in May 1811 Johnston was court-martialled for inciting rebellion. He was convicted and cashiered, but allowed to return to Australia. See Alan Atkinson, 'Jeremy Bentham and the Rum Rebellion', *Journal of the Royal Australian Historical Society*, lxiv (1978), 1–13.

[11] William Bligh (1754–1817), rear-admiral 1811, vice-admiral 1814, governor of New South Wales 1805–8. He tried to reduce the illicit rum trade in which many officers of the New South Wales corps were involved, and was deposed in the coup of January 1808.

[12] No reports of Macarthur's examination have been found in *The British Press* for May–June 1811.

2139

From Étienne Dumont

4 September 1811

I have not forgotten the letter to Gallatin[2]—I wanted to write it. I began it—I applied myself to it two or three times—I could not succeed to my liking. Not succeed? you say—a good letter—a fine piece of eloquence? Nay!—but a reasonable and useful letter—nothing came of it. Have I not said all?—who am I?—what weight have I?—what does it all mean? I do not like to be impertinent—I do not like to labour without hopes of success. Since I talked the matter over with you, divers reflections have assaulted me. Some you saw as well as I did; but there is one we did not think of, and which moves me much. What CAN the President do? What can be done by a moveable magistrate, whose power expires in a year or two? What engagements can he undertake for his successor?

His personal invitation is nothing. There must be a decree of the Senate or the Congress: and how can this be obtained? Will the Senate read your writings? Will they be able to judge of the aptitude of the author? Burr said he knew not four persons in America who had read the *Principes*.[3] What can then be hoped for, as the author is an unknown being—an Englishman—an English lawyer? Every motive of jealousy and national distrust will operate upon the Americans, among whom presumption and conceit of themselves are the most remarkable characteristics. These are my opinions; they are not meant to influence yours. But I must say, a letter from me to Gallatin is a sabre-blow on the water, and especially as, according to Smith,[4] he is on bad terms with Madison.[5]

* * * * *

We are busy here with a do-nothing life. I admire laborious men, but have not courage to imitate them. The Prince-Regent has intimated to Perceval that he would like him to wear his uniform, and has presented him with a set of buttons; a significant caress!

2139. [1] Bowring, x. 463. Translated extracts.

[2] Abraham Alfonse Albert Gallatin (1761–1849), American politician of Swiss descent, congressman 1795–1801, secretary to the US treasury 1801–14.

[3] i.e. the 'Principes de législation', 'Principes du code civil', and 'Principes du code pénal' in *Traités de législation civile et pénale*.

[4] John Adams Smith (1788–1854), secretary to the United States legation in London.

[5] James Madison (1751–1836), president of the United States 1809–17.

2140

FROM JOHN CARTWRIGHT

6 September 1811

September 6th, 1811.

My Dear Sir,

On Sunday I had an interview with the free settler,[2] but, on recollecting it might be the man's ruin, to be followed by an information to the Governor, that he had made any reports to the disadvantage of persons in power, either here, or in New South Wales, I was guarded in my inquiries, leaving him as much as possible to narrate spontaneously. In the course of our interview, he produced the copy of a letter which he himself wrote on the 26th of January last, three months after his arrival in London, to one of our ministers,[3] exhibiting a clear and distinct charge against a military man[4] then in England, of having, while in power in New South Wales, put to death five or six men, mentioned by name, without trial of any kind, and contrary to law—even the law of New South Wales, such as it is; at the same time stating, that abundance of evidence of these facts might be established by the testimony of several persons then in England, attending at the prosecution of Colonel Johnstone, and that he himself was ready to bring forward the matter in a legal way. From that day to this, no notice has been taken of this letter to a Cabinet Minister.

After waiting awhile from the date above-mentioned, he, in the same form of words, addressed himself to one of the Chief Justices, who has to this hour remained equally silent on this account of so many murders.

Having discovered that my informant came home in support of the charge against Johnstone, for divesting Governor Bligh of his office by a military insurrection, and at the head of troops he commanded—a charge exhibited on the part of Government at home, I was cautious not to alarm him, but expressed surprise that his well-intended communication should have been neglected in so extraordinary a manner as he had related, as well as a wish that Lord Folkstone, or Sir Samuel Romilly, had been desired to have noticed the matter in Parliament, which might have driven Minis-

2140. [1] Bowring, x. 465–6.

[2] See letter 2138.

[3] Not further identified, but possibly Lord Liverpool, at that time secretary of state for war and the colonies.

[4] Unidentified.

ters to have done their duty. In his reply, he mentioned one distinguished gentleman in Opposition,[5] to whom he had shown his letter to the Minister and the Chief Justice; and, to my great surprise, that gentleman not only read the letter without any comment, but was ever after silent on the subject. In what an age do we live, when murders by the half dozen are to be perpetrated by a military man in power, while no party politician, either in or out of power, thinks such matters worthy of investigation! or rather, while no such politician will call for the investigation till he have first considered how his own factious purposes are to be affected by it!

As I was very unwell, and my informant was obliged to leave me, I obtained no other information worth noting; which I the less regretted, as he told me that, from Mr Margarot,[6] every sort of information respecting the colony, might be obtained. I do not know Margarot, but am well acquainted with several of his friends. He also promised to call again before he embarked, which he expected to be within the week. I have not, however, seen him, and have been too unwell to seek him at his own lodgings. Besides which, my time has been much occupied about my brother's life-boat invention.[7]

The moulds I returned a few days since, for the use of which I am very thankful, as it enabled me to propose, to my friend the India captain, a superior boat for all the common purposes of his ship, besides being peculiarly well adapted for the purposes of a life-boat. The boat is now building. When we meet, we must talk over this organized system, of murders by wholesale in the regular course of administering the affairs of an English colony.

With every wish for your health, and every hope that you may yet be eminently instrumental in putting an end to the above abomination.

Truly yours

[5] Also unidentified.

[6] Maurice Margarot (1745–1815), first chairman of the London Corresponding Society, was arrested as a delegate to the reformist convention in Edinburgh and convicted of sedition in January 1794. He was sentenced to fourteen years' transportation and returned from New South Wales in 1810.

[7] Probably the Revd. Edmund Cartwright (1743–1823), the reputed inventor of the power-loom.

2141

To Lord Holland

8 September 1811 (Aet 63)

Barrow Green House, near Oxted, Surry:
Sunday 8 Sept. 1811.

My Lord

Last Tuesday sennight, August 27th, if I am rightly informed, were put into two Post Offices, the one at Charingcross the other in Chancery Lane, two masses of paper, each divided into no fewer than five weighed packets, all of them, on information obtained the preceding day at Holland House, directed to Your Lordship at Lord Granville Leveson Gower's,[2] Taxley, Staffordshire, name of Post Town thereon mentioned, but not now remembered.

In addition to a letter marked *Private* and signed by my own name,[3] the contents consisted of no fewer than 18 sheets of 4to letter paper, making 72 pages, whereof 69 (rather loosely) written upon, signed *Ignotus*, and marked, on page 1st in pencil *Ostensible*:— besides a sheet of folio paper, forming a sort of Appendix.[4]

By a concurrence of circumstances, not worth troubling Your Lordship with, I feel myself haunted by two opposite apprehensions. One is—that the aforesaid *masses* have not, either of them, reached Your Lordship's hands. The other is—that, having reached Your Lordships hands, they have, for and by means of a load of lumber, the value of which may have been found to be—not simply = 0 but negative, subjected you to an imposition, from which I had taken such precautions, as I flattered myself would prove effectual, to save you harmless. In the latter case, if Your Lordship will be pleased to give directions to Your Solicitor, to prosecute me, by a civil *action in the case*—(for, being free from malice, an indictment, (I humbly submitt to his better judgment) will not lie for it—) I am ready, with all contrition, to let judgment go by default, paying costs and damages.

In the mean time, if, by your own,—or rather, to save in one case unnecessary addition to already excessive trouble, by any *other*, hand—you would have the charity to favour me with such few

2141. [1] MS in the possession of Professor G. N. Ray, New York. Autograph.

[2] Lord Granville Leveson-Gower (1773–1846), later Viscount Granville and 1st Earl Granville, at this time MP for Staffordshire.

[3] Missing.

[4] Not traced.

words as may be necessary, simply to let me know, whether the nuisance in question has or has not reached your hands, you will much oblige

My Lord,
Your Lordships very respectful
howsoever troublesome humble Servant
Jeremy Bentham.

Lord Holland.

2142

From Aaron Burr

12 October 1811

October 12th, 1811.

I am very glad, and very sorry to falsify your prophecy, for we shall meet, and soon. The story is thus:—After new and infinite vexations, subsequently to my letter by Forbes,[2] I did, on the 19th of July, obtain a passport: set out immediately for Amsterdam, where was the American ship *Vigilant*, waiting to receive me. On my arrival, found the ship ready; but, on the same day, her departure was retarded by order of the emperor.[3] On the 13th of September, the obstacles to sailing being removed, we embarked again: the ship then at the Texel. At the very moment we were about to sail, an express from Amsterdam brought an order for further delay: returned again to Amsterdam. On the 29th September embarked again; wind being a-head, did not propose to sail until it should change. In the evening of that day came on board a company of Police, commanding we should sail in twelve hours, or that our permission should be revoked. Did sail within the twelve hours, *i. e.* on the morning of the 30th: the same day were visited by a British frigate, whose captain, after examination of the ship's papers, took possession of her: took out fourteen of our crew, put in ten of his own, and two officers, and ordered us hither—where?—read on:—We were in the *Vigilant* seventy-three passengers, of all nations, colours, sexes, and ages—add 32 hogs, and various other quadrupeds and bipeds; but *I am afore my story*—to go back a little,

2142. [1] Bowring, x. 466–7.

[2] An American acquaintance of Burr, not further identified. See *The Private Journal of Aaron Burr*, ed. William J. Bixby, 2 vols., Rochester, New York, 1903, ii. 78.

[3] Napoleon.

then: I had taken a passport, and under an assumed name, with no reference, however, to the British Government. When our master (Combes)[4] went on board the frigate, the first thing said to him by the captain was—'So you have got Colonel Burr on board!' Our master, Combes, having no instructions from me, replied that he had no person of that name on board. 'O no, Sir; but you have Mr A. on board, whom, I believe, you know very well.' This looked ominous. We were eight days in making a passage of about thirty leagues—arrived on Sunday evening last. On Monday, wrote Mr Reeves,[5] announcing my arrival, and asking permission to land to go to London; did not write to you, fearing you might move in the matter, and thereby do yourself harm: resolved first to know whether I were to be confined to the ship, imprisoned on shore, or transported anew—the only three alternatives which presented themselves to my mind. By *return of mail*, to wit, on Wednesday, received from Mr Reeves a polite note authorizing me to land and to go to London at my pleasure. This indulgence is the more valuable, as, of the seventy-three passengers, among them many Americans, not one other is permitted even to come on shore. I shall profit by this permission, and to-morrow (13th October) shall leave *Yarmouth*, and propose to see you on Tuesday morning if you should be in London —hope not—if at Godstone, shall get there as soon as possible.

I have a good deal of spleen to vent at you; but can't just now work myself up into a proper humour: will try at London.

2143

To Aaron Burr

16 October 1811 (Aet 63)

16 Oct. 1811.

To Col. Burr

Under the then existing circumstances of the moment, for greater celerity, and better chance of timeliness, H.K. was commissioned to write to you by last night's post, to speak of your Yarmouth letter that instant received,[2] and to express our wishes for your earliest appearance.

[4] Not further identified.

[5] John Reeves (1752–1829), superintendent of aliens 1803–14.

2143. [1] Historical Society of Pennsylvania, Philadelphia. Autograph. Docketed: 'J. Bentham ⟨. . .⟩ Octr 1811'. Addressed: 'Mr Wm Graves / Mercht / 18 Wallbrook / London'. Postmark: '⟨. . .⟩ / 17 OC 17 / 1811'. Stamped: 'GODSTONE / ⟨. . .⟩'.

[2] Presumably letter 2142.

This letter is a postscript to the above.

Our plan is to stay here as long as possible: viz. till driven away by the cold's becoming strong enough to render sojournment in the one [. . .?] of [. . .?] study uncomfortable without a fire. I hope nothing will render it necessary for you to leave this place till we do: and in particular that you will do nothing yourself towards the creation of any such necessity. Last year it was about the last day of the month. We hope it will be at least as late this year.

One object of apprehension with me is—that some Minister—Ld Wellesley[3] for example, to whose department it belongs—will wish to talk with you, and for that purpose, with the customary barbarity, endeavour to keep you, with or without seeing you, to the day of judgment.

But for this, I can scarce conceive that Mr. R.[4] would have written to you or behaved towards you on any such civil terms. It was he that packed you off before, at the suggestion of the foolish man who but a few months ago told me so, for which I gave him my opinion not angrily but not the less decidedly, that what he did had been much better left undone[5]—for the reasons which I mentioned. It was on the information of the woman with whom you lodged,[6] who from the circumstance of your mode of living, having maps before you, and a man sometimes to write for you, and wearing that odd wig, she concluded that you must be either a Swindler, or a Spy, or a Magician or a Devil, or something of that sort. Cut not her throat till I see you, and then we will have a cut at it together.

Reasons exist in abundance—and not of more amusement—why we should see one another without loss of a single day. You will find such an addition to the company, indeed several additions, which you will not be displeased to see.

If you have got *Blodget's* book,[7] pray bring it with you. I have been trying in vain to get it ever since I saw you. One man alone had seen it: no one man knew where a copy was to be found.

If in the confusion consequent upon a little alteration in Q.S.P. House the maps can be come at, it would be desirable that we should have here a Map of North America, the do of South America which latter I believe will however hardly be findable and a portion of a map of South America which had no ⟨. . .⟩ case to it, but used

[3] Richard Colley Wellesley, Marquis Wellesley (1760–1842), the foreign secretary.

[4] Reeves. See letter 2142.

[5] Perhaps Lord Liverpool, home secretary at the time of Burr's arrest on 4 April 1809.

[6] Unidentified.

[7] Samuel Blodget (1757–1814) was the author of *Economica: a Statistical Manual for the United States of America*, Washington, 1806.

to lie upon my combination of d⟨. . .⟩ the station of which was on the table on which I write.

Lest these should not be findable, perhaps either you have of your own, or could contrive to borrow, the aforesaid.

To Mr Graves.

If at the arrival of this, Col. B. should already have set out for the abode of his friend in Surry,[8] Mr Graves will, of course have the goodness to keep it for him, without forwarding it.

2144

From Aaron Burr

16 October 1811

London, October 16, 1811.

Your letter of the 10th is received.[2] I shall at present reply to that part only which relates to General Miranda.

There is not, to my knowledge, any hostility, nor any cause of hostility between us; nor is it easy to conceive how or why there should be. We never, to my recollection, met but once. Then at the house of a common friend in Philadelphia, and at the time he (Miranda) was preparing for his expedition. Nothing unpleasant passed at that interview; on the contrary, I was greatly pleased with his social talents and colloquial eloquence. It is true, however, that I did, from private considerations, studiously avoid anything which might afford him an occasion to disclose his views. The bare suspicion of any connexion between him and me would have been injurious to my project and fatal to his; a circumstance of which he must have been ignorant. He afterward complained to his friend of my coldness and reserve, and he had reason; but I did not dare to explain, not having sufficient assurance of his discretion. As, how-

[8] Presumably either a round-about reference to Bentham himself, or to Mrs Ann Prevost, a relative of Burr's deceased wife Theodosia Bartow Prevost (d. 1794), who lived at Weybridge. See letter 2009, *Correspondence*, vii.

2144. [1] Davis, ii. 254–5. Reprinted in *Political Correspondence and Public Papers of Aaron Burr*, ed. Mary-Jo Kline and Joanne Wood Ryan, 2 vols., Princeton, 1983, ii. 1134–5, where the editors suggest that the letter might have been written on 29 December 1811. They point to an entry in Burr's journal for that date (*The Private Journal of Aaron Burr*, ed. William K. Bixby, 2 vols., Rochester, New York, 1903, ii. 276) in which reference is made to a letter written on that day to Bentham on Miranda. It is possible, of course, that this was another letter, now missing.

[2] Missing.

ever, there never has been, nor, in any probability, ever can be the smallest collision, political or other, between us, I did not suppose that any sentiment approaching to enmity existed on his part; none certainly on mine.

I heard with great pleasure of his return to his native country, and of the consideration in which he is held. My heart and feelings are, as you know, wholly and warmly with the patriots of Venezuela. His advent is, unquestionably, a very great boon to them. His experience in political and military life, and his literary acquirements, justly entitle him to pre-eminence among his countrymen. But that part of Miranda's character which constitutes his greatest eulogy is the purity of his political creed, and the constancy and consistency with which he has persevered in it. On this head he has shown no caprice, no backsliding, that I ever heard; and I have entire confidence that, so far forth as his influence may prevail, the government about to be established in Venezuela will afford as much liberty as is consistent with security and good order.

With these sentiments, you may be assured of my disposition to contribute, if it should happen to be in my power, to the success of Miranda and his patriot countrymen. There is a possibility, perhaps something more, that I may mingle, personally, in the affairs of Spanish America. In such case, a good understanding would be of sound policy, perhaps of mutual necessity. It is also probable that I may be capable of rendering him or his countrymen service in the United States, whither I am now about to return, and certainly I should do it with pleasure and with zeal.

Farther, were it even true that my mind has been impressed with sentiments unfriendly to Miranda, not only would the wishes you express have influenced my conduct, but any prejudices I could have imbibed would have been honestly and cheerfully sacrificed to your judgment, formed on so much better opportunities.

A. Burr.

2145

To James Madison

30 October 1811 (Aet 63)

London 30th. Octr. 1811.

Sir

The offer which it is the ambition of this Address to submit to the consideration of the President of the United States is addressed (you will see immediately) not to the Person but to the Office. By an explanation thus early made some reading will be saved to you. The respect, of which the offer itself is its own best testimonial needs not, I presume, any more words for the expression of it.

To come to the point at once—Give me, Sir, the necessary encouragement, I mean, a Letter importing *approbation* of this my humble Proposal, and, as far as depends upon you yourself—*acceptance* I will forthwith set about drawing up, for the use of the United States, or such of them, if any, as may see reason to give their acceptance to it, a *complete body* of proposed law, in the form of Statute law, say in one word a *Pannomion*—a body of Statute law, including a succedaneum to that mass of foreign law, the yoke of which in the *wordless*, as well as boundless, and shapeless shape of *common*, alias *Unwritten* law, remains still about your necks—a *complete* body or such parts of it as the life and health of a man, whose age wants little of four and sixty, may allow of.

This letter Sir, I mean the letter above stipulated for, when once I have it in hand, I have my *reward*. I have my *employment*: and the honor inseparable from the employment is the only retribution that *can* be *accepted* for the labor of it. I say *accepted*, Sir, not *required* or *expected* but *accepted*: for from this word corollaries will be deduced, the utility of which, with reference to the proposed Service, will, I flatter myself, when brought to view, as they will be presently, not appear exposed to doubt.

The *Plan* of the proposed work,—and therein the supposed *advantageous results*, the prospect of which forms what the proposal has to depend upon for its acceptance,—the circumstances of *advantage* attached to the nature of the *terms* on which the work would be executed,—the declared *objections* which it ought to be

2145. [1] Madison Papers, Library of Congress, Washington D.C. In the hand of a copyist. Endorsed: 'Bentham. Jer: / Octr. 30. 1811 / conveyed thro' Mr. Brougham and Mr Pinkney'. William Pinkney (1764–1822) was resident minister in London 1807–11. A draft or copy of this letter was published in *Papers Relative to Codification and Public Instruction*, London, 1817, pp. 1–65 (partly reprinted in Bowring, iv. 453–67).

prepared for together with the *answers* which those objections seem to admit of, —the latent, but not the less powerful, *obstacles* which it may have to contend with,—the sort of personal *assistance* in the way of information which should it be thought serviceable I should be ready and willing to receive for the purpose of it,—the *advances* already made towards the execution of it,—on all these several topics some sort of explanation may naturally be looked for: on all of them something in the way of explanation shall accordingly be attempted, though in that state of extreme and proportionately disadvantageous compression, without which no reasonable hope could be entertained, of that promptitude of return which may be requisite to success.

Before I come to particulars respecting the proposed *plan* with its supposed *advantages*, it will be necessary for me to make reference once for all, to a view of it which is already in print. I mean the Work in 3 Vols. 8vo. which, under the title of *Traités de Législation Civile et Pénale . . . par M. Jeremie Bentham. etc* was in the year 1802 published at Paris by my Genevan friend M Dumont.

One Copy of it was, upon its publication, sent, I understand, by the Editor to his Countryman Mr Gallatin Secretary of the Treasury to the United States: whether, in your part of America, any other Copies of it have ever been in existence, it has not fallen in my way to know.

Far as these Papers were from being considered by the Author as having attained a state approaching to that of a finished work, yet of the Plan which, on any such occasion as that in question, was then, and still would be, proposed to be pursued, a conception sufficient for the purpose here in question, may, if I do not deceive myself, be obtained from them. Of the *details*, even of the proposed *text*, they exhibit samples more than one, nor those of small account. So much of the plan being already *there*, it might seem that nothing, in explanation of it, could be necessary in this place. But, without some preconceptions, how slight and general soever, of some of its most striking peculiarities, what it will immediately be necessary to say of it in the gross might scarce be found intelligible.

1. Nature and supposed advantages of the proposed *form*.

Matter and *Form*—to one or other of these two heads, whatsoever features whether of excellence or imperfection, may be distinguishable in a Plan, framed for any such purpose, will, it is believed, be found referable.—

1. As to *matter*, in the character of a *test* of, and *security* for, the fitness of the work in this respect, of one constituent portion pervading the whole mass—the rationale it may be termed such will at

first glance be seen to be the efficiency, that of this alone a slight mention may, to the present purpose, be sufficient.

By the rationale I mean (for a sample See 'Traités etc') a mass of *reasons* accompanying in the shape of a perpetual commentary, the whole mass of imperative or regulative matter, to which alone any body of law as yet extant has ever yet been found to give admission.

Not a single point of any importance settled, but that in the *rationale*, the considerations by which the provision made in relation to it was determined, will be to be found: and by the connection which, through the medium of the *all governing principle*, viz the principle of *utility*, these reasons have with one another, and the repeated application made of the *same* reason to different parts of the text, the quantity of space, occupied by matter of this description, will be found much less than could readily have been imagined.

The *constituent part* or *appendage*, call it which you please, this *perpetual commentary* of *reasons*, is what I will venture to propose as a test, and the only test, by which either of the *absolute* fitness or unfitness of any one proposed body of laws taken by itself, or of the *comparative* fitness of each one of any number of bodies of law, standing in competition with each other, and proposed as capable of serving for the same division in the field of legislation, any satisfactory indication can be afforded: a test to which accordingly, by a predetermined and preannounced resolution, every such composition ought to be subjected.

Without this appendage, to draw up laws is of all literary tasks the easiest: power and will, wherever it happens to them to meet, suffice for it, of intellect there is no need. On the other hand, if, *with* this addition, the task is of all tasks the most difficult, it is at the same time *that*, in the execution of which whatsoever trouble may be found necessary to the surmounting it will find itself most worthily and richly paid for, by real and important use.

2. As to form—here again by one word *cognoscibility*, every sort and degree of excellence which, under *this* head, can be given to a body of law, will be found expressible. On the fact of its being *present* to the mind of him on whose part, to the effect indicated, *action* or *forbearance* is, on each occasion, called for,—*present*—that is to say in the degree of *correctness* and *compleatness* necessary to the accomplishment of the legislators purposes depends, on each occasion, whatsoever good effect the law can be, or can have been designed to be, productive of. But on the *form* thus given to the *matter*, will depend the degree of excellence in which the property of *cognoscibility*, as thus explained has been given to it: on the *form* therefore will, in a proportionable degree, depend the practical good

effect of whatsoever degree may have been given to the matter of the law.

Taking *cognoscibility* then for the *end*, the following may serve as a sample of the *means* or *securities* that in the plan in question, have been devised and provided for the attainment of it.

1. Division of the whole *Pannomion* into two separate parts, the *General Code*, and the System of *Particular* Codes.

In the General Code are comprised all such matters, of which it concerns persons in general to be apprised: in the System of Particular Codes, each Particular Code contains such matters only, with which some *one* Class or denomination of persons only have concern: some *one* class or denomination, or in case of correlative classes of Persons, running together in pairs, such as *husband* and *wife*, *Master* and *Servant*, and so forth, some two or other such small number of classes or denominations, whose legal concerns are thus inseparably intermingled.

Merely for illustration sake, number of particular Codes, as above, say 200: average length of each 5 pages.—Consequent advantage, burthen of legal matter to be borne in mind by each person reduced from 1000 pages to 5 pages. Such, in respect of *cognoscibility*, is the advantage which this single arrangement suffices to produce. To more such classes, it is true, than one, will one and the same individual person be commonly found aggregates: I mean of those Classes which as above, would have, each of them its separate Code. From the sort of saving in question, a correspondent deduction would accordingly be to be made: but for illustration thus much without going any further into calculation may it is supposed suffice:—

From *General Code* to *Particular Codes*, and *vice versâ*, frequent references will of course be necessary: nor, in the working up of the one can the texture of the other consistently with clearness and mutual consistency pass unheeded. But all this is a matter of detail, for which no room can be found here.—

2. In each Code, as well *Particular* as *General*, an ulterior distinction noted and acted upon, is the distinction between matter of *constant* concernment, and matter of *occasional* concernment. To produce the effect aimed at in the making of a law,—to produce the effect of *guidance*, that which is matter of *constant* concernment must in all its magnitude, in all its detail, be borne in mind at all times: while in the case of that which is but matter of *occasional* concernment, the bare *knowledge* or *suspicion* of its existence will in general be sufficient, matters being so circumstanced, that before the time for action comes, sufficient time for *reference* to the text of the

law, and for perusal of its contents, may on all occasions be found.
3. In each Code in which it is found requisite, and in particular in the *Penal* branch of the *General* Code, in which it will *throughout* be found requisite, another distinction and division made is that between *Main text*, and *Expository matter* or *Exposition.*

The *Expository* matter consists of explanations given of or on the occasion of, this or that particular word in the *Main Text.* In the *Main text* each word so explained is distinguished by a particular *type*, accompanied by a letter or figure of *reference*, by which means the fact of its having received explanation is rendered manifest to every eye.

In the course of the Pannomion, should this or that same word be employed in ever so many hundred *places*, one and the same explanation serves for all of them, and by the appropriation of the particular type to the expression of these leading terms, of which an explanation is thus given, notice of the existence of such explanation is in every place presented to the eye: care being taken all along to apply the explanation to every such passage, to the end that it may be found conformable to the sense, intended in each such passage to be conveyed.

So moderate will the number of these *essential* terms, these expounded words be found, that the labour necessary to the giving correctness and consistency to the part of the language, the import of which is thus fixed,—fixed by authority of law,—needs the less be grudged.
4. To the *Penal* Code belongs an ulterior distinction peculiar to itself: matter descriptive of the offence in its ordinary state, and matter indicative of the several causes of *justification,*(1) *aggravation*(2) and *extenuation*(3) with the grounds of *exemption*(4) from punishment, which apply to it.

From beginning to end, one object kept in view and aimed at is —that, the whole field of legislation being surveyed,—surveyed and travelled through over and over again in all directions, no case that can present itself shall find itself unnoticed or unprovided for. Of this object the compleat attainment may be too much for human weakness: but by every approach made towards it, the science is advanced, and, in all shapes, the security of the people against suffering,—sudden and unlooked for suffering,—is encreased.

Note.

Examples—(1) *Consent. Self-defence.* Lawful exercise of *Public power.* Lawful exercise of *domestic power* etc. (2) *Premeditation. Confederacy* etc. (3) *Uninentionality Provocation* (contemporaneous or recent) etc (4) *Insanity. Infancy* etc.

5. *Promulgation-paper*: for formularies of all sorts,—*Conveyances* and *Agreements*, as well as instruments of judicial *procedure*,—*Paper*, of a particular size and form and appearance in other respects, provided, with a margin of Letter press, in and by which, in the instance of each such species of instrument, intimation is given of the whole text of the law relative to the species of transaction therein in question: intimation,—Vizt. according to the quantity of room occupied by it, given, either *in terminis*, or in the way of *abstract* with indication of, and with reference to, any such portion, as is found to occupy too much room to be given *in terminis*.

In particular, to the whole business of *Conveyances* and *Agreements* would thus be given a degree of simplicity, certainty, and security, of which, even after the many improvements which, I am certain must have been made in all the United States upon the original chaos, no adequate conception would, I believe, be readily formed, antecedently to experience.

In and by this method, one useful result is looked for and I hope provided for, vizt. that, to such persons by whom in respect of its *matter*, the work may in this or that part of its extent be disapproved, in respect of its *form*, it may still be found of use. Seeing the *reasons*, in which the proposed provision has found its support and final cause, each such disapprover will thereby have before him such a view as, I hope, will not be an indistinct one, of the force which in the shape of reason and argument, he has to combat. On the one side (he may see cause to say) this or that reason seems defective, and taken all together, the whole mass of reasons appear insufficient and inconclusive: or, on the other side the nature of the case affords such or such a reason, no mention of which is, in this work, to be found.

Thus it is, that, even where the reasoning may appear erroneous or inconclusive, and the proposed provision improper or inadequate—even in these places, if the matter be stated with that *clearness*, which it has been the object of the workman to give to every thing that ever came from his pen, and which, on the occasion in question, would, in a more particular manner, be the object of his endeavour and his hope, even his *errors* may, by serving or helping to bring to view the opposite truths, be found not altogether devoid of use.

In this way it is that both in point of *matter* and in point of *form*, his endeavour would be to give to the work such a character and complexion, as shall be found correspondent to the progress, made, in these our times, in every other line of useful science: to the end that, neither in the whole nor in any part, in matters of law any more than in matters dependant on mechanical or chemical science, shall the lot of the present inhabitants of your part of the globe, be determined by the unexperienced and ill considered imaginations of primaeval barbarism.—

As matters of law stand at present, Sir, in *your* Country (not to speak of *ours*) on what sort of basis is it that every man's dearest and most important interests stand or rather fluctuate? On some random decision, or string of frequently contradictory decisions, pronounced in this or that barbarous age, almost always without any intelligible reason, under the impulse of some private and sinister interest, perceptible or not perceptible, without thought, or possibility of thought, of any such circumstances or exigencies, as those of the People, by whom the country here in question is inhabited at the present time: pronounced by men, who, if disposition and inclination depend in any degree on private interest, were as far from being *willing*, as from being in respect of *intelligence able* to render their decisions conformable to the interests, even of the people by whose disputes those decisions were called for, and whose situation alone it was possible that in the framing of those decisions, they should have in view.

Since the year in which the Work, edited by Mr Dumont, was published in French at Paris, vizt. in the year 1802, that same language has given birth to two authoritative codes, the one already a *Pannomion*, or at least designed to become such, published by authority of the French Emperor,[2] the other, confined as yet to the *penal* branch, published by authority of the King of Bavaria.[3] In both instances, the compositors have done me the honor to take into consideration and make mention of that work of mine. On the proposed occasion in question, I should not fail to make correspondent return, and make my best profit of their labours.

The examination of them is what I have as yet postponed, waiting for some particular occassion by which such examination might be applied to some particular use. But to warrant a man in pronouncing, and with confidence, that, in and by each of those Works, a prodigious benefit has been conferred on their subjects, by the respective Sovereigns, it is not necessary to have read so much as a single page. Executed as well as the nature of men and things admits of its being executed, no other literary work can vie with it in usefulness—executed in the very worst manner in which in the present state of society it is at all likely to be executed, it can

[2] *Code civil des français. Édition originale et seule officielle*, Paris, 1804 (the famous *Code Napoléon*).

[3] Bexon's *Application de la Théorie de la législation pénale*, for which see above, letter 2057 n. 11. The king of Bavaria from 1805 was Maximilian I (1765–1825).

scarcely when compared with the chaos to which it comes to be substituted, fail to be productive of clear profit in the account of use.

* Of some of the leading features by which the Work here proposed would be distinguished from both these—a work composed for the use of men who are in use not only to think, but to speak and print what they think, from works composed for the use of men who scarce dare speak what they think, and to whom it has been rendered impracticable to print what they think, a slight sketch, Sir, has just been laid before you.

For securing the aptitude of it in point of *matter*, in the *proposed English* work, the *rationale* above described: in neither of those French works, any security at all in this shape or any other.

For securing the aptitude of the work in point of *form*,—for securing to it the maximum of *cognoscibility*—and thereby the advantage of producing to the greatest extent possible, in respect of number of *observances* compared with number of *non-observances*, whatever effect it purposes to itself to produce,—in the proposed English work, 1. Division into General Code and System of particular Codes:—2 Division of the tenor of the law throughout into *Main text* and *Expository* matter: 3 In the Penal Code, not to insist on any such division as the usual and already familiar one into *General titles* (titles of general application) and Particular titles (each applying exclusively to a particular species or tribe of offences) division of *Main text* and *Expository matter* together, into *definitional* matter descriptive of the main body of each offence, and matter indicative of the several causes of *justification*, *aggravation*, *extenuation* and *exemption*, which apply to it.

For securing, on every imaginable occasion, perfect *notoriety*, to each new set of *rights* acquired and correspondent obligations contracted, vizt. by whatsoever *instruments* of conveyance or agreement contracted, and that not only as soon as contracted, but also before contracted, and thence before the time when repentance would come too late,—in the proposed English work, the already described *Promulgation paper*.

In neither of those French works for the necessary cognoscibility above described is any security at all in any of the just above mentioned or in any shape declared or discernible.

Here, Sir, you see a *memento* given—it was not put to use—here

---

* *Note*

What is here enclosed in a bracket Mr President will be pleased to make public with the rest, or suppress, as in his judgment may be most fitting.—

was even a *gauntlet* thrown down, it was not taken up. Circumstanced as those respectable and truly useful servants of the Public were, causes for such abstention might, without much difficulty, perhaps be found;—causes, however, which it would be more easy to imagine than useful to express.

That in the United States any similar or any other causes should be found, not only operating, but operating with effect, to the neglect of all those securities for the adaptation of law to the only useful ends of law, is a result, the bare possibility of which cannot, by a feeling mind, be regarded with indifference.

The encouragement not only stipulated for, as above, but demanded in advance, is a gem of too high a price, to be cast, either *into* the Sea, or *across* the Sea, without thought, or without such prospect of a suitable return as the nature of the case admits of.

Of the presumable fitness of any person for the execution of a literary work proposed by him, no evidence so apposite can, I suppose, be looked for, as that which is presented by a work or works, where any such happen to be in existence, taking for their subject the subject itself which is proposed to be taken in hand, or any part or parts of it.

An assortment, as nearly complete as could be formed, of such of my printed Works as have taken for their subject any part or parts of the field of legislation accompanies this letter; and solicits the honor of your acceptance. They are the fruit of above 45 years devoted to the study of the science, and, for little less than the whole of that time, without a view to any thing but the improvement of it.

If to a discerning mind, such as that to which this offer considers itself as addressed, any such *loose presumptions* as are capable of being afforded, by tokens of attention and approbation given by foreign authorities, can be of any use, it can only be by contributing to produce, should such be the result, a recurrence to the only *direct* and *proper* evidence.

Citizenship of France, decreed by one of the National Assemblies, on the same occasion on which the like mark of approbation was bestowed on *Joseph Priestly* and *Thomas Payne*.[4] In one of the legislative Assemblies held during the Consulate of the present Emperor, elogium pronounced by one of the Members on the above

[4] On 26 August 1792 Bentham was made a French citizen by the National Assembly. Joseph Priestley (1733–1804), the theologian and scientist, and Thomas Paine (1737–1809), the author of *Rights of Man*, 2 parts, 1791–2, together with other foreigners, were similarly honoured on the same day.

mentioned Work and printed in the official Paper.[5] Nomination (though by subsequent incidents rendered fruitless) to the then existing Institute of France. Translation of that same Work made by Order of the Russian Government and published in the Russian language, besides another published in the same language without authority.[6] Translation of another Work on the mode of providing for the *Poor*, made and published during the Consulate by the municipality of Paris,[7] and (if I have not been misinformed) *since* put in some shape and degree or other to public use—these tokens, together with the notices taken as above in the French and Bavarian Codes, may, it is hoped, have the additional good effect, of rendering it pretty apparent, that Governments of the most opposite forms and characters, have found something to approve, nothing considerable to disapprove, and nothing at all to be apprehensive of, in the views and dispositions with which the task here proposed would be taken in hand.

In a man's writings, the character of the *moral* part is not so clearly delineated as that of the *intellectual* part of his frame.

Artifice, in pursuit of some private end, might give birth to an offer such as the present, unaccompanied with any such intention as that of giving effect to the engagement sought:—levity though pure from original insincerity, might intervene at any time and be productive of the same failure.

On the question concerning *intellectual* aptitude, the evidence lying before you, the judgment, Sir, will be your own. As to what regards *moral* promise, the nature of the Case refers you in course to the gentleman, be he who he may, who, in this Country stands charged with the Affairs of your State. Transmitted to him, your Letter, I mean the necessary letter of authorization above stipulated for, may, according to the result of his enquiries, be delivered or kept back.

§2. As to the *Advantages* that promise to result from the *gratuitousness* of the proposed service, though there is not one of them, that seems much in danger of escaping the observation of the distinguished person to whom the proposal is addressed, yet as it will naturally have to pass through a variety of hands, in all of which it

[5] A reference to the speech made in the Corps Législatif on 8 April 1803 by Jean-Jacques Combes-Dounous (1758–1820), French writer, philosopher, and politician, reported in *Gazette Nationale ou Le Moniteur Universel*, 9 April 1803.

[6] See above, letter 2086 and n. 9.

[7] Adrien Cyprien Duquesnoy (1759–1808) translated Bentham's work on the poor as *Esquisse d'un ouvrage en faveur des pauvres adressée à l'éditeur des Annales de l'Agriculture*, Paris, 1802.

cannot promise itself exactly the same degree of attention, it may not be amiss that these features of recommendation should in this place be distinctly brought to view.

1. In the first place, no *pecuniary* charge whatever being to be imposed on the Public or any part of it, the great and prominent objection which public works in general have to encounter, has here no place: and be the chance for useful service rated ever so low, still, should any the smallest portion be reaped, it will be all clear gain.

2. By supervening imbecillity, by death, or even the levity and caprice on the part of the proposed Workman, should the work be left in a state ever so far from compleatness, still, to the public there would be no positive loss: the situation in which in this respect it would find itself, would, at the worst, be but what it is at present,—be but what it would have been, had no such proposal been made.

3. On these terms the situation of the Workman stands altogether out of the influence of any sinister motive, from which either an undue *protraction* of the business, or an undue *acceleration* of it, might be apprehended: *protraction*, as if a salary were given, to be received during the continuance of it: *acceleration*, as if it were a sum of money to be once paid, or a life annuity to commence at the completion of it.

4. In respect of the *commencement*, and so far in respect of the *completion*, of the work, it admits of a degree of promptitude, the want of which might otherwise be fatal to the whole design. If money were necessary, consents,—I need not set myself to think or to enquire in what number—would be requisite to be obtained: obtained, not only for the fixation of the sum, but for the origination of the measure, and therefore if not for the giving of *any* answer, at any rate for the giving any definitive and sufficient answer to this address. As it *is*, a single fiat, a letter how short soever from the authority to which this address is made, suffices for giving commencement to the work: and whatever subsidiary matters may hereinafter come to be suggested, may without inconvenience wait, in that case, all proper and accustomed delays.

5. It must I think be acknowledged to be a feature of advantage in any proposal, if it be such as to clear from all possible suspicion of sinister interest, all such persons to whom it may happen to take a part in the giving introduction or support to it.

To this sort of advantage, if there be any imaginable proposal that can lay claim, this I think cannot easily avoid being recognized to be thus happily circumstanced.

With or without any particular individual in the character of proposed workman in his eye, suppose the pre-eminent person to whom this proposal is submitted—suppose him bringing forward a Plan, tending to the accomplishment of the proposed work, but accompanied with a plan of *remuneration* in the ordinary shape and mode. What would be, be he who he may, the *motives* to which the proposal would be referred?—referred, by adversaries at least, not to speak of friends?—they are by much too obvious to need mentioning.

Supposing it the good fortune of this proposal to obtain the sort of approbation which it aspires to, I have set myself to consider, by what public token it may be natural and proper for that approbation to declare itself. The inability I have found myself under, of obtaining the documents necessary to secure me against falling into misconception respecting such of the functions of your high Office, Sir, as may be found to have application to the present case, will, I hope, in case of mis-supposal, obtain for me the benefit of your indulgence.

The steps, to any or all of which it may happen to be taken in this view, present themselves to my imagination as follows.

1. To lay the Proposal before Congress at its meeting, with a *recommendation* to take it into consideration, stating or not stating the provisional authorization given or intended to be given to the author.

2. To cause a *Minute* to be made in the books of the President's Office, stating a resolution on the part of the *President* for *the time being* to lay before Congress any such part of the Work as may come to have been transmitted during his continuance in Office, together with a recommendation of the like operation, in the like event, to *future* Presidents.

3. To transmit a Copy of this proposal, accompanied with the like recommendation to the legislative bodies of each of the several particular States.

4. To cause it, on public account, to be printed and published by authority, as other public documents are in use to be.

For affording to me the necessary encouragement, any one of the above testimonies of approbation would, if notified to me by the President, be sufficient: but the greater the number of them that may come united, the greater of course, and the more operative would be the encouragement.

Two things require to this purpose to be distinguished—1. the *design* itself.—2. any work that may come to be presented by me in execution of it.

If, by any approbation bestowed upon the *design* itself, you were to be pledged for the like or any other tokens of approbation to be bestowed on any *work* done in execution of this same design, this would be an objection against the bestowing any such provisional approbation on the design itself. When it comes, the work might appear ill adapted to its purpose, and, on that or any other account, not likely to be approved by the respective constituted authorities, on which the adoption of it would have to depend.

With submission, it appears to me Sir, that, on the supposition that the design itself has met your approbation, it would not be a committal of yourself, were you to undertake for the forwarding either to Congress, or to the several Legislatures, for their consideration, any work that shall have been transmitted by me, in execution of the design so approved. For, contrary to expectation, when produced suppose the work to prove, in your judgment, to ever so great a degree absurd and even ridiculous, nothing will there be to hinder you from saying so: wherever it goes there it will lie: nor will it impose, on any person, any such trouble as that of taking it into consideration, unless some person or other should happen to be to such a degree impressed with the contrary notion, as to make the proper motion for causing it to be taken into consideration, as in the case of any particular law proposed in ordinary course.

As to *the expense of printing*—to any such extent as in the different cases may appear requisite, an expense so moderate would hardly, I should suppose, be grudged, by those to whom it belongs to judge: if it should, it would not be grudged by *me.*

§3. Against an enterprize of the sort in question, an host of jealousies and fears will naturally be springing up and arming themselves with objections. To such as appear best grounded or most plausible, I proceed to submit such answers as the nature of the case presents to me.

Objection the 1st. '*Disturbance to property and other existing rights.*' 'What?' (cries the man of law) 'remove our landmarks?' 'revolutionize our property?' throw every thing into confusion? 'Is this what you would be at?' 'and is this to be the practical fruit of these fine theories of yours?'

Such, Sir, if not where *you* are—such at any rate would be sure to be his language *here.*

My answer is—so far as the objection confines itself to the law of private rights,—when these and any other number of declamatory generalities in the same strain have been expended, the only real mischief which they hold up to view, is that which is reducible to this one expression—to *existing expectations disappointment, productive of the painful sense of loss.*

What then is this mischief, by the apprehension of which this proposed Pannomion is thus to be put aside?

It is the very mischief, under which it is impossible that, for want of a written, and visible, and intelligible, and cognoscible rule of action, in a word for want of a *Pannomion*, the people in your country should not be at present labouring:—the very grievance from which it is the object of this my humble proposal to be admitted to afford them my best assistance towards working out their deliverance: the principal grievance which it would not only be the object, but to a considerable degree the sure effect of a Pannomion to remove.

Throughout the whole extent of the territory of the United States (new acquired dependencies excepted, in which matters cannot but be still worse) what is it that at this moment forms the basis of the rule of action? What but an ideal and shapeless mass of merely conjectural, and essentially uncognoscible matter,—matter without mind, work without an author, occupying, through the oscitancy of the legislature a place that ought to be filled, and exercising in it the authority that ought to be exercised by law?

Nullis lex verbis, a nullo, nullibi, nunquam

Law, in no *words*, by no *man*, *never*, made:—[8]

Law which, having for its authors—not the people themselves, nor any persons chosen by the people but the creatures,—the ever removable and compleatly and perpetually dependent creatures of the King alone,(*) had of course for its main object not the good of the people, but as far as the blindness or patience of the people would permit the sinister and confederated interests of the creator, under whose influence, and the creatures by whose hands it was spun out:—

Law, blundered out by a set of men, who in their course of operation not being at their own command, but at the command of the plaintiffs in the several causes, were all along as completely destitute of the *power*, as, under the influence of sinister interest, they could not but be of the *inclination* to operate in pursuit of any clear and enlarged views of utility, public or private, or so much as upon any comprehensive and consistent plan, good or bad, in the delineation of the rights they were conferring and the obligations they were imposing—and which accordingly never has been, nor, to

(*) Till the revolution this was compleatly true, and even since it has not wanted much of being so.—

[8] i.e. Or, literally 'a law with no words, by no-one, nowhere, never'.

any purpose, good or bad, ever could have been, nor ever can be, the result of antecedent reflection, grounded on a general view of the nature of each case, of the exigencies belonging to it, or the analogous cases connected with it: nor in a word any thing better than a shapeless heap of odds and ends, the pattern of which has, in each instance been necessarily determined, by the nature of the demand, put in by the plaintiff, as above:—

Law which being, in so far as it could be said to be *made*, made at a multitude of successive periods, and for the use and governance of so many different generations of men, imbued with notions, habituated to modes of life, differing more or less widely from each other, as well as from those which have place at present, would, even had it been well adapted to the circumstances and exigencies of the times, in which its parts respectively came into existence, have, to a considerable extent, been thereby rendered not the better adapted, but by so much the worse adapted, to the notions and manners now prevalent,—to the state of things at present in existence.

Law which, by its essential *form* and character, as above indicated, is, so long as it retains that form, altogether disabled from either giving to itself, or receiving from any other quarter, improvement or correction, upon a scale of any considerable extent: which, even upon the minutest scale, can not give to itself any improvement in the way of *particular utility*, but at the expense of *general certainty*: nor even at that price, but by a course of successive acts of arbitrary power, productive in the first place of a correspondent succession of particular disappointments, followed, each of them in proportion as it comes to be known, by those more extensively spreading apprehensions of insecurity, which are among the inseparable concomitants and consequences, of that ever deplorable, howsoever originally necessary and unavoidable, taint of iniquity, inherent in the very essence of *ex-post-facto* law:

Of *ex-post-facto* law did I say? Yes: for that which by common sense, speaking by the mouth of *Cicero*,[9] has been spoken of as the most mischievous and intolerable abuse, of which, in the form in which it is called *Written* or *Statute* law, the rule of action is susceptible, is an abomination interwoven in the very essence of that spurious and impostrous substitute, which, to its makers and their dupes, is an object of such prostrate admiration, and such indefatigable eulogy, under the name of *Common* or *Unwritten Law*.

[9] See Cicero, *Orationes de lege agraria*, III. ii. 5: 'Of all the laws, I consider the most unjust and the most unlike a law to be that one which L. Flaccus the interrex brought in concerning Sulla, so that everything whatsoever that he had done should become ratified.'

Of *unwritten*, or rather of *uncomposed* and *unenacted* law (for of *writing* there is beyond comparison more belonging to this spurious than to the genuine sort) of this impostrous law the fruits, the perpetual fruits, are in the *civil* or *non-penal* branch, as above, *uncertainty*, *uncognoscibility*, *particular disappointments* without end, *general sense* of *insecurity* against similar disappointment and loss:—in the *penal* branch, *uncertainty* and *uncognoscibility*, as before, and, instead of compliance and obedience, the evil of transgression mixed with the evil of punishment: in both branches, in the breast and in the hands of the Judge, power every where arbitrary, with the semblance of a set of rules to serve as a screen to it.

Such are the fruits of this species of mock law, even in the Country which gave it birth: how much more pregnant with insecurity—with unexpected and useless hardship—as well in the shape of *civil law*, as in the shape of *penal infliction* and non-prevention of crimes, must it not necessarily be in a country, into which the matter of it is continually *imported*:—imported from a foreign country, whose yoke the American nation, has, to all other purposes so happily for both nations, shaken off.

Not that I am by any means unaware of the prodigious mass of rubbish, of which on the importation of English Common Law into America part was, on the change of place naturally, or even necessarily, left behind, other parts since the original importation, at different times so wisely and happily cast out of it:—religiously-persecuting laws, manorial rights, tithes, ecclesiastical courts, distinctions between law and equity, in several of the States at least, secret Rome bred mode of extracting tithe money I believe every where, and so forth. Not that I am by any means insensible to the prodigious alleviation, which from the removal of so large a portion of it, the burthen can not but have experienced.

But though, of the whole mass already imported, as well as of each successive mass, as they come respectively to be imported, there is, and will be, so much the less that needs to be *attended* to, yet, from the respective magnitudes of those several masses, no defalcation ever has been made, or can be made. The consequence is—that what alleviation so ever the burthen of the law has ever received, or can ever receive as above, vizt. by successive patches of *Statute* law, applied to the immense and continually growing body of *unwritten* alias *common* law, is confined to the *matter*, leaving the *form* of it as immense, as incomprehensible, and consequently as adverse to *certainty* and *cognoscibility* as ever.

Yes Sir, so long as there remains any the smallest scrap of unwritten law unextirpated, it suffices to taint with its own corruption—its own inbred and incurable corruption, whatsoever portion of *statute* law has ever been or can be applied to it.

So far then as disturbance to existing rights is the disorder in question, the proposed operation so far from producing, or aggravating such the disorder, presents not only the sure, but the only possible remedy.—Disturbance?—a state of disturbance—of perpetual and universally extending disturbance—is the very state in which they have hitherto existed:—have existed, and, until fixed and secured by the application of this sole remedy, are condemned to remain till the end of time.—

All this while, incapable as it is of serving in any tolerable degree, in its present state, in the character of a rule of action and guide to human conduct, nothing could be much further from the truth, than if, in speaking of the matter of which English Common Law is composed, a man were to represent it as being of no use. Confused, indeterminate, inadequate, ill adapted, and inconsistent as, to a vast extent, the provision or the non provision would be found to be, that has been made for the various cases that have happened to present themselves for decision, yet in the character of a repository for such cases it affords, for the manufactory of law, a stock of materials which is beyond all price. Traverse the whole continent of Europe, ransack all the libraries belonging to the jurisprudential systems of the several political states,—add the contents all together,—you would not be able to compose a collection of cases equal in variety, in amplitude, in clearness of statement—in a word, all points taken together, in instructiveness—to that which may be seen to be afforded by the collection of English Reports of adjudged cases, on adding to them the abridgements and treatises, by which a sort of order, such as it is, has been given to their contents.

Of the necessary materials, the stock already in hand is not only rich, but one may venture to say, sufficient: nor, to the composition of a *compleat* body of law, in which, saving the requisite allowance to be made for human weakness, every imaginable case shall be provided for, and provided for in the best manner, is any thing at present wanting but a duly arranging hand.

Objection 2. *Foreign Yoke*. It was to free ourselves from the yoke of foreign law that we took up arms against the Monarch of England, and shall an obscure subject of the same nation fasten another such yoke upon our necks?

It may perhaps appear an idle precaution to bring to view in the character of an objection capable of being urged, an observation so palpably void of substance. But it is not always by the most rational argument that the strongest impression is made. At any rate the answer will, I flatter myself, be found sufficient.

1. The yoke, the foreign yoke, is already about your necks: you were born with it about your necks.

What your proposed Scribe does, if he does any thing, is to facilitate to you the means of relieving yourselves from it.

2. Year by year, or rather *term* by *term*, that is *quarter* by *quarter*, the mass and burthen of it receives, at present, its encrease. What he does, if he does any thing, will be to help relieve you from such encrease.

3. By him, let him do what he may, no yoke will be imposed: nothing like the imposition of a yoke either done or so much as attempted. By him, let him do what he may, no act of power will be performed, not any the minutest particle of power exercised. The honour for which he is suing is that of being admitted to work in the character of a servant. Labor alone will be his part: acceptance, rejection, alteration, decision, choice, with as much, or as little labor, as it may be your pleasure to bestow upon it will be yours.

Yes, if, to have part in the governance and plunder of you for seven years, he were to be occupied in cringing to you, and in flattering you, for as many days or weeks, then indeed there *might* be power for him to exercise, then indeed there might be a yoke for you to take upon you, and to impose: but any such authority is not more completely out of his reach, than it is and ever would be out of his wish.

4. In suing to be thus employed himself, it is no less opposite to his wish, than above his power, to exclude from the same employment any of yourselves. But of this a little further on.

Heavy or light, by your own hands, if by any, will the burthen if any, be imposed.

5. Innumerable are the yokes, the additions to the existing foreign yoke, by which, until you take this only method of securing yourselves against all such nuisances, the burthen you now labour under will continue to be *encreased*.

Not a year, not a quarter of a year, but, here in this Country fresh loads are produced, of the excrementitious matter of which this burthen is composed. Of this matter, this or that portion, will it, or will it not, by such or such a time, have in your Country begun to swell the load? Upon arrivals or non-arrivals—upon winds and waves—upon good or ill humour between the two nations,—will even *possibility* depend in the first place.

Let *possibility* be now converted into fact. The produce of the last twelve months, or of the last quarter, or such other portion as accident may have determined, is now arrived: Upon whom on the occasion of each cause will the acceptance or rejection of it, and of each particular portion of it, depend? Upon yourselves all together? Upon your appointed legislators? upon the aggregate of all your legislative bodies? or upon any one of them? No:—but on each particular occasion, upon the will of some one or other such small number of yourselves, acting as Judge or Judges.—

Take for example any one such Judge, upon this or that case that chance has brought before him, this or that English decision, (let it be supposed) bears:—will it, or will it *not*, be taken by him for his guide? On contingency upon contingency depends the answer. The last cargo, has it, in the whole or any part of it, come into his hands or under his cognizance? if not the whole, but a part only, *what* part? The case produced to him, will he, or will he not pay regard to it? Yes or no depends (for I see not how it should fail of depending) altogether upon his good pleasure. If it be such as suits his views he makes use of it: if it be such as does not suit his views, he turns aside from it.

6. Innumerable, and many of them still more obscure than your proffered servant, are the workmen who at present, bear, each of them a part, in the fashioning of these successive accretions to this your foreign yoke.

At present—under the existing system of blind and sheepish acquiescence, who are they who thus,—in conjunction in each instance with this or that Judge—become respectively the arbiters of your fate? Speaking of individuals to say who, is, in any instance impossible: speaking generally, a Judge or bench of Judges, nominees of a foreign monarch or to speak more correctly, as well as particularly a mixt yet uncommunicating multitude, composed of Judges, Advocates, self appointed Note takers, Law Report writers, Law treatise makers, Law abridgment makers, and publishing Law booksellers.

Suppose on the other hand the proposed work executed, the proposed Pannomion compleated, in what state would the rule of action be among you in that case?—Comprized it would be the whole of it, in a small number of Volumes; the part necessary to each man in some *one* small Volume:—the whole heap of foreign lumber existing and future contingent, as compleatly superseded, rendered as completely useless, as an equal quantity of *School Divinity*, or Rome bred *Canon Law*

Wide in this respect, is the difference, between a situation in which not a particle of labour has place without a correspondent particle of power attached to it, and a task which would have to consist purely of labour without any the least particle of power attached to it.—

But, though thus bare of power would be the Service in question if rendered by an obscure and unknown foreigner, the case not only might be, but naturally would be, very different, if a service of the self same nature were to find the performance of it lodged in the hands of a native. In *that* case, whatever *reputation* and consequent influence it might happen to a man to obtain by the execution of it, would, in his situation, and for his benefit, convert itself into so much *power*. In power in short, not only would the performance of the Service *terminate*, but it is in power that the choice of the person for the performance of it would have *originated*. If therefore the business finds itself in the hands of a foreigner, there will be at least *this* advantage that the judgment to be pronounced upon it will stand so much the clearer of the influence of local, as well as personal, enmities and partialities, and the work stand so much the better chance of being judged and decided upon, on the ground of its own intrinsic merits, its own fitness for the intended purpose.

Discussions of this sort do not, it must be confessed, shed any very brilliant lustre upon human nature; but so it is that we are constituted, and being thus constituted it is impossible for us to act either prudently or beneficially, any further than as we know ourselves for what we are.

As to local jealousies, to my eyes dissention, be the seat of it where it may, is never a pleasing object. But though in some measure it depends on a man's choice what objects he shall fix his eyes upon, it depends not altogether upon his will what objects shall pass before them.

By the words *northern* and *southern*, if my eyes or my memory dó not deceive me, one cause of division more or less active has been indicated as having place, and more or less frequently manifesting its influence in your confederacy. Supposing this to be so, what is then the consequence? For public Service in this or any other line, if a member of the southern division presents himself or is held up to view, jealousy and opposition gather in the northern regions, and so *vice versâ*.

Another source of division, though to my unpractised eyes not so clear and intelligible a one as the foregoing, is that which is brought to view by the words *democrats* and *federalist*.

Under these circumstances, be the nature of the work ever so uninviting, if a hand were to be offered for it, from one of the sides distinguished as above, in the natural course of things it would find on the other side hands drawn up in array, and prepared if possible to repel it. Such at least would be the case *here*: Such in a word would be the case (for such has ever hitherto been the case) wherever there have been parties—wherever there has been either liberty or the appearance of it. If to this rule the land of the United States offered an exception, it is a land—not of men, but angels.

Such then are the perils which, a work of the sort in question would have to encounter, if proposed for a native workman: perils which in proportion to the utility of the work, would, it is apprehended be more likely to receive encrease than diminution: from these perils, at least, it would be saved by acceptance given to a remote and foreign hand.

Objection 3. *Foreigner's necessary ignorance.*

A foreigner by whom the territory has not, any part of it, ever been, or will be visited, who with the population, with the territory, or its local peculiarities, never has had, nor proposes ever to have any the least personal acquaintance—a person so circumstanced a person this ignorant—unavoidably and incurably ignorant—of so many necessary points of knowledge—is he a person who, with any propriety, can be looked to for any such service?

1. To this question one answer may be given by another question. The legislators, such as they are, to whose combined exertions the loads of *writing*, of which our and your *unwritten* law is composed, owe their existence, have already been laid before you and brought under review: Our Advocates, our Judges, our Note-takers, our Report makers, our Treatise and Abridgment makers, our publishing Law booksellers. By how many of all these functionaries, has the legislative System of the United States been ever studied—been ever so much as thought of, or the Country visited?

2. Another answer is—that, upon a closer scrutiny, the points, which present a demand for local knowledge, would not, it is supposed be found to cover, in the field of law, so great an extent, nor yet to be so difficult to discriminate beforehand, as upon a transient glance, general notions might lead any person to imagine.

3. Nor, if I may venture to say as much, would it be easy to find any person, more compleatly aware of the demand, presented by the nature of the case, for attention to those local exigencies, nor more completely in the habit of looking over the field of law in this particular view.

Of this disposition, and this habit, exemplifications of considerable amplitude may be seen in the already mentioned work, which for these nine years has been under the public eye: and by that work Sir, I am saved from the need of attempting on the present occasion to give you any farther trouble on this head.

Thus in the case of Penal Law. Of the *genera* of Offences, as distinguished or distinguishable by their *generic* names—Murder. Defamation. Theft. Robbery and so forth—definitions for the most part the same all the world over. But for particular species, occasion may be afforded, by particular local circumstances: and so in regard to causes of aggravation, extenuation, justification, or exemption, with demand for corresponding varieties in respect of *satisfaction* or punishment. And so in regard to *contracts*.

Accordingly, in any draught which I should draw, care would be taken, not only to keep the distinction all along in mind, but to keep pointed towards it the attention of all those to whom in dernier resort it belonged to judge.—

4. I say *to those to whom it belonged to judge*: for as it never would be by myself, neither by any one else, let it be forgotten; that of any body of proposed laws to which it may happen to have been drawn up by the proposed draughtsman, there is not any part, of which the legislative bodies in the several United States will not take, each of them according to its competence, perfect and effectual cognizance—cognizance no less perfect and effectual than what has been taken of any other portion of the matter of law to which their sanction has respectively been given or refused.

Whatsoever therefore may, in relation to the local points in question, be the ignorance of the proposed and supposed foreign draughtsman, and, in his draught whatsoever may have been the errors produced by these ignorances, all such errors will, for their correction, have the same instruments and opportunities, as any other errors that ever have been, or may ever come to be made and corrected.

5. Not but that, on this as on most other occasions, it is more to be desired, that errors, of whatever kind, should, particularly in such a work, have never been made, than that, having been made, they should be corrected:—and, by original exclusion, not only the time and labour necessary to correction would be saved but the danger of non correction avoided.

And here perhaps, Sir, may accordingly be seen one use in the sort of assistance, the idea of which will come to be submitted to your consideration, a little further on.

Objection 4. *Shame of being beholden to a foreigner.*

But a foreigner.—How necessary soever the work itself may be would it not to American Citizens be matter of just shame, to see a foreign hand entrusted with or so much as employed in the execution of it? America—the whole population of United America—the 8 or 9 millions or whatever may be the amount of it—among such multitudes of hands, constantly occupied in the business of legislation, does it not contain so much as a single one, competent to such a task?

A question this, which will be apt to appear, much more within my competence to *put*, than to find an answer for. I shall venture however to submit answers more than one.

1. In the first place what I believe is certain is—that whatsoever number of persons thus qualified, may, at this time, be in existence, no one such person has as yet at any time made himself known as such, or been recognized as such.

2. In the next place, be the number of persons, in an equal, or by any amount superior, degree, competent to the task in question, ever so great, of the offer here submitted it is no part, either of the design, or tendency, to deprive the United States of the Services of any one. On the contrary, among its tendencies is that of calling forth into action, to this very purpose, and on this very occasion, whatsoever qualifications or capabilities, of the kind in question, may happen to be in existence.

3. Of this sort of national jealousy, if the effect be to call forth into existence any competitors who would not otherwise exist, so far at least, if the work itself supposing it well executed, be deemed a useful one, in such case, as well the utility of this offer, as the propriety of giving acceptance to it, will be out of dispute: and, in such a competition, the danger that the work of a perfect stranger should, to the prejudice of local interests and influences, obtain an undue preference, will hardly appear very formidable.

4. If on the other hand, it should happen to it, either to be the only work produced, or, finding rival works to contend with, to be really, in the judgment of the competent judges, thought better adapted than any other to the intended purpose, any such supposition as that, on the occasion of such a work, these same judges would see their Country less well served, or not served at all, rather than see it served by a foreign hand, and that accordingly, they would put it in the power of any foreigner, to preclude them from the benefit of a good body of law, or so much as a single good clause in a law, merely by being the first to propose it, is that sort of supposition which, if seriously made, would not, I imagine, be very generally well received.

5. Whatsoever disposition toward jealousy it might happen to an offer of this sort to have to encounter, a man, of whom it was perfectly known, that in person he could never be present, to give to any one the sort of offence which such a disposition supposes, should naturally, on this supposition, present such a ground for

acceptance as should give him on this one score at least, the advantage over a native. On affections of this kind distance in respect of place, especially when the continuance of it is certain, produces an effect intimately analogous to, and little different from that of time. In the present case, were the proposed Workman already numbered among the dead, he could not be more effectually placed out of the sight of the people, and in particular of the constituted authorities, in whose Service it is his ambition thus to place himself, than to the day of his death, he would find it necessary to remain, if this his offer found acceptance.

6. So far from operating as an objection, at least in the mind of any Gentleman, who fills the high station to which this offer is addressed, what I should expect is—to find this very circumstance of foreignership placed, and on this very score, to the account of advantage.

There are certain situations, and those highly important ones, for the filling of which, it has been a known maxim among republican States, to resort to foreigners in preference to Natives.

Among the Italian Republics, this sort of policy was applied sometimes by usage, sometimes by positive law—not only to the subordinate situation designated among us by the title of *Judge* but to that of *Podesta*: a sort of supreme Monarchical Magistrate to whose power, while it lasted, it seems not very easy to assign any very distinct limits. My books are not at present within my reach but in the case of the Podesta, instances more than one will be found in Sismondi's lately published history of the Italian Republics;[10] and, in the case of Judge, I have read laws to that effect in the Codes of Italian States more than one: and if I do not mis:recollect, these instances or some of them are mentioned in the *Defence of the Constitution of the United States* by Mr Adams.[11]

Of this preference the cause, the efficient cause seems manifest enough. For any of those great and enviable situations, seldom could a man, whose character was such as to afford him any chance of finding acceptance, offer himself, without raising up against himself, besides a band of rivals, a much larger host of adversaries.

[10] Jean Charles Léonard Simond de Sismondi (1773–1842), Genevan economist and historian, was the author of *Histoire des républiques Italiennes du moyen âge*, 12 vols., Paris, 1809–18. Podestas are mentioned at ii. 106. They did not come from the towns that they were to govern, but they were not necessarily foreigners.

[11] John Adams (1735–1826), president of the United States 1797–1801. Podestas are mentioned in his *Defence of the Constitutions of Government of the United States of America, against the attack of M. Turgot in his Letter to Dr. Price, dated the Twenty-second day of March, 1778*, 3 vols., London, 1794.

Nor was the justificative cause, the reason, much less clear or impressive. In any such powerful situation no native could seat himself, without bringing into it, in his bosom, a swarm of sinister interests, partialities and prejudices.

§4. On the subject of *alienage*. I gave intimation of an expedient, which I will now venture upon the liberty of suggesting, and on which, it being to myself, personally speaking, a matter of indifference, you will be pleased, Sir, to bestow what regard it may seem to merit.

If at any time, supposing me occupied in the work in question, it were thought worth while, by your Government, to Commission any Citizen of the United States, residing for any purpose of his own, or sent hither for that particular purpose, to take a part in it, and give me the benefit of his information and assistance in the execution of it, whatsoever instruction I may be thought capable of affording, on the subject of legislation, should be always at his command: and whatsoever information, not possessed by him, I am myself master of, it should be my study to make him master of as fully and as expeditiously as possible: always understood that the same considerations, which forbid the receipt of the fruits of public munificence, would oppose the same inexorable bar to the acceptance of the individual's mite.

The probability, of my living long enough to put the last hand to such a work, being of course altogether precarious, my endeavours would be, as speedily as possible, to put him in a way of filling up whatever deficiency it might be my lot to leave.

The Gentleman so commissioned would I suppose be a person distinct from him who stood charged with the Affairs of the United States at this Court or in this Country in any diplomatic character, principal or subordinate, and that for more reasons than one.

1. His whole time would not be too much for such an employment.

2. In his instance, a more intimate acquaintance with the general state of the law in the United States might, perhaps, be thought requisite, than for any such diplomatic character would be thought altogether necessary.—

3. In the event of a rupture between the two Governments, (a contingency the calamitousness of which affords no reason why on this any more than on any other occasion, it should be left unprovided for) the general liberality of the times (and I hope this Country will not to this purpose be considered as affording an exception) leaves me little apprehension, that a person whose commission were known, and declared to be confined to this one object, would not be allowed to continue in this country, for that

particular purpose, notwithstanding any interruption of diplomatic intercourse.[(a)]

§5. The degree of advance already made by my labours in the field of legislation and the order of priority in which, if undertaken, the several distinguishable parts of the Pannomion would be proposed to be executed—these seem to be of the number of the topics, on which something will on such occasion be expected, and on which accordingly it will not be allowable for me to be altogether silent.

On these topics on the other hand, any considerable details would, if comprised within the compass of this paper, swell it to such a bulk, as to subject to too great a degree of uncertainty its prospect of finding a reader, in the exalted and busy station to which it is addressed.

The point for your consideration, Sir, supposing the Work itself a desirable one, will, unless I misconceive the matter be found to be, —whether if this proposal should be passed by without acceptance the rejection will leave an adequate probability of seeing the work executed, at any future period, and under other circumstances, to equal advantage? and in particular, whether there be any such probability, that any other person will arise, who, having, without receipt or prospect of pecuniary retribution, made equal advances in the prosecution of such a design, shall, upon the same desirable terms, be ready to undertake to do what depends upon him towards the completion of it?

To enable you to afford to yourself a proper answer to these questions, the following statements, compressed as they are, and consequently, in a proportionable degree, deficient in point of specific information, may yet perhaps be found to suffice:

1. In regard to the *Penal* Code, the work is already in a state of considerable forwardness. That it was so, so long ago as the year 1802, not to speak of a much earlier period, may be seen from the work edited in that year in the French language by Mr Dumont. What may be seen upon the face of that work is indeed a sample but it is no more than a sample: a great deal more had even then been executed than is there exhibited; perhaps the greatest part of the

---

[(a)] Note desired to be kept private.

A Gentleman with whom I am well acquainted, a Russian born, who at the time of the rupture between Russia and this Country had for many years been Chaplain to the Russian Embassy,[12] and whom I have seen doing business at our Secretary of States' and Admiralty Offices, has all along continued here; having done so even in the time of the Mad Emperor Paul.[13]

[12] Iakav Ivonovich Smirnov.

[13] Paul I (1754–1801), emperor of Russia 1796–1801.

whole:—a few months,—indeed a very few, would, if I do not much much miscalculate suffice for the completion of it—I mean *in terminis*.

2. As to the *Civil* Code, in the adjustment of the *terms* of it, but little advance has been made: but, in respect of *leading principles*, of which in regard to *form* as well as matter, a pretty ample view may in that same work be seen, they have long ago been settled.

3. Of the subject of the Judicial Establishment (the *Judiciary* is I think the more concise denomination it goes by with you) a pretty full view may be seen in the printed, but never yet published Papers drawn up about the year 1790 on the occasion of the French Revolution:[14] Copy herewith sent, as per list. To adapt it to the purpose of the United States, if the System actually in force there should be regarded as susceptible of improvement, would of course require considerable modifications.

4. As to *procedure*,—*judicial procedure*—in the adjustment of the principles of that branch of the law, considerable progress was necessarily made, of which the result was brought to view, and may be seen in the course of the enquiry into the subject of the correspondent part of the Official Establishment as above.

Since that time farther advances were made and presented to view in the work intituled Scotch Reform etc published Ao. 1808 Copy herewith sent.

In addition to this, a work compleat or nearly so on the subject of *Forthcomingness*—Vizt. on the most effectual and in other respects proper, means to be employed for ordering matters in such sort that, whether for the purpose (as they say in French) of *justiciability*, I mean being placed at the disposal of the judicial authorities, or for the purpose of *evidence* (I mean being made to furnish evidence) as well all *things* as all *persons* requisite shall, on each occasion, be *forthcoming*, lies by me in manuscript.—[15]

5. The subject of evidence has been examined in its whole extent and sifted to the bottom. A work of mine on this subject under the title of *The Rationale of Evidence* enough to occupy two moderate sized quarto volumes, has been for some time in the hands of another friend of mine, and will be in the Printers' hands in the course of about two months.[16]

[14] *Draught of a New Plan for the Organisation of the Judicial Establishment in France*, printed in 1790. See Bowring, iv. 285–406.

[15] Procedure MSS, dating from 1803 and 1804, entitled 'Evidence' and 'forth comingness' are to be found at UC lxxiv(b). 223–514.

[16] James Mill had been working on Bentham's MSS on evidence. See letters 2050, 2051 n. 2; and 2058 and n. 3.

For drawing up a Code of *in terminis*, grounded on the principles there laid down, very little time would suffice. Of the customary *exclusionary rules*—rules which are not in the law of any Country either consistent with one another, or adhered to with any tolerable degree of constancy—the place would be mostly occupied by a set of correspondent *Instructions*:—Instructions from the Legislator to the Judge, pointing out, *inter alia*, as causes of *suspicion*, those circumstances which in general are employed in the character of causes of absolute and inexorable *rejection*.

On several subjects not included, as well as those which are included, under the above heads, disquisitions may be seen in the subjoined list of printed works. But, to the present purpose, no separate mention of them seems requisite.

The printed but never published fragment on the subject of the *Art of Tactics* as applied to *Political Assemblies*,[17] is but one Essay, out of some *thirty* or *forty*, which were at that time written and which, taken together, did not want much of having gone through the subject in its whole extent.

But this is a subject, I should scarcely myself propose to include in the *Pannomion*. It is a subject on which each political body will naturally feel itself disposed to legislate, or at least act, according to its own views of its own exigencies, meaning exigencies considered with a view to the public good,—the good of that part of the public Service—not to speak of particular interests and prejudices.

As to *constitutional law*, I mean that branch which regards the mode of appointing the several Public functionaries, with their respective powers and obligations—with you I believe the appellation has a sense somewhat more extensive—As to *Constitutional law* thus explained: I mention it for no other purpose than to show that it has not been overlooked. In respect of the *matter* no demand for alteration has presented itself to my view nor should I myself be disposed to look out for any. In respect of the *form* something might possibly be found needful to adapt it to the other parts.

But though it were to be transcribed without the alteration of an iota, still, for symmetry and compactness, it might be necessary it should go through the hands, by which the other parts were drawn up.

As to the order of operation—I mean as between the different parts of the proposed Pannomion—the *Penal* Code is that which I imagine has already presented itself to your thoughts as the part which claims the first place. In respect of the *matter* of it, it is that

[17] The *Essay on Political Tactics* was printed in 1791 but not published. Dumont used Bentham's MSS to produce *Tactique des assemblées législatives*.

in which the demand for variation presented by local circumstances will naturally be least extensive: and the comparative progress already made in it, would, in default of material reason to the contrary, be of itself sufficient to determine the preference.

I know not whether the legal circumstances of your recent territorial acquisitions[18] will be thought to add any thing to the reasons for acceptance. In the character either of subjects or fellow citizens, you have to make provision for the legal exigencies of a new mass of population, differing from you not less in laws and customs than in language. In the state of these their laws, alteration in many points must already have been necessitated,—alteration in many others must be continually in contemplation. Besides the advantage of having the work done, whatsoever there may be of it to be done, upon an already considered and comprehensive plan—might it not, to the new citizens in question, be in some degree a matter of satisfaction, to learn that the preparation of the business was consigned to hands, for whose impartiality there would be such a security as could scarce have been in contemplation otherwise?

To contemplate the matter on the footing of *presumptions* merely and laying out of the case such ground for acceptance as the works themselves may be found to afford,—I wish to be clearly understood, in what I say as to the considerations, which in the present instance, may appear to operate in favour of the experiment, of receiving into the field of legislation the labour of a foreign hand. They are reducible to this simple circumstance vizt. that of the existence of a person, by whom so large a portion of time and study has been bestowed upon the business, coupled with the assumption that, neither in the British Empire nor in the United States, does there exist that other person, by whom, upon any comprehensive plan an *equal* portion of time and study—I might perhaps add *any* portion of time and study—has been employed with any ameliorative views.

One thing I am ready to admit and am fully assured of: and *that* is, that if, on general grounds, and setting aside any such casual opportunity, a resolution were come to, in your Country to set about the drawing up a *Pannomion*, reasons for looking beyond the American States (I mean on the ground of abstract aptitude and setting aside those which have reference to local jealousies and partialities) would not be to be found.

No, Sir: not the smallest doubt have I, but that, if in both Countries, a *Pannomion* were to be drawn up, and in both Countries

[18] Bentham was referring to the Louisiana purchase of 1803, by which the United States acquired from Napoleon a vast tract of land west of the Mississippi.

hands were to be looked out for, in the class of practising lawyers, the hand of an American lawyer would, even for the use of England, present beyond comparison a fairer premise than that of a lawyer of the English school.

What this persuasion has for its ground is,—the observation of the improvements—the prodigious improvements—which in matter and even in stile, since its voyage to America, the law of England has received from American hands.

Laying out of the case those necessary changes, which, in the constitutional branch, have been produced by the emancipation and the change in the form of Government—(subjects to which my attention neither has turned, nor is disposed to turn itself) those which on this occasion I have in view are those which through the medium of materials, as I have been hitherto able to collect, I have had the opportunity of observing in the *Penal* branch, in the *civil* branch, and in the system of procedure.—

Among these, though there may be some, which, being the result of the change in the constitutional branch, could not, consistently with the existing constitutional system, be introduced into the Mother Country, yet there are others—and those the greatest part,—which, with as much advantage, and with as little inconvenience, might be effected in England, as they have been in the United States.

Accordingly, but for the adverse interest of professional men, and the lazy and stupid confidence with which the bulk of the people have resigned their best interests into the hands of these their natural and irreconcilable enemies,—long ago would these same amendments have been made in this Country.

In America, the work would not fall into the hands of any persons, to whom the practice of amendment was not familiar:—who had not been in use not only to see amendments made—and made to a great extent,—but made with manifest and undeniable good effect: whereas in *this* country (saving exceptions in too small a number to be mentioned) any past work would look in vain for operators, to whom the very idea of amendment was not an object of unaffected terror, and undisguised enmity.—

In this state of things, suppose any person, myself for example, after making up a list of these amendments, were to come forward with the proposal to introduce the same amendments here: what would be the reception it would meet with? 'Oh! *You want to republicanize us do you*?' This would be the cry set up by the men of law—echoed by all others (a countless multitude) who have any share in the profit of the existing abuses: and in this cry would be found a full and sufficient answer. Foundation, it is true, it would have none. But, such is still the blindness and indifference of the people at large—so bigotted their admiration, so prostrate their adoration, of their natural and implacable enemies and oppressors.

* (Do you doubt this? Sir,—I will put you in a way to make the experiment. I will find you some fit person, who, without possibility of profit to himself, merely being indemnified against the expense, shall write the book and publish it.—Sir, if you accept the offer you will be a loser by it. I mean of course in the account of *money*: —if you look for indeminification, honour to yourself and country is the only shape, in which you will receive it.)

Such is the bigotry and indifference which in this Country is still prevalent. How long is it destined to continue? This is more than a prudent man will venture to answer. Thus much, however, I will venture to predict, Vizt. that, before this century, not to say this half century, has passed away, this shame to England will likewise have passed away.

I beg your pardon Sir,—no sooner is the proposal made than I have to beg your permission to withdraw it. For without those, or any other conditions, the friend to both Countries, who will do this, is already found. A Periodical publication is chosen as a vehicle for it: the subject to go on from number to number in continuance.[19]

I have the honor to be,
Sir,
With all respect,
Your most obedient
and very humble Servant
Jeremy Bentham

James Maddison Esq
President of the United States.
P.S.

In the event of acceptance I would beg the favor of you Sir, to give the necessary orders for the forming as Speedily as may be, a collection as complete as possible of the Laws of the several States as well as of those of Congress down to the then present time, and transmitting them to me here.

Immediately on delivery the expense (purchase money, freight and

---

* *Note*

Though the fact is true, it is requested that publicity be not given to either of these two passages inclosed in brackets.

[19] This paragraph seems to relate to the earlier one in brackets. Both were excluded from the published versions. The periodical referred to has not been traced.

all other necessary charges included) will be thankfully paid by me to the person by whom delivery is made.

To these I would beg might be added three Copies of the latest statistical account extant of the United States—that by Blodget would I suppose be the book—About 3 years ago I had a momentary sight of it, year of publication I believe 1806 or 1807, but from that time to this, all my endeavours to obtain the property, or so much as a sight of a Copy have been without effect.

Also a Copy of the Works of Genl. Alexander Hamilton lately published at New York 3 Vol. 8Vo.[20]

Also of such Papers as have been published under the name or in the character of official Reports—whatsoever promise to be serviceable in any way to the intended purpose.—

Underneath is a List of all the Books of United States Law I have been able to procure, and for most of them have been indebted to various accidents—enquiries made at the Booksellers for others, and in particular for information of the Laws of Congress have proved fruitless.—

1 Computation of the several Independent States of America—2d Edition by the Revd W Jackson London 1783.[21]

2 A Review of the Laws of the United States of America—the British Provinces and West India Islands Anonymous London 8vo. Printed for Otridge Strand 1790

3 A Defence of the Constitution of Government of the United States of America against the attack of M Turgot in his Letter to Dr Price dated 22nd March 1778 by John Adams Ll.D. etc In 3 Vol 8vo. New Edition London Printed for Stockdale 1794.[22]

4 The Pensylvania State Trials, containing the Impeachment, Trial and Acquittal of Francis Hopkinson and Jn. Nicholson Esqr. 8vo. Vol 1 Philadelphia Printed by Francis Busby for Edmund Hogan 1794.[23]

[20] *The Works of Alexander Hamilton*, 3 vols., New York, 1810. Hamilton (1755–1804), architect of the federal constitution of 1787, was shot dead by Burr in a duel.

[21] *A Collection of the Constitutions of the Thirteen United States of North America*, London, 1783, by the Revd William Jackson (1737?–95), an Irish revolutionary who committed suicide after being convicted of high treason.

[22] The letter from Anne Robert Jacques Turgot (1727–81) to Richard Price (1723–91) was published in Price's *Observations on the importance of the American Revolution, and the means of making it a benefit to the world. To which is added a letter from Mr Turgot . . .*, London, 1785.

[23] Francis Hopkinson (1737–91), American statesman, musician, and author, judge of admiralty for Pennsylvania 1779–89, was acquitted in an impeachment trial after the disciplining of a subordinate. John Nicholson (d. 1800), comptroller-general of Pennsylvania 1782–94, was impeached by the local legislature for financial irregularities, but acquitted by the senate. Nevertheless, he resigned all his offices.

5 A System of the Laws of the State of Connecticut in Six Books by Zephaniah Swift 2 Vol: 8vo. Windhams printed by John Byron for the Author Vol 1—1795.—Vol 2 1796.[24]
6 Acts passed at the First Congress of the United States of America begun and held at the City of New York 4 March Anno 1789 Philadelphia Printed by Francis Child Printer of the Laws of the United States 1795.—
7 Do.—of the Second Congress begun and held at the City of Philadelphia 24 Octr 1791 ibid 1795.
8 Do.—of the Third Congress Do—2 Octr 1793 ibid 1795
9 Do.—of the first Session of the 4th Congress begun and held at Philadelphia 7th Decr 1795. Printed by Thomas Dobson 1797.
10 Do.—of the second Session of the 4th Congress begun and held at Philadelphia 5 Decr. 1796—ibid Printed by T Dobson 1797.—
List of the Works sent with this Letter.
Panopticon 3 Vol
Essay on Political Tactics
Defence of Usury.
Views of the Hard Labour
Sketches relative to the Poor Act.[25]
Draught of a Plan for the Judicial Establishment in France
Address to the National Convention of France, proposing the emancipation of their Colonies.[26]
Escheat vice Taxation.[27]
Protest against Law Taxes[28]
Traités de Législation 3 Vol:
Panopticon versus New South Wales[29] and Plea for the Constitution
Summary view of a Plan for a Court of Lords Delegates[30]

[24] *A System of the Laws of the State of Connecticut*, 2 vols., Windham, Conn., 1795–6, by Zephaniah Swift (1759–1823), American jurist and barrister.

[25] A new (and subsequently discarded) title for his *Outline of a Work entitled 'Pauper Management Improved'*, reprinted from the *Annals of Agriculture* letters and published in 1812 as *Pauper Management Improved: particularly by means of an Application of the Panopticon Principle of Construction*. See the receipt signed by Thomas Beeby, 12 February 1812, BL XIV. 349.

[26] *Emancipate your Colonies! Addressed to the National Convention of France, Anno 1793*, London, 1830 (Bowring, ix. 407–18), was first printed in 1793 as *Jeremy Bentham to the National Convention of France*.

[27] *Supply without Burden; or Escheat vice Taxation*, London, 1795 (Bowring, ii. 585–98).

[28] *A Protest Against Law Taxes, Shewing the Peculiar Mischievousness of all such Impositions as add to the Expense of an Appeal to Justice*, published with the above, London, 1795 (Bowring, ii. 573–83).

[29] What had originally been published in 1802 as *Letters to Lord Pelham*. The title *Panopticon versus New South Wales* was used for the edition of the *Letters to Lord Pelham* published with *A Plea for the Constitution* in 1812.

[30] *Summary View of The Plan of a Judicatory, under the Name of the Court of Lords' Delegates*, London, 1808 (Bowring, v. 55–60).

Scotch Reform
Théorie des Peines et des Récompenses
Works not sent, being out of print and not procurable.
An introduction to the Principles of Morals and Legislation, printed in the year 1780, and first published by J Bentham Esqr of Lincoln's Inn, London Printed for T. Payne and Son at the Moor Gate 1789.
A Fragment on Government.—

2146

From Étienne Dumont

12 November 1811

J'avois bien espéré, mon cher Bentham, vous voir avant mon départ pour Ashdon—mais je n'ai pas osé entamer vos matins et je n'ai pu disposer d'une soirée—

Dr Roget[2] a quelque intention de faire un cours de *lectures* sur la Jurisprudence médicale—*scientific evidence*—il a posé les grandes bases—mais il désire beaucoup, avant d'aller plus loin, de vous consulter—Ce seroit un complément du grand ouvrage—Ce qui lui manque le plus, c'est la connoissance de *cas* qui aient été dans les Cours de Justice, et qui fassent sentir l'utilité de cette doctrine et son application.

Je viens de Holland house—il n'y a pas une petite nouvelle politique—le livre de Trotter est plein d'intentions méchantes et perfides[3]—heureusement le talent de nuire n'a pas été égal à la volonté—j'ai appris nombre de choses sur le personnage qui font preuve de mauvaise tête et de mauvais cœur. Une des causes de son irritation contre les amis de Mr Fox, c'est qu'on lui a refusé de chasser Trail de son emploi pour le lui donner.[4] Il croyoit que tout étoit dû à un Secrétaire de Mr Fox. Après avoir tiré mille livres St de Mrs Fox[5] et 300 de Ld Holland il écrivit à la première des injures atroces parce qu'elle lui refusoit de l'argent—etc etc

2146. [1] BL VIII. 556–7. Autograph. Docketed: '1811 Nov. 12 / Dumont Hay market / to / J.B. Q.S.P. / Inclosing Dr Rogets / Table of Medical Juris- / prudence.' Addressed: 'Jeremy Bentham Esq. / Queen Square Place / Westminster'. Partly-translated in Bowring, x. 467.

[2] For Roget see above letter 2031 n. 1.

[3] John Bernard Trotter (1775–1818), secretary to Charles James Fox (1749–1806), was the author of *Memoirs of the Latter years of C.J. Fox*, London, 1811.

[4] James Trail (1750–1809), MP for Orford 1802–6, was Irish under secretary 1806–8. For his earlier contact with Bentham see *Correspondence*, ii, iii, iv, v and vii, as index.

[5] Elizabeth Bridget Fox, née Blane (1750–1842), who had married Fox secretly in 1795. Their marriage had been revealed in 1802.

Je pars Jeudi matin—Si le Hay-Market étoit demain dans le circuit antéjentaculaire, nous pourrions causer un moment.

Adieu Tout à vous
Et. D.

Mardi

2147

From Lord Holland

18 December 1811

Holland House
Decr 18
1811

Dear Sir

I return you with many thanks your very curious and interesting paper from the perusal of which I have received much pleasure and instruction—There is no question but Names have great influence on Mankind and that those you object to are unlucky. It is however somewhat less certain that it is in the power either of Parliaments or Princes to change names and it is very certain that till the latter changes other things as well as names nothing that you or I could recommend for the conciliation of Ireland would be listened to with any chance of success—

With sincere hopes that you may long enjoy your health and pursue your interesting and useful researches I am

Dear Sir Your obliged friend and Servant
Vassall Holland

2147. [1] BL VIII. 562–3. Autograph. Docketed: '18th Decr. 18 / Ld Holland Holl. House / to / J.B. Q.S.P. / Delivered at Q.S.P. not / till 8 Jany. 1812. / Brith.' Printed Bowring, x. 467, where it is introduced: 'Among plans for producing greater harmony and unity of feeling between Great Britain and Ireland, Bentham proposed that the United Kingdom should be denominated *Brithibernia*.'

2148

To James Mill

[1811? (Aet 63?)]

Nothing can be more frank, more candid, more judicious, more honourable than Brougham's conduct; nothing more satisfactory than his accounts of it.

If, in his dealings towards my brother, Lord St Vincent had been fortunate enough to have Mr B. for his adviser, this favourite plan of his, supposing it capable of standing the test of examination, might have been saved from that opposition, and even that retardation at least, which it has been its destiny to experience.

2149

From Sir Samuel Bentham

4 January 1812

Portsmouth dk yd 4th Jany 1812

Taking for granted you would like to see Kirk[2] and hear from his own lips his account of the Petersburg Panopticon I have given him this note of introduction and as it seems desirable that he should see the *new mint*[3] being perfectly acquainted with that at Petersburg I wish somebody to give him a note to Mushet.[4] I have engaged K to make me drawings of Panopticon and to afford me assistance in other matters private as well as public though I have no hopes of my being allowed to engage him in the public service.

2148. [1] Bowring, x. 462. Introduced: 'In answer to a letter from Mill, suggesting inquiries into some subjects of naval reform, Brougham writes, that he fears Lord St. Vincent would not concur in Bentham's views, and that of Lord St. V. he had formed a high opinion.'

John Jervis, Earl of St Vincent (1735–1823) was first lord of the admiralty when Samuel Bentham was proposing his administrative reforms.

2149. [1] Koe MSS, in the possession of Mrs B. Hyde-Smith, The Old School, Balsham, Cambridgeshire. Autograph. Docketed: '1812 Jan. 4 / S.B. to H.K.' Addressed: 'Jery Bentham Esqr / Queens Square Place / or Mr Koe / Westminster'.

[2] The manager of the wooden Panopticon constructed on Sir Samuel's instructions at Okhta from the summer of 1807. See below, letter 2152 and M. S. Bentham, *The Life of Brigadier-General Sir Samuel Bentham*, London, 1862, p. 246.

[3] The new mint on Tower Hill was built by Robert (later Sir Robert) Smirke (1780–1867) between 1807 and 1812.

[4] Robert Mushet (1782–1828), third clerk at the royal mint.

I have received an interesting letter from Grellier[5] stating the appeal of Bridge[6] plan and furnishing further information. He could not find your chambers but will be in Town again from Sheerness on Tuesday. The proceedings relative to the Bridge are to be according to your wishes. Bukely[7] means to apply to me and G said that he [. . .?] a Committee will come to me when I come to Town. you may moreover urge the expediency of this application being made in the manner most desirable. The communications hitherto have been very confidential not only R's[8] plans but all his ⟨. . .⟩ are sent to me

2150

To Richard Wharton

21 January 1812 (Aet 63)

Sir

Understanding that, on the 24th of this Month in pursuance of an Order of the House of Commons at the instance of the Company formed for the building of the intended Vaux Hall or Princes Bridge, a Bill is to be brought in, having for its object (inter alia) the procuring powers for making some alteration in respect of the spot to be occupied for the purpose of the said Bridge, on and near the Bank, Milbank it is called, on the Middlesex side,[2]—in virtue of which powers if obtained, appropriation will be made of a part more or less considerable of the ground at Milbank aforesaid (53 Acres or

[5] James Grellier, Roman cement manufacturer of Millwall, who was to dine with Bentham in the following month (George Bentham to Lady Bentham, 28 February 1812, George Bentham papers, Linnean Society of London). He appears to have known Sir Samuel as a result of his contracts with the navy board (see letters 2237 and 2238), and at this time seems to have been seeking an agreement with the Vauxhall Bridge Company. See below, letter 2179 and n. 9.

[6] i.e. Vauxhall Bridge.

[7] An undated list of Vauxhall Bridge subscribers at UC cix. 330 includes Henry Buckley of Lawn, South Lambeth. He might be the Henry Buckley that appears in the trade directories as a floor cloth manufacturer of 161 Strand and later of Bridge Road, Lambeth.

[8] Probably John Rennie (1761–1821), the civil engineer specializing in bridge-building and dock construction, who was employed as the original architect for the Vauxhall Bridge. Rennie was a great rival of Sir Samuel, with whom he was to be at odds over various dockyard schemes for many years. See below, letter 2237.

2150. [1] BL VIII. 568–73. Pressed copy, in the hand of a copyist, except for the signature.

[2] On 24 January a petition from the Vauxhall Bridge Company was read in the Commons. The petition asked that the site of the road across Tothill Fields from the proposed bridge to Eaton Street should be moved about 100 yards to the east, through some buildings called the Pest Houses. See *Commons Journals*, lxvii. 71.

thereabouts) purchased Octobr 1799 by the Lords Commissioners of his Majesty's Treasury, for the purpose of the then intended Penitentiary Establishment—purchased viz: in my name and put in my possession in the character of Feoffee,—it appears to me to belong to my duty in that character to do what depends upon myself towards calling the attention of the present Lord Commissioners to the subject, for the purpose of humbly representing to their Lordships the opportunity, which is thus put into their hands of preserving that spot of ground from a *dismemberment*, by which its fitness, in relation to its intended purpose as above, could not but be subjected to very considerable diminution.

Under the powers already possessed by that Company in virtue of an already existing Act,[3] I understand it to be their intention, to carry the road, from the foot of the intended Bridge, in a direction, in which the effect of it would be to cut off from the above mentioned 53 acres at least 13: of which 13 a considerable part, being converted into the intended public road and that a very broad one, would leave the remainder in the state of a narrow *slip*, so compleatly separated and thrown to a distance from the 40 acres which on the other side of such road would thus be left, as to render it—though I should suppose not deteriorated in value with reference to any other use, yet very much so with reference to the use to which by the authority of their Lordships' predecessors in office and by virtue of an Act of Parliament (7 July 1794) it stands appropriated.[4]

What in relation to that spot is at present the intention of their Lordships does not lie within my knowledge: whether it be at present their determination to institute any such establishment, and if yes, whether the ground in question is meant to be appropriated to it, or some other ground obtained for it: in which latter case a natural consequence will be the making by authority of Parliament, some other disposition of the spot actually in hand.

But, even in this latter case, on the supposition that, perhaps, in their Lordships' view it might not seem proper so far to prejudge the pleasure of Parliament, as, for want of any lawful and proper exercise of their authority, to suffer the spot to be rendered comparatively unfit for the purpose, to which it stands as yet appropriated by Parliament, it seems to me matter of duty, to submitt to their Lordships' consideration, the information which the relation I bear to the land puts me in possession of; that by having it thus before them, they may be the better enabled to take any such measures as, to the purpose above-mentioned, the occasion may be considered as calling for at their hands.

[3] 49 Geo. III, c. cxlii (3 June 1809).

[4] Written in the margin: '34.G.3.c.84'.

If carried from the foot of the Bridge, for a short distance, in a direction parallel, instead of *perpendicular*, to the course of the river, the road, when it came to take the perpendicular direction, would be carried on the other side of the spot in question, in which case the abovementioned dismemberment would be avoided. In that case I know of no need there would be to take from the establishment any part of the spot, over and above what would be necessary to form the piece of road, running in a direction parallel to the river as above.—But even if, in addition to this, any part were taken from it, in a direction perpendicular to the course of the river as above, still so it might perhaps be, that only the *extremity* would thus be *pared off* (viz. not exceeding the amount of the breadth given to the road) and no part separated and dismembered from the main body, as according to the design now on foot.—

For preserving—not only from such *division* and *dismemberment*, but from all *defalcation* whatsoever, an establishment altogether *private*, viz. the pleasure-ground occupied by Mr *Elliot* with his *Brewhouse*,[5] a clause may be seen in the existing *Vauxhall-Bridge Act*:—and whether, to a spot of ground appropriated to an establishment of the public nature in question, equal protection at the hands of Parliament may not be due, is a question on which it rests with their Lordships to determine.

Having had the honour in April or May last to attend Mr Holford, then Chairman of the late *Committee on Penitentiary Houses*, and conduct him to the spot (Sir Evan Nepean, another Member of that Committee, being also in company) and having in my hand on that occasion (if I do not misrecollect) a sketch shewing in what place, for the purpose of the above-mentioned Bridge, the dismemberment was, as I understood, intended to be made, I at time took the liberty of calling their attention to the subject; and, both Gentlemen having at that time the matter in full view; and Mr Holford as I learn from the Votes of the House,[6] being one of the Members by whom the Bill now depending in Parliament in relation to the Penitentiary establishment, has been, or is to be, brought in,[7] I

[5] Elliot and Co., brewers, of Pimlico.

[6] Written in the margin: '11 Jany. 1812'. The 'votes' were issued daily. They constituted a record of the previous day's business in the House of Commons. Until 1817 they were as full as the account in the *Commons Journals*.

[7] The Penitentiary House Bill was ordered to be brought in by Holford, Francis Burton, and the home secretary, Richard Ryder. See *Commons Journals*, lxvii. 47. In essence the bill was the legislative enactment of the Penitentiary Committee Report. It formed the basis of 52 Geo. III, c.44, the Penitentiary Act, which authorized the construction of a penitentiary for convicts from London and Middlesex (but not on the Panopticon design) and provided for Bentham to be compensated.

would beg leave humbly to refer their Lordships to those Gentlemen, and in particular to Mr Holford, for any such account of the matter as, in their Lordships view, it may seem to require.

Considering how adequate the information is which is so compleatly not only at their Lordships command but at every moment within their reach, I should hardly have thought it incumbent on me, thus to attempt giving their Lordships any such trouble, but for the circumstance which in the hurry of more important business, might I thought, perhaps escape the attention not only of their Lordships but of Mr Holford: I mean that which, if I do not misconceive the matter, puts it in their Lordships power, if in their judgment the spot in question ought to be preserved from the intended dismemberment, to preserve it accordingly, viz. by refusing their concurrence, or if necessary and proper, by announcing their opposition, to the Bill about to be brought in as above by the Vauxhall Bridge Company, if the change requisite to save the spot from such dismemberment be not consented to on their part.

A map of the land in question lies at their Lordships command in the *Office of Woods* etc at Whitehall, and from that Office was, by order of the aforesaid Committee on Penitentiary Houses, produced, and submitted to the inspection of that Committee.

At the conclusion of this long address, I can not but beg leave to express my regrets, at the thoughts of the trouble which it seemed necessary for me thus to attempt giving to their Lordships and on their behalf, Sir, to yourself, being with all respect,

Sir,

Your most obedient Servant,

Jeremy Bentham.

R. Wharton Esqr.
etc. etc. etc.
Treasury.

2151
From Henry Rhodes

23 January 1812

Office of Woods etc
23d. Jany. 1812

Sir

My Lord Glenbervie[2] and the other Commissioners of His Majesty's Woods etc having had occasion to enquire into the Circumstances of the tenure of a piece of Garden Ground in the Bird Cage Walk Saint James's Park abutting southwards on the Houses in Queen Square Place Westr. now or lately in the respective Occupations of yourself and the Honble Andrew Cochrane Johnstone which piece of Ground extends from the North east angle of the recruit house to the north west angle of Mr. Bracebridge's[3] Premises, they find from the Documents relating thereto that many years ago Application was made by your late father first to Lord Orford[4] and afterwards to Lord Sandwich[5] for permission to inclose a part of the said park for the purpose of preventing nuisances to the two Houses before mentioned—And that on the subject of such Application much correspondence passed between your said father and the Officers who then had the superintendance of the said Park, the result of which was that permission was given by Lord Sandwich to inclose the piece of Ground in Question on your Father's undertaking to pay two Guineas a year as a rent or Acknowledgement of the right of the Crown and in which Arrangement he having signified his acquiescence, an agreement was entered into by him, of which the following is a Copy.

'Whereas I have, lately by leave of the King, inclosed at my own Expense a piece of Ground in St. James's Park lying between Queen

2151. [1] PRO CRES 24/6, pp. 332–3. Letter-book copy. Endorsed in the margin: 'J. Bentham Esqr. / Ground in St. James's / Park'.

Henry Rhodes was deputy registrar, land revenues office 1810–13. The offices of surveyor-general of the land revenues and surveyor-general of the woods and forests had been combined in 1810.

[2] Sylvester Douglas, Baron Glenbervie (1743–1823), surveyor-general of the land revenues and surveyor-general of the woods and forests 1810–14, previously surveyor-general of the woods and forests 1803–6, 1807–10.

[3] Abraham Bracebridge of 14 Queen's Square.

[4] George Walpole, 3rd Earl of Orford (1730–91), ranger of St James's and Hyde Parks 1763–83, ranger of St James's Park 1784–91.

[5] John Montagu, 4th Earl of Sandwich (1718–92), ranger of St James's and Hyde Parks 1783–4.

Square Gate and the Recruit House. Now I do hereby undertake and agree to pay for the same the Clear yearly rent of Two Guineas to the ranger of the Park for the time being Witness my hand this 10th day of Decr. 1783

(signed) Jereh. Bentham'

Witness
R. Burton[6]
Noon

And the Commissrs. having learned that the said piece of Ground which was occupied by your late Father under the above Agreement has been from that time to the present period in his or your own occupation or that of your Undertenants for which Occupancy no rent has hitherto been paid to the Crown, I am commanded by them to request that you will be pleased to pay the Arrears of the said rent—amountg. for 28 years computed from the date of the sd. Agreement to 10th of this inst. Decr. to £58 " 16 to the present Ranger of St. James's Park or to his Deputy within a Month from the date of this Letter. I am etc.

Henry Rhodes

To Jeremy Bentham Esqr.

2152

To George Holford

24 January 1812 (Aet 63)

Queen's Square Place Westminster 24 Jany. 1812.

In obedience to the Orders of the Committee of the House of Commons on Penitentiary Houses, requiring from me duplicates of certain works of mine that had been laid on the Table of the said Committee, on which the Book intituled Panopticon etc printed Ao 1791 was one, these three Plates as being referred to in that Book, are for the purpose of illustration transmitted along with it. But the plan of construction had afterwards received many alterations and it is hoped improvements, some of which were, at my House as above, visible, being rendered so by models, for many successive years; and

[6] Unidentified, but see *Correspondence*, ii. 194 and 203.

2152. [1] BL VIII. 574–5. Autograph draft. Docketed: '1812 Jan. 24 / Panopt. / J.B. / to / Holford / Quere if sent / Answer to his / Letter to Abercromby / asking for J.B.'s / Plans as to Penitentiary / House?'

actually seen by Members of both Houses of Parliament to the number of it is supposed of not less than 100: and of a plan of construction still posterior, a rough outline will be found in another work intituled *Preliminary Sketches relative to the Poor*[2] herewith sent.

Under instructions from my Brother Sir Samuel Bentham Commissioner of the Navy, an Establishment on the Panopticon principle, for educating and employing boys in a variety of trades subservient to the business of the Naval Department, was begun at Petersburgh during his mission there Ao 1807–8, and has since been not only finished, and employed with success, but copied in several other private as well as Government establishments in that Empire. Mr Kirk who till within these four months had the management of it is now in London.

Jeremy Bentham.

2153

From Thomas Beeby

24 January 1812

Sir

I am desired by the Chairman of the late Committee of the House of Commons on Penitentiary Houses to request you will send by the bearer the book intituled 'Panopticon' etc and also the other books referred to in your Evidence the same being continually wanted to refer to by the Members and should have been placed amongst the other papers but the only Copies that had been before the Committee were brought by Sir Evan Nepean and were again taken away by him last Session

I am Sir
Your most obt. hble Servt.
Thos. Beeby.

Ho. of Coms.
Friday Morning
24 January 1812

[2] A provisional title for what was to be published later that year as *Pauper Management Improved: particularly by means of an application of the Panopticon principle of construction*. See above, letter 2145 and n. 25.

2153. [1] BL VIII. 578–9. Autograph. Docketed: '1812 Jany 24 / Panopt. / Beeby. H. of / Commons / to / J.B. Q.S.P. / For duplicates of / J.B.s Panopticon / Works / Answered -and / Sent accordingly / 1. Panopticon. / 2. Preliminary Sketches / relative to the Poor'. Addressed: 'Jeremy Bentham Esqe.'

2154

To Thomas Beeby

24 January 1812 (Aet 63)

Queen's Square Place
24 Jany. 1812
10 o Clock A.M.

Sir,

It is with great concern that I find myself unable to pay immediate obedience to the pleasure of Mr Chairman as signified to me by your letter this instant received,[2] in relation to such books of mine as were laid upon the Table of the Penitentiary Committee. There is not any one of them of which at this instant I have a made-up copy, except that which I keep of necessity for my own use. In the instance of some of them I will send as soon as obtainable from the Bookbinders: but in one instance the copies have been rendered imperfect by the negligence of the printer in whose custody they were:—and how soon it will be possible to have them compleated it is impossible for me at this moment to say:—all that I can answer for is my best diligence.—

In the mean time it being acknowledged by your letter that a copy of each was transmitted by me—that it was laid upon the table—and by one of the Members of the Committee, viz the Gentleman who received it from me, taken from thence it seems scarcely necessary for me to suggest—and yet I know not how to avoid suggesting, the idea of making application to that same Right Honble Gentleman who I have not heard has yet left town, and who is frequently seen in the streets in his way to the India House.[3]

The works rendered imperfect as above are the *Two letters to Ld Pelham* and the *Plea for the Constitution* which three have been put up together in one—A thought that strikes me this instant is—that of the pamphlet thus composed a *perfect copy* was, a little before the sitting of the Committee, presented by me to Mr Secretary Ryder through Mr Under Secretary Becket, at whose hands I delivered it, and some time after, *another*, wanting, if any thing, nothing but the title page, to the said Under Secretary Mr Becket.—It will rest

2154. [1] BL VIII. 576–7. Copy. Docketed: '1812 Jany 24 / Panopt / J.B. Q.S.P. / Beeby. Ho of / Commons / In answer to his / of this date'.

[2] Letter 2153.

[3] Nepean was appointed governor of Bombay in 1812.

with Mr Chairman to judge whether, for the temporary deficiency a temporary supply might not at his instance, be obtainable from one of these quarters.

I am Sir
Your Very obedient Servant
Jeremy Bentham

Mr Beeby
Clerk in the House of Commons

P S. I have this instant had the satisfaction of lighting on a copy of each of the most material works which are accordingly herewith sent—Three plates which belong to Panopticon I will as soon as possible send by a Messenger of my own.

2155

From Wilson and Chisholme

27 January 1812

Sir,

In compliance with your request we beg leave to state that the intended alteration of the line of Road from the Vauxhall Bridge consists in taking the line from the present scite where the Abutment is built directly across in a straight line to the Pest Houses in Tothill fields instead of the old line which is a few yards further to the Westward

We have the honor to be
Your mo Obdt. Servts
Wilson and Chisholme

47 Linc. Inn fields
January 27th. 1812
To J: Bentham Esq.

2155. [1] BL VIII. 580–1. Autograph? Docketed: '1812 Jany 27 / Panopt. / Wilson Lincolns Inn / Fields / for Vauxhall Bridge / Company / to / J.B. Q.S.P. / What part is now proposed / to be taken from Ld / Salisbury's by the Bill / to be brought in 24 Feb. / 1812 / viz. the Road is now to run to "the *Pest House*".'

2156

From George Harrison

3 February 1812

Sir,

I am commanded by the Lords Commissioners of His Majesty's Treasury to desire you will transmit to me the Deeds of Conveyance of the Land at Milbank purchased of Lord Salisbury; and also the Declaration of Trust, if by a separate Instrument and not indorsed upon the Purchase Deeds

I am
Sir,
Your most obedt. Servt.
Geo: Harrison

Treasury Chambers
4 Feby. 1812
J: Bentham Esqre.

2157

To George Harrison

4 February 1812 (Aet 63)

Queen's Square Place Westmr.
4 Feby. 1812.

Sir,

I have to acknowledge the receipt of your Letter of this day's date, in which you say 'I am commanded by the Lords Commissioners of His Majesty's Treasury to desire you will transmitt to me the Deeds of Conveyance of the Land at Milbank purchased of Lord

2156. [1] BL VIII. 588–9. Autograph. Docketed: '1812 Feby. 4 / Panopt. / Secry Harrison Treasury / to / J.B. Q.S.P. / Requiring the Convey- / ance to J.B. / Answered Feby 4th / Mem. This letter / though by mistake / dated 4th was de- / livered on the 3d.' Letter-book copy at PRO T 27/69, p. 194.

2157. [1] PRO CRES 2/675. In the hand of a copyist, with the exception of the signature, valediction, and Harrison's name and address. Docketed: '4th Febry: 1812 / J. Bentham / on Treasury Lre requiring / of him the deeds of / conveyce. of ye land at / Milbank purchased / of Lord Salisbury. / No 1403 / Rd. 6th Febry: 1812.' Draft, part autograph, part in the hand of a copyist, at BL VIII. 586–7, docketed: '1812 Feb. 4 / Panopt / J.B. Q.S.P. / to / Secry Harrison / Treasury / Answering Harrison's / of this date demanding / Title Deeds of Ld Salisbury's'. Pressed copy of the letter sent to the Treasury at BL VIII. 590–1, docketed: '1812 Feb 4 / Panopt. / J.B. Q.S.P. / to / Secry. Harrison / Title Deeds'.

Salisbury; and also the Declaration of Trust, if by a separate Instrument, and not indorsed upon the Purchase Deeds.'[2]

Their Lordships' pleasure being in these terms signified, Sir, by you, and not by Mr Secretary Wharton, with whom, in the months of May and June last, I had the honour of a correspondence on this subject,[3]—what strikes me is—that, perhaps, at the time of writing this your letter, it had not happened to you to have been apprized of that correspondence, or of the result of it.

Of the deeds which your Letter has in view copies are already in possession of that Gentleman, the originals having at his desire been transmitted to him for the purpose of taking such copies, and by him returned.[4]—There being no such '*Declaration of trust*' as your letter speaks of, it is by this circumstance that I am led to suppose, that it is in your not being apprized of it that this application of your's respecting the originals has its cause.—

I have the honour to be,
With respect,
Sir,
Your most humble Servant
Jeremy Bentham

Geo. Harrison Esqr.
etc etc etc
Treasury.

2158

To Aaron Burr

9 February 1812 (Aet 63)

Q.S.P. Sunday 9 Feby
1812

If you do not come to day which would be still better, I hope sincerely and entreat you that you will come tomorrow: the rather as on Tuesday and Wednesday I am engaged at dinner time, though neither day in any such manner, as, after what I find has happened, your imagination many naturally enough be apt to suggest. Yesterday exhibited some whimsical coincidences, the explanation of

[2] Letter 2156.

[3] Letters 2123, 2124, 2129, and 2131.

[4] Letter 2127.

2158. [1] Historical Society of Pennsylvania, Philadelphia. Autograph. Docketed: 'J Bentham 9th Feb 1812' and 'J.B. 9 Feb. 1812'. Printed in Davis, ii. 325.

which, if you have not yourself, from the knowledge of my habits, anticipated it, will occupy three minutes by the watch, before the three other points set down by you for arguing—some of them of rather more importance than the coincidences, are brought upon the carpet.

2159

From Richard Wharton

12 February 1812

Mr Wharton presents his Compliments to Mr Bentham and requests he will have the goodness to transmit to him for the purpose of being copied, the Deed of Conveyance of the Milbank Property from the Marquis of Salisbury to Mr Bentham.

Treasury Chambers 12 Feby 1812

2160

To Richard Wharton

13 February 1812 (Aet 63)

Queens Square Place Westmr 13 Feby 1812.

Sir

I have to acknowledge a note of yours of yesterday's date, expressive of a desire to have transmitted to you 'for the purpose of being copied', the deed of conveyance of the Milbank Property from the Marquis of Salisbury to me.[2] The deed in question having on the 24th of May last been in obedience to your commands transmitted to you for that same purpose and returned to me on the 28th,[3] I am inclined to think that in the hurry of more important business that little transaction had at the time slipped your memory, and that on

2159. [1] BL VIII. 592–3. In the hand of clerk. Docketed: '1812 Feb. 12 / Panopt. / Wharton Treasury / to / J.B. Q.S.P. / For Milbank / Feoffment / Answered 13th.'

2160. [1] BL VIII. 594. Autograph draft. Docketed: '1812 Feb 13 / Panopt. / J.B. Q.S.P. / to / Wharton Treasury / in answer to W.'s of 12th requiring / Milbank deeds / for copying / Answer-Already / copied.' A pressed copy or duplicate in the hand of a copyist can be found at BL VIII. 595, docketed: '1812 Feb 13 / Panopt / J.B. Q.S.P. / to / Wharton Treasury / Milbank Deeds'.

[2] Letter 2159.

[3] Letters 2124 and 2127.

inquiry you will find a copy of the deed in question already taken and waiting your orders in the proper hands.

In answer to a letter of Mr Harrisons of the 4th instant on this same subject, I had occasion to make reference to my correspondence with you, as above.[4]

I have the honour to be, with respect
Sir
Your most obedient Servant
Jeremy Bentham

Mr Wharton Esq
etc etc. etc
I have before me the
receipt given to me
for it by Mr Charles Woodford.[5]

2161

From Charles Woodforde

14 February 1812

Mr Woodforde presents his Compliments to Mr Bentham, and begs to inform him that the Copy of the Deed in question is not now forthcoming. Mr Woodforde therefore at the instance of Mr Wharton requests that Mr Bentham will have the goodness to transmit it to him for the purpose of being copied.

Treasury Chambers 14 Feby 1812

[4] Letters 2156 and 2157.

[5] See letter 2124 n. 3.

2161. [1] BL VIII. 596. Autograph. Docketed: '1812 Feby:14 / Panopt. / Woodforde(C) Treasury / for Secry. Wharton / to / J.B. Q.S.P. / Asking for Milbank / Feoffment without / naming time for return / Answered same day— / sent the next—requiring / a person to be sent to / Q.S.P. to copy it / as per Wharton to / J.B. 23d May 1811'. Wharton's letter to Bentham is letter 2123.

2162

To Charles Woodforde

14 February 1812 (Aet 63)

Queen's Square Place Westmr. 14 Feby 1812

Sir

I have to acknowledge your note of this day's date,[2] in which, speaking of the deed which on the 24th of May you received from me, for the purpose of taking a copy of it and on the 28th returned to me, you inform me that '*the copy is not now forthcoming*:' and that 'therefore at the instance of Mr Wharton' you ask me 'to transmitt it to him for the purpose of being copied.' On that former occasion Mr Wharton having had the goodness at my humble request to name a particular day on or before which I might expect the return of it, I found so much cause for satisfaction in the punctuality with which that expectation was fulfilled, that, on receiving a similar assurance I was prepared, in the event of receiving any further command from him to that effect, to manifest on my part the same liberal obedience.

But considering that it is my *duty* to have *the original*, at all times forthcoming, and in readiness to await the pleasure of Parliament in that behalf, and observing from your note that some how or other the copy, which I suppose had been intended to be forthcoming, is not so, and considering that on that former occasion Mr Wharton in his letter written by 'direction' from their Lordships had the goodness to give me the option of two courses, either of which was by their Lordships considered as equally well adapted to the desired purpose, I take the liberty of here transcribing that passage from his said Letter—[3]

'or in case (says he) you should be unwilling to let the said Feoffment pass from your custody, that you will name an early hour in the course of to morrow when a person may attend from the Treasury at your House, and in your presence take a Copy of the same.'

Under these circumstances I would beg leave to submitt to him whether this latter branch of the alternative may not be most

2162. [1] BL VIII. 597–8. Autograph draft. Docketed: '1812 Feb 14 / Panopt / J.B. Q.S.P. / to / Woodforde Treasury'. A pressed copy or duplicate in the hand of a copyist is at BL VIII. 599–600, docketed: '1812 Feb 15 / Panopt / J.B. Q.S.P. / to / Woodford Treasury'.

[2] Letter 2161.

[3] i.e. letter 2123.

accordant with my abovementioned duty: and, if such should be his opinion, any day and hour that he will have the goodness to name for a person's calling here as above, I will take care that it shall be in readiness, and delivered to him, to be here copied at his leisure.

I am, Sir,
Your very obedient Servant
Jeremy Bentham.

Charles Woodforde Esqr
Treasury Chambers

2163
From Charles Woodforde

15 February 1812

Mr Woodforde presents his Compliments to Mr Bentham and avails himself of the mode suggested by Mr Bentham in his letter of yesterdays date.

The Bearer Mr Adrian[2] writes very quick and will copy the Deed without loss of time—

Treasury Chambers
15 Feby 1812

2164
From James Abercromby

18 February 1812

My Dear Sir—

The reasons which you assign for not sending the models of your Panopticon to the State Paper office are in my mind entirely satisfactory. You will perceive that Mr. Holford's application was limited to having a drawing of your plan at the Office, and of which he

2163. [1] BL VIII. 603–4. Autograph. Docketed: '1812 Feb 16 / Panopt. / Woodforde Treasury / to J.B. Q.S.P. / Sends *Adrian* to / Copy Millbank / Feoffment, in / consequence of J.B.⟨'s⟩ / of yesterday. / Adrian accordingly / is employed in copy- / ing it. Sunday 10[?] ⟨o'⟩ / -clock A.⟨M.⟩' Addressed: 'J. Bentham Esqr. / Queen Square Place'. Franked: 'Treasury'.

[2] T. Adrian was extra clerk to the treasury 1807–57.

2164. [1] BL VIII. 605–6. Autograph. Docketed: '1812 Feb 19 / Panopt / Abercromby Spring / Gard / to / J.B. Q.S.P. / About Holfords Letter / for Panopticon plans.' Addressed: 'J. Bentham Esq / Q. Square Place'.

appears to be in possession, but of this I am not certain. I should suppose that you will have no objection to his having the drawing if he has one, and if he has not one, perhaps you can furnish one without trouble. The suggestion of sending the model was entirely my own, and I seriously regret that those who are about to erect a penitentiary House have no sort of claim upon you, to afford them any assistance whatever. I hope therefore that you will discharge from your mind all Idea of giving either yourself or Genl. Bentham any trouble whatever about the models, and by a reference to Mr. Holford's letter which you have,[2] you will be able to judge what it is that he wishes, and also whether you have either the power or the inclination to gratify him.

I am sorry that I have given you so much trouble about this business and I return with many thanks the letter with a perusal of which you have so obligingly favoured me. I remain

Dr Sir
Yrs. Very faithfully
J. Abercromby

New St
Feby. 18th.

2165

To Aaron Burr

1 March 1812 (Aet 64)

Q.S.P. Sunday 1 March
1812.

Inclosed, according to your pleasure signified by your letter of yesterday's date[2] is a letter which was left this morning by a somebody, who expressed a desire that it should be transmitted to you either today or tomorrow. To *day* not affording any post, it shall, by the earliest hour be transmitted *tomorrow*.

Your secret, at least for any thing that I have ⟨. . .⟩ said or done remains inviolate: and shall so, ⟨. . .⟩ ⟨. . .⟩ would had your first intimation never been followed by anoth⟨er⟩ until you had thought proper to revoke the injunction.

[2] i.e. Holford's letter to Abercromby, mentioned in letter 2152 n. 1.

2165. [1] Boston Public Library, Boston, Massachusetts. Autograph. Addressed: 'To / Mr Arnot / 49. / Clerkenwell Close.' Postmark illegible. Adolphus Arnot was another of Burr's pseudonyms.

[2] Missing.

The letters you speak of shall be looked for, against we meet and I make little or no doubt of their being found.

We were disappointed at not seeing you last Wednesday according to the proposed appointment, of which, from your silence I inferred, as I [. . . ?] and I should, your acceptance. I invited on that day to dinner, half on your account, a man whom I thought you would like to see: In regretting your non-appearance, and expresing a strong *desire*, *ambition* I should have said, to see you, I invited him wholly on your and his account for the then next day. Unfortunately he was then engaged; and as he was about to set out forthwith for the country on his business—he being a man in much business no other day could for the present be found. My Brother and he had business: but ⟨. . .⟩ could have been no hindrance to you and me: we should have retired after dinner upstairs: leaving them below. Next Wednesday I shall expect you at dinner time, unless I hear to the contrary. I do not expect my Brother again, till the day after.

2166

From Sir Samuel Bentham

3 March 1812

March 3d 1812

Partly from an inability proceeding I believe from the change of weather and partly from being very unably [?] engaged in defending myself against Mr Grenfell's attack,[2] I seem totally [?] incapable of stating my case in regard to the relinquishment of Panopticon as I would wish and as I had formed an intention of doing. My assistant[3] being very unwell is nearly as incapable as myself so that what is now sent seems very unfit for the purpose but yet we determined something should go: I should hope that after the Bill has passed for

2166. [1] BL VIII. 607–8. Autograph. Docketed: '1812 Mar 3 / Panopt. / S.B. Hampstead / to / J.B. Q.S.P. / J.B.s Compensat⟨ion.⟩'

[2] On 22 February 1812, in a debate on the naval estimates, Pascoe Grenfell (1761–1838), MP for Great Marlow, stated that the copper-sheet lining manufactured by the navy's establishment at Portsmouth docks was of lower quality and higher price than the article available from private manufacturers. See *Parliamentary Debates*, xxi. 886–7.

[3] Lady Mary Sophia Bentham wrote in her biography of her husband that members of his family acted as his assistants, copying documents, making drawings, and so on. In 1809 family illness meant that Sir Samuel 'had no longer even a single clerk at his disposal'. Perhaps this was the situation in March 1812. See M. S. Bentham, *The Life of Brigadier-General Sir Samuel Bentham*, London, 1862, pp. 258 and 278.

giving the powers to compensate us for our loss opportunity will be afforded of urging our pretentions. Lloyd[4] and Burr[5] seem the fittest persons to be examined as to the profits that might have been made by those of my inventions which they actually practised. What is now sent must not be shewn to any one but it may serve to suggest what might be said on the subject.

2167

To James Abercromby

12 March 1812 (Aet 64)

Q S P 12 March 1812
Thury Eg

Dr Sir

Availing myself of your kind permission I trouble you with a few proposed Amendments with some words of explanation

Another Copy is already in the hands of Sir S Romilly[2]

Your much obliged
J B.

P S. Under the existing circumstances, you will not wonder that my endeavours should be confined to the points in which I am personally interested.

[4] John Lloyd.

[5] James Burr, draftsman in the naval works department 1796–1805. According to Lady Bentham, Burr (or Barr as she called him) was chosen by Sir Samuel 'not on account of any neatness or proficiency in drawing' but because he had served as an apprentice in a dockyard and 'had been for several years accustomed to working machinery of Bentham's invention'. *The Life of Brigadier-General Sir Samuel Bentham*, p. 118.

2167. [1] BL VIII. 611–12. Copy in the hand of a copyist. Docketed: '1812 Mar 12 / Panopt. / J.B. Q.S.P. / to / Hon. J. Abercromby / New Street, / Spring Gar⟨den⟩ / With Proposed A- / mendments to / Penitentiary Bill / -confined to J.B.⟨'s⟩ / personal interest'. The proposed amendments are missing.

[2] Missing. For Romilly's attempts to amend the bill on 20 March, see below letter 2170.

2168

To Lord Folkestone

12 March 1812 (Aet 64)

Q.S.P. 12. March 1812.

My dear Lord,

At the instance of Sir S Romilly I take the liberty of informing you from him that the *Penitentiary Bill* I mean the Commitment of it, will absolutely take place to morrow.[2] He has some curious circumstances to tell you in relation to it.

Mr Holford, Chairman of the Committee and author of the Report that passed sentence on Panopticon had the politeness to write me a letter on Thursday, Friday, or Saturday *last*.[3] (Romilly has the letter) informing me that the Commitment would take place towards the latter end of *this* week whereupon to the no small surprise of Romilly and others, it was set down for last Monday; but at the instance of Romilly Abercromby and others he found himself under the necessity of putting it off till tomorrow, as above. If a report that Romilly has heard speaks true, this Gentleman together with another who in the character of judge[4] were most active in the condemnation of the Defendant (to whom by the bye no opportunity of defending himself against the charge was allowed) are to put themselves in his place and be sharers in the forfeiture.[5]—If ever there were a political composition that lay open to compleat exposure it is surely that Report. But it is the opinion of the friends of the party injured by it, that it would be altogether unadvisable that either he or any of his friends in Parliament should attempt any

2168. [1] BL VIII. 609–10. Copy in the hand of a copyist. Docketed: '1812 Mar. 12 / Panopt. / J.B. Q.S.P. / to / Ld Folkstone / Duke Street Man- / chester Square / For him to be at / H. of. C. tomorrow.'

[2] Holford did indeed move the committal of the Penitentiary House Bill on 13 March. See *Parliamentary Debates*, xxi. 1292.

[3] Missing.

[4] Probably Charles Long, who was a member of the Penitentiary Committee. In letter 2108 Bentham described Long as 'Sitting over me as Judge to pronounce himself guiltless and me guilty'.

[5] In an article in the *Philanthropist*, v (1815), probably written by James Mill, it was pointed out (p. 133) that Holford 'is the person chosen, with very considerable emoluments, to be the superintendent of the new penitentiary. Of Mr Holford there is no ground that we know of to complain. But in the case of those who ruled the appointment, the choice of a man to sit in judgement upon a plan, who was to be disappointed of a great source of emolument by the execution of that plan, looks pretty much like a determination to see it set aside.'

opposition to it, because the success of any such opposition would be hopeless and neither power nor disposition was wanting to take a ruinous revenge.

Believe me with the truest respect
Your most obedt.
Jeremy Bentham

Lord Folkstone

2169

To John Reeves

21 March 1812 (Aet 64)

Q.S.P. 21 March 1812.
Saturday.

Dear Sir

I know not whether you have or have nor received any intimation of the unfortunate issue of the intended arrangement which procured me the honour of your acquaintance. The object of the trouble I am now giving you is—to beg the favour of your interposition for the purpose of obtaining from Miss C.[2] an account of the pecuniary damage which it has been or may be the means of subjecting her to, and to permitt me to pay into your hands the amount. My own entreaties to her have been without effect: and thence comes the necessity I find myself under of giving you this trouble.

Last Monday sennight the 9th instant I think it was—but the day is not material—Miss C. called upon me here: she came from Richmond she said, to see about the apartment and was about to return immediately or very soon. She found me immersed in the most disagreable and important business which called for instant despatch and absorbed all my time and thoughts. I said to her what was but too true, that my business with government (of the nature of which she had had a general intimation) seemed to be taking so unfavourable a turn that I was under the apprehension of seeing so much a year (I mentioned to her the exact sum) cut off from my income, upon which it would be utterly out of my power to continue

2169. [1] D. R. Bentham MSS. Autograph draft. Docketed: '1812 Mar 21 / J.B. Q.S.P. / to / Reeve Duke Street.' Reeves, besides being superintendent of aliens (see letter 2142 and n. 5), was a commissioner of bankrupts resident at 18 Duke Street, Westminster. Bentham had probably met him through Aaron Burr, with whom Reeves had become friendly during the American's stay in Britain.

[2] Almost certainly Amelia Curran, an Irish artist and friend of Burr and Bentham. See Lea Campos Boralevi, *Bentham and the Oppressed*, Berlin and New York, 1984, p. 27.

in this house: and that this was what I was making my mind up to, and planning matters accordingly. Oh then (cries she) there is no use in my going to look at the Pavillion—(this was the name she had christened the place by—) Nay says I pray do look at it—there can be no use in your not looking at it: and if I were obliged to quit my house it would not be immediately—my plan would be to continue in it for a year or some such matter (which in fact was one of various plans I was discussing with my friends). On this occasion very little if any thing more passed than as above: nothing that is any way material. On the subject of furniture in particular nothing was said on either side. Begging her excuse on account of the business with which I was pressed, I left her in the lower room to which I had come down from my upper room to speak to her; and whether she visited the Pavillion as I had begged of her to do I know not: she had been in the habit of vis⟨iting⟩ it she and her friends without seeing me.

On Tuesday the 10th instant, continuing under the same pressure of mind under which she found me and adverting to the circumstance of the furniture, I wrote to her a letter, a copy of which is here annexed:[3] The circumstance which occasioned my preserving a copy of it was—that, understanding from her that the times of her being respectively in town and at Richmond were altogether uncertain, and that she thought of quitting the lodging in Little Ryder Street in which I had seen her, and the direction she had given me for Richmond being to her at the Post Office and no otherwise, I thought it necessary to provide for the accident of its not reaching her there.

Under the abovementioned uncertainty instead of directing my letter to her at Richmond in the first instance I called on Wednesday the 11th with the letter in my pocket at Little Ryder Street; and was there informed that she had gone to Richmond, and was not expected to return to that lodging any more. The letter remained still unsent when I think it was the then next day Thursday the 12th my Brother being with me, and he and I about to sally forth that very instant upon some business which we were then in the discussion of, upon my stepping out of my upper room where we were into the next room my bedchamber to throw open the window, I saw Miss C. in the Park, upon the point of coming in at my gate. Catching her eye that moment I waved my hand to her, for the purpose of giving her to understand that that was not a moment for her and me to meet; which she understood accordingly and departed.

[3] Missing.

This was the circumstance alluded to in a letter of her's to me[4] which you may perhaps see. On my return from the business I was going upon with my Brother I sent off the abovementioned letter directed to her at the Post Office Richmond; having first broken it open, and inserted a postscript explaining to her the cause of what had just been happening as above: but of this Postscript I took no copy.

On Tuesday last the 17th I received from her the letter abovementioned in which she speaks of furniture adverting thereby though without express mention of the receipt of it to what I had said on the subject in my letter dated 10th and sent the 11th or 12th.

On Wednesday last (the 18th) it was that I had the pleasure of seeing you, and then it was that from the circumstance of your not having been applied to, I drew the inference (though I believe an erroneous one) that nothing very material had been definitively done in relation to that little business.

The day before Yesterday Thursday the 19th it was that Miss C. called upon me here. After the mutual enquiries and regrets that may be supposed, I begged to be informed how the business of the furniture stood (impatient as I was to relieve her from all solicitude on that score). All my entreaties were unavailing and then it was that I found (judge, Sir with what affliction and surprize) that by what I had said in my letter about the necessity of a temporary suspension—suspension only—it had been my misfortune to offend her, and to offend her past forgiveness. I was every thing that was bad. It had never been my intention, or at least for months past it had not been my intention that she should be there: what I had said to her about the apprehended catastrophe was a mere pretence. Yet, if so it was that she saw the Pavillion at the time when I begged of her so to do, she could not have opened the door without seeing the floor of the little Hall which I had improved—improved in her absence, and as it were by stealth, and in violation of a sort of promise which she had extracted from me that no addition should be made to that part of the expence which I had prevailed upon her to consent that I should take upon myself in lieu of the whole which of course belonged to me also she refusing to come unless I allowed her to defray the remainder in her own way.

This was but one out of several other similar proofs that I could have given of a sincerity which I little thought could have stood in need of proofs: and as to the story about the apprehended necessity of my quitting the residence and changing my plan of life it so happened that she was but one of several friends to whom I had

[4] Missing.

made the same communication, which is naturally not of the number of those which a man is fond of making without a very real apprehension of it even to the most intimate of his friends.

No: money she would not have howsoever strictly due to her: not even for the repairs which I had been forced to suffer her as above, to take upon herself: repairs done to my own house. What she would have was revenge! and that revenge was to consist in painting me to every body that would hear in those black colours which so justly belonged to me, for which purpose she gave me hints of a plan which she had formed.

A mere suspension, you will observe not an absolute dereliction of the arrangement was all that I had announced. In my letter it was all that I had announced, and for a very good reason, because it was all that I had contemplated as being for the present necessary.

But between the time of my writing that letter and the time of this our last interview circumstances had occurred which it would have been unpardonable in me to have concealed from her, and which when known to her could not humanly speaking have left any possibility of a wish on her part to persevere in coming here. A notion had spread itself in the neighbourhood a public house close to me and seven other houses of my own forming part of that neighbourhood—that I was going to keep a mistress: and that it was for that mistress that the Apartment was preparing. From what exact source or sources it had originated was without the reach of my observation: but the fact of the existence of such a notion had been made known to me by indubitable proofs. While with patient grief and astonishment and almost in silence I was enduring the storm the result of which was the declaration of an implacable enmity, I could scarce find an interval for or see any use in, making communication of this new aflicting circumstance. But after taking her departure and shutting the door, she had not been gone many steps when she entered the room once more I believe it was to express her astonishment at my patience. It then occurred to me that as matters could scarcely be made worse by any thing, it might possibly be a means of diminishing her disappointment if she were to find that the arrangement had been rendered incompatible with her purposes and wishes by incidents in the production of which I had no share, and which were out of the controul of both of us. I therefore took the opportunity of mentioning the circumstance, choosing brief and general terms in preference to details by which so far as they had come to my knowledge nothing but fresh afliction and irritation could be produced. Unfortunately in the state of mind the poor dear lady was in nothing was viewed[?] on that side in which irritation might be diminished by what presented itself to view, everything in this side in which it was encreased.

In the midst of all this distress the most astonishing circumstance was—the contrast between the hostility manifested as above, and the more than friendly disposition expressed in that letter of hers which was written as abovementioned after and in consequence of that letter of mine had been already spoken of, and which now lies before you. Upon my leaving this house, she had 'taken her resolution (she says) to follow me whither soever I might be going'—as if such a step supposing me to concurr with it could have been compatible with the preservation of that character which to her was matter of such anxiety, that, on the occasion of my habit of taking a walk every morning before breakfast she had been led (she had told me) by the opinions she had heard into a peremptory determination never on any such occasion to bear me company either without or even with a third person if of the male sex, at least till after a very considerable lapse of time. In that same letter there were many other expressions of attachment as much beyond my expectation as beyond my desert. It is too long to copy: but if you would favour me with an other call, any day after Monday, informing me of the time that I may be in readiness to attend you, I would shew to you as to her friend and as it were her guardian this mysterious letter and thus enable you to join your wonder and regrets to mine.

To my other regrets I have in conclusion to add that which is occasioned by the thought of the trouble I have been giving you by this unpleasant and tedious communication. It is a trouble I should scarcely have thought it of use to give you, if I had seen before me any other mode of doing what depends on myself towards acquainting myself of these obligations on the score of justice which I set out with stating to you.

Believe me to be, with the most respect and regard,
Dear Sir,
Your most obedient Servant
Jeremy Bentham

J. Reeves Esqr.
etc etc etc.

2170

From Sir Samuel Romilly

21 March 1812

Sat. Morng

Dear Bentham

I did for you yesterday as well as I could, not as well as I wished, but better than I expected. They agreed to alter the Bill to make it imperative on the Treasury to pay the Sum awarded within a Month after the award made and in the mean time to pay you the amount of the Rents which they understand to be 715 a year. They consented to insert in the bill the statement of the grounds on which you claim compensation in the words suggested by you. I am afraid however there may hereafter be found some difficulty in respect to the Interest which the Genl.[2] may have in the Compensn. The Speaker[3] to whom I mentioned the Difficulty thought it might be best to provide that the Compensation should be made to both of you and that the Genl shod. afterwards assign his Interest to you so that the Arbitrs. might make their award in favour of you only. Perhaps another way of enabling the Arbitrators to consider the Genls. claims in the Compensation to be made to you would be to insert in the Bill that Genl. Bentham had given up his Interest to you. in that Case I must be authorized for him to say that he is willing to do so.

Perceval is very willing to have the Arbitrators named in the Bill which I think extremely desirable for you I *believe* he will name Rose[4] on behalf of the Public and he wishes me to be prepared with the Arbitr. on your part by Monday. Who do you think of naming? Will Ld Folkestone accept it and is there any objection to him.

Whatever alterations or additions are to be made should be ready on Monday as the Report is then to be received.

Ever most sincerely
Yours
Saml Romilly

2170. [1] BL VIII. 613–14. Autograph. Docketed: '1812 Mar. 21 / Panopt. / Romilly Russel Sq / to / J.B. Q.S.P. / this [?] [. . .?] / on the Commitment of Bill / last night.'

[2] Sir Samuel Bentham.

[3] Charles Abbot.

[4] George Rose (1744–1818), at this time MP for Christchurch, vice-president of the board of trade, and treasurer of the navy. As secretary to the treasury 1784–1801 he had been in frequent communication with Bentham regarding the Panopticon scheme. See *Correspondence*, iv, v, and vi, as index.

2171

To Sir Samuel Bentham

22 March 1812 (Aet 64)

Q.S.P. Sunday afternoon 22 March 1812.

Just come from Romilly's. By his advice your presence is necessary here to settle a matter of form in relation to the Penitentiary Bill. It comes on again tomorrow: and what is done must be sent to the House at the sitting of the House viz. at four.

But any time before that hour will suffice. Meantimes I have still the form to settle.

There is a strong talk of a change of Ministry, and of a dissolution of Parliament. Great Opposition dinner at Ld Lansdowne's[2] today. Romilly one. But it is clear that rather than take in the Opposition the P.R.[3] will try to make up a Ministry with Marquis Wellesley Canning and Huskisson. Percevals credit so sunk in the Country but more particularly in the City by the bad success of the measure for funding Exchequer Bills that it is thought he can not go on in any way. Parliament to be dissolved in expectation of finding a new one more Anti Catholic. Perceval afraid in that case of taking in the Sidmouths[4] for fear of what the Methodists and Dissenters to whom Sidmouth is so obnoxious may do in the Elections.[5]

In the House t'other night Lord Grey declared positively that Opposition would not come in without the utter destruction of 'secret influence' (Lady Hertford[6] etc.) Therefore if they do come in, the Prince will be in a state of the most abject nullity and subjection.

2171. [1] BL VIII. 615–16. Autograph. Docketed: '1812 March 22. / JB–SB'. Addressed: 'To / Sir Samuel Bentham'.

[2] Henry Petty, 3rd Marquis of Lansdowne, chancellor of the exchequer 1806–7. He had been abroad with Dumont in 1801–2. See *Correspondence*, vi and vii, as index.
vii, as index.

[3] The Prince Regent.

[4] The followers of Henry Addington, 1st Viscount Sidmouth (1757–1844), speaker of the Commons 1789–1801, first lord of the treasury 1801–4. Sidmouth was soon to become lord president in Perceval's administration, and shortly afterwards, on the construction of Liverpool's ministry, he served as home secretary 1812–21.

[5] In the previous year Sidmouth had introduced a bill requiring all dissenting ministers to be licensed and restraining unlicensed preachers. The bill was thrown out by the Lords on its second reading.

[6] Isabella Anne Ingram-Seymour-Conway (1760–1836), the second wife of Francis Ingram-Seymour-Conway, 2nd Marquis of Hertford (1743–1822). For many years she exerted great influence over the Prince Regent.

2172

From Aaron Burr

30 March 1812

Off Deal, March 30, 1812.

We came to anchor here on Saturday. The wind being from the S.W., we must remain here till it shall please to change. I am a little dissatisfied with the levity with which you have put in circulation some of my very trifling letters, particularly the first which I wrote you after leaving London on my visit to Edinburgh. That was eminently a letter fit only for the eye of the most indulgent friendship.[2]

I must again beg that that letter, and also that which I wrote you from Paris,[3] be returned. Any letter or parcel for me may be sent to Mr. Graves, whose punctuality may be relied on. Transmit me a list of the American books you possess, that I may avoid sending you duplicates.

A. Burr.

2173

From Francisco De Miranda

2 June 1812

Head Quarters,
Maracay, 2d June, 1812.

My Dear Sir,

I hope the day is not far distant, when I shall see the liberty and happiness of this country established upon a solid and permanent footing. The appointment I have just received, of Generalissimo of the Confederation of Venezuela, with full powers to treat with foreign nations, etc,[2] will perhaps facilitate the means of promoting the object I have for so many years had in view.

Miranda.

2172. [1] Davis, ii. 379–80.

[2] Probably letter 2020, *Correspondence*, viii.

[3] Missing, but perhaps 30 December 1810. See letter 2098.

2173. [1] Bowring, x. 468.

[2] Miranda was appointed 'general in chief of the soldiers of the Venezuelan Confederation' on 23 April 1812.

2174

From James Mill

c. 5 June 1812

By what I learned from Sharpe[2] on Wednesday, at Ricardo's, I look upon a Whig Ministry as certain. Marquis Wellesley having found it impossible to form an Administration, resigned the task,[3] when it was transferred to Lord Moira; and on Wednesday, at five o'clock, Lords Grey, Grenville, and Wellesley, met at Lord Moira's.[4] Since that time, I know nothing, except that there was no account of this in the papers yesterday. But the certainty of the fact, that Lord Moira is the former, makes an equal certainty, I think, of the Whigs being the material with which the formation will be accomplished,—Wellesley and Canning to be included. This being the case, I cannot imagine but that your proposal about Panopticon—namely, along with their penitentiary house—will be immediately assented to; at least, after the reasons which you can so easily give them. In truth, I suspect Panopticon will bar the way to Devonshire as a residence,[5] and should the Whigs come in, as supposed, I suspect you will hardly feel easy at the idea of being away, till you know what is to be done with you. It is a maxim in politics, says De Retz, '*que l'absent a toujours tort.*'[6]

2174. [1] Bowring, x. 468. Reprinted in Bain, pp. 118–19. Dated from internal evidence.

[2] Richard Sharp (1759–1835), at this time MP for Castle Rising. He was known as 'Conversation Sharp'.

[3] The newly-formed Liverpool government resigned after an address calling on the Prince Regent to secure an efficient administration won a majority in the Commons on 21 May 1812. Wellesley was asked to form a ministry but, unable to win the support of the opposition, he announced his failure to the House of Lords on Wednesday 3 June. See *Parliamentary Debates*, xxiii. 333.

[4] It seems that Mill had been misinformed on this point. Moira met Grey and Grenville (but not Wellesley) on Saturday 6 June, and not, as Mill believed, on the Wednesday before. Moira was no more successful than Wellesley in reaching agreement with Grey and Grenville, and on Monday 8 June Liverpool and his colleagues resumed office. For Moira's interview with the opposition leaders on 6 June see Historical Manuscripts Commission, *Report on the Manuscripts of J.B. Fortescue, Esq., preserved at Dropmore*, 10 vols., London, 1892–1927, x. 286–7.

[5] An indication that Bentham was already seeking a new summer retreat: his efforts were eventually to bear fruit with the renting of Ford Abbey, near Chard.

[6] Jean François Paul de Gondi, Cardinal de Retz (1614–79), French churchman prominent at the time of the *Fronde* of 1648–53. His *Mémoires* were first published in 1717. The phrase appears to be a French proverb, although most authorities cite Philippe Néricault-Destouches (1680–1754) as the first to use it in a literary work. It appears in his play *L'obstacle imprévu ou L'obstacle sans obstacle*, I. vi, first performed in 1717 and published in Paris in the following year.

2175
To Lord Sidmouth

13 June 1812 (Aet 64)

Queen's Square Place
Westmr. 13 June 1812

My Lord

Observing in Yesterday's papers that the Office of Secretary of State for the Home Department is now filled by your Lordship; and it having been my lot for these twenty years and more to bear a sort of relation, in some inefficient and unfortunate shape or other, to the business of the Penitentiary Establishment, I write this to request the favour of a short audience—of your Lordship—I mean in person and not any substitute—on that and possibly another subject or two, at any time most convenient to Your Lordship, so it be before any step or resolution has been taken in relation to that business.

Being more in the habit of declining than seeking interviews with Ministers, and not at all in the habit of wasting words, I dare venture to mention ten minutes by the watch as the utmost quantity which I should attempt to consume, of an article so pretious to the public as Your Lordship's time.

I have the honour to be
with all respect
Your Lordship's most
obedient servant
Jeremy Bentham

Ld Viscount Sidmouth
etc etc etc.

2175. [1] BL VIII. 617–18. Copy in the hand of a copyist. Docketed: '1812 June 13 / Panopt / J.B. Q.S.P. / to / Ld Sidmouth / Secry for Home / Depart⟨ment⟩ / Copy / Original sent this / morning by Walt⟨er⟩ / Marked Private.'

2176

From Lord Sidmouth

13 June 1812

Whitehall.
June 13th. 1812

Lord Sidmouth presents his Compliments to Mr. Bentham, and will be glad to see Him at the Office of the Home Secretary at half past Twelve on Monday Morning.

2177

To Lord Sidmouth

20 June 1812 (Aet 64)

Mr Bentham to the
President of the United States
—Postscript to Lord Sidmouth.

Queen's Square Place,
Westminster, 20th June, 1812.

My Lord,

Your lordship's kindness having impounded the *brouillon* of my letter to the President of the United States,[2] as it were, in a state of nakedness,—apprehensive of the misconceptions to which, when viewed through that medium, the nature of the offer thus submitted by me to your lordship, may have been left open, by a conversation carried on, on my side, with the greatest rapidity which it was in my

2176. [1] BL VIII. 619–20. Autograph. Docketed: '1812 June 13 / Panopt. / Ld Sidmouth / Home Secretary / to / J.B. Q.S.P. / In answer to J.B.s of this / day / Visible on Monday 15⟨th.⟩ / Monday 15th went / accordingly—recei⟨ved⟩ / his promise to read / any thing I should / present, with his as- / surance that the sub- / ject was quite new / to him—that he / received no impressio⟨n⟩ / from any body — / never talked on the / subject even with / Bragge Bathurst.'

Charles Bragge Bathurst, for whom see letter 2120 n. 13, was a member of the Penitentiary Committee and Sidmouth's brother-in-law.

2177. [1] Bowring, x. 469–71. An autograph draft of the latter part of this letter (from the paragraph beginning 'What (I say once more)') is in the Watson Collection, MS 581, fo. 112, National Library of Scotland, Edinburgh, docketed: '1812 June 20 / Codification / J.B. Q.S.P. / to / Ld Sidmouth / under the title of / J.B. to Pres. of U. States / Postscript to Ld Sidmouth / Sent by Walter 21. June'.

[2] Letter 2145. Bentham had evidently provided Sidmouth with a copy or draft.

power to give to it,—I take the liberty of troubling your lordship with a few words of explanation, requesting that *this* letter may be added to *that other*, and considered as forming a sort of postscript to it.

1. What is *there* proposed to the President, as ready to be *begun*, or rather to be *continued*, is no less than what is there termed, for shortness, a *Pannomion*, a complete *body* of law, commensurate in its extent with the *whole field* of law.

What I should propose to your lordship, to call into existence for the purpose of the department over which your lordship now presides, is nothing more than a *Penal Code*: a proposed Penal Code *in terminis*, with a perpetual Commentary of *Reasons* (as per sample in the French book, Mr Dumont's[3]) and Observations, bringing to view all along, and under each head, the imperfections, or supposed imperfections, of the existing rule of action in its present state.

That you should pledge yourself for any such endeavour as that of *carrying into effect* so much as any the smallest part of it when produced, is more than I expect, or—But why do I say expect? It is more than, if it depended upon myself, I would suffer to be done.

That in some point of view or other, some sort and degree of approbation, as prodused by the opinion already before the public, would, in and by any encouragement given to the *continuance* of it, be unavoidably, if not expressed, implied, is more than I can take upon myself to speak of as questionable. But to that general sort of approbation there are not any imaginable qualifications, limitations, reserves, modifications, or exceptions, that would not, on my part, find a ready acquiescence; and when the thing is finished, if from the beginning of it to the end, there should not be a single proposition in it that you saw reason to approve of, you would be just as free to say so, as if you had not contributed in any way to the production of it.

In my own country, and in my own lifetime, the utmost I could expect of any body of proposed law drawn up by myself, is, that it should be received, and employed, and made use of in the character of a *subject of comparison*—a subject or object of comparison, capable, on occasion, of being referred to—referred to for good provision or for bad provision, for good argument or for bad argument, for approbation or for censure. The more insignificant the author, the more entire the freedom with which the work, in every part of it, might be, and would be cavassed. Here would be *a something* which would extend over the *whole field* of the subject, and which, good or bad, would, at any rate, have an existence and *a shape*.

[3] *Traités de législation civile et pénale*, ii and iii ('Principes du Code Pénal').

As to the existing Penal Code—but there *is* no existing Penal Code—(those fragments, those deplorably scanty, as well as frequently exuberant and throughout inadequately expressed—those perpetually incommensurable, never-confronted and ever-inconsistent fragments which are in the state of *statute law* excepted) existence cannot be predicated of it. Be it *law*, be it what else it may, that *discourse* which has no determinate set of *words* belonging to it, has no existence.

Excuse my freedom; but I would beg of your lordship to consider whether this be not that sort of thing from which, in your lordship's situation, a public man has something to *gain*—something, I mean, of course, in the shape of reputation, and nothing at all to lose.

Without expense to the public—without anything which, from any human being, can receive any such name as that of *a job*, on a subject of such importance, a work of such difficulty, brought out by the labour of the only individual in the country who has ever applied himself to the subject;—whatever there be in it that comes to be well spoken of—supposing anything in it well spoken of—Mæcenas, with his superior discernment and liberal views, gets, of course, the credit of: whatever there is in it that is ill-spoken of, Mæcenas washes his hands of it.[4]

Of one thing, I think, I can venture to give your lordship pretty full assurance, viz., that from *opposition*, anything done in this view, and, in particular, if coming from your lordship, would experience not merely a cold acquiescence, but upon occasion, openly and pretty extensively declared approbation and support; and I am even content to put the matter upon this issue, viz., that upon this point a sufficient assurance shall *previously* have been obtained. The grounds of this persuasion would require by far too many words for your lordship to be troubled with in the shape of black and white. But any time I am ready to submit them in the fullest detail, and with that confidential frankness which is so well suited to the subject, and of which, at the very first interview, your lordship's kindness set so encouraging an example.

Since the days of Lord Bacon,[5] the sort of offer I am making to your lordship is what has never, from that time to this, been made to any public man. This is as plain a truth as it is a known one; and in this, if there be anything of flattery at the bottom of it, it is a sort

[4] Gaius Cilnius Maecenas (*c.*70–8 BC) was famous for his patronage of learning and literature at the time of Augustus. Among his protégés were Virgil and Horace.

[5] Francis Bacon, 1st Baron Verulam and Viscount St Albans (1561–1626), philosopher, writer, solicitor-general 1607–13, attorney-general 1613–17, lord chancellor 1618–21.

of flattery which I am not ashamed to give, and which your lordship, I presume, will not be ashamed to receive.

Of the offer made in Lord Bacon's time, that great man, it is true, was the maker, not the receiver,—the receiver being an unwise king,[6] and not the less unwise for the neglect he charged himself with in not profiting by it.

When the object thus solicited for is neither more nor less than the faculty of taking up, for the remainder of life, a course of hard labour, without an atom of what is commonly understood under the name of *reward*,—in a word, without any reward but what is inherent in the nature of the labour itself, (supposing it to be followed with any effect,) and cannot be separated from it, your lordship, I am inclined to flatter myself, will join with me in the opinion, that the solicitation, should it even be deemed importunate, is not of that sort by which anything of dishonour would be reflected either upon the unofficial man who urges it, or upon the official man who should yield to it.

What (I say once more) is NOT necessary, is reward; but what, I cannot but confess is necessary—I mean in my own case—to the execution of the sort of work in question, is ENCOURAGEMENT, meaning by *encouragement, attention*; for the work when executed, assurance of attention, viz. on the part of the public, and to that end, in some shape or other, from office.

What your lordship has to consider is—whether it does or does not promise to be of advantage to the country, and thence to mankind at large, that a work of the sort in question, on the subject in question, by the hand in question, should be executed? Should your determination be in the affirmative, it will then be time enough to consider, in what *shape* the *encouragement* may most suitably be administered—I mean the assurance of attention afforded. This, however, is not a subject for writing, but for *vivâ voce* discussion, and on which I should have more to hear than speak—at least would more willingly hear than speak. One other thing, which your lordship may, perhaps, have to consider, is—whether it would be for the advantage of Lord Sidmouth's fame, that it should go down to posterity, that Lord Sidmouth, having it in his power to cause a work of the sort in question, a sample of which is in the hands of the public, to be brought into existence, and by that same hand, chose that it should *not* be brought into existence?

'But all this while, Sir,' (I think I hear your lordship saying,) 'if

[6] In March 1622 Bacon offered to draw up a digest of the law for James I, but Bacon's dismissal from office for bribery in the previous year had effectively debarred him from further employment by the court and made it impossible for the king to accept.

you really have any such strong desire for executing any such work as you speak of, what is there to hinder you?' My lord, I am perfectly able and willing to explain to your lordship what has hindered me—what does hinder me—and what continues to hinder me. But this is not a subject for black and white.—I have the honour to be, etc.

2178

To John Mulford

9 July 1812 (Aet 64)

July 9th, 1812.

Alack-a-day! how long a trial has your talent at deciphering been already put to! The two or three last pages at least might have been spared; but as you grow stronger and younger, your letters lengthen, while your handwriting improves; and although I should never learn to write as well as you do, though I were to keep on writing to the age of Methusalem,[2] yet I have always been your match in length. Moreover, since you have renewed your lease, your hand seems to have become clearer than it was when I had first the honour to become acquainted with it. What say you to the entering in one of the Inns of Court? In five years you might be called to the Bar, and in about fifteen or twenty years more might become Attorney or Solicitor-general, which would oblige you to come into Parliament: whereupon, in a few years more, you might pursue the track marked out by the late Mr Perceval, and become Minister; but, in that case, lest you should share his unhappy fate, let me recommend it to you, to listen to the voice of prudence, and insure your life.[3]

The member by whom this letter is franked, is the famous Mr *Brougham*—pronounce *Broom*—who, by getting the Orders in Council revoked, and peace and trade with America thereby restored, has just filled the whole country with joy, gladness, and returning plenty.[4] He has been dining with me to-day, and has but

2178. [1] Bowring, x. 471–2. Partly reprinted, under the date 6 July 1812, in Bain, pp. 122–3 n. Bowring added to this letter part of another of a later date, the latter part of December 1812. This second letter is published here as letter 2199.

[2] i.e. Methuselah, who lived to be 969 years old. See Gen. 5: 21.

[3] Perceval was assassinated in the lobby of the House of Commons on 11 May 1812.

[4] The Orders in Council of 1807 had declared the ports of the French and their allies closed and made all vessels attempting to enter them liable for seizure unless they first called at a British port. The orders led to friction with the United States and were held responsible for the depression in trade. Brougham played a leading role in protests against them, securing the appointment of a parliamentary select committee of inquiry in March 1812. Two months later the government agreed immediately to withdraw the orders.

just gone. This little dinner of mine he has been intriguing for any time these five or six months; and what with one plague and another, never till this day could I find it in my heart to give him one—I mean this year: for the last we were already intimate. He is already one of the first men in the House of Commons, and seems in a fair way of being very soon universally acknowledged to be the very first, even beyond my old and intimate friend, Sir Samuel Romilly: many, indeed, say he is so now.

Sir Francis Burdett is still upon my hands, for a dinner he has been wanting to give me, any time these six weeks, offering to have anybody I will name to meet me. In real worth he is far below those others: but being the hero of the mob, and having it in his power to do a great deal of harm, as well as a great deal of good, and being rather disposed to do good, and, indeed, having done a good deal already, must not be neglected.

For society, I have to pick and choose amongst the best and wisest, and most esteemed men in the country, who all look up to me; and yet, having so much to do, and so little time left to do it in, I lead, in this my hermitage, a hermit's life—not much less hermitish than yours. You sometimes, I believe, read newspapers: which paper is it that forms your channel of communication with this wretched world? It will be some weekly one, I suppose: if any, the *Examiner*[5] is the one that at present, especially among the high political men, is the most in vogue. It sells already between 7000 and 8000. Cobbett also, who, through a powerful writer, is almost universally known for a vile rascal—has sunk from between 4000 and 5000, to no more than 2000: in pretty broad terms, he has been vindicating the assassination of poor Perceval, and recommending it for imitation! yet, even he has been, in many respects, the instrument of good; for so, of course, will the vilest rascals be, when they think they see their interest in it.

The editor of the *Examiner*—Hunt,[6] has taken me under his protection, and trumpets me every now and then in his paper, along with Romilly. I hear so excellent a character of him, that I have commissioned Brougham to send him to me.

The Marquis of Lansdowne is going this summer to the family seat at Bowood, in Wiltshire, for the first time since his coming to the title and estate. I am summoned to go and take possession of the apartment there, which, for these thirty years, has gone by my name; but this year I certainly cannot afford time, and others are not likely to be very abundant. Here, my dear Doctor, in hopes of

[5] A weekly periodical launched in 1808.

[6] James Henry Leigh Hunt (1784–1859), editor of the *Examiner* until 1821.

contributing to your amusement, have I been scribbling and scrawling to you as to a father, in confidence that you will not, on any account, let it go out of your hands.

2179

To James Mill

25 July 1812 (Aet 64)

Q.S.P. 25 July 1812 Saty.

You will not die the sooner for any thing I am going to say to you, nor for doing any thing which I may propose to you to do.

What is rather the most eligible result is that the cursed portion of your liver should be carried off to hell by the Great Devil for his own eating, leaving what there is good of it in its proper place, and that this operation having been performed before Wednesday next, on that day you should find yourself here as usual.

But if in the mean time any such thing as dying should happen to you (for we are all mortal!!!!) you having however between the act of such dying as aforesaid and the act of receiving these presents, time to make your *will*, (which to the purpose in question may be done by word of mouth but if you can not write it yourself better have it set down in writing and read to you) if you will appoint me Guardian to Mr John Stewart Mill,[2] I will in the event of his father's being disposed of elsewhere, take him to Q.S.P. and there or elsewhere, by whipping or otherwise, do what soever may seem most necessary and proper, for teaching him to make all proper distinctions, such as between the Devil and the Holy Ghost, and how to make Codes and Encyclopaedias, and whatsoever else may be proper to be made, so long as I remain an inhabitant of this vale of tears: after which— but this must remain for God's providence to determine and this, though written in Contemplation of your not coming, you may put into your will, if it be worth the trouble, notwithstanding your coming, as aforesaid.

It would be more classical and more according to precedent, to have me one of the young ladies for a wife: but as the eldest of them will not be ready for matrimony these dozen years, were I even there, some more eligible legatee for them must be looked out for.[3]

2179. [1] John Stuart Mill papers, Yale University Library, Autograph.

[2] John Stuart Mill (1806–73), James Mill's eldest son.

[3] Mill's eldest daughter was Wilhelmina Forbes Mill (1808–61).

In what Walter told you about Brithibernia[4] he omitted the most material part which was that Ld St Helens of his own motion said he would mention it to Lord Hertford.[5] No: not exactly so: it was of his own motion that he proposed mentioning it to another person for the purpose of its being mentioned by him to the Prince. Ld Hertford was my suggestion and approved of in preference to the other, but for particulars, of which there are various, reference must be made to our next merry meeting, whether it be in this world or the next.

Now were your situation in any proper and suitable spot of this planet of your's, I could between dinner and tea time come and sit with you, and help worship Mistrah,[6] and during the armistice of your arm, help whip Mr John Mill: but you would go a whoring after your own or other people's inventions.

If, being able to read you are not able to read any thing that requires the least degree of attention, now would be a time for reading Voltaire's History of the White Bull[7] which you have of mine. John's reading it to you would not do: there would be by far too much of it requiring, and not admitting of, explanation.

His Generalship is now in very good spirits fifteen shares is to be his fee.[8] Every Tuesday this House is to be converted by him into an office. Wednesday therefore will be the day for you. Next Wednesday is the day for signing and sealing every thing in form between Grellier and the Committee.[9] A negotiation commences this day with another Bridge, viz. the Southwark, that is to lead to Cheapside.[10]

[4] For Brithibernia see letter 2147.

[5] Hertford was lord chamberlain of the household 1812–21. For Lord St. Helens, an old friend of the Benthams, see below letter 2240 and n. 5.

[6] One of the chief gods of the ancient Persians; the supreme being in Sir Thomas More's *Utopia*.

[7] *Le Taureau Blanc* by François Marie Arouet de Voltaire (1694–1778) was published in 1774. In the same year Bentham's own anonymous translation appeared in print.

[8] Probably a reference to Sir Samuel Bentham's business dealings with James Grellier.

[9] Grellier was about to reach agreement with the Vauxhall Bridge Company to supply Roman cement for the masonry construction originally envisaged by the designer John Rennie.

[10] The Southwark Bridge was built to Rennie's design between 1814 and 1819.

2180

From James Mill

28 July 1812

July 28th, 1812.

I am not going to die, notwithstanding your zeal to come in for a legacy. However, if I were to die any time before this poor boy is a man,[2] one of the things that would pinch me most sorely, would be, the being obliged to leave his mind unmade to the degree of excellence, of which I hope to make it. But another thing is, that the only prospect which would lessen that pain, would be the leaving him in your hands. I therefore take your offer quite seriously, and stipulate, merely, that it shall be made as good as possible; and then we may perhaps leave him a successor worthy of both of us.

2181

From John Stuart Mill

28 July 1812

My dear Sir,

Mr. Walker[2] is a very intimate friend of mine, who lives at No. 31 in Berkeley Square. I have engaged him, as he is soon coming here, first to go to your house, and get for me the 3d. and 4th. volumes of Hooke's Roman history.[3] But I am recapitulating the 1st. and 2d. volumes, having finished them all except a few pages of the 2d. I will be glad if you will let him have the 3d. and 4th. volumes.

I am yours sincerely
John Stuart Mill.

Newington
Green,
Tuesday 1812.

2180. [1] Bowring, x. 472–3. Extract. Reprinted in Bain, pp. 119–20.

[2] John Stuart Mill. See letter 2179, to which this is a reply.

2181. [1] BL VIII. 621–2. Autograph. Docketed: '1812 July 29 / John Mill, Newington / Green / to / J.B. Q.S.P. / For Hooke Vols 3 and ⟨4⟩'. Addressed: 'Jeremy Bentham Esq. / Queen Square Place / Westminster.' Printed in *The Earlier Letters of John Stuart Mill 1812–1848*, ed. Francis E. Mineka, 2 vols., Toronto, 1963 (vols. xii and xiii of the *Collected Works of John Stuart Mill*), i. 3. Tuesday was 28 July, not the 29th.

[2] Unidentified.

[3] Nathaniel or Nathanael Hooke (d. 1763) was the author of *Roman History, from the Building of Rome to the Ruin of the Commonwealth*, 4 vols., London, 1738–71.

2182

From Leigh Hunt

31 July 1812

37. Portland Street
31st. July 1812.

Sir,

I beg you to accept my best and most respectful thanks for the publications you have sent me, and for the promised invitation that accompanies them.[2] The approbation of the good and wise has always been one of the highest rewards, which my ambition, in its' most sanguine moments, has held out to itself; and when to that is added the cordiality with which you advance to shake hands with me, I have nothing to do but to be delighted.—Pray, Sir, do not take me for a mere enthusiast who deals in words; but excuse the warmth with which I speak, for the sincerity with which I feel.—Your call will find me ready, whenever you are at leisure; and in the mean time, I shall endeavour to gain all the information from your present, which my unwarrantable ignorance on the subject requires.

Your obliged and obed. servant,
Leigh Hunt

Jeremy Bentham Esqr.

2183

To Leigh Hunt

7 August 1812 (Aet 64)

Queens Square Place
Westminster Friday eveng
6 Aug. 1812.[2]

Sir

On Wednesday next, should that day happen to suit your convenience, ⟨. . .⟩ ⟨. . .⟩ I would beg to be informed, ⟨. . .⟩⟨. . .⟩⟨. . .⟩ glad of the pleasure of ⟨. . .⟩⟨. . .⟩ any, to a Hermits dinner, at this

2182. [1] BL Add. MS 38,523, fo. 11. Autograph copy. Endorsed: 'Copy of my answer to Mr. Bentham's letter'.

[2] Missing.

2183. [1] BL Add MS 38,523, fos. 13–14. Autograph. Addressed: 'To / Mr Leigh Hunt.'

[2] Friday was 7 August.

my Hermitage. At ½ after 5 it is commonly upon table; but if it suits you to be here at 5, rather before than after, I should be glad to take a stroll with you, for the intervening half hour.

Between the gate that opens into Queen's Square from the Bird-cage-walk and the *Barracks*, you will see a low fence, with a gate in it that opens into a garden. Entering at that gate, you will see before you an *iron* one, with a bell to it, which you will ring.

Very truly Yours
⟨Jeremy Bentham⟩

Mr Leigh Hunt

2184

From Leigh Hunt

10 August 1812

37. Portland Street—Bedford Road
Monday Morng. 10th. Augt. 1812.

Sir,

Owing to the absence of my brother[2] from home, and to an illness which prevented me from going to the Examiner office, your letter unfortunately lay there neglected till it was too late to answer it in the past week.[3] This must be my apology for the delay, and I am truly sorry to say, that the illness I mention must be my apology for not taking advantage of an invitation which I have so earnestly desired. When I wrote to you last, I was enjoying an interval from it, and hoped to be as prepared for your call as I wished to be; but the disorder,—a curious and foolish one, which has again attacked me after a cessation of some years,—returned and prevented me; and though I am now mending daily, yet it is by confining myself to such hours and modes of living, as make a man fit for no place but home, and hinder my appearance even at the table of a philosopher. Will you allow me to say however, that *after this week*—the time which I have allowed myself for recruiting,—I shall once more be anxious for your call, and that any day which you may chuse to name will be equally convenient, either next week, or the week after, or any other time;—only not very distant, I hope.—I would venture to name as early a one myself as possible, except that I do

2184. [1] Carl H. Pforzheimer Library, New York, L.H. 206. Copy, part autograph, part in the hand of a copyist.

[2] John Hunt (1775–1848), who founded the *Examiner* with Leigh Hunt.

[3] Letter 2183.

not know upon what arrangements I might be trespassing.—I only trust, that when I do come, you will have the goodness to consider me a hermit as well as yourself, and that you will dispose of my time, both before and after dinner, quite as your please. I am, Sir,

Very sincerely your obliged humble servt.
Leigh Hunt.

Jeremy Bentham Esqr.

2185

From Leigh Hunt

12 August 1812

37. Portland Street
Wednesday 12th. Augt. 1812.

Dear Sir,

(For so you must allow me to call you, after the kindness and cordiality of your visit en passant), I believe that in agreeing with the liberty I took to defer my dining with you till after *this* week, you mentioned that it should be some day *next*; but either you did not fix the day, or it has unaccountably slipped my own recollection. May I beg therefore to be informed by a line, when it is that I am to have the pleasure of waiting on you? I long, I assure you, to make my way to your 'hermitage', and to find how happy I can be there, in spite of your having barracks on one side, and Downing Street on the other.

Yours, Sir, most sincerely,
Leigh Hunt.

Jeremy Bentham Esqr.

2185. [1] Ogden MS. 76, University College London. Autograph.

2186

To Leigh Hunt

12 August 1812 (Aet 64)

Queens Square Place
Westmr Wedny 12 Aug.
1812.

Dear Sir

No—there was no particular day mentioned.[2] Satisfied with having engaged you, spite of nervosities, to be well by a *route* certain, I thought it would be bearing too hard upon ⟨. . .⟩ ⟨. . .⟩ ⟨. . .⟩ ⟨. . .⟩ ⟨. . .⟩ day was therefore left to providence, and therefore, if you or somebody or something else do not, what is so often done, thwart and disappoint its designs, the first wednesday in next week, being convalescent week, will be the great the important day in question: of which *Mr. Mill*—(and from description he is already not compleatly unknown to you) being sitting opposite me now at the time of the writing of these presents has received legal notice ⟨. . .⟩ ⟨. . .⟩ ⟨. . .⟩ ⟨. . .⟩ ⟨. . .⟩

2187

From Aaron Burr

27 August 1812

New York 27th Augt. 1812

You will herewith receive 'The Federalist' 2 vols.[2] and 'Graydon's digest of the Laws of the U.S.' 1 Vol.[3] being all that can now be forwarded—Though I was not charged with your list, yet, having reason to doubt whether it will be executed through any other

2186. [1] BL Add. MS 38,523, fo. 12. Autograph.

[2] See letter 2185, to which this is a reply.

2187. [1] BL VIII. 623–4. Autograph. Docketed: '1812 Aug 27 / Burr New York / to / J.B. Q.S.P. / P.U.S. Letter / Sends Federalist etc / Books requested'. Addressed: 'Jeremy Bentham Esquire / Queen-Square Place / Westminster'. Postmark illegible.

[2] *The Federalist: A Collection of Essays, written in favour of the New Constitution, as agreed upon by the Federal Convention, September 17, 1787*, 2 vols., New York, 1788. The principal author was Alexander Hamilton, who was assisted by James Madison and John Jay (1745–1829), American diplomat and statesman.

[3] A reference to William Graydon (1759–1840) and the first volume of his *An Abridgement of the Laws of the United States. Or, A Complete Digest of all such Acts of Congress as concern the United States at large*, 2 vols., Harrisburgh, Pa., 1803–13.

channel, I have assumed the task—I have not yet heard of the sort of reception which your letter met from Prest. Madison[4]—So soon as I shall be informed on that subject you shall know the result, unless I shall learn that a *direct* and satisfactory communication has been made to you—

I wrote you on ship-board, but though we were several days beating out of the Channel, had no opportunity of putting a letter on shore—my passage was, as usual, short and stormy—on the 6th. July I announced my presence, and my intention to reside, in this City and as yet I see no reason to doubt of my remaining here so long as I shall please or as it shall please God—The Philistines, having business enough of their own on hand, let me alone—

Whatever you may wish to send me must be left with W. Graves—I repeat my demand for the remaining letter which I wrote you from Scotland or on the way from London to Edinburgh and also for that written from Paris—[5]

I have returned this Evening from the Country and just now learn that the Packet will sail at 8 tomorrow Morning; and I have several letters of business to write—perhaps with a few hours of leisure I might have written you something more amusing—but a sad event has deadened all my faculties and spread a gloom over all my hopes and prospects—Theodosias boy, her only child is dead and I have much reason to apprehend that she will not long survive him —[6]

May God preserve you many years

AB

To be sent A.B—

The Book on Evidence[7]
Peines et Récompenses, both
in french and English[8]
'The fragment on Government'—Those who attend
auctions for you may pick up a Copy
Two or three of the Cancelled Copies of the 'Art of Packing'

[4] Letter 2145.

[5] See letters 2165 and 2172.

[6] Aaron Burr Alston (b. 1802) had died of fever on 30 June 1812.

[7] Presumably what was soon to be partly-printed as 'Introductory View'.

[8] Dumont's *Théorie des peines et des récompenses* was not available in English at the time of this letter. A translation (including fresh material from Bentham's MSS) appeared in the form of Richard Smith's editions of *The Rationale of Reward*, London, 1825 (Bowring, ii. 189–266) and *The Rationale of Punishment*, London, 1830 (Bowring, i. 388–525).

2188

From Lord Holland

9 September 1812

My Dear Sir

I received your very interesting packet both safely and cheaply some days ago and only deferred acknowledging it till I could obey your commands and give you my opinion on its contents[2]—The fact however is that I have been so occupied by what Dryden calls a cloud of little businesses[3] since my return from the country that I have had no time to bestow that attention on any work that all that comes from you deserves—Indeed I generally defer as much as I am able all reading on political subjects till the approach of Parliament and was therefore inclined to take the permission you give me and not to read the dissertation till the Month of October. In the mean while however I cannot but express my acknowledgements to you for this mark of your confidence though it is perhaps right to add that whatever may be the substance of your paper I am so situated as to make it not only difficult but actually improper for me to suggest any thing of a political nature to His Royal Highness the Prince Regent—

I am Dear Sir
with sincere respect
Your obliged Hble
Servant
Vll Holland

Hd House
Septr. 9

2188. [1] BL VIII. 626–7. Autograph.

[2] Missing.

[3] Holland was probably thinking of the use made by John Dryden (1631–1700) of the phrase 'flood of little businesses' in a letter of 7 November 1699, published in Edward Malone's *The Critical and Miscellaneous Prose Works of John Dryden . . . grounded on Original and Authentick Documents; and a Collection of his letters*, 3 vols., London, 1800, i. (ii). 92–3.

2189

From Richard Wharton

11 September 1812

Treasury Chambers
11 September 1812

Sir,

I am commanded by The Lords Commissrs. of His Majesty's Treasury to refer you to the Act of the 52d. George 3d. Cap. 44 for the Erection of a Penitentiary House for the Confinement of Offenders convicted within the City of London and County of Middlesex and I am to acquaint you that as Supervisors have been appointed in pursuance of the Provisions of the said Act Sect. 1.[2] the absolute Property in the Lands and Tenements purchased of the Marquis of Salisbury and Conveyed to you in 1796 has become vested in His Majesty by virtue of the said Act Sect.2.[3] their Lordships therefore desire that you will forthwith deliver to the Commissioners of Woods Forests and Land Revenues all the Deeds Muniments and Papers relative to or connected with the same for the use and behalf of the Crown.

I am
Sir
Your very obedient Servant
R Wharton

Jeremy Bentham Esqr

2189. [1] BL VIII. 628–9. In the hand of a clerk, except for the signature. Docketed: '1812 Sept 11 / Panopt / Wharton Treasury / to J.B. Q.S.P. / J.B. to give up all / Deeds and Papers.' Letter-book copy at PRO T 27/70, p. 33.

[2] At BL VIII. 630–3 there is an autograph draft of an intended letter to Lord Sidmouth, which is docketed: '1812 Sept. 11 / Panopt / J.B. Q.S.P. / to / Ld Sidmouth Secry / of State / Not Sent. / Written on receipt / of Wharton's Treasury / Letter requiring the / giving up the Deeds / to the Commrs of / Woods etc.' In this draft Bentham referred to Sidmouth's earlier commitment to give Bentham the opportunity to comment before any further steps were taken relative to the 'Penitentiary business' (see letter 2176 above), and expressed his disbelief that supervisors could have been appointed without Sidmouth's concurrence. In a postscript Bentham suggested that as he had found no mention of the names of the supervisors in any published official sources, 'in the mention made of supervisors in Mr Secretary Wharton's abovementioned letter, there may possibly have been a sort of *anticipation*'.

[3] The Marquis of Salisbury's land had been conveyed to Bentham in 1799, not 1796. 52 Geo. III, c.44 s.2 declared that as soon as the supervisors were appointed the land purchased by Bentham would become the property of the crown 'for the Use of the Public and the Purposes of this Act'.

2190

To Lord Sidmouth

17 September 1812 (Aet 64)

Queen's Square Place Westmr 17th Sept. 1812

My Lord,

Five tracts, begging the honour of Your Lordship's acceptance—all but the *first*, and in some sort the *third*, as yet unpublished—accompany this address:—dates when printed, 1778, 1791, 1797, 1802, 1803.[2]

To give commencement to that part of the history which concerns the *Panopticon* Contract, they are accompanied by copies of two letters, sent to the late Mr Pitt, and answered by acceptance, at the time and in the manner stated in my Evidence as printed in Report 28th of the Finance Committee of 1797–8:—dates, 23d Jany. 1791, and 10th Feby 1792.[3]

To these I was in hopes to have added copy of a short Note, received Ao 1778, on occasion of the tract of that date, from Sir W. Blackstone:[4]—a token, by which it would appear, that, no less than *four and thirty years ago*, in the opinion of that Judge, to which, were it not for the length of the communication, I might have taken the liberty of adding that of his then Collaborator, *Lord Auckland*,[5] my humble and unbidden labours, in this vineyard, were not altogether without fruit:[6]—in this vineyard, from which, after a most maturely considered acceptance, followed by no fewer than twenty years, occupied by an alternation of disappointment and lingering expectation, I have now—and without so much as the slightest suspicion of blame, or unfitness, in any shape—I have now, my

2190. [1] Sidmouth MSS, 152M/C 1812/OH, Devon Record Office, Exeter. Autograph letter, but enclosed 'Advantages' and 'Objections' relating to Panopticon are in the hand of a copyist. A copy of the letter (but not the enclosure) in the hand of a copyist is at BL VIII. 634–9. Part of the 'Objections' are printed in Bowring, xi. 159–62.

[2] Respectively *A View of the Hard-Labour Bill*, London, 1778 (Bowring, iv. 1–35); *Panopticon; or, The Inspection-House*, London 1791 (Bowring, iv. 37–171); the essays on 'The Situation and Relief of the Poor' that appeared in Young's *Annals of Agriculture* in 1797–8, reprinted as *Outline of a Work entitled 'Pauper Management Improved'* and published as *Pauper Management Improved*, London, 1812 (Bowring, viii. 361–439); *Letters to Lord Pelham*, London, 1802 (also known as *Panopticon versus New South Wales*: Bowring, iv. 173–248); and *A Plea for the Constitution*, London, 1803 (Bowring, iv. 249–84).

[3] Letters 738 and 833 (*Correspondence*, iv).

[4] See letter 248 (*Correspondence*, ii).

[5] William Eden, 1st Baron Auckland (1744–1814), had written to Bentham on 27 March 1778. See letter 239 (*Correspondence*, ii).

[6] Isaiah 5: 1.

Lord, been driven out, and unless restored by Your Lordship's justice, without redemption, with my name posted up in the title of an Act of Parliament,[7] in the joint character of a public burthen and a recorded outcast.

I was in hopes, I say, to have added the abovementioned little testimony, the remembrance of which, especially considering my antecedent combat with the departed Sage,[8] is, it may well be imagined, still cherished by me: but, for the present, I know not by what fatality, it has escaped my search. Should I ever be fortunate enough to recover it, I shall take the liberty of transmitting a copy of it by a separate address.

Another little *relick*, which I had been pleasing myself with the thoughts of adding, is a letter of similar brevity from *Lord Auckland*, written on the occasion of the *Panopticon book*, in or some little time after the year 1791.[9] In it would be seen an example of the sort of return, which, from minds such as his Lordship's, may be made, for the freest and closest controversy, when tempered by that respect, to which, in that instance both objects were in so superior a degree entitled. Though some of the terms in his Lordship's letter still vibrate in my ear, I can not for shame pass them through a pen of my own, any otherwise than in the tenor of a copy, which, should it be my good fortune ever to recover the original, will accompany that of Sir W. Blackstone's.

With the good *Howard*[10] my friendship which, at his instance, was produced by the abovementioned tract, and at the time of his last flight was warm and encreasing, has left behind it no written traces, unless it be an inscription or two in those works of his which he gave me.

Of the notice, which, in the *28th Report* of the *Finance Committee of 1797–8*, was taken of the Panopticon plan, and of its mysterious, and from first to last unjustified, and altogether unexplained delays, mention may here be added, *pro memoriâ*. On the late occasion that Report was reprinted.

The quantity of printed matter with which I am thus endeavouring to load Your Lordship's shelves is such as can not be thought of without regret.

But, the first of the printed tracts, as well as the Ms letters, are but matter of history: the use of them is—to shew by what sort of

[7] 52 Geo. III, c.44.

[8] A reference to *A Fragment on Government*.

[9] Letter 836 (*Correspondence*, iv).

[10] John Howard (1726–90), author of *The State of the Prisons in England and Wales*, Warrington, 1777.

inducements the author was led to the subject—what was the complexion of his mind—and what the sort of reception given to his labours by the candour and magnanimity of these Statesmen, in the discussion of whose productions he had allowed himself that latitude, which, in the first place the 'View of the Hard Labour Bill', Ao 1778 and then again the 'Panopticon' book, Ao 1791, will shew.

Perusing is one thing; *consulting* is another.—A *dictionary*—by the bulk of it, be it ever so great, the labour of consulting it is not encreased. In the instance of the tracts in question, with the exception of '*Pauper Management*' the labour necessary to consultation would, by the *running titles* be found reduced (I flatter myself) to little more than what has place in the case of a *dictionary*. Two things at the same time I can venture to state to Your Lordship: viz. that, of whatsoever matter is to be found in these works there is scarce a line, (architectural matter excepted) that does not, in some way or other appertain to the business of the department which is fortunate enough to find itself in Your Lordship's hands: and that, good or bad, there is little indeed, if there be any thing worth mentioning, the equivalent of which is to be found in any other published work.

After so many fruitless laws and other acts of government, as, in the course of twenty years passed in hot water, it has been my misfortune to give birth to, reduced as I am to the condition of a suitor, Your Lordship has not hitherto found in me an importunate one.

Relying with the most implicit confidence on the assurance which on the 15th of June last, Your Lordship had the goodness to give me, that, in relation to the Penitentiary business no farther step should be taken till the opportunity had been given me of being heard, and that too in black and white, coupled with the still more obliging and encouraging assurance, that up to that time Your Lordship's mind was in the state of blank paper on the subject, never having conversed on it so much as with Mr Bragge Bathurst,[11] I should not have been thus troublesome even now, but for the necessity, and on the occasion, of the transmission of these papers.

The business having so happily found its way into hands such as Your Lordship's and Mr Vansittart's[12] (Lord Liverpool will scarce find any time I suppose, to bestow upon it) now that these papers are also in these same hands, I may hope to be understood, when

[11] See letter 2176 n. 1.

[12] Nicholas Vansittart (1766–1851), later 1st Baron Bexley, chancellor of the exchequer 1812–23. Bentham had already corresponded with Vansittart while the latter was joint secretary to the treasury 1801–4. See *Correspondence*, vi, as index.

speaking of my hopes as susceptible of the following gradations—

1. That on perusal even of that *Report*, which had no other object than the setting of the Panopticon plan aside, (First Penitentiary Report Ao 1811) no sufficient reason for taking so extraordinary a step will be found.

N.B. Notwithstanding the late Act (52 G.3.c.44) Government remains as fully at liberty *to give execution to* the *Contract* authorized by the Act of 1794, as *to rescind* it: and, under an existing clause in an existing Act 39. G.3.c.114.[13] £24,000 of the £36,000 therein ordered to be paid to me by name remains due.

2. That if, for the producing of this saving determination, the contents of that Report should not be deemed sufficient, the requisite satisfaction may however be produced, by the perusal of what relates to the subject in the *28th Report of the Finance Committee* of 1797–8.

3. Should *that* too prove insufficient, in that case, and in that case only should I, on my own account, have any need to wish to give Your Lordship any such trouble, as that of looking into any part of the mass of printed matter herewith sent: and in regard to this, it would be matter of some surprize to me, if, of the *Observations*, such as they are, which, in the *recent Report* abovementioned, bear relation to this business, there be a single one, which, in some part or other of these *unnoticed*, tho' called for and delivered papers, would not be found to have received a compleat answer, *before* it was penned.

4. In this particular, should my expectations likewise fail me, in that case, and in that case only it is, that I should beg to be indulged with a full hearing as to all points, unless it were Your Lordship's pleasure to select for that purpose one or more in particular, with an intimation that if, in relation to the points so selected, satisfaction should be afforded, it would be deemed compleat.

5. Should even this hope fail me, then it is that—irksome as would be the task to me—more gratingly irksome than any person would readily be able to imagine—I should deem it necessary to submitt, in the first instance to Your *Lordship*, and in the last instance to *Parliament* and the *public* at large, a compleat examination of the *grounds and reasons*, by which, in that same Report, the propriety of rescinding the Contract in question, depriving the pub-

[13] 'An Act for granting to His Majesty a certain sum of Money out of the Consolidated Fund; for applying certain sums of Money therein mentioned . . .'. The granting of £36,000 to Bentham is provided for in s.22.

lic of the benefit of it, and breaking the public faith, for so many years plighted to me, has been endeavoured to be supported.

Under the idea that, possibly, at the expence of a few more pages scrawled at present, not only a much greater portion of my own time may be saved, but some portion even of a time so much more valuable,—now that the pen is in my hand, I will venture to subjoin in this place, an indication, as brief as I can make it, of some of the topics on which I should have to touch.[14]

A circumstance indeed that renders it indispensable is the occasion I have to make reference to a document, viz. the Estimate of the *Building expence*, £259,725,[15] which has been given in since I had the honour of attending Your Lordship, as well as to submitt to Your Lordship, on my own part, some *eventual offers*, which it seems necessary for me to make, that neither any personal *interests*, nor so much as any *rights* of mine, may ultimately stand in the way of the public Service.

Giving up the contract—giving up all personal emolument giving up all permanency of situation—consenting, so it be after a public hearing, to be dismissed at any time at pleasure—consenting to accept of less than half the land—such are the offers now submitted to Your Lordship, such the offers, which, at an early period—I do not recollect exactly how long, before the fate of the *Contract* was pronounced, my Parliamentary friends were requested by me to make. A copy of the paper put into *their* hands for that purpose is still in *mine*.

No such offers were however made. So inflexible, (it was found), was the determination, to give effect, at any price, to the mysterious resolve, fixt in exalted darkness for these twenty years—so irrevocable the sentence of annihilation, that, for causes unspoken and unspeakable, had, in some inexorable black book, by some invisible hand, been written opposite to my name—so subordinate were all considerations, of justice as well as economy, to the duty of carrying that sentence into effect—such was the peremptoriness of these resolves, such the temper that had grown up under them, that the mention of any such offers would (I was given to understand) be altogether hopeless: the only probable effect of it being the produc-

[14] Printed here immediately after this letter.

[15] This refers to the letter from Thomas Hardwick (1752–1829), surveyor and architect of Berners Street, London, to the supervisors appointed under 52 Geo. III, c.44 to arrange the construction of a penitentiary on the Millbank site. Hardwick's letter, with an abstract of the cost of building a penitentiary, was ordered to be printed by the Commons on 27 June 1812 and appears in the 'Miscellaneous Papers' volume of the *House of Commons Sessional Papers* for 1812.

ing a degree of exasperation, whereby any engagement for compensation, (including restitution of sacrificed property) might either not be entered into, or, if entered into, share the fate of the original one.

Spite of all endeavours to compress it, this address has already swelled much beyond the bounds, which in prospect were assigned to it.

A query or two, which I would beg leave humbly to submitt to the joint consideration of Your Lordship and Mr Vansittart, may serve to close it.

1. Not only in a prison, but in every other place, in which human beings are intended to be kept under rule, *want of inspection* is the undeniable, and even acknowledged, cause of every thing that is amiss:—and still, my Lord, is an *uninspectable* prison to be preferred to an *inspectable* one?

2. As to the *prison itself*, is it sufficiently clear, that by being rendered in the first instance inspectable, it would, in case of *inconvenience* resulting from such inspectability, be thereby rendered *incurably unemployable?*

3. Admitting that this would be the consequence, the effects of an *unlimited faculty of inspection* are they, in prospect, so *pernicious*, that it would be worth while to bestow at this time *£200,000* public money, as above, on the exclusion of it?

As to the *once-appointed Jailor*, is it sufficiently clear, that, before the service could be rid of him, so prodigious would be the mass of mischief done by him, that £200,000 paid to a certainty and in advance, besides some number of years postponement of the intended reformation, and all hope, of addition to be made to the reforming establishment on the same matchless spot, foregone, *plus* the amount of the by-him-ever-abhorred compensation-money, *plus* the recorded breach of public faith, would be worthily employed in securing the country against the *possibility* of it?

I have the honour to be, with all respect
My Lord,
Your Lordship's
most obedient Servant
Jeremy Bentham.

Queens Square Place Westmr.
17 Sept. 1812.

Lord Viscount Sidmouth
etc etc etc.

P.S. Before this reaches Your Lordship's hands my direction will be

Barrow Green House Oxted Surry; where I propose to remain till the first week in November, subject of course to any summons from Your Lordship.

[Enclosure]

1. Advantages obtainable by the making experiment of Mr Bentham's Panopticon Plan, accompanied or not with the suspension of the now intended Non-Panopticon plan.

I. Saving in the article of *capital*, expended antecedently to the commencement of the service.

Upon the now proposed number of 600 certainly not so little as— £200,000[a]

Expence of the Non-Panopticon plan would probably not be less than £400,000—But say no more than— £300,000

Expence, as per Panopticon plan would not be as much as— £100,000[b] See next page[16]

Minimum of saving thereupon as above— £200,000

II. Saving in respect of *time* consumed, antecedently to the commencement of the service— Years—4.

£30,000 and no more having been provided for the expenditure of this first season, the consequence is—that if this rate were continued, then, although the total expence were no more than £300,000, the time consumed would be *ten* years. True it is, that in the future years, when the building season would be entire, the pace of expenditure would be less slow: but at the rate which has been customary in public works, it can hardly be set down at less than 5 years even exclusive of the now current year.

Upon the Panopticon plan, the establishment might, and would, be compleated in *one* year. Witness *Drury Lane theatre*.[17]—Upon an establishment of this kind the allowance of a sum any thing near so large as £300,000 within the space of one year would naturally be grudged.

It might not be grudged, if the £300,000, were reduced to £100,000.[c]

[16] i.e. the next page of the original MS.

[17] Rebuilt in the course of 1812, after earlier rebuilding in 1662 and 1674. A theatre had been on the site since the reign of James I.

III. Saving in respect of the dead *annual* expenditure, composed of *Official Salaries.*

Under this head, the proportion of saving would be found to be at least equal to what it would be under the head No 1. See my Letter to the Penitentiary Committee, Ao 1811, as printed in the Appendix to their First Report.[18]

IV. On the Panopticon plan, supposing the experiment *satisfactory*, the advantage of being able to make provision for the whole convict population, with such graduality of progress as may have been indicated by experience, upon this same spot of *ground*; which, for vicinity to the seat of supreme inspection, is altogether matchless.

On the Non Panopticon plan, any considerable addition seems not to be looked upon as capable of finding sufficient room: and, by the expence, and proposed rate of progress, is, *in intention*, plainly enough thrown to an infinite distance.

N.B. Suppose the experiment of the Panopticon plan *unsatisfactory*, still the expence bestowed upon it would not be lost. For its being, the whole of it, exposed to inspection at one view, there is surely not any part of the covered space that would be in any respect the worse. If it were, there is no difficulty in putting an *end*, to the *inspectability*, whatever may have been the ingenuity necessary to the securing the *existence* of it.

The experiment of the *Panopticon* plan might thus be made, not only *without retarding*, but in such sort as even to *expedite* the *Non Panopticon* plan.

Suppose the *Panopticon* plan to have been tried and proved *unsatisfactory*, the subsequent advance of so large a sum as would be necessary for the *Non Panopticon* plan, would be the less grudged. What would otherwise have occupied five years or more as above, might be effected in two years, added to the *two* occupied (suppose) one of them in the setting on foot the Panopticon establishment, the *other* in affording the supposed experimental proof of it's unfitness.

II. Objections to the making experiment of Mr Bentham's Panopticon Plan obviated: viz. partly by Answers partly by fresh Offers.
Objection 1. You will overwork them, (it has been said,) You will *underfeed* them, (those by the underfeeding of whom there is any thing to be gained,) you will *overfeed* them, (those by the overfeeding of whom there is any thing to be gained) you will pamper them with '*luxuries*', you will work them so that you will not leave time

[18] Letter 2110.

for their receiving any sufficient 'religious and moral instruction'. (Report. pp. 13.14) Ao 1811.[19]

Answer 1. No tolerably intelligent man, howsoever selfishly disposed, would do so in my place. This is what I had pleased myself with the thoughts of having made tolerably clear, and used to be considered as having done so. viz. in and by the *Panopticon* Book, herewith submitted to Your Lordship. Part II S. 2. intituled '*Management Why by Contract*:' from which place Honourable Gentlemen have taken all their *objections*, forgetting to say any thing about the *answers*.[20]

2. As to *underfeeding* them, by the terms of the Contract, I stand bound to give to each man as much as he can eat.

As to luxuries, I really do not understand what there is that can, so it be paid for, be stated as a *pernicious* 'luxury', unless it be *fermented liquors*, which by the contract, *at my own solicitation*, I stand precluded from giving admittance to,—and with such securities against contravention, as had never before been so much as imagined.

Offers. But, if any Honourable Gentleman in whose view of the matter, an '*Index Expurgatorius*' of meals and drinks, would in the situation in question, be an article seriously subservient either to religion or morality, will be pleased to frame one, and obtain the requisite orders, I am ready to pledge myself for its being inviolably observed.

3.—As to the neglecting their 'religious and moral instruction', I should forfeit all my pledges—I should incur reproach by such neglect, and I could not get any thing by it: for I could not work them on a Sunday, without a positive breach of the law of the land, such as, to persons in abundance, besides the prisoners themselves, could not but be of the utmost notoriety.

4. I would humbly entreat Your Lordship's perusal for at least *that* section, together with the antecedent one entituled '*Leading Positions*':[21] the rather as being applicable to *Poor-House* as well as Prison Management.

5. My Brother and I had a favourite Sunday Plan, for the combining *religious edification*, with *public inspection*, and the most perfect and

[19] i.e. *First Report from the Committee on the Laws Relating to Penitentiary Houses. Ordered, by the House of Commons, to be printed, 31st May, 1811.*

[20] *Panopticon: Postscript, Part II*, s. ii (Bowring, iv. 125–34).

[21] ibid. x. (Bowring, iv. 121–5).

universal *facility of complaint*: and the architectural design was, in a most striking manner, adapted to it; as shewn in the *models*, which were seen by Members of the Upper House by dozens, and by those of the lower House by scores.

Ere I could have suffered that feature of the management to fall into neglect, my character must have been compleatly forfeited.

6. (Offer. 2). Taking an unknown—taking an *average* man, were I to give it as my opinion, that he would conduct the business, as much for the advantage either of the *public* or the *prisoner* for a *salary*, or *without* any pecuniary remuneration, as upon the terms of the Contract proposed by me, I should utter a gross untruth. But, after the perusal of these two sections, should this matter present itself to your Lordship's mind in a different light,—to cut up all such objections by the roots, *there should be an end of the contract*, I would conduct the management on account of the *public purse*, without a farthing's worth of pecuniary profit in any shape, direct or indirect,—keeping and regularly delivering in accounts, upon the plan indicated in my work intituled *Pauper Management* (herewith submitted)[22] with any additions or other amendments that may be prescribed to me.

Objection 3. Under Your Contract, you were to have had no fewer than 1000 Prisoners: all worked under your *direction* and for your *advantage*.—This is too great a *power* to be trusted in any individual hand.

Answer 1. In *specie*, It is no greater nor other power, than what, by the law of the land, every *Master* has over his *Apprentice*.

As to the *number*, the *power*, so far from being encreased, is, as to all purposes of *abuse*, lessened by it. Except his own particular relatives, or other friends, where he is fortunate enough to have any, an *Apprentice* has no person engaged by any special tie of *interest* to look to him with a protecting eye. *My Prisoners* would, by the common and most obvious tie of *interest*, as well as bond of *sympathy*, stand engaged to afford, to one another, *this* as well as whatsoever other assistance could be afforded, against *oppression* in every shape, at the hands of the common *master*: and, as to persons without-doors, *each* would, accordingly, have so many friends, in the friends of every *other*.

[22] *Pauper Management Improved*, London, 1812, pp. 99–112 (Bowring, viii. 391–4).

Answer 2. In so far as concerns *sinister profit*, this objection would, together with the preceding ones, be cut up by the roots, by the *giving up of the Contract*, as above.

Answer 3. Independently of all consideration of sinister profit and danger of abuse on that score, can it be, that the magnitude of the power, merely in respect of the *number* of persons subjected to it, is considered as being so great, as to constitute of itself an objection and that a peremptory one?—A Colonel of a Regiment has as much or more.

Answer 4.—If, numbers being the same, this objection, taken from a supposed excess of power, were conclusive against the *Panopticon* plan, how much more ought it to be against the now proposed *Non-Panopticon* plan!

Under the *Panopticon* plan, behold the management in the hand of an *unseated*, *unofficed*, *unconnected*, insulated, individual; whose blameless life, known to have been for little less than half a century devoted to a course of unpaid, yet unremitted, howsoever fruitless toil, in the service of mankind, has not been able to preserve his rights from being an object of neglect, and himself an object of silent oppression, to every Administration for these last eighteen years.

Under the *Non-Panopticon* plan, the management in the hands of a *detachment of the Ministry*, rendering no account but to their *assured protectors*—the body from which they have been detached. Who is there who does not know, or will think it worth while to affect not to know, that in all these cases the whole power is in the hands of some *one* individual, in whom the *confidence* is reposited, and that, of an assortment of *colleagues*, who, to each other, are *a tower of defence*, the use in this respect is—by dividing, and by dividing, dissipating, the *responsibility*, to *encrease* that *power*, which in demonstration they are employed to *reduce*?

What is very true is—that, if the prison were a den of *Cacus*,[23] so that no mischief, which, for the benefit of the tyrant, were done in it, could be *known*, the security, afforded by his being liable to be dismissed for it *if known*, could not be very effective.—

But that this should be urged, as an objection, against *the only*

[23] A fire-breathing monster and brigand of Roman legend who lived in a cave on the Aventine hill, where he hid oxen he had stolen from Hercules. See Virgil, *Aeneid*, viii. 190–267.

plan, which ever had for its *declared* object the *maximum of publicity*, and in proof of the superior wisdom of a plan, in which, neither in *that* nor indeed in *any degree*, publicity is so much as *professed*, seems not very consistent.—

In the one case one tyrant devil, working in impenetrable darkness, in the other a company of Guardian Angels—such is the supposition, on which, though not *declared*, every thing in the Non-Panopticon plan is all along *grounded.*

Objection 4. You may *profess* to desire inspection, and to court gratuitous inspectors; but in these professions of yours either you *are* not sincere, or if you are you *will* not long be so; and, though you should be ever so much so, you might as well be otherwise,—for nobody will come.

Answer 1. On this head at least, as to my sincerity, present and future probable, after what I have said in my *Panopticon* book, (to compare *minute* with *great*, *obscure* with *illustrious*)—with submission, it would be less unreasonable to impute, to *Your Lordship*, a desire to see *Protestantism extirpated* and Catholicism towering in its place,[24] than to impute *to me* the possibility of harbouring any such idea as that of shrinking from inspection.—Your Lordship *has not* professed any such *invention* as that of an *engine* for the *universalizing of Protestantism* in the Christian World: *my Brother and I* have, for these twenty years and more, professed to have invented *an engine* for the *universalizing of inspection* in a Penitentiary House.

Answer 2. *Offer 3.* True it is that if, in numbers sufficient for the purpose, after all that were done to invite them, people would *not* come—let this be *supposed*, all my *sincerity*, and all the *exertions* of which it can be productive, would be to no purpose.—Well then my Lord;—if my schemes for making people come should all *fail*, insomuch that after all people do *not* come,—in short if, in the opinion of the appropriate Judges (—say the King in Council) although no abuse actually appears, yet, *for any thing that appears to the contrary*, there *may* have been abuse, then, and in this case, let the experiment, howsoever free from blame on my part, be pronounced to have *failed*; and, on that ground, let me be dismissed, and, if such

[24] Sidmouth was well known for his staunch opposition to Catholic relief: this had been the primary reason for his replacing Pitt as first minister in 1801. His last recorded speech in the Lords (April 1829) was against Catholic emancipation.

be the pleasure of the said Judges, let my said supposed universal inspection Plan be put aside; and, *for remedy*, let the plan in which *general inspection* is *not* aimed at or so much as professed, be set up in its stead.

Objection 5. Well, Sir, if you please, you *yourself* shall be a '*well meaning*' man;[25] and not only for the moment, but as long as you live: and, for the purpose of the argument, even under so corruptive a plan as yours is, an *honest manager*: all this will not make your *plan* a good one. You live, to commence, and for a time carry on the management:—be it so. Sooner or later however there is an end of *you*: and then, whatsoever be the security afforded by our 'personal character',[26] there is an end of *it*.

Answer 1. If, before the building is finished, *I* die, there is my *Brother*, on whose plan, if *for me*, and in *my life time* it will be built: if, before that time, *he* dies also, there are *others* in this Town, under whose directions a building on this same plan was lately compleated, viz. at Petersburgh, and the management of a correspondent establishment conducted, and to whom the advantages of it are accordingly well known by experience: nor, for the *management*, would there be any want of persons, to whom the principles of management detailed in the Panopticon book, and the book entitled *Pauper management* (herewith submitted) are already familiar, and who are perfectly competent to the purpose of applying them to practice.

Answer 2. If, for a moment, any such supposition be endurable, as that, in my management there can be any thing worth copying, and preserving, the nature of the case affords as good a security as can reasonably be desired, for its being accordingly copied and preserved.

Yes, my Lord, if *I* am what I *ought* to be, such as *I* am, such will my *successors* be. My *rules*, my *practice* according to those rules, will be *public*: public as I, and the *press* and *open doors*, can make them: the moment they cease to be so—I say as before, out with *me*. Being public, what there is *good* in them will be as so many *laws* to my *successors*: or, if they are *not* so—the fault will lie not in *me* and *my* successors, but in Your Lordship and *your* successors:—whenever to any successor of mine it happens to swerve from these (by the supposition) good laws, out with *him*.

[25] Written in the margin: '*best intentions* Rep. p. 13'. This and the following of Bentham's marginal notes refer again to the *First Report* of the Penitentiary Committee.

[26] Written in the margin: 'Rep. p.13.'

True it is, that, by wearing out so many years as have been worn out, of a life of which four and sixty are already past, Honourable Gentlemen have given to this argument of theirs a degree of force, as well as to some other of their arguments and expedients, beyond what *I* could have wished:— and, seconded by such treatment as it has been my lot to experience at their hands, and to which, unless stayed by the intrepidity of Your Lordship's justice, this last measure will have given the crowning stroke, the chances of life and death were certainly in favour of the plan, so perseveringly pursued, for ridding the powers of high seated darkness, of the incumbrances: for already (as may be seen by the calculation, printed in Report 28th of the Finance Committee of 1797–8)[27] it has been my lot to live several years more than according to the Tables I *ought* to have lived. Yet still, considering the counter consideration above submitted, this argument will not, I hope, be found to have so far accomplished its purpose, as to be, in *Your Lordship's* account, a conclusive one.

Answer 3. *Offer 4.* On the *Non-Panopticon* Plan, what the spot of *ground* is, that is deemed requisite for the 600 Prisoners, I do not know. On the Panopticon plan, in case of necessity, I could make less than half what there is, serve for the experiment. On that supposition, should there be also a sufficiency for the Non-Panopticon system, the two could be carried on together.

Here then, if the honour of Honourable Gentlemen could be reconciled to the idea, the benefit of *competition* and *emulation*, a benefit to which, in some cases (for example, that of the highest Courts of ordinary Justice)[28] no small value has been ascribed, might be given to the service.

For my own part, in so far as, all consideration of the public and the prisoners being put out of the question, I myself am alone concerned, were *I* to choose my competitors, I know not of any whom I would more gladly choose, than the Honourable Gentlemen, with whose company in that quality I should, in that case, be likely to be honoured. *Their* desire, to be rid of *me*, can scarce be stronger, than *mine* would be to possess, *in that shape*, the benefit of *their* assistance: and, though my general character were as noted for *insincerity*, as it may perhaps be for the opposite failing, in the present instance my sincerity would be put sufficiently out of dis-

[27] *Twenty-Eighth Report from the Select Committee on Finance, etc. Police, including Convict Establishments. Ordered to be printed 26th June 1798*, p. 81 (Appendix H).

[28] An allusion, presumably, to the competing jurisdictions of the king's bench and courts of common pleas and exchequer.

pute, by the *Observations* which in case of necessity I should have to make on their *Report*, and the plan of management which it has served to introduce.

Objection 2. As, upon your plan, by night as well as by day, several males will co-exist in the same apartment, irregularities of the sexual appetite will, without any wilful neglect on your part, unavoidably take place. Therefore for 600 prisoners, for night residence alone there can not be fewer than 600 separate apartments. Answer 1. If I do not, at any time, make it plain to the satisfaction of the appropriate Judges, *on their view of the spot*, that, in my Panopticon, consistently with moral *probability*, no such incident can be at the time in question, deemed to *have* taken place, or ever be about to take place, let me, though it were on that *sole* ground, be dismissed.

NB With Honourable Gentlemen this I am well assured was the grand argument relied upon and employed, at least in whispers and significant looks, against Panopticon, and the system of economy dependent on it. For, in what manner soever men are grouped in the day time, (all violence and attempt to escape being precluded by actual and unremitted inspection), what possible objection, unless it be *this*, can there be to the *sleeping* hours being passed in the *same groupes*?

Why in an unremittingly inspected prison more than on board an uninspected apartment in a ship?

At *sleeping* hours, in the way of *mischievous discourse*, in whatever shape, of all the things that men can say to one another, is there anything that in the *same* place the *same* men could not just as easily say, and be at least as *ready* to say, in their *waking* hours?

Two measures being predetermined *upon*—viz. the *suppression* of *Panopticon*, and (to diminish the apparent urgency of the demand for it—) *inter alia* the *preservation* of the *Hulks*—while unfortunately on board the Hulks the prevalence of these practices was matter of *notoriety*—of these two measures, in appearance so difficult to reconcile, how was the reconciliation to be accomplished?

In the first place, by insinuations conveyed with the utmost delicacy, an impression was to be produced, that in a *Panopticon*, and without the 600 houses, on which so large a portion of the grand mass of patronage was to be founded, the prevention of such practices is impossible.

Report, p.66.[29] *Question* (to Mr Bentham.)—'Did you mean that

[29] Another reference to the *First Report* of the Penitentiary Committee. Bentham was quoting from the record of his examination by the committee on 27 March 1811.

they should sleep more than one in the same room?' Answer.—'Oh Yes' etc.—*Question thereupon*—'Did it occurr to you that there were any objections to any more than one sleeping in the same room, or had you any means of obviating the objection?' *Answer*—'There would be *very* strong objections . . . were it not for the characteristic principle of my plan' etc.

The answer, of course, was not satisfactory: if it had been, there would have been an end to the *town of 600 Houses*, with the *two or three hundred thousand pounds* worth of needless expence attached to it.

Thus—and with so delicate a touch as scarce to leave a soil on Honourable fingers—thus was *Panopticon blackened.*—What remained was—*to whitewash the Hulks.* Rumours, to the effect in question, there had been it is true: but those rumours, (Parliament was to understand) were groundless.[30] How was this established?—In one or other of two ways:—either by *avoiding to hear evidence*, or, after having heard it, by *suppressing* it. Accordingly, in this *paper*, which calls itself a *Report* on the Hulks, there is not a single *examination* printed: no—not an iota of information, in any shape, but that in which, where it is to be had in the shape of *examination*, information, (as the Lord Chancellor declared and protested in Your Lordship's House but t'other day)[31] is not, even under the sanction of an *oath* fit to be received as evidence.

My Lord, if it had not been determined, not to have evidence in the only shape that is not palpably deceptitious, Honourable Gentlemen knew well enough where it was to be had.—I myself, without ever having looked for it, could have named to them—one person I am sure of, and, if I do not misrecollect, persons more than one, who *to an official person* had confessed the practice, as having been habitual in their own instance, and with numbers whom they would have named:—Confront, My Lord—do my Lord have the justice to confront—this *silence*, with the sort of *interrogativeness*, which, throughout the whole course of the Report just quoted, was exercised upon *me*.

For a foundation, ground was to be made for the assurance, that,

[30] Written in the margin: 'Penitentiary Report 3d. 27 June 1812 p. 139.' A reference to the *Third Report from the Committee on the Laws relating to Penitentiary Houses. Ordered, by the House of Commons, to be printed, 27 June 1812.*

[31] An allusion to an event that took place more than two months before the covering letter was written: the House of Lords was in recess during August and September. In a debate on Catholic relief Eldon had asserted that no oath of allegiance taken by a Catholic could provide adequate security for his loyalty. See 'Parliamentary Intelligence', *The Times*, 2 July 1812; *Parliamentary Debates*, xxiii. 837.

defective as it is in its present state, the *Hulk* system is not, even in its present state so bad as to be *incorrigible*: is not so bad, but that *it ought to be preserved*: a measure which some persons, who might require to be consulted, might have been apt to make objections to, if in the character of *once prevalent*, howsoever *for the present suppressed*, or *not* suppressed practices, the irregularities in question had been suffered to come to light.—Certificates and so forth, of the capability of the system, were accordingly, in all the forms of regularity obtained, and printed in the Appendix.[32] Obtained, and from whom?—From all persons, interested, in possession or hope, in the continuance and extension of it: certificates, some it is true from *neutrals*, but others from official persons bearing testimony *to their own merits*.

For strengthening this foundation, the *next* thing to be done was—to manifest the *impartiality* and *candour* of Honourable Gentlemen; and, accordingly, a confession was made, acknowledging in substance that in those receptacles every thing is not yet, exactly as it should be.

Upon the *present* plan (Third Report p. 144.) . . . '*these persons* (it is said) *must be expected to return into society with more depraved habits and dispositions. . .*'

But when a panacea is at hand, the more desperate the disease, for the honour of the Physician at least, so much the better.— '*Such alterations and corrections as will in a great degree lessen, if not altogether remove the evil.*'—Such are the words, in and by which an intimation thus consolatory is conveyed.[33]

Now, my Lord, what is this panacea? Oh, my Lord, considering who the Physicians are, an answer is almost a superfluity—*Offices*! *offices*! Yes my Lord: the nests of offices promised, with the expences attached to them, innumerable. To begin with, a few thousands a year in offices. (p. 148.)[34]—Reformation is it still tardy? a few thousands a year more to quicken it; and so on till the cure is perfected.—

Yes, my Lord: it is among the *maxims* of Honourable Gentlemen, that if in an establishment of this sort any thing is amiss, it is for want of offices.

[32] i.e. to the *Third Report* of the Penitentiary Committee.

[33] This second quotation from the *Third Report* of the Penitentiary Committee is from p. 145 not 144.

[34] On this page of the *Third Report* the Committee recommended an additional number of chaplains in the hulks, an increased salary for the superintendent, the appointment of assistant inspectors to reside near the hulks, and further officers and guards with better pay.

It is among their *postulates*, that every man who is paid for doing duty will do it in perfection, provided the reality of patronage, and shew of superintendance, is in the hands of Honourable Gentlemen, whose whole time is demanded for *higher* duties, and who have neither *interest* in, nor *affection*, other than that of *contempt*, for this *low* business,—the inspection occasional only, instead of being, as in Panopticon unremitted,—and above all, provided that neither the inventors of the Panopticon system, to whom the faith of government has for these twenty years been pledged, nor any body that would have come after them, shall have any thing to do with it.

Such is the *purity* of Honourable Gentlemen, such is even their *simplicity*—the species of interest constituted by *patronage*, coupled or not coupled with irresponsible power, is among the species of *sinister interest* they have no conception of.

Had it not been the determination to crush Panopticon at *any* price; and, rather than it should not be crushed, to set all *decency* at defiance, pursuing with inflexible constancy, the plan, which began with appointing Honourable Gentlemen, to act as *Judges* for the purpose of *passing condemnation*, under an assurance *of sharing among themselves the predetermined forfeiture*, on a man, in whom no fault was to be found—to speak out, my Lord—had the object been any thing better than accumulation of job, profusion, and arbitrary power, upon the ruins of that system, by which abuse in *all* these shapes would have been put to shame,—but for *this*, the worthy Magistrate, whose services in the character of *Inspector* of the *uninspectable Hulks*, have been so *efficient*, and so *well approved*, why, in a building, of which *universal*, and *simultaneous*, and *perpetual inspectability* is the undeniable characteristic, should their efficiency be less compleat?

[a] Upon the Non Panopticon plan, of Building and 'fitting' alone, expence (as per Estimate confessedly loose)—£259,725.[35] Remain expences of *furnishing* this town, of which 600 separate houses form a part:—item that of *stocking* whatsoever *manufactories* may ever be proposed to be carried on in it.

As to these expences, Parliament remains to this hour in the dark. And thus it is that all comparison, and by that means all exposure, has been set at defiance. At random, and for the present, setting down the whole at £300,000, I set down these three items, together with the unliquidated addition announced as perhaps requiring to be made to the Building Estimate, and the difference between expence as per *Estimate* and expence as per *experience*, at no more than £40,375. and, under the utter impossibility of liquidation, in which I am involved by omissions, with none of which I am chargeable, I must beg of your Lordship to consider the *figures* as remaining in

[35] Written in the margin: 'Mr Hardwick to Penitentiary Supervisors, 26: June 1812. date of H. of Commons Order for printing 27 June 1812. No 303.' See above, n. 15.

some degree *afloat*, and to hold in reserve for me the eventual faculty of submitting any such supplemental information as may at any time present itself. For the purpose for which they are hazarded, the figures, such as they are, will be sufficient, should they be found to afford a sufficient *provisional* support to the practical result here grounded on them.

The fixation of the expence, the whole mass of it together, on whom does it depend? On a multitude of persons of various ranks and classes, but all agreeing in this, viz. that, as usual, it is their common interest to swell it to the very highest amount, which it is supposed that Parliament and the public can be brought to endure.

In the first instance and in the *lower* ground, Architects, and suppliers of labour and materials, all paid by a per-centage on the amount of the expence: on the *upper* ground, and in official language for a *check* upon these underlings, in effect for a *protection* to them, Honourable Gentlemen, men of virtue, whose dignity is much too high, and their time much too valuable, to be expended in any such illiberal operation as that of narrowing and pinching the encouragement due to elegant arts and useful manufactures.

[b] In relation to the estimated amount of Panopticon expence, in the shape of *capital* advanced, it will scarcely be expected, that, without some little ground for supposing that it may not be altogether thrown away, I should impose either, upon myself or any other person, the labour that would be necessary, to enable me to speak with that assurance, with which, if called upon, I would be ready to speak before any thing were to be done in consequence. But, the conjecture by which the above sum of £100,000 is mentioned, is no such *random* one, as might, not unnaturally, be supposed. On a plan, not materially differing, from that, which on the occasion in question, would be pursued, under the direction of my Brother, a Panopticon was but a few years ago, actually erected at *Petersburgh*:[36] and, by his official situation at the Navy Board, he has occasion to keep himself acquainted in this country with the *current prices*.

If the *contract plan* were preserved, whatsoever were the sum settled by the estimate, I would, for the purpose of rendering it manifestly *my interest* to keep within the estimate, bind myself to pay, for every penny expended above the estimate, a sort of *extra* or *penal* rent, payable out of the profits.

Here, my Lord, is a *real* test of sincerity. This on all occasions is my test. Who else is there that will abide it?——Not Honourable Gentlemen.——No, my Lord they will call it *speculative*: and *that*, as well as any other word, where Gentlemen have power, serves instead of *reason*, and is deemed sufficient: or, if not, some such word as *Jacobinical* may be added.

If, according to an offer made below, the *Contract plan* were to be given up, true it is, that, among other disadvantageous effects of such a rescission, the possibility of affording this sort of pecuniary security would be done away. In this case, the only possible resource would be, on the part of my Brother and myself, a public declaration, whereby, as far as in such case character could be pledged, our characters would respectively be pledged to the securing the public purse against any addition to the sum of money originally required.

In regard to the *excess*, the existence of which under the course of proceeding which is *customarily* pursued in relation to public works, and which in the instance of the proposed *Non Panopticon* plan is *actually* pursued, may, however uncertain the *amount*, be looked upon as being to *some* amount matter of absolute certainty, I

[36] See above, letters 2149 and 2152.

would venture to submitt it to your Lordship, and, through your Lordship, with your Lordship's approbation, to *Mr Vansittart*, whether, to assist in forming an expectation in relation to it, it might not be of use to have an account taken of the difference between expence as per *estimate* and expence as per *experience*, in the instance of such public works as have been carried on at the public expence for a certain number of years back.—

[c] In the character of a principle of economy, applicable in practice to no inconsiderable extent, I would beg leave also to submitt, whether the unfrugality of these driblet expenditures might not be found to have some claim upon the attention of Mr Vansittart. Some years ago, my Brother, in his official capacity, found occasion to use his endeavours to point to this subject the attention of his superiors:—I know not with what fruit.—If in a work, capable of being compleated in *one* year, you distribute the expenditure in equal portions among *ten* years, the consequence is—that, for every year but the last, money in the shape of *interest* upon capital advanced, is expended in waste, and every year but the last in the shape of *compound* interest. If I do not misrecollect, my Brother found in this way upon some single article a waste—I am afraid to say how much—I believe some millions: certainly hundreds of thousands.—'If the work be such as is capable of being compleated in a year, rather than begin it immediately and keep on bestowing upon it a tenth part of the same every year, pass a *resolution* relative to it, if you please now, but do not begin upon it, till the same year, though it were the last of the ten, on which you have settled with yourself that you are able to disburse the whole of it.'—In some such words if I do not misconceive the matter, the memento might stand expressed.[37]—End of the Note.

[37] Sir Samuel's concern for losses incurred 'from a disregard of interest on money' is noted by Lady Bentham in *The Life of Brigadier-General Sir Samuel Bentham*, London, 1862, p. 195.

2191

To Richard Wharton

21 September 1812 (Aet 64)

Barrow-Green House Oxted Surry
Sept 21. 1812.

Sir,

I have to acknowledge the receipt of your Letter, dated the 11th instant,[2] in which, speaking of the Act 52 G.3. c. 52[3] whereby, on a certain event, which you speak of as having now taken place, 'the absolute property of the Lands etc purchased of the Marquis of Salisbury and conveyed to' (me) 'in 1796' (it was to me in 1799 as Feoffee) is declared to be about to become vested in his Majesty, you communicate to me on the part of the Lords Commissioners of the Treasury their 'desire that I would forthwith deliver to the Commissioners of Woods etc, all the Deeds Muniments and Papers relative to or connected with the same for the use and behoof of the Crown.'

Upon a second glance at the Act, I flatter myself, Sir, you will join with me in the perception, that, to a very considerable extent, the possession of the documents, as above described, is necessary to me to enable me to comply with a particular requisition in the Act.—For the purpose of deducting my *receipts*, as therein required, from the *compensation* money there spoken of,[4] it will be necessary for me to make up *my accounts*: and, not to speak of '*papers*', such for instance as are expressive of transactions with Tenants, without the *Leases* to *refer to*, and upon occasion to employ as *vouchers*, it will be impossible for me to make up those accounts.—Under this demand will be included every thing but *Title Deeds*.

As to the *Title Deeds*, viz. such of them as came into my possession, of which you have the list and copies, I have not been able to

2191. [1] PRO T 1/1297/565. In the hand of a copyist, except the signature. Docketed: '21st September 1812 / J. Bentham / In answer to a letter from this / Board, desiring him to deliver / up all Papers rel: to Property / at Milbank, purchased of / the Marquis of Salisbury / No: 12132 / Recd. 22d: September 1812 / Read 6 Nov. 1812 / 2d Sheet 5 Division / Write to Solor / W Cotton'. The treasury solicitor 1806–17 was Henry Charles Litchfield; William Cotton was a senior clerk. An autograph draft of this letter is at BL VIII. 610–13. Docketed: '1812 Sept. 21 / Panopt. / J.B. Barrow Green / to / Wharton Treasury / Deeds etc why not / delivered up.'

[2] Letter 2189.

[3] In the MS '52' is underlined in pencil and a note, also in pencil, is inserted in the margin: '*C.44*'.

[4] 52 Geo. III, c.44 s.4.

satisfy myself, which, if any, the Crown would be entitled to the possession of under the Act, which, if any, *I* am entitled to, as neccessary to *my own security*:—ex. gr. for eventual defence on the occasion of any demands that might be made on me, on account of any acts exercised by me during the existence of my interest in the character of Feoffee: of which demands instances have actually occurred.

In regard to the need the *King* may have of them, on the one hand what is clear is that the sort of title given to him by the Act being superior to every other, for *confirmation* of it he can have no need of any *act* which I can *do*, or any *muniment* which I can *furnish*.

On the other hand, the *subject matter*, viz the *parcels*, of land in question, being, in the Act, described no otherwise than by *reference*, viz. by reference to the *conveyance* thereof made to *me* in quality of *feoffee*, what seems not only matter of *right*, but, for *practical purposes*, eventually neccessary, is—that he should have in his possession the *most recent description* of those parcels, in addition to whatsoever, if any, more *antient* descriptions there may be, that never came into my hands.

But, in respect of the *matter of right*, I flatter myself, Sir, you will agree with me that there can be no particular demand for *haste*: and, for practical purposes in general, there can be no difference between the *originals* and the *copies* which *you* have.

Had *Sir Samuel Romilly* been in town, I should immediately have consulted him in relation to these points:—nor will I fail to do so *on his return*. If, in *his* opinion, there should be any I ought to retain, I should suppose their Lordships would not insist upon my delivering them, without taking some *Official opinion*, by which, in matters of this nature, they are in use to be directed.

Mean time, if there should be any purpose, for which in the office in question or elsewhere, the *copies* would not serve so well as the *originals*, and if you, Sir, or Lord Glenbervie, or Mr Rhodes of that Office, (with whom I have communicated on the subject) would have the goodness to name any day, on or after which, they shall on demand be returned, from that office, to me or my order, I will take care they shall be delivered *there*, to any person in the office giving a receipt for them, as per list; having, previously to my departure for this place (at which I propose to continue till the first week in November) taken care to leave them out in the custody of a proper person, at my House in Queens Square Place Westminster.

Meantime, since my arrival here, I have reason to think, that, in consequence of some misconception, *the Leases* have actually been taken to the Office, and delivered to Mr Rhodes.[5] I am however in no pain on that account, not dubious that Lord Glenbervie would, at the first word, see the absolute need I should have of those leases, to enable me to comply with the requisition in the Act, as abovementioned: and accordingly, in the undertaking for the eventual redelivery of the muniments *in general*, as above proposed, that his Lordship would have no objection to the insertion of the *Leases*, supposed to have been delivered by mistake as above.

I have the honour to be,
with all respect
Sir,
your obedient Servant
Jeremy Bentham.

R. Wharton Esqr.
etc. etc. etc.—
Treasury Chambers

2192

To Sir Samuel Bentham

28 September 1812 (Aet 64)

Barrow Green near Godstone 28th Sept 1812

J.B. to S.B.

Something you said in your last[2] about fiddles, an odd fancy that one of them had ever been yours, or called or reputed such. Neither of them are in much danger of going out of the family or far out of your reach: they are both with me here, and will return with me the 1st week in Novr.

Midford Greece[3]—As the volumes are done with, let them be returned. John Mill will be a candidate for them. To assist in reading them the boy had better have the map or two (d'Anvilles) of antient Geography.[4] They are at any time at your service on asking

[5] A list of the leases taken to Rhodes on 18 September 1812 is at BL XIV. 350–1.

2192. [1] BL VIII. 644–5. Autograph. Docketed: '1812 Sepr. 28 / J.B. to S.B.' Addressed: 'To / Sir S. Bentham / or Lady B / Hall Oak Farm / Hampstead'.

[2] Missing.

[3] William Mitford (1744–1827), elder brother of Lord Redesdale, and a contemporary of Bentham at Westminster and Queen's College, Oxford, was the author of *History of Greece*, 5 vols., London, 1784–1818. He was soon to become MP for New Romney 1812–18, having already sat for Newport, Cornwall 1785–90, and Beeralston 1796–1806.

[4] Jean Baptiste Bourguignon d'Anville (1697–1782), French geographer and cartographer. His *Compendium of Ancient Geography* was published posthumously in 1791.

Walter for them who knows where they are. But perhaps he may bring them and if so you might as well keep him and feed him: for till my return he is *upon the pavé* at board wages in Q.S.P. or rather with Tom[5] at Mrs Farr's.[6] If you can find mice to make him catch well and good. But he will probably return hither as soon as Herbert[7] is departed hence which will probably be about the middle of the month.

2193

FROM WILLIAM ALLEN

3 November 1812

London 3 of 11th month 1812

My dear Friend

Thy note of yesterday[2] gave me great pleasure as it proved that I still enjoyed the regard and notice of a Friend whom I have highly valued ever since I have know him, and have only to regret that the opportunities of intercourse are so few—I am delighted with the hopes afforded me, that I may expect a visit before long. If it were in the middle of a week say Thursday and I had previous notice of the day we would dine at any hour and take care to have no other company except Mill or Koe in order that we may have some free converse I intended to have written to Mill while he was at Barrow Green—but have been in such a perpetual whirl of engagements that I have had no leisure I long however to see him on more accounts than one—and hope that by this time he is returned to Newington Green

I have been much chagrined with hearing bad accounts of Miranda[3] and with the defeat we have sustained at Bristol and Liver-

[5] Thomas Coulson junior.

[6] Not further identified, but probably a connection of Bentham's through his stepmother, Sarah Bentham, the daughter of Jonathan Farr of Moorfields. Mrs Farr appears to have been a neighbour of Bentham's. See *Correspondence*, i. 99 n. and vii, as index.

[7] i.e. John Herbert Koe.

2193. [1] BL VIII. 646–7. Autograph. Docketed: '1812 Nov.3 / W. Allen Plough Court / to / J.B. Q.S.P. / H. Coulson ticket for him / etc'. Addressed: 'Jeremy Bentham / Queen Square Place / near / James's Park / Westminster'. Postmarks: '10 o'Clock / No.4 / 1812 EN' and 'Two Penny / Unpaid / Lombard St.'

[2] Missing.

[3] On 12 July 1812 Miranda had proposed an armistice to the royal forces and on 25 July the capitulation of San Mateo was signed.

pool[4]—things however I trust will find their level and settle right at last—

Pray desire Henry Coulson[5] to call upon me—he is sure to find me at ½ past 9 in the Morning at Plough Court on Hospital days I shall feel gratified in doing all in my power to accommodate him—and request his acceptance of the inclosed Ticket for the Natural Philosophy Lectures—only two Lectures have yet been given—the next is on this day week at ½ past 6 in the Evening

I remain very respectfully
thy affectionate Friend
Wm Allen

2194

From Edward Sugden

26 November 1812

Lincolns Inn
26th. Novr. 1812.

Dear Sir

I do myself the pleasure of sending you a copy of a Pamphlet on a subject which you have long since so entirely and happily exhausted as to leave nothing for any future writer to attempt.[2] Truth however requires sometimes to be repeated and this [is] all that I have done. It is not without hesitation that I venture to submit to you my humble production but Mr Brougham assures me that it will be kindly received; and as he justly observed it is a tribute due to the father of the subject. I beg to express my regrets that I have so long delayed to render it

I have the Honor to be
Sir
With great respect
Your faithl and obedient
Edwd. B. Sugden

J. Bentham Esqre.

[4] Romilly was defeated at Bristol in the October 1812 general election. He was later returned at Arundel: see letter 2199 and n. 9. Brougham, obliged to give up his seat at Camelford, had been forced to withdraw from the poll at Liverpool on 16 October.

[5] Henry Tonkin Coulson (1796–1840), the cousin of Walter and Thomas Coulson junior.

2194. [1] Ogden MS 62(2), 27. Autograph. Printed in Bowring, x. 473.

Edward Burtenshaw Sugden (1781–1875), lawyer, politician, and writer, subsequently solicitor-general 1829–30, Irish lord chanccellor 1835, 1841–6, lord chancellor 1852. He was knighted 1829 and created Baron St Leonards of Slaughton 1852.

[2] Sugden was the author of *A Cursory Inquiry into the expediency of repealing the Annuity Act and raising the legal rate of Interest*, London, 1812. He seems to have been referring to Bentham's *Defence of Usury*, London, 1787 (Bowring, iii. 1–29).

2195

To Sir Samuel Romilly

27 November 1812 (Aet 64)

Q.S.P., 27th November, 1812

Dear Romilly,

Nobody can be more fully or feelingly sensible to anything, than I am to the regard for justice manifested by Mr Vansittart throughout the whole course of this business. *Justice* I call it—*favour* I will not call it; for that would not be to do justice either to his probity or his discernment. What he I perceive is as fully sensible of as myself is,—that if by a Chancellor of the Exchequer, without concert with the individual, the arbitrator to act in a case such as that in question for the public, were to be chosen, arbitration and compensation might in that case be converted into a mere form, since by an arbitrator of *his* choice, nothing could be easier than for a minister in his situation, so to order matters, that of the enacted compensation not a half-penny would ever find its way into the individual's pocket.

As to any person to whom the nature and history of the Panopticon plan, from the time when it first found acceptance, and so on through the revolutions it was destined to experience, were *not* more or less known,—you seemed as fully sensible as myself how ill qualified in comparison of one to whom those things *were* thus known, a person so circumstanced would be to form any tolerably well-grounded award.

As to Mr Rose, in addition to a great part of the knowledge *I* had had of the business, he could not have but had knowledge of a great deal of secret history (of some part of it I received from him some obscure intimations at the time) which it was not permitted to me to know. It was this, added to the confidence which, from his political situation, I could not but presume would be reposed in him by the Treasury, and the hope, that, in his dealings by me, he would be so far mindful of former actings and declarations, as well as of the opinion entertained of the plan and its authors by Mr Pitt and Lord Melville, to whose department the business belonged, as to procure for me some small aliquot part, (which was the utmost I could expect or indeed accept of, and which by the breach of the engagement I have been deprived of,)—it was this that gave birth to the idea of casting myself upon his mercy. From what it has happened to

2195. [1] Bowring, xi. 162–4.

me now and then to hear from A and B, I had reason to presume, that, in respect of general character, his opinion was not unfavourable to me. As to partiality, whether I had anything of that sort to expect from a man, who, when I have met him in the street, as I have every now and then done, has never appeared to know me, may be left to be imagined.

After disappointment about Mr Rose, the same principle, viz., the wish of having for my judge a person who, to a presumable absence of hostility or ill opinion, as towards myself, and some acquaintance with the history of the transaction, might, from his situation, be to any such purpose as that in question expected to add the qualification of being regarded as a proper person by the Treasury,—led me to *Lord Glenbervie*. But *once* in my life was I ever in any residence of *his*, and that was at Lincoln's Inn some thirty or thirty-five years ago, when he had chambers there. Not within these twenty years has *he* been in any residence of *mine*, except one morning about eighteen years ago, when he brought some company to see the Panopticon *raree*-show.[2] Since that time, I have never met him in the street but it has been matter of doubt with me, whether I was to know him or no.

Upon your informing me of the disappointment in regard to him, I forget whether I had sufficiently thought of the matter to mention to you any person in particular to mention to Mr Vansittart. What I do remember (if I did not misconceive you) is,—an intimation from you, that you felt a difficulty about suggesting any person to Mr Vansittart without a previous assurance that a proposal from him would find such person already prepared for signifying his willingness to accept it.

Casting my eyes around, with this instruction before them, I have thought of two persons, viz., *Sir Charles Bunbury*, and *Mr Moreton Pitt*. Both of them were in its day well acquainted with Panopticon; and it was that circumstance that pointed them out to me. The names of both of them were (by, or with the approbation of, Mr Holford, etc., I presume,) put upon the late Penitentiary Committee. From that time to the present, I have not had, with either of them directly or indirectly, any the smallest intercourse. Neither of them on that occasion gave me any signs of life. If there could be any need of it, this circumstance would, I suppose, be regarded as sufficient evidence of the absence of any connexion from which partiality might be to be apprehended, even if in other respects their characters had been such as to admit of any such surmise.

[2] For Bentham's earlier contact with Glenbervie see *Correspondence*, ii, iii, iv, and v, as index.

Should Mr Vansittart approve of *either* of them, *which*, it may be, is to me a matter of entire indifference. Should he indulge me with the option, I would have two strings to my bow; and my first application would be made to the first of them I could get the speech of. With his consent, and with the assurance it would enable me to convey *that* application I could make without difficulty. But, without the power of affording any such assurance, the errand (I make no doubt of your agreeing with me) would be rather an unpromising one; for in that case neither of them could yield to my request without exposing himself to the hazard of knowing himself to be rejected.

Mr Moreton Pitt (I think you informed me) is returned again for Dorsetshire. That being the case, though I suppose he has no house in town, (for I happen to know of his having some time ago parted with the house he had,)[3] some time or other I suppose he will be in town to take his seat. Whether he will or no, is, I suppose, perfectly known to Mr Vansittart. For my part I have not set eyes on him, for I know not how many years,—about ten years ago, I think it is,—that for the last time, I saw him in the street by accident for two or three minutes.

As to *Sir Charles Bunbury*, on sending, about ten days ago, to his house in town, I learned that he was expected in town, but that at that time no day had been fixed. It is, I think, about two and a half years since I saw him for a few minutes.

Oh, how grating—how odious to me is this wretched business of *compensation*! Forced, after twenty years of oppression—forced to join myself to the Baal-peor[4] of blood-suckers, and contribute to the impoverishment of that public, to which, in the way of economy, as well as so many other ways, I had such well-grounded assurance of being permitted to render some signal service. Half-a-year's payment of my permanent compensation-annuity was due last Michaelmas;[5] and reduced as I am, I have not yet been able to bring myself to apply for it. Last Sunday fortnight it was that you called on me, and till now I have not been able to drag myself, or to attempt to drag you to this abominable task. If you mention to Mr Vansittart this about the *arbitrator*, will you have the goodness to ask him about the *annuity*, whether a payment on it will now be made; and if not,

[3] In the *Royal Kalendar* for 1810 Moreton Pitt is listed as living at 10 Arlington Street; in the same publication for 1813 at 12 Albermarle Street. In the intervening years he does not appear to have had a London residence.

[4] See Num. 25: 3; Deut. 4: 3; Pss. 106: 28; Hos. 9: 10.

[5] See below, letters 2196 and 2197.

at once, at what other time, and how I should apply for it? Whether by memorial, or how.

After all, besides the breach of public faith—than which surely there never was a grosser one—can such a man as Lord Sidmouth, can such a man as Mr Vansittart, bring himself to put the public to an extra expense of £200,000 plus my miserable compensation, only to make a job for Mr H.?[6] To any such supposition my conception finds itself utterly unable to square itself. Yet, if Lord Castlereagh and Co.[7] insist, how can they refuse. What is it that will be done? Nothing. This is what presents itself to my view as the most natural and least improbable result. Panopticon not gone on with, nor the job neither.

Howsoever canine, is it impossible to the appetite of the enemy to be satisfied by any less expensive means? A compensation, would it not be more suitable to his case than to mine?

Dear Romilly,
yours ever

2196

To Richard Wharton

8 December 1812 (Aet 64)

Queen's Square Place Westmr
8 Decr. 1812

Sir

Understanding that, about 11 or 12 days ago, Mr Chancellor of the Exchequer was pleased to mention to you the subject of the inclosed Memorial, and to desire that immediate steps might be taken for putting the business in train, I take the liberty of addressing it to you for that purpose, waiting the favour of your commands in relation to it, and am, Sir, with all respect

Your most obedient
Servant
Jeremy Bentham.

Mr Secretary Wharton
Treasury Chambers

[6] Holford.

[7] Robert Stewart, Viscount Castlereagh (1769–1822), later 2nd Marquis of Londonderry, foreign secretary and leader of the House of Commons 1812–22.

2196. [1] BL VIII. 681. Pressed copy of autograph letter. Docketed: '1812 Decr 8 / Panopt. / J.B. Q.S.P. / to Secry. Wharton / Treasury / For first ½ yearly payment / of Provisional Compen- / sation Annuity, due / 25 Sept. 1812: inclosing / J.B.'s Memorial of / this date. / Answered by Secry Harrison / 16 Decr 1812: viz. / payment ordered.' Addressed: 'To / R. Wharton Esqre / etc etc. etc.'

For Bentham's memorial see 2197; for Harrison's reply, letter 2198.

2197

To the Lords Commissioners of the Treasury

8 December 1812 (Aet 64)

To the Lords Commissioners of his Majesty's Treasury the Memorial of Jeremy Bentham of Queen's Square Place Westminster humbly sheweth,

That by an Act passed the 20th day of April in the 52d year of the reign of his present Majesty, intituled 'An Act for the erection of a Penitentiary House for the confinement of Offenders convicted within the City of London and County of Middlesex; and for making compensation to Jeremy Bentham Esquire, for the non-performance of an Agreement between the said Jeremy Bentham and the Lords Commissioners of his Majesty's Treasury, respecting the custody and maintenance of Convicts,'[2] after reciting that 'certain Lands and Premises have been purchased of the Most Honourable The Marquis of Salisbury, at Milbank near Tothill Fields and a conveyance thereof made to' Your Memoralist under the authority of an Act of the 34th year of his present Majesty intituled 'An Act for erecting a Penitentiary House or Penitentiary Houses for confining and employing Convicts'[3] the said 'Lands and Premises' became vested in Your Memoralist 'as Feoffee for the purposes of the said Act,' and after power given to 'his Majesty to appoint three persons to carry into execution the purpose of this Act, and to be Supervisors of House and Buildings to be erected in pursuance thereof' it is enacted 'that as soon as such Supervisors shall be so appointed as aforesaid, all the Lands and Premises so purchased by Your Memoralist, or then, viz on the said 20th day of April last past, vested in him for the purpose of the said Act of the thirty fourth Year aforesaid shall vest absolutely and without any conveyance or assignment thereof, in His Majesty, His Heirs and Successors for the use of the public and the purposes of this Act.'

2. That in and by another clause in the said Act of the said 52d Year, after reciting that in virtue of the said Act of the 34th year 'Articles of' Contract and 'Agreement for the management of one thousand male Convicts in a National Penitentiary House to be

2197. [1] BL VIII. 682–92. Pressed copy; original in the hand of a copyist with the exception of the signature and address. Docketed: '1812 Decr. 8 / Panopt Compensat. / J.B. to Treasury / Memorial for / first Payment of / Provisional Annuity.'

[2] 52 Geo. III, c.44.

[3] 34 Geo. III, c.84.

erected by' Your Memorialist upon the said Lands had been 'approved' by Your Lordships and by authority of Your Lordships Your Memorialist had at a large expence taken Measures for carrying such contract and agreement into effect and after making provision for affording compensation to Your Memorialist by two Arbitrators to be chosen for that purpose, one by Your Lordships the other by Your Memorialist according to whose award when made Your Lordships are therein and thereby 'empowered and directed to issue out of the consolidated Fund . . . the net sum so awarded to' Your Memorialist, 'within one month after such award shall have been made', it is enacted and declared that in the mean time Your Lordships are 'authorized and directed to issue and pay out such annual sum as may appear to' Your Lordships 'to be equal to the net annual profit of the said lands in the hands of' Your Memorialist.

3. That, under and by virtue of the said Act not long after the said 20th day of April last past (which was the day of the passing thereof) on some day not known to Your Memorialist, but known as he humbly presumes, to Your Lordships, his Majesty, or on his behalf the Prince Regent, was pleased, as Your Memorialist understands, to appoint such *Supervisors* as above mentioned; whereby and whereupon Your Memorialist's interest in the said 'lands and premises and his means of drawing profit from the same immediately ceased: and that accordingly the last profit, which he has drawn, or been able to draw, from them, consisted of the rents thereupon due from the respective Tenants at Lady day the 25th of March last past, down to which time he has received the whole of Rents due from the said respective Tenants.

4. That, no Arbitrator having as yet been appointed by Your Lordships, nor therefore by Your Memorialist, Your Memorialist has not yet received any thing on the score of compensation as aforesaid.

5. That the profits, received by Your Memorialist from the said Lands, consisted of rents which were made payable quarterly, and which to a considerable amount were actually so paid; and the remainder at such times as Your Memoralist thought fit to demand the same: and that, property tax and a certain small quit rent or fee-farm rent deducted, the total net sum, which, in respect of the said rents, would have been received or receivable by Your Memoralist, as and for the rents of the two quarters then due, would on Michaelmas day the 29th of September last past have been £363: 0s: 7½d:[4] as, by Schedule A hereunto annexed, containing a particular account of the said Rents, as reserved in and by the respective Leases or

[4] The same sum is written in the margin at this point.

Agreements (which or copies thereof, are, all of them, in the possession or otherwise at the command of Your Lordships) will particularly appear.

6. That, if Your Memorialists humble conception of the matter be not incorrect, it was the intention of Parliament as above expressed, that, until full compensation shall have been made to Your Memorialist as aforesaid, Your Memorialist should, in respect of his *means of subsistence*, since for twelve years last past or thereabouts in great part derived from and dependent on his possession of the said Lands, be kept or put in the *same plight*, as if the said Lands and Premises had continued in his possession as aforesaid: in which case (not to speak of the still earlier period at which such part of the said rents as were all along paid quarterly would have been received) the sum receivable by him as and for the half year's rent of the said premises, would, on the 29th of September have been the said sum of £363: 0s: 7½d[5] just mentioned.

7. That though, in respect of a considerable part of the said rents, he actually was in the habit of receiving the same quarterly, and, by the spontaneous punctuality of the Tenants, on the very quarter day, yet, out of respect to Your Lordships time, and his unwillingness to be in any way unnecessarily troublesome to Your Lordships, he forbore making application at the time when the first quarter, as above was due; and, should it so happen that, before full compensation be made to him as aforesaid, by any delay in making of the said award, any further sum or sums on account of *this his provisional Annuity* should become payable, it is his humble intention, Your Lordships not forbidding, to make the like application to your Lordships at the end of every successive half year, and no oftener.

Jeremy Bentham

Queen's Square Place Westminster
8th December 1812

[5] The same sum is written in the margin at this point.

(A) 8 December 1812

Schedule (A), referred to in the Memorial of this day's date, addressed to the Lords Commissioners of his Majesty's Treasury by Jeremy Bentham Esquire.

In this Schedule are shewn, in each instance, 1. the names of the parties—2. the date of the respective Instruments—3. the nature of the instrument, whether Lease or Agreement or Indorsement—4. the day of commencement—5. the time of duration—6. the day of expiration—7. the annual amount of the Rent issuing out of the Lands in the said Memorial mentioned, situated at Milbank Westminster, lately vested in the said Jeremy Bentham as Feoffee for the purpose of the then intended Penitentiary Establishment, but now in his Majesty his Heirs and Successors.

To the account of the *Rents*, so payable to the said Memorialist, is subjoined an account of all *deductions* to which the same are liable the *balance* being the amount of the '*net annual profit*' of the said Lands to which the *net annual sum payable to the Memorialist* by direction of their said Lordships, under the Act of Parliament in the said Memorial mentioned, was and is to be '*equal*'.

N.B. 1. The said several Leases and Agreements were made defeasible at any time by occupat⟨ion?⟩ of the premises by the said Feoffees, for the purpose of their being respectively applyed to the purposes of the said intended Penitentiary Establishment.

N.B. 2. The said several rents were payable, clear of *Land Tax* and all other deductions; except Property Tax and a small annual Quit Rent or Fee-farm rent as hereinafter mentioned.

N.B. 3. In the several instruments the name ⟨. . .⟩ said Feoffee's Brother was added to his own, in respect of the interest which his said Brother had, under the Agreement with their said Lordships, as in the said Memorial mentioned. On this account it is, that the surname of the Memorialist is here put in the plural number.

I. Parties	II. Date of the Instrument	III. Instrument	IV. Commencement	[V.] Duration	VI. Time of Expiration	£ s. d
1. Benthams to Hodges—	20. Decemr 1803.	Lease	25 Dec 1803	21 Years	25 Decr. 1824	107. 0. 0
2. Benthams to Hodges— same premises	31. July 1805.	Indorsement on the above lease—same premises	29. Sept. 1805.		25 Decr. 1824.	18. 0. 0
3. Benthams with Hodges— other premises	1. Aug. 1806.	Agreement for a Lease—	25 Mar. 1805	7 Years	25 Mar. 1812†	18. 0. 0§
4. Benthams to Hodges— other premises.	30 July 1807.	Lease—	24 June 1807	17½ Years	25 Decr. 1824.	20. 6. 0
5. Benthams to White	25 Mar. 1805.	Agreement for a Lease—	25 March 1805.	14 Years.	25 Mar. 1819.	3. 15. 0.‡
6. Benthams to Cooke	28 Aug. 1805.	Lease—	25 March 1805.	14 Years.	25. Mar. 1819.	290. 0. 0
7. Benthams to Cooke same premises.	26. August. 1807.	Indorsement on the above Lease—*same* premises.	24 June 1807	21 Years	24 June 1828.	100. 0. 0
8. Benthams to Cooke— other premises	27. Aug 1807.	Lease	24 June 1807.	21. Years	24 June 1828.	150: 6: 3#
				Carried over		£707. 7. 3.
Benthams ⟨. . .⟩ Baker	30 March 1809	Lease—	25 March 1809	7 Years	25 March 1816	95. 0. 0.
Benthams ⟨. . .⟩ Cooke	2 March 1811	Agreement for Lease—	25 March 1811	8 Years	25 March 1819	5. 0. 0.
						807. 7. 3.

Deductions to be made from the above—

	£ s d	
Annual Fee Farm or Quit Rent, payable and paid to the Honble Thos Brand......	0. 11. 4	
Property tax upon £806. 15s 11d being the balance of the said Rents after deduction of the sd Fee—Farm Rent......	80. 13. 7	81. 4. 11.
Remains payable to the Memorialist under the said Act as and for 'the *net annual Profit* of the said Lands' in the hands of him the said Memorialist—		726. 2. 4.
Do payable to do on the 29th day of Septr 1812, as and for *the sum then due*, being the Rent of *two quarters*, constituting *moiety* of the said *annual* sum......		s. d. £363. 1. 2.

Remarks

† No. 3. By this it appears, that, in this instance, the Rent expired before the premises were taken, as above, out of the Memorialists hands. But, as the Tenant was desirous of continuing in possession for any such term as he could obtain, and at a Rent not inferior to the above, this article is therefore inserted along with the rest.

§ No 3. Under the Agreement here in question, the annual Rent was £63[?] But, in virtue of a clause in the said Agreement, Ao. 1807 as much Land as reduced the annual Rent to the abovementioned sum of £18 was taken from *Hodges*, and allotted to *Cooke*; and is comprized in the Lease to Cooke, No 8.

‡ No ⟨5.⟩ Under the Agreement here in question, the annual Rent was £11. 18s. But, in virtue of a clause in the said Agreement, Ao 1807 as much of the premises as reduced the Annual Rent to the abovementioned sum £3. 15s. was taken from *White*, and allotted to *Cooke*; and is comprized ⟨in⟩ the Lease to Cooke, No 8, as above.

⟨#No⟩ 8. From and after the 24th June 1814, under a clause in this same Lease, the Rent had of the above £150. 6. 3d, would have been £210. 8s. 9d. But the said £150. 6. 3d ⟨be⟩ing the whole Rent as yet payable, is of course the whole of the sum in⟨clu⟩ded in the above account. 1812. 8th Decr.

Jeremy Bentham

2198

From George Harrison

16 December 1812

Sir

I have it in command from the Lords Commissioners of His Majesty's Treasury to acquaint you that a Warrant has been prepared to authorize the Auditor of the Land Revenue[2] to make out a Debenture in your favor for the Sum of £363. 1. 2 and so much more as will cover the Fees upon the issue thereof.

I am
Sir
Your Obed Ser
Geo. Harrison

Treasury Chambers
16th. Dec 1812
Jeremy Bentham Esqe

2198. [1] BL VIII. 698–9. Autograph. Docketed: '1812 Dec. 16 / Panopt / Secry Harrison Treasury / to J.B. Q.S.P. 363 1s. 2d. / Debenture for J.B.s / Provisional Compensation Annuity / First half yearly payment ordered.'

[2] The joint auditors for the relevant circuit were Sir William Henry Cooper, Bt. (1766–1834) and his younger brother Frederick Grey Cooper (1769–1840). They were joint auditors 1795–1832.

2199
To John Mulford

*c.*21 December 1812 (Aet 64)

I mean to send, if I can find it, one of the numbers of the weekly newspaper called *The Examiner*. In it you will find a letter of which your humble servant is the subject; but which, odd as it may appear to you, your said humble servant never has read, and most probably never will read. He has too much use both for eyes and time, to read half the things that are said of him in books and newspapers.[2]

But what will interest you more, when you come to know the little circumstances that are connected with it, is the mention made by the editor, in a paragraph marked as written by himself, of my name in conjunction with those of Brougham and Romilly. Brougham is the sole confidential adviser of the Princess of Wales, in her contest with her husband.[3] The Princess takes in *The Examiner*; and, as being in such pointed hostility against her said husband, reads it with great interest. The Princess Charlotte[4] comes once a-fortnight, on a stated day of the week, I forget which, to dine with her mother, and there she steals a peep at the said *Examiner*. The Princess Charlotte had been taught by her father to be a great admirer of Charles Fox.[5] Upon her father's casting off that party without reason assigned, she would not go with him; but, being disgusted with his behaviour towards her mother, and on so many other accounts, adheres to her mother, and retains her original political feelings in great force. Brougham and Romilly are the Princess Charlotte's two great heroes, whom she is continually trumpeting. If she were on the throne, Romilly would of course be Chancellor, Brougham either Minister, or in some other high office. They are both of them more democratic than the Whigs; and Erskine, having already been Chancellor,[6] would probably have been preferred for that office, to Romilly, by the Whigs, had they

2199. [1] Bowring, x. 472, where it is printed as part of an earlier letter (letter 2178 above).

[2] A reference to the letter in the *Examiner* of 1 November 1812, signed 'A.Z', and dated 15 October, proposing Bentham as legislator for the new government of Sicily, occupied since 1806 by British forces.

[3] Princess Caroline of Brunswick-Wolfenbüttel (1768–1821) married the Prince of Wales in 1795 but separated from him in the following year.

[4] Princess Charlotte Augusta (1796–1817), only daughter of the Prince of Wales and Princess Caroline.

[5] Charles James Fox.

[6] Thomas Erskine, Baron Erskine of Restormel Castle (1750–1823), MP for Portsmouth 1783–4, 1790–1806, lord chancellor 1806–7.

come into power when they were so near it. Romilly's is the only house I go to; and Brougham one of the very few, indeed, that I admit into mine. When the Earl of Dundonald dies, Lord Cochrane, who is his eldest son, will succeed to the peerage; and then it is understood to be certain that Brougham will succeed him as member for Westminster. Lord Dundonald, a few days ago, was supposed to be at the point of death, but is now, they say, a little recovered.[7] It is supposed, however, that he has but a short time to continue in this wicked world. In the same case, would the Prince-Regent, if drinking could kill him; for he is drunk (say the learned) every night, and palsy is hovering over him. Brougham does not seem to have any other more immediate prospect for coming into Parliament, which, of course, I am sorry for. He had a claim for a seat for Scotland, which, on account of the certain expense, and the little chance of success which the bitter hostility of the ministry towards him seemed to leave him, he has determined to give up.[8] Romilly is in Parliament by this time. He went down yesterday, to be elected, to Arundel, which is one of the Duke of Norfolk's boroughs.[9]

2200

From Étienne Dumont

28 December 1812

J'avois tout à fait oublié, mon cher Bentham, un engagement pour Mercredi prochain, dans le cas où je resterois en ville. Si vous le voulez, nous remettrons la partie au Mercredi suivant, et j'en prendrai note pour ne point faire d'erreur.—J'ai vu ce Pce Kostuevsky[2] grand admirateur de Théorie des Peines et récompenses—on alloit la mettre en vente quand il a quitté Ptbg.

Lundi soir. 28.

[7] Archibald Cochrane, 9th Earl of Dundonald, did not die until 1831. Lord Cochrane remained MP for Westminster until 1818.

[8] Brougham was obliged to give up the seat he had held at Camelford when Parliament was dissolved on 29 September 1812. His efforts to secure a seat at Inverkeithing Burghs were unsuccessful and he was out of the House of Commons until July 1815.

[9] Romilly was defeated at Bristol in October 1812 but was returned for Arundel on 21 December. Charles Howard, 11th Duke of Norfolk (1746–1815), who succeeded his father in 1786, was a staunch Whig.

2200. [1] BL VIII. 704–5. Autograph. Docketed: '1812 Dec 28 / Dumont Haymarket / to / J.B. Q.S.P. / Peines et Récompenses / at Petersburgh'. Addressed: 'Jeremy Bentham Esq. / Queen Square Place / Westminster.'

[2] Not identified.

2201

From Samuel Bentham Jr.

2 January 1813

Dear Uncle

If you will be so good to come you shall lead down the first dance with Miss Joanna Baillie

I am
Dear Uncle
Your dutiful nephew
Saml. Bentham

Hall Oak Farm
2nd. Jany. 1813

2202

From Richard Wharton

25 January 1813

Treasury Chambers
25th Jany. 1813.

Sir

I am commanded by the Lords Commissioners of His Majesty's Treasury to transmit to you copy of an Opinion of the Attorney and Solicitor General[2] and to acquaint you that the same was written on

2201. [1] George Bentham papers, Linnean Society of London. Autograph. Docketed: '1813 Jan 2 / S.B. Junr Hampstd / to / J.B. Q.S.P. / Ball Invitation'. Addressed: 'Jeremy Bentham Esq.'

2202. [1] BL IX. 11–12. Autograph. Docketed: '1813 Jan. 25 / Panopt. / Secry. Wharton Treasury / to / J.B. Q.S.P. / Part I / Insisting on surrender of / Deeds Title Deeds and / inclosing Atty. and Solr. Genls. / Opinion as to the right. / Saying nothing of "*Papers*" / Answered Jany. 29 / by Letter I / Part 2. / Calling on J.B. to name / Arbitrator: *Hullock* being / named by Treasury / Answered Jany. 29 / by Letter II.' Letter-book copy at PRO T 27/70, p. 275. For Bentham's letters I and II see 2203 and 2204.

[2] The attorney-general was Sir Thomas Plumer (soon to become vice-chancellor); the solicitor-general, Sir William Garrow (1760–1840). The copy of their opinion, dated 13 January 1813 is at BL IX. 9–10, docketed: '1813 Jan. 13 / Panopt. / Atty and Sollr. General / Opinion (without/Case) as transmitted / from Treasury by Secry / Wharton to J.B. on / J.B.s right to retain / "Deeds" relative to the / Milbank Salisbury Estate / Transmitted to J.B. by / Wharton's Letter dated 29 Jany.' The opinion reads:

'We think Mr. Bentham has no right to retain these Deeds from the King the Lands originally purchased with public Money being by the Act of Parliament vested in the King the right of the Deeds necessarily devolves to His Majesty. The proper mode of recovering these Deeds will be by Information but probably on a further Application to Mr. Bentham such a proceeding will be rendered unnecessary.'

a Case framed upon your letter of the 21st. September last[3] refusing to give up the Title Deeds of the Estate of Millbank of which you were Feoffee in trust for the Crown and my Lords entertain a full confidence that you will conform to the suggestion of the Crown Lawyers and immediately deliver the said Deeds which are necessary in the prosecution of the Reference directed by the Statute 52 Geo: 3. C. 44 upon which my Lords are now ready to enter having appointed John Hullock of Grays Inn Esqr.[4] Referee on the part of the Crown and I am to request that you will nominate a Referee on your part without delay.

I am
Sir
Your most obedient Servt.
R Wharton

J. Bentham Esqr.

2203

To Richard Wharton

29 January 1813 (Aet 64)

Queen's Square Place Westmr Friday
29 Jany 1813.

Sir,

Letter I
Delivery of the Deeds.—

I have to acknowledge the having received last Monday evening Jany. 24th your letter of that day's date.[2]

In relation to *the second* of the two subjects mentioned in it, I thought there might be a convenience in your having my answer in

[3] Letter 2191.

[4] John Hullock (1767–1829), author of *The Law of Costs*, London, 1792, called to the bar 1794. He was made a serjeant-at-law 1816, and a baron of the exchequer and a knight in 1823.

2203. [1] PRO T 1/1301/1636/79818. In the hand of a copyist, except for the address, valediction, and signature. Docketed: 'Mr J. Bentham letter refd to Solicitor.' and '29th Jany. 1813 / Mr. J: Bentham / respecting the Title Deeds / of some Property to be given / up to the Crown for the / Erection of Penitentiary / Houses / No 1330 / R 30th Jany 1813 / Refer to Solicitor / (No.30) W Cotton'. A copy is at BL IX. 17–23, docketed: '1813 Jany. 29 / Panopt. / J.B. Q.S.P. / to / Secr. Wharton Treasury / Letter I / Delivery of Deeds / and Papers.'

[2] Letter 2202.

the form of a separate letter, which you will find accordingly in this inclosure.

As to the *first*, what I have done is this. With the exception of the *Instrument of Appointment*, of which presently, I yesterday transmitted to the Office of Woods' etc, having Mr Rhodes's receipt for them, whatsoever documents could come under the denomination either of '*Title Deeds*' or '*Deeds*'.

They are *six* in number: viz. *Lease* and *Release* constituting together the conveyance, together with three *Assignments of Terms*. To these *five*, I have added a long lease from the Salisbury Family to one of the tenants (Foley)[3] which expired while the land was in my possession—viz. Ao 1803.

These *six*, together with 13 Leases or Agreements for Leases, delivered into the same Office the 18th September, as per Receipt from the said Mr Rhodes,[4] in all 19 instruments, are all I ever had, that could come under the denomination either of '*Title Deeds*' or *Deeds*, or 'Muniments *relative to or connected with*' the Estate of which I was feoffee.

Those which come under the denomination of '*Papers relative to*' etc I have, for the present, taken the liberty to retain. In my letter of the 21st of September, in answer to your's of the 11th,[5] I submitted to their Lordships, that, without having them before me it would be impossible for me to make up, for the use of the Arbitrators, an Account which the Act required me to make up.

In the requisition it makes of Title Deeds your Letter of the 25th instant makes no mention of '*papers*'. My conclusion is—that as to these articles my humble representations above mentioned have been fortunate enough to produce the effect they aimed at.

As to all *deeds* but the *instrument of Appointment*, *self preservation* against eventual *wrongs*, from the apprehension of which the demand found me not altogether free, and that on *specific grounds*, which, if called upon I could produce, was my sole motive for wishing to be allowed to retain them: nor accordingly did my wishes in this respect extend beyond the danger.

As to the *instrument of appointment* itself, in the character of an authentic testimonial of the confidence with which I was honoured by *the late Mr Pitt*, as evidenced by his signature, and as a sort of family memorial to that effect, I must confess that to me the possession of it—the *perpetual* possession—is not a matter of indiffer-

[3] Henry Foley of Codford St Peter, Wiltshire, for whom see *Correspondence*, vi and vii, as index.

[4] See letter 2191 n. 5.

[5] Letters 2189 and 2191.

ence: and, unless (which I have never heard so much as whispered,) any thing has been imputed to me which, if true, would render me unworthy of that confidence, it is my humble hope, that under the misfortunes under which I have been labouring for these twenty years, and to which I am still so far from seeing an end, that consolation, such as it is, will not be refused me. To the King's service that parchment can not be of any imaginable use. That instrument forms not any part of his title. His title is an Act of Parliament; a title which being *paramount* to the one of which that instrument makes a part, has no need of it. For information of its existence and contents, as matter of history, if that be needful, one copy of it, Sir, is—perhaps two are—already in your hands.

In the *other* deeds, a description of the *parcels* is (I take it for granted) contained: a description which may be necessary for ascertaining the situation and quantity of the lands. In the instrument appointing me feoffee for the purpose of treating and purchasing, no such description is contained.

As to this instrument, in relation to the matter of *right*, I have no need of attempting to form a judgment. Should it be ever so clear to me that in the event of a litigation the King would be adjudged to have no right to take it from me, their Lordships commands for the surrender of it should, if persisted in, be not the less submissively obeyed.

I can not bring myself Sir, to close this letter, without expressing my concern at finding, that, by some accident which I know not how to account for, I stand represented to their Lordships, and thence to Mr Attorney and Mr Solicitor General, as having returned a *refusal*—if not *express virtual* at least, (—for '*refused*' is the word—) —and that a compleat and indiscriminating one—to their Lordship's commands, as signified to me by your first Letter. In my answer, for the reasons therein mentioned, I took the necessary liberty of soliciting information: no such information have I received, but instead of it a threat: a threat of prosecution.—What is communicated to me is the *Opinion* of those same learned Gentlemen. But, without the case on which it is grounded, that opinion conveys to me no meaning: the words in it are '*these deeds*': But what '*these deeds*' are is not said.—Your letter, indeed, Sir, says '*title deeds*:' but *that* is in speaking *to me*, not to *them*. My letter to you of the 21st of September—it was *that* letter that constituted the sole and compleat ground of any *Case* which, on that occasion, could have been laid before them: and, till I hear to the contrary, I can not but infer that it was *not* that letter, but some account given of it by somebody else, that formed the *Case* by which that *Opinion* was produced.

It may be thought a weakness, but I really cannot reconcile myself to the idea of standing upon the Treasury records, in the character of one, whom, to bring him to do what was right, it was necessary to threaten with a prosecution at the suit of the crown.

Now, as to that matter, Sir, the case stands thus. By an indiscriminate compliance in regard to *delivery*, but for the⟨ir⟩ *return* or *access*, of which I had not any assurance, I could not have made out my claim to the *provisional compensation annuity*, on which I have already been favoured with one payment, any more than, without the '*Papers*' to the *definitive compensation* itself. This latter position is I hope, Sir, already proved; and, as to the other, the *leases*, which proved eventually necessary to the making up the *Account*, without which the above-mentioned *provisional compensation* could not be claimed, having, (by mistake, as confessed in my former letter[6]) been delivered in at the 'Office of Woods' etc to *Mr Rhodes*, it was to the voluntary civility of that gentleman that I became indebted for that access, without which the business could not have been done.

This letter, with the explanations in it, which it seemed to me thus necessary to give, will, *of course*, I should suppose, be preserved in company with the *Opinion* taken as above: if *not* of course, it is my humble request that I may do so at my instance.

I am truly sorry to have felt myself under the necessity of being thus troublesome, being

With all respect, Sir
Your very obedient Servant,
Jeremy Bentham

Mr. Secretary Wharton
Treasury.[7]

[6] Letter 2191.

[7] Written below this: 'The Lords Commissioners of His Majesty's Treasury are pleased to refer the aforegoing letter to Henry Charles Litchfield Esqr: their Lordships Solicitor who is to consider the same and Report to My Lords his opinion thereon. Whitehall Treasury Chambers the 3d day of February 1813.

Geo Harrison'.

Litchfield replied (5 February):

'In obedience to your Lordships commands signified by Mr Harrison's reference of the 3rd. instant of the annexed Letter from Mr. Jeremy Bentham I most humbly report that it will in my Opinion be proper to request Mr Bentham to transmit to your Lordships a copy of the Instrument of Appointment of himself as feoffee to which he alludes in order that your Lordships may determine whether it is or is not expedient to comply with Mr. Benthams wishes in allowing him to retain the original—Mr. Benthams Letter of the 21st. of September last was set forth at length in the Case upon which the Opinion of the Attorney and Solicitor General was given.'

2204

To Richard Wharton

29 January 1813 (Aet 64)

Queen's Square Place Westminster, Friday 29 Jany. 1813

Letter II.

Sir

Appointment of an Arbitrator.

The present address is in answer to the second and last part, of the letter which I had the honour of receiving from you on Monday the 25th instant.[2] In the last part, speaking of 'the Reference directed by the Statute 52.G.3.C.44' you add 'upon which my Lords are now ready to enter, having appointed John Hullock of Grays Inn Esqr. Referee on the part of the Crown': and conclude with saying 'I am to request that you will nominate a Referee on your part without delay'.

Upon the presumption, that the appointment above spoken of has received, or is designed to receive, it's expression, in and by some written instrument or deed of appointment, the object of this address is humbly to request communication thereof, that the instrument, whereby the appointment of the arbitrator to be named on my part will, I suppose, be to be expressed, may be adapted, and made conformable, to it.

I am, with all respect,
Sir,
Your most obedient Servant
Jeremy Bentham.[3]

Mr Secretary Wharton,
Treasury.

2204. [1] PRO T 1/1301/1603/79818. In the hand of a copyist, with the exception of the valediction, signature, and Wharton's address. Docketed: 'Mr J. Bentham letter refd to Solicitor' and '29th Jany 1813 / Mr. J. Bentham / relative to the Appointment / of an Arbitrator for deciding / Respecting some Property / belonging to him, which / is to be given up to the / Crown for the Execution of / Penitentiary Houses. / No 1331. / R 30th Jany 1813 / Refer to Solicitor / (No. 31) W. Cotton'. Copy at BL IX. 24, docketed: '1813 Jany 29 / Panopt. / J.B. Q.S.P. / to / Secry. Wharton Treasury / Letter 2d. / Appointment of an / Arbitrator.'

[2] Letter 2202.

[3] Written below this: 'The Lords Commrs. of His Majesty's Treasury are pleased to refer the aforegoing letter to Henry Charles Litchfield Esqr: their Lordships Solicitor who is to

2205

From Henry Brougham

9 February 1813

Extract of Letter ⟨fro⟩m Mr Jeffrey[2]—at Edinh.

'Our Clergymen all subscribe the *formula* and *confession of Faith*, at their ordination, and if by any accident that solemnity should have been omitted they are unquestionably liable at any time to be called on to do so—The *formula* is a declaration purporting that the Doctrines in the confession are orthodox and was all, I believe, that ⟨w⟩as at first intended for ⟨su⟩bscription; but the custom has crept in to subscribe the *confession* itself also—All Teachers and Professors in universities are liable to be called on for such subscription, as well as persons in Orders.'

N.B. By Teachers, I presume he means Parochial School Masters—The *confession of faith* is established by *Stat. 1690.*[3]

H.B.

consider the same and Report to My Lords his opinion thereon. Whitehall Treasury Chambers the 3d day of February 1813.

Geo. Harrison'.

Henry Hobhouse (1776–1854), assistant treasury solicitor 1812–17, replied on 4 February:

'In obedience to your Lordships Commands as signified by Mr. Harrison's Reference of the 3d. Instant of the annexed letter from Mr. Jeremy Bentham, I most humbly report, that I am not aware that there is any objection to Mr. Bentham being provided with a Copy of the Instrument by which Mr. Hullock has been appointed a Referee on the part of the Crown, and your Lordships may therefore, if you approve thereof, give the necessary direction for that purpose.'

2205. [1] BL IX. 26–7. Autograph. Docketed: '1813 Feb 9 / Brougham Temple / to / J.B. Q.S.P. / Jeffrey's / of Scotch Subscription'. Addressed: 'J. Bentham Esq. / Queen Square Place / Westminster'. Postmark: '10 o'Clock / FREE / [. . .?]'. Stamped: '[. . .] / Unpaid / [. . .?]. Printed in Bowring, x. 473.

[2] Francis Jeffrey.

[3] The 'Act Ratifying the Confession of Faith and settling Presbyterian Church Government' of 7 June 1690. See *The Acts of the Parliaments of Scotland*, ix. 133–4.

2206

From George Harrison

15 February 1813

Sir

I have it in command from the Lords Commissioners of His Majestys Treasury to transmit for your information the accompanying Copy[2] of the Appointment of W Hullock as a Referee on the part of the Crown for the purpose of settling all Questions between the Public and yourself in respect to some Property belonging to you to be given up for the Erection of Penitentiary Houses.

I am
Sir
Your Obed Serv
G Harrison

Treasury Chambers
15th. Feb 1813
J Bentham Esqr

2207

From Étienne Dumont

22 February 1813

Mon cher Bentham

L.L.[2] a parlé à Ld. S.[3]—il a trouvé qu'il avoit signé le Warrant[4] depuis quelque temps, and that he did not understand himself to be under any engagement to Mr B. not to do so—

Ce n'est pas précisément ce que j'avois dit—j'avois parlé d'une

2206. [1] BL IX. 28–9. Autograph. Docketed: '1813 Feb 13 / Panopt. / Secry. Harrison Treasury / to / J.B. Q.S.P. / inclosing Copy of Treasury / deed appointing *Hullock* their Arbitrator'. Letter-book copy (dated 15 February) at PRO T 27/70, p.320.

[2] Missing.

2207. [1] BL IX. 30–1. Autograph. Docketed: '1813 Feb 22 / Panopt. / Dumont Haymarket / to / J.B. Q.S.P. / Ld. Sidmouth has / signed the '*War* / *-rant*'—i.e. He / determined against / Panopticon and J.B.' Addressed: 'Jer. Bentham Esq. / Queen Square Westm. Place'.

[2] Probably Lansdowne.

[3] Sidmouth.

[4] Presumably the warrant appointing supervisors under 52 Geo. III, c.44.

promesse faite à vous de ne pas signer sans vous en avoir donné information—ou fait une réponse à votre lettre.[5]

He spoke with admiration of Mr Bentham etc. etc. but could not hesitate when a committee of the H. of C. was at variance with him.[6]

Tout à vous
E.D.

Monday.
Je vous renvoye la lettre [. . .?] Ld. S.

2208

From Richard Wharton

24 March 1813

Treasury Chambers
March 1813.

Sir,

I am commanded by The Lords Commissioners of His Majesty's Treasury to refer you to Mr. Harrison's letter of the 13th. Ulto.[2] transmitting for your information a Copy of the appointment of Mr. Hullock as a referee on the part of the Crown for the purpose of settling all questions between the Public and yourself in respect to some property belonging to you to be given up for the erection of a Penitentiary House, and I am to request you will nominate an Arbitrator on your behalf.

I am
Sir
Your very obedient Servant
R. Wharton

Jeremy Bentham Esqr.

[5] See letters 2176 n. 1, 2189 n. 2, and 2190.

[6] The Penitentiary Committee.

2208. [1] BL IX. 32–3. Autograph. Docketed: '1813 Mar 24 / Panopt. / Sec. Wharton Treasury / to / J.B. Q.S.P. / J.B. to name his / Arbitrator'. Letter-book copy at PRO T 27/70, p. 395.

[2] Letter 2206.

2209

To George Harrison

25 March 1813 (Aet 65)

Queen's Square Place Westmr 25 March 1813

Sir,

In obedience to the commands of the Lords Commissioners of the Treasury as signified to me by your letter of yesterdays date,[2] I have to inform their Lordships, that I have obtained the consent of James Whishaw of Lincolns Inn Esquire, one of his Majesty's Commissioners for the Auditing of the Public Accounts,[3] to act on my behalf as the Arbitrator named by me—Mr Hullock the Arbitrator named, as your Letter informs me, on the part of the public, by their Lordships, left this place I understand at the usual time, on the Northern Circuit.[4]

On his return or shortly after, I hope to have in readiness, and to submit accordingly to the two Gentlemen in question in their quality of Arbitrators, the statement of my case.

I am, with all respect,
Sir,
Your very obedient Servant
Jeremy Bentham.

Mr Secretary Harrison,
Treasury Chambers.

2209. [1] PRO T 1/1318/5979/79818. In the hand of a copyist, except for the signature and Harrison's address. Docketed: '25 March 1813 / J. Bentham / Nominating Jas. Whishaw / Esqr to act on his behalf / as Arbitrator / No 4175 / Recd. 26th March 1813 / Read 30 March [. . .?] / 5th. Division 1 sheet / Write to Solicitor / W. Cotton'. Copies at BL IX. 34, docketed: '1813 Mar 25 / Panopt. / J.B. Q.S.P. / to / Secry. / Harrison Treasury / Answer to his of 24 / Whishaws consent / to be Arbitrator' and Robert C. Waterston Autograph collection, vol. I, Massachusetts Historical Society, Boston, docketed: '1813 March 25 / Panopt / J.B. Q.S.P. / Sent to Harrison Treasury / Answer to his of 24th. / Whishaw's consent to / be J.B.'s Arbitrator.'

[2] Letter 2208 (from Wharton, not Harrison).

[3] John not James Whishaw (*c*.1764–1840), originally of Gray's Inn, moved to Lincoln's Inn in 1794, was commissioner for auditing the public accounts 1806–35. For his earlier contact with Bentham see *Correspondence*, vii, as index.

[4] Hullock had joined the Northern Circuit on being called to the bar in 1794. Bentham's letter was sent to the treasury solicitor, and Hobhouse wrote to Harrison on 30 April: 'I take the liberty of informing you that I understand Mr. Hullock will be in London very early in the next week, and submit the Propriety of acquainting Mr. Bentham with that fact, in order that he may be prepared with the statement of his case.'

2210

To George Harrison

31 March 1813 (Aet 65)

Queen's Square Place Westmr 31 March 1813

Sir

In compliance with my humble request, as expressed in my Memorial of the 8th. of December last,[2] the Lords Commissioners of the Treasury were pleased, as in and by a letter of yours of the 16th of that month I was informed,[3] to give order that payment should be made to me of such sum as, after the customary deduction, should leave in my hands the neat sum of £363 : 1s. 2d being the amount of the first half yearly payment due on the 29th of September last on account of the provisional compensation Annuity granted to me in the then last Session by Parliament on the account in my said Memorial mentioned: in consequence of which order, on or about the 23d of January last, I received of Mr. James,[4] as Deputy to the Receiver General of the Land revenue for Middlesex etc. by draught on his Banker so much money as left in my hands neat the abovementioned sum: £390 : 11s : 11d, if I understand the matter right, was the gross amount of the sum, the issue of which was employed in the production of that effect.

At the conclusion of that same Memorial, taking into contemplation the state of things which now have place, I stated it as my humble intention, 'their Lordships not forbidding', to renew the like application half yearly, until such time as my definitive compensation should be awarded, and payment made accordingly. On the 25th of this month March, a second half yearly payment upon that same annuity became due. The object of this address is therefore, to beg the favour of you, Sir, to represent the matter to their Lordships, in such sort that payment may be made accordingly: and I take this liberty the earlier, because in consequence of a temporary deficiency in the abovementioned fund, and some uncertainty which attended the time of its replenishment, it was about five weeks before their

2210. [1] BL IX. 35–6. Copy. Docketed: '1813 Mar 31 / Panopt / J.B. Q.S.P. / to / Secry. Harrison Treasury / For Provisional Compensa- / tion Annuity 2d half yearly / payment due 24 March / 1813 / Left by Mr. Koe 1 April.' The Treasury index records the receipt of this letter (PRO T 2/64, no. 4499 of 1813), and Wharton responded to it on 13 April (see below letter 2213), but the original does not appear in the treasury papers.

[2] Letter 2197.

[3] Letter 2198.

[4] John James, solicitor, of 19 Red Lion Square. See letter 2227.

Lordships intentions and consequent orders in my favour were productive of their effect. I flatter myself that, in consequence of the appointment of the Arbitrators this is the last time that I shall have need to trouble you on this account. But as the making of the Award, and my receipt of the money thereupon are events which in respect of the time as well as in themselves are not altogether in my power, the present application has not, by the abovementioned incidents, been rendered the less necessary to me.

I am, with all respect, Sir, your most obedient Servant

J.B.

Mr Secry Harrison
Treasury.

2211

To Sir Samuel Bentham

7 April 1813 (Aet 65)

Wedy 7 April 1813

Along with this goes the remainder of No 2. 7 or 8 pages.[2]

The boy delivered to me from you No 4: 31 pages. In it I see the passage about Brunel:[3] which however I dare not venture upon till I have the benefit of your verbal explanation.

If it had been No 3, I believe I should have ventured to go on with it, though you say nothing on that subject. But the sight of 31 pages is a sickener: it would take me three days: and you could not perhaps spare that time: I very indifferently, certainly not in addition to No 3 which I should have ventured to attack (as being shorter) had I had it before me.

In No 2 and I believe in No 3 I have I believe, generally given the punctuation. With a view to facility of intellection this is an article of no mean importance direction should therefore be given for the copying of my punctuation in the Ms fair draught.

This Navy Board interruption, whatever it is, I am of course sore vext at.

2211. [1] BL VIII. 63, where it is incorrectly filed as a letter of 1803. Autograph.

[2] Bentham appears to have been looking at the proofs of Sir Samuel's *Services Rendered in the Civil Department of the Navy*, London, 1813.

[3] Marc Isambard Brunel (1769–1849), civil engineer of French origin, knighted in 1841. Many of his inventions were adopted by the British government and he had been in close contact with Sir Samuel. Brunel is mentioned in the fourth section of *Services Rendered*, entitled 'Statement of Services Relative to the Improvement of Manufactures Requisite in Naval Arsenals', pp. 157–65.

If I must occupy myself I had rather it were with No 3 than No 4 as coming earliest.

9 o clock. Just came the inclosed from Lady Spencer[4] which I opened.

2212
To Sir Samuel Bentham

7 April 1813 (Aet 65)

Admitt, I pray, the boy who is the bearer hereof, into the *Curiosity*-room and the garden—that 'in his own phrase' he may edify thereby.

Advertise me of your intended motions

2213
From Richard Wharton

13 April 1813

Sir,

I have in Command from the Lords etc. to transmit to you for your Information the accompanying Copy of their Lordships Minute of the 6th. inst.[2] upon your Letter of the 31st. Ulto.[3] requesting payment of the half years Allowance in lieu of the Rent of certain Lands surrendered to the Crown for the purpose of erecting a Penitentiary House.

13th. April 1813
R Wharton

[4] Lavinia Spencer, Countess Spencer (d. 1831), wife of George John Spencer, 2nd Earl Spencer (1758–1834), first lord of the admiralty 1794–1801, home secretary 1806–7. She had given Sir Samuel's naval reform projects encouragement and support.

2112. [1] George Bentham papers, Linnean Society of London. Autograph. Docketed: '1813 Apl 7th / JB–SB'. Addressed: 'To / Sir S. or Lady Bentham'.

2213. [1] PRO T 27/70, p. 449. Letter-book copy. Endorsed: 'Jeremy Bentham Esqr. / transg. Copy of / Minute–respectg. / payment of / Allowance in / lieu of Lands / Surrendered / to the Crown.' The original letter is not in Bentham's papers.

[2] Missing. The minute of 6 April 1813 is at PRO T 29/122, pp. 505–6. It reads:

'Read letter from Mr: Jeremy Bentham dated 31st Ulto. requesting payment of half a year's Allowance on account of the provisional Compensation granted by the Act of the [*cont. on p. 313*]

[3] Letter 2210.

2214

To Susannah Chicheley Koe

15 April 1813 (Aet 65)

Queens Square
Place Westmr. 15 April
1813

My dear Madam

This will be delivered to you by my worthy old friend and Housekeeper, Mrs. Elizabeth Stoker. I call her my friend, for, in her sphere of life, a true one she has ever been to me. Your kind consent to receive her for a while under your protection calls forth my sincere gratitude. Herbert undertook the management of the business, and has not communicated to me, or seemed very ready to communicate to me, the details: but, the result being such as it is, I, on my own account at least, can have no reason to complain.

As to my good woman, the purpose, for which we have all joined in the wish that she should have the benefit of breathing a little of the reviving air of Barrow Green, will be but too visible on her countenance: but air—even *that* air—would of itself be but an imperfect remedy, without that kind and condescending sympathy,

last Session amounting to £363..1..2 in lieu of the Rent of certain Lands surrendered to the Crown for the purpose of erecting a Penitentiary House the same being due on the 25th ulto [letter 2210].

My Lords resume the consideration of Mr Bentham's Letter of 25th Ulto. containing his nomination of an Arbitrator and read their letter of 15th Feby: last in which My Lords signified their nomination to Mr: Bentham and called upon him for his Appointment [letters 2209 and 2206].

It appears to my Lords that the Annuity secured to Mr. Bentham pending the discussion of his Claims by the Act of the last Session of Parliament is due to him up to 25th Ulto. but my Lords entertain doubts whether the period elapsing between the 15th Feby: and that date, during which the arbitration relative to those Claims might have been commenced and probably terminated had Mr. Bentham used due diligence in fixing on a proper person to act on his part therein, ought not to be taken into consideration hereafter by way of deduction from any Period in respect of which Mr: Bentham may claim the continuation of the said Annuity. For the present reserving that question, my Lords are pleased to direct that a Warrant be prepared requiring the proper Auditor of the Land Revenue to cause paymt: of the sum of £363..1..2 together with such further Sum as may be necessary to cover all charges incident to the issue and receipt thereof to be made to Mr: Bentham by the Receiver of Land Revenues for Middx: out of any Monies in his hands in discharge of this Annuity secured to that Gentleman under certain Limitations by the Act 52nd. G. 3rd Cap 44 up to the 25th March last.

Transmit Copy of this Minute to Mr: Bentham.'

2214. [1] UC clxiii. 9–12. Autograph copy. For Mrs Koe see letter 2049 n. 7.

which at first for *my* sake and afterwards, as you become acquainted with her, for *her own*, I have ventured to give her the assurance of. I will undertake for her being faithful to, and in every respect worthy of, whatever confidence you may be pleased to honour her with. Even in her best health, her manners have ever been as gentle and unassuming as you will find them in the present—I am sorry to find—very precarious state of it. It is to the excellence of her temper, joined to her other good qualities, that I have been indebted for the excellent servants that I have had under her, and for their joint attachment to herself and me. Nothing can be more correct than her behaviour has been in every respect throughout life: but her history you will have much better from herself than you could have it from me. Ever since my return from Barrow Green she was to have paid a visit by invitation to Mrs Mill, to spend a day or two there, had not the state of my family, in one way or other, proved a continual obstacle. She was in high favour with my next door neighbour and tenant Lady Mary Lindsay Crawford;[2] she sent her not long ago in her own equipage to the play in company with her Ladyships upper servant—*Mrs Wickerman*[3] I think her name is—who, not being of the London, but the Scotch breed, is likewise a very excellent woman in her sphere. I asked Mrs Stoker but now, whether she had seen her lately?—No: she had not.—How so?—Because, in the present state of my poor good woman⟨s⟩ health, the talking of the other, though at other ti⟨mes⟩ agreeable, was rather too much for her: and so, for the present she had declined seeing her. I take the liberty of mentioning this my dear Madam, that you may see—what she could not venture to inform you of herself—that much conversation at a time, howsoever kind, might be oppressive to her. What has reduced her so much lower this time than she ever was before, has been the great exertions she was obliged to make, to make up the deficiency of a poor creature of a servant she was obliged to take up with for some time: she looks to a little *rest* and *pure air* as affording her her only chance. A capital recommendation of Barrow Green to her was the solitude which I assured her of: together with the liberty of wandering alone and undisturbed, over the deligh[t]ful spots she had heard so much of.

But it is high time to put an end to this scrawl, which your eyes, my dear Madam, with all their acuteness will find no small difficulty

[2] Lady Maria Frances Margaret Lindsay (1783–1850), later Countess of Crawford and Balcarres, the daughter of John Pennington, 1st Baron Muncaster, and the wife (since 1811) of James Lindsay, Lord Lindsay (1783–1869), later 24th Earl of Crawford, 7th Earl of Balcarres, and 1st Baron Wigan of Haigh Hall.

[3] Not further identified.

in making sense of: the badness of it, which it is ever too late to remedy, is no small plague to myself as well as to my friends. T'other day I received from your old acquaintance of Tadley[4]—aged 92 or 93 I forget which—a letter[5] which, from the direction you would have judged to have been written by a man some thirty or forty years younger than myself: but he talks about his coffin in the inside of it.

Believe me ever
My dear Madam
with the truest respect and
regard
Your most obedient
and obliged humble
Servant
Jeremy Bentham

Mrs. Koe.

P.S. Many thanks for your kind remembrance in the article of *the flowers*: they have been taken care of:—not forgetting the long list of former luxuries.

The dear Princess[6] must have afforded you no small amusement of late.

[4] John Mulford. Bentham had been in contact with members of Mrs Koe's family—the Plowdens of Ewhurst—many years before. In his childhood he had spent time near Ewhurst with his mother's relations at Browning Hill, Baughurst, Hampshire. Tadley was also nearby. See letters 7 n. 1 and 1912 (*Correspondence*, i and vii).

[5] Missing.

[6] Probably a reference to the attempts made by Caroline, the Princess of Wales, to gain access to her daughter, Princess Charlotte. On 14 January 1813 Caroline had written to her husband on the subject but he returned her letter unopened. She then published it in the *Morning Chronicle*. The Prince referred the matter to the Privy Council, which decided that the restrictions imposed on Caroline's meeting Charlotte should continue. Caroline responded by writing to the Speaker on 1 March, who read her letter to the Commons. On 8 March she was then informed that even her limited visits to Charlotte were to be curtailed. Only the death of Caroline's mother on 23 March induced the Prince temporarily to relent and permit a brief meeting between his wife and her daughter.

2215

To Elizabeth Stoker

18 April 1813 (Aet 65)

Q.S.P.
18 April 1813

My good Mrs Stoker

I heard by means of the Gardener (whose arrival by the bye I was not informed of till he was gone) that you had already found sensible benefit from your expedition: you may imagine what satisfaction it gave me, to hear such good news of you already.

I forgot to mention to you the girl you will have seen at Barrow Green, and who is, and very justly—was at least a great favourite. Sooner or later she will quit that place, as she had not when I left Barrow Green any wages. Without saying any thing to her, keep your eye upon her, with the view of taking her here one of these days, should other resources fail us. She was eager to have gone with Mrs Mill, and cried bitterly at the disappointment: but of course Mrs Mill would not take her from Mrs Koe: so she took another girl from thence.

Your ever assured friend
J.B.

2216

To John Mulford

21 April 1813 (Aet 65)

Q.S.P., Wednesday,
21st April, 1813.

In a former letter,[2] you mentioned, I think, your having made an offer to my brother to send him some account of his genealogy by the mother's side,—the Groves. He does not care about these things near as much as I do: anything you could favour me with on that head, would be very interesting to me. What I remember hearing, is, that they came from the *Groves of Wiltshire*, which it was said was a

2215. [1] UC clxiii. 13. Autograph. Addressed: 'To / Mrs Stoker.'

2216. [1] Bowring, x. 473–4.

[2] Missing. Bentham's later remarks suggest it was an earlier letter than the one mentioned in letter 2214.

good gentleman's family.[3] Well do I remember a sword which T. West[4] used to keep in the granary to fight the rats with; it was said to have been employed by an ancestor of mine, when a student at Oxford, in defence of Charles the First.[5]

Would you like to see the 'Book', as it is called, that is, Mr Perceval's 'Defence of the Princess of Wales; including the charges against her'?[6] being printed in one or two numbers of *Cobbett*, I could send it you, as above, *post free*. It so happened that I was a good deal in the secret of that business: being upon the most confidential terms with her chief adviser,[7] his letters to the *Prince* and Officers of State, a good while before they were published, or even sent, were shown to me. *This you will take care not to mention.* So confident were the ministers of being able to ruin her reputation, that they deposited the papers they had against her in Whitbread's hands, that her chief adviser might see them, making sure that he would be intimidated, and that, accordingly, she would keep silence. When he saw them, however, he saw that there was nothing in them that he was not fully prepared for, and so she wrote those letters to the Lord Chancellor and the Speaker;[8] and so, for *our* amusement, everything came out. If you have read any newspaper of late, you must have seen how Lord Ellenborough fell, on this occasion, into one of his passions, and ran into such extravagances as to have had the effect of adding general contempt to the almost universal detestation he was held in before. Though, in general, he is what is called

[3] Bentham was perhaps thinking of the Groves of Ferne House, Donhead St Andrew. This family had provided a number of local MPs in the sixteenth and seventeenth centuries. Their relations, the Groves of Chisenbury and more recently of Zeals, also in Wiltshire, had produced an MP within Bentham's lifetime; William Chafin Grove (*c.*1731–93), MP for Shaftesbury 1768–74 and for Weymouth and Melcombe Regis 1774–81. It has not been possible to trace any connection between either of these families and Bentham's maternal ancestors.

[4] Unidentified.

[5] Perhaps Joseph Bentham (1594?–1671), the royalist clergyman and writer. He might have been the same man as the 'Josias Bentham' listed as BA New Inn Hall 1626, MA 1632.

[6] *The Genuine Book. An Inquiry, or Delicate Investigation into The Conduct of Her Royal Highness The Princess of Wales; before Lords Erskine, Spencer, Grenville, and Ellenborough, The Four Special Commissioners of Inquiry, Appointed by His Majesty in the Year 1806*, London, 1813. Known simply as 'The Book' this was 'superintended through the press' by Spencer Perceval before his death. It had been printed but not published in 1807 as a defence of Caroline.

[7] Brougham.

[8] For Caroline's letter to the speaker, see letter 2214 n. 6. 'Lord Chancellor' was perhaps a slip on Bentham's part (or a misreading by Bowring) for lord president. Caroline had written to the lord president of the council, Dudley Ryder, 1st Earl of Harrowby and Viscount Sandon (1762–1847) on 27 February about the privy council's report. See *Parliamentary Debates*, xxiv. 1127.

a *good lawyer*, on this occasion he fell into an error so gross, that an attorney's clerk might be ashamed of it. It took me, however, two or three long letters to expose it, in the *Examiner*, under the title of a 'Defence of Mr Whitbread,'[9] who was much pleased with it, and asked Brougham, whether he knew whose it was. Brougham, who had never heard from me, or anybody else, whose it was, told him, as soon as he saw it, (he was but just come from Yorkshire,) that he was sure it was mine; and this was the case with a multitude of others, who knew me at once by my style,

When you received the *Examiner*, you were pleased to think you had got a frank of Romilly's direction, though it was no such thing. This being the case, the next time I write to you shall be in that manner; unless he happens to be out of town, as he is at present. When this reaches you, it will find you free of your cough: you confess you were but in the fashion; how could you expect to be always out of it? That last letter of yours,[10] the handwriting, and everything belonging to it, is so provokingly strong and correct, there is no bearing it.

2217

From George Harrison

6 May 1813

Sir

The Lords Commissioners of His Majesty's Treasury having had under their Consideration your Letter of 25. March last[2] nominating Mr. James Wishaw to act as Arbitrator on your behalf; I have it in command from their Lordships to acquaint you it is understood that

[9] These 'long letters' or articles, signed 'An Ex-Lawyer', appeared in the *Examiner* of 28 March, 4 and 11 April 1813. Whitbread had argued in the Commons that in the examination of witnesses by the commissioners of inquiry into Caroline's conduct in 1806 both questions and answers should have been recorded. Ellenborough responded angrily in the Lords on 22 March (*Parliamentary Debates*, xxv. 207–13), claiming that the recording of questions was both unnecessary and contrary to practice. Bentham, in his articles, maintained that it was essential to know the questions to understand the answers, and produced precedents to refute Ellenborough's assertions about normal practice.

[10] Probably the letter referred to in letter 2214.

2217. [1] BL IX. 42–3. Autograph. Docketed: 1813 May 6 / Panopt. / Secy Harrison Treasury / to / J.B. Q.S.P. / Arbitrator Hullock expected / in town next week'. Letter-book copy at PRO T 27/70, p. 492.

[2] Letter 2209.

Mr. Hullock, the arbitrator on the part of the Public, will be in London very early in the next Week, in order that you may be prepared with a Statement of your Case.[3]

I am, Sir
Your obedient Servant
Geo. Harrison

Treasury Chambers
6th. May 1813.
Jeremy Bentham Esqre.

2218

To George Harrison

7 May 1813 (Aet 65)

Queen Square Place Westmr
May 1813

Sir,

Your letter of yesterday's date[2] found me occupied in the drawing up of the 'Statement of my case': a part of it already is in the hands of a Copyist. You speak of the Treasury Arbitrator, Mr Hullock, as being expected in town 'very early in the next week'. I know of nothing likely to prevent my being prepared with my aforesaid Statement by that time.

Your letter does not in express terms call for an answer: but, judging from the purport of it, coupled with that of their Lordships' Minute transmitted to me by the Letter of Mr Secretary Wharton dated the 13th of April last,[3] I thought it might be matter of satisfaction to their Lordships and serve as a token of my respect for their

[3] Harrison had written after receiving the letter from Hobhouse of 30 April quoted in letter 2209 n. 4.

2218. [1] PRO CRES 2/675. In the hand of a copyist, except the signature and Harrison's name and address. Docketed: 'May 1813 / Mr. Bentham / Further rel. to penitentiary / Houses / No 6322 / Recd. 7th May 1813 / Read 11 May 1813 / 2 Sheet 6 Div / Act / Mitford.' Robert Mitford was senior clerk at the Treasury 1812–16. An autograph draft of this letter is at BL IX. 44–5, docketed: '1813 May 7 / Panopt. / J.B. Q.S.P. / to / Harrison Treasury / In answer to his / of the 6th announcing / Hullocks return very / early in next week: / No Press copy taken / The Letter taken by Walter'

[2] Letter 2217.

[3] Letter 2213.

Lordships' implied commands, thus to hear from me that so far as depends upon myself, the business is thus far in it's way to a termination.

I am,
Sir,
Your most obedient Servant
Jeremy Bentham

G. Harrison Esqr
etc etc etc
Treasury Chambers.

2219

FROM ÉTIENNE DUMONT

18 May 1813

Mon cher Bentham, les Edgeworth et en particulier votre favorite[2]—ont la plus grande envie de ne pas quitter Londres sans vous avoir vu—je n'ai pas osé, sur mon grand crédit qu'on suppose, promettre plus que je n'étois sûr de faire—si vous y consentez, pour le temps et le mode, c'est à vous à déterminer. On demeure en Holles Street, Cavendish Square, n. 10—

Vous m'avez dit, je crois, qu'il vous restoit encore quelques papiers sur les Sophismes—Si cela est, ayez la bonté de me les envoyer.—J'ai fini—je vous renverrai les MSS. avant mon départ pour Ashdon.[3]

Adieu.

Mardi

2220

FROM JOHN HERBERT KOE

19 May 1813

Whishaw approves of this altogether and if you think it now right to be copied and will send it to me, I will forth with take measures about it.

2219. [1] BL IX. 46–7. Autograph. Docketed: '1813 May 18 / Dumont 19 Hay M / to / J.B. Q.S.P. / Edgeworths Visuriunt'. Addressed: 'Jeremy Bentham Esq.'

[2] Maria Edgeworth (1767–1849), the novelist, who, with her father Richard Lovell Edgeworth (1744–1817), had written *Practical Education*, London, 1798.

[3] Dumont was referring to what was to become *Traité des sophismes politiques*.

2220. [1] BL IX. 48. Autograph. Docketed: '1813 May 19 / Panopt Compensat. / H.K. Linc Inn / to / J.B. Q.S.P. / Whishaw approves / Compensation Claim'.

2221

From John Hullock and John Whishaw

27 May 1813

We the arbitrators appointed under the 52d Geo. 3d. c. 44. to determine upon a claim made upon Government by Jeremy Bentham Esqr, do hereby appoint our first Meeting on Tuesday next the first of June at Mr Whishaw's Chambers No 7 New Square Lincolns Inn at half past 9 in the morning when we desire to be attended by the Solicitors or Agents of the parties.[2]—

John Hullock
J Whishaw

May 27th. 1813.

2222

From Sir Samuel Bentham

27 May 1813

Hampstead 27th. May 1813

your note has been just brought me by the Postman at ten minutes past one o'clock[2] so that it is impossible for me to reach the Tontine office before two. All therefore that I can do in the first instance is to come to you tomorrow morning about 11 in hopes that by presenting myself at the office you may receive the money. Dr White[3] insisted upon it that his Certificate as he wrote it was proper

2221. [1] BL IX. 53–4. In the hand of a copyist, except the signatures. Docketed: '1813 May 27 Thursday / Panopt. Compensation / Whishaw / and / Hullock / Arbitrators / to / J.B. Q.S.P. / First meeting appointed / for Tuesday 1 June.'

[2] Bentham was represented by William Vizard (1774–1859), solicitor to Princess Caroline 1811–20, later solicitor to the home secretary and secretary of the bankruptcy court. The treasury's representative was Henry Dampier (1758–1816), a barrister of the Middle Temple, who was appointed justice of the court of king's bench on 23 June 1813 and knighted on the following 15 July. He appears to have been assisted by William Cooke (1757–1832), barrister of Lincoln's Inn and the author of a treatise on the *Bankrupt Laws*. (See BL IX. 89, where 'Mr. Cooke' is mentioned as a counsel for the treasury.)

2222. [1] BL IX. 55–6. Autograph. Docketed: '1813 May 27 / S.B. Hampstead / to / J.B. Q.S.P. / Tontine J.B.'s / Compensat. claim. / Venturit locuturus [?]'. Addressed: 'Jery. Bentham Esqr. / Queen Square Place / Westminster.' Postmark: '7 o'Clock / My 27 / 1813 N.T'. Stamped: '[. . .?] Unpaid [. . .?].

[2] Missing.

[3] Possibly Anthony White (1782–1849), of 5 Parliament Street, Westminster, assistant surgeon of the Westminster Hospital, but more probably John White (1756?–1832), the

being similar to what he had been used to give on similar occasions: many thanks for your draft but as you are uncertain how your account stands and as I probably have some credit I hope not to be obliged to make use of it. When your supply comes if mine is not yet come I shall be much obliged by your assistance.

If the papers are ⟨. . .⟩ some of my young ones are much to blame.

The Type should be the same with 'Services'[4] as by cheaper, in short which ever is the cheapest.

2223

To William Collins

28 May 1813 (Aet 65)

Q.S.P. 28 May
1813

My dear Sir

How many ages is it since you and I met? You know my Hermit life, but just now I have a particular reason for wishing to see you, for the purpose of begging from you some information, which may be of very essential service to me. In respect of visiting town, what at present are your habits? If that of a daily visit be among the number, so much the better: for if I could have the pleasure of seeing you *before Tuesday* so much the better for me. If you could not have come to town so soon, and it would be more convenient to you to see me at Greenwich, do me the favour to name a time, and you will take by the hand accordingly

Your grey-bearded old friend
Jeremy Bentham.

W. Collins Esqr.

former surgeon-general of New South Wales, surgeon at Sheerness yard 1799–1803 and Chatham 1803–20, where he almost certainly met Sir Samuel.

[4] Sir Samuel's *Services Rendered in the Civil Department of the Navy*.

2223. [1] BL IX. 57–8. Autograph draft. Docketed: 1813 May 28 / Panopt Compens / J.B. Q.S.P. / to / W. Collins / Greenwich'.

William Collins (d. 1819) had helped the Bentham brothers in various of their schemes. See *Correspondence*, v and vi, as index.

2224

From William Collins

29 May 1813

Mary's Hill Greenwich
May 29 1813

My Dear Sir

I shall be happy to wait upon you any hour of any morning next week—It will give me real pleasure to see you but I did not think it right to break in upon you without some notice on your part and if I can afford any information you want I shall consider myself very fortunate.

I am
My Dr. Sir
yours most truly
William Collins

2225

From Lady Bentham

May 1813

Your brother will be with you by $\frac{1}{2}$ past 10 at the *latest* tomorrow morning, we believe there is not a coach which would take him earlier—You will receive this evening by post an answer to your letter of yesterday,[2] which did not reach this till past one.

Laborers in the Ports yard actually earn more than 5 shillings per day in working your brothers machines, besides which there is a saving to Govt on each man's work of from one to five shillings a day as a difference between work done by machinery or by hand

2224. [1] BL IX. 59–60. Autograph. Docketed: '1813 May 29 / Panopt. Compens. / W. Collins Green- / wich / to / J.B. Q.S.P. / Veniet'. Addressed: 'Jeremy Bentham Esquire. / Queen Square Place / Westminster'.

2225. [1] BL IX. 61–2. Autograph. Docketed: '1813 May / Panopt. Compensat / Lady B Hampstead / to / J.B. Q.S.P. / Portsmouth Labourers / earn 5/- a day in / working S.B.s Ma- / chines'. Addressed: 'J Bentham Esqr'.

[2] Missing.

2226

From William Vizard

14 June 1813

Dear Sir

I send you the Treasury Answer to your claim[2]—No great effort can have been used in preparing such a document—You will find no difficulty in replying to it but remember the reply must be returned on Wednesday.[3]

I am Sir
Your faithful
and obedt Serv
Wm. Vizard

Linc. Inn
14 June 1813

2227

From John James

15 June 1813

Office for receipt of Crown Rents
No. 19. Red Lion Square
15th. June 1813

Mr. James presents his compliments to Mr. Bentham and acquaints Mr. B. that he may receive payment of his Debenture, at any time convenient for Mr. B. to send it to this Office, with *his* Receipt for the amount—

2226. [1] BL IX. 64–5. Autograph. Docketed: '1813 June 14 / Panopt. Compensat. / Vizard Linc. Inn / to / J.B. Q.S.P.' Addressed: 'Jeremy Bentham Esq / Queen Square Place / Westminster'. For Vizard see above letter 2221 n. 2.

[2] Missing.

[3] i.e. 16 June.

2227. [1] BL IX. 66–7. Autograph. Docketed: '1813 June 15 / Panopt Provis Compen / James No 19 Red Lion Sq. / to / J.B. Q.S.P. / Per Special Messenger'. Addressed: 'Jeremy Bentham Esq.'. For John James see above letter 2210 and n. 4.

2228

To William Vizard

15 June 1813 (Aet 65)

Q.S.P. 15 June
1813

Dear Sir

9 o'clock

With this you will receive, in addition to the *13* sent this morning between 10 and 11 through Mr. Koe, the remainder of the half sheets, 9 in number of my Reply to Mr Dampiers[2] paper of Observations. Considering the badness of my hand, lest any non-intended sense should find its way into the copy (for against *nonsense* the attention in your Office will be sufficient security) I could wish you to mention to the Gentleman on the other side, how in that respect the matter stands.

As to the once intended Conclusion, whatsoever may be the indulgence given to it by your opinion and that of Mr Koe, I have settled with myself, for the present at least and forbear forwarding it.

J.B.

2228. [1] BL IX. 82–3. Pressed copy of an autograph letter. Docketed: '1813 June 15 / Panopt. Compen / J.B. Q.S.P. / to / Vizard Linc Inn / With Brouillon of / Reply to Dampier's / Observations on / J.B.s Statement.'

[2] For Dampier see letter 2221 n. 2. His 'Observations' on Bentham's claim were referred to by Vizard in letter 2226.

2229

From William Vizard

16 June 1813

Dear Sir

Your reply is delivered to the Solicitor to the Treasury and I must beg the favour of you to return me Mr. Dampier's observations a copy of which I am to deliver to Mr. Whishaw

I am
Your faithful
and obedt Servant
Wm. Vizard

Lincolns Inn
16 June 1813

2230

To George Harrison

25 June 1813 (Aet 65)

Queen's Square Place Westm
25 June 1813

Sir

The inclosed was delivered to me while I was at dinner: and seeing the word Treasury at the corner of the cover, I hastily opened it, not suspecting that it could be designed for any other than the person at whose house it was delivered: a glance at that one of the two papers which has your signature to it, sufficed to make known to me the mistake. Under the unpleasant reflection of having opened a letter which was not designed for me I have the satisfaction to have seen what is sufficient to assure me that, the

2229. [1] BL IX. 76–7. Autograph. Docketed: '1813 June 16 / Panopt. Compensat. / Vizard Linc. Inn / to / J.B. Q.S.P. / J.B.'s Reply to / Dampiers Observation / on J.B.s Statement / delivered to Treasury / Solicitor / Dampiers Observat. / wanted for Whishaw / Returned the same / day by H.K.' Addressed: 'Jeremy Bentham Esq / Queen Square Place / Westminster'. Postmark: '10 o'Clock / 17 Ju / 1813 FN n'.

2230. [1] BL IX. 80–1. Autograph Draft. Docketed: '1813 June 25 / Panopt. Compensat. / J.B. Q.S.P. / G. Harrison Treas / ury / Returns a letter / delivered at J.Bs / by mistake in- / stead of to the Superintendants / of the Penitentiary / House.'

matter having nothing of heresy in its nature, the disclosure is in no danger of being productive of any unpleasant consequences. I have the honour to be,

Sir

Your most obedient Servt.
Jeremy Bentham

G. Harrison Esqr.
etc. etc. etc.
Treasury Chambers.

2231

To Sir Samuel Bentham

28 June 1813 (Aet 65)

Lincolns Inn 28 June 1813

I was quite unable to go out to Hampstead myself but Mr Ainslie and Mr Stavely[2] had the goodness to undertake the Commission you desired to have executed and the following is the report they have just been giving of their proceedings and communication with Mr Toller.[3] They first went to the Cellar whither they were accompanied by Mr. T. [. . .?] They found it so well stocked with a quantity of Crockery ware in addition to the old Iron and Lead, that Mr. T. said he would not have the things ⟨. . .⟩ disturbed, but would content him⟨self⟩ with the Cellar that was left open ⟨not⟩withstanding that he would thus be⟨. . .⟩ straitened for space. In return ⟨. . .⟩ the k⟨itchen⟩ with him he observed that he could not supply the ovens, and that he should be under the necessity of taking the kitchen grate out, which event he begun upon to day, and substituting a proper range in its place. They were then about to lock the book case door, at this Mr. T. expressed himself extremely indignant and observed that there were already a great many places already locked up in the House that ought to have been left open, and that

2231. [1] BL IX. 84–6. Pressed copy of an original in Koe's hand. Parts of this letter are illegible. Docketed: '1813 June 28 / Panopt. Compensat / J.B.'s [. . .?] Q.S.P. / to / S.B. Portsmouth / He and Burr to come to / give evidence to the Arbtn / on Thursday the 1st July'.

[2] Probably Thomas Staveley, later a clerk at the foreign office. For his role in forwarding mail to Sir Samuel in France see Bentham to Koe, 14 December 1817, Koe MSS.

[3] Perhaps either Edward Toller or Edward Toller junior, both proctors and notaries of Great Knightrider Street, Doctors Commons. The Toller family were to rent Hall Oak Farm until early February 1814. See Joanna Baillie to Lady Bentham, 4 February 1814, D. R. Bentham MSS.

for the accommodation of his family he should find himself under the necessity of opening some of the Cupboards in the course of next week if in the mean time you did not send orders to have them opened for him, and he wished it to be mentioned to you that he was induced to take this step from the directions you sent and have the Book case door locked up and he at the same time expressed himself very much hurt at the little confidence there seemed a disposition to repose in him: he however desired that the Book case might be locked up which was attempted, but unsuccessfully as it could not be done they say without the assistance of a Carpenter. He moreover observed that there were a number of things required, and which he did not find in the House, neccessary for the accommodation of his family, such too as were usually found in houses let as that was, which he should purchase and deduct the cost out of the money that would come to be paid to you—This is all very unfortunate. Nothing was said about the Catalogue for fear of producing a further degree of irritation. They have brought here a quantity of Keys which will be sent to you by tomorrows Coach.

P.S. by J.B. At a meeting of the Arbitrators to day, present H.K. and Vizard it was Voted that you and Burr[4] should be summoned on Thursday [. . .?] Paid[?] for Burr have [. . .?] [. . .?] Hobhouse[5] one of the Solicitors to the Treasury [. . .?] to write the needful [. . .?] [. . .?] Burr to [. . .?]

Wednesday. You will of course advance to him on my account [. . .?] [. . .?] and probably sufficient. You had better see him to prepare him, and tell him what it is for, otherwise a Letter from such a [. . .?] may frighten him. The aspect seems rather favourable than the [. . .?] Hobhouse is a cousin of Sir Benjamin's.[6] He has made advances for a compromise. Unfortunately Harrison the Under Secretary of the Treasury, through whom it is to be conducted, was not at the Treasury [. . .?] being reported indisposed: otherwise Vizard would have seen him to day.

A day or two ago, Ld. Lucan[7] called in my absence to learn your address. Lady Spencers father or Brother he is:[8] I know not which. The printer has called upon me, [. . .?] says it is very inconvenient to him to have the Press so long standing.

[4] James Burr.

[5] Henry Hobhouse.

[6] Sir Benjamin Hobhouse, Bt. (1757–1831), MP for Hindon. For Bentham's earlier contact with him see *Correspondence*, vii, as index.

[7] Richard Bingham, 2nd Earl of Lucan (1764–1839).

[8] Countess Spencer was sister of the 2nd Earl of Lucan.

2232

FROM WILLIAM VIZARD

29 June 1813

Dear Sir

I have just recd. a letter of which I send you a copy[2]—What is to be said to it?

I am
Your faithful
and obedt. Servant
Wm. Vizard

Lincolns Inn
29 June 1813

2233

FROM SIR SAMUEL BENTHAM

30 June 1813

Wednesday evening seven o clock your Letter received but this instant;[2] it is impossible for me to come tonight, but I will come in the course of tomorrow, and bring Burr[3] with me if he has received his notice and is not go⟨ne⟩

MSB from SBs dictation

2232. [1] BL IX. 88. Autograph. Docketed: '1813 June 29 / Panopt. Definitive / Compensat. / Hobhouse Sol. to Treasury / to / Vizard Linc. Inn / for J.B. / Copy'. Addressed: 'Jeremy Bentham Esq / Queen Square Place / Westminster'. Postmark: '8 o'Clock / 30 Ju / 18:3 Mn'. Stamped: '[. . .?][. . .?] / Unpaid / Lincoln's Inn'.

[2] The letter from Hobhouse to Vizard, dated 29 June 1813, is at BL IX. 87. It reads:

'I have this Morning seen Mr. Wharton and am directed by him to say that he does not see that a Conference can be usefully had with you unless you are prepared to state what the reasonable expectations of your client are as to the Amount of his Compensation and that if you can make such a Statement, it would be better that you should in the first instance communicate it to Mr. Litchfield or myself, so that it may—undergo some consideration preparatory to a—Conference.'

Bentham's comments on this letter are at BL IX. 89, docketed: '1813 June 29 / Panopt. Compens. / J.B. / Explanations on Solicit / Hobhouses Letter to Vizard'.

2233. [1] BL IX. 90. Autograph. Docketed: '1813 June 30 / Panopt. Compensat / Lady B. Berry Lodge / Gosport / for S.B. / to / J.B. Q.S.P. / H.K.'s Summoning Letter of Monday / 28 not received till / this day Wedny at 7 P.M. / S.B. arrived at Q. / S.P. Thursday 1 July, about 7 P.M.' Addressed: 'Jeremy Bentham Esqr. / Queen Square Place / Westminster'. Postmark: '6/2 JY 2/1813'. Stamped: 'PORTSMOUTH/1 JY/13'.

[2] Letter 2231.

[3] James Burr.

2234

FROM EDWARD BLAQUIERE

7 July 1813

Utile, North Yarmouth,
July 7th, 1813.

Before I say anything about my own more immediate concerns, I beg to inform you how your works first attracted my attention. Being at Gibraltar in 1805, I saw the critique on the '*Traités de Législation*' in the Edinburgh Review[2] and lost no time in sending to England for a copy of the work. I need scarcely add, that its perusal amply repaid the trouble and anxiety experienced before I could get it sent out. You will probably be gratified to know what effect the book produced on my mind at first: I had previously considered law as involved in such intricacy, that it struck me as being quite useless to attempt entering into the study of a science, so apparently abstruse, and beyond the reach of ordinary capacities: but the word legislation contained an irresistible charm: and no sooner had I seen the plain and simple manner in which you teach men to govern, than a new impulse was instantly given to all my thoughts, and I made the '*Traités de Législation*' a groundwork of future study, in which I have indulged freely, though not very successfully, ever since. From the work having been printed at Paris or Geneva, I forget which, it occurred to me that you were on the continent—in which supposition I have indulged—till meeting Mr Peak[3] here just before I took the liberty of addressing you last.[4] Of the work upon crimes and punishments,[5] I was totally ignorant till my arrival in England, about a year ago. Since that time I have read it twice, and am now going over it the third time. To enumerate the beauties I have discovered in every chapter, would be to exhaust your

2234. [1] Bowring, x. 475–6.

Edward Blaquiere (1779–1832), lieutenant in the Royal Navy 1801, stationed in the Mediterranean 1805–13. He was later described by Bowring (x. 514) as 'a sort of wandering apostle of Benthamism'. For further details of his career see Claire Gobbi, 'Edward Blaquiere: agente del liberalismo (1779–1832)', *Cuadernos Hispano-americanos*, cccl (1979), 306–25.

[2] Jeffrey's 'Bentham, Principes de Législation' appeared in the *Edinburgh Review*, iv (1804), 1–26.

[3] John Peake, who worked under Sir Samuel Bentham as secretary in the naval works department 1796–1807, and then as extra assistant to the civil architect and engineer of the navy at the navy board.

[4] The earlier letter here alluded to is missing.

[5] Dumont's *Théorie des peines et des récompenses.*

patience: suffice it to add, that I consider it, and the preceding work, two of the most important published since the days of the immortal Lord Bacon. This may be thought flattery; but believe me, Sir, it is the language of my heart. Anxious to get hold of anything from your pen, I have been making continual researches, and called at Mr Dulau's, in Soho Square,[6] repeatedly; but he could give me no information. I then inquired for Mr Dumont, but was equally unsuccessful; but, on my arrival here, was more fortunate; for, in the catalogue of a library at Norwich, I found two productions, the perusal of which has given me considerable pleasure. Your 'Defence of Usury' published in 1787, and another, 'Supply, without Burthen', in 1795. In the former I read your letter to Dr Smith[7] with peculiar satisfaction. His indiscriminate expressions relative to prodigals and projectors had often struck me as partaking of that species of irascibility in which his countrymen often delight; but you certainly have the merit of setting him to rights most effectually. I am truly astonished the self-evident truths contained in the last mentioned pamphlet were not adopted by the Ministry: but why should I be surprised at anything?

When on the point of leaving Sicily, where I have still some very valuable correspondence, I received a commission to send out several copies of your work on Legislation, which, of course, I executed. But I very much fear that those in whose hands they are will not have the means of carrying any of your valuable hints into effect. The state of Sicily is not to be described: it is infinitely worse than I have related, in every respect. I beg to call your attention to the character alluded to in the first vol. Lett. XI. p. 350:[8] his name is Agostino Puleo.[9] He is a man of transcendant abilities and uncommon learning. He was bred to the law; and the style his manuscript breathes is precisely in your own way of thinking. His works will, I trust, be given to the world some day or other; but at present he is the object of suspicion, and has long been that of unmerited persecution. Would to God it were possible to take such a man from among the savages he is doomed to live with! I am indebted to him for an infinity of information upon every subject. Had it not been for the '*Traités de Législation*' and 'Agostino Puleo', I do not think my work would have ever seen the light. Amongst many allusions made to

[6] A. B. Dulau and Co., of 37 Soho Square, importers of foreign books.

[7] Adam Smith (1723–90), the famous Scottish economist and moral philospher, author of *An Enquiry into the Nature and Causes of the Wealth of Nations*, London, 1776.

[8] i.e. Blaquiere's *Letters from the Mediterranean*, 2 vols., London, 1813.

[9] This man, described as a scholar, lawyer and orator and one of the 'real friends of England', is never named in Blaquiere's book.

him in the course of my letters, there is one, p. 609, vol. i.,[10] which may have attracted your attention.—Believe me, with utmost respect,

your most devoted and obedient servant.

2235

From Étienne Dumont

13 July 1813

Mon cher Bentham, je suis bien fâché de partir sans avoir eu le plaisir de vous voir—mais je me suis trouvé engagé aujourd'hui et demain—et je suis attendu Jeudi à Ashdon. J'ai appris de Wishaw les termes de l'arbitrage dont il est très mécontent, quoiqu'il pense que vous avez bien fait pour votre repos, *rem prorsus substantialem*,[2] de vous tirer des griffes de la Trésorerie—J'ai toute cela sur le coeur—

Je reviendrai vers le 12 de Juillet[3] mais je suppose que vous serez à Barrowgreen. Je m'en informerai à mon retour. Adieu

Et D.

Mardi

2236

From Richard Wharton

14 July 1813

Treasury Chambers
14th. July 1813.

Sir,

I am commanded by the Lords Commissioners of His Majesty's Treasury to transmit to you for your information a copy of their Minute of yesterday's date[2] on perusal of the award of John Hullock

[10] At this point in Blaquiere's work Puleo, in a long speech, talks, *inter alia*, of the bribery and corruption of lawyers.

2235. [1] UC clxxiii. 10a. Autograph. Docketed: '1813 July 13 / Dumont Hay Mt. / to / J.B. Q.S.P. / Going to Ashdon / *Award displicet*'. Addressed: 'Jeremy Bentham Esq. / Queen Square Place'.

[2] i.e. 'certainly a substantial matter'.

[3] Clearly a mistake if Bentham's dating of this letter is correct.

2236. [1] BL IX. 91–2. Autograph. Docketed; '1813 July 14 / Panopt. Definitive Compensat. / Wharton Treasury / to / J.B. Q.S.P. / Inclosing Minute respecting / the deferring of the payment.' Letter-book copy at PRO T 27/71, p. 107.

[2] The copy of the minute is at BL IX. 93–4. docketed: '1813 July 13 / Panopticon

and John Whishaw Esqrs. the Arbitrators chosen and appointed under the authority of the 52 Geo. 3. C. 44 for the purpose of settling all questions between the publick and you.

I am
Sir
Your very obedient Servant
R Wharton

Jeremy Bentham Esqr.

2237

To Sir Samuel Bentham

15 July 1813 (Aet 65)

Q.S.P. Friday 15 July 1813.

The hue of my yesterday's letter[2] was a lugubrious one: the prospects which suggest the present one have, to my view at least, something chearing in them. Few of your 'Services'[3] will have been better bestowed than the one I put so lately as Friday or ⟨. . .⟩ into

Definitive Compensat. / Treasury minute relative to / the deferring payment / Transmitted by Letter of / Secry. Wharton dated the 14th'. It reads:

'Read Letter from the Solicitor to this Board dated the 10th. Instant enclosing the Award of John Hullock and John Whishaw Esqres. the arbitrators chosen and appointed under the authority of the 52d. Geo.3.Cap.44 for the purpose of settling all questions between the public and Mr. Bentham arising out of an agreement therein referred to—by which the Solicitor states that after deducting from the Claims of Mr. Bentham as well the Sum of £2,000 advanced to him in the year 1794 as the amount of the profits which he has derived from the Lands at Milbank whereof he was Feoffee, the said arbitrators have awarded the sum of £23.000 clear of all Deductions to be paid to Mr. Bentham in the manner prescribed by the said Act as a full compensation to him in respect to all matters and things referred to them by virtue of the said Act. My Lords read also the Act of the 52d Geo 3. Cap.44—It appears to my Lords that in framing the said Act Parliament has not accurately adverted to the Provision of Law under which no issue can be made out of the Consolidated Fund except at the expiration of a Quarter; so that the Enactment that the sum awarded to Mr. Bentham shall be paid to him within one Month after the date of the award entitling him to the same cannot legally be executed.

With a view however to obviate as far as possible any disappointment which may result to Mr. Bentham on this Account My Lords will direct a Warrant to be prepared for paying to Mr. Bentham on the 10th day of October next out of the Consolidated Fund of Great Britain the sum of £23,000 with Interest for the same after the rate of 5 p Cent. to be computed from the 9th. day of August being one month after the date of the said Award.'

2237. [1] BL IX. 95–6. Autograph. Docketed: '1813 July 15 / JB–SB'. Addressed: 'To / Sir Samuel Bentham / Berry Lodge / near Gosport'.

[2] Missing.

[3] Sir Samuel's recently-printed *Services Rendered in the Civil Department of the Navy.*

the hands of Mill. He took it to *Wakefield's*;[4] and he and W. read together the Chapter on Naval Accounts. Yes, cries W. from this has been taken every thing that is good for any thing in this plan about Northfleet.[5]

Now so it happens that this man W. has a good deal to say and to do about this same Naval Arsenal, wheresoever it may happen to it to be situated say Northfleet for shortness.

The connecting threads, as far as I caught them last night in a short conversation with M. are these. Wakefield is upon a footing of considerable and old-established intimacy with Lord Melville.[6] His Brother, now at the Bar[7] (not a very good character)—was for some years private Secretary to the first Lord Melville. He is likewise upon terms of intimacy with two great Merchants both I believe India Directors—*Read*[8] and *Ric*hardson[9] (I think) their names:—if in this there should be error it shall be corrected another time. *Read* is particularly connected with Ld M: Ld M. upon first coming to London (a youth) was particularly consigned to Reads care. (How so, having his own father in Town and in high Office? Not having asked, this I can not answer.) These Merchants are the principally active Citizens in the scheme about Northfleet, and W. knows them all, and all about it; and goes about it from one to another and from them to Lord M. It is to be brought forward next Session: it was put aside this Session—not from any disinclination, but merely for want of time. Of course you must have heard more or less of it: some things probably that are true and that I have not yet heard. The thing to be undertaken by a Company of Merchants to be incorpor-

[4] Edward Wakefield (1774–1854), philanthropist and statistician, employed for a time at the naval arsenal. He was a friend of Mill and a supporter of Lancaster's educational theories.

[5] In 1799 Sir Samuel had proposed the building of a new naval arsenal at the Isle of Grain. Despite initial approval, the site was rejected. In 1810 a pamphlet was published, quoting, without acknowledgement, his arguments for such an establishment, but favouring Northfleet as an appropriate location (see *Naval Considerations Relative to the Construction of a New Naval Arsenal at Northfleet*). After inspecting Northfleet later that year, Sir Samuel was again convinced that the Isle of Grain was a preferable site. See M. S. Bentham, *The Life of Brigadier-General Sir Samuel Bentham*, London, 1862, pp. 268, 273–6.

[6] Robert Saunders Dundas, 2nd Viscount Melville (1771–1851), first lord of the admiralty 1812–27, 1828–30.

[7] Presumably Daniel Wakefield (1776–1846), writer on political economy, called to the bar at Lincoln's Inn 1807.

[8] Thomas Reid, director of the East India Company, the London Dock Company, and the Imperial Insurance Company.

[9] In letter 2238 Bentham corrected this error: he meant Rutherford not Richardson. Abraham Watson Rutherford was a director of the Equitable Assurance Company and of the Imperial Insurance Company.

ated in the manner of the Undertakers of the London Docks: in what precise manner they are to have their profit I have not heard Estimated cost, per Rennie,[10] £4,000,000: the money to be advanced by Subscription the Subscribers of course to have the execution of the business. Why?—because quoth Ld M. to W. '*the Board are altogether incapable of it.*' Between the interest of Government in respect of the public, on the one hand, and that of the Undertakers there seems about to be—how extraordinary so ever it may seem—a sort of connection in such sort that Government / Ld M. at least / had rather see that estimated cost reduced than encreased. In this view a proposition had been made and acceded to some time ago that in case of its coming to more than the £4,000,000, the Undertakers should some how or other be proportionably *losers*. Lately a further clause was proposed, viz. that in case of its coming to *less*, they should proportionably be *gainers*. T'other day this being mentioned to Ld M.—'really' (quoth he) '*this had never occurred to me*:' and of his approbation of it evident marks were visible.

Now if Rennie could do it for £4,000,000, you could, I suppose, do it for considerably less: the difficulty would be in *convincing them* of it. But the curious thing is that *W*—though he has no quarrel with Rennie, but has all along been and still continues to be on terms of intimacy with him—should now be willing as he has all along appeared to be, such is his public virtue—to promote your plans in preference to Rennies. Upon this I gave M. a copy of '*Services*' to give to W. in addition to the one which I had given him for himself, and of which he had made so good a use.

Does not all this present a reason for expediting the intended impression of your Indications etc. about Naval Arsenals?[11] or rather is it not already printed? though I see not that I have got or have ever had a copy of it and H.K. is not here to tell me about it.

Is there not some attack of yours upon Rennie finished though not printed? If so, might it not be of use that W. should see it?[12]

Before I commence my tour, which will not last less than 3 weeks if so little, should I not have W. here, to examine him about the particulars of this Arsenal plan? If so, and you have any *Instructions* to send me, I must have them without loss of time: for I shall set out, if I can, before *ten* days are at an end.

[10] Rennie was involved in the scheme to erect a new establishment at Northfleet; drawing up plans for it took up much of his time at this period. The scheme eventually came to nothing, however, as the site was rejected by the government.

[11] *Desiderata in a Naval Arsenal, or an Indication of several Particulars in the Formation or Improvement of Naval Arsenals; together with a Plan for the Improvement of the Naval Arsenal at Sheerness*, London, 1814.

[12] Apparently not published.

In regard to *Burnham*[13] (is not that the name of the place near the Isle of Foulness?) upon being interrogated W. said that Ld Winchelsea[14] is the principal proprietor and I believe it is of him that he rented the Estate—but that there are several little proprietors. Understanding some how or other of Mill that I had some reason in the way of interest for wishing to learn some particulars about it, he expressed a readiness to go down himself to the spot for the purpose of making enquiries.

If W. gets invited here as proposed, should not provision be made for furnishing him with Copies of '*Services*' for any such Members of the proposed Company as appear to be influential?

Per dictation of H.K.

The Navy Board have just given notice to Grellier to put an end to the Annual Contract, and, by Rennie's directions, the Cement Mills at Sheerness are to be pulled down.

H.K. upon my inquiring said that this could not affect the scheme of employing the Steam Engine in Wheel-making.[15]

Mackintosh,[16] Whishaw and Mill dined here yesterday: Mackintosh appears very friendly and pleased with his visit. It was in the course of the few minutes that Mill staid after they were gone that the above information was collected.

There can be no doubt that W. will embrace every occasion that presents itself of impressing Ld M. with a favourable opinion of you. But probably so much will not depend upon him as upon other wretches[?]. He is said to be not very ill disposed but weak and ignorant.

Upon talking with H.K. I find he has at Chambers a parcel of your *Desiderata etc. etc. Naval Arsenal.* He will bring some hither this afternoon: and tomorrow, having occasion to send to Mill, I shall probably put up one for him to give to Wakefield. Asking H.K. about your attack on Rennie, he said he understood it to have been suspended: but he did not know for what reason. You may now perhaps find reasons for continuing it.

[13] Burnham-on-Crouch, Essex.

[14] George Finch, 9th Earl of Winchelsea (1752–1826).

[15] Probably a reference to one of Sir Samuel's inventions, although no such device appears in the list of his patents.

[16] Sir James Mackintosh (1765–1832), philosopher, judge, and politician. He had just become MP for Nairn.

2238

To Sir Samuel Bentham

18–19 July 1813 (Aet 65)

Q.S.P. Sunday 18 July 1813.

The prospect clears up and brightens. Accident brought Mill here today for a few minutes, and in that time I have got from him what follows.

Who could have thought it? W.,[2] instead of having more or less to do with it in quality of go between and in the way of suggestion, will virtually have the sole management in his hands.

The money being to be found all of it by the private undertakers, is all of it engaged for and in readiness. The acting persons are 1. Read—an E. India Director—on account of his connection with Ld M. as per my last.[3] 2. *Rutherford*—(not Richardson the name erroneously mentioned in my last). Read will have no concern in it without his friend Rutherford. Rutherford will have no concern in it *without* W.—would have had no concern in it but for W. in whom his confidence is. Agreed that the execution shall be vested in three Commissioners: viz. those three. Rutherford is infirm, unwilling—and to his own conviction unable to take an active part in any such business. His principal inducement is the making *a job* (so to speak for shortness) for W. For probity and intelligence Rutherfords opinions of the Ministry and the Offices in general agree exactly with ours: if they were the persons to look to for the money, he would have nothing to do with them. W. read through your Services t'other day as soon as they were put into his hands, one result was an anxious wish to see in print the documents therein referred to.

Rennie, understanding the official part of the business to be about to be vested in his hands is as civil to him as ever Puss was to the travelling-puss and dog-ordinary woman.[4] How then can W. get clear of him?—in this way. As soon as he is in the saddle, he gets his Colleagues to join in an advertisement for a competition. To this no objection can be made. If you then give in a plan, and that plan obtains a preference, W. has his two superior colleagues to stand in

2238. [1] BL IX. 97–8. Part autograph, part in the hand of a copyist. Docketed: '18th July 1813 / JB–SB'. Addressed: 'To / Sir S. Bentham / Berry Lodge / Gosport'. Postmark: 'JY / [. . .?] / ⟨1⟩813'.

[2] Edward Wakefield.

[3] Letter 2237.

[4] Presumably the woman bringing round food for cats and dogs.

the gap and take it upon themselves. If they decide in your favour, he is but one, and can not help it.

About the cost, as per estimate H.K.'s recollection is whether from you or any body else that at one time it was to have been £10,000,000. Now, if I recollect aright from Mill, it is to be but £4,000,000. The suggestion of the additional per centage was from Mill: (originally of course from you): from Mill to W. from W. to R. and R.[5] and from one of them and from W. to Ld. M. and so by him approved of, as by my last.

Now then for your attack on Rennie: viz. (as per H.K.) on the ocasion of the Sheerness business: and observes he, W. could as well read it in Ms as in print.[6]

W. who throws his thoughts around him beholds in the spot the centre of a future town, the houses of which will by degrees crystallize around it; and think about the government of it.

The misfortune of it is—that Northfleet being the place fixed upon, nothing can safely be said against it by W., howsoever his opinion about it may agree with yours. Untill the Act is passed, and his appointment is actually made out, prudence requires him to keep in the back ground.

Whether after he and his colleagues are appointed it will be possible for him, should he be so disposed, to propose any change of place is a thing not to be spoken to at present.

This day Mill was pressed for time. On Tuesday he dines here: and then I shall talk to him at large about getting a sight of any papers that may as yet have passed upon the business.

If the complection of the business turns out favourable, I shall naturally be disposed to lay out some of my money in that way; viz. if there is any room for Subscribers. H.K. is afraid of your setting yourself to kick against the pricks, and fight the existing situation, instead of swimming with the stream, and setting yourself to plan how to do what is to be done: which said *faciendum* you shall learn almost as soon as I do, and I will learn it as soon as I can.

If not for you, here may be work for Stevens.[7]

At any rate W. is fully impregnated with the Panopticon principle, and will make what application he can of it.

When I saw Mill today he had not yet had time to look at your Arsenal paper,[8] nor consequently had W. read it.

[5] Reid and Rutherford.

[6] See letter 2237 and n. 12.

[7] Perhaps John Stevens (d. 1857), surveyor of 54 Green Street, Grosvenor Square.

[8] *Desiderata in a Naval Arsenal, or an Indication of several Particulars in the Formation or Improvement of Naval Arsenals*. See letter 2237.

W. will of course be glad to have the Act (the Act of Parliament that must be passed) looked over by Bentham the Great: who in that case will be as careful to keep his interference a secret in this case as he was in that of the Thames Police Act.[9]

The manner of concluding the Cement Contract, as I am told, was this. Mr Rennie attended at the N Bd[10] and told them that the situation of the Mill at Sheerness interfered with the carrying into execution the proposed plan for the yard and that it must in consequence be pulled down. In obedience to this declaration and without requiring any specific reason for the removal of the Mill, the N Bd have given notice, dated a few days back, to Grellier that the Contract is to be considered as determined at the expiration of 6 months from the date of the notice. As it is a Contract from which profit might be, though very little in point of fact has been, derived, Grellier proposes the offer to the N Bd to take down and rebuild in any spot that may be allotted for the purpose, the Mill at his own expence and to supply Government thereafter from thence at 2s /4d per Bushel, and in the meantime until the Mill is rebuilt he offers to supply whatever quantity may be wanted, at the same price (viz 2s /4d per Bl) from his own manufactory. There seems howev⟨er⟩ very li⟨ttle⟩ probability, unless properly backed, tha⟨t⟩ this pro⟨pos⟩al should be accepted, as the inducement for pulling down the existing Mill seems not unlikely to have been the getting rid of the existing Contractor and the substituting in his place the more worthy Mr Wyatt,[11] who, I understand, has a very large stock of Cement Stone on hand with the use of which he would of course be very happy to oblige his Majestys Government. I gave long ago to Romilly a copy of Services for himself and another for G. Wilson[12] which he engaged to forward to him. The Vauxhall committee begin already, I am told, not to be very well satisfied with their new Engineer,[13] and a very great majority of them would there seems every reason to suppose were they not in dread of the imputation of fickleness be extremely willing to return to the mass plan.[14] But however that

[9] For Bentham's role in the preparation of the Thames Police bill see *Correspondence*, vi. 91–2, 122 and n., 354 and n.

[10] Navy board.

[11] Charles Wyatt (*c*.1751–1819) of Parker and Wyatt, the firm that originally manufactured Roman cement, which had been patented in 1796 by his partner James Parker.

[12] George Wilson (1755–1816), barrister, who had known Bentham since 1776, but was no longer close to him. He had retired to Edinburgh in 1810 after an attack of palsy. See *Correspondence*, i. 293 n.

[13] James Walker (1781–1862), the civil engineer who took over the building of Vauxhall Bridge from Rennie, substituting an iron structure for the masonry construction originally envisaged.

[14] See letter 2113 and n. 3.

may be, contrary to the determinations they had taken upon engaging with Walker and contrary certainly to Walkers wishes, Seven out of nine of them are determined that the two first Piers shall not be disturbed, as was communicated to Grellier in confidence at their last meeting with a recommendation to stand staunch with them in resisting the common enemy. Buckly, as having introduced him, is still the firm adherent of Walker. He has lately made the trifling addition of Seven hundred tons to the quantity of Iron intended to be employed—and that too since the drawings and Contract were made and signed.

Monday morng 19th Just received your letter[15] if my former was a spear, the present one will be a spike. What a scrawl do you scribble! not half the strokes that a word has a right to! This is *calligraphy* to it. Ask your reprobates what that means. W.'s offer I never had a thought of accepting. I only mentioned it to shew his devouement.

The *Times* came here yesterday for the first time, and was forwarded in due course. A very good Letter from Vetus (25)[16] The direction they had taken down from you was a wrong one. H.K. called and set them right.

P.S. Should any demand for personal intercourse between you and W. present itself, before hollow tree is open to receive you again, your betters being absent either on the tour or at Barrow Green, you might come here with all your incumbrances springing upon said betters, as said betters did upon you.

2239

From Sir James Mackintosh

20 July 1813

July 20, 1813.

My Dear Sir,

I have been so exceedingly struck with a reperusal this forenoon, that I begin to doubt whether I was not wrong in advising delay. If

[15] Missing.

[16] *The Times* of Saturday 17 July 1813 contained the 25th letter of 'Vetus' on the subject of the war against Napoleon and the conduct of various British politicians. 'Vetus' was Edward Sterling (1773–1847), a military writer who subsequently became a regular member of the staff at *The Times*.

2239. [1] Bowring, x. 476. Introduced: 'I find this note from Sir James Mackintosh on the subject of "Swear not at all".'

it were to be published separately,[2] I should venture to suggest a preface, with two objects: 1. To state that the discussion may be considered as speculative, from the distance of possible application. 2. To disclaim any attack on individuals, in the Oxford case chosen only as a strong illustration.[3]

2240

To Sir Samuel Bentham

24 July 1813 (Aet 65)

Q.S.P. Saty 24 July 1813

Reced Your's i.e. Lady B's letter this morning,[2] and observe the contents. H.K. of course not now at home, but at Linc. Inn.

Yesterday or the day before came a man from Lloyd's[3] to take any thing there might be to send to be packed up in the Oven, but so long as he staid nothing could I recollect. When he was gone, I recollected an inclination you had expressed to have Captn Beavers Account of the Settlement at Bulama on the African Coast:[4] if you had mentioned it you would have had it: as you forgot it, no wonder I should, startled as I was by the unexpected visit of the company, in the middle of my scribble.

Yesterday made a trading voyage—left a 'Services' with Ld St Helen's[5]—got an invitation to a family party there to dinner on that day—could not have accepted it if I would, Brougham being engaged to dine with me. On Monday he goes off for the North, and returns not till Octr. 28th.

[2] *'Swear not at all:' Containing an Exposure of the Needlessness and Mischievousness, as well as Anti-Christianity, of the Ceremony of an Oath* (Bowring, v. 187–229), was printed in 1813 but not published until 1817. It was originally intended as an appendix of 'Introductory View of a Work now in the press entitled The Rationale of Evidence, for the use of Non-Lawyers as well as Lawyers', partly-printed in 1812 (UC xlv. 2).

[3] Oaths at Oxford are dealt with in section 11 of *'Swear not at all'*: 'Mischief 6—Corrupting the National Morals and Understanding—Oxford University Oaths' (Bowring, v. 209–12).

2240. [1] BL IX. 99–100. Autograph. Docketed: '1813 July 24 / JB–SB'. Addressed: 'To / Sir Samuel Bentham / Berry Lodge / near / Gosport.' Postmark illegible.

[2] Missing.

[3] John Lloyd.

[4] Captain Philip Beaver (1766–1813) of the Royal Navy was the author of *African Memoranda: Relative to an Attempt to Establish a British Settlement on the Island of Bulama, on the Western Coast of Africa, in the year 1792*, London, 1805.

[5] Alleyne Fitzherbert, Baron St Helens (1753–1839), diplomat. He retired in 1803 but was an old acquaintance of the Benthams. See above letter 2179.

In his way, he spends three days at Whitbread's near Bedford.[6] He takes 2 Services, one for his own reading, the other to leave with Whitbread. He says he will read *his* Copy there, that he may talk to W. about it, or make him read it. H.K. I don't know very well why, opposed in Br.'s presence my adding a Copy of Naval Arsenal Indications:[7] his reason was that being so obvious many of the Indications (admitting that there are others that are not so) they would be in danger of appearing trifling—it being inconceivable that they should have so much of novelty as they have.

Got from Ld St Helens his incompleat Copy of Services P. Carew not at home—left Services at his House. In consequence of a verbal message left by me with his Servant, he called this morning and bored me for one hour or more in the middle of my breakfast—Does not go to Antony this summer,[8] knows of no house in particular to be let—is to send me the Sherborn Mercury for the chance of advertisements of Houses. Half spontaneously or more than half mentioned Sr J. St Aubin's[9] places either of them as probably haveable by me: if so it would be Gratuitously.

You Mr Sir S.B. You know two people at Dartmouth or thereabouts, who might catch mice for me viz. both Contor Duncan[10] and a somebody else—To one or other or both you might send me a letter of introduction mentioning my errand—Place taking-and-viewing—and my being your brother, if you think I am, and are not ashamed of me. If what you write to each is contained on one side of half a sheet, so much postage will thereby be saved.

At King's Bridge (did I tell you?) there are certain *Prideauxs*[11] Quakers intimate with Grellier and his 'Jumps',[12] and certain of whom H.K. saw at Grellier's. To them the Grelliers or the Jumps are to give me Letters

I think to set off on Thursday morning. Ergo, not much time to spare for your letters.

For not going to Antony P. Carews reasons are 1. business 2d his

[6] Whitbread's estate was at Southill, Bedfordshire.

[7] See letter 2237 and n. 11.

[8] Antony was Pole Carew's house in Cornwall.

[9] Sir John St Aubyn, 5th Bt. (1758–1839) of Crowance, Cornwall, and Devonport, Devon; man of science and MP for Truro 1784, Penryn 1784–90, and Helston 1807–12.

[10] Perhaps Henry Duncan, deputy controller of the Navy Board 1801–6, for whom see *Correspondence*, vii, as index.

[11] There was a strong contingent of Quaker Prideauxs at Kingsbridge: notably Walter (1740?–1829), George (1774?–1841) and Charles (1781?–1869).

[12] Grellier was an acquaintance of the Jump family of Appledore. Anne Jump (1793–1862), the daughter of Lt. Robert Jump (1761–1837), was to marry John Herbert Koe on 24 August 1815. Lt. Jump was an investor in Grellier's enterprises.

wife about to lie in.[13] Sorry he was not to be there—but made no offer of or concerning his House. Aware of his [. . .?] [. . .?] I asked him not for any letter from him to any body. Indeed had he been otherwise, it was for him to have offered it, not for me to have asked it. I do not wonder there is something sarcastic and not pleasing in his manner. He has no portable map of Devonshire. Stevens has not sent his as he was to have done. A two Sheet abridgement of the Corp Ordnance Map[14] is expected in a few weeks or days.

Take this and copy from it, to improve your hand. I scorn to cheat any man of a single stroke: you do not give half the number.

The Speaker[15] has been seriously ill so say Brougham and Ld. St Helens, but is now pretty well recovered. This may account in some measure for your not hearing from him.

Your Rye packet went two or three days after you left this place.

2241

To The Lords Commissioners of the Treasury

28 August 1813 (Aet 65)

To the Right Honourable the Lords Commissioners of His Majestys Treasury
The Memorial of Jeremy Bentham Esqr
Humbly Sheweth

That an Act of Parliament was made and passed in the 52d year of the Reign of His present Majesty intitled 'An Act for the Erection of a Penitentiary House for the confinement of Offenders convicted

[13] Pole Carew's second wife, whom he married in 1808, was Caroline Anne Lyttelton, the daughter of William Henry, 1st Baron Lyttelton.

[14] *A Topographical Map of Devonshire including all the Adjacent Counties Reduced from the Survey made by Order of the Board of Ordnance under the Direction of Colonel Mudge*, published 4 June 1813, the same day that William Mudge (1762–1820), later major general of the Royal Artillery, was promoted brevet colonel.

[15] Charles Abbot. His published diary gives no indication that he had been ill at this time.

2241. [1] PRO T 1/1349/14128/79767. In the hand of a copyist, except the signature. Docketed: '28 Augt. 1813 / Jeremy Bentham / For paymt. of Costs incurred / in respect of Arbitration for / settling his claim upon the / Public / No. 12764 / Recd. 28 Augt. 1813 / Refer to Solicitor / (No.342) W. Cotton'.

This memorial was passed on to the treasury solicitor on 21 September by Charles Arbuthnot (1767–1850), MP for Orford and joint secretary to the treasury. Litchfield replied on 28 September:

'In obedience to your Lordships commands signified by Mr. Arbuthnot's reference of the 21st. instant of a Memorial of Jeremy Bentham Esqr. (herewith returned) praying That

within the city of London and County of Middlesex, and for making compensation to Jeremy Bentham Esquire for the non-performance of an Agreement between the said Jeremy Bentham and the Lords Commissioners of His Majesty's Treasury respecting the Custody and Management of Convicts', whereby after reciting a proposal made by your Memorialist to contract with the Lords Commissioners of the Treasury relative to the execution and establishment of a National Penitentiary House, and that Articles of Agreement founded on such proposal had been approved of on behalf of the Lords Commissioners of the Treasury, which Articles of Agreement, although not formally executed, had been acted upon and considered as binding; and further reciting that it was not then deemed expedient that the said Contract should be carried into effect but it was just and reasonable that your Memorialist should be repaid certain sums which he had expended, and should receive a liberal compensation for the loss and damage which he had sustained by reason of

your Lordships will be pleased to give directions for the payment of the Costs reasonably and properly incurred by the Memorialist in respect of an Arbitration directed by the 52.Geo 3.c.44. the amount of such Costs to be ascertained by the Solicitors to your Lordships Board. I most humbly report That as the Arbitrators were appointed for the purpose of Settling all Questions between the Public and Mr. Jeremy Bentham arising out of the agreement or intended agreement referred to in the act, and to make Mr. Bentham a liberal compensation in addition to the Sums Expended by him for all loss and damage by him sustained by reason of the nonperformance thereof, Mr. Bentham ought to have contended before the Arbitrators that the Costs of the reference were a part of the damage which he had sustained by reason of the Non fulfilment of the said agreement, if he had intended to make any Claim to compensation on that Account. How far the Arbitrators might have deemed themselves competent to take those Costs into their Consideration, it appears to me in the present stage of the Business superfluous to Enquire, but if they had deemed themselves incompetent for want of Express words in the Act, it is to be observed that the necessity of incurring such Costs must have been foreseen by Mr. Bentham when the Bill was before parliament, and therefore the omission of any provision on the Subject gives him no claim to ask payment at your Lordships Hands; It is also to be remarked that as the Grounds on which the Arbitrators made their Calculation are not stated, it is by no means clear that they did not advert to such Costs, as must necessarily have been incurred by Mr. Bentham, in Estimating the aggregate Sum which they have awarded to be paid to him: But however these matters be, as all questions upon this Subject between the Publick and Mr. Bentham have in pursuance of the Act been finally closed by the decision and award of the Arbitrators and Mr. Bentham is certainly mistaken in supposing, that there is any Established Usage, that the Costs of a Reference should be paid to the party who succeeds in Establishing a claim to such an amount as he has done, I have great doubt whether your Lordships would be warranted in directing the Payment of his costs which would in Effect be granting to Mr. Bentham a further Sum in addition to the Sum so awarded—

All which is nevertheless
most humbly submitted
H.C. Litchfield'.

the nonfulfilment of the said Contract; It was enacted that the two Arbitrators should be appointed in manner therein mentioned for the purpose of settling all questions between the Public and your Memorialist arising out of the said Agreement; and the Lords Commissioners of the Treasury were empowered and required by the said Act to issue to your Memorialist out of the Consolidated fund in manner therein directed the net sum to be awarded by the said Arbitrators—

That Arbitrators were accordingly appointed agreeably to the directions of the said Act; who by their Award dated | | July 1813 adjudged and directed that the clear sum of £23,000 free from all deductions should be issued to your Memorialist in full compensation of his claims under the said reference; in consequence of which Award your Lordships have pleased to signify to your Memorialist (by a Letter of Mr Wharton dated 14th July 1813[2]) your intention of causing the said sum of £23,000 to be issued to him from the Exchequer in the Month of October next—

That for the purpose of making good your Memorialists claim to the said Compensation your Memorialist was under the necessity of employing a Solicitor and Counsel to attend the said Arbitrators; and also of producing divers Witnesses to be examined before them touching the matters in question in the said reference—

That in the course of the said proceedings your Memorialist has incurred considerable Costs for the trouble and attendance of his Solicitor and for fees to Counsel, and he has also incurred certain costs on account of the attendance and travelling charges of several of the Witnesses whom he produced; all which expences have been paid by your Memorialist; except Mr James Burr of His Majesty's Dock Yard at Portsmouth, who came up to London at the request of your Memorialist, and in consequence of directions from your Lordships, to attend the said Arbitrators; and whose travelling expences (as your Memorialist understands) have been defrayed at the public charge—

That the Arbitrators in making the said Award did not, and as your Memorialist apprehends, could not legally take into consideration whether your Memorialist was entitled to the Costs of the said Reference; the Act of Parliament, under which they were appointed, having given them no authority on that subject: But your Memorialist nevertheless humbly submits that it is just and reasonable and within the spirit and intention although not within the strict letter, of the said Act, that such Costs should be allowed to your Memorialist; inasmuch as the said Costs will operate as a deduction from the

[2] Letter 2236.

full amount of the compensation awarded to him, and he will not, in effect, receive the full benefit which was intended for him by the legislature—

That your Memorialist also submits that according to the established course and usage of Arbitrators, a party who succeeds in establishing a claim under a Reference to so large an amount may be considered as having a just and undeniable claim to the Costs of the Reference, and no doubt can reasonably be entertained but that the said Arbitrators would have awarded Costs to your Memorialist—

Your Memorialist therefore humbly prays that your Lordships will be pleased to give directions for the payment of the Costs reasonably and properly incurred by Your Memorialist in respect of the said Arbitrators; the amount of such Costs to be ascertained by the Solicitors of Your Lordships Board—

And your Memorialist etc
Jeremy Bentham.

Queen Square Place
Westmr
28 Augt. 1813

2242

From Charles Arbuthnot

2 September 1813

Sir

All discussion between you and the Lords Commissioners of His Majesty's Treasury relative to the Erection of a Penitentiary House being closed, I have received their Lordships commands to acquaint you that it is in their opinion expedient that you should deliver up to this Board the Deeds which concern the Premises at Milbank

I am
Sir
your most obednt. Servant
C Arbuthnot

Treasury Chambers
2d Septemb. 1813
Jeremy Bentham Esqr.

2242. [1] BL IX. 101. Autograph. Docketed: '1813 Sept.2 / Panopt. Deeds / Rt. Hon. C. Arbuthnot Treasury / to / J.B. Q.S.P. / Reced. at Barrow Green.' Letter-book copy at PRO T 27/71, p.222.

2243

To Charles Arbuthnot

6 September 1813 (Aet 65)

Barrow Green House near Oxted Surry
Monday 6th Sept. 1813

Sir

Last evening and not before, your letter dated the 2d instant[2] reached my hands. In it you speak of yourself as having received the commands of the Lords Commissioners of his Majesty's Treasury to acquaint me that 'it is in their opinion expedient that I should deliver up to their board the Deeds, which concern the premises at Milbank.'

In answer, what I have to observe is—that, with the exception of a single one, all those deeds were, in obedience to their Lordships commands, delivered up by me several months ago, and that among my papers in town, I have a receipt for them, as per list, signed by the person to whom on their Lordships behalf they were delivered.[3] With regard to *that one*: it had been my humble hope, and from their Lordships silence, my inference, that on the considerations submitted to their Lordships I had their permission to retain it. It was the instrument, by which, under the signature of Mr Pitt and two other Lords of the Treasury Board, I had been appointed Feoffee for the purchase of those premises.[4] From this your letter I now infer, that, in respect of this deed—the only one to which it can have any practical application—that humble conception of mine has not been fortunate.

My removal from this place to London had been fixed for the first week in the month after next. In the course of that week, if not

2243. [1] PRO CRES 2/675. In the hand of a copyist, except the signature and Arbuthnot's name and address. Docketed: '6 Septr 1813 / Mr Bentham / Rel. to deliverg up deeds which / concern certain Premises / at MilBank / No 13296 / Recd 8 Septr. 1813 / Refer to Solicitor / (No 330) W Cotton'. Copy at BL IX. 104–5, docketed: '1813 Sept. 6 / Panopt. Ld. Salisbury / J.B. Barrow Green / to / Rt. Hon. C. Arbuthnot / Treasury / Promise to deliver the / only remaining Deed the / first week in Novr. / In answer to A. of the 2d.'

Arbuthnot forwarded Bentham's letter to Litchfield on 15 September, asking for his opinion. Litchfield replied on 18 September 'that there is not that I am aware of any necessity for requiring Mr. Bentham to come to Town for the purpose of delivering up the Appointment in question, but he may be requested to transmit it at his Earliest Convenience'.

[2] Letter 2242.

[3] See letter 2191 n. 5.

[4] See letter 2203.

earlier, I will not fail to deliver up to any person authorized by their Lordships that only remaining deed. Between this and then, I expect several opportunities of meeting with some proper person, who, with my keys, by the help of my directions, will be able to find it for that purpose: and the earliest of such opportunities that presents itself I shall not fail to profit by. I should hope their Lordships would have the goodness not to insist upon my going to town for that single purpose: but should such be their pleasure, they have but to cause a day to be signified to me, and on that day my respect for their commands shall be testified by my obedience.

I have the honour to be
Sir
Your most obedient Servant

Jeremy Bentham

Right Honrble
C. Arbuthnot
etc etc etc
Treasury Chambers.

2244

From Lord St. Helens

17 September 1813

My dear Sir,

The present Lord Aylesford[2] has no court employment: neither am I much acquainted with him. Sufficiently however to authorize my forwarding to him your inquiry concerning his House at Fryars which I have accordingly done (suppressis supprimendis)[3] and will communicate his answer as soon as received. Which however can hardly be in less than a week or ten days: so that if you should

2244. [1] BL IX. 108–9. Autograph. Docketed: '1813 Sept 17 / Ld. St. Helens Hinkley / to / J.B. Barrow Green / House / Ld Aylesford's House / at "*Fryars*" near Maidstone'. Addressed: 'Jeremy Bentham Esqr / Barrow Green / Oxted / Surry'. Franked: 'Hinckley Seventeenth September / 1813' and 'Free / St. Helens'. Postmark: 'FREE / 18 SE 18 / 1813'.

[2] Heneage Finch, 5th Earl of Aylesford (1786–1859), MP for Weobley 1807–12. He had succeeded his father, Heneage Finch, 4th Earl of Aylesford, in 1812.

[3] i.e. 'having suppressed the things that ought to be suppressed'.

purpose quitting your present place of residence within that time, you will be pleased to apprize me of your change of address by a line directed to me in Grafton Street.[4]

Ever, my dear Sir,
very truly yours
St. Helens

Hinckley
17th Septr 1813
Jeremy Bentham Esqr

2245

From George Harrison

28 September 1813

13790[2]

Treasury Chambers
28th. September 1813.

Sir,

I am commanded by The Lords Commissioners of His Majesty's Treasury to acquaint you in answer to your letter of the 6th. Instant[3] that there is no necessity for your coming to town for the purpose of delivering up the Instrument under which you were appointed Feoffee for the purchase of certain premises at Milbank, but that my Lords request you will have the goodness to transmit it to them at your earliest convenience.

I am
Sir
Your very obedient Servant
Geo. Harrison

Jeremy Bentham Esqr
Barrow Green House Oxted
Surry

[4] St Helens lived at 19 Grafton Street.

2245. [1] BL IX. 112–13. Autograph. Docketed: '1813 Sept 28 / Panopt Deeds / Secry Harrison Treasury / to / J.B. Q.S.P. / Reced. at Barrow Green / Deed of Feoffment / Not necessary to come to / Town.' Letter-book copy at PRO T 27/71, p. 256.

[2] This number refers to the treasury solicitor's report on Bentham's letter of 6 September (see letter 2243 and n. 1 and the treasury index for 1813, PRO T 2/64, entry under date of receipt, 9 September).

[3] Letter 2243.

2246

To Martin and Co.

early October 1813 (Aet 65)

Gentlemen

On the 10th instant or rather (that day being Sunday) on the 11th I am assured that a Warrant for £23,000 with some odd money in the name of interest will be delivered to me from the Treasury,[2] payable in course at the Exchequer which I am told will be within a week from that date. I write this for two purposes—1st for the purpose of learning by your favour whether it lies in the way of your business upon receiving a Warrant of that sort to receive payment on it at the Exchequer? If yes, my friend Mr Koe of Lincolns Inn who has all along communicated with you about my business will as soon as the warrant is obtained by him deliver it at your House: if not, he or I or somebody on my behalf must be in town for that single purpose

The other purpose of this letter is to direct the application of the money when received by you.

1. of £2,400 the destination is already determined, by three Bills to that amount in the whole drawn on me by Mr Grellier and accepted payable on the 20th instant

. . . . 2,000

2. For a number of years past I have been indebted to your kindness for a loan of £300. the extinction of this debt, with whatsoever may be due for interest you will be pleased to apply the sum requisite Say 700

3. £18,000 I propose to invest in the funds, viz. in the Navy 5 per Cents: and for this purpose I must beg the favour of you to transmitt to me at this place for my signature the requisite powers of Attorney, including one to your House to enable you not only to receive the Dividends but to sell the Stock itself. As to the particular day or days of purchase, I would beg the favour of you to use your discretion. And if it can be done without inconvenience I had rather leave some even sum than a fractional one: and for this purpose as far as £300 or £400 may be added.

2246. [1] BL IX. 126–7. Copy. Docketed: '1813 Oct. / J.B. Barrow Green / to / Martin and Co Lombard / Street / Compensation money / -disposal of / Answered by theirs of Oct.' The reply from Martins is missing; letter 2250 below appears to be a reponse to another letter from Bentham, which is also missing.

[2] See letter 2236 n. 2.

2247

From Lord St. Helens

6 October 1813

Grafton Street 6th Octr. 1813

My Dear Sir

I had almost despaired of obtaining an answer from Lord Aylesford;[2] but it is at length arrived, and, as you will see, seems to bid fair towards a prosperous issue of your negociation for the House. But you will observe that I have effaced an *Epithet*: which I thought it right to do, because, tho' it would not have been displeasing to yourself, it might perhaps have produced an unfavourable impression on the John-Trot[3] understanding of his Lordship's Steward, should you produce this letter to him as I suppose you will, in the way of a *Credential*. In like manner, and from similar motives I took care to leave out several passages of your letter in the copy of it which I sent to his Lordship. Tho' by the way this may perhaps lead to a slight future inconvenience; since he seems to have taken the said copy for an original; and therefore, should the treaty go forward and lead to a direct correspondence, must be somewhat surprized at the difference of the hand-writing. More especially as that of the Copy was a young Lady's, and uncommonly beautiful.

Failing this project (tho I sincerely hope and trust that it will succeed) I beg leave to mention that I have a house at my disposal, not far from Dorking in Surry which will be vacant at Christmas next, and which I consider as not unlikely to suit you on many accounts; and most especially from its being in the close vicinity of our friends the Romillys.[4]

ever, my Dear Sir,
very truly yours
St Helens

2247. [1] BL IX. 120–1. Autograph. Docketed: '1813 Oct. 6 / Ld St Helens Grafton / Street / to J.B. Barrow Green / Aylesford and / Dorking Villas'.

[2] See letter 2244.

[3] An eighteenth-century expression for a man of slow intellect, a bumpkin.

[4] At this time Romilly lived at Tanhurst, Leith Hill, Surrey.

2248

From George Harrison

9 October 1813

Sir,

The Lords etc. having had under their Consideration your memorial of the 28th. August[2] last praying payment of the Costs reasonably and properly incurred by you in respect of an Arbitration directed by the Act 52d. Geo.3.C.44 the amount of such Costs to be ascertained by the Solicitors to this Board, I have received their Lordships command to acquaint you that as the Arbitrators were appointed for the purpose of settling all Questions between the Public and you arising out of the Agreement or intended Agreement referred to in the Act, and to make you a liberal Compensation in addition to the Sums expended by you for all loss and damage by you sustained by reason of the nonperformance thereof, you ought to have contended before the Arbitrators that the Costs of the reference were a part of the damage which you had sustained by reason of the Non fulfilment of the said Agreement, if you had intended to make any claim to compensation on that account.—How far the Arbitrators might have deemed themselves competent to take those Costs into their Consideration it appears to their Lordships in the present Stage of the business superfluous to enquire, but if they had deemed themselves incompetent for want of Express Words in the Act, it is to be observed that the necessity of incurring such Costs must have been foreseen by you when the Bill was before Parliament, and therefore the ommission of any provision on the subject gives you no Claim to ask payment at their Lordships Hands; It is also to be remarked that as the grounds on which the Arbitrators made their calculation are not stated, it is by no means clear that they did not advert to such Costs, as must necessarily have been incurred by you, in estimating the aggregate Sum which they have awarded to be paid to you; But however these matters be, as all questions upon this subject between the Public and you have in pursuance of the Act been finally closed by the decision and award of the Arbitrators and you are certainly mistaken in supposing that there is any established usage that the Costs of a Reference should be paid to the Party who succeeds in establishing a Claim to

2248. [1] PRO T 27/71, pp. 270–1. Letter-book copy. Endorsed: 'Jeremy Bentham Esq. / appn. for payt. / of Costs on Reference / of his Claims refused'.

[2] Letter 2241.

such an amount as you have done, my Lords do not think they should be warranted in directing the payment of your Costs which would in effect be granting to you a further Sum in addition to the Sum awarded.

I am etc. 9th. October 1813
Geo. Harrison.

2249

To Sir Samuel and Lady Romilly

17 October 1813 (Aet 65)

Barrow Green House Sunday 17 Oct. 1813.

Dear Romilly

Presume not to read a single line further, but hand the paper over *instanter* to your betters.—

Dear Madam

Profiting by Your Ladyships most imperative—and the more imperative the more gratious—commands,—we propose—all three of us[2]—to present ourselves at Tanhurst—two of us bolt upright —the other, after due preparation, if the stiffness in his back will suffer him, at your feet—on Thursday next. As to the hour, recollecting that the last time I had the honour of dining with you it was as late at six, I shall venture to take for granted that *that* hour late as it may be for the country, will not be inconvenient to you. The case is—that *that* same morning Mr Koe will have to come hither from the neighbourhood of Maidstone, after waiting there (as it is necessary he should do) for the coming in of the post: after which there will be certain packings to perform here. But the hour of 6 we can be sure of. Dear Madam, with the truest respect

Ever Your most devoted
Jeremy Bentham.

2249. [1] UC clxxiv. 109. Autograph. Docketed: '1813. / J. Bentham.'

Anne (1773–1818) eldest daughter of Francis Garbett of Knill Court, Herefordshire, had married Romilly in January 1798.

[2] Presumably Jeremy, Sir Samuel and Lady Bentham.

2250
From Martin and Co.

19 October 1813

Lombard St. 19th. Octr. 1813

Sir

In consequence of your Letter of the 15th. Inst[2] we have this day received £22456 . 12 . 6 from the Exchequer on your account deductions being made at the Office as follows.

Received	£22456 . 12 . 6
Fees at Pell Office	949 . — —
Do. Tellers Do.	172 . 10
	23578 . 2 . 6

We wait your further directions as to the investment and are

Sir

Your obedt Servs.
Martin Stone and Martin

J Bentham Esqr

2250. [1] BL IX. 122–3. Autograph. Docketed: '1813 Oct 19 / Panopt-Compensat / Martin and Co Lombd / Street / to / J.B. Barrow Green / £*22*,456:12:6 / reced from the Exchequer'. Addressed: 'Jery. Bentham Esqr. / Barrow Green House / Oxted / Godstone / Surry'. Postmark: 'OC / 19 / [. . .?]'.

[2] Missing.

2251

To George Harrison

26 October 1813 (Aet 65)

Queens Square Place Westminster 26 Oct. 1813

Sir

In obedience to the commands signified by your Letter of the 28th last,[2] I herewith transmit the Instrument therein mentioned. The Indorsement on it is in the following words

'Dated 10th October 1799

The Lords Commissioners of the Treasury to Jeremy Bentham Esqr.	Appointment of feoffee of Lands at Milbank for the scite of A Penitentiary House.'

It is *the last* of all *the deeds* I ever had, bearing relation to the Penitentiary business; the others having been already delivered up by me, as appears by the correspondence on the subject, and the receipt or receipts for them which I have in my possession.

I have the honour to be
Sir
Your Most obedient Servant
Jeremy Bentham

G. Harrison Esqr
etc etc etc
Treasury Chambers.

2251. [1] PRO CRES 2/675. In the hand of a copyist with the exception of the signature. Docketed: '26 Octr. 1813 / Mr Bentham / With a Deed respg Lands / at Millbank for the Scite / of a Penitentiary House / No 15569 / Recd. 27 Octr. 1813 / Read 30 Novr. 1813 / 4th. Div: 1st Sheet / Write to Commr. Woods'. A copy is at BL IX. 125, docketed: '1813 Octr 27 / Panopt / J.B. Q.S.P. / to / Harrison Treasury / Sending Appointm / of J.B. as feoffee / 10 Octr. 1799 / being the last deed / remaining.'

[2] Letter 2245.

2252

From William Hill

27 October 1813

dated 10 Octr 1799

The Lords Commissioners of the Treasury to Jeremy Bentham Esqr.	}	Appointment of Feoffee of Lands at Milbank for the scite of a A Penitentiary House.

Received of the said Mr Bentham an Instrument endorsed as above

W Hill

Treasury
27 Octr 1813

2253

To George Harrison

27 October 1813 (Aet 65)

Queen's Square Place Westminster, 27 Octr. 1813.

Although, on account of the £23,000 Compensation money, awarded to me by award dated on the 9th. of July 1813, under the act of the 52 Geo.3. Ch.44 (the same being under the Act to be paid

2252. [1] BL IX. 124. Autograph. Docketed: '1813 Oct 27 / Panopt / Hill Treasury / to J.B. Q.S.P. / Receipt for Appointment / of Feoffee for Milbank / being the last Deed / remaining undelivered.'

William Hill was assistant clerk of revenue at the treasury.

2253. [1] PRO T 1/1354/15598/79863. In the hand of a copyist, except the signature and Harrison's name and address. Docketed: '27 Octr. 1813 / Mr. Bentham / For issue of further Sum / of £779.3. to pay the fees etc on / the Sum awarded to him as a Compensat / for his Claim upon Government / No 15598 / Recd. 27 Octr. 1813 / Read 30 Novr. 1813 / 6. Div: 2d St. / Prepare Warrant'. Copy at BL IX. 116–19, docketed: '1813 Oct 27 / Panopt / Definitive Compensation / J.B. Q.S.P. / to / Secry. Harrison Treasury / for Interest £233:3.0 / Deficiency of fees £546:0:0'. At BL IX. 128–34 there is an autograph draft of another letter to Harrison, started at the end of September and continued in October 1813. In this letter Bentham requested another payment of the provisional annuity granted under 52 Geo.III, c.44. The draft is docketed: 'J.B. Q.S.P. / to / Harrison Treasury / Proposed letter for / 3d and last ½ yearly / payment. / ☞ Oct 26. Discontinued / being supposed useless / this being included in / the award of the defi / nitive Compensation.'

net) I received, some days before the 19th Oct. 1813, a Treasury Warrant for the sum of £23,578″2″6—(the odd £578″2″6 being upon the issue thereof to pay fees)—yet, in order to give their full effect to the intentions of Parliament and the Lords Commissioners of the Treasury in my favour, the circumstances of the case have rendered it necessary for me to make this my humble application for a further sum of £779 odd money to be paid *net* on the following grounds.

I For *interest* at 5 per cent. from the day when the money ought to have been paid to the day when paid .... £233″3″0[2]

II For difference between the sum *received* as above to pay fees, and the amount of fees actually required and paid .... £546″0″0[3]

Together .... £779″3″0

To which will be added whatsoever may be further necessary to pay the fees upon this £779″3″0 in such sort as to render the payment *net.*

On the subject of each of these two items something in the way of explanation may perhaps be necessary—

I. As to the £233″3.″0 for *interest*, it arises out of the Treasury Minute of the 13 July 1813: which, after stating that by certain legal considerations their Lordships regard themselves as precluded from paying the said compensation money within the time prescribed by the Act (52 G.3.C.44), proceeds to declare that 'with a view to obviate as far as possible any disappointment which may result to Mr Bentham on this account, My Lords will cause a warrant to be prepared for paying to Mr Bentham on the *10th* day of Oct. next (1813) out of the consolidated fund of Great Britain the sum of £23,000 with Interest for the same after the rate of 5 per cent to be computed from the *9th* day of August being *one month* after the date of the said Award.'[4]

The *principle* being thus plainly declared, to warrant the claim of the exact sum of £233″3″0 on the score of Interest a few words may be necessary respecting the arithmetical application made of that principle.

1. When the *9th* of August is stated as the day on which the principal should have been paid, the species of *month* assumed as the proper one is the *Calendar Month.* But on reflection, and if necessary, on enquiry, you will, I flatter myself, Sir, concur in the opinion that on all occasions of this sort, the Month considered as

[2] Written in the margin at this point: '£233..3..0'.

[3] Written in the margin at this point: '£546..0..0'.

[4] See letter 2236 n. 2.

the proper sort of month is the LUNAR of *28* days: and this for one reason among others viz. that the Lunar is the only one *the length of which is always the same*: the Calendar Month being composed, as it may happen, of any number of days from 28 to 31 inclusive: thence it is that, for the computation of the interest, instead of the *9th* the proper *terminus a quo* is the *6th* of August.

2. Next as to the *terminus ad quem*. The day mentioned in that character is the *10th* day of October: *that* being the day on which it is assumed that payment *will be* made. But, in the *event*, all the solicitation I could use was not able to obtain payment till the *19th* of October. On so considerable a principal sum as £23,000, the interest for 12 days, (viz. as above, *3* in respect of the *terminus a quo*, and *9* in respect of the *terminus ad quem*) is itself a sum too considerable to be neglected. As to *power*, it is as completely in their Lordships *power* to allow not only *this* but a much more considerable *addition*, as it is to allow the sum which would be the result of a *literal* compliance with the above minute. The *very* day of the date of the award viz. the 9th July 1813 was a day on which they would have been warranted in ordering payment of the money, had such been their pleasure: and, in deferring it till the *last* day of the *month in question*, they took the utmost latitude that was allowed them by the terms of the Act.

As to the *terminus ad quem*, the day on which the relief to the claimant, and with it the burthen to the public takes place, is *not* the day *for* which the *promise* of payment is made, but the day *on* which that promise is actually *performed*.

'To obviate *as much as possible* any disappointment which may result', is the so graciously declared object of the allowance which their Lordships thereupon proceed to declare their resolution of making. From this same disappointment, a loss has in fact befallen me, which, it not being in their Lordships power to order reparation for it, I forbear troubling them with. But the above little arithmetical adjustments will (I flatter myself) not experience any difficulty.

II. As to the deficiency in respect of the money paid on the score of *fees*, it stands thus—

1. Money paid by Martin and Co. (my Bankers)
19 Oct. 1813 at the *Pell Office* .... £949″ 0″ 0
2. Do by do (Oct. 19 1813) at the Tellers' Office £172″10″ 0
3. Do by another hand on my account
12 Oct. 1813, to Mr *Vernon* of the Treasury
in his quality of...[5] ....£ 2″12″ 6.
Total .... £1124″2″6

[5] Joseph Vernon was receiver of fees at the treasury 1794–1834.

Deduct money received from the Exchequer for the purpose of paying fees..	578″2″6
Remains due, to complete the allowance necessary, on the score of fees, to render the sum *net* according to the Act	546″0″0
Add as above, due on the score of *interest*	233″3″0
Total remaining due to me (besides so much as is requisite to render the payment of it *net*)	779″3″0

To this, to render the compensation complete, would require to be added *interest* upon the above sum of £546 from the 19th day of this month (October 1813) down to the day on which the money hereby prayed shall have happened to be actually paid, and perhaps interest on the other sum of £233″3″0. But, as on both these sums together, the interest would scarcely amount to so much as a pound, on this score it is not my wish to make any addition to the trouble unavoidably occasioned by this my humble address.

I have the honour to be
Sir,
Your most obedient Servant
Jeremy Bentham.

G. Harrison Esq
etc. etc. etc.
Treasury Chambers.

2254

To James Pillar

30 October 1813 (Aet 65)

Queens Square Place Westmr 30 Octr. 1813

Sir

To exempt myself from the imputation of a concurrence, which on my part, besides the illegality of it, would have been on many accounts singularly improper, I thought it necessary just now in conversation to state to you the fact of *a course of pavement just laid down*, or nearly so, *in the plot of ground adjacent to the Dwelling House of my tenant Lady Mary Lindsay Crawford,*[2] *fronting the BirdCage walk* in St. James' Park. But, should any representation

2254. [1] D.R. Bentham MSS. In the hand of a copyist, with the exception of the signature and Pillar's name and address. James Pillar was secretary for crown lands at the crown estates office, Whitehall.

[2] See above, letter 2214 n. 2.

be made to her Ladyship from your Office, I would beg leave to propose it for consideration, whether, to constitute the more regular ground for any such representation, it might not be proper that some person from your Office should *take a view* of the spot, so as to be able to make a Report, descriptive with official accuracy of what has been done in it; in which case there will be no need of stating the information as coming from *me*, who, tho' an informant, am so from necessity and not from choice

I am
Sir
Your Most obedient Servant
Jeremy Bentham.

James Pillar Esqr
etc etc etc
Office of Woods etc

2255

From William Vizard

1 November 1813

Dear Sir

I return you a book which you lent me during the proceedings upon your late Reference and I have to thank you for the account of our bill which has been paid by Mr. Koe to whom I have given a receipt

I am Dear Sir
Your faithful
and obliged Servant
Wm. Vizard

Lincolns Inn
1st. Novr. 1813

2255. [1] BL IX. 135–6. Autograph. Docketed: '1813 Nov 1 / Panopt Compensat / Definitive / Vizard Linc Inn / to / J.B. Q.S.P. / Returning book and / acknowledging payment / of his Bill'. Address: 'Jeremy Bentham Esq / Queen Square Place / Westminster'.

2256

From James Mill

3 December 1813

Newington Green 3d. Decr. 1813

Yesterday I complied with an entreaty of Wm. Allen to dine at his house, in order to meet with Owen,[2] who is just come up from the Lanark Mills.

I took occasion to put to Mr. Allen the questions respecting the mines, which you had directed me to put, and the answer was such as, I think, I had better send you. As soon as the questions were out of my mouth, he began—'Do entreat Friend Bentham, to have nothing to do with mines'—he added, 'or at any rate to wait till I can write to Cornwal, where I have friends upon the spot, and can get him accurate information.' He said that he himself had embarked several years ago about £700 in a Cornwall mine, and that it had never produced any thing. He said, that as far as his information or experience went, more had been lost by the Cornwal mines than had been gained.

Hearing all this, Owen then spoke, and said, if Mr. Bentham wants to lay out a sum of money, to greater advantage, than on any opportunity that almost ever occurs, he should buy a share of the Lanark Mills, which are to be sold at the end of this month.

The price Owen says, will not exceed £100,000 for the whole—and that he himself will buy one half—that the raw produce, and the goods which they have on hand, with the materials of the buildings, would sell for nearly the whole sum which the concern is likely to fetch—that he has now brought the manufactory to so great perfection particularly the rational machinery, that even last year, when other manufactories of the sort could make little or nothing, they have cleared 20 per cent. upon their whole capital, and that now (viz. the continent open) they will clear a great deal more—that in short he knows not of any occasion within his memory, when so profitable a speculation was to be made.

An obvious question was, why then on the present profile, so willing to get out of it? To this the answer was, that they had in

2256. [1] Bowring, 'Memoirs', at p. 46. Autograph. Docketed: '1813 Decr 3 / J.Mill Newington / Green / to / J.B. Q.S.P. / Disposal of the / £23,000. / Ricardo's Advice.'

[2] Robert Owen (1771–1858), early socialist and manager and part-owner of the New Lanark Mills.

general got soured with him on account of his perseverance in his endeavours (to which they were averse) to improve the population of the mills; and that even now, though they felt the advantage of his proceedings, they would not acknowledge them—that they were also in some measure bound by their repeated declarations to him, of a readiness to quit the concern, upon even the purchase money of their shares being made good to them—and that it was now his earnest desire to get such partners, as would go along with him, in his efforts to shew what can be done to make a manufacturing population, virtuous, and happy, and far more productive than they have yet been.

Such is the conversation that passed. Of the subject I know so little, that I am hardly entitled to have an opinion, much less to give an advice.

Under that ignorance, had I to determine for myself, it would certainly be to prefer good security with little produce, to almost any prospect of produce, where there was a risk.

2257

FROM LORD HOLLAND

3 December 1813

St. James Square
Decr: 3

Dear Sir

I know that you admire or at least approve some of the works of my late excellent friend Dn. Gaspar Melchor de Jovellanos[2] and I know also that he set the highest value on your commendation and good opinion—He would have considered it no small honour to have been admitted into Mr Benthams study and would have solicited that favour with as much earnestness as you did a passport to Mexico from him[3]—Will you therefore allow me to beg your acceptance of a cast from his bust which bears a strong resemblance and which I hope you will allow to stand in some part of your library—Lady Holland begs me to present her compliments and I am Dear Sir

with sincere respect
Your obliged
Vassall Holland

2257. [1] BL IX. 143–4. Autograph. Docketed: '1813 Dec 6 / Ld Holland St James Sq / to / J.B. Q.S.P. / With a bust of Jovellanos'. Printed in Bowring, x. 477.

[2] Jovellanos had died in 1811.

[3] See above, letters 2030, 2048, and 2055.

2258

To Lord Holland

6 December 1813 (Aet 65)

Q.S.P. 6th Dec., 1813.

My Lord,

Valuable on its own account, as well as that of the worthy original, the bust deserves a yet higher value from the hand it comes from. Your lordship's commands are already obeyed: Señor Jovellanos has already taken his station. It is, in every sense, an obscure one; but it is the best my narrow and crooked workshop, which is my constant sitting-room, can afford.

As a small return, made according to the measure of my small faculties, do me the honour to accept of an imperfect sketch just made of a venerable lady, who, by the blessing of God, is as much alive as ever she was, even my own *alma mater*:[2] whether, speaking to your lordship, I should have been entitled to say *ours*, is more than I recollect at present.[3] By the inscription, without looking any further, your lordship will see that I am, now in my old age, drawing near to the meeting-house—yea, even to the Quakers. I should be too proud even for a Quaker, could I be permitted to amuse myself with any such imagination as that of having drawn your lordship any part of the way along with me.

2259

From Lord Sidmouth

13 December 1813

Lord Sidmouth presents his Compliments to Mr. Bentham, and returns, with many Thanks, the inclosed Copy of a Letter to the President of the United States,[2] with the Perusal of which Mr. Bentham had favor'd Him

Home Department

Decr: ye: 13th: 1813

2258. [1] Bowring, x. 477.

[2] Bowring recorded that this letter was accompanied by a copy of *'Swear not at all'*, which included an attack on oaths at Oxford. See Bowring, v. 209–12 and letter 2239.

[3] Holland had attended Christ Church, receiving his MA on 20 June 1792.

2259. [1] BL IX. 145. In the hand of a copyist. Docketed: '1813 Decr 13 / codification / Ld Sidmouth Secry. of State / to / J.B. Q.S.P. / Returns J.B. to / P.U.S. in compliance / with J.B.s of Decr 1.' Bentham's letter to Sidmouth is missing. For Bentham's providing Sidmouth with a copy of his letter to Madison, see letter 2177. [2] Letter 2145.

2260

From Joseph Vernon

20 December 1813

Mr Vernon's Compliments to Mr Bentham the Warrants are now ready for paying him £238. 10s.
Treasury
20th Decr 1813

2261

To Sir Samuel Bentham

25 December 1813 (Aet 65)

Q.S.P. 25 Decr. 1813

Received yours of yesterday,[2] and maturely and sufficiently considered it. I am much concerned to think of the trouble you must have given yourselves. Hall-Oak[3] is not divisible. My dear Sam, I will not be a clog upon any of your arrangements.

Received also the parcel. I. Parochial Education.[4] 2 Magazines, *namely* (I will not use the forbidden word) Monthly and Gentlemen's, with Letter for Miss Baillie do for Lee,[5] do for H.K. with pocket-book to be returned to . . . and slip of Paper Hangings.

H.K. Has taken himself into his own hands till Tuesday or Wednesday. This is rather unfortunate, in relation to a jar of Salted Cucumbers which is come from Smirnove[6] and is represented by him as a present from Tchitchagoff. 'They must be soon eaten' (says he) 'otherwise they will become mouldy and get spoiled:' Time and seasons are adverse to them. This is Xmas day: tomorrow is Sunday.

2260. [1] BL IX. 146–7. Autograph. Docketed: '1813 Decr 20 / Panopt compensat / Definitive / Vernon Treasury / to / J.B. Q.S.P. / with Memorandum of Fees by H.K.' Added later in another hand: 'Paid to Mr Vernon / at Treasy £8.6s.' Addressed: 'J. Bentham Esq / Queen Square'. Franked: 'Treasury'.

2261. [1] BL IX. 148–9. Autograph. Docketed: '1813 Decr. 25th. / J.B. / to / S.B.' Addressed: 'To / Sir Samuel Bentham K.S.G. / Berry Lodge / Gosport / Hants.' Postmark: 'DE / 25 / 1813'.

[2] Missing.

[3] Sir Samuel's farm at Hampstead.

[4] Unidentified.

[5] Probably James Lee the younger (1754–1824), nursery man of Lee and Kennedy of the Vineyard, Hammersmith. For Sir Samuel's earlier contact with his father, James Lee the elder (1715–95), see *Correspondence*, iii, as index.

[6] Iakov Ivanovich Smirnov, chaplain of the Russian embassy. See letter 2045 n. 4.

All that Harry[7] recollects of a former parcel containing certain keys is that being directed to you at Berry Lodge, it was left at the White Horse Cellar. It being Xmas day Henry[8] has taken himself into his own hands, returnable I suppose not till dinner. I have cough and cold: lay abed in hopes of curing it, but without curing it, weakened myself and destroyed my appetite for the day—the sure effect of bed-lying. After directions about covering the paper with leather, I have assigned the matter over to Mrs Stoker, and the delivery must depend partly upon Mrs. Stokers skill and care, partly upon that upon which every thing depends in this sublunary and other worlds.

Great ire at finding the boys and the periodicals gone, and no list of the *latter* left by the former. At sight of a list purporting to be a list thereof (sent in a letter to Mr Koe) I suffered myself (weak as I am) to be half appeased. But how do I know, or can I ever know, how many of them over and above those which were thought fit to be comprised in the list, may have been employed as a foundation for Mutton or other pies? For the sake of the general rule, let them understand, that these things should be considered.

A letter designed for Emp. Alexander[9] was taken to Smirnove t'other day by H.K. and objected to in some parts as not plain and plump enough. At the expence of a good deal of delicacy, it was altered and returned by him with full approbation. But (to make sure) he recommends its going to Dumont to be put into French.[10]

On being asked, Sm. gave it as his opinion, that even circumstanced as Tchitchagoff is with Alexander, his efforts might be of very considerable use, if the business needed them, and he were disposed to exert them. It is rather the Emp. that is in disgrace with him than he with the Emperor.

The misfortune is that substituting blunt statements to allusions requires *poring* and takes up time and trouble.

Let Lady B. know, that I have pinned the bit of paper hanging upon the note to the alas! absent H.K.

[7] Probably Henry Tonkin Coulson.

[8] Presumably Coulson again.

[9] Alexander I (1777–1825), emperor of Russia 1801–25.

[10] See letters 2262 and 2263.

2262

From Étienne Dumont

17 January 1814

Voilà mes notes, mon cher Bentham—vous voyez que j'arrange les choses de manière à se passer du *mémoire additionel* sur le plan, c'est qu'il est très obscur pour ceux qui ne connoissent pas l'ouvrage,—il faudroit le faire beaucoup plus long pour le rendre intelligible à sa M.I.[2]—et si on ne peut pas le lui rendre intelligible, il vaut mieux s'en tenir à des généralités qui ne lui présentent que des résultats.

Adieu.

Lundi

d/ à supprimer—c'est faire naître l'idée qu'on doit éviter.
c./*for a commencement—the completion of it*—cela n'est pas clair—*humbly* n'est pas du bon genre.

Mais quoique les Rédacteurs de ces Codes aient cité mes ouvrages, quoiqu'ils en aient emprunté quelques idées, la base de leur travail est l'ancienne Jurisprudence romaine et n'a rien de commun avec le mien. Le Code pénal de Napoléon, ce qu'on a fait de mieux en ce genre, me paroît encore bien loin de ce qu'il devroit être. Mais je ne pourrois montrer tout ce qu'il a de défectueux qu'en présentant tout mon système.[3]

2. In my above-mentioned work a sample of a penal code is exhibited.[4]

le code pénal que j'ai préparé et qui pourroit à ce que je présume être complet en moins d'un an, est par rapport au *texte des lois* d'une brièveté remarquable. La cause de cette brièveté est dans la méthode que j'ai suivie—par exemple, j'ai fait entrer dans des chapitres généraux toutes les matières applicables à une grande variété de délits. Ainsi les circonstances d'aggravation et d'exténuation sont dans un titre séparé auquel on se réfère partout et cela seul épargne

2262. [1] BL IX. 152. Autograph. Docketed: '1814 Jan: 17 / Codif. to Alexander / Dumont Haymarket / to / J.B. Q.S.P. / Proposed Emen- / dations'. Addressed: 'Jer. Bentham Esq.' Dumont's apparently uncompleted notes are at BL IX. 153–4, docketed: 'Dumont to J.B. 17 Jany 1814', and '17 Jany: 1814 / Haymarket.'

[2] Majesté Impériale; Alexander.

[3] The whole of this paragraph is lightly crossed in pencil, presumably by Bentham.

[4] This sentence is deleted in ink, again probably by Bentham, who wrote in pencil underneath: 'Brevity'.

une multitude de répétitions. Mais chaque disposition du Code est accompagnée de ses raisons. Tout est justifié. Tout est fondé sur des principes. Cette espèce d'instruction, étrangère[5] à tous les Codes, motive la volonté[?] du Souverain. Monarque et Père, il commande et il éclaire, il prescrit l'obéissance, mais il ne veut pas être obéi par l'autorité seule, il veut l'être par la conviction.

Cette nouvelle manière de donner des lois est une de celles, Sire, qui me donnent le plus de confiance en offrant ce travail à V.M.

Dans les *Traités de législation*, il y a un modelle de tout le Code dans un article sur les injures personnelles. Tous les délits sont traités sur le même plan. L'unité de méthode est un des caractères de l'ouvrage.

In the midst of war etc

(Je supprimeroi l'article in brackets et substitue)[6]

Le séjour que j'ai fait en Russie m'a déjà mis à profit de connaître les principales circons⟨ta⟩nces qui peuvent servir à diriger la législation dans l'application locale des principes généraux. D'ailleurs ceux que V.M. chargeroit de m'envoyer des informations, ou des notes sur les parties du Code qui leur seroient transmises, éprouveroient de ma part toutes les dispositions nécessaires pour perfectionner de concert avec eux un ouvrage où la connoissance du caractère national est d'une grande importance.

As to remuneration etc

2263

From Étienne Dumont

22 January 1814

J'ai relu deux fois—je n'ai plus d'objection essentielle—et quant aux bagatelles, nous n'en finirions jamais,—je n'aime pas par ex. le paraghr. *this sample was a challenge* etc. cela importe peu à Alexandre.

Je ne vous envoye point de traductions—je suis décidé—il faut une lettre angloise—il lit l'Anglois comme le françois—et il aura plus de respect pour l'Anglois—cela est machinal mais cela est—j'en suis sûr.

[5] At this point Bentham wrote in pencil: 'Reasons'.

[6] Much of this paragraph is lightly crossed out in pencil.

2263. [1] BL IX. 155. Autograph. Docketed: '1814 Jan 22 / Codification / Dumont / to / J.B. or S.B. / On J.B. to / Emp. Alexander / before it was sent'.

encore un mot—*without apointment* from any Govern.—je crains un peu le double sens du mot en françois où *apointement* signifie salaire—

Je fais demander l'adresse de Mill.

2264

FROM MARTIN AND CO.

29 January 1814

Sir

Our Clerk, who received your Exchequer Payment having been served with the enclosed Notice[2] to refund a Part of the Money, We beg your Authority so to do.

We are Sir
Your obedt Sts
Martin Stone and Martin.
London 29 Jany 1814

Jeremy Bentham Esq

2265

FROM MARTIN AND CO.

31 January 1814

Lombard St. 31 Jany. 1814

Sir

In answer to your Letter of this morning[2] we beg to assure you that you are perfectly welcome to the advances you may require on your account with us We shall therefore not sell any part of the Exchequer Bills.—

2264. [1] BL IX. 158–9. Docketed: '1814 Jany. 29 / Panopt. Compensat. defin. / Martin and Co Lombard Str / to / J.B. Q.S.P. / Inclosing Exchequer / demand for refunding / Property Tax on / Interest on the Com- / pensation money £23,000'.

[2] Missing.

2265. [1] BL IX. 160–1. Docketed: '1814 Jany. 31 / Panop Compens. Definitive / Martin and Co / Lombard Str. / to / J.B. Q.S.P. / Will enclose draught / till 26 Feby when / Grellier's Note is payable / Will pay the Property / Tax to Exchequer tomorrow'. Addressed: 'Jeremy Bentham Esqr / Queens Square / Westminster'. Postmark: '[. . .?] o'Clock / FE I / 1814 Mn'. Stamped: 'Two Py Post / unpaid / Lombard St.'

[2] Missing.

The payment you direct shall be made into the Exchequer tomorrow.

We are
Sir
Your obed Servt.
Martin Stone and Martin

J Bentham Esq.

2266

To Alexander I

January 1814 (Aet 65)

Queen Square Place, Westminster,
London Jany 1814.

Sire!

The object of this address is to submit to Your Imperial Majesty an offer relative to the department of Legislation.

My years are sixty six. Without commission from any Government, not much fewer than fifty of them have been occupied in that field. My ambition is to employ the remainder of them, as far as can be done in this Country, in labouring towards the improvement of the state of the branch of Government in your Majesty's vast Empire.

In the year 1802, a work, extracted, as therein mentioned, from my papers, was, by *M Dumont of Geneva*, published at Paris in 3 Volumes 8.vo under the title of *Traités de Législation Civile et Pénale etc.*

In the year 1805 a translation of it into the Russian Language, was published at St. Petersburgh, by order (if I am rightly informed) of Your Majesty's Government.[2]

Since the publication of that work, Europe has seen *two* extensive bodies of law promulgated within its limits: one by the *French Emperor* the other by the *King of Bavaria.*[3] These two are the only bodies of law of any such considerable extent, that have made their

2266. [1] Central State Archives of Ancient Acts, Moscow. In the hand of a copyist, with the exception of the signature. Another copy or a draft of this letter formed the basis of the version printed under the date 'May 1814' in *Papers Relative to Codification and Public Instruction*, London, 1817, pp. 83–8 (Bowring, iv. 514–15) and *Memoirs of Prince Adam Czartoryski and his Correspondence with Alexander I*, ed. Adam Gielgud, 2 vols., London, 1888, ii. 290–4.

[2] See letter 2086 and n. 9.

[3] See above, letter 2145 and nn. 2 and 3.

appearance *within the last half century*. Of the one promulgated by the *French Emperor* a complete *penal* code formed a part. In the preface to that authoritative work, my unauthoritative one is mentioned, with honour: among the *dead*, *Montesquieu*, *Beccaria* and *Blackstone*;[4] among living names, (unless it be for some *matter of fact*) none but *mine*. In the Bavarian Code, drawn up by *M Bexon*, much more, *particular as well as copious mention* is made of that work of mine, much more *eulogy* bestowed upon it.—[5]

In *France* under the immediate rod of Napoleon, in *Bavaria* under the influence of Napoleon, the generosity displayed by the notice thus taken of the work of a living Englishman, could not but call forth my admiration.

Approbation is one thing; *adoption* is another. With mine before them, both these modern works took for their basis the jurisprudence of *ancient Rome*. Russia at any rate needs not any such incumbrance.

In the texture of the human frame, some fibres there are which are the same in all *places* and at all *times*: others which vary with the *place* and with the *time*. For these last, it has been among my constant and pointedly manifested cares to look out and provide. Of the particularities of Russia I am not altogether without experience. Two of the most observant years of my life were passed within her limits.[6]

Codes upon the *French* pattern are already in full view. Speak the word, Sire, *Russia* shall produce a pattern of her own, and then let Europe judge.

To Russia, it is true, I am a foreigner. Yet to *this* purpose scarcely more so than a *Courlander*, a *Livonian*, or *a Finlander*. In point of local knowledge to place me on a level with a native of Russia—to *me* as to *them*—information in various shapes could not but be necessary. Any such assistance no person could ever be more ready to supply than I should be solicitious to receive and profit by it.

In my above mentioned work, a sample of a *Penal Code* is exhibited. In the first place, what I should humbly propose is—to do what remains to be done for the completion of it. For this purpose not many months would I hope be necessary.

Sovereign and father—in this double character it is on all occasions Your Majestys wish and delight to shew yourself to your

[4] For Montesquieu and Blackstone, see above, letter 2098 and nn. 9 and 10. Cesare Beccaria, Marchese de Beccaria-Bonesana (1738–94) was the author of the influential *Dei delitti e delle pene*, translated into French in 1766 as *Traité des délits et des peines*, translated and edited by André Morellet (1727–1819).

[5] See above, letter 2098 and n. 11.

[6] From January 1786 to December 1787.

people. In this same character—even on the rough and thorny ground of penal law—in this same happily compounded character, addressing them through my pen Your Majesty would still shew yourself. The Sovereign by his *commands*; the father by his *instructions*; the Sovereign not more intent on establishing the necessary obligations, than the father on rendering the necessity manifest; manifest to all men, and, at every step he takes, thus justifying himself in their sight.

Reasons—Yes, it is by *reasons* alone, that a task at once so salutary and so arduous can be accomplished—reasons—connected, and *that* by an undiscontinued chain of references, on the one hand with the *general principles* from which they have been deduced, on the other hand with the several *clauses* and *words* in the text of the law for the *justification*, and at the same time for the *elucidation*, of which they have respectively been framed. An accompaniment of this kind would form one of the peculiarities of my *Code*:—a sample is given in my above mentioned *Treatises*.

All comprehensiveness, *conciseness*, *uniformity*, *simplicity*—qualities, the union of which is at once so desirable and so difficult such, as far as concerns the choice of words, are the qualities for which the nature of the work seems to present a demand. To infuse them into it, each in the highest degree which the necessary regard to the rest admits of, would, on this, as on all similar occasions it has been, be to my mind an object of unremitting solicitude. With what promise of success let the above mentioned sample speak. Whosoever sees that *one part*, sees, to all such purposes, the *whole*.

In the midst of War, and without interruption to the successes or to the toils of war, a line or two from Your Majesty's hand would suffice to give commencement to the Work:—to this the greatest of all the works of peace.

As to *remuneration*, the honour of the proposed employ, joined to such satisfactions as would be inseparable from that honour, compose the only reward which my situation renders necessary, the only one which my way of thinking would allow me to accept.

With all the respect, of which the nature of this address conveys so much fuller an assurance, than can be conveyed by any customary form of words, my endeavour would be to approve myself,

Sire,
Your Imperial Majesty's
ever faithful Servant,
Jeremy Bentham

2267

From John Cartwright

16 February 1814

Wed. 16. Feb. 1814

My dear Sir

The much injured Mr. Wilson,[2] who has been shamefully used in the two naval departments, who are indebted to him for unrequited services, has reason to believe they are now actually invading his patent right in the insubmergible gun boats of which he put into their hands one or more. He understands they are now cutting out the frames and planks of a large number of these gunboats to be sent to Canada, for the Lake service. He employed a friend at *Chatham* to give him information of the fact, but the work is done in secret, and nobody allowed to see what is going on. He thinks your friend Mr Peake, must know if the fact be as above stated, that, at Chatham, the Builders are at work on such frames of his patent boats, or any boats of the models *he has furnished*, and he believes Mr. Peake at your request would have no objection to say how the fact is.—

Sir F.B.[3] is detained by Lady B. being near her time and not very well, which makes her unwilling to part with him. Yours truly

J. Cartwright

2268

From Leigh Hunt

3 March 1814

Dear Sir,

I must beg pardon for subjecting you to the perusal of a long letter, but as the subject is a good and useful one, I have no doubt you will hear me, without lifting up your stick, like the philosopher

2267. [1] UC clxxiv. 110. Autograph. Docketed: '1814 Feb 16 / Cartwright James Str. / to / J.B. Q.S.P. / Navy Board employs / Wilson's invention sans / récompense.' Addressed: 'Jeremiah Bentham Esq'.

[2] Probably Christopher Wilson, inventor of machines and systems applicable to naval architecture patented 1795–1806.

[3] Sir Francis Burdett's wife Lady Sophia (1775–1844), gave birth to Angela, later Baroness Burdett-Coutts (1814–1906) on 21 April.

2268. [1] Bowring, 'Memoirs', at p. 474. Autograph. Docketed: '1814 Mar 3 / Leigh Hunt Horsemonger Lande / Prison / to / J.B. Q.S.P. / For Elton Hammond / that he may be

of old.[2] There is a young man,—the friend of a friend of mine,—who from *family* misfortunes, has fallen from a state of prosperity into indigence, and who cannot find it in his heart to bear a state of dependence with good spirits. He has been for some time past very uneasy, and is willing, he says, to do any thing and encounter any fatigue so that he can, in any shape, be useful to his fellow-creatures and a little so to himself. His particular object is, if possible, to get a situation, however humble, in some such society, as the Lancasterian[3] or African,[4] where while he was procuring *bread*, he could be conscious of doing essential service to the community. He is zealous and enthusiastic, and it ought to be mentioned, that he was once employed in mercantile business and *did not like it*,—being fonder, it seems, of books than accompts. Since that time, however, he has a great and heavy lesson, and is now anxious to put his knowledge of accounts to use. It struck me, that such a young man, so lessoned, so unfortunate, and so enthusiastic, would be one of the very best persons for an assistant in some such society as above-mentioned; and accordingly, I wrote yesterday to Mr. Brougham, with little compunction on the score of making interest, to ask him whether he could point out any thing to be done. Mr. Brougham favoured me with a visit this morning, and tells me that the other day there was a letter written by Mr. Fox[5] to the West London Lancas. Society,[6] recommending a young man to the office of Secretary to that institution, but requesting at the same time that they would not enquire too narrowly into his capacity for the situation. To this Mr. B., as a trustee, thought himself bound to object, as you may well suppose; and the consequence is, that after having received my letter, he is willing to transfer his good wishes to the person of whom I speak, and to mention the subject to Mr. Place[7] and Mr. Brooks[8] (names, of

employed / by the Lancasterians'. Hunt had been convicted of libelling the Prince Regent and sentenced to two years' imprisonment in February 1813.

[2] A reference to Antisthenes, the fifth-century BC Athenian philosopher, and his pupil Diogenes the Cynic. See Diogenes Laertius, *Lives and Opinions of Eminent Philosophers*, vi. 21.

[3] The Royal Lancasterian Society (later the British and Foreign School Society) had been founded in 1808 to popularize Joseph Lancaster's educational ideas and maintain Lancaster's model school in the Borough Road.

[4] Probably the African Education Society, founded in 1800.

[5] Joseph Fox (*c.*1776–1816), a surgeon dentist and secretary to the British and Foreign School Society.

[6] In 1813 the West London Lancasterian Association had been established as an offshoot of the Royal Lancasterian Society. Its aim was to provide 'schools for all' in London.

[7] Francis Place (1771–1854), master tailor and radical reformer, former leading figure in the London Corresponding Society, supporter of Sir Francis Burdett, and member of both the British and Foreign School Society and the West London Lancasterian Association.

[8] Samuel Brooks (d. 1822), glass manufacturer, founder member, treasurer and frequent chairman of the Westminster committee of electors 1807–22.

course, with which you are acquainted); though under the circumstances, he felt that he could not in delicacy recommend the person himself; but he wished me, at the same time, to write to yourself on the business, and perhaps, he said, you would mention it to Mr. Mill, and Mr. Mill, if he had no person better qualified in view, might offer his good wishes too. It might be as well perhaps, in consideration of the feelings of a young man well educated and unfortunately situated, to use his name as little as possible till it became necessary to mention it; but he is a Mr. Elton Hammond,[9] and once, I understand, in the days of his prosperity had the pleasure of paying his respects to yourself, from a feeling which I need not mention. The friend who mentioned him to me is a very worthy and intelligent man, Dr. Gooch,[10] my physician. Dr. G. has given me expressly to understand that Mr. Hammond's wishes were of the humblest kind, provided he could be doing something and feel himself of some use:—a Secretary's place, I suspect, would be much more than he looks for; but were there any thing less to be had, I have no doubt it would be welcome.

You will be good enough to observe, my dear Sir, that though I am bound to do what I can for a fellow-creature who is unfortunate, yet I should not think myself justified in recommending him to others, if I were not persuaded that he had a proper claim to their good offices; and as I am not acquainted with the person in the present instance, (whatever may be my reliance on the word of his friend), I say all that I have said with a *reserve*, that if he be not found *fit* for the situation which might be open to him, it is far from my intention to wish him in it. Indeed, I believe it would be equally so from his own. With my best remembrances to Mr. Mill, and the other friends round your table (if you will be good enough to take them in charge for me), believe me,

My dear Sir,
Your affectionate servant
Leigh Hunt.

To
Jeremy Bentham Esqr.

[9] Elton Hammond (1786?–1819), a former merchant, whom Burr described as 'A very intelligent young man; admiring of the works of B.' (Davis, i. 94). For his earlier contact with Bentham, see *Correspondence* vii, as index.

[10] Perhaps Dr Robert Gooch (1784–1830), a physician who practised in Surrey 1808–11 and then in London, also lecturing in midwifery at St Bartholomew's Hospital.

2269

To William Salisbury

11 March 1814 (Aet 66)

Queen's Square Place Westmr.
11 March 1814

Mr Bentham would be obliged to Mr Salisbury if he would have the goodness to return this paper with the addition of the figures expressive of the answers to the subjoined queries.
1. What has been the *total* number of the days in which a course—*one* course—of lectures has been delivered at the Botanic Garden in Sloane-Street?
2. What has been the length of time employed in the lecture on each day?
3. What has been the length, in number of *days* and *hours*, as above, of the longest course of Botanical Lectures that has ever come to Mr. Salisbury's knowledge?

2270

From William Salisbury

March 1814

No. 1. Twelve. Lectures were usually read 2 in a Week making 6 Weeks.—
2 From 1 hour and half to 2 hours—
3 Mr Salisbury believes Mr Curtis[2] used to deliver his course in Sixteen days. four in a Week for a month. he does not remember a course having been longer atended.

2269. [1] UC clxv.1. Autograph. William Salisbury (d. 1823) was the owner of the London Botanic Garden, Cadogan Place, Sloane Street, described in his *Botanists' Companion*, London, 1816.

2270. [1] UC clxv.1. Autograph. Salisbury wrote his replies on the inside of Bentham's letter of 11 March (letter 2269). Docketed: '1814 1814 March / Chrestomathia / Salisbury / Information / about No. of Lectures / on Botany'.

[2] William Curtis (1746–99), botanist, founder of the *Botanical Magazine*, partner of Salisbury at the garden at Queen's Elm, Brompton.

2271

To Sir Samuel Bentham

2 April 1814 (Aet 66)

Q.S.P. 2 April 1814

Dined yesterday Mill Koe and I at Cartwrights—Wakefield there also. Wakefield having through Mill derived some information from you relative to the Portsmouth Marine Academy[2] with a view of endeavouring to get placed therein his son[3] who was with the late Capt. Beaver[4]—thinking you would be glad to see him *I* invited him accordingly, and he will be with you on Tuesday to dinner unless in the mean time I hear from you to the contrary. He asked your dinner hours, and I could not tell him, if you have need to write to me in the mean time tell me. If he comes, you make a Porter of him for these Geometry papers of yours and some which we spoke about; and which he may bear at Mills or may take to his (Wakefield's) Brother's[5] Chambers at or near Linc. Inn, whence Koe may bring them hither. Before we parted, he told me he was perfectly satisfied of the eligibility of the thing, though fears otherwise of the probability of his obtaining it. He was to try to see Ld. Melville about it on this day. Just now comes a man from a man of the name of *Evans*? is it? or Edwards?[6] or who else about a Bill of £13. odd due from you for Floor Cloth, saying that Lady B. had said to this man he being at Hampstead that I would pay the Bill on demand. I recollect nothing of your having said any thing to me on any such a subject: I recollect your making me give you a piece of paper, and your drawing a draught thereon, but I have no recollection of your leaving it with me. I think if you had made any such attempt I should have resisted it, as being a burthen upon my memory, which is not in a condition to take upon itself unnecessary burthens. I offered to the man to write about this, but he said I need not as he should soon revisit Hampstead. The Women below say that

2271. [1] D. R. Bentham MSS. Autograph. Docketed: '1814 April 2 / J.B. / to / S.B.' Addressed: 'To / Sir Samuel Bentham / Hall Oak Farm / Hampstead.' Postmark: 'Two Py Post / Unpaid / [. . .?]. Stamped: '[. . .?] / by 10 o'Clock / on Sun'.

[2] Established in 1729, this institution became the Royal Naval College in 1806 and was transferred to Greenwich in 1872.

[3] Probably Arthur Wakefield (1799–1843), second of Edward Wakefield's four sons, who entered the navy in 1810.

[4] For Captain Philip Beaver see above letter 2240 n. 4.

[5] Probably Daniel Wakefield, for whom see letter 2237 n. 7.

[6] Perhaps Elliot. John Elliot and Son were House-painters and floor-cloth-manufacturers of 22 Friday Street, Cheapside.

you had said something about this debt to Koe, and that there was a danger in paying it to this man, he being a Bankrupt or suspected of being so.

2272

FROM JOHN PICKTON

6 April 1814

Royal free School,
Borough Road,
April 6th 1814.

Sir,

I have drawn out a paper of the Commands used in this School, which you will find enclosed.[2] I have done it in much haste, and am not sure it is sufficiently explicit, if you find it so and will give me a line stating where I have not been perspicuous enough, I will endeavour to give you a more clear explanation in writing, or will wait on you at any time for that purpose.

I am Sir
Your obedient Servant
J Pickton

2273

TO PAVEL CHICHAGOV

early May 1814 (Aet 66)

After what you have said, I shall depend upon your ascribing to the true cause, and thence regarding with complacency rather than displeasure, my availing myself to the full of the liberty you give me, and submitting to your consideration a few suggestions in the

2272. [1] UC clxv. 3. Autograph. Docketed: '1814 Apr 6 / Picton, Borough Road / to J.B. Q.S.P. / Inclosing list of / words of command'.

John Pickton was superintendent of the Royal Free-School, Borough Road.

[2] Missing.

2273. [1] Bowring, x. 477–8, where it is undated and introduced: 'Admiral Tchitchagoff consulted Bentham on the publication of a history of the Russian campaign. From a long letter of Bentham's on the subject, I copy an extract, which contains valuable suggestions to any writer engaged in similar literary undertakings.' This letter appears to have been written while Chichagov was still in Russia, and we know he left St Petersburg on 22 May 1814 (see letter 2274). Letter 2278 mentions Chichagov's arrival with documents, 'in pursuance of my advice'.

way of advice. Addressed by a man who is so much in the habit of literary composition, to one who has been so much more honourably and efficiently employed, they will stand clear (I flatter myself) of any such imputation as that of officiousness or impertinence.

1. Whatsoever *papers* you have in your possession, of a nature to serve as *proofs*, or (as we say) as *vouchers*, for the propositions you advance, relative to matter of *fact*—be careful to transmit them in company with the *narrative*: for example, the daily and other periodical *military reports*, such as you received them from day to day, stating the number of *men* of all ranks, in and out of condition for service: *horses*, *cannon*, *carriages*, and so forth. If in *French*, so much the better; though, if there should not be time to get them translated into French, *my brother's children* would, (I suppose,) among them, find Russ and French enough for the purpose.

2. Send, if possible, either in print or manuscript, a *map* of the route pursued by the armies, as particular as may be, accompanied with *references* from the *narrative*. If stated as being *original*, such map, besides *explaining* the narrative, will help the sale of it.

3. Remember, on every occasion, to render as well the narrative of military *movements*, as the description of *fixed objects* and *states of things*—as *particular* as possible. Trust as little as possible, to any such expectation as that *assertions*, conceived in *general terms*, unsupported by *particular proofs*, will make the wished for impression on the bulk of readers. Consider that *your own knowledge*, or *interior persuasion*, of the truth of the several assertions, cannot of itself operate as *evidence* on the minds of *strangers*; and that, in default of particular vouchers, for judging of the truth of any such assertions, what an impartial reader will look to, will be their consistency with such facts, as either are established by *especial evidences*, or are in their own nature sufficiently notorious.

2274

To Albert Gallatin

16 June 1814 (Aet 66)

Queen's Square Place Westmr
Thursday 16 June 1814.

Dear Sir

Circumstances have reduced me to the necessity of being once more, and in this manner, troublesome to you.

When the Emperor Alexander, and my Proposal to him, were the subject of conversation between us, I was mentioning to you, that it was not my wish to have any personal communication with him, and that my wish was rather to avoid it. Such it continues to be still, but, considering that by one accident or other, he might, with or without having received my Proposal, happen to hear of my existence, and in consequence command my attendance, on that supposition I could not but be anxious, to have in my pocket, a recommendation so persuasive, as the letter which you have so obligingly and repeatedly led me to expect.

Amongst the incidents, which might possibly render my personal attendance on the Emperor unavoidable, is the arrival of Admiral *Tchitchagoff*, who, after obtaining a letter of leave from his master, conceived in very gracious terms, left Petersburgh on the 22 of last month, in the declared intention of reaching this country as soon as the post could carry him. He is accordingly expected every hour: and I had been flattering myself with the imagination, that in the event of his arrival before your departure, you might perhaps be able to find time to give him a meeting at my house.

Another object of my call of this morning was eventually to disburthen you of that pamphlet from the title-page of which the name of the author is cut out.[2] When I had first the honour of seeing you,—no, I believe it was the second time—it being at that time a matter of uncertainty whether your departure might not take place almost immediately—I said that, if it were worth the carriage as far as *Ghent*,[3] it would be time enough for me to receive it back again, when any occasion of sending a packet from *that* place to *this*

2274. [1] Gallatin MSS, New-York Historical Society, New York. Autograph. Autograph copy at BL IX. 164–71, docketed: '1814 June 16 / J.B. Q.S.P. / to / Galatin 9 Orchard / Street'.

[2] Unidentified.

[3] Gallatin was one of the American representatives in the negotiations leading to the signing of the treaty of Ghent, which ended hostilities between Britain and the United States.

presented itself. So it would be *still*. But as, except one that I have written in, I have but that one copy, and know not where to get another, and as that one was rather borrowed by me than begged, I should be much obliged by the return of it before you leave England, if by that time you have either given up all intention of making use of it, or already made any such use of it as you may have intended.

With regard to the letter from you to the Governor of Pennsylvania,[4] my sending to the press mine to the P.U.S.[5] has been waiting for my receiving it, and will finally depend upon that event. You see therefore how material it is for me to know what, in relation to that subject, I have to expect. For this purpose, that any addition which I may have to make, to the trouble which I have already been led to occasion to you, may be as small as possible, it has occurred to me to put the matter to this issue. If I receive back from you the abovementioned pamphlet, without finding it accompanied with any written communication from you to me, my conclusion will be— that whatsoever intention you may have had, in relation to any such letter, exists no longer.

To prevent all misconception, I will state to you the circumstances which led to the conception that such a conclusion as above might be acceptable to you. This morning, when, upon the opening of your door, I asked your black Servant whether you were within, his answer was in the affirmative: therefore you had no objection to see at *that* time any person whom you would choose to see at *any* time. I mentioned my name to him: he knew me, having twice before let me in etc. I had scarce seated myself in your drawing room, into which, as before, he had conducted me, when he entered the room again with these words—'*My Master*' (or '*Mr Galatin*', I forget which) '*is engaged,*' *Sir*: whereupon, taking out of my pocket a card with my name and address on it, I put it into his hand and withdrew. On Monday or Tuesday it was that, upon my sending to know whether you were still in London, my Messenger learnt at your house that your departure was expected at the latter end of this week. In this state of things, from the tenor of the above verbal message, in which no disposition to see me, or to communicate with me, in any other manner, at any other time, was expressed, I knew not how to avoid drawing, provisionally at least, a conclusion, the

[4] Simon Snyder (1759–1819) was governor of Pennsylvania 1808–17. Gallatin's letter to Snyder, dated 18 June 1814, is printed in *Papers Relative to Codification and Public Instruction*, pp. 71–3 (Bowring, iv. 468–9).

[5] Letter 2145.

erroneousness of which no one could be so well pleased to learn, as the drawer of it.

The importance of the design which led to the trouble I have been giving you being considered, I can not but flatter myself with your concurring with me in the opinion, that it would not have been excusable in me to have risked the extinction of it altogether, for want of any such endeavours as it might be in my power to use for the removing of any misconception, if any such there may have been, that has stood in the way of it.

Believe me, with the truest respect,

Dear Sir,
Your most obedient Servant
Jeremy Bentham.

Mr Galatin
etc. etc. etc.

P.S. In expectation of the pamphlet in question, at 11 o'clock A.M. tomorrow, or soon after, a messenger will call at your House to ask whether there be any packet directed to me.

P.S. It was perfectly understood between us, and for very obvious reasons, that any letter of yours in which I were mentioned to the Governor of Pennsylvania was not to be printed by me, nor in any sense made public, if at all, till it had reached his answers. Eventually shewing it to the Emp. Alex. was a special exception for that special purpose.

2275

To Albert Gallatin

25 June 1814 (Aet 66)

Queen's Square Place Westmr
Saturday morng 25 June
1814.

Dear Sir

Proportioned to the alarm under which I had been suffering, was the satisfaction produced by the receipt of your very obliging letter.[2] These few words will, I flatter myself not be displeasing to you: the

2275. [1] Gallatin MSS, New-York Historical Society, New York. Autograph.
[2] Missing.

many more that I had actually written I spare you the trouble of reading under your present pressure.

I am, My dear Sir
Most truly yours
Jeremy Bentham.

Mr Galatin
etc etc etc

2276

From Henry Brougham

27 June 1814

These are to give notice that Prince Czartorinsky will call on you today at *one*.

Yrs ever truly
H Brougham

Monday
27 June 1814

2277

From Joseph Lowe

3 July 1814

Caen, in Normandy 3d July 1814.

My dear Sir

I embrace an opportunity of giving you a report of our proceedings. We left Ludlow on the 12th inst. and after calling on Mrs Mackintosh[2] at Tenbury, travelled to Southampton which we reached without difficulty on the morning of the 14th. There we found the competition to have us as passengers so great that there

2276. [1] BL IX. 174–5. Autograph, apart from the date, which is in Bentham's hand. Docketed: '1814 June 27 / Brougham / to / J.B. Q.S.P. / Prince Czartorinski (Admiral) / to call on Q.S.P. / at *1* / Reced ¾ after 12. / He called accordingly / at ½ after 1 staid / till ½ after 3: it was / to ask J.B.'s leave / eventually [?] to put questi- / ons to him in relation / to a Polish Code.' Addressed: 'J. Bentham Esq / Queen Square Place / Westminster'.

Prince Adam Jerzy Czartoryski (1770–1861), Polish patriot and Russian deputy foreign minister 1804–6, was hoping to see a restored Poland emerge from the negotiations at the end of the Napoleonic wars. He was in Britain seeking support. For Bentham's earlier contact with Czartoryski see *Correspondence*, iv. 131 and n., 256 and n.

2777. [1] BL IX. 188. Copy. Endorsed by Bentham: 'The following is from Mr | | Lowe, a fellow countryman, school-fellow and intimate of Mr Mill's: he was with us for about a week at Barrow Green the summer before last, or the summer before that.' Whether this letter was to Bentham, or to Mill, or to another of Bentham's associates, is unclear.

[2] Not further identified.

was no difficulty in making a bargain to land us at the mouth of Caen river instead of going to Havre de Grâce. We went on board on the morning of the 15th, and passed Portsmouth about 2 o'clock. The wind being westerly, we were enabled to accomplish the passage speedily, and were landed next morning by a French boat at the place of our destination. Here, having shewn our trunks to the Custom House officers, and procured some very homely refreshment, we travelled over execrable roads, but thro' a pretty country, to Caen, a distance of eight miles, and were put down by dinnertime at the Hotel d'Angleterre, where we soon partook of a sumptuous repast.

Caen is built of stone, and the houses, to outward appearance, surpassed our expectations: but the inside presents a very different picture. Imagine to yourself a number of large buildings with stone stairs, wandering and gloomy passages, and what is more uncomfortable still to our eyes, stone or brick floors in the rooms. Add to this, a strange want of taste in the appropriation of a building, the ground floors of a spacious mansion being frequently occupied by a cooper or joiner, surrounded with all the insignia of his trade. As to the streets of Caen, some of them are close and dark; others, particularly the late buildings, would do honour to an English City. The situation of the town is good; and parts of it are sufficiently elevated to have a fine prospect. The chief division of the town is on a plain, but a plain enlivened by fine walks, and a navigable river. Never was there a more motley group than that exhibited every day in the streets, particularly in the one in which our quarters are. The dress of both sexes is so varied, as to bid defiance to all attempts to reduce it to a standard. The men figure away in coats, jackets, great coats, and hats round or cocked, as it suits the fancy or the pocket of the wearer. The women have a still greater variety, but the predominant feature of their dress is a cap ending in a point, after rising like a pyramid, 6, 8, or 10 inches from the forehead.

You see from this report that this country is of a mixed character, the people being extremely civil, the climate good, and provisions abundant, but the state of progress in point of comfort, greatly behind England. Yet a short time, we are told, is found sufficient to bring round English families to an acquiescence in local habits: but as few towns in France present the accommodation of furnished lodgings, it is expedient for every family designing to come here to have arrangements made before hand, by a friend on the spot.

I employ myself chiefly at present in looking around and collecting information both by letter and otherwise, and comparing the merits of different residences. Our great object is to have no further change to make, a French dwelling requiring so much to render it comfortable to an English family that removal is a very serious affair—In two things we have experienced some disappointment—In the want of furnished lodgings, and in the inconvenient structure of the houses.—In other respects, such as the aspect of the country, the disposition of the people and the facility of book supplies, our expectations have been surpassed. As to the price of provisions, without finding it so low as stated by Pinkney,[3] we see that a family may be maintained at the half of a Shropshire, and less than the third of a London expenditure

Butcher's meat 5d the lb. of 18 oz.
Bread______ $1\frac{1}{2}$ do.
Butter______ 8______ do.
Milk______ $1\frac{1}{2}$ the Quart
Women Servants wages £4 a year
Fuel nearly as at Ludlow (very cheap, the mines being near)

		s	.	d
Poultry a goose (larger than in England)		2	"	6
Turkey______	do. ______	2	"	6
Couple of fowls______	do. ______	2	"	–

Eggs 5 d per dozen

Game—a hare 2 s/. a brace of partridges 2 s/.

House rent not much less than at Ludlow where it is little more than half the London. but taxes trifling

Wine 1 s/3 d a bottle

Potatoes and vegetables about half the Ludlow prices which are very cheap

Sea fish plenty and cheap

A fine turbot 2 s/6
Macharel 1d or 2d each.

[3] Ninian or Nathan Pinkney (1776–1825) was the author of *Travels through the South of France, and in the interior of the provinces of Provence and Languedoc, in the years 1807 and 1808*, London, 1809 (2nd edn. 1814).

2278

To Sir Samuel Bentham

4 July 1814 (Aet 66)

Q.S.P. Monday 4 July 1814

As Tchitchagoff was to dine with me on Saturday, you will expect I suppose or at least wish to hear something of the result. Six was the time appointed for dinner; ½ *after* 5 the time for his coming, settled at his desire by our watches; *5*, the time he came. Finding him a walker, I took him the walk by the Brushouse, and then till dinner was ready seated him in the state chair in my work-shop. Alexanders head he represented to me as a perfect '*vacuum*:' that was several times his word: fickle as a weathercock: when a plan for any purpose had been proposed to him, and even established, let him be ever so well satisfied, when the back of the person who proposed it is turned, the first person who finds any thing to say against it drives it off the stage. More, a good deal, than I can stay to write about the same character, the general result is—that under such a man, and with such people about him, all chance of the establishment of any such Code as I should pen, and hence of any immediate good to Russia, is altogether out of the question. Yet, when I asked him about getting the letter conveyed, he undertook to do it with the utmost readiness: this accordingly is what it will be my object to get him to do: presuming from a Letter of acceptance from his vacuity various good effects, though his vacuity were to think no more of it: unfortunately, the conversation was unavoidably brought to a close, before there was time for settling any specific arrangements for the purpose.

He told me of his having, in pursuance of my advice, brought with him to England an ample provision of documents: to Q.S.P. he brought but two, viz. a narrative written by a French General whom he captured, and a small MS Map drawn by the same General for the illustration of that same narrative.[2] To all appearance it redounds highly to T.'s honour: and whereas 70,000 I think was the number stated by him in his Letters to you as opposed by Bonaparte to his 35,000 whereof but 16,000 Infantry, upwards of 90,000 is the

2278. [1] BL IX. 176–7. Autograph. Addressed: 'To / Sir Samuel Bentham K.S.G. / Berry Lodge / near Gosport.' Postmark illegible.

[2] General Frédéric-François Guillaume de Vaudoncourt (1772–1845) was captured at Vilna on 10 December 1812. His narrative was *Relation impartiale du passage de la Bérézina*, Paris, 1814, which was translated into English in the following year as *Critical situation of Bonaparte in his retreat out of Russia*.

number reckoned up by this Frenchman. The dinner party H.K, Mill, and (more Rustico) Henry:[3] who / which last / immediately after dinner decamped. As soon as the Ice was swallowed, at my proposal the Narrative was produced: it lasted us till ½ after 10, soon after which he departed. What I was surprized at, is—that though my stay in Devonshire whither I expected to go in a week or a little more was not likely to be for less than 4 months, still he *was*, and I believe *is*, for putting off till that time all arrangements about his work: so likewise my obtaining for him admission to divers sights; and interviews with divers persons whom yet he expressed himself desirous to see. Having learnt his hours (breakfast at 11—*exit* not till 12) I reserved in my own mind for this morning, divers explanatio⟨ns⟩ that about Letter to A.[4] among the rest: but the bird was already flown, viz to Woolwich from whence he was not expected till at the end of four days. I have just been writing to him.[5] I don't know what he has been saying or will say to you: he said, he wished you to come to town to see him, rather than to go into the Country to see you. He says he shall stay in this country as long as he can: i.e. till the further deterioration of the Government finances makes such a deterioration in his, as to prevent his living here any longer. I have a suspicion—though it is but a suspicion, that he is taking my advice, and looking out for another English Wife.[6] He talks of taking a small House half way between where his daughters[7] are at School (Brentford?) and Woolwich, where his late wifes sister is No. 9. Quebec Street Oxford Street is his present residence.

Among T.s documents are a number in Russ; which he proposes to get translated. You and yours I told him, could I suppose help him: but this of course depends upon the time of your stay.

[3] Henry Tonkin Coulson, who had been admitted as a sizar at Queens' College, Cambridge on the previous Friday 1 July 1814.

[4] Alexander.

[5] Letter 2279.

[6] Chichagov had married Elisabeth Proby shortly after the death of her father Capt. Charles Proby (1752–99), commissioner of Chatham dockyard.

[7] His daughters Adelaide and Catherine, who were both later to marry French noblemen.

2279

To Pavel Chichagov

4 July 1814 (Aet 66)

Queen's Square Place Westmr.
Monday 4 July 1814

Dear Sir

This morning at ½ after 11 I called at your House, making sure from what you had told me about your hours, of catching you at home. I had then and there the mortification of hearing that you were already gone to Woolwich, and that you were not expected here for four days to come. I write this for the purpose of learning what it may be your pleasure to communicate to me about your motions. Were I to call on Friday, at the commencement of your breakfast hour (par parenthèses I never breakfast from home myself) should I be more successful, and at the same time find you alone? or if not on that day on what other day. Of my own departure for the place I have taken in Devon[2] there the day is not—could not be—as yet, fixt: all that I know is—that it can not be earlier than Monday next: and that on various accounts it is necessary that it should be as soon after as possible. Sooner than not see you again before your departure, if you would give me an hour, I would run down to Woolwich, hoping it might be such as would enable me to be back by 12 or ½ after. But, for reasons too long to explain, I would much rather it were at your own house than any where else, even than at mine.

I am, Dear Sir, with the truest respect and regard,
Your's
Jeremy Bentham

Admiral Tchitchagoff.

P.S. Did you see Prince Czartorisky as you expected? if not, I must perforce write an answer to his note. Cutting to pieces one of the few mornings that at my time of life I can expect, would do me some harm, and unless it promised to do him and his some specific good, I would avoid it.

Favour me, in black and white with the names of two persons 1. The French General (mentioning his friend to whom we were so much obliged for our Saturday evening's entertainment).[3]

2279. [1] BL IX. 178–80. Pressed copy of an autograph letter. Docketed: '1814 July 4 / J.B. Q.S.P. / to / Tchichagoff Woolwich / Vaudincour'.

[2] Ford Abbey.

[3] Frédéric-François Guillaume de Vaudoncourt.

2. The Polish General, Governor of Minsk,[4] to whom we have been so much obliged for the share he contributed to the ruin of Bonaparte.

Over and over again, every body heard both these names, nobody remembers either of them.

2280

From Pavel Chichagov

5 July 1814

Woolwich july the 5
1814

Dear Sir

I am particularly sorry that a man who knows to make so good a use of his time as you do should have lost so much of it on my account. I thought I had told you that I would leave the town Monday at eleven a clock. Whoever it is now irreperable and remains only the satisfaction I have to find that you think of me. I have not met P. Czartorisky but begged Count Orloff[2] who was to see him to deliver the message and thereupon think that he wont trouble you any more unless it is with the purpose you admit.

Friday I shall certainly be in town and will be very happy to receive you at breakfast or any other way. I breakfast at 11 and shall be quite alone for you, that morning. Whatever you will intrust me with, shall be done with the greatest exactness and as much to your satisfaction as possible. I shall only hope that you will help me to give you proofes of the regard and esteem I entertained for you allways and how much it is encreased by my being personaly acquainted with you.

The name of the French general is Guillaume de Vaudancourt but I will give it you more correctly in town. The governor of Minsk is Bronikovsky. I should like to know What you want to make of them.

If you had been so much pleased with what I read to you as I have been with the Conversation and all together with the party I found in your house it would do great honour to the French general.

[4] Nicolas Deodatus Cajetan Bronikowski, count of Oppeln (1767–1817), governor of Minsk July–November 1812.

2280. [1] BL IX. 181–2. Autograph. Docketed: '1814 July 5 / Tchitchagoff / Woolwich / to / J.B. Q.S.P.'

[2] Probably Count Mikhail Fedorovich Orlov (1788–1842), a Russian army officer who had taken part in the war against Napoleon and been a member of the force that occupied Paris. At this time he was engaged in various diplomatic activities for the Russian government.

Let me see you there on Friday or else fix me any time to come to you I will be contented with either and particularly so I am with the friendly words you give me

yours most truly
P. Tchitchagoff

2281

To Simon Snyder

14 July 1814 (Aet 66)

London, July, 1814.

Sir,

In transmitting the herewith inclosed Letter addressed to your Excellency by Mr. Gallatin, together with some copies of a now first printed Letter of mine, addressed and sent in October, 1811, to President Madison,[2]—it will be necessary for me to accompany them with some account of the incidents that have led to this my respectful address. From a common friend of Mr. Gallatin's and mine,[3] I understood, not long ago, that for some time past he had been expressing a desire to see me. I accordingly called upon him at his then residence in Orchard Street. Thinking the opportunity a favourable one, for learning whether my abovementioned letter to the President, a printed copy of which is here inclosed, had come to hand,—I went with the MS. brouillon of it in my pocket. I was received, with the most unequivocal tokens, of that favourable opinion, which is so gratifying to me, and of which that letter of his to you contains the expression. I found him almost at the very moment of his then expected departure from this country. Under these circumstances, in the course of a conversation carried on on both sides with the necessary rapidity, I took out of my pocket the MS. abovementioned, speaking of it as a thing which, had time permitted, it *had* been my wish to have submitted to his perusal. Understanding the drift of it, he insisted upon my leaving it: and a plan of future intercourse on the subject, adapted to the various

2281. [1] *Supplement to Papers Relative to Codification and Public Instruction*, London, 1817, pp. 1–30. Reprinted in Bowring, iv. 468–75. A letter from Snyder to David Meade Randolph (1760–1830) of Williamsburg, Virginia, of 31 May 1816, reveals that Bentham's letter was dated 14 July 1814. See *Papers Relative to Codification and Public Instruction*, p. 75 (Bowring, iv. 475).

[2] Letter 2145. For Gallatin's letter see letter 2274 and n. 4.

[3] Probably Aaron Burr.

contingencies to which his own local situation stood for some time exposed, was settled between us. I had the scarce expected pleasure of seeing him two or three times after *that*, though no more than once only for any continuance. He was, I believe already gone, when this of his to you was delivered to me: so that, had it been my wish,——though I know not why it should have been,——to have seen it in any manner altered, whether by omission, addition, or substitution, it has not been in my power. In this account of it is implied the circumstance of its having been sent to me open. To this circumstance I owe the faculty of submitting to you some of the following explanations.

I found him well acquainted——not only with those two works of mine, which he spoke of as having been edited in French by my friend Mr. Dumont——the first at Paris anno 1802, the other in London anno 1811,——but with a preceding one in English, edited in my own name by the title of *An Introduction to the Principles of Morals and Legislation*, London, 1789; which was the forerunner, and, as far as it extended, formed the basis, of the earliest and most extensive of the two in French. Being in English; I regret that, on the present occasion it is altogether out of my power to find a copy to present to you: it having for many years been out of print. About five and twenty years ago (he said) it was put into his hands by Colonel Burr: and from that time (he was pleased to say) he considered himself as my pupil.

It was in October, 1811, as above, that my letter addressed to the President was dispatched out of my hands. It went, accompanied with two recommendatory letters, from a person of eminence here,[4] to two persons of very high eminence in the United States,[5] with whom he was well and personally acquainted. From that time to this, no tidings of it have ever reached me. At the time of its going out of my hands, being at a distance from London, several circumstances concurred in preventing me from being precisely informed of the details of its transmission. Supposing it received, various circumstances presented themselves as capable of warranting the President in leaving it unnoticed. Mr. Gallatin, however, could not bring himself to believe that, being thus unnoticed, it could have been received.

The President of the Union being the person addressed, an observation of Mr. Gallatin was——that it belonged not to a person in that office to *originate* so much as a single law, relative to the *internal* concerns of any one of the United States. My answer was

[4] Brougham.
[5] Unidentified.

—that that circumstance was completely in my view: but that, on a subject of that nature and importance, in the character of an instrument of *communication*, to any proper person in any one of those States, the highest of all persons comprised in the Union might serve, at any rate, as well as any other person: and if so it were, that in the number of those States there were any one or more, to which the proposition were regarded as capable of being of use, no one person could, in respect of situation, be more likely—few equally likely—to be informed who they were: and that what, in my obscurity, it had fallen in my way to hear, of the character of the person by whom that office was at that time filled, could not but plead in favour of that choice.

Had the opportunity, which has produced to your Excellency the trouble of this address, fallen in my way at the time of writing that letter,—it would, of course, have been to *The Governor of Pennsylvania* that it would have been addressed, and not to *The President of the United States*.

In that case, in several points of form, as determined by the difference between the two official situations, it would have, of course, been different: but in substance, the difference, if any, would have been so inconsiderable, that, to save the eventual waste of more labour,—in addition to that which, hitherto with so little fruit, has already been expended—I have, with the concurrence of Mr. Gallatin, taken the liberty to send it to you under its original address.

While thus sitting at the feet of my Gamaliel,[6] in a few minutes I saw before me, a map of the whole Union: of three compartments, one seemed to present rather an inviting prospect; another, but a faint one; a third, none at all. In the foreground stood *Pennsylvania*, placed there for specific reasons: in addition to such as are of a *permanent* nature, I beheld two *temporary* ones: one derived from the character of *the present Governor*, of which, at the same time (if I do not misrecollect,) he stated his conceptions as derived rather from general reputation, than from personal intercourse; the other, from the circumstance of his (Mr. Gallatin's) having, when a member of the legislature of that State,[7] had the satisfaction of seeing an individual, (*Judge Wilson*,[8] by birth and education a Scotchman, in

[6] Acts 5: 34 and 22: 3.

[7] Gallatin was a representative of Fayette County, Pennsylvania 1790–3.

[8] James Wilson (1742–98), politician, writer, and lawyer; born in Scotland, he came to America in 1765, was admitted to the bar in 1767, and appointed associate justice 1789. He was commissioned to make a digest of the laws of Pennsylvania but did not live to complete it.

consequence of *his* recommendation, both as to the *measure* and as to the *person*,) appointed, for the very service here in question: to which *satisfaction* was added the *expectation* of finding, that,—although, on *that* occasion, the performance of the service was prevented, by the death of the person, by whom it was to have been performed,—yet the sense of the *utility* of it remains unchanged; and the *hope*, that upon his return (which he spoke of as probably not far distant,) to his residence in that State, the considerations, which he should have to present on that subject, to the minds of his fellow-citizens, would prove not to have been deprived of any part of their efficiency by any intervening incidents.

Inclosed (No.   .) is that letter of Mr. Gallatin to myself, by which this of his to you was announced and accompanied.[9] From him I have no authority for making any such communication: since the time of my receiving it, I have neither seen nor heard from him. Yet, in making it, I can not charge myself with any such imputation as that of breach of confidence. Of a transaction, of which the welfare of mankind in general, and of your State, Sir, in particular, is so manifestly the object, and the sole object,—(unless any personal satisfaction, derivable from the contemplation of the eventual success of the proffered labour, be worth considering as a distinct object)—an object, the pursuit of which is so perfectly and manifestly free from all mixture of what is commonly understood by *personal* interest, and at any rate, from every thing included under the denomination of *sinister interest*,—of such a transaction it seems to me, that the circumstances can not be too particularly, distinctly, and extensively open to view: and as to the obscure individual himself, who thus has the honour of addressing you,—of the favourable opinion thus testified to be entertained of him by such a man, should a proportionable measure of public regard be the eventual, as it can not but be regarded as a natural consequence,—you will judge, Sir, whether, from an advantage of this sort, accruing to an individual, any just reason can be deduced, for depriving the public at large,—and that portion of it in particular, over which you preside,—of any benefit, of which the contemplation of such an end, pursued by such means, may naturally be productive.

In the too short intercourse, which it has been my lot to hold with that illustrious citizen of your State, and servant of your confederacy, there was not a single word, to which on his own account in respect of present honour, as well as on the account of

[9] Missing: perhaps the letter referred to in letter 2275. For Gallatin's letter to Snyder, 18 June 1814, see letter 2274 and n. 4.

mankind at large, in respect of eventual profit in all imaginable shapes, it would not have been a satisfaction to me to see every degree of publicity given, of which human language is susceptible: there was not a word, the publication of which, could be unto me, on my own particular account, a source of regret. In regard to an event, the importance of which, supposing it to take place, will be of such conspicuous magnitude, scarcely can even the present, much less can any future generation, be altogether incurious to know the origin: and surely for such a work, a purer origin could not so much as be *wished*.

In relation to my Letter to the President,—after such apologies as his politeness suggested, Mr. Gallatin, (it being agreed between us that it should be printed,) favoured me with two pieces of advice: observing at the same time, that he had read the Letter over but once, and that his wish and intention had been, before he gave, to that or any other effect, any *definitive* advice, to read it over a second time: unfortunately for any joint consideration of the subject between us, no such time could be found. At that same meeting, to express my determination to make my utmost profit, of an advice, of the value of which I was so fully sensible, was all that the time allowed of.

Of these two recommendations, one was of a general cast, embracing all that part, in which, in considering what observations might be likely to present themselves in the character of objections to the whole proposal, I brought to view, in company with my answers, that which regards the circumstance of my being *a foreigner*. What was said in relation to *that* topic, had presented itself to his view (he said) as superfluous: in *the United States*—in *Pennsylvania*, at least—that circumstance, he thought, would not be likely to present itself *of itself*, in the character of *an objection*: and that it was better not to *raise up* phantoms, which would not have appeared of themselves, and in regard to which, when once raised up, there was more danger of thus raising up, or furnishing arms to those who disapproved of the design, than assurance of their being *laid* by those who approved of it.

In relation to this suggestion,—penetrated with that respect for the authority of my adviser, which every thing that I had ever seen or heard of him contributed so strongly to impress, I set myself to work but now, to expunge all such passages as it should appear to me that he had in view. But, when it came to the point, I found all that related to that circumstance,—considered as likely to be brought forward in the character of an objection,—so intimately, and, as to me it seemed, inextricably, interwoven with other matter, which, consistently with the requisite explanation, could not, without considerable disadvantage, as it appeared to me, be left out,—that I determined to let it stand untouched. How the separation could be made, I saw not, without taking a considerable part of the whole, and writing it anew. And for this task, destitute of that information, as well as encouragement, which his presence would have afforded me,—loaded too as I found myself with a variety of occupations, and with the additional weight of almost three years, which since the writing of it have elapsed,—my courage failed me.

But, if you, Sir, who on various accounts, can not but be still better qualified for determining what is best to be done—what it would be advisable to expunge, and what to leave—if you, Sir,—on the supposition of the proposal's appearing to be, on public grounds, worth the labour,—would be pleased to take in hand, at this my humble request, and apply, the censorial spunge,—be assured of my grateful sense of the honour done me, as well as of my cheerful acquiescence.

In his letter to yourself, Sir, speaking of my works, 'in most of them,' (Mr. Gallatin, I observe, says,) 'you will find peculiarities both of matter and style, and some suggestions which you will condemn as inadmissible or inapplicable.'

In the letter that accompanied it to myself, he moreover says,—'Permit me to suggest, with respect to your intended labours for Pennsylvania, that she stands in much greater need of a system of civil or non-penal law than of a penal code, which is already much improved, and naturally daily improving. In the other branch, I include procedure, and even organization of Courts, as well as *substantive* law:' (these terms, *non-penal* and *substantive*, the necessity of the case obliged him to take from me:) 'and there,' (continues he) 'lies the great difficulty, both intrinsic and artificial.'

Concerning the peculiarities above alluded to, at this distance from your State, my position has not enabled me to form so much as the slightest conjecture: and, most unhappily for me, from my Mentor, from whom I could have learnt every thing, time admitted not of my learning any thing.

On this subject,—on which, had time admitted, I might, with the greatest ease, have poured out my whole mind to *him*,—I am thus reduced to the necessity of addressing myself to *you*, Sir, at the risk of being found troublesome.

Notwithstanding what you have seen above, I can not but flatter myself, Sir, with the hope, that you will agree with me in the opinion, that, for reaping the greatest profit from whatsoever service it may be in my power to render, the most promising course you can take, is to leave me as *free* as possible:—free, and not only in respect of the *manner* of treating each part of the subject, but also in respect of the *priority* as between part and part:—free, not only in respect of *matter*, but in respect of *form*: free, not only in respect of absence of *restraint*, but in respect of absence of *constraint*: 'free,' (as the Poet says) 'as air,' in every respect.[10] In and by so doing, there would be no precise limits, to what, in respect of the *use* capable of being made of the work, you may gain: and,—should there be any the smallest benefit, which, if left free, it might have been my good fortune to contribute to put you in possession of,—its not being as yet in the contemplation of any of you, will hardly be deemed a sufficient reason for your depriving yourselves of it. On the other hand, by any such freedom on my part, not a particle either of loss or risk will you on your part be exposed to.—Yes: if in the hands of this your proffered servant, there were to exist any the least particle of *power*,—of *power*, or so much as of *influence*,——such influence alone excepted, as by such *reasons* as you will see, may come to be exercised on your minds.—'*Silence*,' fellow Citizens, '*I understand better what is best for the commonwealth than you do*.'[11] Such, with all the frankness of undisguised self-sufficiency, is the recorded speech, of I forget what *Roman*, in whose instance, the consciousness of that intellectual authority,—which is the inseparable accompaniment of superior ability as demonstrated by conspicuous service,—might serve as a cloak, and in some measure as an excuse—for a degree of arrogance, from which nothing whatsoever could have afforded him, or any one, a justification. In the present case,—being as far from any propensity, as from any title or pretence, to employ any such language,—that which the individual who is now addressing you, desires at your hands, is—not that you *should* condemn *yourselves*, but that you should *not* condemn *him*, to silence.

If then, on the one hand, my wish is—that, for your own sakes, (for no interest can I have that is not your's) my service, as rendered to you, should, at this *earliest* stage, be a service of perfect freedom, —at a subsequent stage, you may depend upon me for a degree of obsequiousness, such, as will be more likely to exceed your expectations, than to fall short of your wishes. Freedom at the one stage, obsequiousness at the other,—both are the result of one and the same principle, so far as sincerity admits. My intellectual faculties,

[10] An allusion to the first line of *On a Goldfinch starved to death in his cage*, by William Cowper (1731–1800). This poem was written in 1780 and published in 1782.

[11] i.e. 'tacete, quaeso, Quirites . . . plus ego enim quam vos quid rei publicae expediat intellego', said in a speech to the people by P. Cornelius Scipio Nasica while consul in 138 BC. See Valerius Maximus, *Facta et Dicta Memorabiles*, III. vii. 3.

such as they are, are altogether at your service: but such, to any good purpose, they cannot be, any further than as they are free. *Will*, so far as you are concerned, I have none. To yours, in the execution of this my supposed office, I will accordingly pay the most unreserved—a more than passive—an unreservedly active obedience.

Explanation is here necessary. Most assuredly, to a considerable extent—it is impossible to me to say to how great an extent—what I find to propose to you will appear erroneous.—Again, for the most part, what has thus presented itself to you as erroneous, you will *yourselves* find no difficulty in correcting—in finding for the amendment of it, (whatsoever be the mode of amendment—omission, insertion, or substitution)—such entire provisions of detail, as well as such words as, in your own judgment, will be apt and sufficient for the purpose.—But,—should it be the good fortune of my proposed work, in the general complexion of it, to prove acceptable to you,—a case that may also happen is—that, on the occasion of this or that correction, for this or that reason, it may be your inclination to *remit* the subject to me; to the end that, in respect of the necessary details, I may propose such particular words, or even such particular expedients, as may seem to me to be best adapted, to the purpose of giving the most thorough effect, say to the *will*, say to the *principle*, be it what it may, which, in general terms has been expressed by you. Should the general method, and mode of expression, for example, as employed in the work, stand approved by you,—such as above, in regard to matters of detail, may, perhaps, be the course approved of by you: viz. under the apprehension, lest, if made by any other hands than those of the original draughtsman, the alteration, made in this or that part, should prove in some way or other repugnant to, inconsistent with, or detrimental to, the provision made and approved of in this or that other part. I say, if made by any *other* hand: for to myself, working according to my own method, I can not bring myself to regard it as in any degree probable, that, in the penning of any one part, the purport of any other that has any bearing upon it, should escape me: a sort and degree of command, which, at least, unless it be after a very long course of practice, it can scarcely be expected that any one man should possess, over a work so voluminous, composed by a different hand.

Well then—on the occasion of such supposed error in such my Code, and thereupon for the correction of it,—or say, in the first instance, and without reference to any such Code,—a certain effect—no matter what, or in which of two characters, viz. that of an *end*, or that of a *means*, presents itself to you as fit to be produced. Referring to me the choice, either of the mode of expression alone, or—matter and expression together, of the expedients—the provisions of detail—by which the effect shall be produced—you require me to perform my part towards the production of it. Of this effect, in whichever of the above two characters considered, the production (suppose) is directly repugnant and irreconcileable to that, which, in my own view of the matter, is *fit* and *right.* Such being the effect, shall I, in my supposed position, refuse or decline to employ my pen towards the production of it? Not I indeed. *On one condition*—a condition which you, Sir, (I speak here in the plural as well as the singular number) will, I am sure, not refuse your subscription to—in my own view of it be the effect ever so unfit to be produced, I will not on that account, so much as decline doing that which belongs to my supposed employment, towards the production of it.

This *condition* is neither more nor less, than the being suffered to possess and use, in this supposed *second* stage, the same liberty, which, without absolutely stipulating for it, I made my humble request for, in the above supposed *first* stage: the liberty of making known my opinion, whatsoever it may be, with the reasons on which it grounds itself. In this liberty will be included—if it be in the character of an *end* that the production of the effect in question appears to me unfit,—the bringing to view the considerations, by which, in the character of *reasons*, that opinion has been produced: if it be in the character of a *means*,—the like liberty, with the addition of that of proposing any *other means*, by which, in my view of the matter, the same end may be produced on more advantageous terms.

In a word—on this condition, by which is saved from violation that *sincerity*,—the violation of which, could not, in this my supposed situation at any rate, on any imaginable occasion, be of any the smallest use,—there is not that imaginable effect, which in that my supposed position, I shall not at all times be ready, in the way in question, to employ my labours towards the production of. Try me—examine me—for the purpose of the experiment, set imagination to work, to paint the effect in any the most terrific colours—my answer is still the same.[a]

[a] To avoid starting, at this premature period, any subject, capable of being found pregnant with doubts and differences,—for the experiment, let us take such cases, as being among the strongest that can be imagined, are thereby among those which are surest not to happen. Descending then from these elevations, we shall, by force of the argument *à*

Taking this course, in this way, (it seems to me) and in no other, can a man, in my supposed position, steer clear of two opposite errors:—*over-scrupulosity*, and *insincerity*.

Take the case of the over-scrupulous man. In his judgment the measure given to him to shape is, to a certain *degree*, an unfit one. —What follows?—He turns his back upon it, declaring that he will have nothing to do with it. Of ill humour thus expressed, a merit is commonly, at the same time, made. Such is his purity, nothing will he have to do with evil in any shape.—Nothing to do with *evil?*—then nothing will he have to do with *government*. For what is government but a *choice of evils?* Government operates not but by coercion: coercion can not be produced but by punishment. Coercion —punishment—are they not evils? if they are not, then what else is? Employed to produce a more than equivalent good, or to exclude a greater evil, does *an evil* change its nature? No more than a sum of money does, by being carried to the one or to the other side of an account.

Most compleatly incompatible would any such scrupulosity be, with the performance of the sort of service, for which I am thus offering myself. For, if, after having been in the first instance presented by me, my proposed Code were to be returned to me,—for me, in pursuance of certain instructions, to propose amendments to it,——how could it happen, but that, among the provisions thus required at my hands, there should be a considerable number that would in my sight be unfit ones?—comparatively at least, if not absolutely *evil* ones?

The other error is *that* of *insincerity*. In any other position than my supposed one, this, of the two errors, is *that*, of which it is scarce necessary to say, that it is the one most frequently exemplified, and every where most likely so to be. Not only by their votes, but by their discourses, do men give their support in public to that one of

fortiori, be able with the greater ease, to clear the ground, of all such difficulties, as might otherwise have presented themselves.

We call upon you (say you) to draw up for us a law, for attaching to this or that species of offence, the punishment of the *wheel*, as employed till t'other day in France—to this or that other, that of *dismemberment* by four horses, as also then and there employed:—is there that imaginable case, in which you would lend your hand to any such atrocity?—Oh yes, (say I) *that* there is, and with gladness: yes, and not only so, but even advocate it, and give my vote for it, if I had one:—if, for example, by so doing, I could prevent the attaching, to those same offences, the punishment of *impalement*, still employed in the Turkish Empire. In the case of the *wheel*, the torment always might be, and commonly was —in the case of the *dismemberment*, it always was—at an end in a very few minutes: in the other, it frequently lasts for days.—Yet, in my own mind, I am against the employing death as a punishment in any case.

two opposite measures, which in their own eyes,—as privately confessed, or otherwise demonstrated,—is least beneficial, or most pernicious. This is what, in *every* country, the man of *law*, who has a piece of gold for his fee—confessing it, for how can he deny it?—does for the *half* of his public life. That is what, in *this* country, the man of *politics*—more particularly the legislator, who, lest sincerity or probity in any shape should be possible, has an *office* for his fee—does for the *whole* of his public life. Whether in this *our* legislature, such a course is necessary,—consistent with utility—consistent with probity,—I stay not—I need not stay—to enquire. Sure I am—and to the present purpose this is quite sufficient—sure I am, that,—in a situation such as that here in question, in the situation in which the acceptance of this my offer would place me,—no such vice would either be necessary, or of any use. In this supposed situation—such is the felicity of it—without any the least particle of insincerity, it would, on every occasion, be in a man's power to render every particle of service, which it would be in man's power to render, with the most consummate contempt for the law of sincerity. Whatsoever is required of him, *that* he does: laying before the eyes of his employers for their choice, as well that which in his own eyes is *unfit*, as that which in his own eyes is *fitting*, to be done.—This being the case, in what way would his employers be the better served,—any more than his own mind and conduct be the more pure,—if—to save himself from being seen to be working in contrariety to his own opinion,—he were to misrepresent his own opinion—to give an untrue account of it—stating it as being favourable to that to which it is really adverse,—adverse to that to which it is really favourable. Here would be a *cloak*—a most costly one—and where would be the *use* of it?—Yet, in the ordinary situation of a member having speech and vote in a legislative assembly,—as often as it happened to him to propose for adoption a measure, or any the least particle of a measure, which at the same time were in his eyes an unfit one, this would be his only alternative; viz. either to put on and wear a cloak of this kind, or take that course, for the liberty of taking which, I am here stipulating:—viz. the preparing for expected adoption a measure, which, by his own confession, is, in his own eyes, an unfit one.

Sir, you now see—and I hope in a pretty strong light, one of the effects—a happy one, I think, you will acknowledge it to be—of the position in which, with reference to you, I should stand. Obsequiousness,—of the sort and in the degree here in question—to carry it to the length above described, would, in this my supposed position, cost a man much less, working for you at your distance, and such as you are, than it would to carry it to any thing like an equal length, working for government here. Working for you, he would be working for a master, who has not so much as a penny—no, not so much as a ribbon to give. Doing any such work here, he could not work but under a master, who has pence to give in abundance:—pence, which men in abundance are at all times so ready to earn—to earn at any price. At the same time,—even in favour of the particular—the personal interest—of this master,—even an honest man's judgment could not but lead him to do many things; the necessity of such his situation many more. So many of these things as he should thus have been doing, so many are the occasions, on which, lips there would be—lips not a few—to open and cry aloud—*All this is for the pence!*—But between you and me, Sir, not a penny can be so much as supposed to pass. For the like reason, even among yourselves, working under you, one of *yourselves* could not be so free,—so free, I mean from all suspicion, from all danger of disrespect on the score of obsequiousness,—as I should be. Why? Because, for one of yourselves, (not to speak of *power*, still less of *ribbons*) thriftily and wisely as your pence are distributed—you, even you, have always *pence*.

Sir, it is to a feast that I am thus bidding you. Join hands with me, you and I will govern the world. Sir, I will shew you how we will govern it. Independently of the *reasons* on which it is grounded, and by the contemplation of which it has been produced,—my own opinion not being, even in its own estimation, worth any thing, never do I declare it, (you understand the sort of occasion, of which I am speaking) without declaring at the same time these *reasons*. If then you have a Code from me, the Code you thus have, will be one that is a Code accompanied with *reasons*. Of this Code, some part, I may hope—hope without much overweeningness—some part, however small—will be sanctioned by your concurrence. Here then will be, in authority as well as in existence, a Code supported throughout by *reasons*. Hereupon, seeing that neither to establish, any more than to pen, a Code, supported throughout by reason, is a thing impossible, government will, in this or that other state, become ashamed of giving out codes, altogether destitute of this support. But it is by the nature of things, that *reasons*, in so far as they are good ones, are made: made *they* can not be, as laws may be and are, by any man that has *power*—by any such man at pleasure. Giving *reasons* every where, rulers will not, every where, without giving such as they would be ashamed to give, be able to give *reasons*, nor therefore to give *laws*, altogether different from *ours*: and thus, you see, our empire spreads itself. To be sure, even for the earliest of these conquests, there is one of us that must wait till he is dead. But this is no more than what he has always been prepared for: this is that, of which no man could ever be more fully aware than he is. As for you, Sir, over some of *your neighbours*, at least, *your* reign—I see not what should hinder it—may commence in your life-time. Over Morocco, or China, or even over Russia (not to speak of the empire, with the long-winded and round-about name, called by the Greeks in one word *Holophthoria*)[12] I dare not promise you, that you will thus speedily cast forth your shoe: but, for any delay, which human perversity may oppose to you in these distant regions, I flatter myself you will have made up your mind. In the mean time, the men of superior wit and wisdom all over the world,—in whose nomenclature *utility* and *mischievousness* are synonymous terms, and to whom the idea of any increase to human comfort, would, but for the matter it affords for derision, be an afflicting one,—will make their sport of us: and even this effect so far as it goes, even this effect, taken by itself, will, in my estimation at least, be a good one.

As on the one hand, if the observations above submitted be just, in instructions of the *obligatory* kind you can not, in the first instance, be too sparing,—so, on the other hand, in instructions of the *informative* kind, you can not be too liberal. For keeping my *will* in the right path, nothing can be wanting to me: for to *you*, Sir, (I speak in the plural number) a *will* such as mine is nothing. For proving and keeping my *understanding* in the right path, I have no less *wish* than *need* for every thing that you can give me. Information I mean, as correct and compleat as can be given, on the subject of all those circumstances, by which your country is distinguished from that in which I write, and thence the mind of the people of your country stands distinguished from that which is the most familiar to me: and, as to documents, besides those, if any, which, though in existence, never having been as yet made public, are consequently not only out of my power, but even out of my knowledge,—those which, though published in America, not being as yet published in this country, would, all of them, be, for some time, out of my power to obtain, and, with few exceptions, are as yet out of my knowledge.[b]

On this subject, besides the above *general* requests, I have two or three *particular* ones to trouble you with. *One* is—that whatsoever

[b] Forms of conveyance—such as are most in use,—and forms of judicial procedure in every sort of judicatory,—would be particularly useful, not to say necessary, to me; of these, a considerable part at least, must (I should suppose) be in a print.

[12] i.e. ὁλοφθορία, a word apparently coined by Bentham to mean 'utter destruction'.

parts of the mass of information are purchaseable, may be set down to my account, whereupon as soon as received, the whole amount shall be promptly and thankfully repaid; and that, in case of acceptance, the transmission of the letter informing me of it, may not be made to wait a *moment*,—or, to speak more pertinently, a *ship*,—for the collecting of any part of this documentary mass.

The case is—that, at my age, and with my *constitution*, there is no time to lose. Memory, and capacity for *dispatch*, have already, I perceive, undergone considerable enfeeblement: and the state of my *eyes* is already such as forbids the using them for any purpose of entertainment:—for any sort or quantity of *reading*, beyond what is necessary for the purpose of what *I write*. If whatever aptitude for the task in other respects I may be thought to possess, were already, or threatened to be, in any similar degree diminished,—no such offer as the present would have escaped from me. But, by every day, during which, without sickness, life may be continued to me,—as far as I or my friends can judge, that aptitude, instead of being diminished, not only has been, but promises to be increased. Why?—because it depends upon those logical arrangements, which, being already consigned to paper, enable me, as if by an algebraic process, to discover on each occasion, so far as the *facts*, that bear upon the case, are known, whatsoever requires to be discovered: and, in the application of which, the more frequently and thoroughly the mind is exercised, the more perfect it is made.

For these same reasons, *another* request that I have to make is—that if in your individual judgment, Sir, the offer should seem to possess a chance more or less considerable, of obtaining acceptance at the hands of the legislature, information to that effect may be transmitted to me by the earliest opportunity, no opportunity being suffered to be lost, by waiting for the determination of the legislature.

After a declaration, the frankness of which will, I hope, stand excused by the necessity,—postponement and rejection will be the same thing.—If, after having commenced, I live not to compleat the service, the very last of my thoughts will be at any rate devoted to it.

From the pen of a man already far advanced in his 67th year, marks of eagerness and impatience, such as these,—impatience to be set down to a task of assiduous, and, in the ordinary sense of the word *pay*, *unpaid* labour, to the end of his small remnant of life, may perhaps provoke a smile. But I know not to what worthier object the labour of any Being in human shape could be directed: and,—being, with or without sufficient grounds, impressed with the hope of my having, by the already bestowed labour of near half a century, rendered myself better qualified than a man unexercised, or even a man much less exercised, in the same time, is likely to be, for rendering to a political state, and thence to mankind at large, service, intellectual and moral, in this its most important of all simply human shapes,—it would be but an ill conclusion of such a course of labour, to leave untried or undone any thing that promised to contribute, in any degree, to the accomplishment of the object of it.

Penetrated with that respect, which your eminent situation, and the reports that have reached me of your conduct in that situation, could not fail to inspire, I have the honour to subscribe myself, Sir,

Your faithful,
though as yet unbidden Servant,
Jeremy Bentham.

His Excellency, Simon Snyder,
Governor of the State of Pennsylvania.

2282

From David Ricardo

15 July 1814

Mr. D Ricardo is very much obliged, both to Mr. Bentham and Mr. Mill, for the perusal of the MS, on the subject of the proposed school.[2] He will be happy to give his assistance, as far as a subscription in money will promote the object desired.

Upper Brook Street
15 July 1814

2282. [1] UC clxv. 5. Autograph. Docketed: '1814 July 15 / Chrestomathia / D. Ricardo / to / J.B. and Mill / Promises Subscription / to Chrestomathic.' Printed in *The Works and Correspondence of David Ricardo*, ed. P. Sraffa, 11 vols., Cambridge, 1951–73, vi. 112.

[2] By this time Bentham had produced a MS version of part of what was to be published in revised form in 1817 as *Chrestomathia*. This set out the curriculum and teaching methods to be employed in a secondary day school for children of the 'middling and higher ranks' of London society. The idea of the school seems to have originated with Edward Wakefield and Francis Place, and to have been taken up by Bentham early in 1814. On 24 February of that year, Mackintosh, Brougham, Mill, Allen, Fox, and Wakefield were named as trustees of the proposed school and plans were made to raise £3,000 by means of three-hundred £10 shares. See the editorial introduction to *Chrestomathia* (*CW*), ed. M. J. Smith and W. H. Burston, Oxford, 1983, pp. xi–xv.

2283
To Sir Samuel Bentham

19 July 1814 (Aet 66)

Ford Abbey Devonshire
$3\frac{1}{2}$ miles from *Chard*, Somersetsh.
Tuesday 19 July 1814

To Sir S. Bentham

If the recent Codicil should not be a serious one,[2] you will be as rich as a Jew, rolling in paper guineas. A few of them, for the purchase of amusement could not be better employed than in coming down to this odd and venerable place: a various mixture of antiquity of various ages with modern elegance By *you* I mean of course *the Admiral* and you: for without him, you, in the singular would find the doors shut against you. We would sit him down, Mill and I, to the History of his campaign, and make him work at it.[3] You would not be in my way in the least. Between the public breakfasting and mine, conjunct walking for as long as you liked: then I breakfast alone, working from thence till dinner time: after dinner Mill and I always walk in a duet, to digest what we have written: tea, conjunct or separate, as it may happen: at 11 I must go to bed: before 11, i.e. from 10 to 11 I generally steal an hour for working: those who choose to sit up all night are free to do so.

Two such places in England: not one in the whole Russian Empire. Salloon, 60 feet long or thereabouts with copies of five of Raphael's Cartoons in Tapestry:[4] a printed book about them, but though I have seen the Gobelin Tapestry,[5] I never saw any in which to my unlearned eye the figures seemed more like human. Glazed Cloister, they say 400 feet. Hall 50 or 60, and of a loftiness more than in proportion. Gravel walk running parallel to the front of the

2283. [1] BL IX. 183–4. Autograph. Addressed: 'To / Admiral Tchitchagoff / 5 Quebec Street / Oxford Street / London / or Sir S. Bentham.' Postmark: 'A / 21 JY 21 / 1814;. Stamped: 'CHARD'.

[2] The codicil of the will of John Mulford, who had recently died in his ninety-fourth year. The *Gentleman's Magazine*, lxxxiv. 302 reports that he was thought to have left about £20,000.

[3] See letter 2273.

[4] The Mortlake tapestries at Ford Abbey depicting the life of St Peter and St Paul after the cartoons by Raffaelo Sanzio (1483–1520), the celebrated Italian painter. The tapestries are said to have been given to Francis Gwyn (1648?–1734) by Queen Anne. See Royal Commission on Historical Monuments, *An Inventory of the Historical Monuments in Dorset*, 5 vols., London, 1952–75, i. 244.

[5] A tapestry made at the factory in Paris named after Jean Gobelin (d. 1476). The works were purchased by Louis XIV and run by the state from the seventeenth century.

House, half the length of the Mall at least—say $\frac{1}{4}$ of a mile: breadth 28 or 30 feet: all the way, either the front of the house or water, stationary or running: some of it making a noise in little waterfalls running over rocky stones or artificial steps bowling green with slope over slope rising above it. Statues and pictures—every thing of this kind indifferent or execrable: of the furniture the antique part mostly in tatters, but not the less curious: in several of the rooms, old tapestry. Large trees a moderate sprinkling. In a Park of no more than 50 Acres, 130 head of deer, but the grass still luxuriant. There will, I suppose, be a buck to kill when you come: but at any rate you will not starve. If your French peregrination is put off for a week, what matters it? Probably enough, it may be the last time we ever spend together: and it could not be in a better place.[6]

If economy be the order of the day, there are two Coaches which at different days of the week set out from Piccadilly for Exeter etc, and pass through Chard: fare to Exeter, 3 Guineas an inside passenger: one of them carries 4 inside, the other 6: in each of them there is one night, in neither more than one night, passed in travelling, without stopping at an Inn to sleep.

Some things being at present at an uncertainty, I fear I must tax you to bring with you the bedlinnen you would sleep upon if you were in London: item a dozen of napkins if you have any. Some little shifts ⟨. . .⟩ may possibly have to make: but none that your Russians are likely to be shocked at.

I suppose the Admiral would like to bring a Servant: every thing else for him there will be plenty: but for him too I fear, sheets would be to be imported, as above.

From Chard $3\frac{1}{2}$ miles your own legs could bring you: I mean your *persons*: a conveyance might unquestionably be found hereabouts for your *things*. Mr. Elswood,[7] *Attorney* at Law at Chard, but a person of no small magnificence, is the *Fac-totum* of my Landlord, Mr. Gwyne:[8] and prodigously civil to me. On your arrival at Chard, call on him for directions: he will treat you, I am certain, with condign respect, and do every thing desirable for your accommodation. Fail not to answer by the very earliest opportunity: and if you desire, tell me whatever you know about your motions

Furniture and tapestry, just discovered more features of whimsical and antique magnificence: have ready your money to pay me for shewing it.

[6] The end of hostilities in Europe meant that Sir Samuel was free to go to France with his family. They remained there until 1827.

[7] Azariah Elswood.

[8] John Fraunceis Gwyn (1761–1846), owner of Ford Abbey since the death of his father in 1789.

If you come post, in which case you will come I suppose in the Admirals Chariot, you might take Baghurst and Ewhurst on your way, coming to Reading (38 miles on the Bath Road) and from thence by a cross road, to Basingstoke 45 miles on the way on this road: it will be out of your way but 7 miles at most. If I live and flourish, I propose to take that route next year. Salisbury, Shaftesbury and Yeovil—all beautifully situated towns in your way.

Dead or alive, you *must* come you villain, if you don't come, I'll cut you off with a shilling,—and *that* shall be a bad one.

Horner will be here in his way to the Assizes at Exeter,[9] on Saturday or Sunday sennight—sleeping a night, or at most two nights.

2284

To Sir Samuel Bentham

4 August 1814 (Aet 66)

Ford Abbey near Chard
Thursday 4 Aug 1814

To Sir S.B.

The Buck is condemned to be shot on Thursday next.[2] You rascal, know that there are lock-up places in this mansion for younger Brothers as well as for Russian Admirals. You can not stay till the flesh is eatable? Yes: *that* you shall, till it is not only eatable but eaten. The Gamekeeper says, that, this weather, it is matter of uncertainty whether it will keep for more than two or three days. Half, including one haunch and half which is to be reserved for this place: the other goes somewhere else to fetch money. You do not tell me whither you return from hence: whether to Berry Lodge, or to London. I suppose to London: for I do not suppose you can be assured of any means of embarkation at Portsmouth.

You must not leave England till the money transactions between us are settled. I have not learnt either from H.K. or from you how these matters stand. Authority to enable your Bankers to receive from Mulford's Exors your legacy: thereupon out of that to pay your debt to me: it must be such an authority as they will be satisfied

[9] Francis Horner was a barrister and practised on the western circuit.

2284. [1] BL IX. 185–6. Autograph. Addressed: 'To / Admiral Tchitchagoff / 5 Quebec Street / Oxford Street. / London / If gone from thence, / to be forwarded to / Sir S. Bentham's / Berry Lodge near / Gosport. immediately.' Postmark: 'A/6 AU 6/1814'. Stamped: 'CHARD'.

[2] See letter 2283.

with. I discussed this matter with H.K. Authority (such as they will be satisfied with) to direct and empower them to transfer into *your* name the whole of the £3.170 Navy 5 per Cent from Mulford's, instead of half only to you, and the other half to me.

I ought to have sent this from hence yesterday. It will not now (I find) be distributed so as to reach Quebec Street before Saty morning, and by that time, should the intentions declared in your letter be fulfilled, you may have set out from thence for Berry Lodge. I must provide for that contingency by the direction.

If you arrive at Berry Lodge on Saturday evening, it seems to me that Sunday and Monday will be long enough for you to stay there, and that on Tuesday you may set out from there for this place and reach it the same day. Mr. Mill says you must at any rate come through Dorchester: but when there you may either come through Axminster or through Chard. From Axminster it is barely 8 miles. Horner t'other day paid for that number: from Chard it is barely 4 miles. Horners notion was that Chard would have been the shorter way. You had better take counsel at Dorchester. If you come through Chard you may as well call at Mr. *Elswood's* there, to ask whether he has any thing to say of this place, or to say or send to it. Though an Attorney (my Landlord Gwyne's Agent) he seems in his dealings a liberal man: he is very respectful and very serviable: Mill who has seen his house and garden says they are very comfortable and even splendid. In ideas however he seems not to abound. A Sister in law of his[3] will be glad some how or other to come with him to play upon a good organ which is here.

Napkins and Sheets: yes: and pillow cases to the sheets. You know or do not know that Henry Coulson leaves me in October to go to enter himself at Queen's College Cambridge[4] That will make a gap which must be filled up. I must have a boy capable of reading to me at all times: and in particular at rising and going to bed. He must at least ought to be capable of reading Latin: though it is not absolutely necessary that his acquaintance with it should be very intimate: as it will be only for quotations, of course if French so much the better. I would not have him under 12 nor more than 15. The poorer his friends *are* at present, the better, as also the richer they *have been*. Know you of any means of my getting one? Your friend the Irish Surgeon[5] is there any chance of his knowing of any such an one?

P.S. If the course of the post permitts, fail not to give us the most precise pre-intelligence of the time of your intended arrival here.

[3] Not identified.

[4] See above letter 2278 and n. 3.

[5] Perhaps John White (see letter 2222 n. 3).

2285

To Sir Samuel Bentham

10 August 1814 (Aet 66)

Ford Abbey, near Chard Somersetshire 10 August 1814.

Sadly disappointed and sore vexed was I at the receipt of your's of Saturday the 6th[2] received here yesterday the 9th: not till the 9th because a Sunday intervened. Before you can receive this—indeed several days before, you will have left London: I direct therefore to Berry Lodge. I have written a letter—(I don't know whether I shall send it or no) to the Admiral,[3] abusing him for not coming with you, and trying to force him for very shame to come though it be without you. As for you, if you will come, and stay though it be but for two whole days exclusive of the day of advent and the day of departure, bringing with you your two boys,[4] I will pay all charges: and so the pecuniary part of the objection is compleatly done away. I reckon it at about £20, or a little more: but that I shall not grudge: the reprobates will be in the 7th. heaven.

Nevertheless, as it is not you who have taken 'le mord aux dents,' that you may not for the Admiral's sin lose the business of *Lowe's* instruction, on the other half is a transcript of his letter.[5] He was originally a mercantile man: but having commenced without capital, and saved up a small one, he has for some few years been retired from business, and in the character of *man of letters*, though but a feeble writer, with the assistance of two journeymen-writers whom he keeps, and with whom he spent some months this year at Oxford, rummaging libraries, he makes in that way a regular addition to the one income which without it would be barely sufficient for the maintenance of himself with a wife and three daughters. Mill continually speaks of him as being brimfull of honesty, as well as of mercantile intelligence. Being in the neighbourhood, he was much in the society and even intimacy of Lucien Bonaparte[6] while in

2285. [1] BL IX. 187. Autograph. Docketed: '1814 Augt. 10 / J.B. / to / S.B.' Addressed: 'To / Sir Samuel Bentham K.S.G. / Berry Lodge / near / Gosport / Hants.' Franked: 'Single Sheet'.

[2] Missing.

[3] Sent but missing: Chichagov mentioned the receipt of a letter of 9 August from Bentham in letter 2287.

[4] Samuel junior and George (1800–84).

[5] Letter 2277.

[6] Lucien Bonaparte (1775–1840), Napoleon's second surviving brother. He was exiled from France after breaking with Napoleon and captured by the British while travelling

Shropshire. He was a little mortified, I believe. and Mill for him and with him; at his never when in London being invited to Q.S.P. But the case was that though when at Barrow Green he knowingly took H.K.'s bed, sending him down to a Couch, I could hardly get him out of the House, he staying beyond the term at first announced. I not asking him to stay, but rather going giving him hints to the contrary: and moreover there was an appearance of self-sufficiency and pomposity that seemed above his merits. But Mill states him as being eminently serviable: and I see no reason for doubting it. Should you ever be disposed to make the experiment, this letter of his will serve you for an introduction and a certificate.

To him I have determined to address myself (of course through Mill) for a French Boy: M. says the young men whom he chose as abovementioned turn out very well, and are attached to him to a surprizing degree. I would wish you, however, whenever you are in France, to be on the same look-out. *His* instructions are already drawn up by you: and one of them is that any boy whom he may send is to be warned beforehand he and his friend that the pleasure of the journey and a short visit to England at free cost is all that he is to look upon as sure of. I would not have your's quite so little as 12, nor quite so much as 15 at most not many months before: below the earliest age he would know nothing and be a plague: above the latest his character might be mannish, with mannish and incorrigible French vices. As for the rest, without further instructions you could judge what would suit me. By speaking and writing French he would have that advantage over every English boy. A fine opportunity for a French boy with connections and prospects, to learn legislation. An essential part of his duty will be to read to me as Henry does while undressing for bed and dressing of a morning. Meliorated as my eyes are, I venture not as yet to read any thing for amusement. I rejoice to hear your eyes have been cut and slashed: they would not have been so, without a fair prospect of relief

Though this place is a very delightful one, I look forward to one that in many respects is likely to be still more delightful——a place called Buckland Monachorum, (one of the Houses of the late Lord Heathfield)[7] not far from Tavistock. *Wakefield*, if it be let, will have the letting of it. If so, in October when he will be this way, M. and I

from Italy to the United States. He remained under surveillance in England until the peace of 1814, when he returned to Rome.

[7] Francis Augustus Eliott, 2nd Baron Heathfield, died in 1813, whereupon the peerage became extinct. The 1st Baron, George Augustus Eliott (1717–90), governor of Gibraltar during the great siege of 1779–83, had obtained Buckland Abbey as a result of his marriage to Anne Pollexfen, daughter and heiress of Sir Francis Henry Drake, Bt.

shall go and look at it. It is likely to be had cheaper than this. This is in some particulars out of repair, and the Gardening part has its imperfections. I have a power of quitting it next Midsummer. This power if I do not quit it then I shall make use of to make the owner let it me as from year to year only. I look forward to a time when being grown indolent, and wanting the bustle of London to help amuse me I should not care to go more than half a day's journey's distance from it.

As for Martins,[8] I shall not have the smallest need to apply to them before Mulford money has been received on your account

2286

To Sir Samuel Bentham

11 August 1814 (Aet 66)

Ford Abbey, Chard Somersetshire
Wedny. 11 Aug. 1814

I sent from hence for you yesterday a letter including a letter of information from Caën in Normandy[2]—and a fresh invitation hither which I fear can not be accepted.

I received yesterday a letter from H.K.[3] saying amongst other things that he imagined the Admiral if properly pressed would not be finally inexorable: and that he might be prevailed on to accompany H.K. hither. The pressing as I told you or at any rate a pressing letter[4]—went from me yesterday along with mine to you.

It is not about the above that I write now: it is to entreat you, if it be necessary not to omitt to let me have the Geometry papers:[5] that being among the subjects which I have need to touch upon not only for Chrestomathia, but now for Logic,[6] which is making Giant's

[8] Bentham's bankers.

2286. [1] Keynes MS 77, King's College Library, Cambridge. Autograph. Docketed: '1814 Augt 11th / JB / to / SB' Addressed: 'To / Sir Samuel Bentham KSG. / Berry Lodge / Gosport / Hants.'

[2] Letter 2285, enclosing the copy of Lowe's letter (letter 2277).

[3] Missing.

[4] The letter to Chichagov of 9 August, referred to in letters 2285 and 2287.

[5] Perhaps the Bentham brothers' early writings on mathematics, dating from the 1770s and 1790s, now in UC cxxxiv and cxxxv.

[6] Bentham was probably thinking of papers now in UC ci and cii that were to form part of what was to be posthumously published as 'Essay on Logic' (Bowring, viii. 213–93). In this work Ch.VIII, s.5 is entitled 'Misapplication of the terms Synthesis and Analysis to Geometry and Algebra'.

strides or rather Dragon's, brushing in and gathering up with its tail as it goes on every part of the field of thought and action.

Journal—Who is it, or who are they that will keep one? Virtue, supreme virtue will consist in keeping one, and sending it off to me sheet by sheet[7]—postage whatever it may come to will not be grudged. Bank post paper,[8] I hope and suppose is provided. Now you are so rich, you will call I presume on Cox,[9] and keep one.

Fail not to leave at your departure, a letter apprising me of it. likewise one, upon your first setting foot on French ground

Fourteen Visitors to see the place in one company this day 5 or 7 in another: scarce a day passes without some company at least: generally two; yesterday there were three. If you have a mind to get rich, come here, put on a livery, and attend them.

You will bless me on the wrong side of your mouth should you have already taken measures about the Mathematical papers, whereby this letter will have been rendered superfluous.

2287

FROM PAVEL CHICHAGOV

15 August 1814

London 15 August 1814

Having been out of town for 8 days, allways within the 30 miles prescribed by the alien act,[2] I returned home only to day and found to my great satisfaction your *angry* letter of the 9th. upon my table.[3] I was certainly not less disapointed than you, when I was apprized of the bounderies that were put to my excursions, the first effect of which was to deprive me of the pleasure of going to you, a pleasure that I so much enjoyed before hand. But what could I do? Transgress the laws, or expose myself to be sent back or kept under a custody as it is already happened to one of my countrymen some

[7] Presumably a journal of Sir Samuel's experiences once he arrived in France.

[8] A special paper for foreign correspondence.

[9] Probably Thomas Cox of Elizabeth Cox and Son, booksellers and stationers of 26 and 27 St Thomas's Street, Southwark, and later of 39 Borough High Street.

2287. [1] BL IX. 189–90. Autograph. Docketed: '1814 Aug 15 / Tchitchagoff London / 25 Cumberland Street / to J.B. Ford Abbey / Visiturit.' Addressed: 'Jeremy Bentham Esqr / Ford Abbey near Chard'. Postmark: 'AU / B15 / 1814'.

[2] 43 Geo. III, c. 155, the act that came into force after the renewal of war with France in 1803. The first Alien Act had been passed in 1793, amended in 1798, and replaced at the Peace of Amiens in 1802.

[3] See above, letters 2285 and n. 3, 2286 and n. 4.

time ago.[4] I am to much acquainted with vexatious systems as to expose myself to some new one. when I left a prison of 30,000 miles around it was certainly not with the idea of confining myself to one of 30 miles. And therefore as soon as the discovery was made nothing remained to do but to guard me against its inconveniences and leave the country as soon as possible. whoever matters are settled otherways now. To my great joy the act is repealed, at least sufficiently so to give to foreigners as much liberty as they can wish for.[5] Now when I come to you in this lawful manner, I will enjoy your offers in all purity. Your meadows will look beautiful, your walks charming, your air fragrant, your fruits sweet. But how and when shall I come. I am engaged till the end of this month for different country visits, after which if I am not obliged to go to some bathing place I would like very much to repair my losses. The best will be to let you know when I am free and if it suits you I am yours—

No body values more the advantage of possessing your friendship or being in your society than I do. I am aware also of the good it would do to the Beresina affair, but this would not be my chief object for I know to well how military reputation, and fame are acquired now to run after it. If one had to choose out of a foolish glory and a foolish-calumny I dont know which would be preferable perhaps the last. I must not omitt to tel you that the general which wrote the *memoir* of the passage of the Beresina[6] is arrived to paris and tells me that he wishes to come to London. He would be of great use to me for putting it alltogether and facilitate by that means the translation of it in to the english.

I am very sorry to have missed making acquaintance with the gentleman you have had with you.[7] It would be interesting to talk to him about all sorts of things from the mediteranean to the north seas. I perfectly understand and agree with you that o⟨ne⟩ may have much honour without honours, I know even that which honour is allways and every where precious and honourable, honours on the contrary are but to often degrading and dishonourable. What do you think of this?

[4] Not identified.

[5] The 1803 Aliens Act was repealed on 29 July 1814 by 54 Geo. III, c.155, the provisions of which continued certain restrictive and coercive powers, including that of deportation.

[6] Frédéric-François Guillaume de Vaudoncourt.

[7] Probably Joseph Hume (1777–1855), former MP for Weymouth, at this time out of parliament. Hume had served in the land and sea services of the East India Company, and on his return to Britain he toured the country and travelled extensively in the Mediterranean and Egypt. He is mentioned by Chichagov in letter 2289.

I long to make acquaintance with your ghosts, for I believe that by the means of the profane ones, we can get to the holy.

Your brother must have told you that we parted one day sooner than it might be as something has detained him wheil my arrangements were made according to his first intention. I hope to see him soon here or meet him at geneva.

I must also tell you that I have changed house and am at present in No 25 Cumberland Street.

My best Compts to Mr Mill I conceive very well how good it would be for me to be with you and I will endeavour to get at you. only don't be angry if I come and be very much so if I dont, that will please me extremely—

2288

From George Bentham

27 August 1814

Le Havre de Grace
1814 Augt 27th

Dear Uncle

We are lodged at the Auberge de la Vierge *au deuxième et troisième* on the Quay The floors are stone and most of the walls wooden Our room door is about 18 inches broad Thursday was Louis's birthday[2] The whole town was illuminated (as the Mistress of the house tells us) There is to be a ball here today.

I am Dear Uncle
Your dutiful nephew
G Bentham

2288. [1] George Bentham papers, Linnean Society of London. Autograph. Docketed: '1814 Aug 28 / S.B. and Children Havre / de Grace / to / J.B. Ford Abbey'. The docket suggests that this was enclosed in a letter from Sir Samuel, now missing.

[2] A reference to the feast of St Louis, Louis IX (1214–70), king of France, which took place on 25 August.

2289

From Pavel Chichagov

30 August 1814

London 30 august 1814.
25 Cumberland Street portman square

Though I have not been able to determine the day of my setting out for Chard yet I can not have the patience to remain silent any longer in expectation of that time and must tell you something about me for my own sake. Before I begin with any thing new I will reply to some of your *Satirical* observations to me. I might have been obliged to go to a bathing place, not by a particular act of *a government which is as reasonable as any government can be, as I am as reasonable a man as any man can be,* but 1st by a most natural and even not unusual an obligation to accompany my Children which I came to see and to which it has been recommended to go to the sea side for the benefit of the air and bathing. 2ndly as my leave of absence was granted to me by our *most Constitutional government* on account of my bad health it might therefore have been prudent of me to try some remedy for the purpose of justifying my former application for leave of absence. These foreseen uncertainties have been since increased by an unforeseen one, *viz,* I have been unwell, a giddiness came on in the morning and kept me in bed all day. I immediately returned to town, for it attacked me in one of my excursions in the country, and waited for relapses which whoever did not come. I learned since that almost all the foreigners that come here have, besides the tiresome formalities of the alien act, to go through the proces of giddinesses and fainting fits by way of introduction or naturalising themselves to the climate. Having also fulfilled all what your excellent government and still more excellent climate require I think I may dispose of my future movements to my greatest satisfaction. As during the interval of my decision to conform to your alien regulations and the repeal of the alien act, which in fact is not repealed at all, I have contracted some engagements, I must fulfil them. These dont go beyond the midle of September at which time if you dont send me any thing to the contrary I mean to set out for Ford Abbey. Kow sent me the *marche route* from London and also from Portsmouth as I may perhaps call there in my way for few hours to see the isle of white.

2289. [1] BL IX. 194–5. Autograph. Docketed: '1814 Aug 30 / Tchitchagoff 25 Cumberld. / Str. Portman Squr / to / J.B. Ford Abbey / Veniet medio mense'. Addressed: 'Jeremy Bentham Esqr / Ford Abbey near Chard / Somersetshire'. Postmark: 'AU / B30 / 1814'.

I hope Mr. Hume will still be with you at that time for he may also come later than you both intended.

So you know that all this time I am much oftener with you than you imagine. your works delight me. Now I am reading the fragment on government and am sorry it is not more extensive. I was very much pleased with an expression of the Examiner who says in his weekly paper speaking of the Emperor, that it must have done him good to have seen the *greatest philosopher of England*.[2] I subscribed for that paper, for it recommended itself to me by that word more than any thing else he could have said.

The french general did not fix the time for his comming but we can very patiently wait for him. I suppose your brother left you for france and I think if our change goes falling as it does now, for it is at 11 and even below it, I shall soon be obliged to follow him and go to some less expensive Country.

I long to see you and enjoy your society undisturbed by the tumult of the town or untimely interruptions.

My best Complts to those who know any thing of me is Mr Mill's son with him. they say it is a prodigy of talent I should like to see him——

2290

From Pavel Chichagov

15 September 1814

London 15th September 1814

I am just returned to town from my excursions and hasten to inform you of my further proceedings. Will you say many thanks to Mr. Hume for the marche-route and his observations of which I mean to profit. To morrow the 16th I set out for Portsmouth and the isle of weight which will take at least two days to see, then I proceed to Salisbury and Wilton. You know perhaps that Lord Pembroke[2] is married to Countess Woronzki[3] which is a very good

[2] The *Examiner*, 12 June 1814, in an article entitled 'Emperor Alexander and the English People', stated that 'His Majesty has seen our greatest warrior,——the Duke of Wellington; perhaps he has seen our greatest philosopher, who resided, we believe, some time in Russia,——Mr. Bentham'.

2290. [1] BL IX. 196–7. Autograph. Docketed: '1814 Sept 15 / Tchitchagoff London / to / J.B. Ford Abbey / Scripture from Wilton / Sept. 20'. Addressed: 'To / Jeremy Bentham Esqr / Ford Abbey near Chard / Somersetshire'. Postmark: 'SE / 15 / 1814'.

[2] Gen. George Augustus Herbert, 11th Earl of Pembroke and 8th Earl of Montgomery (1759–1827).

[3] On 25 January 1808 Pembroke married for the second time. His bride was Catherine

friend of mine her Father being my best friend. She is to be confined to her bed in october[4] for which purpose she returns to town and wanted me very much to be there before she leaves Wilton. This makes a little uncertain the day of my leaving Wilton therefore I propose to write to you from Salisbury fixing the day and perhaps the hour when I can be with you. You see how many things in this world subject me to very involuntary delays.

Since the alien act is in some way, at least nominaly or seemingly repealed I could not help going to Countess Pembroke who can not put off her lying in and must accomplish it at a certain time. that is not the case with you your children come in to the world at all places, at all seasons and without great efforts and preparations therefore one need not be so very exact with you as with her. Besides you are much farther to the south than any body that I know and therefore I expect to find warm and fine weather with you after it has left our Hypoaborian[5] climates. At last in whatever manner it may happen I shall be extremely glad when I reach you and this you will know exactly by a note from Salisbury about the 20th. or a little after. I have been at Cambridge and made acquaintance with Doctor Parr[6] and some other methaphysicians which in the best greak and Latin don't know what they say, nor what they are about. Upon other subjects they are very good kind agreable people

To Jeremy Bentham Esqr.

2291

From James Mill

19 September 1814

My dear Sir

I think it is necessary that we should come to some little explanation—and that, according to your most excellent rule, not with a view to the past but the future, that we may agree about what is

Vorontsov (1783–1856), only daughter of Count Semën Romanovich Vorontsov (1744–1832), Russian ambassador at London 1784–1800, 1801–6. For earlier mention of Count Vorontsov see *Correspondence*, iii, iv, and v, as index.

[4] In October 1814 the Countess gave birth to a daughter at Arlington Street, London.

[5] i.e. Hyperborean.

[6] The Revd Samuel Parr (1747–1825), Latin scholar. For his earlier contact with Bentham see *Correspondence*, v and vii, as index.

2291. [1] Mill Collection, Keynes MS 172, King's College Library, Cambridge. Autograph. Docketed: '1814 Sept 19 / J. M. Ford Abbey / to / J.B.' Printed in Bain, pp. 136–40, and with omissions in Bowring, x. 481–2.

best to be hereafter done. I have made some attempts to join you for the purpose of explaining to you, but as you plainly declined, I have chosen this method, as what may be less disagreeable to you.

I see that you have extracted umbrage from some part of my behaviour; and have expressed it by deportment so strongly, that I have seriously debated with myself whether propriety permitted that I should remain any longer in your house. I considered, however, that I could not suddenly depart, without proclaiming to the world, that there was a quarrel between us; and this, I think, for the sake of both of us, and more especially of the cause which has been the great bond of connection between us, we should carefully endeavour to avoid. The number of those is not small who wait for our halting. The infirmities in the temper of philosophers have always been a handle to deny their principles; and the infirmities in ours will be represented as by no means small, if in the relation in which we stand, we do not avoid shewing to the world that we cannot agree. Where two people disagree, each tells his own story, as much to his own advantage, as much to the disadvantage of the other, at least as he conceives the circumstances to be, that is in general as much as the circumstances will permit. The rule of the world, I observe, on these occasions is, to believe much of the evil which each says of the other, and very little of the good which each says of himself. Both therefore suffer.

In reflecting upon the restraint which the duty we owe to our principles, to that system of important truths of which you have the immortal honour to be the author, but of which I am a most faithful and fervent disciple, hitherto I have fancied, the master's favourite disciple—in reflecting, I say, upon the restraint which regard for the interest of our system should lay upon both of us, I have considered that ⟨. . .⟩ was no body at all so likely to be your real successor as myself. Of talents it would be easy to find many superior. But, in the first place, I hardly know of any body who has so compleately taken up the principles, and is so thoroughly of the same way of thinking with yourself. In the next place, there are very few who have so much of the necessary previous discipline, my antecedent years having been wholly occupied in acquiring it. And in the last place, I am pretty sure that you cannot think of any other person whose whole life will be devoted to the propagation of the system. It so rarely happens, or can happen, in the present state of society, that a man qualified for its propagation, should not have some other occupation, some call or another, to prevent his employing for that purpose much of his time, that without any overweaning conceit of myself, I have often reflected upon it as a very fortunate coincidence, that any man with views and propensities of such rare occurrence as mine, should happen to come in toward the close of your career, to carry on the work without any intermission. No one is more aware than yourself of the obstacles which retard the propagation of your principles. And the occurrence of an interval without any successor whose labours might press them upon the public attention, after you are gone, and permit no period of oblivion, might add, no one can foresee how much, to the causes of retardation. It is this relation then in which we stand to the grand cause, to your own cause, which makes it one of the strongest wishes of my heart that nothing should occur which may make other people believe there is any interruption of our friendship.

For this purpose, I am of opinion, that it will be necessary not to live so much together. I cannot help perceiving, either that you are growing more and more difficult to please; or that I am losing of my power of pleasing; or perhaps there is something in being too much in one anothers company, which makes people stale to one another and is often fatal, without any other cause, to the happiness of the most indissoluble connections. I should contemplate, therefore, with great dread, the passing another summer with you. I think that we ought by no means to put our friendship to so severe a test. I am desirous of staying with you this season, as long as you yourself remain in the country, both for the sake of appearance, and because you have had not time to make any other arrangement for society; and I shall remain with so much the deeper an interest, that it is a pleasure not to be renewed; for I can most truly assure you that at no moment was you ever more an object to me of reverence, and also of affection, than at the present; and nothing on my part shall be left undone while I here remain to render my presence agreeable to you, perhaps I ought rather to say as little disagreeable as possible.

There is another circumstance which is of a nature that is always painful to me to speak of it. My experience has led me to observe that there are two things which are peculiarly fatal to friendship, and these are, great intimacy, and pecuniary obligations. It has been one of the great purposes of my life, to avoid pecuniary obligations, even in the solicitation or acceptance of ordinary advantages—hence the penury in which I live. To receive obligations of any sort from you, was not a matter of humiliation to me, but of pride. And I only dreaded it from the danger to which I saw that it exposed our friendship. The only instances of this sort which have occurred are,—first that a part of my family, while with you in the country, have lived for a small part of the year at your expence, this year the whole of them were destined to live a considerable part of it,—and secondly that at your solicitation, that I might be near to you, I came to live in a house, of which, as the expence of it was decidedly too great for my very small income, part of the expence was to be borne by you. The former of these obligations of course will now cease; and I reckon it still more necessary that the other should. And as it would be ruinous for me to bear the whole expence of the house, of course I must leave it. I shall explain to you the course which I have planned in my own mind, and hope that you will approve of it. Next summer I shall go to Scotland with my family, on a visit to my relations and friends, which for the sake of being with you, I have deferred till I have offended them all; and as my friends have long been apprised of an intention I had formed, of residing, as soon as peace should permit, for some time in France, I shall go there before the winter, which will not be a matter of surprise to any body, both as I long ago declared the intention, and because the growth of my family and the smallness of my means, render a cheap place of residence more and more desirable for me, and even indispensible. I shall, therefore, propose, if it is agreeable to you, that I should keep the house in Queen Square for the next half year after Xtmass,[2] which will both afford you time to dispose of it, and me to make my arrangements.

As I propose all this most sincerely with a view of preserving our friendship, and as the only means, in my opinion of doing so—the explanation being thus made—I think we should begin to act towards one another, without any allusion whatsoever towards the past; talk together, and walk together looking forward solely, never back; and as if this arrangement had been the effect of the most amicable consultation. We can talk about our studies, and about every thing else, as if no umbrage had ever existed; ⟨. . .⟩ thus we shall not only add to the comfort of each other during the limited time we shall be together, we shall also avoid the unpleasant observations which will be made upon us by other people. For my part I have been at pains to conceal, even from my wife, that there is any coldness between us. I am strongly in hopes, that the idea of the limitation will give an additional interest to our society, and overbalance the effects of a too long, and uninterrupted intimacy, which I believe to be the great cause—for there is such a disparity between the apparent cause, my riding out a few times in the morning with Mr. Hume, to take advantage of his horses in seeing a little of the country, instead of walking with you, and the great

[2] i.e. Christmas.

umbrage which you have extracted; that the disposition must have been prepared by other causes, and only happened first to manifest itself upon that occasion.

I remain, with an esteem which can hardly be added to, and which I am sure will never be diminished.

My dear Friend and Master
Most affectionately Yours
J Mill

Ford Abbey
19th. Sept. 1814

2292
From Lady Bentham
20 Sept–13 Oct. 1814

Tours 20th Septr 1814

One letter was sent to you on our arrival at Havre,[2] another by post from hence yesterday.[3] We continued three days at Havre, delighted with the surrounding country, and desirous of seeing something of the manners of the people, as it was not likely we should return there. Our first days expedition was (Bentham on a bidet,[4] the rest walking) to the heights above the Town. The Town itself has a spacious Quay and two or three broad streets in the heart of the Town; the houses 5, 6 and 7 stories high. We went along the middle Street, Rue de Paris—through the gate there is a large suburb of tradesmens houses and shops, having passed these on ascending the hill, the most enchanting view presented itself I ever beheld of scenery in which houses formed a principal part. Conceive the side of a rocky hill cut into terraces each forming the residence of a wealthy merchant or shopkeeper, the houses painted fresh with green venetian blinds and ornaments, each in the midst of a garden with fruit trees, flowers, shaded terraces and alcoves of forest trees, some of their natural growth, but most cut so as to afford shade to the allées and cabinets de verdure without injuring the fruit, all

2292. [1] Koe MSS. Autograph. Docketed: '1814 Oct 13 / Lady B. Saumur / to / J.B. Q.S.P. / Ford Abbey / Reced at Ford Abbey / Oct. 26.' Addressed: 'Jeremy Bentham Esqr. / Queen Square Place / Westminster / England'. Redirected: 'Ford Abbey / near Chard. Somersetshire'. Postmarks: '2 o'Clock / OC⟨. . .⟩ / 1814 A.M.' and another illegible.

[2] See letter 2288 n. 1.

[3] Missing.

[4] i.e. a small horse or pony.

kept in the highest order: the form of the hill too was the most beautiful, being hollowed out as an amphitheatre, and so steep that every house completely looked over those below it. Ascending the road the first of these houses we came to had written on the window of a gardeners cottage by the entrance gate that there were green-house plants for sale: we went in, it was a merchants house and garden the gardener allowed to sell certain plants that he reared. The garden was excessively neat, all the fruit trees bearing such a profusion of beautiful fruit as I never saw. The longest pears hanging in clusters of 6 or 8 at every bearing spur, and spurs left very close together. The whole stone wall surrounding the garden was so covered. In the parterres were apples and pears trained in pyramids, and others as dwarfs, all loaded with fruit; a dwarf apple of a foot high and 15 inches in diameter had 14 or 15 apples upon it. I saw no single flower that we have not commonly in english gardens, and the general observation I made afterwards was that the variety in english gardens is usually far greater than in these french ones: the green house plants were common geraniums and myrtles, all the sweet jasmines, fine orange trees much loaded with fruit and flowers, the prices much the same as in England, rather higher generally for large trees. The view from this garden was in another way no less fine than that of the houses and gardens on looking up to them. The Basin, the Harbour, the mouth of the Seine, the sea, rocks, wood, chalky hills, gardens Towns and villages. There are many English families who have already established themselves in this delightful suburb; and to many no better a situation need be sought; house rent is cheap, bread 3 sous a pound, meat 8, chickens 20 sous each, fish in abund[ance] and very cheap, masters cheap and good, the french language well spoken—par contre a long cold and moist winter, no good society, that is the only society is that of mercantile and seafaring people. We proceeded up the road till we arrived at the brow of a hill, some parts of it Timber trees, others copse, others heath and turf, here we sat down and feasted on the provision of cakes and fruit we had brought with us, looking down upon the Paris road, with other country houses on each side of it on the flat ground, beyond this a great extent of perfectly flat low ground in the highest state of cultivation to all appearance, beyond the mouth of the Seine and the high ground on the other side. One naturally looks for new wild plants in a new Country; here there was not one to be found; the only striking circumstance was the perfect verdure of the foliage. I should have said that the first business in the morning was the getting our plate stamped, and our medicine case (the same we had taken to Petersburgh) liberated, which by the intercession of our bankers son[5] was effected and to my great satisfaction for it contained bark in *powder* which is *prohibited*, though the french cannot pound bark fine enough, nor have they much of it that is good—there were also a few *compound* medicines which are likewise prohibited—we had also been to see the preparations for a grand ball, to be given in honor of the Fête de St Louis.[6] For this purpose the Exchange, a room of about 50 feet long or more, between 30 and 40 wide, was prepared for dancing—it was lined with a drapery of—do not disdain the material—*buntine*, green and orange in large curtain like folds, between and round the open windows on one side, round looking glasses or medallions on the other, round the room at top festoons of green with an orange border as if a fringe. The medallions were inscribed 'Vive Louis XVIII' 'C'est Louis qui nous donne le Pain' 'Faisons hommage à la beauté' and so forth. A door opens from the window side of the exchange to a garden consisting of four alleys divided by cut lime trees—this space was covered over from one row of trees to the other with ships colours, festoons of coloured lamps were suspended from tree to tree, the ground was sanded to form a promenade, and benches and tables for refreshments were placed at the end. The effect of the whole was very gay—But we were sitting on the turfy bank looking down on the Seine—we had not time to remain for ever, beautiful as it was—we had other things to see—we proceeded along the road up hill and down amongst corn fields, the oats reaping, abundant crops; the operation of reaping with a basket scythe performed in a manner far more neat and expeditious than *I* had ever seen in England, though B says he has seen the same mode—above the scythe taking the same curve with it were three wooden prongs affixed to the handle which prongs caught the corn as mowed and laid it down regularly on the next ridge. We saw a good deal of clover, some for hay other fields eaten green, in most cases by cows tethered very short, the tether moved three or four times a day. Some of the fields open, others inclosed as is common in Normandy by banks of from four to 8 feet high, upon the top of which two rows of forest trees are planted and trained up to a great height before they are cut that is from 20 feet high, to their greatest growth, the branches are left down to nearly the bottom, for a year or two's growth it would seem, cutting one year the brush wood from one row the next year from the other: this mode of enclosing seems particularly in use for surrounding and sheltering orchards,

[5] Probably Daniel Ancel, son of the M. Ancel mentioned below.

[6] See letter 2288 and n. 2.

of which there are a great number exactly like those in your neighbourhood; apples and pears for cyder and perry: other enclosures were excellent hedges of hawthorn and all the other shrubs employed in England for the same purpose; the hedges as well made and as well kept as english ones; some, indeed many clipped regularly in width and height, especially round farm house and cottage gardens. The narrow bye roads stony and bad enough like Devonshire ones, but there is always for foot passengers the accommodation of a path between the two rows of trees on the bank. The trees all the common forest trees, as oak, lime, hornbeam, elm etc. The manner of cutting up the trees seems to induce them to make very long shoots; I noticed some from lime trees that must have been 5 or 6 feet long of this years growth. The farm houses and cottages are dispersed about as in Devonshire, and much resemble the better sort of Devonshire stone buildings for the same purposes. I have been into cottages in many different parts of England, none surpass those I saw about Havre in size, cleanliness, or abundance of necessary common utensils and furniture. We were all much struck with the extraordinary cleanliness of the persons and cloathing of the lower orders of people both in the Town and in the Country. There was one dirty woman with two dirty children at a fruit stall near our lodgings at Havre, otherwise I do not recollect to have seen either woman or child with a dirty face, even the baby of the poorest looking woman we passed on the road, had its face so clean that I could willingly have kissed it. The women, especially the younger ones were remarkably pretty, and spoke with an air of modesty and mildness of voice we little expected from french women. Men and women chearfully ceased from working to answer our questions; when the object was to enquire our way, they went on with us as far as necessary to point it out; if we asked explanations of the operations going on, the form of a plough, the use of this that or the other, they took pleasure in explaining what we wished to know, and almost always in their turn enquired how we performed the same business in England: the very superior mowers of oats, seemed conscious of their savoir faire, otherwise I do not recollect any appearance of a desire to boast. I accosted one beautiful girl who was turning oats over with a stick, laying them down as regularly as they had been at first deposited by the scythe; she curtsied, answered my question of how much she earned a day, by telling me the field was their own, never omitting to introduce 'Madame' into the reply, and this with a modesty and softness that was fascinating: the instant I was satisfied she returned to her business without once looking up to examine the strangers. There were marks of heavy rain having recently fallen; we were told the season had been extraordinarily cold wet and backward. Grapes still small and perfectly hard, peaches beginning only to ripen. We wandered through green lanes and green fields till near six o'clock, then returned to our inn to dinner. During dinner M. Ancelle, Père,[7] made us a visit; he is the Banker on whom B had a letter of credit from Martin and Co. M Ancelle is one of the principal people of Havre; at present he is *Adjoint* du Maire: he told us a story of himself which might have been intended as an apology by anticipation in case we should hear it from other quarters—When Louis XVIII was to be proclaimed, the Maire being ill, it fell to Mr Ancelle to read the Proclamation; he did so, he said, surrounded by the Official people of the place, by the Military etc etc in grand parade, but when he came to the conclusion 'Vive' '*L Em*'—he said he had uttered, when some one beside him jogged his elbow, and Ancelle recovered himself time enough to say *le Roi* without his involuntary mistake being discovered by the crowd. He and all others we have asked here, express great joy at the change, but say the Military are discontented—(It has been the same up to this time through all the country we have passed, but there is at the same time an appearance of the greatest confidence on the part of the people, rich and poor, that the discontents of the military are not in the least to be feared)—Ancelle said the King had secured the Generals and other leading Men of the military; that the inferior officers and privates could do nothing therefore—After dinner, the entrance to the Ball room being opposite our window, and perceiving that there was but little crowd and that orderly, I was tempted to take out the little girls,[8] that they might see the splendid equipages of Havre—with the fine ladies they conveyed. There was an old mishapen green coach and a yellow one, two machines that I must I suppose call chariots, perhaps as many vehicles a good deal like the best of the country bakers carts that have covers of wood—the *ladies* came successively in the coaches and chariots as fast as the[y] could put down one load and as the gentlemen in the cart like conveyances; 5, 6, 7 or 8 ladies in a coach at once. A large covered way had been prepared with sail cloth under which the carriages set down the company, and where guards were stationed. The lookers on some of them were allowed to come to the edge of this covered space; by degrees I and my little companions were induced to get amongst these people, almost all of them women and children, many of them well dressed, and they

[7] The father of Daniel Ancel, alluded to above.

[8] The daughters of Sir Samuel and Lady Bentham were Mary Sophia (1797–1865), Clara (1802–29), and Sarah (1804–64).

principally of their own accord, some with a very little solicitation passed the little girls on quite to the entrance door of the salloon: every time a carriage came up the guards cleared the way for it, the crowd closing in behind it immediately, some of the guards even invited the 'petites anglaises' *within* the door, all allowed them to stand close to it excepting *one* of the guards, who repeatedly exclaimed 'Retirez vous: il n'y a pas de place pour des *Anglaises*', but the others all endeavoured to soften his ill humour with our nation and completely overpowered his wish to send away the girls. This was the only instance that I have seen of ill will towards us as english people, or to the English as a nation. Amongst the crowd a sailor had pressed in and two ladies fair his companions; the guards as soon as they discovered the party, came and ordered them away; the sailor resisted, he was shown the nearest way of retirring by a couple of the guards who took him by the shoulders, 'il n'y a pas de place pour des polissons'. The ladies not thinking themselves included in the prohibition, endeavoured to remain they were soon forced away: it surprized me much to see that even on the Quay of one of the greate[st] seaports in France, ladies of this description were not suffered to mix with the other inhabitants, indeed, excepting these two ladies, and perhaps two or three more, I did not see any of this description in Havre; how different at Portsmouth, Plymouth and all the rest of our english seaports. The children were afterwards taken into the Salloon, where they saw all the company and what was most worth seeing of the whole, the immense bunches of full blown cabbage roses and other flowers of equally noble dimensions which were worn by the ladies in their heads and bosoms. It would not be amiss if our countrywomen could adopt another of the french fashions if not this of the enormous head dresses, I mean that of covering the neck; even at this ball though the gown was made very low behind, there was a gauge or a lace or a something quite sufficient that was made up to the throat. The bustle during the night prevented my sleeping much, so that I was up and looking out of [the] window when the last of the company went dancing home by day light and the guard was drawn up to be discharged before the guard house opposite my window. Whilst waiting for their officer their gestures showed that they were all making comments on the dancers; but one of the soldiers in particular with his musket on his shoulder imitated the swimming motion and languishing air of some of the dancers and the capers of others, most amuzingly. I question whether an *english* soldier would have had the inclination, I am sure he would not have had the power to execute the various movements which this Frenchman performed with the most perfect ease.

In the forenoon of Sunday[9] we again set out on a riding and walking expedition, taking the Paris road, which is quite flat at the bottom of the hill we went up the preceeding day. There was nothing remarkable in the culture of this valley excepting the crops of harricot for ripe seeds for stewing soups etc.

Our walk extended to the village of Greville, where there is a church on the summit of a rocky hill, the view beautiful from it. At the foot of the hill we asked a woman some question concerning the road, she told us we could return to Havre straight through the Wood to which Bentham pointed, but as she concluded we were taking a walk to amuse ourselves, she recommended that we should go up to the church, walk round the church yard, and then through the wood. The peasants came out of church whilst we were in the Church yard, the cleanliness of their persons and the tightness and goodness of their apparel surprized us much. Our walk was delightful amongst cottage gardens, woods, and country roads where the peasants were walking in parties of two or three to two or three dozen. We came to a copse in which were many nuts; we strolled in different parties through the cross paths; whilst I was in one too narrow for two persons, I met twenty or thirty peasant women and girls, I retired in a part where there was a green turfed recess to let them pass; as they came up, they bowed successively, 'Bon jour Madame' 'Remercie Madame' every one had something to say in words, besides her smile of thanks. nearer the Town hundreds were assembled, walking in the Paris road, or sitting on the turfy banks besides it, showing themselves and their finery, all in good humour, but none of the dancing or singing which were were all led to expect as of course in France.

2d of October at Saumur. My journal if it can be so called proceeds but slowly; the lateness of the season makes us desirous of settling for the winter, so that our whole time is occupied in looking for houses. We had determined to fin at Tours; fifteen hundred english (including irish) have driven us away. There does not seem to be a householder in or about Tours who would not quit his house to let it at prices that the *english* are willing to pay, one, two to four hundred a year we have had asked us. I told you that we liked Genl Donadieus[10] house much; alas the *Masters* we required for the

[9] 28 August.

[10] Baron Gabriel Donnadieu (1777–1849), French general, made commandant of the department of Indre-et-Loire by Louis XVIII on 3 June 1814. He remained loyal to the king during the Hundred Days and was created vicomte in 1816.

children do not—there are english enough at Tours to more than employ all masters fully at double their former charges; there were two months ago six man servants in want of places at Tours, there were a fortnight ago *fifty* english families in want of men servants —the same in regard to females. The people of Tours find that the English are willing to pay greater prices for every thing than the customary ones and of course the price of every thing is rising— these considerations were enough to induce us to seek our fortune elsewhere, especially as our children have already had enough of *english* french, and as *irish* english does not enter into our plans for their course of studies for this year—accordingly here we are at Saumur—Here at Saumur a week ago there were good Masters of all kinds—the day before we came the master of mathematics went to Tours to teach the English, the dancing master followed the next day, and now the Piano Forte master is gone—no wonder—these masters can *now* get two francs a lesson at Tours, the price at Saumur of the most costly is 8 *sous*, four pence farthing at the present exchange. We had determined to give the children sixteen or twenty penny worth of music three times a week, that is five hours each day, and of dancing still more time, for that accomplishment is to be obtained here for about two pence halfpenny an hour. The English are driving us into the sea, tomorrow B and I are to set out for Angers to try our fortune there. Saumur is of all the places I have seen the most desirable for a family of young children to be brought to for education. The french language is well spoken, there is a College. The Town is upon the whole the airiest and best built of any I have seen, the surrounding country excessively beautiful— provision of all kinds in the greatest profusion, excellent of all kinds—salmon, oysters 30 sous a hundred, sea fish very cheap in winter, trout, carp, tench, pike, eels etc. etc, game chickens 16 to 20 sous a *couple*, the largest fowls 30 sols a couple—*peaches* good flavored and for from 14 a penny, 13 very large apples for six liard, pears ten twenty to 40 a penny—the finest vegetables of all kinds, —the meat looks good from 6 to 8 sous a pound. A bidet from four to five pounds. A cow forty to 100 francs, butter excellent 14 sous a pound. One house that has been offered to us, in one of the best of the suburbs, has a fine hall and staircase a dining room and drawing room each 19 feet by 20, a kitchen cooks room, butter pantry, a bed room and dressing room on the ground floor, rooms over all of these and above these the *grenier*, prepared for plaistering as servants rooms but not plaistered all kinds of outhouses, four stall stable double coach house, with a garden a very small one its true, rent and taxes would be 25£ a year—It might be furnished for from 100 to 300 pounds according to the elegance of the furniture, and at the end of a year the upholsterer would take back the furniture at four fifths of the original cost. To us the town itself, as every other *town* would be very disagreeable, and the immediate environs through which the Thouet runs would be as objectionable to us being marshy as to the few houses that are near the town. Unfortunately it is not the fashion to build houses on the very beautiful hills that every [where] rise on both sides of the Thouet.

Saumur 13th Octr. Returned from Angers to Saumur, the only house that would be suitable near Angers having been let a month ago; but we have been fortunate enough to find one near this place, that is at about a league and a quarter from the Town (a league is 2 and $\frac{1}{2}$ miles). We have settled a place for Masters and hope to be in the house on Monday. The house itself is farm house looking, it is furnished, the garden and grounds in which we have the privilege of walking superlatively beautiful in the stile of Sweedish beauty woods, water, vines, meadows, rocks. I say Sweedish beauty because nothing is on the large scale which could give an idea of grandeur.

We would beg you to write to us at Saumur, Department de Mayenne et Loire.

Mr Koe did I request the favor of you to send 10£ to Bishop Stortford? If not you would much oblige me by doing it now.[11]

[11] Presumably money for the maintenance of Mrs Maria Burton, the mother of Sir Samuel's illegitimate daughters. Mrs Burton was later to write to Koe from Bishops Stortford complaining, *inter alia*, that Lady Bentham had threatened to have her money stopped if she tried to move nearer to London. Mrs Burton to Koe, 24 April 1816, Koe MSS. See also *Correspondence*, v. 244 and n.

2293

To Jean Antoine Gauvain Gallois

September 1814 (Aet 66)

Ford Abbey, Devonshire, near Chard, Somersetshire
Sept. 1814.

Dear Gallois

Thanks for your '*Opinion*':[2] still more for your remembrance of me. 'Friend to Sir Philip Davy' was, by I forget what vain man, assumed as his highest title:[3] 'Master of the White Elephant' was the King of Siam's: Master to Gallois (have you not conferred it on me?) shall be mine.

As to your *Opinion*, through Romilly, it was directed hither by Providence. You know *Brougham*: every body knows him who reads English Newspapers, that is who reads Newspapers. The same post which brought your '*Opinion*', brought a letter from him,[4] announcing a work of his 'on the liberty of the press':[5] aussi-tôt off went your Opinion to him, wherever he is, or at least was, viz. at Lord Grey's, in Cumberland, or Westmoreland,[6] or some such county in the extreme north. Supposing it written, which I rather think it will be, and *that* in a few weeks, his pen being that of a ready writer[7] (the allusion is as religious as it is beautiful—but, I fear, will be lost upon you, your religion being confined within the Romish pale, therefore regard it as *non avenue*) and, going back to the abovementioned supposition, expect from it a copy of the abovementioned work, when the fulness of time shall be accomplished. Not that by *liberty of the press* you and he mean the same thing. The liberty which *you* want *we* have: it consists in the *absence* of that *security*,

2293. [1] Archives Daru, 138 AP 213, dr.2, Archives Nationales, Paris. Autograph. Endorsed: 'Lettre / de Jeremy Bentham'. Addressed: 'A Monsieur / Mr Gallois / Membre de la Chambre / Députés / Paris.' Franked: 'single sheet'. Postmark: 'FOREIGN / 30 / 1814'. Stamped: 'ANGLETERRE' and 'DÉBOURSÉS [?] / CHAMBRE DES DÉPUTÉS'.

Jean Antoine Gauvain Gallois (1761–1828) was a French politician and translator of the works of Gaetano Filangieri (1752–88), the Italian lawyer and writer. For his earlier contact with Bentham see *Correspondence*, iv. 459.

[2] *Chambre des Députés, opinion sur la liberté de la presse, par M. Gallois Séance du 6 août 1814*, Paris, n.d.

[3] A mistake, surely, for Sir Philip Sidney (1554–86), soldier, statesman, and poet. The words were those of Sir Fulke Greville, 1st Baron Brooke (1554–1628), forming part of the epitaph he wrote for himself on his monument at Warwick.

[4] Missing.

[5] Probably a reference to the article that was to appear the following June; 'Liberty of the Continental Press', *Edinburgh Review*, xxv (1815), 112–34.

[6] Earl Grey's residence was at Howick, Northumberland.

[7] Psalms 45: 1.

which would be afforded to authors by a licenser: the assurance of not being punished for any thing they write. What we possess is (subject to being punished for the use of it) the full liberty of publishing whatever we please. But if there be a man who finds in any thing we publish any thing that he does not like, he applies to the Lord Chief Justice of the King's Bench: whereupon his Lordship considers whether *he* likes it: and if he does not, he gives the Jury to understand as much: and the Jury, being, though not openly yet not the less effectually named by his Lordship, the consequence is, if not pillory imprisonment for a few months or years, *fine* a few hundreds of pounds, besides costs of prosecution, to the amount of a few hundreds more: this last *item* attaching upon a man whether he is convicted or acquitted. Private man or public man, if what you publish is understood to cast an imputation upon a man's character, the *truth* of it (say all the Judges) is an *aggravation* of your guilt. What Brougham is to contend for, is—that it shall be a *justification*. Good, so far, were he to succeed, which he will not. This however would not satisfy *me*, unless '*a libel*' were defined, which, with the consent of any one lawyer, it will never be: I mean, of course by the only competent authority—the legislature. The subject is as stale, as ever fish was: no reason against *continuing*, which would not have been as good against *beginning*: and the like, at this distance, for all the rest of politics.

On this subject I mean *libels* and *Juries* together—several years ago I printed a large pamphlet:[8] just as the last sheet but one was printed, the Printer took panic, and would not let me have it to publish: twelve copies I obtained with great difficulty: and gave to as many hands: one of them I can get back by extortion, and (together with whatever else I have *printed* since you saw me for I *publish* nothing) I will *send to you*, if you will let me know how. The Prince of Benevinto[9]—think you he would ever look into any thing more of my writing? if yes, I would put up another copy of every thing for *him*. In that case to whom should I address the packet? to yourself, or to him? or to each his own? Does not he go to the Vienna Congress? If he does, he may see a copy in the hands of Galatin—Nonsense—Galatin will not be there.

Remember me tenderly to Father Morellet.[10] May he live for ever!

[8] *The Elements of the Art of Packing*. See above, letters 2050, 2056, 2057, 2058, 2059, and 2070.

[9] Charles Maurice de Talleyrand-Périgord (1754–1838), French diplomat and statesman. He was granted the title Prince of Benevento by Napoleon in 1806. Gallois had accompanied Talleyrand to England in 1792.

[10] Abbé Morellet, for whom see above letter 2266 n. 4.

that his Memoirs[11] may go on encreasing for ever:—item, may he die before I do, that I may have the reading of them.

Now for a commission: should Chance enable you, perhaps you might not be displeased to execute it for me. For some years, such has been the state of my *eyes* I have been able to read just as much as is necessary for what I write, but no more: for amusement, nothing. While dressing and undressing, I have always somebody to read to me: the care of my eyes, together with this or that little infirmity incident to old age, makes my toilette as long as a fine lady's. For reading, as above, and other odd jobs of the literary kind, for these twenty years past I have always had some youth or other living in the house with me. He sleeps in the same room with me. The one whom I have here at present leaves me early in next month. He is going to the University of Cambridge,[12] in expectation of a *Fellowship* there: a sort of Protestant Canonry, amounting to a comfortable provision for life. Boys exist in France as well as in England. A French boy, if he speaks any thing, speaks French, and if he reads any thing, reads it. Now, if so it be, that you can think of any animal of that description, that, you think, would suit me, what he and his friends for him may be assured of, is—a trip to England and back again at free cost: the rest must depend upon Providence. At my own table he would always dine: except possibly once in a fortnight or so, when he might have to dine alone: at other times whatever company I have, which is very small and select, he would have. For my own part *I* do not *visit* anybody: but it would not follow that *he* would not. *Auctions of Books* are in London numerous and almost continual: all my boys have attended occasionally to bid for books, and, if the cargo bought has not been to heavy to bring in hand or under arm, have brought it home for me, as I need to do for myself. In London, Lawyers and their Clerks walk the streets with bags of a particular kind, in which they carry books and papers: bags of this sort my boys have always been provided with for such purposes. My London residence continues where you remember it. My present residence, as above, is a very aristocratical ⟨one⟩ much above my cut, in point of expence, but that I have it by the year and have it *ready furnished*: (for country residences, a very convenient custom, which has sprung up within these few years.) It includes the remains of an old Abbey,[13] enlarged and decorated with posterior, though still antique, magnificence: it has attached to it a small Park

[11] Morellet's *Mémoires* were published in 2 volumes at Paris in 1821, two years after his death.

[12] Henry Coulson.

[13] The original Ford Abbey dated from the twelfth century: see Bain, p. 130.

well stocked with deer: and is itself well stocked with *ghosts*: for which the tapestry hangings, and many uninhabited rooms, afford harbour in abundance. I have been in it about six weeks. I have it for 7 years, with liberty to quit it at the end of the first. It is 145 miles from London. I give £490 a year for it. If France could spare you, I should wish you here. *Geese* you would find in ⟨suf⟩ficient plenty: and undefended by any such obstacle, as the law of property opposed, 21 years ago at *Hendon*, to your concupiscence. The boy in question, how would he do to live? *Fruit*, at stated times not altogether absent: but not existing in such plenty as to be accessible all day long without stint, as in France. *Wine*, none of those light and pleasant sorts, to which alone he has been accustomed: our heavy sorts not unaccessible: but I, liking none, drink none: and for one reason or other, *indifference*, or regard to *health*, very little is drunk in any house of mine. Beer at *this* house very good. At both houses, scenery more than ordinarily delightful: the Master generally gay, never melancholy, never angry: none of his servants ever had an angry word: in London, he has none but females. None of his boys ever experienced any thing in the name of punishment, one excepted, who was once ordered to leave the room for impertinence. Boyish exercises, for exercise, I have scarce yet left off. But, the conversation being wholly of the intellectual kind, if Monsieur neither has nor can be made to have a relish for it, he will be ennuié à la ⟨. . .⟩ Of four boys I have had, the first was the son of a man of good fortune: he was with me a year instead of going to University: 2 or 3 years ago he married an accomplished girl with £20,000 in possession, and £85,000 more in prospect.[14] The 2d was in perfect indigence. I got him the Pursership of a Man of War: he has been for some years married to a Widow with a handsome Chateau, and a good estate for life.[15] The third, whom you saw with me at Paris was in equal indigence. He still lives with me and manages my affairs: is called to the Bar, well respected and coming into business, with a provision from other sources.[16] The 4th is not yet *twenty*: with me he qualified himself for the function of Parliamentary Reporter for Newspapers, for which he left me above a year ago, and is paid 4 Guineas a week all the year round:[17] the 5th is leaving me for the cause abovementioned.

[14] Edward Collins, second son of William Collins. Edward was Bentham's amanuensis *c.*1795–6. He later joined the army and as a captain in the 21st Light Dragoons married on 9 April 1810 Margaret, daughter of the late William Wood of Charlotte Street, Fitzroy Square. See *Correspondence*, v, as index, and Bowring, x. 572.

[15] John Heide Koe.

[16] John Herbert Koe.

[17] Walter Coulson.

As to Monsieur, his age should be between 12 and 15: the fairer and quicker the *hand* he *writes*, the better: also if he has some acquaintance with the Latin, sufficient to enable him to read short passages in that language, such as quotations, with some conception of the import: and an acquaintance with the rules of grammar, as applied, if not to the Latin, to his own language. *La physique*, the more he possesses, the better: but if he does not already, with me he soon will: he will attend lectures.

Whether by *noblesse*, *station* or *opulence*—I should rather have said *by habits of life*—his situation should be somewhat above the vulgar: but, in any case, better than *at present*, his friends should be in straitened circumstances (à l'étroite) whether from *scantiness of means*, or multitude of children. In every particular, the *less* satisfied he is with his *present* situation, the *more* likely he will be to be satisfied with the *proposed one*. Let not any boy be sent who is not *himself desirous* of it—He should not be *lame* in any way, nor have a forbidding aspect. I should be sorry he were *nearsighted*. Point d'esprit militaire. I hate murder upon the smallest scale: much more upon a large one. Monsieur's stay with me would be liable to be put an end to, by other incidents besides disagreement this he and his friends should be fully apprised of, to prevent disappointment. With what views would he be sent to me? To save expence of maintenance? or to acquire information in some shape not so easily obtainable at home? You have read and heard of the recent inventions for shortening and cheapening the process of *instruction*: a new and very extensive plan is likely to be carried into effect for apply⟨ing⟩ these inventions to the higher branches of instruction. It will be managed by Committees of the Association They look to me for guidance; Monsieur might observe and bear a part in the whole of the business

Mode of conveyance for Monsieur. There are Inns (I hear) in London at any of which on paying £4. 8s.0d a person is conveyed to Paris. Mode and expence probably the same from Paris to London. Be it what it may, *De Lessert*[18] would, I doubt not advance, drawing for reimbursement on *Romilly*, as being at or near London. At London, Monsieur should enquire for *Mr Grellier*, Queens Square Place, Westminster (You know the place) who will take charge of him.

[18] Probably Gabriel Étienne Delessert, for whom see letter 2098 n. 25.

2294

From Thomas Northmore

1 October 1814

16 Orchard St. Portman sq.
Octr. 1. 1814

Dear Sir

'Mine host' of the abbey is all politeness, and the Ladies say irresistible. So that, I suppose, come I must—but the Exeter people are so knowing, that they are much better acquainted with the affairs of others, than the individuals themselves—otherways they never could have told you that my arrival is fixt for the 10th. In fact my Builder tells me that he hopes the house will be ready for my reception by *the 20th.*[2] and I shall think myself in high luck if I get there by that time, or even a week later. My children (except the nursling) will be sent before me, so that if I can possibly contrive to spend a night at your hospitable abbey on my way, (and I shall be happy in so doing) I shall bring only Mrs. N.[3] and the nurse and infant with my man servant—of course we shall not require more than 3 beds—and I will write again to inform you more exactly of our arrangement.

The worthy Major, I am sorry to say, has had another bad attack[4]—and I much fear his constitution is severely shaken—but thank god he is considerably recovered now, and if the winter be not severe I trust he will recruit himself in Devonshire next season—Perhaps you will also give me the pleasure of your company; so many patriots at Cleve will inspirit the weak nerves of the Devonshire man. They already talk of returning me for Exeter—but my

2294. [1] Bowring, 'Memoirs', at p. 480. Docketed: '1814 Oct 1 / Northmore(Ths) 16 Orchd Str / Portman Sq / to / JB. Q.S.P. / Accepts invitatn to Ford'. Addressed: 'Jeremy Bentham Esq. / Ford Abbey / Chard / Somersetshire'. Postmark: 'OC / 1 / 1814'. Stamp illegible.

Thomas Northmore (1766–1851), inventor, geologist, and miscellaneous writer, was a radical in politics.

[2] Northmore's family seat was at Cleve House, near Exeter.

[3] Emmeline (d. 1850), daughter of Sir John Eden, Bt., of Windlestone Park and Beamish Park, County Durham, had married Northmore on 9 November 1809. She bore him a son, Eden Shafto Northmore (d. 1838) and eight daughters. By his first wife, Penelope (d. 1792), eldest daughter of Sir William Erle Welby, Bt., of Denton Hall, Lincolnshire, Northmore had one son, Thomas Welby Northmore (1791–1829).

[4] Cartwright.

resolution is taken—I will not *buy* because I will not sell—if therefore they return me—it must be *free* of expense à la Burdett—[5]

I remain my dear Sir
yours truly,
Ths. Northmore

P.S. you don't say how you like the Abbey—nor do you speak of certain *aerial* co-tenants—Have you, or *yours* seen any white-sheets yet walking by mid-night

2295

From Lady Romilly

9 October 1814

Tanhurst Octr. 9.

Dear Mr. Bentham

Romilly is busy or idle and will not write to you and therefore I his unworthy substitute hope to make a merit in your eyes of thanking you for the interesting letters you have been so good as to send us and petitioning for further indulgence whenever you are disposed to favour us and this without any return on our part as to Dumonts letters we have had but two since those you saw and they have related entirely to William[2] his studies his amusements his good qualities and his defects, all of which could be alone interesting to Parents. The illness of his Sister[3] had detained him almost entirely in the Country. William writes us word that he went to the Theatre to see Talma[4] with Madame de Staël[5] and that she was greeted with the greatest enthusiasm and cries of Viva viva—Sir

[5] Burdett was returned at Westminster in 1807 without personal expense, the cost of the election being met by the local committee. In 1812 Burdett and Lord Cochrane were returned unopposed. Northmore stood unsuccessfully at Exeter in June 1818.

2295. [1] Bowring, 'Memoirs', at p. 186.

[2] William Romilly (1799–1855), eldest of the six sons of Sir Samuel and Lady Anne Romilly. At this time he was staying with Dumont at Geneva.

[3] Probably Marie-Louise, or 'Lisette', Dumont's sister who had married Louis-David Duval. She was to die in the following year.

[4] François-Joseph Talma (1763–1826), French actor.

[5] Anne Louise Germaine de Staël (1766–1817), writer and novelist, daughter of Jacques Necker, French finance minister under the *ancien régime* and during the early stages of the Revolution. She married in 1785 baron de Staël-Holstein, Swedish ambassador in Paris, but was subsequently separated from him.

Humphrey[6] and Lady Davy[7] have been at Geneva but return to pass the winter in Italy (at Rome) where Lady Davy is a very great favorite of *his holiness the Pope.*[8] William is going on in a way to give us very great satisfaction and to entirely recompense us for our resolution in parting with him. Geneva is beginning to be inundated with English which is a pity but I hope they may only be summer birds. Tours is likely to be very full I know several families going to settle there, I regret very sincerely that we cannot be of any use to Sir Samuel and Lady Bentham about a correspondent at Paris poor Madame Gautier[9] is gone to Switzerland to watch over her Son who is in a state of health that gives her the greatest apprehension, she is the only person that we could have applied to for Romilly has never been in the habit of corresponding with the Baron de Lessert and he desires me to say that he should be more likely to write to Gallois to enquire after him than the reverse but if he should have occasion

2296

From Henry Tonkin Coulson

October 1814?

The influx of fresh men, has sent those last entered into the town. My tutor, (Mr Barnes,)[2] to whom I introduced myself, when I had provided myself with a cap and gown, is a fat, jolly, athletic man, about 50, looking good humour, full of jokes, but with a stock of bitter jibes and taunts for those who come to his lectures unprepared. His subordinate[3] is a tall, grave personage, of solemn demeanour, exceedingly devout, but withal rather pleasant, unless he sus-

[6] Sir Humphry Davy (1778–1829), scientist. He is mentioned in correspondence between Bentham and Peter Mark Roget in 1800. See *Correspondence*, vi. 225 and n. and 349 and n.

[7] Lady Davy, née Jane Kerr (1780–1855), who had married Davy in 1812.

[8] Luigi Barnabà Chiaramonti (1740–1823), pope as Pius VII 1800–23.

[9] Madame Madeleine Gautier, for whom see letter 2098 n. 26.

2296. [1] Bowring, x. 483. Introduced: 'A letter from one of Bentham's young friends, gives rather an unfavourable description of Cambridge University a quarter of a century ago.' The writer was almost certainly Henry Coulson, admitted as sizar at Queens' College on 1 July 1814, who was at Cambridge from the beginning of October of that year. See letters 2278 and n. 3, 2293 and n. 12. The information conveyed in this letter suggests that it was written shortly after Coulson's arrival.

[2] George Barnes (1769?–1846), admitted sizar at St. John's 1792, BA 1796, MA and fellow of Queens' 1799, BD 1808, rector of Grimston, Norfolk 1816–46.

[3] Probably William Mandell (d. 1843), admitted sizar at Queens' 1799, BA 1803, MA 1806, BD 1815; a fellow of Queens' 1803–43, senior proctor 1811–12, and leading figure among the Cambridge evangelicals.

pects that meet reverence is not paid him. Bows and prostrations are therefore much in demand, though latitudinarian irreverences has somewhat curtailed them. It is a heinous offence to laugh at his lectures; and an eminent virtue to admire his lamp, on whose construction he greatly prides himself. When proctor, he exhibited most exemplary diligence in recovering the frail ones of both sexes, and particularly in sending certain damsels to the spinning-house, and of sending under-graduates to rural meditations. Men rejoice here in visiting the chapel nine times in seven days: at 7 o'clock in the morning,—stay half-an-hour: mathematics at 8,—out at 9: classes at 10,—out at 11 o'clock: dine at 3: sup at 9. We don't care for classics. At Trinity they are honoured,—at St John's respected,—at the smaller Colleges despised. Reading men occupy themselves with mathematics exclusively: these alone can bring them with honour through the senate house. The claim of a wrangler to the substantial honours of a fellowship is seldom rejected. So classics are for the most part voted a bore. Others are scarcely ever mentioned,—a little of Locke and Paley, but little indeed. Some even read hard,—one man reads thirteen hours a day,—but seven or eight hours are the golden mean. Study and success then, bring, through a four-years' vista, the prospect of £250 per annum.

2297

To An Unknown Correspondent

9 November 1814 (Aet 66)

No shuttlecocks but these tawdry ones; all glitter, no worth; just like the age, and a startling exemplification, and conclusive proof of the degeneracy. Pointed epigrams, yes; but pointed shuttlecocks never were, nor ever will be, good for anything. These, indeed, have not yet been tried; but trial is not necessary to condemnation in the case of such a set of shuttlecocks. The balls, by the eye of faith, I perceive, are orthodox,—the primitive firmness is perceptible to the touch, and Horace's *totus teres atque rotundus*[2] may, with truth, be predicated of them.

2297. [1] Bowring, x. 480. An extract of a letter concerned with the sending of a supply of shuttlecocks to Ford Abbey.

[2] Horace, *Satires*, II. vii. 86: 'et in se ipso totus, teres atque rotundus' ('and complete in himself, smooth and round'). Bentham appears to have missed out the comma, allowing the phrase to be translated as 'completely smooth and round'.

2298

To John Herbert Koe

24 November 1814 (Aet 66)

Ford Abbey Thursday 24 Novr 1814. P.M 8.

Yours of the 22d just received.[2] None of yours have missed. What made you suspect as much was my insisting about enquiries from Brougham about Gallois: but the reason was your recollection about the matter was not mentioned as positive. You still talked of enquiries at the Post Office: *cui bono* if the letter was received. Thereupon it seems I am a letter in pocket: which I do not grudge—especially the good news it brought about stone-saws.

Search here after the 4to Oxford Statutes fruitless.[3] Fabri has taken them to himself.[4]

Much good may it do you with your bad weather. We have none such here: though to be sure one night did procure us frost all over the ponds perhaps $\frac{1}{4}$ of an inch thick. The worst was it *pinched* the poor dear plants that were looking so beautiful in the porch, two tier on each side in as high perfection as in the middle of Summer—I hope not to *death*. The others are still in high perfection facing the Sun in the Great Hall. The Cloisters are now the Orangerie, with room for vibrating—an operation performed regularly every day after dinner. Every body is in high health: even Mrs Stoker can scarce find any thing to complain of.

The Roof at Mill's—to patch or renew? How can I tell which is best, I a poor ignorant mortal, and at this distance. Your own scientific discretion—let that be used in the name of goodness, to a creature so ignorant as myself, your discretion is what Ld Camden calls all discretion—the law of tyrants.[5]

When the periodicals or any thing else is sent, time enough Mill says for the parcel to Mrs Mill.

2298. [1] UC clxxiv. 108. Autograph. Docketed: '1814 Novr. 24 / J.B. to H.K.' Addressed: 'To / J. Herbert Koe Esqr. / Lincoln's Inn / London.' Postmark illegible. An extract of this letter is printed in Bowring, x. 480.

[2] Missing.

[3] Probably *Corpus Statutorum Universitatis Oxoniensis*, Oxford, 1768–70, the most likely quarto edition.

[4] Apparently Bentham's word for what we would now call a Gremlin. He used it in later letters. See Bentham to Sir Samuel Bentham, 14 January 1820, BL IX. 380.

[5] Charles Pratt, 1st Baron and 1st Earl Camden (1714–94), in *Reports of Cases Argued and Adjudged in the King's Courts at Westminster*, ed. George Wilson, 3 vols., London, 1770–5, ii. 137–8. Bentham had made reference to this in 'Law Versus Arbitrary Power: or A Hatchet for Dr. Paley's Net', written in 1809 (UC cvii. 272–5).

Along with periodicals send me I pray a Copy of *Lindley Murrays* English Grammar.[6] Being a thing to turn over and over, I had rather have a bound Copy if *well* bound, than in boards You remember the passion you were in at the view of the Abbey from the iron railing in front of it that separates the lawn from the park. What will you give me to make not only a walk for you there but a shrubbery by the side of the same? viz. one part of the belt coming in continuation of the walk recently cut, and the other coming at right angles to it (only with a curvilinear elbow) to join the broad gravel walk, thereby running in parallelism to the Vegetable Cloisters? breadth of the belt about 15 or 16 feet, made to slope upwards by as steep a slope as may be so that the top may be as high perhaps as the top of the railing. One use of it, to plant out that insipid field, so that the first object that meets the eye in looking from the house may be some of the Timber and other scattered trees in the field next beyond. To prevent your seeing through, a line of young beeches thickly planted, let in to the slope that slopes downwards to the rails, in such sort that nothing but the foliage may be seen: for the parcel of sticks through which you hid the day form a miserable prospect. This for a back and screen, between that and the walk rows of flowering shrubs in *quincunx* two or three. N.B. Per Mill, even in Scotland Beeches when young preserve their foliage through the winter, though discoloured. Pray measure the shrubbery at Q.S.P. between the lawn and the cross walk, at the broadest and narrowest part, and let me know the result.——Well but this is not all.——Wakefield when last here told us he had just seen an advertisement in an Exeter paper of date about *October 27th* a Nursery which was to be quitted at Lady Day next, and of which the stock was consequently to be sold off before that time, with a list of prices at which various articles were to be sold. Enquiries thereupon of Elswood produced a West Country paper in which were one or two Nursery Advertisements but this not among them. Do of Northmore produced an Exeter paper viz Truemans Exeter Flying Post with Nursery Advertisements, but this not among them. Now you know at Peeles Coffee House Fleet Street all Country papers without exception are taken in: and supposing this true were you to call there, if Wakefields account be not incorrect, you would be sure to find it. The use of this advertisement would be great: the prices would probably be cheaper than at any other Nursery hereabouts: and at any rate I should by the rule of addition know my expence

[6] Lindley Murray (1745–1826), American-born grammarian, who settled in England in 1784, the author of *English Grammar, Adapted to the Different Classes of Learners*, York, 1795, which went through many editions.

beforehand. The measure is between 600 and 700 feet in length: breadth say 15. Under the grass a gravel walk was and therefore is in existence: the gravel pit not more than a few yards off. The belt of grass parallel to the walk by the brick wall has already been dug up for a similar purpose. The *beech* as above to serve for a screen will be composed of suckers from shrubs already in existence: and some evergreens if you remember exist there already. Oh yes, and the belt of grass which is at right angles to them and joins them will be disposed of in the same manner. The border along the brick wall that runs in a line with the house is widened, and stocked with flowers from the kitchen Garden. The lists in question were said to be lists of trees and flowering shrubs. Suppose 50 sorts that will be 100 words to copy besides the prices, and the Nursery mans name and the name and date of the paper.
P.S. Mrs Stoker is intriguing for her friend Mrs Langston[7] that now keeps Q.S.P. to keep the Abbey during our absence.

Nails for nailing trees to walls. Cast iron. Per Mill none such known here, tho' better and 6 times as cheap as wrought iron. Requested with the periodicals, 3 lb. if of divers sizes, the middling: or for experiment $\frac{1}{2}$ lb of those larger, $\frac{1}{2}$ of those of smaller, size than the middling These will drive into the brick itself: *secus*[8] the wrought. But if too small they are apt to break under an inexpert hand. Item a sliding pencil, if square so much the better.

2299

To An Unknown Correspondent

13 December 1814 (Aet 66)

Nobody that could stay here would go from hence. Nobody is so well anywhere else as everybody is here.

Fogs—he asks—fogs? What is the meaning of the word Fog? No such word is to be found in the vocabulary of Ford Abbey. Rains and sunshine *à la bonne heure*. April weather, except that it is warmer than April is with you: about 56°, I think it was, out of doors.

[7] Mrs Langston appears later in Bentham's letters as one of his tenants in London. See Bentham to J. H. Koe, 20 September 1820, Koe MSS.

[8] i.e. 'otherwise'.

2299. [1] Bowring, x. 480–1. An extract.

2300

To John Herbert Koe

15 December 1814 (Aet 66)

Ford Abbey, 15th December, 1814.

Thanks for your about-nothing-at-all letter.[2]

Ricardo and Say[3] came here yesterday to dinner unexpected; whether they go, however, or no, to-morrow, as was originally intended, I know not. Both very intelligent and pleasant men, and both seem highly pleased. There are two or three long letters to friend Allen,[4] from Clarkson,[5] giving an account of his negotiation at Paris for the abolition of the Slave Trade, in September and October last, extremely curious, and not a little hope-inspiring. By Wellington[6] he was received with the utmost appearance of frankness and cordiality: Louis XVIII.[7] not only consenting, but zealous, acknowledging himself terrified into what was done, but determined that the trade shall not outlast the five years. He gave an account of interviews with a multitude of the negotiating people at Vienna, and of the measures taken by Clarkson, with the assistance of Louis and several of his Ministers, for disseminating truth to inform and govern the public mind in France.

2301

To John Herbert Koe

20 December 1814 (Aet 66)

Ford Abbey, 20th December, 1814.

I have been consuming two or three days in indexing 'Bell's Elements of Tuition.'[2] But I am all admiration at the genius and

2300. [1] Bowring, x. 484.

[2] Missing.

[3] Jean-Baptiste Say (1767–1832), French economist and political philosopher, who visited Britain between September and December 1814.

[4] William Allen.

[5] Thomas Clarkson (1760–1846), anti-slavery campaigner.

[6] Arthur Wellesley, 1st Duke of Wellington (1769–1852), British commander in chief in the Peninsula war, later prime minister 1828–30 and, briefly, 1834. He had been appointed ambassador to Paris in July 1814 with the primary objective of negotiating the ending of the slave trade.

[7] Louis XVIII (1755–1824) the king of France from the restoration of the monarchy until the Hundred Days and then again until his death.

2301. [1] Bowring, x. 484.

[2] Dr Andrew Bell (1753–1832), who was claimed by Anglicans to be the founder of the

talent displayed in the work, (when I came into the marrow of it, which was mismatched by the quantity of introductory quisquilious matter,) and at the inestimable utility of it.

2302

From William David Evans

20 December 1814

Sir

Permit me to express the thanks of myself and the other gentlemen acting in the commission at this Place for your obliging attention to our application for the benefit of being assisted by your valuable works[2] in the alterations which we are about to make in the prison.

The addition of your treatises respecting parochial police[3] will be also peculiarly acceptable as the magnitude of the expences which in this country are incurred in the maintenance of the poor renders it highly important to pay all possible attention to administering them in the most advantageous manner.

I have the honour to be
Sir
Your most obliged
and obedt. Servt.
W. D. Evans

Manchester
20 Decr. 1814

monitorial system of education, was the author of a book originally entitled *An Experiment in Education, made at the Male Asylum of Madras*, London, 1797, subsequently republished as *The Madras School*, and as the first part of *Elements of Tuition*, 3 parts, London, 1813–15.

2302. [1] UC cxxii. 534. Autograph. Docketed: '1814 Decr. 20 / Panop / W.D. Evans Manchester / to / J.B. Ford Abbey / Thanking for Panopt Book / N B Evans per H [Koe?] He / is Chairman of the / Manchester Magistrates / and a Provincial Coun / -sel of eminence.'

William David Evans (1767–1821), called to the bar 1794, practised on the northern circuit; based at Liverpool until 1807, when he moved to Manchester. He was appointed stipendiary magistrate for Manchester 1813 and vice-chancellor of the County Palatine of Lancaster 1815. He held both offices until 1818 and was knighted in 1819 on becoming recorder of Bombay.

[2] Presumably Bentham's *Panopticon* and its *Postscripts*.

[3] Apparently a reference to *Pauper Management Improved: particularly by means of an application of the Panopticon principle of construction*, London, 1812.

2303

From Lord Holland?

December 1814

Rome, December, 1814.

For those who require a good climate, Rome is not a place to spend the winter in. The houses are falling into decay, and the streets are filled with wretchedness and filth; but the antiquities are more easy of access than formerly; and, in spite of all that has been removed, the monuments of architecture, painting, and sculpture, are more numerous than in any country in Europe. The society is chiefly that of strangers; and a large, not unpleasant, English colony. One has, too, an opportunity in contemplating fallen grandeur in men, with the ruins of the greatest empire in the world; for here are nearly as many dethroned monarchs as crumbling palaces: Charles IV.,[2] the Queen of Etruria,[3] King of Holland;[4] and Joseph[5] and Jerome,[6] it is said, have expressed a wish to swell this number, but both have been refused. Lucien is a man of sense, and very much attached to his wife and family:[7] ambitious of the character of a man of letters, and pleased with any allusion to his poem, which he seems to think has, by this time, made its appearance in England.[8] He is a Romish prince, but has, I suspect, accepted that title more as a mark of protection, and a sort of earnest for the security of his person than from any value he attaches to so empty a title. He lives on good terms with his brother Louis and Cardinal Fesch.[9] I do not know whether he has any communication with Napoleon. Several

2303. [1] Bowring, x. 483–4. Introduced: 'I find this letter from Rome, without a signature. I suspect the writer to have been Lord Holland.'

[2] Charles IV (1748–1819), king of Spain 1788–1808. After abdicating his throne he received a pension from Napoleon and went to Rome in 1811.

[3] Maria Louisa, queen of Etruria, the widow of Louis I (*c.*1786–1803), king of Etruria. She was dethroned by Napoleon in 1808 and governed the duchy of Lucca 1816–24.

[4] Louis Bonaparte (1778–1846), Napoleon's third surviving brother, king of Holland 1806–10.

[5] Joseph Bonaparte (1768–1844), Napoleon's elder brother, king of Naples 1806–8, king of Spain 1808–13.

[6] Jérôme Bonaparte (1784–1860), Napoleon's youngest surviving brother, king of Westphalia 1807–13.

[7] Lucien married his second wife, Madame Joubert, née Marie-Alexandrine-Charlotte de Bleschamps (1778–1855) in 1803. She bore him six sons and four daughters.

[8] *Charlemagne; ou l'église delivrée. Poème épique, en vingt-quatre chants*, 2 vols., Rome, 1814. This was published in Paris and London in the same year, and appeared in English translation in 1815.

[9] Joseph Fesch (1763–1839), French cardinal, archbishop of Lyons. He was the half-brother of Napoleon's mother.

English have lately visited the latter at Elba,[10] and he talked to them in the most open, cheerful, and intelligent manner, chiefly on past events, with great clearness, for two or three hours; and spoke with a calmness, amounting to insensibility, of many past transactions, as if he had seen them from an eminence, but as if they reflected neither credit nor discredit upon himself. He was only animated in relating battles, especially those of Egypt; and was highly diverted at hearing one of the Pacha's[11] secretaries had assumed his name—*Ainsi il s'appelle Buonaparte.* and then laughed excessively. They would find great difficulty, he said, in settling affairs at the Congress, '*mais cela ne me regarde pas; mon rôle est fini; Je me regarde comme mort.*' He was, he added, at Elba, because he wished to be too powerful. England was now at her height, and must soon begin to decline; he did not know how, or when, but decline she must. He spoke good humouredly of Madame de Staël: said she was always in opposition, but always disinterested.

2304

To An Unknown Correspondent

1814?

A visiter is expected from London, who has some notion of taking the holy place. Should the rascal—any such rascal—come, I am determined to do one of two things—either to murder him, or to treat him well. The latter course would have the advantage of smoothing the path to a number of little negotiations for which there may be a demand. How to murder the fellow I don't understand—never having seen or read the German play which gives instructions, it is said, on that subject.[2]

[10] Napoleon was confined to Elba after his first abdication.

[11] Mohammed (or Mehemet) Ali (*c.*1769–1849), pasha of Egypt 1805–48.

2304. [1] Bowring, x. 480. Introduced by a passage concerning Ford Abbey which concludes: 'his attachment to it was greatly strengthened, and he was very unwilling to think of being forced to leave it. In one of his letters he says:—'

[2] Bentham was probably thinking of Act II, sc. i, of *Die Raüber* by Johann Christoph Friedrich von Schiller (1759–1805). This play was first published at Frankfurt and Leipzig in 1781, and performed at Mannheim in the following year. It was translated into French in 1785 and into English in 1792.

2305

To Albert Gallatin

28 January 1815 (Aet 66)

Ford Abbey Devonshire near
Chard Somersetshire 28th Jany 1815.

Dear Sir,

Having been resident at this antique and remote mansion, ever since the 17th. of July, I know nothing about the world at large, except what I glean from a few newspapers, and therefore write to you at a venture.

The hopes you were kind enough to give me, in relation to certain printed but unpurchaseable documents, will, I flatter myself, should they happen to have slipt out of your memory, be recalled by these lines. If, since I took my leave of you, any thing has been transmitted from you addressed to me, I have not been fortunate enough to receive it, or to hear of it. In relation to my letter and packet with yours for the Governor,[2] after fruitless endeavour in abundance, my friend Mr Koe (John Herbert Koe, of Lincolns Inn, Esqr.) who has all along resided in my House at Queens Square Place Westminster, in a letter dated the 18th. Octr. 1814,[3] writes to me as follows.

'The Parcel of Books for the Governor has, by the medium of Mr. Randolph,[4] got itself dispatched to America. It has been consigned to the care of a friend of his, who goes out Passenger in a cartel, that sails in a few days; and this friend of his is also a friend of the governors.'

With this parcel, I *hope* (for some how or other having concluded as much, I omitted to enquire more particularly) went the two letters, yours and mine. If they did not, perhaps they were sent to you at Ghent by Mr Koe: for, in a former letter, dated 30th. Augt. 1814,[5] which lies before me, such, at that time, under the difficulties Mr K. and he had encountered, was the project they had formed.

In relation to this business, a whimsical enough accident (I hope not an unfortunate one to boot) happened, a little before my depar-

2305. [1] Gallatin MSS, New-York Historical Society. Part in the hand of a copyist, part autograph. Endorsed: 'Somersetshire 28 Jany. 1815 / Jeremy Bentham'. Addressed: 'To / Albert Gallatin Esqr / etc etc etc. / 16 Hanover Street / Hanover Square.' Postmark and stamp illegible.

[2] Simon Snyder. See letters 2274 and 2281.

[3] Missing.

[4] David Meade Randolph, for whom see letter 2281 n. 1.

[5] Also missing.

ture. On or near my table, along with a letter or two designed for the post, lay that letter of yours to the Governor, which, for some purpose or other, I forget what, I had been casting my eye upon. A young gentleman,[6] who, at that time, was living with me, and whom I had desired, as usual, to take charge of my letters for the post, took up, without instructions from me, *this* along with the rest, sealed it, and put it into the nearest post office. On my missing it, he told me what had happened. Repairing to the General post office, he got them, not without some difficulty, to return it to me: not through *his* hands, but through their own messenger, first *stamping* it with one of their *marks*. On one of his attendencies, he heard one of the clerks say to another—'this is a letter of great consequence.' Here am I unhanged and now unprosecuted: But I should be sorry that, making a political mystery of a transaction so remote from politics, they should have mentioned it to the secretary, he to the acting postmaster general, and so on. Might it not be of use that the odd appearance of the Lombard St. Post mark should be explained to the Governor?

After the happy termination of your grand business, my delight at which will be much better conceived than it could be expressed, have we any chance of seeing you once more, and when, in this part of the world?

I forget whether it was before or after I last saw you that the person who has the principal direction of the affairs of Poland (of course *sub lege graviori*)[7] applied to me for leave to consult me about the constitution for that country.[8] Constitutional law is a subject I am not very fond of meddling with: but, under the uncertainty what it might prove to be that would be desired of me, I saw no reason for declining, at that time, a proposition, to the honor of which I could not be insensible. Of the whole result of that business my expectation is far from sanguine.

I know not whether I mentioned to you a work I had partly in hand partly in contemplation, for the extension of the *Bell Instruction system* over the whole field of *art and science learning, language learning included*. It now draws to a close.[9] Among the results, if I am right, is this: viz. that this of Bell's is *one* of the most useful, if not *the* most useful of all the products of inventive genius (printing excepted) that this globe has ever witnessed: and that it may be

[6] Probably Henry Coulson.

[7] i.e. 'under a more oppressive law'.

[8] See letter 2276. A reference to Czartoryski.

[9] *Chrestomathia*, the first part of which was printed in 1815 and again in 1816; the whole being published in two parts in 1817.

applied to every the *highest* branches of useful learning with as much advantage as it has already been to the lowest. When printed if you would favour me with the names of such persons in the different states of the Union to whom you think it might be communicated with the best prospect of its being employed to advantage, I would send copies accordingly. The institution of the experimental school for the purpose in Westminster (I am ashamed to think it) to all appearance waits only for me: I mean for the completion of the above mentioned work.

I think of leaving this for London about the middle of next month (Feby) proposing to return hither for the summer and Autumn the latter end of April or beginning of May: but any foreign letter would at all times be better directed to me at my House Queen's Square Place Westminster than any where else.

Believe me ever, with the truest and most cordial respect.

Dear Sir
Yours
Jeremy Bentham

Albert Gallatin Esqr.
etc etc etc.

2306

To John Frauncеis Gwyn

28 January 1815 (Aet 66)

Ford Abbey 28 January 1815

To John Frauncеis Gwyn of George Street Bryanston Square London and Ford Abbey in the County of Devon Esquire

Sir

Whereas by Articles of Agreement, entered into between yourself and me, and bearing date on the sixth day of July last, 1814, relative to my renting of you the said Abbey with the appurtenances, for the term of seven years, reckoning from the twenty fourth day of June then last past, it was, amongst other things, provided, that, if I should be 'desirous of quitting the said premises at the end of the first year of the said term, then I should be at liberty so to do,' 'upon giving to' you 'three months previous notice in writing, of such desire (meaning not less than three months)' and 'that thereupon at

2306. [1] BL IX. 198–9. Draft. Docketed: '1815 Jany 28 / J.B. Ford Abbey / to / J.F. Gwyn / George Street / Bryanston Square / London / Notice to quit 24 June / 1815 / Fair copy sent same / day to J.H. Koe / to be made use of / by him.'

the expiration of the said three months the said term' should 'cease,' Now therefore in virtue and in pursuance of the said provision, I do hereby give you notice, that it is my desire to quit the said premises on the twenty fourth day of June 1815 next ensuing, being the day on which the said first year of the said term will cease.

I am, Sir
Your most humble Servant
Jeremy Bentham

Witness

2307

From Pavel Chichagov

2 February 1815

London 2d February 1815

To my great and most agreable surprize Mr Koe delivered to me your letter this morning.[2] It was the more wellcome as I had given up not only the idea of hearing from you but even seeing Mr Koe again, who disapeared for a month instead of the few days which he intended to spend with you. I thought you had laid an embargo upon him. I Share very much your distress in not having compleated the work you meant to have done, and that more perhaps for posterity's sake than for your own and here is my reason for it. One good book is sometimes sufficient to immortilize a man, to make his reputation, and satisfy him, but you can't make to many good books for posterity. The more they have, the better they like them and the more they want, as the frenchman says, l'appétit vient en mangeant.[3] Is not it a good reasoning? I have observed it allways is, when it derives its arguments from the stomach. So much for the influence of the physic upon the morals. I am very glad to find that the opinion I have adopted upon the nature of our intellect is so perfectly consonant with yours. I can not imagine any thing between matter and vacuum, unless you put fools there, either something or nothing. You see that with such disposition I should certainly have profited by your advice to attend the physical lectures of Mr

2307. [1] BL IX. 200–1. Autograph. Docketed: '1815 Feb / Tchitchagoff London / to / J.B. Ford Abbey'. Addressed: 'Jeremy Bentham Esqr / Chard Ford Abbey / Somersetshire'. Postmark: 'PAID / 7 FE 7 / 1815'. Stamped: 'MORE TO PAY'.

[2] Missing.

[3] The Frenchman was François Rabelais (1494?–1553); the quotation from *La Vie treshorrifique du Grand Gargantua*, Lyon, 1534, I. v.

Walker[4] if I had received your letter a little sooner and if I had not suspected them of being to superficial. I have been allways fond of that study and as I have had an opportunity of familiarizing myself a great deal with mathematics they made me allways dissatisfied with public lectures which in general are inncompleat. I have had the curiosity of looking in to Mr Stewarts philosophy of the human mind,[5] expecting to find some thing of a *physical metaphysic* in it but was very much mistaken and left it about the midle where he acknowledges that neither he nor his predecessor Dr Reid[6] know themselves anything about what they write. He is neither clear enough to instruct nor absurd enough to amuse. But when will you come to town? Can one trust to the midle of this month? as you got over the great cold I see no reason for leaving the country now and yet I wish you very much to come. I want to have clear ideas about the *influence*, the *reform* etc. etc.[7] in short in spite of your principle I think it much more virtuous to read what you have written than be writing oneself, and this for most people.

I have not heard from Czartorisky but I think as you do that he must be very much at a loss to guess, what if it comes out of an *empty head*, upon so important an article as the existence or non existence of a whole nation, of which he is a part. As I have heard lately that the Emp. has about him almost all the Chancery I have had the last campain I shall be able to reinforce my claims and in the same time find out what Czartorisky is about.[8]

You wish to know something about the Congress[9]—1., Do you know that it has not begun? 2. do you know that they have no general principle no acknowledg⟨ed⟩ plan and therefore dont know

[4] Perhaps Adam Walker (1731?–1821), author and inventor, who lectured on natural philosophy from 1778, or one of his sons, William Walker (1767?–1816) or Deane Franklin Walker (1778–1865), both of whom assisted their father in his popular discourses in London.

[5] Dugald Stewart (1753–1828), professor of moral philosophy at Edinburgh University 1785–1820, was the author of *Elements of the Philosophy of the Human Mind*, 3 vols., London, 1792–1827.

[6] Thomas Reid (1710–96), appointed professor of moral philosophy at Glasgow University 1764; the same year in which his *An Inquiry into the Human Mind, on the Principles of Common Sense* was first published at Edinburgh.

[7] Apparently a reference to Bentham's writings on 'Parliamentary Reform', which formed the basis of many of his published works on the subject. The MSS were arranged in three parts: 'I, Necessity; II, Influence; III, Plan.' 'Influence', written mainly in 1809–10 but with additions in 1811, 1814, and 1815, deals with corruption.

[8] Chichagov was probably thinking principally of Ioannes Antonios Capodistria (1776–1831), a native of Corfu who had entered the Russian service in 1809. In 1812–13 he served as director of Chichagov's diplomatic chancery while the admiral was commander in chief of the army of the Danube.

[9] The Congress of Vienna, which had assembled in September 1814 to settle the borders of the European states after the Napoleonic wars. It continued until June 1815, when the final treaty was signed.

what to do, having no more reason to do one way than the other at last I dont think it can finish unless they put the European estates in lottery tickets and have it drawn by the most innocent of them, which is easily found, and settle accordingly.

Now if you understand the meaning of my scramble you must be as clever as I am in understanding the caracter of your writing though you kept me rather out of practice—

What is your brother doing? have you heard from him? is he satisfied with the french magna charta?[10] good by, god preserve your physic and the moral will preserve itself

2308

From Sir Samuel Bentham

26 February 1815

I have not received any copies of my 'Sir W. Petty's Plan'[2] of which some copies were to come in the ⟨. . .⟩ which followed me via Portsmouth and 2 or 3 copies were to have been sent to Ld Spencer, Lansdowne etc. By a short note I have received from Secretary Nelson[3] I am given to understand that several of the N Bd. are likely to be *pensioned off*, but I am left to guess *who*. It seems as if the public was dissatisfied with some naval concerns.

as you have never acknowledged the receipt of a letter I wrote on leaving England[4] telling you among other things of payment of my russian accounts having been stopped[5] and as three letters I put in the post at the same time one to the Comptroller[6] one to Mr Carr[7]

[10] The French charter of 4 June 1814, by which Louis XVIII granted a bicameral parliamentary system on the British model.

2308. [1] Koe MSS. Autograph. The first part of this letter is missing. Docketed: '(1) 1815 Feby. 26 / S.B. Saumur / to H.K. (2) Saumur 26 Feby. 1815 / Recd. March 6th / Answd. March 10th.' Addressed: 'Jeremy Be⟨ntham Esqr⟩ / or Herb⟨ert Koe Esqr⟩ / Queen ⟨Square Place⟩ / ⟨. . .?⟩.' Postmark: 'FOREIGN / MR 6 / 1815'.

[2] A work of Sir Samuel's printed but not published. No copy has been traced. A letter from Jeremy Bentham to Koe of 28 August 1817 in the Koe MSS indicates that the work related to 'Petty's Plan for Naval Instructions.' This might be a reference to 'A Treatise of Naval Philosophy' by Sir William Petty (1623–87), the political economist, which appeared in Thomas Hale's *An Account of Several New Inventions and Improvements Now Necessary for England*, London, 1691, pp. 117–32.

[3] Richard Alexander Nelson, secretary to the navy board 1796–1820.

[4] Missing.

[5] i.e. money Sir Samuel had claimed for his expenses during his visit to Russia. See M.S. Bentham, *The Life of Brigadier-General Sir Samuel Bentham*, London, 1862, pp. 302–4.

[6] Sir Thomas Boulden Thompson, comptroller of the navy 1806–16.

[7] Thomas William Carr, solicitor to the excise, who later acquired Sir Samuel's portion of the Hall Oak Farm estate.

and one from some of us to Miss Baillie[8] have neither been answered and the last we are told did *not* reach its destination we suspect they may have all miscarried—pray tell me if you received any such letter and perhaps you may have indirect [?] opportunity of enquiring if Mr Carr received his. your commission for an *intelligent boy* has not been forgotten.[9] as yet not success but you will hear of our endeavours in the next letter. I must employ the remainder of this sheet to give you or rather Mr Koe the contents or rather a copy of the letter I have at length received from Attorney Foss urging the giving up the Pianoforte.[10]

2309

To Robert Owen

25 March 1815 (Aet 67)

Queens Square Place Westr. 25 March 1815

Dear Sir

In spite of my endeavours to the contrary, I am reduced to employ this informal mode of signifying my desire to receive from the Lanark Mill concern on the 1st of July next the £1,000 stipulated for in *one* of the articles, (I have no means of saying *which*) of the Deed of Partnership.

On Saturday last, on the occasion of my return to London on the preceding day, Mr Koe, at my desire, wrote to friend Allen[2] to beg the favour of him (the article being a short one) to cause it to be copied and sent to me, that I might ground upon it a *Notice* in proper form: such notice being to be delivered three months before the said 1st of July, to each of the Partners. To this having received no answer, but hearing from Mr Mill two or three days ago that Mr Allen was to call upon him the next day, I took that opportunity of expressing my desire to see him at that time. So it has happened,

[8] Joanna Baillie.

[9] See letter 2285.

[10] After this there is a copy of a letter from Edward Smith Foss, solicitor, dated Essex Street, 31 January 1815, claiming that Miss Fordyce, perhaps Lady Bentham's aunt, shortly before her death, had expressed the wish that her grand piano should pass to Foss's youngest daughter Fanny.

2309. [1] MS in the possession of Mr Hamish Riley-Smith, Swanton Abbot Hall, Swanton Abbot, Norfolk. Autograph draft. Docketed: '1815 Mar 25 / J.B. Q.S.P. / to / Rob. Owen Esq. Lanark / Copy in James Hume's / hand (signed by J.B.) / Sent same day by Post'. James Hume, the nephew of Joseph Hume, was Bentham's secretary at this time.

[2] William Allen.

that being called off by some business into the country at no great distance, he excused himself by letter from calling at Mr Mills on that day, but said he should in a few days, expressing great satisfaction at the thoughts of seeing me.

Another matter, in respect of which by these circumstances I am left still in the dark, is the whole state of the concern—By one of the Articles, according to my recollection of it, a Statement of this sort was to be sent, on the first day of every month (*sent* to or *received by*—I forget which) to each of the Partners: and I believe by Post. No such statement has ever reached me: though it was before the end of Jany: that my signature to the deeds was affixed, and the money paid to Friend Allen in consequence.

It was not less to my own regret, than it naturally was to that of the other partners, that it was such an enormous length of time before that money of mine was paid. The reason and sole reason of the delay—you have always been sufficiently apprized—was the delay in reducing the Deeds to a determinate shape: a delay of which *that* which took place in the office of the professional men, was I take for granted, the cause.

My money has all along, been as I told you it would be—as ready to be paid, as on the day on which it was paid. The ground of the determination I took (as mentioned to you) not to pay it till the Partnership Deed was brought into a determinate shape; was—the alteration to which I saw it so frequently subjected: so that, at length, it might happen to it to have received such a shape, and *that* so different an one from that in which it was first represented to me, that I might not think it advisable to accede to it: and so, instead of such a share as I looked for, purchase, at the expence of so large a portion of my property, a law suit of the termination of which there could be no material prospect, during the short remainder of my life. This determination received no inconsiderable sanction from the event: for, my surprize, I must confess, was not small, upon finding that, in respect of his last sum of £10,000, which was not agreed for nor thought of, till long after the terms of mine were settled, Mr Walker[3] was to have his partnership Share, without any such obligation of lending other money at common interest as was imposed upon me. Of this change no intimation was given to me, till it was concluded upon: however, taking for granted that it had not been introduced, but on considerations which were regarded as *cogent*, I acquiesced.

You heard, I suppose, at the time, how it was that the pleasure I

[3] John Walker (d. 1824) of 49 Bedford Square and Arno's Grove, Southgate, who had taken three shares in the Lanark Mill.

had so long been promising myself of paying you a visit at Lanark, was lost to me.

Believe me ever, with the truest respect and regard

Dear Sir Yours,
Jeremy Bentham

P.S. Since writing the above, I learn by note from Mr Allen to Mr Mill that the reason why the partial transcript in question was not sent to me is—that the whole Deed is in Lawyers hands to be copied.

2310

From John McCreery

25 March 1815

Black Horse Court
25th March 1815

J MCreery's Compts wait on Mr Bentham, and the *Proofs* were sent with the Revises to Mr Koe's chambers some days since—As the heads of all Tables *depend upon their size when made up into their proper shape*, J MC. is quite at a loss how to set this head until the proofs are finally returned, and the matter put into the proper form—However, he will proceed to do it in any manner Mr Bentham may point out, if the explanation be not satisfactory.

2311

To John McCreery

25 March 1815 (Aet 67)

A

Q.S.P. 25 March 1815

Chrestomathic Table

To the Printer

When the Title comes to be printed, let the N.B. and all that follows it be in a considerably smaller type, to distinguish it the better from the matter which alone properly belongs to *the Title*. If

2310. [1] UC clxv. 6. Autograph. Docketed: '1815 Mar 25 / Chrestomathia / McCreery Printer / to / J.B. Q.S.P. / Title'.

John McCreery (1768–1832) printed both editions of part I and also part II of *Chrestomathia*.

2311. [1] UC clxv. 7. Autograph copy. Docketed: '1815 Mar 25 / A. / Chrestomathic / J.B. to Printer.'

in Italics, this effect would, I suppose, be the more perfectly produced.[2]

I am sorry not to see any *spacing* to the titles of the several sets of *Principles*,[3] as directed in the Proof

J.B.

2312

To John McCreery

25 March 1815 (Aet 67)

B

25 March 1815

For the short title at the top in capitals, instead of Chrestomathic Bill Instruction Table print in one line as follows—[2]
No. II. Chrestomathic Mesophantic i.e. Means-shewing, or Exercises-and-Principles-of-Management Shewing Table.

Then before the N.B. print as follows: viz. in Italics, as mentioned in the accompanying paper marked A.[3]
☞ This Table has for its accompaniment No. 1 Chrestomathic Telophantic, i.e. Ends-shewing or Subjects of Instruction shewing, Table

2313

From Alexander I

22 April 1815

Monsieur, c'est avec un grand intérêt que J'ai lu la lettre que vous m'avez écrite et les offres qu'elle contient d'aider de vos lumières les travaux législatifs qui auroient pour but de donner un

[2] Bentham was apparently referring here to the first of the 'Chrestomathic Instruction Tables' that were to appear in the 1815 edition of the first part of *Chrestomathia*.

[3] The second table contains the exercises to be performed in the school, and the principles upon which the teaching and management were to be based.

2312. [1] UC clxv. 8. Autograph copy. Docketed: '1815 Mar 25 / B / Chrestomathic / J.B. to Printer'.

[2] Bentham seems to have been referring to the second Chrestomathic Instruction Table, but the words he wanted to include do not appear in the table as printed in the 1815 edition of *Chrestomathia*. Alternatively, Bentham might have been giving McCreery directions for the 'whole sheet Table' designed to accompany *Chrestomathia*. See below, letter 2325 and n. 2.

[3] Letter 2311.

2313. [1] BL IX. 206–7. Copy. Docketed: '1815 Apr 22 / Emp. Alexand⟨er⟩ / Vienna / to / J.B. Q.S.P. / Copy.' Printed in *Papers Relative to Codification and Public Instruction*, London, 1817, p. 89 (Bowring, iv. 515).

nouveau code de loix à mes sujets.[2] Cet objet me tient trop à coeur et J'en connois trop la haute importance pour ne pas désirer pendant sa confection de profiter de votre savoir et de votre expérience. Je prescrirai à la commission qui en est chargée[3] d'avoir recours à vous et de vous addresser ses questions. Recevez en attendant mes remercimens sincères et le souvenir ci-joint comme une marque de l'estime particulière que Je vous porte[4]

Alexandre

Vienne
le 10/22 Apl. 1815

2314

FROM PRINCE ADAM CZARTORYSKI

25 April 1815

Vienne, le 25 Avril, 1815.

Monsieur,

Les courses continuelles que Sa Majesté l'Empereur a faites, après avoir quitté l'Angleterre, et les grands intérêts qui L'ont occupé depuis quelque tems, ne m'ont permis que dans ce moment de remettre à Sa Majesté Impériale la lettre que vous Lui avez addressée, Monsieur.[2] C'est avec un plaisir particulier que je m'empresse de Vous transmettre, ci-joint, la réponse de Sa Majesté Impériale.[3]

Veuillez recevoir également de mon côté l'assurance de la haute estime que je ne cesserai de Vous porter, et permettez moi d'avance de me flatter de l'espoir que Vous ne refuserez pas de nous éclairer aussi de vos lumières dans tout ce qui pourrait avoir rapport à la législation que Sa Majesté Impériale daignera accorder à la Pologne. Je ne manquerai pas, lorsqu'il en sera tems, de m'adresser à Vous, Monsieur, et de vous rappeller les promesses amicales que Vous avez bien voulû me faire à ce sujet.

Je profite, en attendant, avec un grand empressement de cette

[2] Letter 2266.

[3] A reference to the commission appointed by Alexander in 1801 to draw up a new code of laws for the Russian empire.

[4] This, according to Bowring, iv. 515 n., was a small ring enclosed in a packet bearing the imperial seal.

2314. [1] *Supplement to Papers Relative to Codification and Public Instruction*, London, 1817, pp. 82–3. Reprinted in Bowring, iv. 528.

[2] Letter 2266.

[3] Letter 2313.

occasion pour Vous prier d'agréer l'assurance de mes sentimens, et de la considération la plus distinguée avec laquelle j'ai l'honneur d'être,

Monsieur,
Votre très humble
Et très obéissant Serviteur,
A. Czartoriski.

2315

From Sir Samuel Romilly

30 May 1815

Dear Bentham

Mr. Galatin has no Recollection of having received your Packet while he was at Ghent[2] but he received there a good many Letters and packets to be forwarded to America and he thinks it very probable that yours was amongst them. All he received were sent to America. He supposes that the Letter having been from Mr. Koe whom he does not recollect may be the Cause of his not remembering that he received the Packet. Your Letter from Ford Abbey[3] Mr. G. received but not till he arrived in England Probably however you know all this already for he told me that it was his Intention to call on you

ever most sincerely
yours
Saml. Romilly

Russell Sq.
May 30

2315. [1] BL IX. 208–9. Autograph. Docketed: '1815 May 30 / Romilly Russel Sq. / to / J.B. Q.S.P. / Galatin's receipt / of J.B.s Letters— / non receipt of H.K.'s / G. Visitaturus at Q.S.P.'

[2] See letter 2305.

[3] Presumably letter 2305.

2316

To Lazare Carnot

8 June 1815 (Aet 67)

A M. le Ministre de l'Intérieur
Imprimé Ao. 1791, le présent Essai n'a jamais été publié,

8 June 1815

Un ouvrage en François, extrait des Mss. dont cet Essai fait partie, doit paroître dans peu à Genève. M. Étienne Dumont / Pierre Louis Etienne Dumont / avant son départ, au mois de Mai 1815, pour cette République, déclara l'intention, òu il étoit, d'y faire paroître cet ouvrage.[2] Il y avoit 'déjà mis' (disoit il) 'la dernière main'. Cependant son extrait, tiré d'un tas de papiers, jamais complette, n'a pas été revû par l'*auteur*, non plus que les autres ouvrages qui portent les deux noms: savoir I. *Traités de Législation Civile et Pénale:* 2. *Traité des Peines et des Récompenses.*

S'il avoit raison d'en espérer quelque utilité pour la France, il n'est pas à douter, que *M. Dumont* (bien que dans sa qualité de Citoyen de Genève, il a été couché (il n'a jamais sçû pourquoi) il y a quelques années, sous le Gouvernment François, sur la liste des *proscrits* soit Émigrés) trouveroit, dans cette espérance, un motif suffisant pour faire son possible pour hâter la publication de cet ouvrage.

M. le Ministre de l'Intérieur est prié de vouloir bien faire passer cet exemplaire au Président de la Chambre *des Députés*:[3] s'il en arrive deux exemplaires, l'un des deux au Président de la Chambre *des Peers*.[4] De l'autre côté se trouve une traduction à la hâte, en mauvais François, de la Note, écrite ce moment, au bas du *titre* de l'ouvrage Jeremy Bentham Juin 1815

Ces règles, dont le tout ensemble a été déduit de la pratique qui s'observe en Angleterre, et dont (à ce que l'on croit) la plupart lui appartient exclusivement,—règles dont une esquisse raisonnée ne se trouve encore publiée dans aucune ouvrage,—sont celles à l'observation des quelles (à ce que l'on croit) le Parliament Britannique est principalement redevable (de même que les Assemblées Anglo-

2316. [1] Letter in copyist's hand in the British Library copy of *Essay on Political Tactics*, London, 1791 (shelf mark 80006 f. 10).

Lazare Nicolas Marguerite Carnot (1753–1823), French military engineer and statesman, was minister of the interior during the Hundred Days.

[2] What was to be published as *Tactique des assemblées législatives*, with *Traité des sophismes politiques*, 2 vols., Geneva, 1816.

[3] Jean-Denis, comte Lanjuinais (1753–1827).

[4] Jean Jacques Régis de Cambacérès, duc de Parma (1753–1824).

Americaines) pour sa capacité d'agir librement et avec effet, et par là pour son existence. Et c'est sur ce modèle-ci, que les opérations et les débâts de toutes les Assemblées, tant soit peu nombreuses, tant volontaires (soit non-officielles) qu'officielles, s'y conduisent toujours.

2317

FROM JOHN HERBERT KOE

17 June 1815

Lincoln's Inn Saty. 17 June 1815.

By mistake I took these papers away with me, and thinking you might want them, I send them back.[2]

Sir S. Romilly calculates then on seeing you on Monday and has made it a $\frac{1}{4}$ past 6: and he mentioned to me, as I will tell you, why before he thought he should have been unable to prevail upon you to come.

2318

TO PRINCE ADAM CZARTORYSKI

21 June 1815 (Aet 67)

To Prince Czartoryski.
Queen Square Place, Westminster,
21*st June* 1815.

Dear Sir

—For one thing I must begin with casting myself upon the Emperor's forgiveness as well as yours; that is the enormous length of time (upwards of a month), that has intervened between my

2317. [1] UC clxv. 9. Autograph, with the exception of the date, which was added by Bentham. Docketed: '1815 June 17 / Chrestomathia / H.K. Linc Inn / to / J.B. Q.S.P. / Sends the 2d. Proposal / drawn by Mill / Romilly visurit.' Addressed: 'To / J. Bentham Esq / Queen Sq Place / Westmr.'

[2] The docket suggests that the papers were drafts of the proposals for a prospectus of the Chrestomathic school published as *Proposals for establishing in the Metropolis, a Day School, in which an example may be set of the application of the methods of Dr. Bell, Mr. Lancaster, and others, to the higher branches of education*, London, 1816.

2318. [1] *Memoirs of Prince Adam Czartoryski and his Correspondence with Alexander I*, ed. Adam Gielgud, 2 vols., London, 1888, ii. 294–301. This version must have been based on the letter Czartoryski received. Bentham used a copy or draft for his *Supplement to Papers Relative to Codification and Public Instruction*, London, 1817, where this letter appears on pp. 86–96 (Bowring, iv. 528–30).

receiving of the two letters,[2] and the despatching of these my answers. Another thing for which, likewise, I must beg your indulgence, is—the rough state in which I am reduced to send a copy of mine to the Emperor, for your use.[3]

Both trespasses have their source in an engagement under which the letter found me: viz. that of drawing up for this country, for the use of a voluntary association, a plan of National Education,[4] in relation to which I may perhaps take the liberty of troubling you with a few words before the close of the present letter; or at any rate by the next messenger: the whole business was in danger of being put a stop to for an indefinite length of time had I not devoted myself exclusively to it. As to your copy (I mean of my letter to the Emperor) I hope you will find it legible, as consistently with my engagements, time could not be found for the copying and revisal of another fair one.

As to the original, you, as well as he, will (I fear) be sadly annoyed by it, were it only for the length of it. It was, however, absolutely necessary I should speak out, and I saw no hope of being able to do so, to my purpose, in any lesser compass. I hear it said everywhere that he is a good-natured man: by what you will find me saying to him, that quality will be put to the *test*. From me, if he has patience enough, he may thus *read*, what from a man in any other situation, it is not in the nature of things that he should either *read* or *hear*.

A bandage on his eyes—leading strings on his shoulders—on this part of the field of Government, such has hitherto been his custom. My aim is to rid him of those appendages: is it possible he should forgive me? Forgive me or not, that is not the point: that he should suffer himself to be rid of them, *that* is the one thing needful.

I hope this will not draw *you* into a scrape; a scrape on your part so perfectly undeserved: for no such thing as a *tale out of school* have I ever heard from *you*.

If, by any thing I have said, an end should be put, not only to *that* correspondence, but to another which is so truly flattering to me, I shall be truly sorry; but it was necessary to run the risk, for I think you will agree with me that whether *with* it anything be done or no, without it nothing was at any rate to be done.

The letter addressed to his Majesty, I put into a separate packet. I avoid purposely any such attempt as that of making it pass through *your* hands. In relation to an official person there so frequently alluded to, it was absolutely necessary I should speak without

[2] Letters 2313 and 2314. [3] Letter 2319.

[4] *Chrestomathia*.

reserve: and there seemed neither use nor necessity for *your* being involved in such business.

Even if it should be in the *constitutional* part of the field of law that my labours, such as they are, should be desired by you (though for reasons already given, *that* is the part in relation to which my hopes of being of use are least sanguine) I repeat my promise to put them under your command:

I. Because I do not absolutely despair of being able to do some good—here a little and there a little—even in relation to that branch.

II. Because (as I say to the Emperor) that is the branch which I imagine *you* had more particularly in view. But my expectations are much more *extensive*, as well as sanguine, in relation to the *Penal* and *Civil* branches: including, in both cases (though so far as concerns the organisation of the *Judicial Establishment* it belongs to the *constitutional* branch) the *system* of *Procedure.*—Why? Because in the *Civil* branch there will be a good deal of matter, and in the *Penal* a good deal *more* applicable, with little or no difference, under *any form of Government.* So far, therefore, I could myself *propose* matter, with a tolerable expectation of its being received, and thence with a proportionable degree of facility and alacrity: whereas in regard to *constitutional* law, in which is included the *form of Government*, it would be folly for me to pretend to originate anything considerable.—What is the monarch willing to *leave* or to *concede* to you nobles and the great body of the people, taken together? What are the monarch and you nobles, taken together, willing to *leave* or to *concede* to the great body of the people? What are the people at present in a condition to *receive*, if the powers, on which it depends, were willing to concede it to them? What more, within a moderate space of time, may they be *expected* to come of themselves to be *in*, or to be capable of being put *into* a condition to receive,—and by what means? All this, if known to anybody, is known to you:—not a particle of it to me.

When, near the close of the reign of poor King Stanislaus,[5] a constitutional code for Poland was drawn up,[6] *Bukati*[7] (I think it was he that was then resident here) sent me a copy of it. What is become of it I do not exactly know. But what I remember is—that people in general were here much pleased with it: myself among the

[5] Stanislaus Augustus Poniatowski (1732–98), last king of independent Poland as Stanislaus II 1764–95.

[6] On 3 May 1791 the Polish *Seym* issued a new constitution, but this was withdrawn after the Russian invasion of 19 May.

[7] Francis Bukati (d. 1797), secretary to the Polish agency in London *c.*1773–80. See *Correspondence*, ii. 344 n.

rest, as far as I had looked at it; which was very slightly; for being deeply embarked in other pursuits at the time, nothing called upon me to suspend them for any such purpose as the study of it.

On the present occasion, *that* paper, is it intended to form the *basis*? Here would be a field for experimenting in: and to a monarch with the whole Russian Empire under such entire command, what possible danger can there be from any such experiment? Under the Great Turk was not Ragusa even a Republic?[8] In such a case more real efficiency than what he would lose in the shape of *coercive power*, the Autocrat of Russia would gain in the shape of gentle *influence*: loss, were there any would be all of it to the successor,— who, not having been the author of the *boon*, would not be a sharer in the gratitude:—But, even by him, he being used to the comparatively new state of things, the loss, if there were any, would not be felt.

It is now about forty years since I began to lift up my prayers for Poland. The most intimate friend I had was John Lind,[9] privy councillor to the King, and under his Majesty, original institutor, as well as director, of a school for 400 cadets at Warsaw, and Governor of Prince Stanislaus,[10] nephew to the poor king, whose business at our Court he did for a number of years, writing a letter from London every other post day. Bukati being all the while the resident kept for show, because our King would not see in that character one of his own subjects.

Lind's first appearance at Warsaw was in that of reader of English to your father[11] or your uncle, I forget which it was. Oh, how he used to talk and talk of Poland! And how he used to curse the Fredericks[12]—great as they were—not to mention other persons.

Being of all connections and of no party, I have just sent off to Paris a large packet of printed copies of a part of the educational scheme to leading men there, Bourbonnites, Napoleonites, and Republicans promiscuously,—some of them old friends of mine.

[8] Suleiman I (1496–1566), the 'Magnificent', was sultan of Turkey 1520–66. Ragusa (now Dubrovnik) was subject to the Venetians, the Hungarians, and then the Ottomans, but remained a city republic with considerable autonomy.

[9] John Lind (1731–81), a close friend of Bentham in the 1770s, when he was unofficial Polish minister in London, undertaking Bukati's duties. For Lind's relations with Bentham see *Correspondence*, i and ii, as index.

[10] Prince Stanislaus Poniatowski (1754–1833).

[11] Prince Adam Kazimirez Czartoryski (1731–1823).

[12] Frederick the Great of Prussia (1712–86), who had seized part of Poland in the first partition of 1772, and his successor, Frederick William II (1744–97), who took still more in the second and third partitions of 1793 and 1795. Lind, of course, was not alive at the time of the last two partitions.

If you follow the camp, perhaps you may make prizes of them: yet I should be sorry you should; were it only because while you are at Paris, you would not be at *Warsaw*; and whether you are so or no, I am of the number—and that I believe not a small one—of those who are impatient for your being there.

Well, but about this education scheme: were it only to account for the delay, a few words I find I must trouble you with about it even here:—

An experiment of it is about to made in a part of that garden of mine which you saw. It has for its object the applying to the higher branches of learning, and the higher as well as middling ranks of the community, that *new* system of instruction, of the success of which you can not but be more or less apprized.

Brougham, *Sir James Macintosh*—and if I can persuade him to lend his *name*—for that is all he can have *time* to lend—*Romilly*, will be at the head of it. For the *details* of the management there will be some very efficient men, with whose names you can scarcely be acquainted. For reasons not worth troubling you with, my fixed determination has been from the very first, not to be of the number. In the *Executive* department, I accordingly bear no part: but of the *Legislative* the *initiation* has fallen entirely to my share. My labours in that field had (I believe) already commenced, when I had the honour of receiving you: and, for want of their being completed, the business was at a stand, and by a few days more of delay, the season might have been lost—(I mean the time when the expected *contributors* are in town)—and the execution of the plan deferred for a whole twelvemonth; and thereby perhaps finally defeated.

It is now in such advance, that everything which it is necessary to publish in the first instance, is either already in print or in the printer's hands. A copy or two will, I trust, be brought to you by the next messenger. On this field, at any rate, in doing what I have done, I consider myself as being at work not less for *Russia* and *Poland*, than for London. For the elementary branches, as taught upon the Bell and Lancaster system, *Paris* is already provided with a schoolmaster from hence. The son of a Protestant clergyman—Martin,[13] I think, is his name—was in Louis XVIII's time sent from the south of France to a Lancasterian school for the express purpose of learning the method, and is now at Paris; and (I understand) much caressed there.

His business there is to *form* Instructors. The salary offered to

[13] Francis Martin, a Swiss Protestant clergyman who came to London in September 1814 to study the Lancasterian system and was appointed director of the Lancasterian school on Rue St Jean de Beauvais, Paris, May 1815.

him was £200: for such a station, a very considerable salary at Paris. No, (says he) *that* would be too much. Success or failure depends upon the degree of economy. Such a sum (naming it, perhaps a quarter as much) is all that you need give. By this the price will be set to those who succeed me. If in my instance, in consideration of my being the first institutor, you see any claim to extraordinary remuneration, let *that* come by and by, when by experience you see what I have done. Just the same thing might the Emperor do for Petersburg and Warsaw. The expense—I mean the *necessary* expense—would be next to nothing; and if this can not succeed with you, I am at a loss to think what else can.

For this purpose you will see how necessary it has been for me to take a fresh peep into every nook and cranny of the whole field of art and science. My business having been to apply the new method of instruction to every part of that field that is deemed capable of receiving it. My endeavour has been to reduce the whole sketch into as narrow a compass as possible: and the narrower the compass the greater the quantity of time which it has cost me. Locke's Essay (so he tells us in his preface) is too long—Why? 'Because' (says he) 'I had not time to make it shorter.'[14]

If upon the field of codification, it be in my power to throw any *light*, you see the terms upon which it is in the power of your Alexander to have it? Exactly the terms upon which God Almighty had *His*: a couple of words the whole of the expense.

I hope the Emperor will not be angry with me for returning his ring;[15] if it had been a *brass* or a *glass* one, I would have kept it. If he will send the value of it, and no more, to my masters and employers, as above, for their *school*, I as well as they will be all gratitude. But of this in that ensuing letter with which this threatens you. Believe me ever, with the truest respect, dear sir, your most obedient servant.

Jeremy Bentham.

Prince Adam Czartoryski.

[14] John Locke, *An Essay Concerning Human Understanding*, ed. Peter H. Nidditch, Oxford, 1975, p. 8 ('Epistle to the Reader').

[15] See letter 2313 and n. 4.

2319

To Alexander I

June 1815 (Aet 67)

London, June, 1815.

Sire,

I open this moment the letter in your own hand, with which Your Imperial Majesty has been pleased to honour me.[2] Through another channel, I receive, in the words *bague de prix*, the interpretation of the word *souvenir*.[3] My endeavours to make myself understood on that subject, have I fear, not been altogether successful. The same pacquet which conveys to Your Majesty this expression of my gratitude, will bear witness for me, that, in my eyes,—after the proof afforded me, as above, of the place which I am fortunate enough to possess in Your Majesty's good opinion,—money's worth as well as money, is in this case, without value. The Imperial seal will be found unbroken.

Your Majesty's *wish* is—to turn my humble services in some way or other to account. In that view it is, that Your Majesty has been pleased to point out a particular *course*. But, so it happens, that if this and no other were the *course* pursued, it is not in the nature of the case, that that *wish* should in any degree take effect. The impossibility is the result of circumstances, which to Your Majesty are not known, and which it is therefore necessary for me to bring to view: which done, I will take the liberty of submitting *two courses*, in either of which, the opinion Your Imperial Majesty is pleased to entertain of me, might be productive of public benefit.

'Je prescrirai,' (says the Letter) 'Je prescrirai à la Commission d'avoir recours à vous, et de vous addresser ses questions.' The course is a perfectly regular one, and nothing is more natural than that it should have been suggested, or even that it should have suggested itself, to Your Majesty. Yet if this were all, Your Majesty's intentions, it will be seen, would be altogether frustrated.

In my former letter,[4] a proposal I took the liberty of submitting was, that I should receive Your Majesty's orders for the drawing up, upon a plan of my own, and submitting to Your Majesty, a *Projet de Loi*, on the subject of some large portion of that *compleat* body of

2319. [1] *Supplement to Papers Relative to Codification and Public Instruction*, London, 1817, pp. 31–81. Reprinted in Bowring, iv. 516–28.

[2] Letter 2313.

[3] See below, letter 2337 and n. 24.

[4] Letter 2266.

law, which has so long been in contemplation: and in particular, of that which belongs to the *penal* branch: upon the closer view, which the present occasion has obliged me to take of the subject, the course which, as above, had at that time presented itself simply as an eligible one, now presents itself to me as the *only* eligible one.

The *penal*—I understood from good authority a little more than a twelvemonth ago—was the branch, on the subject of which, at that time, or a little before that time, the greatest advances had been made. From the Commission alluded to, questions relative to this branch (suppose) are addressed to me. For giving answers to those questions, with any prospect of being of use, there is but one course which I could take: and this is—to draw up as above, the proposed *Projet de Loi*, and so transmit the *tout ensemble*. Yes, Sire: upon the *tout ensemble*, in a case like this, every thing depends. The points to which the questions would point, would be such and such particular points. What, in such case, I should have to say in answer, I well know.—'It will not be possible for me (I should say) to determine within myself what is best to be done in relation to those points in particular, until it is understood by me what is proposed to be done in relation to such and such other points, with which those are necessarily connected.'

In an all-comprehensive body of law, such as that in question, each provision requires to be adjusted to, and for that purpose confronted with, every other. In no other way should I ever think, in no other way did I ever think, of drawing up the *Projet* of a *Code*. Thence it is, that if not in the first instance, at the long run, any papers sent by me in the shape of answers, would, if they amounted to any thing, fall into that very shape, in which I ventured to propose they should be presented in the first instance, and in which the course in question would not admit of their being presented, if at all, till at the end of an indefinitely greater length of time.

On a subject such as this, it is only in proportion as a man is himself master of it, that he is qualified for putting questions to others. On a subject such as this, in the situation occupied by the persons alluded to, if men are perfectly qualified for putting questions, they are pretty well qualified for doing the business without putting questions: at any rate, if, in their own opinion, they are qualified for putting any such questions, in that same opinion they can scarcely fail of being qualified for doing the business without putting any such questions.

But, the better *qualified* they are in their own opinion, for doing the business, and thence for putting questions in relation to it, the less will they feel *disposed*: and assuredly so long as by any means it could be avoided, no such questions would ever be put.

Suppose them however put—put by the persons alluded to—the questions are still *their* questions. In relation to those questions, before they are sent, the determination will have been already taken: taken by the very persons by whom the questions will have been penned.

The transmission of the question will be matter of *form*. Supposing answers sent, the reception given to the answers will be matter of form. If the acknowledgement of their being received can be avoided, avoided it will be.

If it can not be avoided, the matter of the answers divides itself into two parts. In this or that part, does it happen to be *conformable* to the predetermination, taken as above? in that part it is of course *needless*: useless therefore,—in any other character, than that of a testimony, in favour of the wisdom, by which the predetermination was made:—as to the *unconformable* remainder, coming as it does, from a foreigner, who, if he has some notion of the business taken in general, at any rate does not understand the state of the particular country in question, it is of course *inapplicable*.

Sire, this is not surmise: it is certainty—certainty, derived from reiterated experience.

The business being, under Your Majesty's government, as the like businesses are with us, in *form* put into the hands of a *Commission*, or, as we say here, a *Board*,—Your Majesty's letter to me, could not, with strict propriety, have spoken of it in any other terms. But, so far as concerns original penmanship, this same business (it is no secret) is,—as in the first instance every such business ought to be, or rather can not but be,—in the hands of one and but one person. Now this one person is generally known:[5] the others being *figurantes*, and, except to the readers of Your Majesty's Court Calendar, not known. Of this one person, and no other, I must therefore speak, on pain of being unintelligible.

Of this person, though near two years in Your Majesty's dominions, (it was in the years 1786 and 1787) not having visited either Capital, I have not any personal knowledge. But of *his* writings *I* know a great deal more, and of *mine he* knows a great deal more, than it is agreeable to *him* to think of. Ever since he began his career, he has beheld in my name an object of terror: an emotion, which, at several distinct times, in the view of several different

[5] Baron Gustav Andreevich Rosenkampf (1764–1832), head of the working staff on the law commission, president of the tribunal of justice at Dorpat, Livonia. See letter 1851 and n. 7, *Correspondence*, vii.

persons, has betrayed itself: betrayed itself by symptoms, such as would figure in a Comedy. Your Majesty has no time for gossiping anecdotes, or I could furnish written proofs.

Sire, I shall as soon have answers to send to the Emperor of Morocco, as to a Commission so *headed*. But if you have a mind for a laugh, tell him you have received papers from me, and that they are satisfactory. But salts and smelling-bottle should be at hand.

Sire, I should ill warrant the good opinion entertained of me, if I hesitated to pronounce him *radically* incapable: for, supposing this to be a truth, I am perhaps the only person, from whom, with any chance of good effect, Your Majesty could receive it. The persons, by whom on such a subject, any judgment at all could be pronounced, are extremely few: of these few, probably not one, how intimate soever his persuasion were, could dare to avow it to Your Majesty: unless, perhaps, it were some *rival*, whose suggestions would be liable to be referred altogether to the motive indicated by that name.

Meantime, from the person in question, with his colleagues and supporters, Your Imperial Majesty will have received the assurance, that no such assistance, either from myself or from any other foreigner, is necessary: and that not being necessary, it would be but an incumbrance: for that no foreigner has or can have any tolerable acquaintance with the business: while *they* are become compleat masters of it. In relation to this matter, I will venture to submit to Your Imperial Majesty the following observations.

When, from any country, a compleat body of law, such as appears to be proposed,—or any one of its largest divisions, such as a Penal, a Civil, or a Constitutional Code,—is in contemplation,—in respect of publicity, two modes of going about the business—the *close* and the *open* mode—require to be distinguished.

Carried on in the *close* mode, it is carried on as in ordinary cases, by a single person, or some small number of persons, appointed by the sovereign; and not made public at all, till it comes out *armed with the force of law*.

Carried on in the *open* mode, the work, antecedently to its coming out armed with the force of law, is made public, viz. in the way in which literary works in general are made public: and this, for the purpose—if not expressly declared, at least implied and generally understood—of its being taken for the subject of observations, such as any person (keeping his expressions of course within the bounds of respect and decency) may, in a manner alike public, feel disposed to communicate. The mode, which, in the present case, will, in course, be recommended by the Commission, is the close mode.

Why?—because in this mode, their inaptitude, be it ever so compleat, will be screened: screened, till exposure comes too late for obviating and preventing mischief, with which it is pregnant: whereas, by the *open* mode, it would be brought to light in time.

In regard to the demand for previous publicity, altogether different is the present case from that of *ordinary* legislation; i.e. legislation taking for its subject matters of detail, as they happen to present themselves. In *that* case, the business is, of course, and must be carried, and cannot but be, carried on in the *close* mode. This closeness is what follows from the constitution of the Government: as that does from the extensiveness of the territory, and the state of society among the great bulk of its inhabitants. By want of time, if by nothing else, previous publicity is in that case rendered generally impracticable. The demand for legislation being, in this case, the result of sudden exigency,—such exigency requires to be provided for as it occurs, and without loss of time.

Quite *different* in this respect—not to say opposite—is the present case:—the case (it may be called) of *Codification*: where, of the entire field of *law*—a field little less extensive than the whole field of human action—some very large portion—(a third, a fourth, a fifth, or some such matter)—and which, in some way or other, is—and for ages has—in some shape or other, at successive times, though, hitherto, as to a large proportion of it, in a bad enough shape—lain covered with law,—is to receive an entire new covering all at once. The field having already its old covering, hence comes the *facility* of waiting, and that without any more than the accustomed inconvenience, for whatsoever lights may be capable of being collected, for the elucidation of the ground: and thence, during whatsoever length of time may, for so important a purpose, be found necessary: *waiting*, viz. before final enactment; the formation of the new one, if as yet unformed, or the examination of it, if formed, being all the while going on. But, of this same new covering, whatsoever may be the sort of matter which it substitutes to the old, one sure effect will be, (unless in so far as this or that particular exception comes to have been made and declared) to reduce the old matter, in its whole extent, to a non-entity. And, along with the *facility*, hence comes the *demand* for a delay—a precaution at once so necessary and so safe.

In a case like this, answers from me received or not received, when, by Your Majesty's authority, the Code as penned by the Commission first comes out, will it come out already armed with the force of law? or only in the shape of a *Projet de Loi*, continued thereupon in that state, for a length of time more or less considerable,—to the intent that, by that means, the sense of the public at large, or of a determinate portion of the public, may, in the mean time be, in some shape or other, taken upon it?

On the first of these plans, in case of an ill-penned Code, the mischief would commence immediately, and without so much as the appearance of a chance of its being prevented.

In the other case, an appearance there will be, of a chance of prevention: but very little more than an appearance will there be. —From the calling into question, in any one particular, the more or less explicitly declared excellence of it, what inducement in any shape can any other person find? what prospect of advantage, either to himself, or to Your Majesty's service? At Your Majesty's ear, stands the official adviser,—seen to have been in possession of it for these dozen years or some such matter,—by whom you will be assured, that the observations are nothing worth, and the author an impertinent, from whom no good service, in this or any other shape, is ever to be expected.

Such is the sort of retribution, and the only one, which, in this *close* mode, every one could entertain a reasonable *expectation* of receiving,—for any labour, which, on so important and vast a field, he might otherwise feel disposed to bestow.

Sire, the mischiefs which,—from so prodigiously extensive, and at the same time new, a body of law, drawn up by such hands,—the population of your Majesty's vast Empire will stand exposed to, are such as I tremble but to think of.

In detail, a great deal of bad legislation, the work of a variety of hands, all of them very indifferently qualified, may be endured, and the mischief flowing from it may continue to flow without much notice. Why?—because, being composed of additions gradually made to an original stock, under the influence of which every body was born,—while, of the mischief which is the result of it, a part more or less considerable, in consequence of the observation taken of it, comes sooner or later to be put a stop to,—the rest is imputed to the imperfections inseparable from human nature.

But, of a body of new law, such as that proposed, the effect is, in some very large proportion, as above, to annihilate the whole body of that fabrick upon which every thing which is valuable or dear to man depends: and, when the gap thus made in the old matter comes to be filled up with the new,—then it is, that, of any one of the inadvertences, or ignorances, or wrong judgments, which in this *close* mode, may with so full an assurance be expected,—ruin, to thousands and tens of thousands, will be but the too probable consequence.

At the same time it will be known—for it is known already—that the labours of an Englishman—of an Englishman, whose labours in this line stand approved, not only by other governments,—by the Bavarian—by the French, at several different periods—but by your Majesty's,—and even by your Majesty in person—that these labours have, to this very purpose, been for these dozen years at your Majesty's command: and, all that while, those who, on this part of the field, have been in possession of your Majesty's ear, have been successful in their endeavours to keep the fruit of those labours from making its appearance.

In the hands of several different persons,—all unconnected with each other—all occupying, at different times, in their respective departments, the highest posts in your Majesty's service,—I could give your Majesty reason to be assured that my being occupied in a task of this nature, would be a result in no small degree advantageous to your Majesty's Empire: in this or that instance, matter to this effect, addressed to myself: in other instances, to other people. If such had not been their real persuasion, what could have been their inducement for declaring as much, to or concerning an unconnected, and in most instances personally unknown, foreigner?—Then why not say as much to your Majesty?—Sire, they were no longer in office: or, if they were, it had not been, or was not at that time exactly within their province; or if it was, confidence was, as the event proved, on the decline.

The disappointments which, in this same ground, your Majesty has already experienced, are no secret. Now by what cause is it that these disappointments have been produced?—By this one circumstance;—by the adoption of the *close*, to the exclusion of the *open* mode: by the omitting to take the benefit of such lights, as the world at large might be capable of affording: by exclusive confidence, placed in a small number of persons, or rather in a single person, of whose aptitude for the task no proof has ever seen the face of day: a task in which the whole field of government is included, and for which the whole stock of genius, knowledge, and talent, which the civilized world affords, would not be too great.

Sir, there exists not, even in this country, that man, or that limited number of men, who in the eyes of the public, or even in their own, would be competent to such a task, without receiving all such lights, as, after publication made for that declared purpose, the public in its utmost amplitude should be disposed to furnish. In the Commission in question, is it possible your Majesty should continue to see any such matchless combination of genius, intelligence, and wisdom—to say nothing of probity—as should render superfluous in Russia, those precautions, which in England are so indispensable?

As to *competition*,—in the close mode, of course there could not be any such thing:—competition I mean as between two or more entire *draughts*, i. e. *proposed Codes*—drawn by different hands: unless it were between member and member of that same *Commission* or *Board*; which, in the present instance, I take for granted, is not to be expected. By possibility, the *open* mode might be preserved, *without* admitting competition. In the state of a *Projet*, antecedently to its being armed with the force of law, one work, and no more, being admitted, such one work might be made public, with liberty to persons at large, or to particular descriptions of persons, to make observations on it:—to point out any such imperfections of detail that might seem imputable to it, but not *to* propose another *Projet*, in the whole or in part, in lieu of it: in a word, to point out here and there a symptom of weakness, but not to present any thing like a general and radical remedy.

But, in this case, in so far as the mode of proceeding can with any propriety be said to be open, its *openness* will, comparatively speaking, be of little use. Let the badness of the only work exhibited be rendered ever so manifest, no better will be produced. Let the disease be shewn to be ever so desperate, no remedy will be at hand to be administered. The utmost good, which, in this way can be done, will be—the putting an end to the design altogether, by shewing the unfitness of the hands, who have been employed in it. But, even out of this good—negative as it is, and no better—a great evil would be but too apt to arise. Instead of the incapacity of the workman, the cause of the bad performance may be looked for—and being willingly looked for, may be found—in the nature of the *sort* of work: in its supposed incapacity of being well performed: and, supposing the unfitness of the *individual* work sufficiently recognized, this of course is the hypothesis, which by the strongest ties of interest, the unskilful workman will stand engaged to advocate.

So much for the *close* mode. Now as to the *open* mode, competition as above, being supposed admitted. What are its advantages?

In the first place, all that incalculable mass of mischief just alluded to, is avoided.

In the next place, the greatest probability is obtained, of the best possible code: a probability, the greater the number of the competitors on the one hand, and of the critics, in the character of advocates and judges, on the other.

In the third place, the comfort and satisfaction, which so unequivocal a proof of the sincerest regard for their feelings, their wishes, their good opinion, their lasting welfare, could not fail to afford to the thinking part of the people. A more unequivocal one it surely is not in the power of a sovereign to give. *Without* this token,—the best possible code, suppose it even a perfect one, will want much of producing the good effect, which, by means of a work of that sort is capable of being produced: *with* so expressive a token, any inconvenience, of which the change may, in spite of every care, happen to be productive, will receive no slight compensation, as well as reduction, from the proof afforded of the goodness of the intention that gave birth to it.

In the last place comes, as the effect of all these several causes, the ease to your Imperial Majesty's conscience. Think, Sir, of the responsibility—the tremendous responsibility—which you would incur, by setting the destiny of forty millions of souls, to hang, as it were, by a thread, upon a work of such vast extent, drawn up—I can not but repeat it—by such ill-qualified hands. Yes, Sir, this would be responsibility indeed. Pursue the *open* mode—receive—not from mine only, but from every other hand, that can find such an offering to make, whatsoever it shall have to give—plan for the whole, plan for this or that part—miscellaneous observations,—no such burthen will, in that case, press upon your Imperial Majesty's conscience. The consciences, upon which whatever burthen there is will press, will be—in the first place, those of the volunteer workmen themselves: in the next place, those of the *thinking*, though not *working*, part of the public, whose suffrages, by another application of the same all-preserving principle—the *principle of publicity*, it will have been your Majesty's endeavour to collect. At the door of this many-seated tribunal, should its judgments prove more or less erroneous, will all blame from the error lie. Your Imperial Majesty,—having towards the avoidance of error, done all that it is in the power of man to do,—will stand clear from all self-reproach, as well as from all censure.

Your Imperial Majesty has seen, on the one hand, the *close* mode, with its mischiefs: on the other hand, the *open* mode, with its advantages. Let the course, which, from the first, I ventured to point out, be adopted,—your Imperial Majesty will see all those mischiefs avoided—all these beneficial results secured.

In my proposal, as above,—the *open* mode, with all the advantages naturally attached to it—the open mode, with the benefit of *competition*—was implicitly included.

My *Projet*, I took for granted, would be presented to your Imperial Majesty ready printed. Produced thus to the world before it had ever met your Imperial Majesty's eye,—the work might be ever so inapplicable, or even absurd, your Imperial Majesty would not be subjected to any imputation on that score. The only source of responsibility would be the choice thus made of the person, to whom the encouragement would thus have been given: but, from all imputation of improvidence on that score, your Imperial Majesty stands, it is hoped, sufficiently exempted, by the testimonies, which in my first letter, were submitted to your Imperial Majesty's notice.

In this state, let me suppose it published (I mean my *Projet*) at St. Petersburgh. Over and above any particular degree of aptitude which it may be found to possess,—the advantages which result from the circumstance of its coming from a foreign hand, will presently (I can not but flatter myself) appear manifest.

Of any such publicity given to the work, the object or end in view can be no other, than the receiving from the thinking part of the public, indication of any such imperfections, as it may be in the power of any person to point out in it,—with or without the indication of correspondent remedies, or supposed remedies: unless for a distinct object be to be taken the enabling and encouraging them, to give indications of the like nature, in relation to whatsoever body of law may have been the final result.

In this view, when the publication is announced,—*notice* given in some shape or other to the public at large,—notice, having for its object the obtaining, from all such as in their own conception are qualified to furnish it, communication, of the sort just mentioned,—seems to follow as a matter of course.

Publication, it is true, might have place, without any such *notice*. Moreover, the notice being given, the purport of it might confine itself to simple permission; without any direct and positive invitation. But, without positive invitation,—very limited, and even precarious, would the effect of the notice be in the way of *encouragement*. So, on the other hand, the warmer the invitation, the stronger the encouragement: the stronger the encouragement, and therefore the greater the probability thus afforded, of the accomplishment of the object thus supposed to be in view.

In so far as, in any imperfection or supposed imperfection having place any where in the proposed body of law, it happens to any person to see a probable cause of mischief, to himself or any other person or persons, in whose welfare he feels an interest—in so far, to engage him to do what depends on him towards making known such mischief, to those in whose power it is, or to him seems to be, to afford relief, *motives* can not be wanting: all that can be necessary is the removal of *restraints*. By the invitation above supposed, this necessary removal will, at least, be strongly promoted, if not universally accomplished: I say, *if not universally accomplished*; for, in so far as, in the event of his making any such communication, an individual, by whom it would otherwise have been made, sees reason for apprehending injury at the hands of any subordinates,—in so far the invitation, given by the sovereign, can not but, in the instance of that individual, fail of such its intended purpose.

But *motives*, how adequate so ever, suffice not without adequate *means*: and, for the purpose of giving publicity in this way to all such useful information as, if *means* were not wanting, might be afforded,—the stock of necessary means at the command of individuals, would, I cannot but apprehend, be very far from sufficient, unless *facilities* were for this purpose afforded by the hand of government.

By the following very simple arrangement, if I do not much deceive myself, not only may the facilities necessary to this purpose be afforded,—but, in the only way in which it can be either necessary or conducive to the service, *encouragement* may be afforded, and *that* without any unproductive or superfluous expense; and moreover—and still without any additional expense—a *School of legislation* formed, out of which, for filling offices belonging to this department, individuals may be chosen, distinguished by the most conclusive proofs of that aptitude, of the deficiency of which the recorded confessions lie before me: proofs, such as the nature of things will not suffer to be afforded by any other means.

In the whole or in part, let the author of every such communication be eased of the expense of *printing*: in the whole or in part, let him moreover be eased of the expense of *printing-paper*: viz. to the extent of a limited number of copies: but with permission to add, at his own expense, paper for as many additional copies as he thinks fit:—and so in regard to *advertisements*: money, received on account of the sale, to be paid, either all of it to the author, or all of it to the Treasury, or in this or that proportion divided between the individual and the Treasury, according to circumstances.

But an essential precaution, without which, mischievous deception instead of useful information will be the result, is—that this facility be afforded indiscriminately to every one that offers. If, under the notice of a selection to be made of the most deserving, the choice be left to any one man or body of men,—the consequence will be—that, to such communications alone as suit the personal purposes, of these Judges whoever they are, will the facility be afforded: in every instance, in which, either in the *matter*, or in the *author*, there is any thing that does *not* suit these personal purposes,—suppression, not publication, whatsoever be the merit of the work, will be the almost sure result.

To whom then shall the facility be afforded? To every offerer, without distinction, so long as any press remains unoccupied: he who first offers being all along first served.

But, suppose every press thus occupied, who is it that shall then determine?—I answer, *Fortune*. Fortune has no sinister interest: *men*, will in such a case, be almost sure to have such interest, and to be more or less swayed by it.

Deception—the result of partial information—will not be the only mischief: instead of *reward*, he by whom a communication—useful in itself, but to the Judge or Judges in question unacceptable—is tendered, will in return for it receive *punishment*. As long as he *can* be kept, he will be kept in a state of expectation and anxiety, dancing attendance, and wasting—perhaps his *money*, and certainly his *time*: when at last his patience is exhausted, then it is that he will discover, or not discover, that from the very first he had no chance.

Another result, altogether natural, is—that, by persons on whom the decision depends,—with or without other persons on whom, though erroneously, it will be supposed to depend,—*bribes* will in some shape or other be received: and the candidates from whom they are extracted will be—as well those, to whom it was predetermined to deny the facility, as those to whom it was predetermined to afford it.

The expense of such a facility—even if granted to the utmost extent of the demand—will it be considerable enough to be felt as a burthen by Your Majesty's Treasury? Glorious indeed will be the burthen—auspicious the sign—in such a case.

Here then, Sir is your *School of Legislation*: and presently I shall have to shew you, that,—among the Scholars, thus performing their exercises in this School,—persons will be to be found, better qualified than any others could be for doing that for you, which, in my situation, the most consummate wisdom would not qualify a man for doing for you.

My proposed Code will be but an *Outline*. Why? because in my situation, the most consummate ability could not furnish—moderate wisdom would not suffer a man to profess to furnish—any thing more.

Among the circumstances by which a demand for legislation is produced, some are of *universal* growth, others only of *local* growth: to such only as are of universal growth, could a foreign hand undertake to afford *in terminis* an adequate supply of legislative provision, with any sufficient ground for confidence. In this Outline will accordingly be contained so much of the proposed Code as can be proposed to stand *in terminis*. For the filling up of this Outline, notwithstanding the utmost degree of ability with which it can possibly be penned, whatsoever matter of detail, adapted to circumstances of *local* growth may be necessary, must be prepared by some *native* hand: at any rate by some person, to whom those circumstances have been made sufficiently known by *residence*.

For this matter of detail, the demand will be produced—in the first place, by the widely different condition of different provinces; in the next place, by the different condition of different classes of persons in the same province.

Meantime, even in regard to these details, what I could do, what I am accustomed to do, and what in my proposed Code I should make a point of doing, is—to furnish suggestions, having for their object the affording *guidance* and *assistance* to the local penman, in the adjustment of the details: in such sort, that the general principles exhibited and pursued in the *Outline*—the principles adapted to such circumstances as are of universal growth, and such circumstances of local growth as are generally notorious—may likewise in the *filling up* be pursued. Accordingly, in this way likewise,—the microscope being, in this field, not less familiar to me than the telescope,—I should hope to be of use.

For shortness, I have said *filling up*; aware at the same time, that, to put the work in a state fit for use, not only *addition*, but *subtraction* and *substitution* may occasionally be necessary.

Now then, Sir, comes the grand use—the immediate practical use—of Your Majesty's *Legislative School*, formed as above. For the filling up, of the *Outline* thus drawn, whether by my own or any other *foreign hand*,—matter of detail, as above, will be necessary, —I might add perhaps even *native hand*: for, in Your Majesty's vast Empire, such in many instances, are the differences between province and province, that the native of one will be little other than a foreigner to another. By whom then shall this business be performed?—I answer—by some scholar or scholars, by whom proof of qualification for the function has been exhibited,—exhibited by exercises, performed as above, in that School, by him or them, in preference, by whom,—according to the best grounded judgment that can be formed,—the proofs of greatest aptitude have thus been furnished. Among them all has no one been found, by whose works proof sufficient of this species of aptitude, has, in a sufficient degree, been thus furnished?—If so, I am truly sorry for it: for, this being the case, then not in the whole of Your Majesty's vast Empire, does there exist any person sufficiently qualified for the business. In the scale of aptitude,—that person, by whom proof of any degree of aptitude, how low soever, has been furnished,—stands, at any rate, above all those by whom no such proof has been furnished.

Will it be said, by way of objection, that the same difficulties, as those just represented as attaching upon the choice of works for publication, will attach upon every choice to be made, among the authors for the filling of situations such as those in question, *after* the works are published? Not, surely, on any sufficient ground. For, of a selection made for publication, the consequence is—that, by every work not selected (except in the instances in which the author may have the resolution to publish at his own expense—instances which, under such discouragement, do not promise to be very numerous) the public sustains a loss: and, on that plan, among those who upon the open plan would have produced and given in their works, some there may be who, by despair of acceptance, may be deterred from applying their thoughts to the subject. A work thus stifled or nipt in embryo is dead to every purpose: whereas a work, which, through the medium of the press, has once been brought to light, remains upon the carpet, capable at all times of being taken for the subject of an *appeal*, by which every injustice, done to it in the first instance, may be repaired.

In this way, how unfortunate soever the choices made should eventually prove, still what will at the same time be seen—seen by all eyes—by Your Majesty—by Your Majesty's subjects,—by foreign sovereigns—by foreign subjects—is—that those choices have not been altogether groundless: on the contrary, that, for the securing the best choices possible, the best adapted and most promising means have been employed.

By every such contributor—the authenticity of the production being supposed to be out of doubt—I mean the fact of its having been composed by him whose name it bears—(for this is a point that must not be overlooked) proofs of *attention*, bestowed upon the subject, will at any rate have been furnished: and this is more than will have been furnished by any one else.

Behold now the advantages, from the circumstance that the hand, by which the Outline has been drawn, is a *foreign* one.

1. No restraint whatsoever on the liberty of criticism. The hand, by which the work is presented, is one from which no man has any thing to fear, any more than to hope. From such a hand, whatever comes is, as the sportsmen say, *fair game*. Not disfavour, but favour rather, will be looked for from the hunting it. Imperfections, and not merits, will be the objects, looked out for with most alacrity, by every native eye.

2. Suppose it put to use:—in the ultimately sanctioned Code, suppose as considerable a portion of this outline employed, as the nature of the case will suffer to be employed. How pure will in such case be the satisfaction of the people! Here cannot have been any undue partiality:—any thing like *favoritism*. The author all the while at a distance, without connexion, and,—with the exception of that mutually honourable influence, which is exercised by understanding on understanding,—altogether without *influence*: to the Sovereign, not so much as his person known: and all this, matter of universal notoriety. Under such circumstances, by what imaginable cause can any preference that has been given to the work, have been produced, but the *opinion* at least—the unbiassed opinion—of its suitableness to the purpose?

3. In this case too,—howsoever it may be in *other* Countries foreign to Russia,—an Englishman being the workman, critics can never be altogether wanting in England. From Your Majesty a simple invitation would, I make little doubt, suffice to produce works undertaken expressly for this purpose. But, at any rate, *Reviews* exist, by none of which, consistently with their interests, could a work, executed under these circumstances, be passed by unexamined. And well may your Majesty be assured, that for discovering in it imperfection in every shape, imagined as well as real, adequate motives can not be wanting here.

Compare, Sir, with the Legislation or Codification School thus sketched out, the unschooled Codification-Establishment, at present or lately in existence.

The Report made to Your Majesty of the 28th February, 1804,[6] lies before me. Whatsoever may be its character in any other point of view,—in an *historical* point of view, it is of no small value. From 1700 to 1804—a space of 104 years,—Commission after Commission—Office upon Office—Salary upon Salary—and still nothing done. Thereupon, in 1804, a Commission in a new form:—eleven years more, and still nothing done. Why?—because the only sort of means, by which, in the nature of the case, any thing could be done—or at least tolerably well done—(I mean those above submitted) have never yet been taken. *So that money is but spent, no matter how it is applied*. So far as concerns salaries, in Russia (I can not but suspect)—in England (I can not but see)—such has all

[6] The report from the Russian ministry of justice on the organisation of the commission for compiling a code of laws appointed in 1801. Alexander confirmed the report on 28 February 1804 and it was published in French and English at St Petersburg in the same year.

along been the principle acted upon: the consequences have been—those which by the nature of things are attached to such principles.

According to this Report, in the time of Catherine II., the whole field of legislation was divided amongst 15 *Commissions*, composed all together of now fewer than 128 members. By each of these Commissions, a mass of paper was covered with written characters: masses 15, (p. 12) not one of them found fit to make its appearance. How should it have been? where should any of them have got their skill—these Codificators? What motives, what means had they for the acquiring of it? Seven years of hard labour, real or supposed, on the part of this set of Commissioners (p. 12) and then, if I understand the matter right, seven more years of the like labour on the part of another set—(p. 13) and still nothing done. Publicity—the most unlimited publicity—the only possible means of doing any thing,—and still nothing but the closest secresy put in practice!

Always the same failure—always from the same causes, and to the last the same hopeless course pursued. Ah, Sir, with what regret did I not see (it was in the Report of 28th February, 1804, p. 35) the long list of offices, with pecuniary appointments, all of them to last—(for how in common compassion could it be otherwise?) to last for the lives of the official persons. Official persons, 48: total of annual expense, Roubles 100,000. But in these salaries were not included those of either of two personages,—each of them lending his name, neither of them any thing else,—*High Excellencies*, the amount of whose appointments in that quality, shame, it should seem, kept out of the list.[7]

By what portion of that multitude of salaried workmen has any thing been done? and by such of them by whom any thing has been done, in what quantity, and to what value, has work been done?

Not but that, in the way of collecting *materials*, and putting them in order,—workmen, even in that multitude, may have been, and for aught I can know to the contrary, have been, usefully employed: materials, consisting of dispositions of existing law, distributed under heads. Few perhaps are the occasions, on which,—to the forming a sufficiently grounded judgment on the question,—what, in relation to this or that head, *ought to be* law,—it is not necessary to know what actually *is* law. Statements, showing what *is* law, are therefore among the *materials*, which he to whom it belongs to say what *ought to be*, and thence what *shall be* law, must have to work with. But, the workman by whom materials of this sort are collected and brought to the spot, is but the *hod-carrier*. And where are the *Architects*, or so much as the *Bricklayers?*

[7] Not identified.

By any one of the *volunteer* workmen whom I have thus been labouring to introduce into Your Majesty's service,—not a penny can be received, but for work, which, well or ill done, will, at any rate, have been done: no, nor in any other *proportion* than that of the quantity actually done: and, among those will be—not only Bricklayers, but under-Architects:—whichsoever function each man feels or fancies himself most fit for. *After trial*, if this or that man does not prove fit, so much the worse: but it is only *by* trial, that he, or any one, can have had *much* chance of being *made* fit, or any chance at all of being *proved* to be fit.

Where, work or no work, salary is received, what you are well assured of is—a man's affection for the *salary*. Where, in the way here proposed, without salary, or pecuniary allowance in any other shape, work is done,—what you are pretty well assured of, is—a man's affection for the *work*.

Affection indeed, is not itself *aptitude*: but, in every case it is one cause of aptitude, and, in the present case in particular, there can not be a more efficient, not to say a more indispensable one.

Meantime, if I have not been misinformed, one Code at least—and *that* on the Penal branch—if not already in print, is already in more or less forwardness, from the official hand.—Now for a few suppositions.—1. It is out already: 2. It is not out yet, but comes out, before any *Outline* from me is at St. Petersburgh:—3. It comes out, but not till after one Outline from me has been for some time out at St. Petersburgh:—4. It never comes out at all. In these several cases, what may be the effect expected from my work?—From my work, including *School of Legislation*, built on the *Tribunal of free criticism*, which, as above, I consider as an *accompaniment* to it, or as one *fruit* of it.

Case 1. *It is out already*. But at any rate not with the force of law already given to it: for, had this been the case, I should have heard of it. I should not expect to find that it is so, even in the *probationary* state. If it is,—then, before it receives the force of law, it will rest with Your Majesty to determine, whether the *Tribunal of free criticism*, above proposed for my own work, shall not take cognisance of it. But, in case of the affirmative, on which I cannot help reckoning—in that case, Your Majesty's declaration on that head had need to be explicit.—'*L'Original est confirmé de la propre main de sa Majesté Impériale dans les termes suivans: ainsi soit fait.*' Thus in French. In English, *Woe to all gainsayers!* Such was the ægis, with which the authors of the Report of 28th February, 1804, thought it adviseable to provide themselves.—*Critics be dumb! Woe be to all gainsayers!*

At any rate, if it be Your Imperial Majesty's pleasure to cause a copy to be transmitted to me,—*observations* on it from me,—or, with Your Imperial Majesty's permission, (that my work may not be stopped,) from some friend of mine,—shall be submitted to Your Majesty with all possible dispatch. It will then rest with Your Majesty's pleasure,—what delay, if any, to allow for the delivering in of my work, before the sanction of law is given to *that*, or any other.

Case 2. *It is not out yet, but comes out before any Outline from me has reached St. Petersburgh.*—In the mean time, shall I have been useless? No, Sir—all this while, though I were all the time asleep, I shall have been rendering to Your Majesty useful service. To the official hand, have been all the while applied the *spur* and the *rein*, formed by the idea of the *Tribunal of free criticism*, which is waiting for that work: and, in conjunction with this idea,—the idea of the rival work, from the hand, by the shadow of which, at this distance, the official hand hath, as above, been so often made to tremble.

Case 3. *My Outline has reached St. Petersburgh, and from the official hand no Projet hath as yet been delivered in, but comes out afterwards.* The official faculties will now have been put to their utmost stretch. The enemy—the foreign enemy—has been seen already on the field. For this his work, here will be at least one Critic, by whom the virtual challenge can scarcely have been refused. Against the intruder's work, whatsoever can be said,—here at least is *one*,—and, at his back, others by dozens and by scores,—who, all of them, have had the strongest interest in saying it.

And now, the fresh subject being come in, the Legislative School finds a fresh recruit of Scholars:—Scholars, as many as can descry for themselves any the least chance of advancement, from their exercises as performed in it.

Let me not here withhold the acknowledgement, which even already seems to be due. What from that hand I should expect to find, is—a work not unsusceptible of criticism,—of examination. In it I foresee a work, in which the forms of method will have been observed: in it will be found distinguishable parts. This I collect from what I see in the above *Rapport*. A point (mathematicians tell us) has no parts: a *Chaos*, how vast soever, has not any more. The fifteen masses of proposed legislative matter, spoken of in the *Rapport*, had not, any one of them, any thing like method:—had not any *distinguishable parts*:—thus much I collect from the *Rapport*. By this methodicalness, the sketch given in that same *Rapport*,—and, I should suppose, whatsoever may have been shewn to Your Majesty since,—stands distinguished, I take for granted, *from*, or at least *above*, all that had gone before it. Here was one step, towards the one thing needful. This, I suppose, is that which gained for the author,—and as far as it went, on grounds, the justice of which is above dispute,—Your Majesty's favourable opinion and acceptance.

Altogether above dispute, are the importance of good arrangement to legislation, and the importance of a set of *Synoptic Tables*,—(*Systême figuré* is the word used by the *French Encyclopedists*)[8] to good arrangement: good arrangement and good tables are at once *effect* and *cause*. A man,—who, feeling the need of it, is able to frame an implement of this sort,—is beyond comparison better qualified for the main work, than one, who is either blind to the use of such a security for good arrangement, or unable to produce it.

This then is one step made towards the one thing needful: but it is not *itself* the one thing needful. Here are so many *drawers* or *boxes*. But the *contents?*—what will *they* be? Every thing depends upon the contents: and, from nothing that I have ever seen or heard, can I entertain any favourable expectation, in regard to the contents, with which, if with any thing, those same boxes are destined to be filled.

Your Majesty was well advised, in the acceptance given to those services. I see not well, how they could have been refused. But the misfortune was—the yielding to that anxiety, which on the part of a person in that situation was at once so natural, and so pernicious:—the anxiety to preclude the Sovereign, according to custom, from receiving, from any other quarter, services, of which the whole civilized world could not afford a supply too large.

Case 4. Lastly—suppose that *notwithstanding the spur so applied, as above, a reasonable time has elapsed, and still no work has appeared from the official hand.* Inwardly felt conviction, of at least the comparative goodness of the already published work,—self-conscious inability to produce a better, if any at all,—such, it will have become manifest, is the state of mind, which the silence has had for its cause. Meantime, here,—by the supposition—here, at

[8] *Encyclopédie, ou Dictionnaire raisonné des sciences, des arts et des métiers, par une société de gens de lettres*, 17 vols., Paris, 1751–65, was produced under the direction of the philosophers Denis Diderot (1713–84) and Jean le Rond d'Alembert (1717–83). In the introduction d'Alembert wrote a paper entitled 'Explication détaillée du systême des connoissances humaines, (i. pp. xlvii–li) to accompany a table entitled 'Systême figuré des Connoissances Humaines'. Bentham reproduced this (from d'Alembert's *Mélanges de littérature, d'histoire, et de philosophie*, 5 vols., Amsterdam, 1767, i. 250) in his 'Essay on Nomenclature and Classification', published in 1817 as Part II of *Chrestomathia*.

any rate, is a something in hand: I mean my own work whatever it may be found to be:—a something, which, but for this my humble proposal, would never have had existence.

To the number of commentators—under the assurance that, where the author is an unconnected foreigner, they will be critical ones,—and thence of self-appointed Judges, under the assurance that they will not be favourably partial ones,—your Majesty sees plainly enough, that it is not without concern, that I should see any limits.

But,—in regard to the sort of a work itself, which is to be the subject of this criticism,—one *condition*, I must confess I should not be sorry to see required,—whatsoever, in the way of *limitation*, might be the effect of it.

This is—that, to each considerable mass of matter,—nay even to each single word where the importance of it required as much,—considerations, destined to serve in the character of *Reasons*,—stated, in proof of the propriety of whatever were so proposed to be established,—should all along be annext.

This subject was touched upon in my former letter:—I cannot too earnestly solicit your Majesty's attention to it.

Sir, it is only by the *criterion*—it is only the the *test*—thus formed,—that talent can be distinguished from imbecillity, appropriate science from ignorance, probity from improbity, philanthropy from despotism, sound sense from caprice,—aptitude, in a word, in every shape, from inaptitude.

Reasons these alone are addresses from understanding to understanding. *Ordinances* without reasons, are but manifestations of will,—of the will of the mighty, exacting obedience from the helpless. Absolve him from this condition—rid him of this check,—not only the man, who presents a Code to you for signature,—but the man who presents your shirt to you,—is competent to make laws. The man who *presents* the shirt? Yes, Sir, or the woman who *washes* it.

Give up this one condition,—Germany alone, on any one subject that you please, will furnish you with as many hundred Codes as you please:—all of them faithfully copied from the chaos, which for a different part of the world was put together, some twelve or thirteen hundred years ago:—all of them composed upon the most economical principles:—all of them written at the rate of so many pages an hour:—all of them, without any expense of thought.

No reasons! No reasons to your Laws!—cries Frederick the Great of Prussia, in a flimsy Essay of his, written professedly on this very subject.[9] Why no reasons? Because, (says he) if there be any such appendage to your law,—the first puzzle-cause of a lawyer, (le premier brouillon d'Avocat)—that takes it in hand, will overturn it. Yes, sure enough: if so it be, that,—a text of law pointing one way,—a reason that stands next to it points another way,—that is, if either the law or the reason is to a certain degree ill constructed,—a mishap of this sort may have place. But, is this a good reason against *giving reasons?*—no more than it would be against *making laws*. As well might it be said—*No Direction Posts!*—Why?—Because, if, coming to a Direction Post, a *mauvais plaisant* should take it into his head to give a twist to the index, making it point to the wrong road,—the traveller may thus be put out of his way.

Suppose now a Code produced, as usual, without any such perpetual commentary of Reasons: prefaced, for form-sake, and to make a show of wisdom—prefaced, as hath so repeatedly been done, by a parcel of vague and unapplied, because inapplicable, generalities, under the name of *principles*. It may be approved, and praised, and trumpeted. But on what grounds? If, in regard to this or that particular provision or disposition of law, any distinct and intelligible *grounds* for the approbation are produced,—they will be so many *Reasons*. Why then, (may it be said to the draughtsman)—why, if you yourself know what they are,—why, unless you are ashamed of them—why not come out with them in the first instance?—Why not spread them out, at one view, before the public at large,—instead of whispering them, one at one time, another at another, in the ear of this or that individual, pre-engaged by interest or prepossession, in quality of trumpeter?—But if no *such* grounds—that is if no grounds at all—can be produced, where is the truth or value of any such praise?

On the other hand,—suppose a body of law produced, supported, and elucidated, from beginning to end, by a perpetual Commentary of Reasons: all deduced from the one true and only defensible principle—the *principle of general utility*—under which they will, all of them, be shewn to be included.—Here, Sir, will *indeed* be *a new æra*:—the æra of *rational legislation*: an example set to all nations:—a new institution:—and your Majesty the founder of it.

The *Penal* is the branch of law, with which in contradistinction to the *Civil*, I in a manner took for granted that it would be deemed most proper to commence. Reasons are obvious, and seem conclu-

[9] Frederick's *Dissertation sur les raisons d'établir ou d'abroger les lois*, Frankfurt and Leipzig, 1752. Bentham appears to have been thinking of a passage on p. 39.

sive. In the penal branch for instance, circumstance of univeral growth have place in a larger proportion than in that other. On that account, it lies, in a more extensive degree, within the competence of a foreign hand. In the penal branch too, changes to any extent may be made,—and, so they be but for the better in other respects,—neither danger nor alarm be produced by the change.

Not so in the case of the *Civil* branch. Of *that* branch, the grand and all-pervading object is—*to keep out change*:—to prevent as much as possible, those *disappointments*, which are the result of *actual* and *unexpected* change, and those *alarms*, which are produced by the tremulous *expectation* of change. In this case, general uncertainty in the state of the law—that perpetual source of unexpected changes, in individual instances, to an unfathomable extent—is the grand source of evil: and uncertainty is the inherent disease of that wretched substitute to law, which is called *unwritten* law, and which, in plain truth, is no law at all. For this disease, *written* law—the only sort of law which has any other than a metaphorical existence,—is the only remedy.—A remedy of this sort, Napoleon had the merit of giving to France. With what degree of skill it is made up, I have never yet seen any use in the inquiring. But, wretchedly bad indeed must this remedy have been, if it has not been in a signal degree better than none.—Happy had it been for mankind,—if, in this way alone, he had set an example to its rulers.

It remains for me to speak of the way alluded to at the outset, as the *other* way, in which, with Your Imperial Majesty's approbation, such services as it may be in my power to render, may, in some sort, be put to use; and in some degree, though not an equal degree, the objects, above spoken of, attained.

By the same conveyance with the letter from Your Majesty, came one from Prince Adam Czartoriski. It is to remind me of an eventual promise I had made to him, and to call upon me for the eventual performance. *Poland* was of course the subject of this promise. What gave occasion to it, Your Majesty may, perhaps, have heard already from that Prince. All that passed between us on either side was in generals: things were not at that time ripe for entering upon particulars. Your Majesty's intentions were not sufficiently known. But, from the nature of the case, an inference I was led to draw, was—that in relation to that country, the *Constitutional*,—antecedently at least to every other,—was the branch, with relation to which, my services were in view. But, of all branches of law,—the Constitutional is *that*, in relation to which, so far as concerns the drawing of a general *Outline*, a foreign hand seems less competent than in relation to any other. Why?—Because Constitutional law depends throughout upon *localities*. Here then, the plan of giving answers, as above, to incidental questions, is the only one that seems suited to the nature of the case.

Not that in this case, any more than in the other, there could be any use in sending answers,—any further than as, in the place to which they were sent, they found a disposition to put them to use. But if, in the present instance, there be any deficiency on that head,—the application, so obligingly reiterated to me by that Prince, is an effect without a cause.

Meantime, if it were Your Majesty's pleasure to give me orders for an Outline of Penal and Civil law, commencing with the Penal law, for Poland,—my labour, although the field of it were confined to Poland, would find motives altogether adequate to the production of it.

My purpose would thus be answered, but not that which I can not but hope to find Your Majesty's. For Russia,—no competition, no tribunal of free criticism, no School of Legislation, no nursery for functionaries, employed in the department of legislation. Nothing but a faint telescopic view of those establishments, as existing in Poland: the destiny of Russia delivered over to a single hand,—such as every thing I have either seen or heard, concurs in forcing me to regard as an insufficient one.

Your Majesty sees my importunity?—Why should I be ashamed of it?—It is not for money: it is not for power: it is not for dignity: it is not even for favour:—it is for a chance of being of use:—of use?—and *to whom* of use?

Not inconsiderable, either in extent, or number, or importance,—are the subjects of consideration, which I have thus ventured to submit to Your Majesty's decision. But, so far as regards any thing to be done by me, few points there are of any importance, in which the decision can be—at once so simple, so easy, and so safe.

To set me at work, all that would be necessary would be—an intimation of Your Majesty's pleasure to that effect. English must be the language in which I write. It is accordingly in that language, that in the first instance, it must be printed. But sheet by sheet, as fast as it comes out in English, Mr. Dumont, serving upon the same terms that I do, would—I am as certain as if he were here, and told me so—be happy to render it into French: in which case, the French translation would be in print nearly as soon as the original. The expense of the work in English would be *my* concern: with regard to the French, it would be as Your Majesty pleased. To Petersburgh, as many copies,—in English, in French, or in both,—as Your Majesty pleased to order, should be transmitted. What should be done in relation to them when *there*, would of course depend altogether upon Your Majesty's pleasure. But, I hope Your Majesty will have no objection to the giving me a promise, that when there, *they shall see the light.* The work will not be a libel: and, if disapproved,—and, with or without reason assigned, the disapprobation declared,—any such disapprobation will not, naturally speaking, experience much difficulty in making itself respected. I have the honour to be, Sir,

Your Imperial Majesty's
Ever faithful Servant,
Jeremy Bentham.

2320

To John Herbert Koe

6 July 1815 (Aet 67)

Ford Abbey, 6th July, 1815.

I see the Ministry have got the lawyers to quash the D. of C.'s marriage.[2] Oh, rare lawyers! If the public money had been got for it, it would have been good enough; nobody would had meddled with it. This affair must, I think, make a fine sensation where you are.

Mill and I are mourning the death of all hopes of a free government in France. The name of a man who has cut so many French throats as have been cut by Wellington, will serve as an essential cover for the most flagrant violation of any the most sacred and universally beneficial engagements.[3] In pursuance of the proclamation of Louis, Carnot, with a multitude of *et ceteras*, all who could have operated most effectually in the character of checks, will lose their heads. Carnot had better have left poor Louis XVI.'s on its

2320. [1] Bowring, x. 485.

[2] Bowring identifies 'the D. of C' as the Duke of Clarence; but this seems to be a slip for the Duke of Cumberland. Ernst Augustus, Duke of Cumberland (1771–1851), subsequently King Ernst I of Hanover, married on 29 May 1815 his cousin, Frederica Caroline Sophia Alexandrina, daughter of the Duke of Mecklenburg-Strelitz and widow of Prince Frederick of Prussia and Prince Frederick of Solms-Braunfels. The marriage was solemnized according to the rights of the Church of England in August 1815, but was not popular, and the Commons refused to increase the duke's income.

[3] Bentham was perhaps thinking of Joseph Fouché, duc d'Otrante (1759–1820), former minister of police and the interior under Napoleon, minister of police again during the Hundred Days, and head of the provisional government established after Napoleon's defeat at Waterloo.

shoulders.[4] Brougham will lament his friend; but, perhaps, he was not of the number of conspirators. All that has been done since Louis XVIII.'s Hegira,[5] will be as void as the Cumberland marriage.

2321

From Pavel Chichagov

13 July 1815

London 13 July 1815

Mr Koe called upon me with your packets for the Emp. and P. Cz.[2] Had he called one day sooner they would have been in their hands by this time for I had then the best opportunity of sending any thing through the hands of a confidential person. Now I shall do my best to forward them by the first opportunity. Mr Koe left the day before yesterday your letter at my house in my absence and though I have not been able to decifer without his assistance every thing I wished to know yet I read enough to understand that you have been so good and friendly to me as to recollect my plans of traveling and help me to make them more interesting useful and agreeable for me. At the same time that I return my sincerest thanks for your attentions to me I must confidentially tell you that in the present state of things when the continent is going to be open to all those who have sufficiently admired and enjoyed English liberty with the alien act, Her riches without guineas and an immense debt, Her ruinous dearness and the abundance in getting the minimum of things for the maximum of money, those I say who have sufficiently tired of all these luxuries and delights may like by way of a change to see the countries where a shilling will do as much as 6 and after having satisfied their sublime mental desires live a little for the satisfaction of their bodies. What I tell you is a secrete for no body knows it here nor thinks so and therefore you must not compromise me. Now the fact is that in few weeks I am going to leave this country and shall procede wherever some attraction or some reason

[4] Carnot had voted for Louis XVI's death without appeal or postponement in January 1793. He was exiled by Louis XVIII after the second restoration.

[5] i.e. Louis XVIII's departure from France during the Hundred Days.

2321. [1] BL IX. 210–11. Autograph. Docketed: '1815 July 13 / Tchitchagoff London / to / J.B. Ford Abbey / J.Bs Letters to Alexr. / and Czartoriski sent / T. [. . .?] to Italy / Poland ill provided for / by treaty between Russia / and Prussia'. Addressed: 'Jeremy Bentham Esqr / Ford Abbey near Chard / Somersetshire'. Postmark: 'JY / 13 / 1815'. An extract is printed in Bowring, x. 485.

[2] i.e. Alexander and Czartoryski: letters 2318 and 2319.

or other that may prevail at the moment will direct me. The general plan is to reach Italy and see Rome and Naples but how and when I cant say.

Do you know what our constitutionalists have done for Poland? Here is a specimen and as a philosopher you dare not refuse me to explain what it means and I require that explanation. The treaty between our Emp. and the King of Prussia[3] says, Le duché de Varsovie à l'exception de la ville libre de Cracovie et de son territoire, ainsi que du rayon, qui sur la rive droite de la Vistule retourne à S. M. L'Emp. d'Autriche,[4] et des provinces dont il a été autrement disposé en faveur *du roi de prusse* en vertu des articles ci-dessus est réuni a l'Empire de Russie.[5]

This is a new partition of the Dutchy in my opinion. Now again, il y sera lié irrévocablement par sa constitution pour être *possédé par S. M. l'Emp. de Russie, ses héritiers et ses successeurs à perpétuité*. This is for the independance now for the government: S.M. Impériale se réserve de donner à ces États jouissant d'une administration distincte, l'extention intérieure qu'elle jugera convenable. So much for representation. Elle prendra avec ses *autres titres celui de Czar, roi de Pologne*. What this means is realy to deep for me to understand. Now for the nationality and the integrity of the Kingdom after having parceled it sooner than ever it says the treaty I mean:

Les polonais, sujets respectifs des hautes parties contractantes obtiendront des institutions qui *assurent* la *conservation* de leur *Nationalité*, d'après les formes d'existence politique *que chacun des gouvernements auxquels ils apartiennent, jugera convenable de leur accorder*. What a variety of advantegeous. Some will have polish nationality in the prussian way some in the austrian and some in the most consistent with freedom in the russian mode.

This master plan amused me so much that I could no⟨t⟩ help treating you with it and how delightful is the idea that these same heads are farther to settle the interest and happiness of France and all those honourable nations who want and expect like children to have hapiness secured to them by the first commer.

[3] Frederick William III (1770–1840), king of Prussia from 1797.

[4] Francis (1768–1835), Holy Roman Emperor as Francis II 1792–1806, emperor of Austria as Francis I 1804–35.

[5] This and the following passages in French are quotations (or near quotations) from Article III of the Russo-Prussian treaty of 3 May 1815 appended to the final act of the Congress of Vienna. See *Le Congrès de Vienne et les Traités de 1815*, intro. M. Capefigue, 2 vols., Paris, n.d. [1863?], ii. 1156.

With my best wishes for the successful application of your labors to the advantages of humanity and may you see them in practice I remain unalterably your sincere

admirer
P.C.

My Cts to Mr Mill your companion and associate

2322

From John Herbert Koe

24 July 1815

Lincolns Inn
24 July 1815—

Mills packet being the most bulky I took compassion upon that and have been unable to obtain another frank.

With respect to Chrestomathic. I think in order effectually to vest the management exclusively in the Managers / Conductors / and to exclude the Subscribers from all power of interference it will be necessary to have three separate papers or instruments—
1. The Lease to the Conductors—which may be quite in the common form and the same as if it were to be granted to ordinary tenants—
2. A Paper containing the Outline of the proposed Plan of Management—which might have some such title as this—Outlines of the Plan of Management for the Chrestomathic School—and then it may be proceeded to impose upon them whatever duties it is deemed expedient they should take upon themselves—such as the building the School as soon as a sufficient sum of money shall have been collected for that purpose and so forth—and reserving to them (the Managers) a power of making any such alterations in that plan of management as they may from time to time deem expedient.
3. A Paper to be signed by the subscribers which might be in some such form as this—Chrestomathic School—Subscription Paper—Each of us undersigned Subscribers to the Chrestomathic School agree to pay when required so to do (having a proper receipt) to A B C D etc. or as they shall direct the several sums set opposite to our names: and each of us consents that such several sums when so paid shall be subject to their absolute disposal and controul each of us

2322. [1] UC clxv. 10. Autograph. Docketed: '1815 July 24 / Chrestomathia / H.K. Linc. Inn / to / J.B. Ford Abbey / Papers what to be / signed by Chrestomathic / Subscribers.' Addressed: 'J. Bentham Esq / Ford Abbey / Chard / Somerset'. Postmark: 'JY / 24 / 1815'.

renouncing, in consideration of the great confidence we feel in them, all interference in the expenditure of the money so subscribed.

I dont know how the purpose can be answered in any other manner than some such as the above—the Lease is obviously necessary—the 2d paper would be to obtain Subscriptions and the 3d to keep the disposition of the funds free from all controul of the crowd. There may perhaps be objections to the last paper on account of the possibility of its operating as a repeller of contributors: but I see not how it can safely be avoided. Without notice, by simple subscription, their faculty of meddling would be clearly let in: verbal notice cannot be trusted to and almost as little written without Subscription / signature / —for the master of the Rolls decided a few nights ago a case relative to notice which upon principle would go this length—that though such a paper as the 3d had been left with a Subscriber, and it could not be proved that he had read it, it would not oust of him of a controul over the employment of his money.[2]

There is a very little technicality in this—the Lease can be drawn at any time in half a day—the Proposals already prepared with some trifling modifications will do for the second the 3d will be very short—

2323

From Jean-Baptiste Say

2 August 1815

Paris, 2d August, 1815.

I have received, honoured master, your Chrestomathic Tables.[2] I am studying them, but could not delay telling you how much I am honoured by your remembrance and your gift. You will labour to your last day for the improvement of the human race; and the human race will not know the extent of its obligations to you, till it has learned your lessons—that is, till we are gone. Our fate is to die at our labour—but our labour will not be lost.

I have just published a little Catechism of Political Economy,[3] for the better circulation of a few important truths. It is short—it is

[2] The decision to which Koe was referring has not been traced.

2323. [1] Bowring, x. 485–6.

[2] See letters 2312 n. 2 and 2325 n. 2.

[3] *Catéchisme d'économie politique, ou Instruction familière qui montre de quelle façon les richesses sont produites, distribuées et consommées dans la société*, Paris, 1815.

clear—it is in dialogues; and the principal difficulties are solved in a manner accessible to all minds and all fortunes. If little books like this were circulated in all countries, these ideas would gradually make their way; and it would be soon seen whether governments are really such a necessary part of society; and if they will then be able to make nations pay so dearly for benefits which they do not confer.

They are trying to build up here a rotten throne. It cannot stand. Your ministers are throwing dust in vulgar eyes; but in the eyes of the thoughtful they are playing a miserable game. Out of this frightful chaos freedom will spring. Meanwhile what sufferings and sins! I write to you in the midst of tears. There is no satisfaction anywhere but in the newspapers, which are written by the police of the Bourbons, and dictated by the Allied Powers.

2324

From Joseph Jekyll

4 August 1815

Dear Bentham,

My Cæstus and Arms on the Western Circuit are laid aside, as I was appointed, in June last, a Master in Chancery. This will account for the disappointment I must bear in not accepting your kind and hospitable invitation to Ford Abbey, where I should have felt sincere pleasure in taking so old and so valuable a friend by the hand.

This summer, I too am to play the part of the London Hermit, as it is the lot of the newly-appointed Master to reside in town during his first long vacation. To so inveterate a metropolitan as myself this is no grievance; but I have two Westminster boys[2] who 'babble of green fields,'[3] and desire a surburban villa for their holidays. Miss V—[4] and Miss F—[5] have aided my inquiry, but it has hitherto been fruitless, and I adopt other resources among friends resident in the vicinity of London.

With the aforesaid most excellent and amiable persons I sat under

2324. [1] Bowring, x. 486.

[2] Joseph Jekyll (1802–41) and Edward Hill Jekyll (1804–76), admitted to Westminster School on 29 April 1811 and 22 May 1815 respectively.

[3] *Henry V*, II. iii. 16.

[4] Presumably Elizabeth Vernon (1762–1830). Her elder sister, Caroline (1761–1833), had married Robert Percy Smith in 1797. For the Vernon sisters see *Correspondence*, iii. 49 n.

[5] Caroline Fox.

a great tree in the gardens of little Holland House last Sunday, and discoursed of happy times in former days at Bowood.

Dumont, I trust, will not take root in Switzerland, notwithstanding his public functions. Your infant Grecian I should like to have seen;[6] and I wish you would use your pen to convince mankind it is not wise to consume the whole period between infancy and manhood, at a public school, in acquiring two dead languages and nothing else.

Good Father Abbot, give me your benison; and if a Master in Chancery should be desirous at any time of taking sanctuary in the west, I rest well assured Ford Abbey would grant it.—Believe me, dear Bentham, most truly yours.

Spring Gardens,
August 4, 1815.

2325

From The Comte De Lasteyrie

23 August 1815

Paris, ce 23 Aout, 1815.

Monsieur,

J'ai reçu votre 2d Table Chrestomathique sur le système de Lancaster.[2] L'ordre systématique et précis, avec lequel vous tracez les avantages, l'importance, et les applications, que présente ce nouveau moyen d'instruction, apprendra à l'Europe à mieux connoître toute son importance, et vous contribuerez ainsi à lui donner un plus grand dévelopment.

Nous faisons des efforts pour parvenir au grand but que se proposent tous les philanthropes éclairés de l'Angleterre. Nous ne pouvons pas y parvenir avec la même rapidité, vû les circonstances

[6] Probably a reference to the young John Stuart Mill, who was educated by his father and Bentham. He started to learn Greek at three years old and by the age of eight had read many Greek works. He would have been nine when this letter was written.

2325. [1] *Papers Relative to Codification and Public Instruction*, London, 1817, p. 109. Reprinted in Bowring, iv. 532–3. Charles Philibert, comte de Lasteyrie du Saillant (1759–1849), was a French writer on education, philosophy, politics, and agriculture.

[2] In his circular letter to the various governors of the United States (June 1817), Bentham described the 'whole sheet Table' he had sent to de Lasteyrie as a 'summary view of the system or mode of instruction, termed sometimes *the new system of instruction*, sometimes, from the inventors, the *Bell and Lancaster System*, . . . In the sheet in question, there is very little that can be called mine, except the compression and arrangement which I have endeavoured to give to the matter of it.' See *Papers Relative to Codification and Public Instruction*, pp. 105–6.

désastreuses qui accablent la France, et le système de destruction et de ravage qui y règne. Mais les mauvaises choses n'ont qu'un temps, et espérons que celui des bonnes arrivera un jour.

Je suis bien flatté que cette circonstance me procure le plaisir de vous témoigner les sentimens d'estime et de vénération que m'ont procuré depuis long-temps vos travaux, si utiles à l'humanité.

C. P. de Lasteyrie.

2326

From Pavel Chichagov

31 August 1815

London the 31 August 1815
34 Upper Berkely Street Portman Square.

The surest way of doing nothing is to undertake a great deal. I was going to Scotland, to Ireland, to Switzerland, to Italy and therefore I remain in my lodgings in London. There is no inducement and no chance of my leaving England now and I expect to spend the winter here after which I may with fewer plans accomplish something more.

your last letter[2] was an evident proof of the divine interference with the affairs of this world and particularly when it concerns such good christians as you and I. You addressed the letter to woolwich, I have not been there this two month's, but I just happened to go there for few hours as if on purpose to receive that letter, which came while we were at dinner. of course I must hasten more than ever to answer such miraculous mark of divine benevolence and must tell you the first thing that I expect with great impatience in the bottle or bundle, I don't know which, of methaphysics, which I hope will be a palpable one for I like to feel what I am about. I shall wait for it till the 10th or 11 of September after which time I set out for Wilton[3] and so to be a little nearer to you in the most tantalising manner as I can't come as near as I would wish to it to be. [. . . ?] your letters to the Emp. and Cz. and the ring have been sent to paris

2326. [1] Bowring 'Memoirs', at p. 486. Autograph. Docketed: '1815 Aug 31 / Tchitchagoff Upper Berkely / Street Portman / square / to / J.B. Ford Abbey'. Addressed: 'Jeremy Bentham Esqr. / Ford Abbey near Chard / Sommersetshire.' Postmark illegible. Extract in Bowring, x. 486.

[2] Missing.

[3] The home of the Earl of Pembroke. See letter 2290.

a little before the time that Mr Koe called upon me. I have heard nothing of them since. Cz. is at Warsaw but your letter will be forwarded to him as I hoped to do it.

After the receipt of your former letter[4] I had an intention of entering in to some details about the political part of it, but having gone to Tunbridge Wells with a party of friends my time has been so much employed in nothingnesses and idlenesses that I never could find an opportunity of making a better use of it. Now what shall I say. We differ intirely, unfortunately for me, upon the subject of poland. You think as well as some poles do, that something good has been done for them. I see nothing but the extreme weariness on the side of those who did it, and an extreme degradation for those who it has been done for. All is a complete failure in the general plan; instead of restoration partition upon partition. Instead of liberty the greatest and the most shamefull Slavery for the future. Those abuses and misaplications of the most sacred words and sentiments. A Kingdom cut out of a dutchy.[5] Submission to the most arbitrary power, tyranical by nature imbecil by circumstances. A Nationality dispersed, over country's the most inimical to that sentiment and put under their fatal yoke. I may as well say that the nationality of the jews is in existence. They enjoy free commerce every where borrow a variety of light and civilisation and preserve the patriotic feeling in their hearts With the seat of their nationality in their breaches indelibly impressed by the circumcision—At last constitutions according [to] my way of thinking can not be given at once and particularly by a set of beings that neither have it themselves nor understand the meaning of it. If the extract of Cz. letter to Mr B.[6] which you send me is not an oppen avowal of all these things in your eyes then I am quite out of the true path and dont wish to be brought upon it. Some time more and you will come I expect a little nearer to my way of thinking.

Now tell me what is Samuel doing, is he the only priviledged being that can remain quite in the midst of a Chaos.[7] Let me know something of him when you write to me again, which I will be very glad of.

[4] Also missing.

[5] The new Kingdom of Poland was based on the Duchy of Warsaw, Napoleon's client state.

[6] Brougham.

[7] Samuel Bentham was still in France, having been near Tours during the Hundred Days and going to Paris after Napoleon's downfall. See M. S. Bentham, *The Life of Brigadier-General Sir Samuel Bentham*, London, 1862, pp. 310–11.

2327

From Madelaine Gautier

August 1815

Paris, August, 1815.

Our position is dreadful. The question is nothing less than 'To be or not to be.'[2] Passions are excited even to the height of despair, and reason is no longer heard.[3] The Allied Monarchs are, I fancy, much embarrassed. We hardly know what to decide on. The oppressions of the foreign troops are terrible; but this is not the worst—for our internal dissensions are far more afflictive.

2328

From Arthur Taylor

11 September 1815

J. Bentham Esqre.

Mr. Taylor presents his respects to Mr. Bentham. If Mr. B. has corrected and will return the Proof of the *Table* part of the 'Springs of Human Action' the other matter shall be added to it, and a complete impression sent to Mr. Bentham—
Shoe Lane
Septr. 11
1815

2327. [1] Bowring, x. 486.
[2] *Hamlet*, III. i. 56.
[3] The August 1815 elections produced an Ultra (extreme royalist) majority in the Chamber of Deputies, and persecution of Bonapartists and Revolutionaries was at its height.

2328. [1] Common Place Book of James Mill, ii. 55, London Library.
Arthur Taylor was a member of the firm of Richard and Arthur Taylor of Shoe Lane, which printed *A Table of the Springs of Action* in July and August 1815. The work was published in 1817. See *Deontology together with A Table of the Springs of Action and Article on Utilitarianism* (*CW*), ed. A. Goldworth, Oxford, 1983, pp. xii–xvii.

2329

To Sir Samuel Romilly

3 October 1815 (Aet 67)

Ford Abbey 3 Oct. 1815.

Dear Romilly

At the eve of your departure for the Continent you received I hope and believe certain copies of my Spring of Action Table 6, 7 or 8 I forget which. They were put up for fear of missing you in the utmost hurry, before the last sheet or two had been revised by me. A revision has since then produced the following list of Corrigenda,[2] six copies of which you will find in this paper, sent to the end that if it be not too much trouble to you one may find its way to each of the persons to whom a copy of the papers may have been delivered —All well here: viz. Mr and Mrs Mill with their four actual children.[3] Mr. and Mrs Herbert Koe with their future contingent ones.

2330

From Pavel Chichagov

12 October 1815

London the 12th October 1815
34 Upper Berkeley Street portman Square

Having left wilton house much sooner than at first intended On account of the Pembroke family going to Paris, I returned to town some time ago and have been since employed in several other excursions of short distance and duration. Moving about is necessary to one who knows that nature is nothing but matter in motion and therefore one must move wheil belonging to it or forming a particle of it. During this time I received two letters directed to me with Mr

2329. [1] Dumont MSS 72 (5)/(f). Autograph. Addressed: 'A Monsieur / Mr. le Chevalier Romilly / à Genève / Ou bien / en son absence / M. Étienne Dumont.' Stamped: 'ANGLETERRE'. Postmark: 'F / 180 / 15'.

[2] This list, in the hand of a copyist, is with this letter in the Dumont MSS.

[3] There were in fact five Mill children at this time: John Stuart, Wilhelmina Forbes, Clara Esther (1810–86), Harriet Isabella (1812–*c*.97), and James Bentham (1814–62).

2330. [1] BL IX. 212–15. Autograph. Docketed: '1815 Oct 12 / Tchitchagoff 34 Upper / Berkeley Str. Portman Sq / to / J.B. Ford Abbey / Self-biography.' Addressed: 'Jeremy Bentham Esqr / Ford Abbey near Chard / Somersetshire'. Postmark: 'OC / 13 / 1815'.

Brougham name upon the covers and containing your brothers letters to you.[2] After an attentif perusal I thought best to keep them till you require me to send them to you and in the mean time I return my most sincere thanks for the communication. They have been read with all the eagerness, interest and attention that the subject the writers and my friendship for them could have inspired. But for all that it does not follow that I should be entirely of their opinion. I can't suppose for instance that the french are realy so fond and so devoted to the King as it is represented. I don't believe also that in that part of france no bitter fruits should be found as it is mentioned in the leters all the rest apears just and above all very agreable to read and useful to know. As you are required to write to them, at least once in 4 month's, I intreat you, when that period comes to do me the favour to remember me kindly to them all and to say that should they continue in france an other year most likely I shall see them; but they wont be able to stay there.

yesterday I was surprised, very much delighted and as much flattered by the long letter which came to my hands through wilton house, writen by you,[3] I dont know when, but as it contains things that are good at all times, so the want of date does not signify, provided you dont scruple about exact answers. Every thing you say is convincing of many thruth's and of the great goodness of your heart. It shews that philosophy has taught you not only to reason right but also to care for other peoples good, or in other words it has made you better than men generaly are even the many pretended philosophers. You are then very right *almost* in every thing and that is as much as I can say, for the best arguments of a member of a free government should find no application at all to an individual of the most arbitrary and the most hateful one. But yet let me speak out my observations, you say that I have a reputation to vindicate. Before who? is there a public opinion in China, in turkey in India and particularly in russia? Will you tell me what public opinion is composed of? what elements are necessary to constitute it? The greatest analyzer of thoughts and ideas must know that better than any body. Is it before a parcel of old women and men worse than old women, who all tried to fly in the woods of archangel at the aproach of the enemy and who sudenly returned from the extreme terror to the extreme arrogance and imagined every thing that was impossible or absurd and required it to be

[2] Missing. These might be the letters Brougham first sent to Earl Grey in August 1815. See *The Life and Times of Henry Lord Brougham*, 3 vols., Edinburgh and London, 1871, ii. 288–9, and below, letter 2331.

[3] Missing.

done? or is it before the deaf and blind calumniators and their echo the ignorant and stupid idlers that I am to justify myself. But perhaps before the admirers and the Enthousiasts of the weak, the profligate, the debauched and the drunk that it is necessary to justify oneself or before the reviewers among whom there is not a *single* impartial or candid one. Should I imitate the author of certain memoirs who has lately undertaken to answer every one of the thousand reviews of this country.[4] But suppose even such thing should be undertaken can there be any hope of succeeding to open peoples eyes when they are determined to keep them shut. What can be better than the pamphlet written by the french general.[5] Every thing that could be expected from a vindication is united in it to a supreme degree—Impartiality from the very situation of the author, proofs incontestable, evidences unequivocal, what has it then produced? Hardly any body cared for it, very few would read it and notice was taken by those who wanted to add to their former animosity to me that for the author. The best is to say with *seneca* if I remember well, That whoever fears the opinions resembles a general frightened at the sight of the dust risen by the catle.[6] You say further, the country has a claim upon me. Do I belong then to any society of thinking beings who have political institutions that bind me to them? If such institutions or contracts—between me and any sort of men exist, I should like to know them and then see how far our mutual claims can go. But in this instance again an Englishman can have no language or expressions fit to apply to despotism and Slavery. Now I come to my last observation which should have been the first and the all sufficient that is the total want of ability for such an undertaking as a Byography that should be interesting. you observe yourself, how few of them are extant. Selfishness would engage many to do it, was it not of an extreme difficulty—

It is true that I have many materials and such ones that would be very difficult for any body else to collect. Great many events and causes of events are also known to me better than to most people but still I dont suppose that the publication of these could be of any real use either to the present or the future generations. Barbarity, blunders, madness, folly, weakness worse than all the first put

[4] Almost certainly a reference to Sir Nathaniel William Wraxall, Bt. (1751–1831) and his *An Answer to the Calumnious Misrepresentations of the 'Quarterly Review', the 'British Critic', and the 'Edinburgh Review' Contained in their Observations on Sir N.W.W.'s Historical Memoirs of His Own Time*, London, 1815. Wraxall's *Historical Memoirs of My Own Time* had been published in two volumes earlier in the year.

[5] General Frédéric-François Guillaume de Vaudoncourt's *Relation impartiale du passage de la Bérézina*, Paris, 1814. See letter 2278 and n. 2.

[6] Lucius Annaeus Seneca (c.4 BC–AD 65), *Ad Lucilium Epistulae Morales*, II. i. 8.

together, would constitute the ground work of such memoirs and surely no utility could be derived from such information not even of the negative kind, for we dont see that past follies prevent the repetition of the same. They only excite contempt or horror, the best of them indifference if represented with truth. Whoever to shew that your arguments are not entirely lost upon me I promise to try to put together something in the way you advise and then present it to your approbation. But when and how god alone knows. I remember to have read the hystory of the jews by Jos.[7] I read it with pleasure because I found that he never try's to persuade people of the supernatural things that he is obliged to relate as having heard off. he even very often leaves every one to judge for himself and believe as much as will apear credible. As for his biography[8] I never mett with it, but this as well as any other that you would recommend I would read with pleasure.

I am very much obliged for all your kind and agreable proposals but to my true regret I can not conveniently absent myself from here for I am often obliged to be with my poor children who very often wish and want me to be with them. I went to day to Mr place and got a copy of your work.[9] I have no doubt that this production is equal to the former and that I shall read it with great pleasure and profit. Accept my thanks for it. I see already that your ideas about interest are the most correct. I allways thought that it was the main spring of all our actions and that there is so much even as the interest of the disinterestedness. provided that spring is properly, usefuly and honestly directed that is all that is wanted and that makes the difference between good and bad.

The person through whom I have send your letters is one of the Emperors secretary of state and a good friend of mine by some particular chance because he was my secretary two years ago.[10] He wrote to me since informing me now particularly of this business. He says that as Cz. has been the principal agent in it he thought proper to sent to him to warsaw both the letters, and as the Emperor is now gone there also, he will soon get it. we shall presently hear of balls, dancings, reviews and Constitutions for the poles.

You were very right when you promised to send me metaphysics.

[7] The *Jewish Archaeology* or *Jewish Antiquities* (as it is usually known) of Flavius Josephus (37–*c*.98), a history of the Jews down to AD 66.

[8] A reference to the autobiographical *Life of Josephus*.

[9] i.e. *A Table of the Springs of Action*.

[10] Capodistria. See Letter 2307 and n. 8.

Your last work[11] is realy methaphysical without being chimerical and entirely coincides with the ideas which I have found in a french author about it I think it was in Mirabeau[12] who says—A proprement parler la métaphysique est le seul guide de l'homme: sans elle il n'éprouverait que des sensations isolées, il ne les comparerait jamais, il ne tirerait aucun résultat de ses observations. La métaphy. de Lock, d'Helvetius,[13] de Condillac[14] n'est que l'art de juger dont la nature nous enseigne elle même les élémens. Toutes les fois que nous comparons et concluons, nous faisons de la métaphysique; nous en faisons lorsque de plusieurs faits épars, nous comparons des notions générales; que de certaines observations individuelles, nous tirons des règles ou des principes: c'est de la métaphysique que l'art de cultiver les champs, d'élever de [. . . ?], de soustraire les chaumières, en un mot de pourvoir au moindre de nos besoins, et c'est d'elle seule que le genre humain peut attendre l'agrandissement de son existence, sa perfection, et son bonheur. Thank god we are in a fair way. This sort of metaphysic will be of real use and I have no doubt but you will extend the field of it as well as trace all the paths that lead through its sinuosities.

I have endeavoured to return you the Compliment of a long letter if not by the value at least by the bulk of it and now it is time not to trespass any more upon yours—adieu—

My best Compts. to your Compagnions.

[11] Probably another allusion to the recently-printed *A Table of the Springs of Action.*

[12] The passage from which Chichagov was quoting has not been traced. By 'Mirabeau' he probably meant either Victor de Riqueti, marquis de Mirabeau (1715–89), the political economist; or Honoré Gabriel Riqueti, comte de Mirabeau (1749–91), the French Revolutionary statesman.

[13] Claude Adrien Helvétius (1715–71), author of *De l'Esprit*, Paris 1758 and *De l'homme, de ses facultés intellectuelles et de son éducation*, London, 1773.

[14] Étienne Bonnot de Condillac (1715–80), French philosopher, author of *Essai sur l'origine des connoissances humaines*, 2 vols., Amsterdam, 1746, and *Traité des sensations*, London and Paris, 1754.

2331

From Pavel Chichagov

3 November 1815

London 3d November 1815
1, george Street portman square

It is now about a week since I have had the pleasure, allways very great, to recieve your letter beginning the 20th and ending at the 23d of October.[2] I have perused and reperused it and very well understand every thing you say, for I think you write a better hand since you have to do with worse heads. Watching if a parcel was sent to me either by Mr Koe's brother or any body else, intended for Czartor and as I have a very excellent opportunity of writing and sending to warsaw I shall be very sorry if this is lost again. The person going that way set off next tuesday, if I dont recieve any thing before that I don't know When I shall meet with so good an opportunity afterwards. That you might continue to call me a good boy I have done on my side all I could to do your commission, I went to see Mr. place: told him all about it and he promised to help me as far as he could, whoever only 3 copies of Chrestomatics are come to my hands and some of the second tables, but no springs of action to this time, nor any other parcel—

you shew rather a bad disposition in suspecting me of being too political to trust you with a name which I never meant to keep secret, but it did not occur to me before to mention it. The person I have applied too for the last business of yours is Count Capd'istria,[3] whose name you will see in the papers every time it is spoken of the paris negociations for he is one of our negociators in a transaction in which no body knows what to do. The leters you mentioned from Lady Bent. have been send to me through Lord grey who had them from Mr. Brhm.[4] I think her accounts of facts are as curious as well sellected and well related but most of the conjectures seem partial and those that I can the best judge off are quite wrong. for inst. all

2331. [1] BL IX. 216–17. Autograph. Docketed: '1815 Nov 3 / Tchitchagoff. No 1 / George Street / Portman Squr / to / J.B. Ford Abbey / To go off 7 Nov J.B.-s / packet for Warsaw for / Emp. and Cz. / Tch's intended self-biography / Pleased with Ensor'.

[2] Missing.

[3] See letters 2307 and n. 8 and 2330 and n. 10. Capodistria, as Chichagov went on to say, was at this time involved in the negotiations leading to the second peace of Paris (20 November 1815), which reduced France to her borders of 1790 after the Hundred Days.

[4] i.e. Brougham. See letter 2330 and n. 2.

what she says of Richelieu[5] and Langeron[6] may be good to produce water melons and any other wont comparatively as good but nothing else. Whoever I may mistake also and therefore the best method is that adopted by your freedom of thought and speech in full length.

I am glad to find that the time of your return to town is so near, but mind you keep your word, that I may praise you also. Franklin's life[7] I know very well for I have read it many times over and over. By reading him it seems that any body may do the same, only take a quire of paper, pen and ink and write what happens to you and yet upon a trial that very work becomes very difficult nay in general impossible. I think the best model for me according to my honour would be the confessions of Rousseau.[8] There is the pleasure of abusing every body and every thing one likes or rather one does not like. The other books you mention I don't know at all and will be glad to see them when you have the means of getting at them yourself. At this moment I am delighting myself in Mr Ensors work upon national government.[9] The begining of it and some parts that I have been looking in too please me excessively, the first day I got it he kept me awake till three a clock at night. I am so glad to have made his acquaintance, thanks to you. It is peculiar to this country only, to find very often that people that you meet are much more worth, I dont mean in guineas, than they at first apear. On the contrary in other parts of the world where dancing and speaking French and making Compliments is prefered to a Classical education, you expect every thing from people at first sight and find nothing but an automotion [?] at last. The immense reading and the liberality of Mr. Ensor's ideas is every thing that would be unexpected in that way

I have read with pleasure Mr de Lasterie's letter to you.[10] There

[5] Armand Emmanuel Sophie Septemanie du Plessis, duc de Richelieu (1766–1822), who had recently become first minister of France. He had been in Russia 1790–1814, serving in the Russian army and as governor of Odessa from 1803. He was described by Sir Samuel Bentham in May 1791 as 'an intimate Russian Army comrade'. See *Correspondence*, iv. 274.

[6] Andrault, comte de Langeron (1763–1831), another Frenchman in Russian service. He had risen to the rank of lieutenant-general. He too was an old associate of Sir Samuel. See *Correspondence*, iv. 203, 222.

[7] Benjamin Franklin (1706–90), American statesman, philosopher, publisher, and writer. His autobiography appeared in many forms; first in French as *Mémoires de la vie privée de Benjamin Franklin, écrits par lui-même*, Paris, 1791, then in an English translation as *The Private Life of the late Benjamin Franklin, . . . originally written by himself*, London, 1793.

[8] The first part of *Les Confessions* of the Genevan philosopher Jean-Jacques Rousseau (1712–78) was published at Geneva, Lausanne, and London in 1782. The second part followed in 1788.

[9] Chichagov was referring to George Ensor (1769–1843), the radical writer, and to the first part of his *On National Government*, 2 vols., London, 1810.

[10] Letter 2326.

is no doubt that this plan will teach Europe how to teach children but I should wish that governments should extend the bell's method to improve the grown up subjects necessary for the action of governments. They should see from the example of children how knowledge of any kind may best and quickest be spread and instead of having recourse, as the most stupid and the most absurd of all governments does, to [. . . ?] rebuke of people to charlatans and adventurers, endeavour to rise and form out of their own subjects, scholar-teachers and scholar tutors and monitors and so rise the whole nation successively and rapidly to knowledge, use and happiness.

There is no other reason for the degradation of man but his government. Neither the Climate nor his own nature never hinder the progress of his improvements if the want of good institutions does not prevent it and the existence of arbitrary acts does not brutalize him. I am sure if the master was good for any thing Scholars would be found presently to teach one another and civilise the whole. But this is not the case, the very reverse exists.

If you can in any manner hasten the arrival of the intended parcel before tuesday it would be as well to do it for I realy can't answer for an other so good an oportunity.

Pray present my Cts to Mr and Mrs Mill and the young philosopher Master John and dont forget that you have promised to be in town in the midle of this month or else have the goodness to let me know when you come.

2332

To John McCreery

13 December 1815 (Aet 67)

Ford Abbey, near Chard, December 13th, 1815.

You have heard, I hope, from Mr. Hoe[2] why I wish to delay the printing of the last half sheet that you sent till my arrival in town, which, by some unlooked-for disappointments, perhaps, will be delayed for these ten or twelve days. I send you now about half of the matter intended for No. V. of the Appendix to Chrestomathia.[3] It is an enormous long article; the others will, in comparison, be, some

2332. [1] *The Collection of Autograph Letters and Historical Documents formed by Alfred Morrison*, 2nd series, 3 vols., London, 1893–6, i. 224.

[2] A mistranscription of Koe.

[3] Appendix V of *Chrestomathia* as published in 1817 consisted of 'Essay on Nomenclature and Classification'. It formed the second part of the work and appears as appendix IV of the 1843 Bowring and *CW* editions.

of them, very short ones. For Chrestomathia the greatest dispatch that can be given will be essential to the business; though I send only a part at present, you may depend upon the press's not stopping for a supply.

As to type, that which served for the letters No. 3 and 4, neither of which had notes,[4] seems too small for this, which has some very long notes. I leave it to you to choose a somewhat larger one.

The paging may go on or recommence. When the day of my departure for town is fixed, I will give you notice, to prevent the proof from coming to this place during my absence. But, in default of such advise, you will send them here as usual.

The other will not be published till this is finished.[5]

2333

To John Herbert Koe?

18 December 1815 (Aet 67)

Ford Abbey Monday 18 Decr 1815

Well—the business is now settled: Gwyn having signed a paper to the effect mentioned in my last to you.[2] His Attorney (Gould of Honiton[3]) was here to day, brought me that paper, and I signed before him he witnessing both duplicates of the parchment Agreement, kept one of them, and gave him the other. I have the little close by the dog-kennels and not the other. W. Baggs[4] and the Gardener very happy. And now you will say I ought to fix a day, and take Coaches. But then there are certain arrangements to be taken here about Terasse and [. . . ?] Ground, and Ice House and River Walk etc. that could not be taken before, because of the uncer-

[4] Appendices III and IV of the first part of *Chrestomathia* were letters from James Pillans (1778–1864), rector of Edinburgh High School, to Joseph Fox, and from James Gray (1770–1830) teacher at the same school, to Edward Wakefield. They appear as appendices II and III of the 1843 Bowring and *CW* editions.

[5] The first part of *Chrestomathia* had been printed in 1815 and again in 1816, but was not published until the second part was ready, when both parts appeared together.

2333. [1] Yale University Library. Autograph. Inserted in a copy of Henry Crabb Robinson's *Diary, Reminiscences and Correspondence*, 3 vols., London, 1869, i. 124. There is no indication for whom this letter was intended, but the reference to the distribution of copies of *Chrestomathia* suggests that the recipient was Koe, since he was later to be charged with this task. See below letter 2353.

[2] Missing.

[3] *Clarke's New Law List* for 1815 records that Daniel Gould was an attorney at Honiton.

[4] Gwyn was later to describe Baggs as 'the Carpenter'. See Gwyn to Bentham, 13 August 1818, UC. clxiii. 20.

tainty. G. is married without making a jointure So Madam[5] is entitled to *dower* of every thing (paying off mortgages) Elswood is in Upper Canada under the name of *Sir Azariah Elswood*.[6]

Kiss every thing kissable—What can I say more. Joseph Hume has postponed his intended continental ramble So he will be in the way for sending Chrestomathia

2334

To an Unknown Correspondent

1815?

Don't tell anybody of it, for I should never hear the last of it. I am in love with Mrs N.[2] She is a most accomplished creature, bearing her faculties most meekly, at least to your humble servant. M.[3] says (but it is jealousy) that she is not handsome enough for me.

2335

To John Herbert Koe

2 January 1816 (Aet 67)

Ford Abbey 2 Jany. 1816

At receipt of these presents you will either be, or pretend to be, both of you[2] in a great rage. Mrs Stoker, for want of warning which could not be given to her, has in store provisions sufficient for a fortnight: such good things must not be wasted. Therefore at the earliest we can not leave this place earlier than this day fortnight nor therefore appear at Q.S.P. till the next day. But even of a day so

[5] John Fraunceis Gwyn's first wife had died in 1807 and on 11 November 1815 he married Dinah, only daughter of R. Good of Winsham, Somerset. She died in 1831.

[6] This appears to have been a false title: there is no record of Elswood's having received a knighthood.

2334. [1] Bowring, x. 485. An extract, introduced: 'He [Bentham] spent one day with his friends, the Northmores, at Cleve, and says in one of his letters—'. In October 1814 (letter 2294) Thomas Northmore had invited Bentham to visit him at Cleve, apparently during the 'next season'. Bentham remained at Ford Abbey until the following February and returned some time in late June or early July 1815. It was probably during that summer that he visited the Northmores.

[2] Emmeline, Northmore's second wife, for whom see letter 2294 n. 3.

[3] Presumably Mill.

2335. [1] BL IX. 218–19. Autograph. Docketed: '1816 Jany 2 / J.B.' Addressed: 'To / J.H. Koe Esqr / Lincolns Inn / London'. Postmark: 'A / 4 JA 4 / 1816'. Stamped: 'CHARD / 142'.

[2] Koe and his wife Anne.

early as that no absolute assurance can be obtained. Various arrangements, domestic and horticulturan, remain still unconcluded. You know who it was in concert with when certain measurements were taken necessary to the laying out of Terrasse and ordering of shrubs for the same: you know what became of said measurements. The ground being covered with the contents of the bottom of the pond, access has not yet been haveable for taking first measurements: and then what with weather what with languor and inaptitude, it is not every day will serve. Then again as to Ice. Poor dear Pretious,[3] when she revisits this chilly place, might almost as well be without bread to eat, as without ices and certain consultations and enquiries respecting that important subject are but just concluded: operations not yet commenced.

Practical inference from the above premises *Periodicals! Periodicals!* including Missionary Register,[4] which though Church of Englandist proves virtuous, and Edinburgh Review which J M says is out.

Letter from the Admiral dated 25 last.[5] He has been at death's door with a fever, but is now alive and lusty. He mentions Prince Czartoriski's receipt of the recipienda accompanied with a letter of Tchitchagoffs own to him, which of course if the end be furtherable will not fail to further it.

Four Column paper is all consumed: Composition converted into it. Composition not enough for the fortnight: if your providence has provided a supply, half a dozen quires may accompany the periodicals.

In the Great Hall Music on Christmas and New Year's Days, according to the ritual: yea, and moreover dancing on the latter day. At the suggestion of Mrs. Mill, Mrs. Stoker at top led by his Reprobacy.[6] Mrs Stoker in all her glory. From [. . . ?] virtuous peach-yielding and apple-yielding Quality to drink tea with her.

Antient Appledorian[7] [. . . ?] on the point of being exhausted, starvation would be our state, were it not for the genius of Mrs Stoker, which has invented and provided a supply of modern ones. ⟨. . .⟩ such is the demand of the necessary merchants to supply ⟨. . .⟩ one.

[3] Presumably Mrs Koe.

[4] *The Missionary Register . . . containing an abstract of the proceedings of the principal Missionary and Bible Societies throughout the World* ran from 1813 to 1855.

[5] i.e. Chichagov. The letter is missing.

[6] Probably James Hume. Bentham was in the habit of calling his secretaries 'reprobates'.

[7] Appledore in Devon was the home of Mrs Koe's parents. See above, letter 2240 n. 12.

2336

To Francis Place Jr.

January 1816 (Aet 67)

Mr Bentham begs the favour of Mr Place Junr at Paris to deliver into the own hands of Sir S. Bentham the letter or letters addressed to him—and not into any other hands whatever: and to ask from Mr B. to see them opened and begun to be read: saying that they are of consequence.

2337

To Aaron Burr

23 February 1816 (Aet 68)

Q.S.P. 23 Feby 1816.

I am still alive: I hope you are. I am in good health and spirits: I hope by this time so are you. I promised to write to you from hence. Not two days together has my promise been ever out of my mind. But when or how to fulfil it? Once I was setting about it: then came a report that you were dead. True or not true, but t'other day I heard that the report was at any rate groundless So now I take my chance

Some time ago American books three or four came to me from you with a letter.[2] I took it kindly of you this remembrance: but grievous was my disappointment at not finding Blodget among

2336. [1] UC clxxiv. 120. Autograph draft. Endorsed: 'Request from Jeremy Bentham to F Place Jun to present or deliver certain / letters to Sir Saml Bentham in Paris—(January 1816)'.

[2]Francis Place jnr. (b. 1798) had been sent to the banking firm of Messrs Mallet at Paris in 1814 and remained there until November 1816. See *The Autobiography of Francis Place*, ed. Mary Thale, Cambridge, 1972, p. 227.

2337. [1] Charles Roberts Autograph Collection, Haverford College Library, Pennsylvania. Autograph. Endorsed: 'Bentham 23 febr 1816'. Addressed: 'To / Colonel Aaron Burr / New York'. Printed, with minor omissions and many errors, in Davis, ii. 447–53. A memorandum on the contents of the letter is at BL IX. 220–1, docketed: '1816 Feb 23 / J.B. Q.S.P. / to / Col. A. Burr / New York / sent by Oldfield and / Cobbet Printers / and [. . .?] to / Philadelphia / Topics touched upon / J.B.'s works sent to / them for do. / 1. Evidence / 2. Swear not / 3. Springs of Action / 4. Chrestomathia / latter proof / 5. Do. table with / allowance to reprint / N.B. This not directed / to him / but them.' This suggests that the letter to Burr went with another to Oldfield and Cobbett, enclosing the Bentham works listed.

[2] Probably letter 2187.

them.[3] Ever since your departure I have been trying in vain to get it. Dont you trouble yourself however about it now: for now I have doubtless the means: viz. by a Nephew of Cobbet: who with a friend is going to set up a Printing Office etc at Philadelphia? is it not? principally for reprinting his weekly periodical work (Political Register) as it comes out.[4]

Grievous was my vexation at not being able to do but in so imperfect a manner what you seemed so desirous of in relation to the return of some of your letters.[5] Just at that time there was in the room of your friend Ann[6] a very stupid female. At the same time that I missed those letters of yours I missed some papers of mine the loss of which was very distressing to me. I do believe the creature took them to light fires with. She was soon after packed off: and Ann reinstated in her place where she still continues.

The time is extremely short—I know not what I shall be able to send you of things of mine printed since you saw. Every thing small or imperfect: stopped by some incident or other (some consideration or other): for I have always—unless it be for my own amusement—too many irons in the fire.

I have at last got one spare copy of that thing which you were so eager to have another of in addition to the one you said you had lost.[7] I don't know whether I shall send it you. I would if I were sure of your giving it publicity there. But how can I when I am not sure of your being alive: and perhaps by this time if alive you may be not only grimgribberizing for the one thing needful, but indifferent to every thing else. I looked to see your name at the head of some of the levies assisting the Spanish Americans: not finding it I conclude that grimgribber has sent empire out of your head.[8]

When you left me I was as I apprehended at the eve of a comparative ruin: singing nos dulcia linquimus arva; nos patriam fugimus:[9]

[3] Bentham had asked Burr for Samuel Blodget's *Economica: a Statistical Manual for the United States of America* in October 1811 (letter 2143) and later the same month also requested President Madison to send him a copy (letter 2145).

[4] William Cobbett sent his nephew Henry Cobbett and Granville Sharp Oldfield to New York to publish an American edition of the *Political Register* which would include material dangerous to release in Britain. See George Spater, *William Cobbett: The Poor Man's Friend*, 2 vols., Cambridge, 1982, ii. 360, 570 n. 30.

[5] See letters 2165, 2172, and 2187.

[6] Presumably Ann Lay, a servant at Queen's Square Place.

[7] See letter 2187, where Burr requested many books, but none that he said had been lost.

[8] By 'grimgribber' and 'grimgribberizing' Bentham meant talking technical or legal jargon, or learned gibberish. For Burr's imperial ambitions, see letter 2023 n. 1. The 'levies' referred to were foreign troops helping the South Americans in their fight for liberation.

[9] i.e. 'we are leaving the sweet fields; we are fleeing from our fatherland', an adaptation of Virgil, *Eclogues*, i. 3–4.

meaning Q.S.P. Now, though after disappointments many and grievous, I am in a state of comparative prosperity. In town Q.S.P. as whilom. In Devonshire, Ford Abbey, not as Boarder but as Housekeeper on lease: a furnished house uniting antique with modern magnificence Gardens picturesque and luxurious. Servants viz for the garden, for so small a person numerous: neighbours cordial though unvisited. Barrow Green a doghole to it. Inmates at the Abbey half the year Mr. and Mrs. Mill with their four children: at Q.S.P. H.K. and his wife, a very amiable person (reading every thing I write or read) with a child upon the stocks.[10]

H.K. took a world of pains for your Randolph.[11] R. Promised him £50 together with the books (statistical)[12] which I wanted. Come neither money, books nor so much as letter. The shoemaking scheme failing him or the hands of his partners, R. I suppose is poor. But if not a book or two, he ought at any rate have sent a letter.

Galatin when here expressed a desire to see me. They told him he could not, as I saw nobody. Hearing of this I called on him. He told me he considered me as his Master in the art of Legislation. I told him of my wish to codify for U.SS any of them. He told me how the land lay in that respect in the different states: and of the scheme he had had for that purpose, and taken steps towards the execution of. Pennsylvania (where his own property is) he mentioned as being one of the likeliest. I asked him whether he had any objection to say in black and white, to persons capable of forwarding the matter any part of what he had been saying viva voce. None whatever: thereupon he sent me a letter highly recommendatory for me to send to Sneyder[13] (or some such name—no time for turning to papers) then Governor. Asking him about books giving an account of U. S. finances—he knew of none published. But he happened to have a spare copy of some official ones never published.[14] He had taken it to Russia[15] and would have left it there could he have found any man there capable of profiting by it: now he had found one: it was with his papers at Ghent, and from there he would send it to me. Along with his letter I sent to Sneyder a copy of every work of mine I could procure from any of my friends most being either out of print

[10] John Herbert and Anne Koe's first child, Bentham Dumont Koe, was born on 18 June 1816.

[11] David Meade Randolph.

[12] Another reference to Blodget's work.

[13] Gallatin's letter to Snyder of 18 June 1814 is published in *Papers Relative to Codification and Public Instruction*, London, 1817, pp. 71–3 (Bowring, iv. 468).

[14] See letter 2305.

[15] Gallatin was in Russia from October 1813 to January 1814 as a member of the American commission invited to St Petersburgh by Emperor Alexander, who had offered to mediate in the Anglo-American war.

or unpublished: together with a letter stating conversations between myself and Galatin.[16] The books went from some port in this Island. Not being able to find any conveyance for the Epistles, viz. J.B. to Sn.[17] and Gal. to J.B.[18] H.K. when I was at the Abbey addressed it to Galatin with a letter saying he could find no other more promising mode of conveyance.[19] Of this letter when he was afterwards in London (I in London likewise) acknowledged the receipt to Romilly (whose letters I have on the subject) and others: but never did. As to the not sending the finance papers, he said that after the burning of Washington[20] there might perhaps be a demand for the spare copy for the service of the State, under which circumstances it was not proper he should part with them. This seemed reasonable. But how he came to Shy me and leave me thus in the dark I can not imagine. The packet for Gov. Sn. did he open it take out his own letter read mine, in which I had said nothing of his conversation with me that was not strictly true, nor had he informed me secretly about any one thing? Had the state of affairs in Philadelphia undergone any change? Would he ask Ministerial people about me and accept vague vituperations as true characters; and true for the purpose of extinguishing such a scheme?

By the bye I think (yes I certainly did) I mentioned to him my scheme of codifying for Russia and obtained permission from him to make some letter of his to me subservient to it. Never did I meet with any man in appearance more respectable and trustworthy. I brought him to Mill, and Mill was quite charmed with him. From Romilly, Dumont etc he could not have heard of any thing but what would have justified any confidence he could have had occasion to repose in me.

Some 8 or 10 months ago, Pr. Adam Czartariski applied to me to assist Poland in Codification.[21] It was then, and till very very lately universally understood that he was to be Viceroy, and in his conversation though he did not say so, it seemed to be implied. Before this

[16] Letter 2281.

[17] Letter 2281.

[18] The letter referred to in Snyder to Randolph, 31 May 1816, where the Governor described the packet that contained Bentham's letter to him as also holding 'a letter from Mr. Gallatin to me, and another from him to Mr. Bentham, both dated in July, 1814'. See *Papers Relative to Codification and Public Instruction*, p. 76 (Bowring, iv. 475).

[19] See letter 2305.

[20] The public buildings in Washington, DC, had been burned by British forces in August 1814.

[21] Bentham appears to have been confused about dates here. Czartoryski visited him on 27 June 1814, some twenty months before, to ask Bentham about a Polish code. See letter 2276 n. 1. Czartoryski may of course have discussed the matter more thoroughly with Bentham at a later date.

I had written to the Emp. Alexander offering my services in this line on condition of these being altogether gratuitous.[22] After I had seen the Prince came a gratious answer in the Emps own hand accepting my offer saying that he had sent orders to his people to consult me, and desiring my acceptance of a 'souvenir'.[23] In a letter to a friend of mine[24] which I saw, Count Capo d'Istria who was then in attendance about him said the souvenir was a 'bague de prix.' In a long answer I sent him back the ring in a packet as it came with the Imperial seal unbroken telling him that after what I said I could not accept of any thing in any shape, and that in comparison of such a letter from him all such things as rings were without value in my eyes.[25] As to his people consulting with me I was sure they would do no such thing: that the man he meant (Rosenkampt or Rosenkampf[26]) (I did not name him) was jealous, and would turn pale at my name: that he might be fit for collecting materials, but was but too well known to be useful for any thing better: that what he ought to do was to invite competition, and I showed him line on line of a Scheme which had cost about 200,000 Roubles a year in Salaries without producing any benefit,[27] he might establish at Petersburgh at Warsaw, or in both places a permanent School of Legislation with scarce any expence. Of this letter I sent a copy to the Prince: telling him I knew very well he was in earnest, and glad I should be to find other people so too. From Cz. I did not expect an answer till his Vice Royalty was settled. About a month ago (being at my Holy place) Newspapers with a list of sub potentates appointed at Warsaw and instead of Cz. a man that nobody had ever heard of.[28] A man with whom I am intimate and whom I will not name for fear of accidents knowing the person most perfectly and knowing the whole matter said he was not at all surprised.[29] Every man who had ever placed any confidence in him was deceived by him: that his head and heart were upon a par: no—but the fault lay most in the head: that the state of that country was most deplorable: that the man

[22] Letter 2266.

[23] Letter 2313.

[24] Probably Chichagov, for whom Capodistria had worked in 1812–13. See letter 2307 n. 8 and 2330 and n. 10.

[25] Letter 2319.

[26] Baron Gustav Andreevich Rosenkampf.

[27] See letter 2319.

[28] In November 1815 Alexander appointed Joseph Zaionczek (1752–1826) viceroy of Poland. A Polish general who had fought against the Russians and served under Napoleon, Zaionczek was soon criticized as too compliant towards Russia.

[29] The 'man with whom I am intimate' was almost certainly Chichagov; 'the person' whom Chichagov knew 'most perfectly' was the Emperor Alexander. For Chichagov's remarks on Alexander's inconsistency see letter 2278.

who happened at the time to be at his elbow (he might have added or the woman especially if an impostor, pretending to be a bigot[30]) was at all times inventor of his resolutions. And to tell the truth I had been furiously blamed before hand for taking any sort of trouble on the supposition that any possible good could come out of him. But Cz. I understood was always at his elbow, and it was in him I put my trust.

If Chrestomathia comes to you (it will be fragmentical it being now / still / on its way through the press) know that the principal persons of name engaged are Brougham, Sir Js Mackintosh, and I hope Romilly—Your friend Allen etc. I will not be of the number of the Managers but Mill will, and others on whom he and I think we can depend for not spoiling it. I furnish ground for it which they could not get elsewhere. viz a part of Q.S.P. garden gratis, and some money besides. I have some thoughts of sending to Cobbets own House a copy of Packg[31] with a request to ask you whether you will procure from N.York an engagement from any person to reprint it without profit or loss to me, and if you do by a certain time, then to send it you: otherwise to be at liberty to print it himself. Do what you will about Chrestomathia: only do not mention any of the above names, the matter not being as yet settled.

Great would be my satisfaction to find that you are still good for any thing. I had little expectaion of continuing thus long at my time of life: 68 the 15th of this, My Abbey has a Court in which I play every morning at fives (beating a boy of 18)[32] instead of taking physic.

I have in print some copies of my letter to President Maddison[33] not yet distributed any of them so much as to intimates. I know not whether it is exactly as you saw it. I think I shewed it (whether in print or Ms I forget) to Galatin. I should have sent you a copy but that I think of adding some account of my transactions with Galatin

[30] Bentham was probably thinking of Baroness Julie von Krüdener (1764–1824), the evangelical prophetess who met Alexander in 1815. She was widely believed to be a fraud, but was thought to have inspired Alexander to pursue his scheme of the 'Holy Alliance', an agreement signed by Russia, Prussia, and Austria in September 1815 which sanctioned the principle of intervention to crush revolutionary and liberal movements in other states.

[31] Apparently *The Elements of the Art of Packing*, printed in 1809 but not published until 1821. In January 1810 Romilly had advised against publication owing to the risk of prosecution. See letter 2070.

[32] John Flowerdew Colls (1801–78), Bentham's secretary who later became an Anglican clergyman, described playing fives with Bentham before breakfast at Ford Abbey in his *Utilitarianism Unmasked*, London, 1844, p. 13. It seems likely, however, that Bentham was referring to James Hume, since Colls was only fourteen at this time, and does not appear to have arrived at Ford Abbey until later in 1816. See below, letters 2357 and 2358.

[33] Letter 2145.

including his letter on my behalf to Gov. Sn. which he gave me open that I might see it: mentioning his name always with respect but with expressions mingled with surprise and regret. Before I printed this letter to Pres. Maddison I sent it in Ms all but a page or two to Ld Sidmouth Secry for Home department[34] who had been an openly declared Admirer of Dumonts book. He acknowledged in black and white the having read it. But being a man of whom it is said that he does nothing of his own opinion, I think it not improbable that he may have hoped with the rest of the Ministry to whom I am in the highest degree obnoxious for the injuries they and their predecessors have done me, and it is nothing but natural that they should have given it in charge to oppose everything of mine to the diplomatic men at all places. Galatin could not but be aware of this. Is it possible that he should have been efficiently influenced by vague vituperation, and not apply to any one of my friends to learn whether if any such vituperation was uttered there was any ground for it?

This is as much perhaps as I shall have leave to write about myself. Now; if you receive it write to me quickly about yourself. Do you still continue a man of *bonnes fortunes*?

To my account of my transactions with Galatin I should probably add do with Emp. and Cz.[35] Kosciusko[36] I am informed is without hopes. How stand you about Constitutional despotism under yourself is not Federalism or Antifederalism the best?

If you are good for any thing, try to set up a Chrestomathia at New York. Depend upon me, in that case, for every assistance in my power.

[34] See letter 2177.

[35] Czartoryski.

[36] Tadeusz Andrzej Bonawentura Kosciuszko (1746–1817), Polish patriot and soldier, who had served with the American army during the war of independence.

2338

FROM SIR SAMUEL BENTHAM

18 March 1816

Hotel de Rivoli 17th March 1816[2]

at $\frac{1}{2}$ past 5 in the afternoon I lost my boy[3] my friend and companion from whom for the last twelvemonth I had no secret and in whom I found the most correct judgement. his mother and I having nursed him ourselves that is I to relieve her to allow her to sleep a few hours having taken her place sometimes entirely I cannot yet become quite reasonable. about two hours before his death I was called out to Mr Place[4] and received your packet[5] as one of my children was present when Place enquired how Sam was I did not acknowledge him to be in danger for till all was over we concealed all apprehensions from the other children as well as from himself so that to the last he looked forward to enjoyments of every kind. he had no mental suffering nor scarcely any pain till the moment when he told us 'my breather pipe is stopt' which were his last words. just before he had asked what letter I was reading though it was behind the curtain that being alone with him I opened your packet. I had read the first 3 or 4 lines when having seen the continuation of the subject by complaint I for the first as well as last time deceived him by my answer assured him that the reason of our not having heard from you was that you supposed us at Tour but that I was confident I shd hear from you in a week. Mary only knows that your packet contained a power of attorney and that only since she wrote what I now send.[6]

It may be use that before I have read your letter I should mention that I have been prevented writing often of late by the apprehension of your suffering from a connection with Grellier and the difficulty I found on that account of writing to you on the affectionate proposal you made to me about the Quarry.[7] desirable as the terms of your

2338. [1] Koe MSS. Autograph. Addressed: 'Jery Bentham Esqr. / Queen Square Place / Westminster / Angleterre'. Postmarks: 'FOREIGN / MR 22 / 1816' and '4 o'Clock / MR 22 / 1816 EV.'

[2] Letter 2340 reveals that this was actually written on 18 March.

[3] Samuel Bentham junior.

[4] Francis Place junior.

[5] Missing, but see letter 2336.

[6] Lady Bentham's letter (2339) was enclosed in this one.

[7] James Grellier had obtained a lease on a marble quarry at Babbacombe in Devon in December 1813. Bentham invested money in the quarry and in Grellier's cement manufactory at Millbank.

offer appeared, I could not be easy in any course depending on Grellier, yet I feared the displeasure my telling you so would give.

If feelings and affections in cases where there is taken any friendly interest can possibly be wholly independent of them those that I and all of mine bear to you are most truly so. If I have erred by withholding anything from you it has never been but for fear of displeasing you. I am prepared for the most which your letter may contain as I have long been preparing my self for my recent loss. I shall soon be quite certain and I have hopes that even poor George may the better bear the loss [of] a brother to whom the attachment was as strong as can be on account of his having already kept so long separate as to diminish the force of secure habits.

2339

FROM LADY BENTHAM

18 March 1816

17th March 1816[2]
5 in the morning

At midnight between Saturday and yesterday[3] an artery broke in a fit of coughing, the boy again recovered so far as to speak to us to eat and even to ask to be read to till about four oclock yesterday afternoon when hemorhage again came on and suffocated him. he was in his perfect senses to the last, died without a single groan.

Expecting this termination for months past, worn out with fatigue neither B nor myself yet feel otherwise than a stupid sen⟨se?⟩ that great as is our loss the dear boy has suffered less ⟨than?⟩ was to be apprehended. Happily for you you have not known the improvement he had made in the last year. We have still four other children, we are determined for their sakes to bear up to the utmost of our ability against this heavy loss.

B has determined to go as soon as possible southwards, we may set out even this week, letters therefore must be addressed to us at Perigaux and La Fittes[4]

But you will never write to us again surely. no notice from you or

2339. [1] Koe MSS. Autograph. Enclosed in letter 2338.

[2] Written in fact on 18 March, see letter 2340.

[3] Saturday was 16 March, 'yesterday' Sunday 17th.

[4] The Parisian banking firm of Perregaux, Laffitte et Cie, headed by the French financier and politician Jacques Laffitte (1767–1844).

Mr Koe yet of any of our letters. Oh do not let us also have the sorrow of fearing we may have offended you; sincerely do we love you and important to our happiness is your affection.

2340

From Sir Samuel Bentham

20 March 1816

Paris 20th March 1816

I write this at the Bankers[2] where I have brought the power of Attorney to be witnessed, they as well as I were at a loss as to the date on account of the impossibility of the two signatures being made at the same date all I could do was to insert the present date. What I have to say on the subject I h⟨ . . . ⟩ to be able to prepare for tomorrow when by ⟨ . . . ⟩ dr Hume[3] it will be sent with the d. of Wellingtons[4] letters in a manner perhaps more expeditious than the post yet—I thought it best to send this power and the notice that the sum you mention will be at your disposal by the ordinary conveyance. only one hour's sleep and under my present circumstances I may be supposed not very calm but the stimulus is great and that is the most essential for me to act. I must only add that I and I only have now read your letter nor is it my intention that any one else shall read it indeed my present idea is to return it to you as soon as I have answered it.

I misdated my letter the day before yesterday it should have been 18th it was on the 17th that Sam died.[5]

2340. [1] Koe MSS. Autograph. Addressed: 'Jery Bentham Esqr. / Queen Square Place / Westminster / Angleterre'. Postmarks: 'FOREIGN / MR 23 / 1816' and '12 o'Clock / MR 23 / 1816 Nn'.

[2] Probably Perregaux, Laffitte et Cie; see letter 2339 and n. 4.

[3] Dr. John Robert Hume (1781?–1857), Wellington's surgeon.

[4] Wellington was in command of the allied army of occupation in France 1815–18.

[5] See letter 2338 and n. 2.

2341
From Étienne Dumont

23 March 1816

Geneva, 23d March, 1816.

Mad. de Staël has been reading in society the Book of Fallacies, and with great success. The division into *Ins* and *Outs*, and *Eithersides*, does not suit the continent, at least so thought Sismondi, and so I changed it.[2] We are diligently labouring at the organization of our judiciary establishment. But we have all to do, and few fitting doers. You would not believe—I could not believe till I had experience of it, how these fifteen years of French vassalage and continued war have turned men away from study, and lowered the tone of the public mind. We were rapidly hastening to be nothing but a degraded provincial town. In another twenty years, and our ancient Geneva would not have been to be recognised. Only four or five distinguished men had the French régime left. All besides was idleness, mediocrity, and military passion. It is fearful to think how easily mankind may descend from an enlightened civilisation to a position where the culture of the intellect is no longer a necessity. We may hope to rise, if not so high as we were, yet higher than we are. Our constitution has not the stimulants of our old republic,—but our distinction was dearly purchased by dissensions,—and we gain something if we lose much. Besides, after long agitation, men seek intellectual and physical repose. I am not popular here,—I am considered the man of opposition: not that the accusation is true, but that I insist on the need of inquiry, and inquiry displeases the ruling people. But this is a general law, influencing us here,—as it influences everybody elsewhere.

2341. [1] Bowring, x. 487. A translation.

[2] *Traité des sophismes politiques* was published with *Tactique des assemblées législatives*, 2 vols., Geneva and Paris, 1816. Parts of it appeared in English as *The Book of Fallacies* in 1824.

2342

From James Mill

11 April 1816

One of the enclosed is from the Duke of Kent[2] on Chrestomathia

The other is from the Society to whom you sent Defence of Usury,[3] containing a proposal for you. When you have read them, you may send them to me—as I shall return them to Place, when I go to meet Brougham between 3 and 4

2343

From John Cartwright

17 April 1816

My dear Sir

I return your four books with thanks,[2] and have now to apply for another assistance.

Thinking I recollect that you are regularly supplied with the *votes*, which I imagine contain all the matter of which the Journals consist, I shall be greatly obliged, if you will let your young friend[3] examine the said Votes for *the first two weeks* in April 1813, and to pick out for me the Votes in which is noticed the tendering of a *printed* Petition from Nottingham for Peace.[4]

On Easter Monday I put into the hand of the Lord Mayor[5] a Card

2342. [1] UC clxv. 13. Autograph. Docketed: '1816 Apr 11 / Chrestomathia / Mill Q.S.P. / to / J.B. Q.S.P. / Inclosing Duke of Kent / to Joseph Hume on /Chrestomathia / and / Place to Mill / on the Society for / Mutual Reformation / and their notice of / J.B.'s present of / Defence of Usury.' Addressed: 'J. Bentham Esq.'

[2] Edward Augustus, Duke of Kent and Strathern (1767–1820), the fourth son of George III and a field marshal, was patron of the British and Foreign School Society, the successor of the Royal Lancasterian Society. His letter to Hume, dated 5 April 1816, agreeing to be a subscriber of the Chrestomathic school and giving permission for his name to be mentioned in communications with other peers, is at UC clxv. 12.

[3] Missing. A Calendar of correspondence in the Place Papers lists a letter dated 10 April 1816 received from the Society for Mutual Improvement. See BL Add. MS 35,152, fo. 136.

2343. [1] UC clxxiii. 13. Autograph. Docketed: '1816 Apr 17 / Cartwright James / Street / to / J.B. Q.S.P. / Wants Parliamy / document / Spoke for Lieut. Jump / to Lord Mayor Wood / Subscription for Westr / meeting.' Addressed: 'Jeremy Bentham Esq'.

[2] Not identified. [3] Perhaps Koe or Hume.

[4] Cartwright seems to have confused two different petitions. On 7 April 1813 a petition for peace from Warwick was presented and read in the Commons. On 30 June 1813 a motion to bring up a printed petition from Nottingham calling for parliamentary reform was defeated by seventy-five votes to eleven. See *Commons Journals*, lxviii. 388–9, 623–4.

[5] Matthew Wood, lord mayor 1815–17, for whom see letter 2062 n. 2.

to keep Mr. *Jump*[6] in his remembrance, in which I related a sort of second-sighted observation of my niece,[7] who has much skill in physiognomy. On Mr. Jump's leaving my room she broke out— 'Lord, uncle, did you not see *Harbour Master* legibly written in the honest Lieutenant's weather beaten chearful face'?—

your's truly
J. Cartwright

Can you put me in a right channel, without troubling a member, of getting sight of the Petition from the Mayor and a few other members of the *rotten borough* of Lymington received on the 15th. of March,[8] together with a prior petition against the Income Tax from the *Inhabitants*?[9]

Our careful Treasurer Brookes[10] hangs back, in respect of our Meeting in Palace Yard for Economy, for radical Reform, and for furnishing the speaker with Spectacles, for preventing future mistakes in reading on the *Rules* and the *Practice* of the Hon. House, until we have a sufficient fund for the Expence; wherefore I must play the beggar for your contribution towards those Spectacles. Our Subscription as follows

Mill	1.0.0
Long[11]	1.0.0
Wishaw	1.0.0
Cartwright	2.0.0
A visitor	1.0.0
Ditto.	1.0.0
Dickenson[12]	1.0.0
Place	1.0.0
Jones Burdett[13] in Marylebone	1.0.0
Sir F. gives	10.0.0

[6] Lt. Robert Jump, the father of Anne Jump, John Herbert Koe's wife.

[7] Frances Dorothy Cartwright (1780–1863), who was adopted by Cartwright and his wife on the death of her mother in 1786. She was to edit *The Life and Correspondence of Major Cartwright*, 2 vols., London, 1826.

[8] A petition from 'the Mayor and Gentlemen of the Borough of Lymington' assuring the Commons that they disapproved of an earlier petition from the town against the property tax, was presented to the House on 18 March 1816. See *Commons Journals*, lxxi. 210 and *The Times*, 19 March 1816.

[9] The petition from the inhabitants of Lymington against the property tax was presented on 5 March. See *Commons Journals* lxxi. 137 and *The Times*, 6 March 1816. Bentham himself lent Cartwright the Votes containing this petition. See BL XXVIII. 43.

[10] Samuel Brooks, treasurer of the Westminster committee of electors, for whom see letter 2268 n. 8.

[11] Perhaps Richard Godolphin Long (1761–1835), MP for Wiltshire.

[12] Perhaps William Dickinson (1771–1837), MP for Somerset.

[13] William Jones Burdett (1775?–1858), brother of Sir Francis.

2344

From James Madison

8 May 1816

Washington May 8. 1816.

Sir

I have a greater debt of apology, I fear, than I can easily discharge, for having so long omitted to answer your letter of 1811.[2] I flatter myself however that you will not do me the injustice to believe that the failure has proceeded from any insensibility to the importance of its contents, or to the generous motives which dictated it; and as little from a want of respect for the very distinguished character you have established with the world, by the inestimable gifts which your pen has made to it.

It happened that your letter was received in the midst of occupations incident to preparations for an anticipated war, which was in fact the result of the anxious crisis. During the period of hostilities, which apparently became more and more uncertain in their duration, there could not be leisure, if there were no impropriety, in opening a correspondence. On the removal of these difficulties, by the happy event of peace, your letter was among the early objects of my recollection. But a variety of circumstances, which it would be tedious to explain, deprived me of an opportunity of bestowing the proper attention on it, until the recent busy Session of Congress became a further obstacle which has just ceased with the adjournment of that body.

On perusing your letter, I see much to admire in the comprehensive and profound views taken of its subject; as I do everything to applaud, in the disinterested and beneficent offer which it makes to the United States; and it is with the feelings naturally flowing from these considerations, that I find myself constrained to decide, that a compliance with your proposals would not be within the scope of my proper functions.

That a digest of our laws on sound principles, with a purgation and reduction to a text, of the unwritten part of them, would be an invaluable improvement, cannot be questioned; and I cheerfully accede to the opinion of Mr. Brougham, that the task could be

2344. [1] BL IX. 222–5. Autograph. Docketed: '1816 May 8 / President Maddison / Washington / to / Jeremy Bentham / London'. Printed in *Papers Relative to Codification and Public Instruction*, London, 1817, pp. 67–70 (Bowring, iv. 467–8).

[2] Letter 2145.

undertaken by no hand in Europe so capable as yours.[3] The only room for doubt would be as to its practicability, notwithstanding your peculiar advantages for it, within a space and a time such as appear to have been contemplated.

With respect to the unwritten law, it may not be improper to observe, that the extent of it has been not a little abridged, in this country, by successive events. A certain portion of it was dropped by our emigrant forefathers as contrary to their principles, or inapplicable to their new situation. The Colonial Statutes, had a further effect in amending and diminishing the mass. The revolution from Colonies to Independent States, lopped off other portions. And the changes which have been constantly going on since this last event, have every where made and are daily making, further reductions.

To these remarks I may be permitted to add, that with the best plan for converting the common law into a written law, the evil can not be more than partially cured; the complex technical terms to be employed in the text, necessarily requiring a resort for definition and explanation, to the Volumes containing that description of law.

These views of the subject, nevertheless, should they have the validity attached to them, still leave sufficient inducements for such a reform in our code, as had employed your thoughts. And altho' we cannot avail ourselves of them in the mode best in itself, I do not overlook the prospect that the fruits of your labors, may, in some other, not be lost to us; flattering myself that my silence will have no wise diverted or suspended them, as far as the United States may have a particular interest in them. It will be a further gratification if it should experience from your goodness, the pardon which I have ventured to ask. Whatever may be the result, I pray you, Sir, to be assured of my distinguished esteem for your character, and of the due sense I entertain of your Solicitude for the Welfare of my Country.

James Madison

Jer: Bentham Esqr.

P.S.

Be pleased to accept my thanks for the valuable collection of your works which accompanied your letter. I have directed a copy of Blodgets Tables and of Hamiltons works[4] to be procured and forwarded to you, and will endeavour as some further return for your favor, to have added to them a few other publications

[3] A view expressed in Brougham's covering letter to Madison of 1 November 1811, Madison Papers, Library of Congress.

[4] Bentham had requested Blodget and *The Works of Alexander Hamilton* in Letter 2145.

2345
To Étienne Dumont
26 May 1816 (Aet 68)

Q.S.P. 26 May 1816

My dear Dumont

It is impossible for me to write to any body—therefore even to you, anything that can entitle itself to the name of a letter: but I imagine a few words under my own hand just to certify to you my existence and my ever affectionate remembrance of you, will produce a sensation not altogether unpleasant in your legislatorial mind. I am so impressed with the joint conception of the shortness of the utmost hours I can have to live, and the immensity of the work which I see before me, and which I could and would execute if it were God's pleasure to allow me time, that it is not without a sensation of melancholy that except for necessary exercise, I bestow a moment of time on any other object. Since you left us I have produced in brouillon no small quantity of matter that you would like to see me occupied about interlarded with no small quantity of matter that you would not be so well pleased to see me occupied about—prudence here stops my pen.

The gentleman, Mr Walker of Bedford Square,[2] by whom or through whom this will be delivered to you, will form an addition, I flatter myself, of no small value to the small quantity of estimable Society which it appears the misfortunes of the times have left or suffered to grow up in your neighbourhood. I need say the less of him—or rather I need not have said even that much of him, considering how well you will know him through the means of Pictet[3] and your Botanist what is it—Decandol is it not?[4] I please myself with the thought that you will not be displeased to see a man who can give you such fresh accounts of my existence and manière d'être, as well as of Mill's, who is I trust occupied this moment or thereabouts in writing to you. You will hear—or perhaps you have heard already by what accident the pleasure which at last we derived from your letter to him of the 7th Oct. 1815 was lost to us for so many months. Romilly and his beautiful daughter for such she is really grown,[5] have just left me: and it is to me you will be

2345. [1] Dumont MSS 33/1, fos. 154–5. Autograph.
[2] John Walker.
[3] Marc Auguste Pictet (1752–1825), Swiss writer and scientist.
[4] Augustin Pyramus de Candolle (1778–1841), the Genevan botanist.
[5] Romilly's daughter Sophia. She was to marry Thomas Francis Kennedy in 1820.

indebted for any letter which you will have from that quarter by this opportunity, it being from your humble servant that it is procured for him, and by your humble servant that he is informed of it.

With this I hope you will receive the remainder of with the exception of the Table my long and tedious Essay on Nomenclature and Classification forming No. V of the Appendix to Chrestomathia: together with my second Preface to that commenced and alas! not yet finished work: for though the brouillon has been gone through, yet I find that the revisal *always* takes me up a much longer time than the brouillon: some of the dry stuff which you will see have been scribbled over three four, five or six times. It is only within these two or three days that I have had the pleasure of reading your letter of March to Whishaw who dined with me in company with Admiral Tchitchagoff, Mill, and an interesting Irishman of the name of Ensor[6] on Friday last.

You will hear with regret the weakness of your Marquis of Lansdowne.[7] Chrestomathia, if set up, will, he is convinced, supersede and empty the Schools at Eton and Westminster: and for that very reason he will have nothing to do with it. So he says in black and white as well as viva voce. Romilly who is one of us has laughed at him for it, but I fear in vain.

I long to see—not so much what you have been able to do with my own stuff about Tactics,[8] as what you have been able to reduce from the state of *theory* into that of practice, at Greece and in Helvetia. Some of this must surely be in some shape or other in print. Being a man of business and of the mercantile class, as well as of large property, large family, and extensive connection I hope Mr. Walker will in some way or other give facility to the intercourse betwixt this part of the world and your's.

In respect of misrule, and in particular bad economy the state of this country is become so bad, and moreover so hopeless that I keep my eyes turned aside from it as much as possible. £600,000 already spent on the Penitentiary House so people say who have looked into the accounts—and the expence not finished: and just as there is going to be another such under the same management![9]

Some hope of Panopticon (in respect of construction) at Bristol

[6] George Ensor.

[7] Henry Petty, 3rd Marquis of Lansdowne.

[8] Bentham's *Essay on Political Tactics* had been printed in London in 1791; a more extensive body of his writings on the subject was edited by Dumont and appeared as *Tactique des assemblées législatives*, 2 vols., Geneva and Paris, 1816.

[9] No record has been found of plans to build a second penitentiary, despite Bentham's claim in letter 2347 below that he had seen 'it resolved on by the Votes'.

possibly at Manchester.[10] laws against usury likely to be abolished next Session. My book referred to in the house as a true book by the man who brought in the Bill etc.[11]

H.K.'s little wife is no small comfort to me. Without the smallest pretention of any kind she reads with pleasure not only every thing I read, but every thing I write: is quiet, good tempered, free from all female weaknesses. She fends for me, eyes, hand, and even in some respects mind. This house holds them both: she is about to Kitten: will you stand Godfather?[12]

Much edified by the contemplation of your *res gestae et Conatae*:[13] not merely for the sake of the public, present and future, but for the sake of your own health and bien être which I am convinced is much improved by it. In the observation of every body, you were become plethoric, lethargic, and but for the so happily applied remedy, paralytic and apoplectic. Now you have recovered your Lease. But how much longer it would be could you but become a *Rechabite*,[14] as I am!

[10] A bill for building a new gaol at Bristol had been presented and read to the Commons in March 1816. The bill passed the Commons on 31 May, the Lords on 11 June, and received the royal assent on 20 June. See *Commons Journals*, lxxi, as index. Bentham's hope for a Panopticon-type prison was probably based on the work of Miss Morgan of Clifton, the Quaker philanthropist who wrote *The Gaol of the City of Bristol compared with what a Gaol ought to be. By a Citizen. With an appendix containing a brief account of the Panopticon, a prison upon a new plan proposed by Jeremy Bentham*, Bristol and London, 1815. His hopes for Manchester were perhaps based on his contact with William David Evans, stipendiary magistrate for the town (see letter 2302).

[11] Arthur Onslow (1759–1833), sergeant-at-law and MP for Guildford, brought forward a motion for a bill to repeal the usury laws and mentioned Bentham and his *Defence of Usury* on 22 or 23 May 1816. (*The Times* of 24 May reported Onslow's motion as being put on the previous day, but it is recorded in the business of 22 May in *Parliamentary Debates*, xxiv. 723–32.)

[12] The Koe's first child, named Bentham Dumont Koe in honour of Jeremy Bentham and Étienne Dumont, was born in June 1816.

[13] i.e. 'things done and attempted'. What Bentham was referring to is unclear.

[14] A non-drinker. See Jeremiah 35: 5–6.

2346

To An Unknown Correspondent

May 1816 (Aet 68)

Queen's Square Place Westminster
May 1816

Dear Sir,

Permitt me to recommend to your patronage the embryo of an Institution,[2] the nature of which is explained in the inclosed sheet, together with the accompanying tract. The originators, among whom however I can scarce number myself, are ambitious of the benefit of your assistance, in the character of one of the select, and comparatively small, number of Managers. A Glance at the list will, I trust, save you from any such apprehension, as that of finding yourself in bad company. I may say so the more freely, not being of the number. In addition to that of contributor to the expence, (taking twenty shares, half in my own name, half in my brother's) together with the ground for building, and an et cetera or two, the relation I bear to the Institution is, as the paper will shew, that of literary Drudge.

So far as concerns money, with the exception of the trifling difference between five p cent and what might be made in funds, I consider myself (I must confess) as contributing under the terms which you will see, nothing more than the mere advance: this not being an affair of Charity—a comparatively small sum sufficient, and a return, though without profit, expected and reckoned upon.

2347

To Sir Samuel Bentham

late May 1816? (Aet 68)

Books from S.B?

Who the rest can have been designed for we cannot conjecture. Not yourselves unless you were coming hence. Not me, for there are none which you could I think have much expectation of finding of any use to me. Though a book of La Crois on Mathematics Essai sur l'Enseignement etc. 8v.[2] with a view to Chrestomathia, I have found

2346. [1] UC clxv. 15. Autograph draft. Probably a circular letter.
[2] The proposed Chrestomathic school.

2347. [1] BL X. 608–9. Autograph draft. Dated from internal evidence.
[2] Silvestre François Lacroix (1765–1843) was the author of *Essai sur l'Enseignement en Général, et sur celui des mathématiques en particulier*, Paris, 1805 (2nd edn. 1816).

not altogether without use. They are I think all of them without exception bound and gilt.

S.B. Maps at Sheerness.

H.K. from whom alone I know any thing about them will give you the history of their being put for completion into the hands of Mr Hurd.[3] You may imagine the consolation which so unexpected a piece of intelligence afforded me. Who knows but after all the matter might be turned to some account?

S.B.s. Services

Can there be any objection now to their being published? What use can they be of, lying as they do buried? Surely the expence of a little advertisement might be repaid by the Sale.[4]

T'other day Brougham in the House went out of his way to pay the Admiralty Board a foolish general compliment for something I don't know what it was that was lately done by them and that had very little relation to Shipbuilding.[5] Mill thereupon went to him with a copy of your Services telling him if he wished to have a little acquaintance with Naval affairs before he spoke about them, that was the only source from which he could acquire it. He spoke of a particular occasion then future on which he might hold forth in a different key and perhaps mention your name etc. but nothing came of it and indeed that is the way with him as towards every body. But as to you I should not wonder if he had received unfavourable impressions through Earl Grey by means of his Brother the Commissioner.[6]

Those who have looked into the matter, Mill Place etc say that the Milbank Penitentiary has already cost £600,000: if it had been £6,000,000 nobody would have found a word to object to it: in respect of disregard of economy—in a word every thing that is bad, between Ministry and Opposition there is scarce a shade of difference.

Now they are going to have another blessed Penitentiary so

[3] Probably Thomas Hurd (1757?–1823), Royal Navy captain, chart-maker, and hydrographer to the admiralty 1808–23.

[4] Sir Samuel's *Services Rendered in the Civil Department of the Navy* had been printed in London in 1813 and copies distributed to parties likely to be interested or helpful. See letter 2237.

[5] Probably a reference to Brougham's remarks in the debate on naval estimates of 5 April. See *Parliamentary Debates*, xxxiii.1009.

[6] Capt. the Hon. Sir George Grey (1767–1828), Earl Grey's brother, resident commissioner at Portsmouth dockyard.

pleased they are with the first. I see it resolved on by the Votes:[7] and I see a Bill for the establishment of the plan of management for the existing one[8]—I have never seen it nor shall ever if I can help it. That and the Vauxhall Bridge are Buggaboo's neither of which shall I ever face if I can help it

New South Wales has swelled to such a pitch as to cost £200,000 a year: and now even the Ministry I understand feel sore upon it. I am tantalised every now and then with the expectation of a prison on the Panopticon plan at Bristol and another at Manchester:[9] but God knows how they will end either of them.

The Revenue of Ireland wants a great deal of being equal to the interest of her debt, the remainder, with the whole of the amount thus falls upon Britain.[10] The E. India Company has for many years been in a state of Bankruptcy To Pay the dividends money is obtained every year of Government under the name of loans.

2348

To Sir Samuel Bentham

1 June 1816 (Aet 68)

1st June 1816

Here follows copy of a letter of Chichagoffs[2] which I thought you would be pleased to see—I don't know whether I have before this mentioned to you my having been at him to make him write his life.[3] You will see my labour has not been altogether in vain.

[7] See letter 2345 and n. 9.

[8] On 21 May 'A Bill to regulate the General Penitentiary for convicts, at Millbank, in the County of Middlesex', was brought before the Commons and ordered to be printed on the next day. See *Commons Journals*, lxxi. 386.

[9] See letter 2345 and n. 10.

[10] During a debate in the Lords on the Marquis of Buckingham's motion on the state of Ireland (2 April 1816), figures were produced which revealed that Irish debt repayments were well in excess of revenue. See *Parliamentary Debates*, xxxiii. 811 and *The Times*, 3 April 1816.

2348. [1] BL IX. 228–9. Autograph, apart from the copy of Chichagov's letter, which is in the hand of a copyist. Addressed: 'To / Sir Samuel Bentham / K.S.G. / Arcueil / near Paris.' At this time Sir Samuel and his family were staying with Claude-Louis, comte Berthollet (1748–1822), the celebrated French chemist. See M. S. Bentham, *The Life of Brigadier-General Sir Samuel Bentham*, London, 1862, p. 312.

[2] Original missing.

[3] See above, letters 2330 and 2331.

I am going out of town next tuesday, my Dear Friend, and, as in that quality I must be a man of honor, I propose, by way of keeping my word, to dine with you on Monday the 3d. of June, provided we are as much alone as possible, I will bring along with me some of my scrawl, quite convinced that if it is very often weak and foolish for people to have a passion for writing when they think themselves good writers, it is the more so to do it when one feels oneself quite incompetent to the task. But, such is the force of the persuasion of a benevolent philosopher that I will do any thing for you, even shew my incapacity.

If that day should not suit you in the least, make no scruple to say so. I shall see you when I return to town, and there will be no loss whatever; for I must see you once more before I leave this country for good.

Most truly and affectionately
yours
Chichagoff

1 June, Saturday
1816

2349

To Étienne Dumont

1 June 1816 (Aet 68)

Q.S.P. Saturday 1 June 1816

A few days ago, Whishaw had flattered me with the hope of seeing a letter of yours to Mallet[2] giving an account of some of your res gestae.[3] Yet now he says 'I am sorry to find that Mr Mallet has received no letter whatever from Dumont either on politics or any other subject Friday May 31st'[4] In company with this goes a letter from Mill, which to save time and preserve liberty I would not see and have not seen.

2349. [1] Dumont MSS 33/I, fo. 156. Autograph. Addressed: 'A Monsieur / Monsieur Étienne Dumont / à Genève'.

[2] John Lewis Mallet, secretary to the audit office 1807–48, was the son of Jacques Mallet Du Pan (1749–1800), a Swiss publicist resident in Britain from 1798, who had founded the anti-French journal *Mercure britannique*. Mallet Du Pan had been in contact with Dumont both before and during his stay in Britain.

[3] See letter 2345 and n. 13.

[4] Missing.

I know not whether I have told you that about 2 Months ago my poor Brother lost his eldest son:[5] and is in sad affliction etc. and was apprehensive about one of his three daughters.[6]

2350

To The Managers of the Chrestomathic School

7 June 1816 (Aet 68)

Queen's Square Place Westminster
7 June 1816

1. As to the Proposed reservation of the use of the School to the Granter of the Lease of the ground

Observations from Mr. Bentham

When by some of the Managers, mention was made to me of an idea as having been started at the last meeting, that in addition to the Chrestomathic School there was a probability that the same Building might be employed with success in giving reception to an Evening School on a similar plan for the use of adults, it was altogether new to me

To hear of it, and to entertain an ardent desire of seeing the scheme carried into effect—was the affair of one and the same moment: a desire as ardent as any which could have accompanied the original conception of it But in regard to days what I could wish is—to see excepted from that use one day in the week viz Saturday: an exception which I have the satisfaction of not finding myself singular in regarding, as not obstructing the scheme of instruction in any respect, and even as promoting it in so far as concerns persons of the Jewish persuasion, whom, were it only for the sake of the principle I should be sorry to see excluded.

2. As to the duration of the term of the lease.

The scheme had but just been mentioned to me when—such was the sensation it produced—I offered at once three things—1 a contribution in money such as I should expect to find at least equal to what the richest contributor, by how many times so ever his

[5] Samuel Bentham junior, who had died in March 1816. See letters 2338 and 2339.

[6] Lady Bentham's biography of her husband mentions the 'illness of a daughter' without specifying which one. See M. S. Bentham, *The Life of Brigadier-General Sir Samuel Bentham*, p. 312. However, a letter from Lady Bentham to Koe of 5 February 1816 in the Koe MSS, explains that the whole family except George had been attacked by influenza, but that Clara had been the most seriously affected.

2350. [1] UC clxv. 70–3. Autograph draft. Docketed: '1816 June / Chrestomathia / J.B. Q.S.P. / to / Managers / Copy left by H.K. / with the Committee / at Wakefield's / Pallmall'.

opulence might exceed my mediocrity, would be disposed to furnish. 2. for the site of the building the use of a piece of ground, more eligible, as it seemed to me, than would be likely to be procured for any money that could be raised, and 3 my personal labours for the devising and bringing to issue the most promising plan of instruction, that my faculties would enable me to form a conception of: in which labour I have accordingly ever since employed myself, and with a degree of assiduity, which considering the apparent smallness of the fruit, of which it has as yet been seen to be productive, I am quite ashamed to think of

When as above, the scheme was first mentioned to me, I had for some time a sort of contest to maintain with the person by whom it was mentioned. I insisting that as the ground was not producing to me any present pecuniary advantage, I could not charge the proposed institution with any payment on that score: they insisting that the object being to ascertain by experiment that one institution of the sort in question might be set up and kept on foot upon commercial principles—the only assuredly permanent foundation, which that or any other institution could to any considerable extent be kept up, I ought to receive money for my ground as well as those who furnished bricks for their bricks, those who furnished mortar for their mortar, and so forth. What put an end to this contest was an observation of mine, viz. that whatsoever the use of the ground for this purpose for the time in question might, upon commercial principles be worth, might be ascertained with equal correctness whether I received the money or did not.

As yet nothing about the duration of the lease was mentioned on either side. In my own mind, I must confess, no more than one conception as to this point had ever occurred to me: and that was to sacrifice to the institution the longest duration of interest which it would be in my power to obtain in the spot (for it is mostly if not the whole Dean and Chapter ground) of which the ground in question made a part. When the term desired came to be mentioned to me, it was not without surprize that I then learnt, that, though it was for building upon, no longer a time than one and twenty years was proposed. How so? Answer—This quantity of time will be abundantly long enough to try the experiment in: and that is all that is wanted. If it succeeds, the country will be covered with such Schools, set up and kept on foot upon commercial principles. This spot of yours will be no longer wanted.

To hear this was, I must confess, not unwelcome to me. Persons are not wanting who are no less dear than they are near to me. I have no such superfluity of wealth to leave to them as to prompt me to cast it away without use. The observation made on this side by the persons whom I was treating with appeared no less reasonable to me than the observation made by me on the other side, as above had appeared to them. This, if I do not misrecollect, was not much little less than a twelvemonth ago. I looked upon these points as concluded upon, and have continued to do so ever since.

In communicating the matter to these relatives, from whose expectation in respect of a patrimony of fifty years standing I had taken upon me to make their defalcation, it was no small satisfaction to me to have to assure them, that the difference between the remainder of my life and the term of 21 years would be the limit of the sacrifice I had thus agreed to make at their expence. Under this assurance they have been reposing ever since: and I must confess, it is not without very considerable reluctance that I should find myself under the necessity of giving disturbance to that repose.

2351

From Pavel Chichagov

9 July 1816

Woolwich 9 july 1816

Your letter[2] caught me on my way to Ramsgate, where I am going to embark for Ostend. I was very happy to have heard from you once more before I leave this country. The History of Mr Norberg is: that you brother saw him in his travels through Russia, he thought him an intelligent and good mecanic.[3] When I saw your brother at petersburg he recommended Mr N. to me for the works of an artificial harbour that was going to be build at Reval. Norb. has been since employed in that business and performed it with great hability, economy, order, honesty and success. The moulds were finished as to the works under water the rest is nothing, presents no difficulty and requires no particular skill. I have received through the same medium of Mr Whitlock[4] two drawings of the works performed and the method of performance. It is this two drawings with a bad french

2351. [1] BL IX. 230–1. Autograph. Docketed: '1816 July 9 / Chichagoff Woolwich / to / J.B. Q.S.P. / Norberg and his drawings / of the Harbour at / Revel'. Addressed: 'Jeremy Bentham Esqr. / Queen Square Place / Westminster'. Postmark: '2 o'Clock / 10 JY / 1816 AN'. Stamped: 'Two Py Post / Unpaid'.

[2] Missing.

[3] Johan Erik Norberg (1749–1818), Swedish engineer, who worked from 1807 on the harbour at Revel.

[4] Not further identified, but possibly Lt. James Bulstrode Whitelock (or Whitelocke), RN.

explanation to them that he wanted your brother to have engraved and published adding that I was the planner of it and that it was begun and partly executed during my administration.[5] Your brother not being at hand and I going away we can do nothing and I am glad of it for I dont whish to be mentioned any where with any praises as I dont care if I am abused. This is all that I know about Mr Norb. as for his distilleries I heard of his exertions about it but I never took any notice of it as I don't understand any thing about them and think not that he can improve it at least in the eyes of the distillers of this country—

To morrow I am setting out for Ramsgate after having stopped two days at Woolwich where my children are at present and as on purpose to get your Letter. I proceed to Ostend and Brusels, Spa and Switzerland etc etc as far as Naples but before I get there I hope I shall be able to inform you of some of my moves. I am very sorry that your brother is not going towards the same part of the world I wish you would advise him to see Switzerland and Italy, we would then meet which would give me the greatest pleasure. Now let me thank you for your invitation which I am very sorry not to be able to accept. as for Mr Whitlock I think he is already gone back to Russia a thing that I dont envy him but I sincerely regret; to leave so many of my english friends behind me.

To console me I hope you will promise not to change and to be to me the same as hitherto that is an excellent friend a wise adviser to your true admirer

P.C.

2352

From An Unknown Correspondent

14 July 1816

14th July, 1816.

This day, at five minutes past one in the morning, my beloved master, Don Francis de Miranda, resigned his spirit to the Creator; the curates and monks would not allow me to give him any funeral rites, therefore, in the same state in which he expired, with mattress, sheets, and other bed-clothes, they seized hold of him and

[5] i.e. while Chichagov was Russian minister of the navy.

2352. [1] Bowring, x. 487–8. Introduced: 'On 14th July, 1816, Bentham's friend, General Miranda, also died, at Cadiz, after having been imprisoned four years, in violation of a capitulation. His death was thus announced:—' Reprinted in Bain, p. 156.

carried him away for interment; they immediately afterwards came and took away his clothes, and everything belonging to him, to burn them.

2353

To John Herbert Koe

26–8 July 1816 (Aet 68)

Ford Abbey 26 July 1816
10 pm

Much ado to make a mark: writing tackle not yet arrived. *Portfolio* left in the Coach and gone on to Exeter: much distress accordingly, and some anxiety. But per Mill, those on whom it depends are honest and careful: your friend *Mrs Locering*[2] so in particular. This (per Sam)[3] the first dry day these three weeks. The hay in the fields I let cut was nearly if not altogether spoilt: injury in abundance consequently in the Garden, which thought not destitute looks I must confess rather bare of flowers. Given the cause: measures remedial taken. The tout ensemble certainly prodigiously improved: yet, owing to the shabbiness of most of the new shrubs not altogether equal to my expectation.

The silk and velvet beds per J. H.[4] magnificently and compleatly repaired. But particulars may well wait your inspection.

28th July 4 o'clock. No tidings of Portfolio come. Thus the continuance of Cat.[5] experiences a deplorable delay: for in that are the papers thereto belonging.

27 July

At my desire, Mill has written this day to Joseph H. about his Nephew's[6] going to Mill wall with a view to Partnership—He has read it to me: it seemed to me a perfectly proper one. He refers him to you for particulars, nothing said of Babycomb:[7] Mill understood you to have avoided the mention of it to Ricardo. Mill mentions

2353. [1] Koe MSS. Autograph. Docketed: '1816 July 26 / J.B.' Addressed: 'To / J.H. Koe Esqr / Lincoln's Inn / London.' Postmark illegible.

[2] Presumably a servant at Queen's Square Place.

[3] A servant at Ford Abbey.

[4] Perhaps James Hume.

[5] Probably a reference to the work published as *Church-of-Englandism and its Catechism Examined*, London, 1818. Manuscripts relating to this work, dated 1816 and headed simply 'Catechism', are to be found in UC vii. Marginals, dated 1813–16, are in UC clviii.

[6] James Hume.

[7] The marble quarry at Babbacombe. See letter 2338 and n. 7.

your Brother alone as interested in it: says nothing of your interest or mine[8] ⟨ . . . ⟩⟨ . . . ⟩⟨ . . . ⟩

Chrestomathia—Additional persons to whom books are to be sent.
1. Dr Hyde Wollaston (Sec.R.S.) with J.B's name[9]
2. Sir Humphrey Davy with J.B.'s name
3. Strutt of Derby[10]—the true one i.e. known to S.B. (when discovered Owen[11] knows which it is). Mention any others that occur to you with J.B.'s name
4. Give to any one where you think it may draw subscriptions: but not in my name without notice. '*From the Author*' might however be just without the persons (the *donee's*) name.

Papers relative to Gardening[12]—a parcel of them, to be put out of the way, were suddenly hustled up and put by somewhere. I believe in one of the drawers under the middle window in my sitting-room. If not there, possibly in that one of the new paste-board boxes marked Miscell.Mss. If found virtue would consist in sending them by Mrs Mill.

Cartridge Paper. James[13] could not find time for getting any. Distress for want of it: no distress not intolerable: blue paper a makeshift. But whenever Plan of Chrestomathic building is sent it should be rolled up upon the cylinder that Mercers employ for their silks etc: and then a dozen of sheets of Cartridge paper may roll over it.

Hat-brush. Here is nothing better than a comb. Desired—such an one as the Q.S.P.ian one: Mrs Mill to be begged to bring it. Sub poena ducat secum[14]

My head and flesh-brush—its abode is in the throne-room cupboard: I suspect it was forgotten: if so, like request as to that.
5 Chrestomathia for Perry.[15] My name with P.s to be written in it: ie. To P. from the Author as in the other cases: and Romilly to be asked (by you) to send it to him with his R's name [on] the cover. Place to be desired to mention the matter to Bennet[16] and desire him

[8] John Heide Koe had a become a partner in Grellier and Co. in May 1815.

[9] William Hyde Wollaston (1766–1828), physiologist, chemist, and physician, secretary of the Royal Society 1804–16.

[10] William Strutt (1756–1830), inventor and fellow of the Royal Society, eldest son of Jedediah Strutt (1726–97), Derbyshire cotton-spinner.

[11] Robert Owen, who was a friend of William Strutt.

[12] No longer to be found in the UC MSS.

[13] James Hume.

[14] i.e. 'she is to bring it with her under penalty'.

[15] James Perry of *The Morning Chronicle*.

[16] The Hon. Henry Grey Bennet (1777–1836), MP for Shrewsbury. He was the second son of Charles Bennet, 5th Earl of Tankerville (1743–1822).

to recommend it to P. P. may ⟨ . . . ⟩ puff it as he has Owen's Prospectus,[17] one or more to be put up with it. This was mostly Mills suggestion: approving.

Wax none: pray send me a couple of sticks by Mrs M. What a plaguey pen! The unfortunate portfolio contained your's.

2354

To John Herbert Koe

29 July 1816 (Aet 68)

To Mr Koe Copy 29 July 1816 Monday

I Sent you off a letter yesterday—forgot a commission to Mr Colquhoun.[2]

Some time after having sent me the Danish Reconciliation Court Books[3] he wrote for at my desire: in the envelope nothing else: no letter: no account of charges. Not improbably he means not to let me pay them, but to give them as a present: but it is not for me to deal by him on that presumption. Pray call upon him as soon after receipt of this as you find convenient, thanking him in my name, asking for the account, and apologize for my not calling on him myself to thank him—I being at that time in the last agonies of removal, under the apprehension of not having time for completion of the things needful.

2. Handel's Concertos not found here: if found at Q.S.P. desired to be sent hither by the first or any other opportunity.[4]

3. Remember Bristol Panopticon and Miss Morgan.[5]

[17] Presumably a reference to Owen's *A New View of Society; or, Essays on the Principle of the Formation of the Human Character, and the Application of the Principles to Practice*, London, 1813, a pamphlet designed to win support for his New Lanark Mill.

2354. [1] Koe MSS. Copy, part in the hand of a copyist, part autograph. Docketed: '1816 July 29 / J.B.'

[2] Probably Patrick Colquhoun (1745–1820), metropolitan police magistrate 1792–1818, who had known Bentham since 1796. See *Correspondence*, v, vi, and vii, as index.

[3] Which books is unclear. Bentham appears already to have owned the standard work on the subject, Andreas Bjørn Rothé's *Mémoire sur l'origine et l'organisation des Committés Conciliateurs en Dannemarc*, Copenhagen, 1803. He lent this to Romilly in 1805 and to Horner in 1807. See BL XXVIII. 39.

[4] Immediately after this there is a deleted passage: '2. The little articles I wrote for—what étourderie to think of desiring them to be sent by Mrs Mill! when they would go so much better by the first packet sent by Macreary.' This is followed by an insertion: 'N.B. the articles here alluded to have arrived.' The 'little articles' are presumably those listed in letter 2353. McCreery would have been sending Bentham the proofs of *Chrestomathia* at this time.

[5] Miss Morgan of Clifton, for whom see letter 2345 n. 10.

2355

To Samuel Hoare Jr.

1 August 1816 (Aet 68)

Ford Abbey, (Devonshire) near Chard
Somersetshire 1 August 1816

Sir

It was not till last evening that your letter, bearing date the 27th July,[2] and written 'by order of the Committee of the Society for investigating cases of juvenile delinquency' reached my hands at this place, at which I am fixed for some months to come. It is matter of no small personal regret to me, that my local situation will not admitt of my profiting by the honour which was intended me. Had the letter reached my house in town a few days earlier, my departure would, for the purpose in question, have been postponed. On the part of the institution however there will be no cause for regret. Among the names of the Members of the Committee is (I understand) that of my particular friend Mr Koe of Lincolns Inn, who is in perfect possession of all my ideas on the subject, and in a variety of ways could be more immediately useful to the Institution than I myself could have been. If since the date of your letter the Committee had been sitting, I expect to find that he has by this time been attending it, and thus, for every purpose but that of the expression of my respectful acknowledgments, rendered this letter superfluous. It is through him (and under cov⟨er⟩ from Sir Samuel Romilly,) to whom I take for granted the matter has been communicated, that I received yours: and I find that Mr Koe has already set himself actively to work entirely in the hope of giving assistance to the business. The Report[3] you speak of as being sent to me in town not having yet reached me here, nothing that I could as yet say on the subject could present a chance of being of use: but as soon as it reaches my hands, I shall not fail to look into it with that degree of

2355. [1] Staatsbibliothek Preussischer Kulturbesitz, Berlin. Copy.

Samuel Hoare junior (1783–1847) was a Quaker banker, a partner in the firm of Hoare, Barnetts, Hoare, and Co. of 62 Lombard Street.

[2] Missing.

[3] The report of the Committee for investigating the Causes of the alarming increase of juvenile delinquency in the Metropolis. Besides Koe, its members included William Allen, Basil Montagu, Mill, and Ricardo. The report identified 'The existing system of prison discipline' as one of the causes of the problem, and recommended the adoption of a better one. Hoare's letter seems to have invited Bentham to attend the committee to explain his Panopticon proposals with a view to their being used for a juvenile penitentiary. See the report as printed in the *Philanthropist*, vi (1816), 199–210, and Bentham's comments in letter 2356 below.

interest which the subject and the character of tho⟨se⟩ who are occupying themselves with it, can not fail to inspire. The Committee may learn from Mr. Koe, during the portion of time the course of his professional business will admitt of his giving to attendance.

I have the honour to be
Sir,
Your most obedient Servant
Jeremy Bentham.

2356

To John Herbert Koe

1 August 1816 (Aet 68)

Ford Abbey 1 Aug. 1816

Reced last night yours of the 30th[2] enclosing the Juvenile Delinquency preventing society's.[3]

Ainslies[4] 'drawing', if 'proper' (say you) will serve 'as well for the Bristol Prison as for this.' Yes, mutatis mutandis: but, I should not expect to find, without some change. The *annular area* for example for boys how delinquent so ever, no older than from 6 to 14 would it be necessary? At any rate it need not be so wide. Then in the Bristol Prison there are separation walls between convicts and Debtors: here superfluous.

The next day after sending off yours of the 30th you received I suppose mine of the | | th from this place.[5] Yesterday went from Mill to Place a letter in which were a few words to you about a visit which I wished and wish you to pay to *Colquhoun* to thank him for the Books and settle with him for the charges.[6]

While these letters were on hand I was under no small anxiety: yesterday and not before I was relieved from it by the return of Mill from Illminster to which he went o' cock-horse, bearing my lost sheep. Think of wicked Ms of all sorts—I thrown a twelvemonth back by the want of them—them dispersed in various hands some of them Parsonical ones![7]

2356. [1] Koe MSS. Autograph, with the exception of the last paragraph, which is in the hand of a copyist. Docketed: '1816 Aug 1 / J.B.' Addressed: 'For / Mr Koe.'

[2] Missing.

[3] See letter 2355.

[4] George Ainslie, for whom see letter 2111 n. 2.

[5] Probably either letter 2353 or 2354.

[6] See letter 2354.

[7] Probably a reference to MSS on the Church of England, for which see letter 2353 and n. 5. These might have been passed on by Dumont to the Revd John North.

Now, being viewed with other eyes, the place—the improvements—answer expectations compleatly inside and out, making in the latter case allowance for bad weather and ravages of cursed geese and peacock, who are become florists, and in particular carnation-fanciers. Their wings clipped they have been banished to the upper pond, where it is hoped so long as flowers continue, they will. Mill and I have been shivering ever since we have been here. The defect in the Ice house is supposed discovered, and if yes will be easily remedied.

In your's to S.B. and Dumont I hope you mentioned the Delinquency-preventing Society's business. Seal, secure direct, and transmitt to the Committee the enclosed.[8]

You say nothing about your having written to Miss Morgan.[9] Cognizance of the application made by the London Society would probably be of use in Bristol: and so vice versâ. Moreover at Bristol it would be of use they should know that the London Society acts with encouragement from *Administration* (for I can not bring myself to give into the abominable serpent of saying *Government*).

No time by this post to give instructions about how many Prospectus's and Whole Sheet Tables[10] should accompany my Chrestomathias. The list has been in my but just recovered portfolio.

Place will tell you where to get sealing wax by the pound better as well as cheaper then elsewhere: he got $\frac{1}{4}$ lb for Mill: treat me with another such.

Secretary for the Committee, later I see Samuel Hoare Junior. Is he not of the Hoares from whom you were in hopes of money for Chrestomathia through the Baillies?[11]

Cargo of people here t'other day in Baroch and four . . . . . At parting, question to Lucy,[12] who the occupant. Answer Mr B—'Ah, what a pity, that we did not know of it that we might have taken a more particular view of him. And so was that he that was sitting in the saloon? how good, to let us see him notwithstanding! Oh yes—that was just what might have been expected of him: that is just his character.'—Such hearings are not unpleasant.

From Brougham[13]

[8] Letter 2355.

[9] See letter 2345 n. 10.

[10] For the 'Prospectus' for the Chrestomathic School see letter 2317 n. 2; for the 'Whole Sheet Tables' letter 2325 and n. 2.

[11] Samuel Hoare junior was the son of Samuel Hoare (1751–1825), another Quaker banker and philanthropist, who had purchased Hampstead Heath House in 1790. The Baillie sisters lived nearby.

[12] Bentham's servant since at least 1801. See *Correspondence*, vi, as index.

[13] Original missing.

I have seen a good deal of Dumont—who is extremely well—I dined with him to day to meet their eminent men—of whom I like Pictet and Bonstetten[14] the best—next to D. himself—I have his Tactics and Sophisms[15]—and shall forthwith set about doing it for Jeffrey.[16] The Sophisms is a very magnificent work indeed. The Tactics are for foreign consumption rather than the home market.

July 14th 1816

2357

To John Herbert Koe

7 August 1816 (Aet 68)

Ford Abbey Wedny 7 Aug, 1816

Reced the packet yesterday with your letter of the 3d.[2] All right: except that there is no mention of the Sub-Reprobate.[3] This makes me fear you have forgotten the putting him to Peacock's[4] to write: and it is for this purpose that I write thus early after the receipt of your's.

By the same conveyance Mill has received a letter from Mrs M saying that all is well and that she hopes to set out for this place the beginning of this next week. That will be Monday or Tuesday: say Tuesday: if so Sub-Reprobate can not set out till either that same day or the next, according to the choice his parents make. If you send for him without loss of time here will or may still be a few days for him to see the upright and square hands of the Writing Stationers see how they manage to form such writing, and get some copies to imitate here. The state of my comfort in respect of eyes and facility of reading, in no inconsiderable degree depends upon it: he should therefore be apprized of the importance I attach to it: and that I shall require (shall it be half an hour in every day or will a quarter of an hour suffice?) to be employed in writing after copies:

[14] Charles-Victor de Bonstetten (1745–1832), Swiss politician and writer, particularly interested in educational reform.

[15] *Traité des sophismes politiques* appeared with *Tactique des assemblées législatives*, 2 vols., Geneva and Paris, 1816.

[16] Francis Jeffrey, editor of the *Edinburgh Review*. Brougham does not appear to have reviewed *Tactique* and *Sophismes*.

2357. [1] Koe MSS. Autograph. Docketed: '1816 Aug 7 / J.B.' Addressed: 'To / J.H. Koe Esqr / 19 Lincolns Inn'.

[2] Missing.

[3] John Flowerdew Colls.

[4] Mrs Peacock ran a juvenile library at 259 Oxford Street. See *Correspondence*, vii, as index.

besides taking pains for some time in the making of such copies of various matters for use which however will not in general take up much time.

On looking over Monthly Mag. M.[5] observed a paper there with the running title of *Mr Benthams Plan of Education* New School for liberal Education[6]—I have glanced at it: it seems to be taken from Mills Proposals,[7] with a paragraph or two by Philips[8] at the beginning, and a note afterwards for puffing Blair's Univ. Precept[9] which has been said to be his. I imagine he is angry at its not having been mentioned. Pray let him have without loss of time a copy with the Whole Sheet Tables.

I hope Lady-ship's Honour is alive and lusty. Give her a good hearty kiss, and set it down to my account. Flog the brat[10] whenever you have nothing better to do, and tell him that it is all for his good, and that I advised it. A propos of his Bratship, I told you I could not endure to take a part in that abominable ceremony, but if you have a mind to give him my name—my surname—for a Christian name well and good. You will then have a Bentham to tyrannize over, as you yourself have been tyrannized over by one: and, according to Juggical justice you may revenge yourself on the young one for what you have suffered under the old one.

Learn as soon as you can the day Mrs Mill will have fixt on for her setting out, that the Sub-Reprobate's may conform to it: it should not be earlier, but if the instruction at Peacock's renders the delay of a few days material, no matter: but whatever be the day fixt upon for his coming, I should be glad to have the earliest notice.

Do, may it please your Ladyships honour make up to Mrs. M. a little and combine with her before departure—things may go on the more smoothly here. Every body has an interest in being surrounded by cheerful countenances: no matter whether some deserve to have of them, so there are any that deserve to see them.

Mill received yesterday a letter from Hume to the same effect as that to you.

[5] Mill.

[6] *Monthly Magazine*, xlii, Pt.ii (1816), 26–8.

[7] *Proposals for establishing in the Metropolis, a Day School, in which an example may be set of the application of the methods of Dr. Bell, Mr. Lancaster, and others, to the higher branches of education*, London, 1816. For the drawing up of these proposals by Mill see letter 2317 and n. 2.

[8] Sir Richard Phillips, the owner of the *Monthly Magazine*.

[9] A note in the article refers the reader to the Revd. David Blair's *The Universal Preceptor; being an easy grammar of arts, sciences and general knowledge*, London, 1811, 'where a similar course is described and recommended, and has long been adopted in several hundred independent schools in town and country'. The Revd David Blair was a pseudonym of Phillips himself.

[10] Bentham Dumont Koe.

Item an excellent letter from Place, *inter alia* giving an account of the meeting at the London.[11] I have obtained permission to inclose it to you, that, if you see no objection, you may show it to Romilly, who seemed pleased with a former letter of Place's. I think this will contribute to raise P. still higher in Rs estimation, and thence serve Chrestomathia, which I told him would for details be in great measure under P's management.

I have desired Macreery to let you know as often as a parcel comes from him to this place: you may on a like occasion give him similar information. At the same time with the parcel from you came a packet from him, for which of course I had to pay separately.

I fear I shall not now have time to give final instructions about distribution of Chrestomathias.

'Allen[12] to write to Miss Morgan for all the information etc.' So far so good: but without some graphical sketch, all the information conveyable by verbal description, would, I fear, be insufficient.

Weather here still deplorable. Ripening of Autumn fruits, still as Peaches and Nectarines depend on future change for the better. Grapes in a great degree abortive Apricots plenty and ripening. On Table as good a melon as ever was tasted.

Supposed cause of failure in the ice house discovered: thence a hoped-for remedy more Peafowls from Lady Bridport[13]—who is thankful for beautiful and virtuous Geese. Bills of Carpenters and Plaisterers and Masons etc. for the recent work, came in: and compared with the work done, cheapness perfectly astonishing. When here, you shall guess.

[11] i.e. the meeting at the City of London Tavern on 29 July to consider the distressed state of the lower classes and how to extend relief to them. See *The Times*, 30 July 1816. See also the copy of Place's letter to Mill, 2–3 August 1816, in the Place Papers, BL Add. MS 35,152, fos. 199–200.

[12] William Allen.

[13] Maria Sophia, Viscountess Bridport (1746?–1831), second wife and widow of Alexander Hood, Viscount Bridport (1727–1814), who lived at Cricket St. Thomas, Somerset, some two miles from Ford Abbey.

2358

To John Herbert Koe

12–17 August 1816 (Aet 68)

Ford Abbey 12 Aug. 1816

Reced on Saty.[2] yours of | |[3]
I don't recollect Dumont's mentioning in his letter to me[4] his having received any Spring of Action. I certainly sent him a parcel of them viz. six by Romilly:[5] and afterwards a list of Errata by post. Pray ask Romilly about this.

Saty. 17th

They all came safe on Thursday. Subreprobate[6] now saved from drowning and falling off and breaking his neck at night by the charity of Mrs. M.[7] By 〈. . .〉 injunction he wrote his letter to his mother certifying his existence yesterday: but it will not be delivered sooner than this will be if I dispatch it this day as I intend. By bad schooling he is much more deficient in general instruction than I expected: but he reads well beyond expectation, which is a great comfort: incomparably better already than Super-Reprobate.[8] Writing I have not yet tried him in. He is under Mill's schooling, and I doubt not will progress as fast as Super Reprobate.

The Organ has been taken to pieces and I hope put to rights, by assistance from a sort of Gentleman-Malster 5 miles off an acquaintance of the Gardener's. The fault which is now discovered being clearly out of the Carpenter's power to end. The whole busines is the result of a special providence, but too multifarious to be detailed here. James Hume took an active and useful part in it.

Stat.53 G.3 c.149 Curates' Pay etc.

Per § 13. Clause narrowing the operation of the Act by confining to *future Rectors* and Vicars the power given to Bishops to take money out of their pockets and give it to Curates; alias to *exempt actual Incumbents* from the operation of it. Marginal Content—'Not to empower Bishops to assign the Curates of persons holding Benefices before passing of the Act *or of certain persons*', any greater stipend than before. Who are these '*certain persons*'? Pray transcribe and send me by Ladyship's honour the words by which they are described.[9] I take for granted that neither in this clause *nor any*

2358. [1] Koe MSS. Autograph. Docketed: '1816 Aug 17 / J.B.' Addressed: 'Herbert Koe Esq / 19 Lincolns Inn / London'. Postmark: 'A/19 AU 19/1816'. Stamped: 'CHARD/142'.

[2] 10 August. [3] Missing. [4] Missing. [5] See letter 2329.

[6] Colls. [7] Mrs Mill. [8] James Hume.

[9] Bentham was quoting the marginal summary of s.14 of the act, not s.13. The '*certain persons*' were non-residents by licence or exemption.

other part of the Act is included any exemption in favour of *existing Patrons*, to prevent the value of the Livings destined for their sons etc. from being reduced to nothing. No certainly: this can not have been d⟨one⟩.

Stemmatic Laticulata [?][10]—Two tall thin volumes—a new purchase of mine. Mill would be glad to receive it by any opportunity that occurs.

Books not to be forgotten by Ladyship's Honour when she comes—
1. Neal's Histy. Vol. 4 and 5[11]
2. The Botanical books left for her at Q.S.P. viz.
Salisbury[12] and Keith.[13] Lee[14] is not here. May it not perhaps have been sent to Appledore?[15] Enquiry at any rate can do no harm.
3. Item the striped Phlox which being exonerated of pot and greatest part of the earth will tie up in a couple of outside Cabbage-leaves.
4. Item. Siberian Flax, if seeds are ripe and saved, or ripening becomes hopeless.
5. Q.S.Pian perennials to be saved, and noted, that in due season (say latter end of Octr.) specimens of such as are not here, or are rare here, may be transferred hither.

Ford Abbey 17 or 18 Aug. 1816 Saturday[16]

Panopticon—I hope and believe we shall have one good one—and that in the most publickly inspectable place in England; viz. the Juvenile.[17] But it grieves me to think of the unpromising state of the Bristol one.

I hope your letter to Miss Morgan will have been written before this reaches you.[18] All depends upon the Bristol people: Justices in Sessions are they, or governing corporate body of the City. We know nothing about them: and as little of the sort and degree of influence this philanthropic and public spirited Lady has in relation to them. I should be happy to see her here, if it afforded any promise of being of use; and perhaps she would not be averse to come.

[10] Not traced.

[11] *History of the Puritans* by Daniel Neal (1678–1743), first published in four volumes 1732–8, and republished in five volumes 1797 under the editorship of Dr. Joshua Toulmin (1740–1815).

[12] William Salisbury was the author of two works published in 1816: *Hints Addressed to Proprietors of Orchards* and the two-volume *Botanists Companion.*

[13] Revd. Patrick Keith (1769–1840) was the author of the newly-published *A System of Physiological Botany*, 2 vols., London, 1816.

[14] James Lee the Elder was a correspondent of the Swedish botanist Carl von Linné (1707–78). He translated part of Linné's work as *Introduction to the Science of Botany*, London, 1760.

[15] Koe's parents-in-law, Robert and Lucy Jump, lived at Appledore, Devon, at this time.

[16] Saturday was 17 August.

[17] See letters 2355, 2356, and 2359.

[18] See letters 2354 and 2356.

Nobody can be more decidedly against all intercourse between Criminals and debtors than we all are: and that Debtors ought not to be subject to inspection, unless it be at their own desire, or in ⟨. . .⟩ of misbehaviour on their part, i.e. on the part of any one, for a time to be limited and by way of punishment for the misbehaviour of that one, and the prevention of future misbehaviour during that time, in the instance of that one. Supposing the disposition of the building suitable, i.e. the simple annular plan adhered to throughout, all this might be secured by a piece of canvas to each apartment, in form of a curtain, which the Debtor might draw aside at pleasure, (in case of sickness for example) and the governing body —the ruling powers whoever they are cause to be removed for a time, for punishment, as above: but in no case without making entry of the act done, and of the justifying cause of its being done.

The great advantage of this plan is that by this means provision will be made in as effectual degree as possible, against the uncertainty attendant upon the numbers of the individuals, in the instance of both classes: whereas but for this you may have the Debtors part crowded to the great distress of all of them, and yet though the Criminals part be not half full no means of affording relief to the distress produced by crowding in the instance of the debtors: and so vice versâ: and thus if health be not injured, productive industry more or less impeded in one part, for want of that relief—that supply of room, which in case of an appropriate construction might so easily be afforded by the other. But even though it should be determined that no such relief shall be capable of being afforded, in which case the quantity of room allotted to both classes together and consequently the expence must be much greater than otherwise it need be, still what use would there be in deviating from the simplicity of the *annular* construction? On the plan you have delineated as collected from the accounts you have heard here would be a portion of the whole mass of building thrust aside out of the ring: of which extrusion it is clear by inspection that a very considerable addition would be made to the quantity of matter and consequently expence of the walls.

I hope in both instances I mean Juvenile and so far as concerns criminals Bristol Ainslie and you have paid due attention to that contrivance of Places, which seems to be an admirable one, in relation to the Necessaries: viz. in including them in the ring but in such manner as to make them be capable of being exposed to inspection (viz. by drawing aside or removal of a curtain as above) yet perfectly air tight,—the windows not opening, and thence no possibility of annoyance by bad smell. Two different ones for the two sexes, that one may be accessible at all times to each sex; and it should seem that one should be over the other, rather than by the side: since in the latter case, what was going forward in the one might be more or less perceptible in the other, conversations might even be carried on etc. etc. in various ways adverse to comfort or decorum or both.

2359

To John Herbert Koe

19 August 1816 (Aet 68)

Ford Abbey, Monday 19 Aug. 9 a.m.

Reced yours yesterday.[2] This morning you will I hope receive one from me.[3]

1. Juvenile Depredation. Huzza! Panopticon for ever! Yes—to beat about they seemed doomed for aye as hitherto, unless we take them in tow. A plan must be formed for them if any thing be done. But 1. their powers *pecuniary* what are they? 2. Powers political—on what foundation do their expectations of getting any rest? on any thing better than a few smiles, commendations and vague-generally promises from Sidmouth? I suppose not. Even supposing him sincere,—driven into sincerity by importunity, upon the principle of the parable of the unjust Judge,[4]—it can not be either expected or wished that he should settle any thing, till he has seen the plan. But this plan of management remains to be drawn up. Yes and ere it can be brought into effect, there must be an Act of Parliament, ergo a *Bill*: and in that Bill will, in great measure, be contained the particulars of the Plan. To this end what is in their power to give, that alone can we extract from them: and that is an assurance of the sums they are respectively willing to contribute: viz. 1. for the expence of the building (capital): 2. for do of management: (annual income).

Who are the persons among them to go to Lord Sidmouth?—The only use of this is to prevent them from going, any of them, to Ld Sidmouth any more, till the plan is drawn up and ready to present to him. No one, I suppose, so competent as friend Allen: and he is

2359. [1] Koe MSS. Autograph. Docketed: '1816 Aug 19 / J.B.' Addressed: 'To / J.H. Koe Esqr / Lincoln's Inn / London.' Postmark: A/21 AU 21/1816'. Stamped: 'CHARD/142'.

[2] Missing.

[3] Probably letter 2358.

[4] Luke 18: 1–6. See especially verse 5, where the unjust judge decides to avenge the widow, but only 'lest by her continual coming she weary me.'

out of the way,[5] and as for you, besides you being out of the way too till the latter end of October, the less you appear at the offices the better, on account of your connection with me. They ought to be particularly cautioned never to mention my name at the Offices: or should it be mentioned there to them, never to speak of it but with indifference.

In consideration of what they are willing to bestow in money and time, Government, I suppose, besides *political* powers, is disposed to give them something in the shape of money, viz. capital or Income or both. In each case it would I should suppose—or at least it ought to be—acceptable to Government to be at a *certainty* as to its own part. But if so this is neither more nor less than a *Contract*: in short my plan: only for the execution of it a plurality of pious and virtuous persons, instead of a single reprobate, such as myself. In conversation perhaps if the word *Contract* can be avoided, so much the better.

As to the footing on which and name under which the favourites are to be engaged. *Apprenticeship* the best possible: a name known to every body and that frightens nobody. Be the age as early as it may, no reason why the Apprenticeship should cease before 21: and if the age be to a certain degree an advanced age say from 14 to 21: they might remain bound as honest Apprentices sometimes are, as late as 24: especially if any thing of actual delinquency be imputed to them. The best bad characters in the kingdom are not in their own power before 21: much less ought these depraved ones. Here you see is our work for nice legislation: a description of the *persons* liable to be consigned, with or without their consent, to this receptacle. We will not call up out of the grave the penman of the *Vagrancy Acts*.[6] N.B. The older the more formidable and difficult to keep confined: therefore to the extent of the number built for, the younger the better. An enclosed airing ground will be indispensable.

The *spot* where is it proposed to be? Is any fixed upon—in hope or so much as wish? Hardly will they get it without compulsory powers. Here then is the original Panopticon business to do over again: with only this difference, viz. the juvenility of the persons to be maintained, and the inoffensiveness of those under whose management they are to be maintained and the comfortable thought that in return for their risk and labours they will not have any recom-

[5] Allen was on the continent, on one of his periodic visits to inspect schools and disseminate reforming views.

[6] The Vagrancy Act of 1744 (17 Geo. II, c.5), which formed the basis of the law on the subject until 1822, made more precise than before the different categories of vagrants, dividing them into 'idle and disorderly persons', 'rogues and vagabonds', and 'incorrigible rogues'. Much space was devoted to the definition of each of these categories.

pence, at least in a pecuniary shape, which is all that the powers above have any comprehension of: and with regard to those exalted vulgars, these differences taken all together are certainly not inconsiderable.

As to the different descriptions of persons whom it is wished to comprehend in the system some lights may surely be to be collected from the observations your colleagues can not but have made. Either they have done this or they have done nothing: this then you will endeavour to get from them. The duration of the contract what should it be? *Minimum*, the earliest time at which the set of boys first taken in are discharged. *Females*? any to be admitted?

What is above is all that occurs to me as promising to be of any use, in any part of it, before we meet. But now as to *Bristol Prison*. The Juveniles being many of them Quakers, and Bristol having Quakers, might not an approbation given to the plan (of construction) by the Juveniles be of use at Bristol? If so, could not you get them to sign a form of yours drawing expression of such their approbation, and of their determination to adopt the plan in consequence? The more subscribers the more imposing. The stile and title of the Society being I suppose fixt upon should stand at the head of the paper.

Though probably like the governing body of the National Society[7] self-elected, they (the signers) will I suppose (for such appears to be the fashion), sign themselves without scruple *the Committee*. This being done collectively, the individual Quakers might be desired to write individually to their individual Bristol Quaker Friends, to the like effect. By these individual writers some account may be given of their expectations from Government: and the more substantial these appear, the greater of course will be the weight with which the recommendation will come.

Meeting at friend Allens on Wednesday, could not you then see what you could make of Martin the Printer for Chrestomathia?[8]

You have heard I suppose from *Place* how shabbily *Butler*[9] has behaved in regard to Chrestomathia. Romilly perhaps, with or without Montague,[10] might get more out of him.

[7] The National Society for the Education of the Poor in the Principles of the Established Church, founded in 1811 in response to the non-sectarian Royal Lancasterian Society.

[8] Probably George Martin, printer, of 6 Great St. Thomas Apostle, Bow Lane.

[9] Charles Butler (1750–1832), the Roman Catholic barrister and specialist in conveyancing who had been a friend of Bentham since the 1780s. See *Correspondence*, iv, v, vi, and vii, as index.

[10] Basil Montagu, for whom see letter 2029 n. 5.

Angerstein[11] my letter to him for Chrestom should go before you go: he will return before you return. I mentioned it to you as a precedent from whence in writing to others in my name matter might be extracted. *Parr*[12] you should if possible treat with a letter on the subject, mentioning the anxiety of my desire to have his powerful assistance, and saying that except for matters of absolute necessity I had absolutely given up writing to any body. Montague may perhaps be of use as to Parr. Somebody was speaking of a suspicion that M. was not just now in good circumstances: if so your expectations *abort*: if any body could, Romilly could extract money from him.

From some of the people the Chrestomathia I distribute may possibly be productive of letters to myself. On this account during your absence somebody should have a general commission to open all my letters, those from S.B excepted; which being known by the postage marks may be forwarded hither at once. The first person I thought of was your Brother:[13] but his dishonor is great: and the possible effect in regard to Chrestomathia will render it acceptable to Place: by whom in case of need answers in his quality of Secretary[14] might be given.

Macreery to J.B.[15] I gave you the Draught of the letter for him to write on Sunday[16] in a copy of *Cat*:[17] forget not to settle that matter with him. Item, about the *Bookseller*. Hunter[18] is the man we fix upon, unless M.[19] suggests any conclusive objection which is not expected. Supposing Hunter to refuse, M. to think of some other. Authors name must not on any account be mentioned to Bookseller. Between M. and Bookseller must the whole transaction be—neither Place nor in a word any body. With the exception of the concluding Nos Appendix IV and V all is now printed off except the 4 last pages of the *Plan* of the work (li to liv)[20] which are reserved to be printed with Title-page etc. but are composed and I have a proof of them. Therefore the work may be already ripe for shewing to the Book-

[11] John Julius Angerstein (1735–1823), merchant, financier, art-collector, and philanthropist. Bentham had been in contact with him in 1795. See *Correspondence*, v. 152 and n.

[12] Revd. Dr. Samuel Parr.

[13] John Heide Koe, who was arrested around this time for debt.

[14] i.e. secretary of the Chrestomathic school committee, established on 16 May 1816.

[15] Missing.

[16] Also missing. Sunday was the day before, 18 August.

[17] What was to be published as *Plan of Parliamentary Reform, in the Form of a Catechism, With Reasons for Each Article*, London, 1817 (Bowring, iii. 433–557).

[18] Rowland Hunter, of St. Paul's Church-Yard.

[19] Here 'M' stands for McCreery.

[20] i.e. 'Plan of this Essay', which forms the first section of the 'Essay on Nomenclature and Classification'. See *Chrestomathia* (*CW*), ed. M. J. Smith and W. H. Burston, pp. 140–2.

seller, and for fear of prosecution he will naturally be for reading it all through. By this means so much time will be saved. As to Nos IV and V though offensive enough they will not be so personally and libellously offensive as what is printed. Number of pages already printed 479 all parts taken together. Those to be added may perhaps swell the number as high as 560: this though large will not for an 8o be excessive.

☞ Forget not to bring with you this letter that it may serve for jabberation.

☞ M.[21] desires to have back again by Mrs. K Place's letter that was shown to Romilly.

Mind Madison's letter:[22] highly gratifying, and opening new prospects which I have not room to detail. His declining any official step was no more than expected: but in substance this is a recommendation to the several states, and had that for its object or view. I am thus confirmed and accelerated in my intention of sending to the U.S. what you know is printed,[23] for the purpose of being sent to the leading men in each State, together with this letter of Madison's, correspondence with Alexander and Czartoriski and perhaps other etcaeteras. If you can find time I wish you would endeavour to see the American Minister here,[24] to desire him to acknowledge to Madison my receipt of his letter, and to convey to him a copy of Chrestomathia as far as printed also one of Springs of Action. You must supply him with Springs: Macreery on a word from you will send to him a Chrestomathia when the copy of Part II is put together. It were highly desirable this should be done by you, if you can find time: it will be so long before it can be done by you otherwise: but if not, assign it over to Place, enjoining his secrecy, till absolved by one of us. If you observe any tendency on the part of the Minister (Adams M. says it is) to a personal intercourse with me, encourage it. Give him a Chrestomathia for himself, if you think there will be any use. If the promised books from Madison[25] come during your absence, let them come to Q.S.P. Place may then be desired to open the packet and send them with the then next periodicals.

Yes—I have so little time to lose—whatever can be done in this way, the sooner done the better. In one of the small drawers on the

[21] Here 'M' seems to be Mill rather than McCreery.

[22] Letter 2344.

[23] Presumably those of Bentham's printed works that were available.

[24] John Quincy Adams (1767–1848), American minister at London 1815–17; subsequently secretary of state 1817–25, and president of the United States 1825–9.

[25] i.e. Samuel Blodget's *Economica* and *The Works of Alexander Hamilton*. See letter 2344.

left hand on the ⟨. . .⟩ chest of drawers in my sitting room, you will ⟨. . .⟩ something of my correspondence with Alex⟨ander⟩ and Czartoriski and perhaps with Galatin: whatever of that ⟨. . .⟩ you find, send by Mrs K. I fear there is little or nothing there about Galatin: for what concerns him and Czartoriski it will be necessary to rummage over my letters from 1811 to the present time: they are all tied up and docketed: what are not on the Great Carochio,[26] are in the left hand upper drawer of my chest of drawers in my bedroom. A copy of Madison's is taking to send to S.B: another may perhaps be of use to be sent to Dumont, to give support to his legislative labours. A considerable parcel of my letters are here and must be looked over in that view by myself. Alexander's original letter is either lost or locked up in the lock-up drawer of the chest of drawers under the window near the bed-room.

Is there an American Consul here?[27] Perhaps, in default of the Minister, he might be the man through whom to receive or send parcels from and to Washington. In talking to the Minister about Chrestomathia you might make general offers of eventual service from me: such as having an eye to any American youth who at the recommendation of Madison etc. might be sent to be instructed in the Chrestomathian methods. The customary number of the 'Proposals'[28] should accompany the Book for Madison.

Pencils—one bundle by Mrs K.

☞ Forget not this for Cat. On the *Carochio* is an Edinburgh Almanack 12 mo. Wanted out of it the number of the Parishes in Scotland: item of the Professorships in the 4 Universities.

List of persons to whom Chrestomathia *Table* as well as Book are to be sent, together with any others to whom in respect of either or both you or P.[29] may think it of use. N.B. M.[30] desires of P. that with each Book of Chrestom. 3 copies of Proposals at least be sent, together with any greater number in particular instances.

1. Ld St Helens
2. Ld Viscount Folkstone.
3. Dr Baillie

[26] A piece of furniture Bentham later described as 'the moveable bookcase' in the sitting room at Queen's Square Place. See Bentham to Place, 12 December 1817, Jacob Hollander MSS, University of Illinois.

[27] The American consul-general was Robert Beaseley; the consul in London, Thomas Aspinwall.

[28] i.e. *Proposals for establishing in the Metropolis, a Day School, in which an example may be set of the application of the methods of Dr. Bell, Mr. Lancaster, and others, to the higher branches of education*, London, 1816.

[29] Place.

[30] Mill.

4. Miss Baillie
5. | | Strutt Esq Derby — Which is S.Bs particular friend?[31] If not known, send it 'To Messrs. Strutt and say from Sir. S. and Mr B.'
6. Rt H.G. Rose
7. W. Moreton Pitt Esqr
8. Rt Hon Sir W. Scott[32]
9. Rt Hon Sr W. Grant[33]
10. Rev Dr Parr
12. Rev Dr Andrew Bell
13. Rt Hon. Sr Joseph Banks
14. Dr Hyde Woolaston
15. Ld Grenville
16. Countess Spencer — on the outside / cover / 'With Mr. Bentham's respects'
17. J. Julius Angerstein Esqr. (already in the packet?)
18. Rev Dr Lindsay[34] Grove House near Bow.
19. Mr Leigh Hunt
20. Right Hon. Ch. Abbot
21. Sir James Mackintosh
22. Ld Viscount Sidmouth
23. The Lord Bishop of Gloucester[35] at the Earl of Harrowbys[36]—on the cover With Mr Bentham's respects the Book: *not* a Table: as he has one.
24. The Lord Bishop of London[37]
25. His Grace the Archbishop of Canterbury[38]
26. Ld. Erskine (Book and Table)[39]
27. Sir Humphrey Davy.

[31] William Strutt.

[32] Sir William Scott (1745–1836), later Baron Stowell of Stowell Park, at this time MP for Oxford University. He was Lord Eldon's brother.

[33] Sir William Grant (1752–1832), solicitor-general 1799–1801, master of the rolls 1801–17.

[34] Revd Dr James Lindsay (1753–1820), minister of the Presbyterian congregation at Monkwell Street from 1783 and in charge of an academy at Bow from 1805. He was a friend of James Mill.

[35] Henry Ryder (1777–1836), bishop of Gloucester 1815–24. In 1816 he established the Gloucester Diocesan Society for the education of the poor.

[36] Dudley Ryder, 1st Earl of Harrowby and Viscount Sandon, lord president of the council and brother of the bishop.

[37] William Howley (1766–1848), bishop of London 1813–28.

[38] Charles Manners-Sutton (1755–1828), archbishop of Canterbury 1805–28, one of the founders of the National Society for the Education of the Poor in the Principles of the Established Church.

[39] Thomas Erskine, 1st Baron Erskine (1750–1823), lord chancellor 1806–7.

28. Sir Everard Home[40]
29. The Very Reverend the Dean of Westminster[41]
30. Saml Hoare Junr Esqr the Banker, if a School-financier
31. Hon. Henry Grey Bennet.

Such plague and delay about determining and the shortest and best way, (now it is seen) would have been to have sent a Table to every one to whom a book was sent.

32. James Pillans Esqr. Rector of the High School Edinburgh
33. James Gray Esqr. High School Edinburgh
34. Francis Jeffrey Esqr Edinburgh
35. Dugald Stewart Esqr near Edinburgh to the care of Mr Constable[42] Bookseller Edinburgh

☞ With a Spring of Action. To care of Longman and Co. London.

36. John Playfair Esqr[43] Edinburgh College

All together in one outer envelope directed to Constable, through Longman.[44]

Lamps the two last—neither of them will do: instead of 12 hours which the former ones burn, one burns but $1\frac{1}{2}$ hours the other 3 or 4 hours. Yet these were the same, that were at Q.S.P.: the one that burns least badly the only one there tried: and, the time being short, it stood the trial. The fault is reported to be in the *outer* cylinder: it is considerably shorter than that into which the wick is inserted: the effect is that if more than a small quantity of oil is put in, it overflows. Sole remedy—the furnisher to send a pair properly made, on receipt of which, these to be returned. For eventual additional ones, a pair of the cheapest sort would serve. Look at them provisionally.

De Boffe.[45] While at Q.S.P. came a Bill of £6 more or less. It is unpaid, I mislaid it. I wish to have it paid: as also to stop the Journal Général's[46] several of which have still come.

☞ Tomorrow I may perhaps send to you in the same sheet a copy

[40] Sir Everard Home (1756–1832), surgeon and professor of anatomy and surgery at the College of Surgeons 1804–13, and again in 1821.

[41] John Ireland (1761–1842), dean of Westminster 1816–42. He helped to finance and remodelled Ashburton Grammar School.

[42] Archibald Constable (1774–1827), bookseller and publisher of London and Edinburgh. He published the *Edinburgh Review*.

[43] John Playfair (1748–1819), joint professor of mathematics at the University of Edinburgh 1785–1805, professor of natural philosophy 1805–19.

[44] Perhaps a reference to Thomas Norton Longman (1771–1842), rather than to his firm. Longman owned half of the *Edinburgh Review* and Longmans became the sole proprietor in 1826.

[45] Joseph De Boffe, importer of foreign books, of 10 Nassau Street, Soho.

[46] *Journal général de l'Europe* had been published at Liège since 1788.

of Madison for S.B. and another for Dumont. Let me know whether you communicate it to Place. One will certainly go without an *envelope*: the other is bungled.

☞ How to send to S.B.? Through Sir C. Stewart?[47] or through Place? How astonishing his silence!!!

2360

From Payne and Foss

2 September 1816

Messrs Payne and Foss's respects to Mr Bentham—and having been applied to respecting his new work Chrestomathia—and understanding that it is announced as to be had of them—beg to be informed where they may apply for copies to meet the demand

88 Pall Mall
Sept 2. 1816

2361

From John Bragge

29 September 1816

Dear Sir

I am as yet unable to give you much intelligence from Pool, but the following Extract of a letter I this morning recd. enclosed in a

[47] Sir Charles Stuart, later Baron Stuart de Rothesay (1779–1845), British ambassador extraordinary and plenipotentiary to France 1815–24, 1828–31.

2360. [1] UC clxv. 24. Docketed: '1816 Sept 2 / Chrestomathia / Payne and Foss / Pall Mall / to / J.B. Q.S.P. / Reced at Ford Abbey / Sept.7 / Asking for copies / of Chrestomathia / 7 Oct. 1816 (or thereabouts) / Sent orders to Macreery to deliver / to Payne and the / other Booksellers / 100 copies each'. Addressed: 'J. Bentham Esq'.

Thomas Payne the younger (1752–1831) had taken his apprentice Henry Foss into partnership in 1813. Payne and Foss were to be the principal booksellers dealing with *Chrestomathia*.

2361. [1] BL IX. 232–3. Autograph. Docketed: '1816 Sept 30 / Bragge Ford Abb⟨ey⟩ / to / J.B. Ford Abbe⟨y⟩ / American Bentham / Intelligence approachi⟨ng⟩'. Addressed: 'To / J. Bentham Esqr. / Ford Abbey'. Although the docket reads 30 September, Sunday was the 29th.

John Bragge of Sadborow House was a near neighbour of Bentham's at Ford Abbey. It appears that Bentham had asked him to make enquiries about a suspected American relative, James Bentham (1749–1811), a merchant of Charleston, South Carolina, who had been born at Wimborne, Dorset.

Frank of Lord Eldons,[2] will convince you I have not slept in yr. Commission

'If my letter is worth noting, remember it costs nothing, and my next a few days hence, I make no doubt will contain all the Intelligence your Neighbour can wish for. Boswell of Dorchester[3] knows the Relation enquired after, and the Elder Mrs. Farquaharson[4] is supposed to be well versed in the Pedigree of the Bentham family, the latter has been applied to on this occasion by the Basketts of Wareham,[5] and the former, promised me the little History in writing but as I told him I was making the Enquiry at yr. request, may probably have directed his letter to Sadborow instead of Corfe Castle—I shall certainly see him in ye next week and by that time have recd. Mrs. Farquarsons report'—

Mrs. F. being a Lady of considerable Age, and Mr. Boswell being officially perfectly well acquainted with the Inhabitants of the County of Dorset I have no doubt from either one or the other of obtaining every necessary information—

Boswell is a right hand Man of Mr. Pitts[6] is resident in Dorchester and could give Mr. Koe every information respecting the Gaol shd. he think proper to call on him for that purpose

I am
Dear Sir
Yr. most obedt. Servt.
John Bragge

Sunday Afternoon

[2] In 1807 Lord Eldon had acquired Encombe House in Corfe Castle parish. The writer of the letter quoted by Bragge seems to have been living or staying at Corfe Castle.

[3] Edward Boswell (1760–1842), antiquary and solicitor, author of *The Civil Division of the Country of Dorset*, Sherborne, 1795.

[4] Probably Mrs Ann Farquharson, only daughter of the Revd Samuel Staines, rector of Winfrith, Dorset, and widow of James Farquharson (1728–95), an East India merchant of Gough Square, London, and Littleton, Dorset.

[5] For the Baskett family see letter 2373 n. 2.

[6] William Moreton Pitt. He had established a hat factory in Dorchester Gaol.

2362

From Joanna Baillie

13 October 1816

Hampstead Octber 13th

Mrs Baillie presents her best respects to Mr. Bentham, with many thanks for his very gratifying present of his last work Chrestomathia which she values highly for the excellent matter it contains and also as a mark of his obliging notice

2363

From John Bragge

27 October 1816

Sadborow Sunday Noon

Mr. Bragge is sorry he cannot yet send Mr. Bentham all the intelligence he wishes to obtain respecting his name sake in America, but the concluding part of the letter which he receiv'd last night affords reasonable hopes he may soon be able to afford him all the information to be wish'd for.

—'I have at last heard from Mrs. Farquarson but her intelligence is only negative. None of the Wimbourne or Wareham Basketts ever intermarried with ye Benthams.

I have seen Boswell twice since I wrote last to you, who says Business has hitherto prevented his attention to our request, but feels confident he shall supply you very soon with a satisfactory answer—Mr. Bentham who emigrated he told me was s⟨uppo⟩sed to be very rich in consequence of a lucky marriage with a Widow and that he acted as Colonel during the War in the American Militia[2] and as he intimated that he considered himself entitled to a

2362. [1] UC clxv. 25. Autograph. Docketed: '1816 Oct 13 / Chrestomathia / Mrs Baillie Hampstead / to / J.B. Q.S.P. / Reced at Ford Abbey / Novr 7th. / Thanks for Chrestomathia'.

'Mrs Baillie' was Miss Joanna Baillie: Bentham had asked Koe to send her a copy of *Chrestomathia* on 19 August (See letter 2359). 'Mrs' was a prefix commonly used by and to describe unmarried as well as married women.

2363. [1] BL IX. 236–7. Autograph. Docketed: '1816 Oct 26 / Carolina Benthams / Bragge Sadborough / to / J.B. Ford Abbey / Devonshire and / Carolina Bent / -ham's intelligence'. Addressed: 'To / J. Bentham Esqr. / Ford Abbey'. Despite Bentham's docket, this letter appears to have been written on Sunday 27 October.

[2] James Bentham married, first, Mrs. Eleanor Phillips, on 5 May 1773, and secondly, on 4 June 1775, Mary Hardy. He was a lieutenant in the Charleston militia regiment in 1775 and later rose to major in the same corps. See Bobby Gilmer Moss, *Roster of South Carolina Patriots in the American Revolution*, Baltimore, 1983, p. 65.

share of ye Sweet Meats, if any should arrive in England,[3] and seem'd to say that other Mouths besides his own would water on this occasion, I think as soon as he begins to set his Enquiries on foot, Mr. Bentham will find cousins enough'—

2364

To John Herbert Koe

27 October 1816 (Aet 68)

Ford Abbey 27 Oct. 1816

Facienda for J.B. by H.K. in London

I Mittenda from Q.S.P.

1. History with Portraits of the Dutch Governor of Batavia. French 4to on Shelf over the door[2]
2. Hutton's Court of Requests[3]
3. Macries Life of Knox, if findable.[4]
4 Omer Talon's works—Vol containing his Journal—not more than the two first[5]
5. Act 53 G. 3 or thereabouts for stopping Wrights Prosecutions[6]

5+ Macreery to be paid for the Acts

---

6. De Boffe to be paid for his Bill for Journal Général de l'Europe etc[7]

[3] James Bentham's father, also called James, had married Elizabeth Boswell in 1740. Edward Boswell, who was born in Piddletown, was presumably related to Elizabeth Boswell, who seems to have come from Piddletown too. See below, letter 2373 n. 2.

2364. [1] Koe MSS. Autograph. Docketed. '1816 Octr 27 / Facienda'.

[2] J. P. J. DuBois, *Vies des gouverneurs généraux, avec l'abrégé de l'histoire des établissemens Hollandois aux Indes Orientales*, The Hague, 1763.

[3] William Hutton (1723–1815), the historian of Birmingham, wrote *Courts of Request; their nature, utility, and powers described*, Birmingham, 1787.

[4] Dr Thomas McCrie (1772–1835) was the author of *The Life of John Knox*, Edinburgh, 1812.

[5] Omer Talon (c.1595–1652), avocat général of the Paris parlement. His *Oeuvres* had not been published at this time; Bentham was probably thinking of *Mémoires de feu M. Omer Talon*, 8 vols., The Hague, 1732.

[6] William Wright, a former secretary to four bishops, had written a series of letters on the non-residence of clergymen which were published in the *Morning Chronicle* between November 1813 and March 1814. He had brought actions against delinquent clerics under 43 Geo.III, c.84 (for which see letter 2365 and n. 3); but by 54 Geo.III, c.6 and 54 Geo.III, c.44 a stay was put on all such prosecutions, and by 54 Geo.III, c.54 they were discontinued. 54 Geo.III, c.175 limited the liability of non-residents and vested in their bishops the power of enforcing penalties. Wright's letters and one of his petitions to the Commons are mentioned in *Church-of-Englandism*.

[7] See above, letter 2359 and nn. 45 and 46.

7. Greenal[8] to be settled with for the lamps.

7* For Abbey. Such plants as are not at Abbey specimens to be sent at proper time: Periwinckle large quantity disembarassing the other plants: item Sumacs: many straggling ones have been saved.

At Q.S.P. Facienda.

8. The hot-air Trunk in J.B.s bedchamber to be thoroughly *caulked*, and a non-conducting coat (suppose of felt?) to be put over it that no hot air may escape into the bedroom.
9. Seeds of bladder Senna and Everlasting Peace and Laburnum to be collected for the Abbey. From Payne and Foss with the next periodical Lives of Newton, Pearce and the two others just published 2 Vols 8vo boards.[9]

Mittenda continued

*6 J.B.s defences of Economy against Burke and Rose[10]

*7 From Biographia Britann.[11] Account of Cardinal Wolseys[12] Benefices viz. the number of each class: Bishopricks so many, Deaneries so many etc. but particularly the *Parochial* Benefices. If not in Biograph they are for certain in a Life of Wolsey in 8vo 2 or 4 Vols[13]

[8] W. Greenall, dealer in curiosities, 32 Old Compton Street.

[9] The collection of biographies and autobiographies edited by Alexander Chalmers (1759–1834), entitled *The Lives of Dr. Edward Pocock, the celebrated Orientalist, by Dr. Twells; of Dr. Zachary Pearce, Bishop of Rochester, and Dr. Newton, Bishop of Bristol, by themselves; and of the Rev. Philip Skelton, by Mr. Burdy*, 2 vols., London, 1816.

[10] The works which were to appear as 'Defence of Economy Against the late Mr. Burke', *The Pamphleteer*, ix (1817), 1–47 and 'Defence of Economy Against the Right Hon. George Rose', ibid., x (1817), 281–332. Both were republished in 1830 in *Official Aptitude Maximized; Expense Minimized* (Bowring, v. 278–328).

[11] *Biographia Britannica: or, the Lives of the Most Eminent Persons who have Flourished in Great Britain and Ireland, from the Earliest Ages Down to the Present Times*, 6 vols., London, 1747–63.

[12] Thomas Wolsey (1475?–1530), English cardinal and statesman.

[13] Probably *The History of the Life and Times of Cardinal Wolsey, Prime Minister to King Henry VIII*, 4 vols., London, 1742–4, by Joseph Grove (d. 1764).

2365

To John Herbert Koe

31 October 1816 (Aet 68)

Ford Abbey Thursday 31 Oct. 1816

The undermentioned Act desired *without fail* by the next conveyance whether with Periodicals or through Macreery.

Act 36 G. 3 c 83. 'for the further support and maintenance of Curates' etc.[2]

Wakefield taking in *Quarterly* as well as *Place*, Mill thinks *Place* may perhaps have no objection to spare us the new number along with the Periodicals.

All well: no news.

The conversation with Mrs Stoker gave her one of her fits, and they thought at one time she would have died. Mill being called in saw her in a horrible state; but she is now pretty well recovered.

By the same conveyance I wish much to know who it was brought in the Bill for the Church-reforming Act 43G. 3. c.84[3]—whether it was not *Sir W. Scott*: and who else was most active in it. Upon occasion the Votes of that year (1803) might I should suppose be seen at Romilly's. I know not whether we have Debates that come so far: but any rate we have Annual Registers that do. I have a notion that it was in consequence of a sort of force put upon him in the House that Sir W. Scot took the matter in hand.[4]

In this or that Act relative to the Army I have seen a clause authorizing *false musters* and disposing of the produce—a clause to this purpose I should suppose to be in every Mutiny Act. If you could find such an [one][5] for example in the last Mutiny Act, though it would be still better if it were in the first of those Acts in which such clause was ever inserted, you would oblige your humble servant.[6]

2365. [1] Koe MSS. Autograph. Docketed: '1816 Octr 31 / J.B.' Addressed: 'To / J.H. Koe Esqr / Lincolns Inn / London.' Postmark illegible. Stamped: 'CHARD/142'.

[2] 36 Geo.III, c.83, 'An Act for the further Support and Maintenance of Curates within the Church of England', which received the royal assent on 14 May 1796.

[3] 'An Act to amend the Laws relating to Spiritual Persons holding of Farms; and for enforcing the Residence of Spiritual Persons on their Benefices in England' (7 July 1803).

[4] Sir William Scott introduced his bill on 6 April 1803. See *Parliamentary Register*, n.s., iii. 583–90.

[5] MS 'a'.

[6] Bentham seems to have made a mistake here. False musters were expressly prohibited in the Mutiny Act (see 55 Geo.III, c. 108 ss. 43–6). He might have been thinking of the old practice whereby an officially-sanctioned 'Stock Purse' or non-effective account was formed in each regiment from the pay of men that did not exist, in order to finance recruiting and

P.S. Under the new system we had the *most exquisite* Rice-pudding today beyond all comparison that ever was tasted.

Mill had a letter just now from Grey Bennet, who speaks of one from Brougham dated Florence in which he says he shall for a certainty be here by the Meeting,[7] but mentions a place at which a letter will reach him in the mean time.

2366

To John Herbert Koe

8–9 November 1816 (Aet 68)

Ford Abbey Friday Novr. 7th 1816

Blank Sheets case and Pens

Hunted in vain in the cargo for the *Ulteriora*[2] promised by your letter[3] franked by Romilly and inclosing Lady B's:[4] disappointment attributed to some sudden and undisobeyable call from Grimgribber:[5] thanks for the Acts and other documents. Upon the strength of those / antecedently / before sent, I have found myself obliged to send to Macreery in the compass of 5 Ms pages, succedanea to two paragraphs of the last section of copy sent viz. § 7. Discipline continued viz. four pages in the room of paragraph 4[6]

Present Marginal content '*These Returns how produced*' etc and one page in the room of paragraph 11 Content beginning '*By 25 H.8. c.13' etc.*[7] I hope the Printer will understand of himself my directions given to the above effect: if not the resort must be to you.

In what I have now sent as above, upon the strength of an old

the clothing of the troops. Any balance remaining from this fund was divided between the regimental captains. The 1782–3 pay reforms transferred the cost of recruiting directly to Government, and thereafter the 'Stock Purse' was abandoned. See Charles M. Clode, *The Military Forces of the Crown*, 2 vols., London, 1869, ii. 2, 20.

[7] Presumably the next meeting of the Chrestomathic Committee, which did not take place until 24 February 1817. Alternatively, the reassembling of Parliament, on 28 January 1817.

2366. [1] Koe MSS. Part autograph, part in the hand of a copyist. Docketed: '1816 Novr 7 and 8 / J.B.' Friday was in fact 8 November, and Saturday the 9th.

[2] i.e. 'additional matter'.

[3] Missing.

[4] Missing.

[5] See above, letter 2337 n. 8.

[6] A reference to the printed version of what was to be published—by Effingham Wilson rather than McCreery—in 1818 as *Church-of-Englandism and its Catechism Examined*, appendix IV, s.vii, 'State of Discipline, as exhibited by Authority, and elucidated by a Diocesan Secretary' (pp. 305–52). The inserted material seems to have related to 43 Geo.III, c.84, on which Bentham requested information on 31 October (letter 2365).

[7] In the 1818 published version, 21 (not 25) Henry VIII, c.13 is mentioned on p. 311.

recollection of the Newspaper Accounts of the Debates, I have given to Sir W. Scott the credit of being the Draughtsman of the 43. G.3.c.84 being the grand Residence-enforcing and otherwise reforming Act; should this prove incorrect, I shall find myself in a proportionable scrape. I cast myself upon your diligence for relief from this anxiety.[8]

Not found in the parcel the work desired in my *facienda* which you took viz, the 4 lives just published: this I attribute to the above cause.[9]

Nor yet Macrie's Life of Knox.[10] I have what seems to me a recollection of its having been borrowed for Appledore:[11] do write to ask by the next letter that goes thither.

Whether I send Lady B's letter to you or Romilly first it may be as well for you to have in a separate state the following extract from it about a demand from a certain Mallard.[12] Put me in a way of paying it: if it can not be done by Michaelmas rents received by you from Tenants, I must send you a draught from hence.[13]

We received Mr Koe's letter in which he mentions Mallard's bill —I had no idea but that B had paid it last time he was in London. We have no means here of ascertaining its correctness—but as there can be little doubt of it we beg that it may be paid. I have no means either of knowing whether there is a sufficient balance of money remaining in your hands to discharge it—but trust that at any rate you would be kind enough to advance what is necessary till B can send on hearing from you a draft to pay it.

Their direction is Au petit Girac, près et par Angoulême, Département de la Charente.

A few lines from my Brother saying that they are all free from medicine, and as happy as we can expect to be. *They* have a letter to the Prefect there from Richelieu[14] and in consequence of another from the same to a Prefect on the road, viz. Marquis d'Argenson[15] were fêted by him for three days.

[8] See letter 2365.

[9] Alexander Chalmers's two-volume collection requested on 27 October. See letter 2364 and n. 9.

[10] See letter 2364 n. 4.

[11] See letter 2358 n. 15.

[12] Probably Stephen Mallard and Son, plumbers and painters of Hampstead. In August Lady Bentham had mentioned earlier (and unsatisfactory) work by plumbers on the roof at Hall Oak Farm. See Lady Bentham to J. H. Koe, 18 August 1816, Koe MSS.

[13] The following paragraph, in the hand of a copyist, was presumably taken from Lady Bentham's letter to Bentham.

[14] Lady Bentham enclosed copies of two such letters of introduction in her letter to Koe of 18 August 1816.

[15] Perhaps Marc-René, Marquis d'Argenson (1771–1842), French liberal politician.

Your hurry to read it will not be great. When I want to write to you again, I may perhaps do so through Romilly sending for the edification of the Ladies etc this of Lady B's.

Lady B. in her letter takes for granted that we have received the packet which we never have received: she says nothing of the receipt of my supplemental copy of the Chrestomathia which I believe you sent or were to send through the Ambassador[16] immediately upon our leaving here which was the 25 of July.

F. Abbey Saty Novr 8th 1816

Herewith you will receive a sheet of Column paper contents of which you will be pleased to communicate forthwith to the Pamphleteer Editors,[17] unless any particular objection should occur to you. No 3. Reform Catechism[18] I would not have come out till after the others: I am afraid of its coming out as yet for fear of its hurting Chrestomathia.

No I Defence of Economy against Burke and No II do against Rose,[19] though not legible enough for their compositor (N.B. they stipulate in their proposals for a fair copy) may be sufficiently so for them to read so as to determine whether to print or no: if they desire it it shall be had for that purpose.

The Defences of Economy were preceded by a part in which my principles are stated. But I do not expect to find that part ready for the press: and even if it were besides that it would make the whole affair too bulky it would not so well suit the Pamphleteer: not being so *piquant* as these attacks upon personages promise to be.

To account for the temporary suppression of that first and principal part, a page or so of Advertisement would be necessary: possibly a slight alteration at the beginning.[20]

When they applied about the Defence of Usury, the Pamphleteer people sent me a copy of their printed Proposals, addressed to Authors. I don't believe I have it here. They would probably give you one for me. Perhaps for all these works you might make them either offer or consent to give me a copy of their Pamphleteer from the beginning.

You are apprized I suppose, by Place of the application in form for me to become Patron of the Mutual Improvement Society and of

[16] Sir Charles Stuart. See letter 2359 and n. 47.

[17] The editor and printer of *The Pamphleteer* was Abraham John Valpy (1787–1854).

[18] i.e. what was to be published in 1817 as *Plan of Parliamentary Reform, in the Form of a Catechism* (Bowring, iii. 433–557).

[19] See letter 2364 n. 10.

[20] See Bowring, v. 278–81 for this 'Advertisement', which is dated November 1816.

their having sent me through him a copy of their laws for my revision.[21]

I believe I shall send you with this copy of the letter in question that you may make use of that sheet to write to my Brother at Angoulême.

2367

From John Bragge

10 November 1816

Sadborow Sunday Noon

Mr. Bragge recd. the enclos'd[2] from Dorchester this morning—It is much at Mr. Benthams service and tho' he cannot agree with the Writer respecting his lapse of ten years betwixt 1759 and 1770—yet it certainly contains some intelligence and promises more respecting the Family of the American Benthams—

2368

To John Herbert Koe

16 November 1816 (Aet 68)

16 Novr. 1816

Herewith you will receive Defence of Economy against Burke, I could not spare time for reading it through. But the sections with their titles have now for the first time been settled, and in here and there a place it has been slightly touched up. God grant the compositor may be able to read it: perhaps though not in a former instance, your taking the trouble to read it to him might be of use. As to its being copied here *in* time, James Hume gone, that is compleatly out of the question. I must beg the favour of you to correct the press. An Advertisement or Preface to account for the keeping back what was designed for the first part has appeared necessary. I have sketched out one which will occupy 5 or 6 pages:

[21] For Bentham's agreement to become patron of the Mutual Improvement Society see Bentham's reply to the Society's secretary, Thomas Tucker, of 31 July 1817 (Bowring, x. 488–9).

2367. [1] BL IX. 242. Autograph. Docketed: '1816 Nov 10 / Bragge Sadborough / to / J.B. Ford Abbey / inclosing Boswell of / Dorchester to Bragge / about the Carolina / Bentham's. / Dorchester Benthams'. Addressed: 'To / J. Bentham Esqr. / Ford Abbey'.

[2] Missing.

2368. [1] Koe MSS. Autograph. Docketed: '1816 Novr 16 / J.B.'

but I would not keep the packet the day longer which would have been necessary for the correction of it. It will be time enough to print it when the main body is printed.

Now as to conditions. In all these cases I understand from Mill it is universally understood that the copy right is not parted with: but for certainty this may as well be mentioned to Valpy[2] as from yourself. If as mentioned in the intended advertisement I received sufficient encouragement I might be disposed to publish the originally intended first part now suppressed. In this case I should probably deem it advisable to republish the Defence or Defences now proposed to be published in the Pamphleteer. I forbear taking up time with looking at the Defence against *Rose* till I know for certain whether Valpy chooses to have it to publish in this number.

If he publishes both or either what I very much want, and indeed must insist on is—some copies to give away. These will not any one of them interfere with the sale of the Pamphleteer. What I want them for most is to send as present to the headmen in the several United States. Besides Madison and his successor in the Presidentship[3] and two or three of the other Metropolitan official persons, such as Secretary of State, Financier General etc. I could send two at least to each State of which by this time I believe there are upwards of twenty. For this purpose less than 50 copies could not serve. This destination with the circumstances that have called it forth you need make no secret to Valpy—any more than to any body else: to Valpy particularly, as serving to convince him that the Pamphleteer could not be hurt by it—and perhaps on other accounts to augment his eagerness. The paper I would pay for of course: and so I suppose it could be necessary I should for the additional press work. If of the 50 there were a few to spare, I should like to send copies to some of the Orators who have distinguished themselves at the late partriotic meetings.[4]

Ford Abbey 16 Novr 1816

Lost sheep found.

Sore vexed to think of your vexation at the apparent loss of it: was just sitting down to write to inform you of the discovery: but was stopped by the consideration that nothing I could then send would arrive time enough to prevent your sending what succedaneous

[2] For Abraham John Valpy see letter 2366 n. 17.

[3] James Monroe (1758–1831) succeeded Madison in 1817.

[4] Bentham seems to have been referring to the radicals who addressed the Spa Fields meeting on the previous day, 15 November 1816. Prominent among the speakers was Henry Hunt (1773–1835), who had stood as candidate for Bristol in the 1812 election. The meeting was reported in *The Times* of 16 November.

matter might have occurred to you as necessary. Yes: it was stuck in somehow or other between the brown paper and the packing-bag that covered it: and its being covered up in whity-brown paper not much different from the colour of either was the reason that it was sent off with the bag without being observed. Two letters received from you since that time.[5]

Lost sheep 2d discovered; viz *Lee's Botany*[6] Lucy at parting had locked it up somewhere very carefully: whereby her husband had been deprived of whatever use he might have proposed to himself to make of it.

1. *Plain Fools Cap paper* desired by next conveyance through Macreery. You see in this paper the distress for want of it.[7] Two or three quires will be sufficient.

2. *Holcroft's Life*——a copy from Paynes.[8]

In two or three days off goes James Hume. He has been highly lucky. His Uncle has contrived in a manner too long to relate to get for him the promise of an appointment to a surgeoncy in the East Indies to take place this time two years if in the meantime he can learn enough of the business to pass an examination. He commences by attending Carpue——then to Edinburgh.[9]

Matter relative to *Defences* etc continued from p.2.[10] I wish you may be able to find time to read over what I have sent, so as to encrease the security against omission or other errors affecting the sense, as also against getting into a scrape: though I have little apprehension of your finding any thing that would even by Ld Ellenborough be deemed libellous.

If I have not a compleat set, you might at any rate get from them gratis, if not to keep to look at, a copy of some No. or Nos. of the Pamphleteer such as they could best spare. Having never seen a copy I have no conception of the type, mode of printing——or any thing belonging to it.

[5] Apparently a reference to the items mentioned as missing in letter 2366, where Bentham refers to another letter from Koe.

[6] See letter 2358 and n. 14.

[7] This letter is written on a rough kind of paper, quite different from that usually used by Bentham.

[8] Thomas Holcroft, *Memoirs Written by Himself and Continued down to the Time of his Death, from his Diary, Notes and other Papers*, ed. William Hazlitt, 3 vols., London, 1816. Holcroft (1745–1809) was a dramatist, novelist, and translator.

[9] Joseph Constantine Carpue (1764–1846), surgeon and anatomist, was a distinguished anatomical teacher in London, known as the 'chalk lecturer' on account of his frequent use of chalk illustrations. Of Hume's subsequent career little is known, but a James Hume is listed as an assistant surgeon on the Bengal medical establishment in 1819; his date of appointment was sometime after August 1818.

[10] i.e. page 2 of this letter.

Thanks for your news. Past 11 o'clock! If there be any thing else to write, no time to write it by this conveyance.

The promised copy of the Pamphleteer Proposal not yet received.[11]

By this conveyance Mill by my desire writes to Place to desire him by means of *Waithman*[12] who you know had long ago promised it to me—to get an introduction to the omniscient man who knows all about the City of London Constitution for the purpose of obtaining a list of the offices now or lately venal: enquire of Place. This is to fill up the gaps (eventually) in Hints respecting Economy.[13] Place may be told of the purpose.

2369

To John Herbert Koe

18 November 1816 (Aet 68)

Ford Abbey Monday 18 Novr. 1816

This will be delivered or forwarded to you by James Hume.

Yea—I am moreover out of 4 column paper. By the next opportunity pray send a competent portion: say three or four quires.

By Saturdays or rather Sundays Coach I sent you a packet containing Defence of Economy against Burke it was directed to you at Lincolns Inn.

Had I thought that James would have gone on so early a day as this, I might have sent it by him. But no matter.

Bladder Senna and Laburnum seeds and Everlasting Peace do. Are there any?[2] The sooner you can gather the whole harvest of them, the better: send by any opportunity, the sooner they are here: that we may form our plans accordingly.

To day I determine with a window washing man who has cured

[11] See letter 2366.

[12] Robert Waithman (1764–1833), political reformer. He had unsucessfully contested the City of London in 1812, but was to be MP 1818–20, 1826–33, sheriff of London and Middlesex 1820, and lord mayor 1823–4.

[13] In his 'Advertisement' to the 'Defence of Economy' papers, Bentham explained that the works were originally designed 'to form a sequel to a tract of no great bulk, having for its title *Hints respecting Economy*. For its subject, it had taken the whole of the official establishment, and for its objects, two intimately connected practical operations, viz. *minimizing official pay*, and *maximizing official aptitude*'. See Bowring, v. 278–9 and below, letter 2370.

2369. [1] Koe MSS. Autograph. Docketed: '1816 Novr 18 / J.B.' Addressed: 'To / J.H. Koe Esqr / 19, Lincolns Inn / London.'

[2] See letter 2364.

all manner of Ice-houses in the neighbourhood. He has much experience but talks nonsense. The earth around is digging for *data* to proceed upon. It is a mystery.

2370

To John Herbert Koe

24 November 1816 (Aet 68)

Ford Abbey 24 Novr 1816

Received this day yours of the 21st inclosing Pamphleteer Proposal.[2] To all the conditions stipulated for by the Editor including the extra pay for the compositor I accede except that I can not bind myself as to any determinate time for delaying the republication of the Defences or either of them. That which was designed for the first part viz. the Hints respecting Economy wanting more or less of being finished, it is altogether uncertain whether with so many irons in the fire I shall be able to find time for finishing it: but if I should it would be very awkward to send it abroad without the two Defences which were designed for sequels to it: still more so with one of them above: so that nobody who had the one part could have both the others without having both or one of them in the shape of an odd volume of the Pamphleteer.

This goes through Macreery with an immense mass of between 40 and 50 pages in two sections. §7 and 8 occupied in the exposure of Excellent Church as per *Returns* and *Wright*.[3] Mill will not let me omitt any part of it: some pages are to be added others substituted to matter already sent in §7. Virtue will consist in your taking cognizance of them for the purpose of removing any difficulties should any occurr.

Opposite sits Wakefield who came here to dinner from Exeter, and is to sleep here to night but goes to Taunton I think it is tomorrow and will not be in town till tomorrow sennight.

I wonder I have heard nothing from you respecting this packet or whatever it is that has been directed to you or me from my Brother. It is fit he should know that no such *parcel* is come as he speaks of in one of his last letters:[4] but I believe it is the letter I received before I left town in July.

2370. [1] Koe MSS. Autograph. Docketed: '1816 Novr 24 / J.B.' Addressed: 'To / J.H. Koe Esqr / 19 Lincolns Inn / London'.

[2] Missing.

[3] A reference to what was to be published as *Church-of-Englandism*, appendix IV, ss.7 and 8. For Wright see above, letter 2364 n. 6.

[4] Missing.

2371

To John Herbert Koe

26 November 1816 (Aet 68)

Tuesday
Ford Abbey 26 Novr. 1816

Reced. yours of the (23d.?)[2] in which you inform me of your giving out Defence to be copied: cheap indeed if feasible.

This is to inform you that I shall send by tomorrows conveyance an Advertisement or Preface consisting of 7 or 8 pages which will be to be copied likewise.[3]

2372

To John Herbert Koe

27 November 1816 (Aet 68)

Ford Abbey Wednesday night 27 Nov 1816

No packet yet received from you and Macreery.

This is written—not that I have anything to say—it being almost an hour past my bedtime—but lest you should be expecting to receive a letter and for want of receiving one suppose it missing.

The inclosed which alas! is sadly illegible will speak for itself: It has been a sad bore to me, but seemed a necessary one.[2]

I shall soon be in want of *Composition paper*.

2371. [1] Koe MSS. Autograph. Docketed: '1816 Novr 26 / J.B.' Addressed: 'To / J.H. Koe Esqr / 19 Lincolns Inn / London.' Postmark: 'A/28 NO 28/1816'. Stamped: 'CHARD'.

[2] Missing.

[3] i.e. the advertisement to preface the 'Defence of Economy' articles for *The Pamphleteer*. See above, letters 2366 and n. 20 and 2368.

2372 [1] Koe MSS. Autograph. Docketed: '1816 Novr 27 / J.B.' Addressed: 'To / J.H. Koe Esqr / Lincolns Inn / London'.

[2] The 'Advertisement' for the 'Defence of Economy' articles. See letter 2371.

2373

From John Bragge

4 December 1816

Mr. Bentham will perceive by ye enclosed Copy[2] that the Boswells having once caught Scent of, what they think, an American Fortune, will not easily be persuaded to relinquish the chace; a circumstance not much to be wonder'd at, as they have both Families and no great landed Property on this side the Atlantic

2373. [1] BL IX. 244. Autograph. Docketed: '1816 Dec 4 / Boswell Dorchester / to / Bragge Sadborow / Dorsetshire Benthams'. Addressed: 'To / J. Bentham Esqr / Ford Abbey'.

[2] Bragge's letter was written on the same sheet as the letter he had received from William Boswell, Edward Boswell's nephew. Boswell's letter enclosed a letter from Humphry Leer, an attorney at Blandford, to Edward Boswell, dated 2 December 1816 (BL IX. 243). Leer's letter stated:

'On searching the register of Marriages from 1730 I cannot find the marriage of James Bentham, but I am informed by a Mrs. Cox, a Widow Lady of Wimborne now in her 86th Year that she knew James Bentham and also his Wife, who was named either Betty or Elizabeth, that her maiden name was Boswell, and that she came from Piddletown. Mrs. Bentham lived two or three years with Mrs. Cox, and she often heard her speak of her sons James and John, who went to America, but never heard of a Daughter. There are other persons in Wimborne who well knew James and John but I cannot learn that there was a Sister. It appears by the register for Baptisms that "Bentham James son of James was baptized Sep. 4. 1749." "Bentham John son of James was baptized Jan. 23. 1752." I cannot find any Jane in the register, or any account of the burials of James Bentham, or his Wife. There was a Mr. Samuel Baskett, who was the son of "Baskett Thomas and Ann Russell married 30 Aug 1739" "Baskett Samuel son of Thos. Baskett, baptised June 7. 1740." Saml. Baskett, son of Thos. Baskett, when a young man, went abroad, and it is reported to me by the Revd. J. Baskett, one of the present Clergymen of Wimborne, that he was lost at Sea, the ship having caught fire, and nothing more was ever heard of him. It is not believed he ever married—no account in the register of Wimborne of such an event.

It appears from the report of several Persons at Wimborne with whom I have communicated, that James was the eldest son, and being a gay young man, and very idle, was through the means of Mr. Fitch of High-hall, and the opportunity of a ship belonging to a Mr. Peter Jolliffe of Poole, sent to Carolina in America, where he did well, and married a person of the Country, who was very rich, which enabled him to live there, which was about the time of the Revolution, and it was reported he was an Officer in the Rebel Army.

John, the second Son, went from England as a common Soldier, and was supposed also to go to America, as his Wimborne Friends never heard more of him.

The mother of James and John Bentham wa⟨s⟩ by the Fitch Family—but it does not appear that James was registered "James Fitch"—only "James".'

2374

To John Herbert Koe

14 December 1816 (Aet 68)

14 Decr. 1816[2]

Desiderata

1. No. of Parishes in England and Wales, as per Population Returns.[3]
2. Date of Bishop Watson's Letter to the Archb. of Cant. It is in a Volume of his Tracts: in the *Carrochio*[4] mention whether 2d Edition or no Edition on the Title page.[5]
3. In the Votes and Debates of the year 1809—the first year in which the annual £100,000 for Poor-Living Augmentation was granted. See the General Appropriation Act. Desired the names of the persons who took part in the measure and of any who opposed it—with the reasons on both sides and any particulars worth remark.[6]

I perceive from some of the Parliamentary papers that the first grant was made in pursuance of a message from the Crown: inquirendum whether it was included in the General Appropriation Act, or whether there was an Act on purpose.[7]

14 Decr 1816

Poor as we are I can not well brook the thoughts of finding Q.S.P. house at my return in the melancholy state in which I left it. I mean in respect of the want of painting.

2374. [1] Koe MSS. Autograph. Docketed: '1816 Decr 14 / J.B.' Addressed: 'To / J. Herbert Koe Esqr / 9 Lincoln's Inn / London'.

[2] Written above this: '3 Decr 1816 Ford Abbey'.

[3] A reference to the 1811 Census returns. See *Abstract of the Answers and Returns Made Pursuant to an Act, Passed in the Fifty-first Year of His Majesty George III, . . . Ordered, by The House of Commons, to be Printed, 2 July 1812.*

[4] See letter 2359 n. 26.

[5] The letter from Richard Watson (1737–1816), bishop of Llandaff, to the archbishop of Canterbury, Frederick Cornwallis (1713–83), was published as *A Letter to Archbishop Cornwallis on the Church Revenues*, London, 1783. It does not appear in Watson's *A Collection of Theological Tracts*, 6 vols., Cambridge, 1785 (2nd ed. 1791).

[6] On 7 June 1809 the then chancellor of the exchequer, Spencer Perceval, proposed that the Commons vote £100,000 for the augmentation of poor clerical livings. His resolution was unanimously agreed to, although some MPs—including Lord Henry Petty—expressed concern at the prospect of rich pluralists sharing in the augmentation. See *Parliamentary Debates*, xiv. 920–2.

[7] The grant was made in consequence of a message from the king, read by the speaker in the Commons on 26 May 1809 (not 20 May as stated in *Church-of-Englandism*, Appendix V, p. 437). See *Parliamentary Debates*, xiv. 716–17.

A day or two before the meeting of Parliament is the time I look to. I wish you would see the Painter as soon as convenient, and get from him a rough estimate of the expence of painting, upon the existing plan, the following rooms etc. (Entrance-Hall being so latterly painted will not I hope be wanted.)

1. Study. 2. Lobby between do and passage. 3. ⟨. . .⟩ 4. Dining Parlour. 5. Hall between do and do. 6. Staircase up to my sitting room. Do up to your room: viz. at least so high as company coming up to my room will see. If I have these jobs done as I probably shall, better it may have had three weeks or so to dry before I arrive.

INDEX

Note. This is an index of names of persons mentioned in the text and notes. References throughout are to page numbers, except in the case of Bentham's correspondents, where the figures in italic type after the sub-headings 'Letters to' and 'Letters from' refer to the serial number of the letters. The abbreviation 'biog.' indicates a biographical note on the person indexed.

In the case of Bentham himself, only references to his works are indexed.

INDEX

INDEX